HOLLYWOOD'S AMERICA

Figure 1 *My Little Chickadee* (1940). Universal Studios. Directed by Edward F. Cline. Courtesy of Jerry Murbach, www.doctormacro1.info.

HOLLYWOOD'S AMERICA

TWENTIETH-CENTURY AMERICA THROUGH FILM

Edited
with an Introduction
by

STEVEN MINTZ and RANDY ROBERTS

WILEY-BLACKWELL

A John Wiley & Sons, Ltd., Publication

This fourth edition first published 2010
© 2010 Blackwell Publishing Ltd

Edition History: Brandywine Press, 1994; 2nd edition, 1997; 3rd edition, 2001.

Blackwell Publishing was acquired by John Wiley & Sons in February 2007. Blackwell's publishing program has been merged with Wiley's global Scientific, Technical, and Medical business to form Wiley-Blackwell.

Registered Office
John Wiley & Sons Ltd, The Atrium, Southern Gate, Chichester, West Sussex, PO19 8SQ, United Kingdom

Editorial Offices
350 Main Street, Malden, MA 02148-5020, USA
9600 Garsington Road, Oxford, OX4 2DQ, UK
The Atrium, Southern Gate, Chichester, West Sussex, PO19 8SQ, UK

For details of our global editorial offices, for customer services, and for information about how to apply for permission to reuse the copyright material in this book please see our website at www.wiley.com/wiley-blackwell.

The right of Steven Mintz and Randy W. Roberts to be identified as the authors of the editorial material in this work has been asserted in accordance with the UK Copyright, Designs and Patents Act 1988.

Library of Congress Cataloging-in-Publication Data

Hollywood's America : twentieth-century America through film / edited with an introduction by Steven Mintz and Randy W. Roberts.
    p. cm.
  Includes bibliographical references and index.
  ISBN 978-1-4051-9003-9 (pbk. : alk. paper)
1. United States–In motion pictures.   2. Motion pictures–United States–History–20th century.   I. Mintz, Steven, 1953- II. Roberts, Randy, 1951-
  PN1995.9.U64H55 2010
  791.43'658–dc22
                                       2009045863

A catalogue record for this book is available from the British Library.

Set in 10/12.5pt Galliard by SPi Publisher Services, Pondicherry, India
Printed and bound in Malaysia by Vivar Printing Sdn Bhd

01 2010

Contents

List of Illustrations   ix

Preface   x

Introduction: The Social and Cultural History of American Film   1

PART I   THE SILENT ERA   29

Introduction: *Intolerance* and the Rise of the Feature Film   29

1   Silent Cinema as Social Criticism   31
    Kay Sloan, "Front Page Movies"

2   Silent Cinema as Historical Mythmaker   43
    Eric Niderost, "*The Birth of a Nation*"

3   The Revolt Against Victorianism   52
    Lary May, "Douglas Fairbanks, Mary Pickford, and the New Personality"

4   Primary Sources   63
    Edison v. American Mutoscope Company   63
    "The Nickel Madness"   65
    Mutual Film Corp. v. Industrial Commission of Ohio   67
    Fighting a Vicious Film: Protest Against *The Birth of a Nation*   69
    Boston Branch of the National Association for the Advancement
        of Colored People, 1915   69
    Analysis by Francis Hackett   69

PART II   HOLLYWOOD'S GOLDEN AGE   71

Introduction: Backstage During the Great Depression: *42nd Street*,
    Gold Diggers of 1933, and *Footlight Parade*   71

5   Depression America and its Films   75
    Maury Klein, "Laughing Through Tears"

6   The Depression's Human Toll   82
    Peter Roffman and Jim Purdy, "Gangsters and Fallen Women"

7   Depression Allegories   91
    Thomas H. Pauly, "*Gone with the Wind* and *The Grapes of
    Wrath* as Hollywood Histories of the Great Depression"

8   African Americans on the Silver Screen   100
    Thomas R. Cripps, "The Evolution of Black Film"

9   Primary Sources   112
    The Introduction of Sound   112
    "Pictures That Talk"   112
    Review of Don Juan   113
    "Silence is Golden"   113
    Film Censorship   116
    The Sins of Hollywood, 1922   116
    "The Don'ts and Be Carefuls"   118
    The Motion Picture Production Code of 1930   119

PART III   WARTIME HOLLYWOOD   **129**

Introduction: Hollywood's World War II Combat Films   129

10 *Casablanca* as Propaganda   133
    Randy Roberts, "You Must Remember This: The Case of
    Hal Wallis' *Casablanca*"

11 Bureau of Motion Pictures Report: *Casablanca*   142

12 John Wayne and Wartime Hollywood   144
    Randy Roberts, "John Wayne Goes to War"

13 The Woman's Film   163
    Jeanine Basinger, "When Women Wept"

14 Primary Sources   170
    US Senate Subcommittee Hearings on Motion Picture and
    Radio Propaganda, 1941

PART IV   POSTWAR HOLLYWOOD   **175**

Introduction: *Double Indemnity* and Film Noir   175

15 The Red Scare in Hollywood   179
    Peter Roffman and Jim Purdy, "HUAC and the End of an Era"

16 The Morality of Informing   187
    Kenneth R. Hey, "Ambivalence and *On the Waterfront*"

17 Science Fiction as Social Commentary   198
    Stuart Samuels, "The Age of Conspiracy and Conformity:
    Invasion of the Body Snatchers" (1956)

18 The Western as Cold War Film   207
    Richard Slotkin, "Gunfighters and Green Berets:
    The Magnificent Seven and the Myth of Counter-Insurgency"

19 Popular Culture in the Age of White Flight   219
    Eric Avila, "Film Noir, Disneyland, and the Cold War
    (Sub)Urban Imaginary"

20 Primary Sources   234
    United States v. Paramount Pictures, Inc. (1947)   234
    **Hearings Regarding the Communist Infiltration
       of the Motion Picture Industry**   235
    US House of Representatives Committee on
       Un-American Activities, 1947   235
    US House of Representatives Committee on
       Un-American Activities, 1951   235
    The Miracle Decision   238
    *Joseph Burstyn, Inc. v. Wilson, Commissioner of Education
    of New York, et al.* (1952)   238

PART V   HOLLYWOOD AND THE TUMULTUOUS 1960s   **241**

Introduction: *Bonnie and Clyde*   241

21 A Shifting Sensibility   243
    Charles Maland, "*Dr. Strangelove*: Nightmare Comedy
    and the Ideology of Liberal Consensus"

22 Films of the Late 1960s and Early 1970s   255
    Michael Ryan and Douglas Kelner, "From
    Counterculture to Counterrevolution, 1967–1971"

23 Reaffirming Traditional Values   264
    Daniel J. Leab, "The Blue Collar Ethnic in Bicentennial America: *Rocky*"

24 Presenting African Americans on Film   272
    Aram Goudsouzian, "The Rise and Fall of Sidney Poitier"

25 Coming to Terms with the Vietnam War   281
    Randy Roberts and David Welky, "A Sacred Mission:
    Oliver Stone and Vietnam"

26 Primary Sources   301
    The Hollywood Rating System, 1968

PART VI   HOLLYWOOD IN OUR TIME   **305**

Introduction: A Changing Hollywood   305

27 Feminism and Recent American Film   309
    Aspasia Kotsopoulos, "Gendering Expectations: Genre
    and Allegory in Readings of *Thelma and Louise*"

28 Hollywood Remembers World War II   329
    John Bodnar, "*Saving Private Ryan* and
    Postwar Memory in America"

29 East Meets West   340
    Minh-Ha T. Pham, "The Asian Invasion
    (of Multiculturalism) in Hollywood"

30 Immigration at the Movies   354
    Carlos E. Cortés, "The Immigrant in Film: Evolution
    of an Illuminating Icon"

31 Movies and the Construction of Historical Memory   364
    Steven Mintz, "Movies, History, and the Disneyfication
    of the Past: The Case of *Pocahontas*"

Bibliography of Recent Books in American Film History   371
Index   395

List of Illustrations

1   *My Little Chickadee* (1940)   ii
2   *Intolerance* (1916)   2
3   *A Corner in Wheat* (1909)   32
4   Douglas Fairbanks in *The Black Pirate* (1926)   53
5   *Footlight Parade* (1933)   72
6   *Public Enemy* (1931)   77
7   *The Grapes of Wrath* (1939)   92
8   *Objective Burma!* (1945)   130
9   *Casablanca* (1942)   134
10 *Mildred Pierce* (1945)   165
11 *Double Indemnity* (1944)   176
12 *On the Waterfront* (1954)   188
13 *The Magnificent Seven* (1960)   208
14 Photograph of the real-life bank robbers Bonnie Parker and
    Clyde Barrow   306
15 *The Immigrant* (1917)   356
16 Portrait of Pocahontas, from a painting by William Sheppard (1616)   368

Preface

Anyone who wishes to know about the twentieth-century United States would do well to go to the movies. Films represent much more than mere mass entertainment. Movies – even bad movies – are important sociological and cultural documents. Like any popular commercial art form, movies are highly sensitive barometers that both reflect and influence public attitudes. From the beginning of the last century, films have recorded and even shaped American values, beliefs, and behavior.

This book has two fundamental aims. The first is to use feature films to illuminate the central themes of twentieth-century American cultural history. The book begins with a concise introduction that traces the history of American film against a backdrop of broader changes in late nineteenth- and twentieth-century popular culture. It is then followed by a series of interpretive essays that examine how classic films treated important aspects of American political, economic, and social life, supplemented with primary sources that illuminate film history. It concludes with an up-to-date bibliography of American film history.

As we shall see, the history of the movies is inextricably intertwined with broader themes and issues in American cultural history, such as the transition from a Victorian culture, with its emphasis on refinement, self-control, and moralism, to modern mass culture. Popular films offer a valuable vehicle for examining public responses to the social disorder and dislocations of the Depression; the fears of domestic subversion of the late 1940s and early 1950s; the cultural and moral upheavals of the 1960s; and the meaning and significance of the Vietnam War. Through their plots, their characters, and their dramatization of moral issues, movies have captured the changing nature of American culture.

The book's second aim is to help students develop the tools to read and interpret visual texts. In a society in which visual images have become a dominant mode of entertainment and persuasion, used to promote presidential candidates as well as sell toothpaste and deodorant, visual literacy may well be as important as facility with written words and numbers.

Film is, as we shall show, a type of communication with its own rules and grammar, which demands the same skills of critical thinking and analysis one uses to read written texts. To analyze a poem, one must understand patterns of rhyme and rhythm and a poet's use of sound and imagery. Likewise, to interpret a film, one must understand the techniques that filmmakers use to construct their texts: camerawork, editing devices, lighting, set design, narrative, and others.

The films examined in this book are feature films – not documentaries or avant-garde or underground films. These are the classic films that engaged Americans emotions, and made them laugh and weep, shriek with terror, and tremble with excitement. They offered wit, suspense, romance, thrills, highlife and lowlife. Highbrow critics might dismiss most Hollywood films as schlock – but these films gave audiences more pleasure than any other art form and taught truly fundamental lessons dealing with intimacy, tenderness, initiation, lust, conflict, guilt, and loyalty. It was from the silver screen that Americans received their most intensive – if highly distorted – picture of their country's past, the lifestyles of the rich and famous, and the underside of American life.

Throughout the twentieth century, films have been the most influential instrument of mass culture in the United States. As America's "dream factory," which manufactures fantasies and cultural myths much as a Detroit automaker produces cars, Hollywood has served a vital ideological role: shaping the very way that Americans look at the world. Hollywood's films have played a pivotal role in "modernizing" American values. They have been instrumental in shaping Americans' deepest presuppositions about masculinity, femininity, race, ethnicity, and sexuality. Movies have helped form Americans' self-image and have provided unifying symbols in a society fragmented along lines of race, class, ethnicity, region, and gender. In certain respects subversive of traditional cultural values, movie culture created a mythic fantasy world that has helped Americans adapt to an ever-changing society.

Introduction

The Social and Cultural History of American Film

One night a year America shuts down. All across the United States tens of millions of people press the buttons on their remote controls, sit back in their easy chairs or recline on their couches, and become the world's largest congregation, watching a key event in the country's civic religion – the Oscars. Even though movie attendance has fallen steeply – to just one-third of what it was at the time of the first Academy Awards ceremony in 1927 – Americans still gawk at the limousines as they pull up to the Dorothy Chandler Pavilion in Los Angeles, gaze at the stars' tuxedoes and gowns, and wait impatiently for a memorable moment – a naked streaker racing across the stage or perhaps Jack Palance performing one-handed push-ups.

Americans watch the Academy Awards presentations for many reasons: to briefly see a more human side of their favorite movie stars; to pit their judgment against that of the 5,000 members of the Academy of Motion Picture Arts and Sciences; to partake in the trashy pleasure of watching the glitziest extravaganza that Hollywood is capable of producing. But the Academy Awards ceremony also offers something more: it gives Americans a chance to recognize the movies that entertained them, engaged their emotions, expressed their deepest hopes and aspirations, and responded most successfully to their anxieties and fears. From *All Quiet on the Western Front* – a graphic portrait of the horrors and futility of war that came to embody the pacifism of the late 1920s and early 1930s – to *Unforgiven* – a bleak revisionist Western that deglamorizes the mythic western frontier and its violent traditions – Oscar winners and nominees have offered a vivid record of shifting American values.

Of all the products of popular culture, none is more sharply etched in our collective imagination than the movies. Most Americans instantly recognize images produced by the movies: Charlie Chaplin, the starving prospector in *The Gold Rush*, eating his shoe, treating the laces like spaghetti. James Cagney, the gun-toting gangster in *Public Enemy*, shoving a grapefruit into the side of Mae Clarke's face. Paul Muni, the jobless World War I veteran in *I am a Fugitive from a Chain Gang*, who is asked how he lives and replies, "I steal." Gloria Swanson, the fading movie goddess in *Sunset Boulevard*, belittling suggestions that she is no longer a big star: "It's the pictures that got small." Even those who have never seen *Citizen Kane* or *Casablanca* or the *Treasure of the*

Figure 2 *Intolerance* (1916). Wark Producing Corp. Directed by D.W. Griffith. Courtesy of Jerry Murbach, www.doctormacro1.info.

Sierra Madre respond instantly to the advertisements, parodies, and TV skits that use these films' dialogue, images, and characters.

Movies are key cultural artifacts that offer a window into American cultural and social history. A mixture of art, business, and popular entertainment, the movies provide a host of insights into Americans' shifting ideals, fantasies, and preoccupations. Like any cultural artifact, the movies can be approached in a variety of ways. Cultural historians have treated movies as sociological documents that record the look and mood of particular historical settings; as ideological constructs that advance particular political or moral values or myths; as psychological texts that speak to individual and social anxieties and tensions; as cultural documents that present particular images of gender, ethnicity, class romance, and violence; and as visual texts that offer complex levels of meaning and seeing.

This book offers examples of how to interpret classic American films as artifacts of a shifting American culture. As backdrop, the book begins by offering a concise summary and interpretation of film history that locates the evolution of the movie industry against a broader backdrop of American cultural and social history.

The Birth of Modern Culture

Toward the end of the nineteenth century, a New York neurologist named George M. Beard coined the term "neurasthenia" to describe a psychological ailment that afflicted a growing number of Americans. Neurasthenia's symptoms included "nervous dyspepsia, insomnia, hysteria, hypochondria, asthma, sick-headache, skin rashes, hayfever, premature baldness, inebriety, hot and cold flashes, nervous exhaustion, brain-collapse, or forms of 'elementary insanity.' " Among those who suffered from neurasthenia-like ailments at some point in their lives were Theodore Roosevelt, settlement house founder Jane Addams, psychologist William James, painter Frederic Remington, and novelists Owen Wister and Theodore Dreiser.

According to expert medical opinion, neurasthenia's underlying cause was "over-civilization." The frantic pace of modern life, nervous overstimulation, stress, and emotional repression produced debilitating bouts of depression or attacks of anxiety and nervous prostration. Fears of "over-civilization" pervaded late nineteenth-century American culture. Many worried that urban life was producing a generation of pathetic, pampered, physically and morally enfeebled 98-pound weaklings – a far cry from the stalwart Americans who had tamed a continent. A sharply falling birth rate sparked fears that the native-born middle class was committing "race suicide." A host of therapies promised to relieve the symptoms of neurasthenia, including the precursors of modern tranquilizers (like Dr. Hammond's Nerve and Brain Pills). Sears even sold an electrical contraption called the Heidelberg Electric Belt, designed to reduce anxiety by sending electric shocks to the genitals. Many physicians prescribed physical exercise for men and rest cures for women. But the main way that late nineteenth-century Americans responded to the pressures, stresses, and restrictions of modern life was by turning to sports, outdoor activities, and popular culture for release.

Few Americans are unfamiliar with the wrenching economic transformations of the late nineteenth century, the consolidation of industry, the integration of the national economy, and the rise of the corporation. But few Americans realize that this period also saw the birth of modern culture – a culture that Americans still live with.

The last years of the nineteenth century witnessed a profound shift in American values: a shift away from Victorian values toward a distinctive set of modern values. A Victorian emphasis on self-denial and self-restraint was replaced by a new culture geared to personal self-fulfillment, leisure, and sensual satisfaction. A culture oriented toward words was supplanted by a new visual culture oriented toward images. A genteel culture, stressing eternal truths and high moral ideals, was overtaken by a new emphasis on realism, energy, and excitement. Above all, a culture deeply divided by class, gender, religion, ethnicity, and locality gave way to a vibrant, commercialized mass culture that provided all Americans with standardized entertainment and information.

The revolt against Victorianism

The 1890s witnessed a momentous change in American values. During that decade, Americans were engaged in a full-scale revolt against a stifling Victorian code of propriety and the confining routine of urban, industrial life. This revolt was apparent, as historian John Higham has shown, in a growing preoccupation with strength, virility, and energy. Victorian values, stressing self-control and domesticity, gave way to a craving for what Theodore Roosevelt called "the strenuous life." The new mood could be seen in a rage for competitive athletics and team sports. It was in the 1890s that boxing became the nation's most popular sport, that basketball was invented, that football swept the nation's college campuses, and that golf, track, and wrestling became popular pastimes. The celebration of vigor and virility could also be seen in a new enthusiasm for outdoor activities, like hiking, hunting, fishing, mountain-climbing, camping, and bicycling.

A new bold, energetic spirit was also apparent in popular music, in a craze for ragtime, jazz, and patriotic military marches. The cult of toughness and virility appeared in the growth of aggressive nationalism (culminating in 1898 in America's "Splendid Little War" against Spain), the condemnation of sissies and stuffed shirts, and the growing popularity of aggressively masculine Western novels, like Owen Wister's *The Virginian*. Toward the end of the century, the New Woman – personified by the tall, athletic Gibson Girl – supplanted the frail, submissive Victorian woman as a cultural ideal. The "new women" began to work outside the home in rapidly increasing numbers, to attend high school and college, and to press for the vote. During the 1890s, American popular culture was in full-scale revolt against the stifling Victorian code of propriety.

The shift in values from a Victorian emphasis on civilized cultivation to a new stress on leisure and self-fulfillment is dramatically illustrated by the rise of the modern amusement park. During the mid-nineteenth century, urban reformers responded to the rapid growth of cities by pressing for the construction of parks to serve as rural retreats in the midst of urban jungles. Frederick Law Olmsted, the designer of New York City's Central Park, believed that the park's bucolic calm would instill the values of sobriety and self-control in the urban masses.

But by the end of the century it was clear that the urban masses wanted more excitement. This was clearly seen at the World's Columbian Exposition of 1893 in Chicago, where the most popular area was the boisterous, rowdy Midway. Here, visitors rode the Ferris wheel and watched "Little Egypt" perform exotic dances. Entrepreneurs were quick to satisfy the public's desire for fast-paced entertainment. During the 1890s, a series of popular amusement parks opened in Coney Island. Unlike Central Park, Coney Island glorified adventure. It offered exotic, dreamland landscapes and a free, loose social environment. At Coney Island men could remove their coats and ties, and both sexes could enjoy rare personal freedom.

Coney Island also encouraged new values. If Central Park reinforced self-control and delayed gratification, Coney Island stressed the emerging consumer-oriented values of extravagance, gaiety, abandon, revelry, and instant gratification. It attracted working-class Americans who longed for at least a taste of the "good life." If a person could never hope to own a mansion in Newport, he could for a few dimes experience the exotic pleasures of Luna Park or Dreamland Park.

Even the rides in the amusement parks were designed to create illusions and break down reality. Mirrors distorted people's images and rides threw them off balance. At Luna Park, the "Witching Waves" simulated the bobbing of a ship at high sea, and the "Tickler" featured spinning circular cars that threw riders together. At the end of the nineteenth century, Americans, in revolt against stifling Victorian norms and the restrictions of urban and industrial life, felt a craving for intense physical experience. In part, this desire be would met through sports, athletics, and out-of-doors activities. But it would primarily be met vicariously – through mass culture. Craving more intense physical and emotional experience, eager to break free of the confining boundaries of genteel culture, Americans turned to new kinds of newspapers and magazines, new forms of commercial entertainment, and, above all, the movies.

The rise of mass communications

The 1890s and 1900s were critical decades in the emergence of modern American mass culture. It was in those years that the modern instruments of mass communication –

the mass-circulation metropolitan newspaper, the best-seller, the mass-market magazine, national advertising campaigns, and the movies – emerged. It was also in those years that American culture made a critical shift to commercialized forms of entertainment.

The urban tabloid was the first instrument of modern mass culture to appear. Pioneered by Joseph Pulitzer's New York *World* and William Randolph Hearst's New York *Journal*, these popular newspapers differed dramatically from the staid upper-class and the staunchly partisan political newspapers that dominated late nineteenth-century journalism: They featured banner headlines; a multitude of photographs and cartoons; an emphasis on local news, crime and scandal, society news, and sports; and large ads, which made up half of a paper's content compared to just 30 percent in earlier newspapers. To make them easier to read on an omnibus or street railway, page size was cut, stories shortened, and the text heavily illustrated with drawings and photographs.

Entertainment was a stock-in-trade of yellow journalism (named from the "yellow kid" comic strip that appeared in Hearst's *Journal*). Among the innovations introduced by yellow journalists were the first color comic strips, advice columns, women's pages, fashion pages, and sports pages. By using simple words, a lively style, and many illustrations, the yellow journalism could reach a mass audience that included many immigrants who understood little English. By 1905, Pulitzer's *World* boasted a circulation of 2 million.

Also during the 1890s, the world of magazine publishing was revolutionized by the rise of the country's first mass-circulation national magazines. After the Civil War, the magazine field was dominated by a small number of sedate magazines – like *The Atlantic*, *Harper's*, and *Scribner's* – written for "gentle" readers of highly intellectual tastes. The poetry, serious fiction, and wood engravings that filled these monthlies' pages rigidly conformed to upper-class Victorian standards of taste. These magazines embodied what the philosopher George Santayana called the "genteel tradition": the idea that art and literature should reinforce morality, not portray reality. Art and literature, the custodians of culture believed, should transcend the real and uphold the ideal. Poet James Russell Lowell spoke for other genteel writers when he said that no man should describe any activity that would make his wife or daughter blush.

The founders of the nation's first mass-circulation magazines considered the older "quality" magazines stale and elitist. In contrast, their magazines featured practical advice, popularized science, gossip, human interest stories, celebrity profiles, interviews, "muckraking" investigations, pictures, articles on timely topics – and a profusion of ads. Instead of cultivating a select audience, the new magazines had a very different set of priorities: by running popular articles, editors sought to maximize circulation, which, in turn, attracted advertising that kept the magazine's price low. By 1900, the nation's largest magazine, the *Ladies' Home Journal*, reached 850,000 subscribers – more than eight times the readership of *Scribner's* or *Harper's*.

The end of the nineteenth century also marked a critical turning point in the history of book publishing, as marketing wizards like Frank Doubleday organized the first national book promotional campaigns, created the modern best-seller, and transformed popular writers like Jack London into celebrities. The world of the Victorian man of letters, the defender of "Culture" against "Anarchy," had ended.

In 1898, the National Biscuit Company (Nabisco) launched the first million-dollar national advertising campaign. It succeeded in making Uneeda biscuits and their waterproof "In-er-Seal" box popular household items. During the 1880s and 1890s, patent medicine manufacturers, department stores, and producers of low-price, packaged consumer goods (like Campbell Soups, H.J. Heinz, and Quaker Oats), developed modern advertising techniques. Where earlier advertisers made little use of brand names, illustrations, or trademarks, the new ads employed snappy slogans and colorful packages. As early as 1900, advertisements began to use psychology to arouse consumer demand, by suggesting that a product would contribute to the consumer's social and psychic well-being. For purchases to be promoted, observed a trade journal in 1890, a consumer "must be aroused, excited, terrified." Listerine mouthwash promised to cure "halitosis"; Scott tissue claimed to prevent infections caused by harsh toilet paper.

By stressing instant gratification and personal fulfillment in their ads, modern advertisers helped undermine an earlier Victorian ethos emphasizing thrift, self-denial, delayed gratification, and hard work. In various ways, advertising transformed Americans from "savers" to "spenders" and told them to give in to their desire for luxury.

The creators of the modern instruments of mass culture tended to share a common element in their background. Most were "outsiders" – recent immigrants or Southerners, Midwesterners, or Westerners. Joseph Pulitzer was an Austrian Jew; the pioneering "new" magazine editors Edward W. Bok and Samuel Sidney McClure were also first-generation immigrants. Where the "genteel tradition" was dominated by men and women from Boston's Brahmin culture or upper-class New York, the men who created modern mass culture had their initial training in daily newspapers, commerce, and popular entertainment – and, as a result, were more in touch with popular tastes. As outsiders, the creators of mass culture betrayed an almost voyeuristic interest in what they called the "romance of real life": with high life, low life, power, and status.

The new forms of popular culture that they helped create shared a common style: simple, direct, realistic, and colloquial. The 1890s were the years when a florid Victorian style was overthrown by a new "realistic" aesthetic. At various levels of American culture, writers and artists rebelled against the moralism and sentimentality of Victorian culture and sought to portray life objectively and truthfully, without idealization or avoidance of the ugly. The quest for realism took a variety of guises: it could be seen in the naturalism of writers like Theodore Dreiser and Stephen Crane, with their nightmarish depictions of urban poverty and exploitation; in the paintings of the "ashcan" school of art, with their vivid portraits of tenements and congested streets; and in the forceful, colorful prose of tabloid reporters and muckraking journalists, who cut through the Victorian veil of reticence surrounding such topics as sex, political corruption, and working conditions in industry.

The most influential innovations in mass culture would take place after the turn of the century. Although Thomas Edison first successfully projected moving pictures on a screen in 1896, it would not be until 1903 that Edwin S. Porter's *The Great Train Robbery* – the first American movie to tell a story – demonstrated the commercial appeal of motion pictures. And while Guglielmo Marconi showed the possibility of wireless communication in 1895, commercial radio broadcasting did not begin until 1920 and commercial television broadcasts only started in 1939. These new instruments of mass communications would reach audiences of unprecedented size. As early as 1922, the movies sold 40 million tickets a week and radios could be found in 3 million homes.

The emergence of these modern forms of mass communications had far-reaching effects upon American society. They broke down the isolation of local neighborhoods and communities and ensured that for the first time all Americans, regardless of their class, ethnicity, or locality, shared standardized information and entertainment.

Commercialized leisure

Of all the differences between the nineteenth and twentieth centuries, one of the most striking involves the rapid growth of commercialized entertainment. For much of the nineteenth century, commercial amusements were viewed as suspect. Drawing on the Puritan criticisms of play and recreation and a Republican ideology that was hostile to luxury, hedonism, and extravagance, American Victorians tended to associate theaters, dance halls, circuses, and organized sports with such vices as gambling, swearing, drinking, and immoral sexual behavior. In the late nineteenth century, however, a new outlook – which revered leisure and play – began to challenge Victorian prejudices.

During the first 20 years of the new century, attendance at professional baseball games doubled. Vaudeville, too, increased in popularity, featuring singing, dancing, skits, comics, acrobats, and magicians. Amusement parks, penny arcades, dance halls, and other commercial amusements flourished. As early as 1910, when there were 10,000 movie theaters, the movies had become the nation's most popular form of commercial entertainment.

The rise of these new kinds of commercialized amusements radically reshaped the nature of American leisure activities. Earlier in the nineteenth century, as Kathy Peiss has shown, leisure activities were sharply segregated by gender, class, and ethnicity. The wealthy attended their own exclusive theaters, concert halls, museums, restaurants, and sporting clubs. For the working class, leisure and amusement were rooted in particular ethnic communities and neighborhoods, each with its own saloons, churches, fraternal organizations, and organized sports. Men and women participated in radically different kinds of leisure activities. Many men (particularly bachelors and immigrants) relaxed in barber shops, billiard halls, and bowling alleys; joined volunteer fire companies or militias; and patronized saloons, gambling halls, and race tracks. Women took part in church activities and socialized with neighbors and relatives.

After 1880, as incomes rose and leisure time expanded, new commercialized forms of cross-class, mixed-sex amusements proliferated. Entertainment became a major industry. Vaudeville theaters attracted women as well as men. The young, in particular, increasingly sought pleasure, escape, and the freedom to experiment in mixed-sex relationships in relatively inexpensive amusement parks, dance halls, urban nightclubs, and, above all, nickelodeons and movie theaters, free of parental control.

The transformation of Coney Island from a center of male vice – of brothels, saloons, and gambling dens – into the nation's first modern amusement park, complete with Ferris wheels, hootchie-kootchie girls, restaurants, and concert halls – symbolized the emergence of a new leisure culture, emphasizing excitement, glamour, fashion, and romance. Its informality and sheer excitement attracted people of every class.

If Coney Island offered an escape from an oppressive urban landscape to an exotic one, the new motion picture industry would offer an even less expensive, more convenient escape. During the early twentieth century it quickly developed into the country's most popular and influential form of art and entertainment.

The Birth of the Movies

Beside Macy's Department Store in Herald Square in New York City there is a plaque commemorating the first public showing of a motion picture on a screen in the United States. It was here, on April 23, 1896, at Koster and Bial's Music Hall in New York City, that Thomas Alva Edison presented a show which included scenes of the surf breaking on a beach, a comic boxing exhibition, and two young women dancing. A review in the *New York Times* described the exhibition as "all wonderfully real and singularly exhilarating."

The pre-history of motion pictures

For centuries, people had wrestled with the problem of realistically reproducing moving images. A discovery by Ptolemy in the second century provided the first step. He noticed that there is a slight imperfection in human perception: the retina retains an image for a fraction of a second after the image has changed or disappeared. Because of this phenomenon, known as the "persistence of vision," a person would merge a rapid succession of individual images into the illusion of continuous motion.

The first successful efforts to project lifelike images on a screen took place in the mid-seventeenth century. By 1659, a Dutch scientist named Christiaan Huygens had invented the magic lantern, the forerunner of the modern slide projector, which he used to project medical drawings before an audience. A magic lantern used sunlight (or another light source) to illuminate a hand-painted glass transparency and project it through a simple lens. In the 1790s, the Belgian Etienne Gaspar Robert terrified audiences with fantasmagorie exhibitions, which used magic lanterns to project images of phantoms and apparitions of the dead. By the mid-nineteenth century, illustrated lectures and dramatic readings had become common. To create the illusion of motion, magic lantern operators used multiple lanterns and mirrors to move the image.

The first true moving images appeared in the 1820s, when the concept of the persistence of vision was used to create children's toys and other simple entertainments. The thaumatrope, which appeared in 1826, was a simple disk with separate images printed on each side (for example, a bird on one side and a cage on the other). When rapidly spun, the images appeared to blend together (so that the bird seemed to be inside the cage). In 1834 an Austrian military officer, Baron Franz von Uchatius, developed a more sophisticated device called the "Phenakistoscope." It consisted of a disk, with a series of slots along its edge, which was printed with a series of slightly differing pictures. When the disk was spun in front of a mirror and the viewer looked through the slots, the pictures appeared to move. A simpler way to display movement was the flip book, which became popular by the late 1860s. Each page showed a subject in a subtly different position. When a reader flipped the book's pages, the pictures gave the illusion of movement.

These early devices were not very satisfactory. The slides used in early magic lanterns had to be painted by hand. The pictures displayed by the Phenakistoscope or flip books could not be viewed by more than one person at a time. The solution to these problems lay in photography. In 1826, a French inventor named Joseph Nicéphore Niépce made the first true photograph. He placed a camera obscura (a box with a tiny opening on one side that admitted light) at his window and exposed a metal plate coated with light-sensitive chemicals for eight hours. During the 1830s another French inventor, Louis Daguerre, improved Niépce's technique and created the daguerreotype, the first popular form of photography.

Unfortunately, the daguerreotype was not very useful to the inventors who wanted to produce motion pictures. The process used expensive copper plates coated with silver and required a subject to remain motionless for 15 to 30 seconds. During the mid-nineteenth century, however, two key technical advances radically improved the photographic process. The first was the replacement of copper plates with less expensive glass plates, light-sensitive paper, and, in 1880, flexible film. The second advance involved the development of new film coatings which significantly reduced exposure time and gave photographers greater mobility. By the late 1870s, the introduction of "dry-process plates" using gelatin emulsion reduced exposure time to just $\frac{1}{25}$th of a second and freed photographers from having to immediately process their prints.

The first successful photographs of motion grew out of a California railroad tycoon's $25,000 bet. In 1872, California Governor Leland Stanford hired a photographer named Eadweard Muybridge to help settle a bet. An avid horse breeder, Stanford had wagered that a galloping horse lifts all four hoofs off the ground simultaneously. In 1878, the English-born photographer lined up 24 cameras along the edge of a race track, with strings attached to the shutters. When the horse ran by, it tripped the shutters, producing 24 closely spaced pictures that proved Stanford's contention.

Four years later a French physiologist, Etienne-Jules Marey, became the first person to take pictures of motion with a single camera. Marey built his camera in the shape of a rifle. At the end of the barrel, he placed a circular photographic plate. A small motor rotated the plate after Marey snapped the shutter. With his camera, Marey could take 12 pictures a second.

In 1887, Thomas Edison gave William K.L. Dickson, one of his leading inventors, the task of developing a motion picture apparatus. Edison envisioned a machine "that should do for the eye what the phonograph did for the ear." Dickson initially modeled his device on Edison's phonograph, placing tiny pictures on a revolving drum. A light inside the drum was supposed to illuminate the pictures. Then he decided to use the flexible celluloid film that George Eastman had invented in 1880 and had begun to use in his Kodak camera. Dickson added perforations to the edge of the film strip to help it feed evenly into his camera.

To display their films, Dickson and Edison devised a coin-operated peepshow device called a "kinetoscope." Because the kinetoscope could only hold 50 feet of film, its films lasted just 35 to 40 seconds. This was too brief to tell a story; the first kinetoscope films were simply scenes of everyday life, like the first film "Fred Ott's Sneeze," reenactments of historical events, photographed bits of vaudeville routines, and pictures of well-known celebrities. Nevertheless, the kinetoscope was an instant success. By 1894 coin-operated kinetoscopes had begun to appear in hotels, department stores, saloons, and amusement arcades called nickelodeons.

Eager to maximize his profits, Edison showed no interest in building a movie projector. "If we make this screen machine," he argued, "… it will spoil everything." As a result, Edison's competitors would take the lead in developing screen projection.

In devising a practical movie projector, inventors faced a serious technical problem: the projector had to be capable of stopping a frame momentarily, so that the image could be clearly fixed in the viewer's retina, and then advance the film quickly between frames. Two French brothers – Auguste and Louis Lumière – were the first to solve this problem. They borrowed the design of their stop-action device from the sewing machine, which holds the material still during stitching before advancing it forward. In 1894, the Lumière brothers introduced the portable motion picture camera and projector.

Finally recognizing the potential of the motion picture projector, Edison entered into an agreement with a Washington, DC realtor, Thomas Armat, who had designed a workable projector. In April 1896 the two men unveiled the Vitascope and presented the first motion pictures on a public screen in the United States.

Competition in the early movie industry was fierce. To force their competitors out of the industry, moviemakers turned to the courts, launching over 200 patent infringement suits. To protect their profits and bring order to the industry, Edison and a number of his competitors decided to cooperate by establishing the Motion Picture Patents Company in 1909, consisting of six American companies and two French firms. Members of the trust agreed that only they had the right to make, print, or distribute cameras, projectors, or films. The trust also negotiated an exclusive agreement with Eastman Kodak for commercial-quality film stock.

Led by Carl Laemmle, later the founder of Universal Pictures, independent distributors and exhibitors filed a restraint of trade lawsuit under the Sherman Anti-Trust Act. A court ruled in the independents' behalf in 1915 and the decision was affirmed by a higher court in 1918. Yet even before the courts ruled in their favor, the independents broke the power of the trust in the marketplace. The trust viewed movies, in the famous words of director Erich von Stroheim, as so many sausages to be ground out as quickly as possible and rented at 10 cents a foot. But the independent moviemakers succeeded in defeating the trust with two potent weapons: the introduction of longer films that told complex stories, and the emergence of the star system.

During film's first decade – from 1896 to 1905 – movies were little more than a novelty, often used as a "chaser" to signal the end of a show in a vaudeville theater. These early films are utterly unlike anything seen today. They lasted just 7 to 10 minutes – too brief to tell anything more than the simplest story. They used a cast of anonymous actors – for the simple reason that the camera was set back so far that it was impossible to clearly make out the actors' faces. As late as 1908, a movie actor made no more than $8 a day and received no credit on the screen.

In 1905, hundreds of little movie theaters opened, called nickelodeons, since they sold admission nickel by nickel. By 1908 there were an estimated 8,000 to 10,000 nickelodeons. Contrary to popular belief, the nickelodeon's audience was not confined to the poor, the young, or the immigrant. From the start, theaters were situated in rural areas and in middle-class as well as working-class neighborhoods. Nevertheless, the movies attracted audiences of an unprecedented size, as a result of their low admission prices, "democratic" seating arrangements, convenient time schedules (films were shown again and again), and lack of spoken dialogue, which allowed non-English-speaking immigrants to enjoy films.

By 1907, narrative films had begun to increase in number. But most films still emphasized stunts and chases and real-life events – like scenes of yacht races or train crashes – and were rented or sold by the foot regardless of subject matter. Exhibitors were expected to assemble scenes together to form a larger show.

The formation of the movie trust ushered in a period of rationalization within the film industry. Camera and projecting equipment was standardized; film rental fees were fixed; theaters were upgraded; and the practice of selling films outright ended, which improved the quality of movies by removing damaged prints from circulation. This was also a period of intense artistic and technical innovation, as pioneering directors like David Wark Griffith and others created a new language of film and revolutionized screen narrative.

With just six months of film experience, Griffith, a former stage actor, was hired as a director by the Biograph Company and promised $50 a week and one-twentieth of a cent for every foot of film sold to a rental exchange. Each week, Griffith turned out two or three one-reelers. While earlier directors had used such cinematic devices as close-ups, slow motion, fade-ins and fade-outs, lighting effects, and editing before, Griffith's great contribution to the movie industry was to show how these techniques could be used to create a wholly new style of storytelling, distinct from the theater.

Griffith's approach to movie storytelling has been aptly called "photographic realism." This is not to say that he merely wished to record a story accurately; rather, he sought to convey the illusion of realism. He used editing to convey simultaneous events or the passage of time. He demanded that his performers act in a more lifelike manner, avoiding the broad, exaggerated gestures and pantomiming of emotions that characterized the nineteenth-century stage. He wanted his performers to take on a role rather than directly addressing the camera. Above all, he used close-ups, lighting, editing, and framing and other cinematic techniques to convey suspense and other emotions and to focus the audience's attention on individual performers.

By focusing the camera on particular actors and actresses, Griffith inadvertently encouraged the development of the star system. As early as 1910, newspapers were deluged with requests for actors' names. Most studios refused to divulge their identities, fearing the salary demands of popular performers. But the film trust's leading opponent, Carl Laemmle, was convinced that the key to financial stability lay in producing films featuring popular stars. As one industry observer put it, "In the 'star' your producer gets not only a 'production' value … but a 'trademark' value, and an 'insurance' value which are … very potent in guaranteeing the sale of this product." In 1910 Laemmle produced the first star; he lured Florence Lawrence, the most popular anonymous star, away from Biograph, and launched an unprecedented publicity campaign on her behalf. As the star system emerged, salaries soared. In the course of just two years, the salary of actress Mary Pickford rose from less than $400 a week in 1914 to $10,000 a week in 1916.

Meanwhile, an influx of feature-length films from Europe, which attracted premium admission prices, led a New York nickelodeon owner named Adolph Zukor to produce four- and five-reel films featuring readily identifiable stars. By 1916, Zukor had taken control of Paramount Pictures, a movie distributor, and had instituted the practice of "block booking" – requiring theaters to book a number of films rather than just a single film. Within a few years, Zukor's company had achieved vertical integration – not only producing films, but distributing them and owning the theaters that exhibited them.

During the second decade of the twentieth century, immigrants like Laemmle and Zukor came to dominate the movie business. Unlike Edison and the other American-born, Protestant businessmen who had controlled the early film industry, these immigrant entrepreneurs had a better sense of what the public wanted to see. Virtually all of these new producers had emigrated to the United States from central Europe and were Jewish. Not part of the Victorian ethos that still held sway in "respectable" Protestant America, they proved better able to exploit ribald humor and sex in their films. Less conservative than the American-born producers, they were more willing to experiment with such innovations as the star system and feature-length productions. Since many had come to the film industry from the garment and fur trades – where fashions change rapidly and the successful businessman is one who stays constantly in touch with the latest styles – they tried to give the public what it wanted. As Samuel Goldwyn, one of the leading moguls, noted,

> If the audience don't like a picture, they have a good reason. The public is never wrong. I don't go for all this thing that when I have a failure, it is because the audience doesn't have the taste or education, or isn't sensitive enough. The public pays money. It wants to be entertained. That's all I know.

With this philosophy the outsiders wrestled control over the industry away from the American-born producers.

During the 1920s and 1930s, a small group of film companies consolidated their control. Known as the "Big Five" – Paramount, Warner Brothers, RKO, 20th Century Fox, and Lowe's (MGM) – and the "Little Three" – Universal, Columbia, and United Artists – they formed fully integrated companies. With the exception of United Artists, which was solely a distribution company, the "majors" owned their own production facilities, ran their own worldwide distribution networks, and controlled theater chains that were committed to showing the company's products. And at the head of each major studio was a powerful mogul – such giants as Adolph Zukor, William Fox, Louis B. Mayer, Samuel Goldwyn, Carl Laemmle, Harry Cohn, Joseph Schenck, and the Warner brothers – who determined what the public was going to see. It was their vision – patriotic, sentimental, secular, and generally politically conservative – which millions of Americans shared weekly at local movie theaters. And as expressed by such producers as Irving Thalberg, Darryl F. Zanuck, and David O. Selznick, it was a powerful vision indeed.

American film in the silent era

Some film historians, like Lewis Jacobs and David Robinson, have argued that early silent films revolved around "characteristically working-class settings," and expressed the interests of the poor in their struggles with the rich and powerful. Other scholars maintain that early movies drew largely upon conventions, stock characters, and routines derived from vaudeville, popular melodrama, Wild West shows, comic strips, and other forms of late nineteenth-century popular entertainment. Given the fact that thousands of films were released during the silent era and relatively few have survived, it is dangerous to generalize about movie content. Nevertheless, certain statements about these films do seem warranted.

American films were born in an age of reform, and many early silent movies took as their subject matter the major social and moral issues of the Progressive era: birth control, child labor, divorce, immigration, political corruption, poverty, prisons, prostitution, and women's suffrage. The tone of these films varied widely – some were realistic and straightforward; others treated their subjects with sentimentality or humor; and many transformed complex social issues into personal melodramas. Yet there can be no doubt that many silent films dealt at least obliquely with the dominant issues of the time.

Although many Americans today think of the films of the silent era as relics of a simpler, more innocent age, in fact more serious social and political themes lurked "behind the mask of innocence." As Kevin Brownlow has demonstrated, despite their well-dressed tramps and child-like waifs, many early silent films were preoccupied with such broad issues as the causes of crime, the nature of political corruption, shifting sexual norms, and the changing role of women. The silent screen offered vivid glimpses of urban tenements and ethnic ghettoes; gangsters, loan sharks, drug addicts, and panderers populated the screen and provided a graphic record of "how the other half lives."

In addition, many early films were laced with anti-authority themes, poking fun at bumbling cops, corrupt politicians, and intrusive upper-class reformers. Highly physical slapstick comedy offered a particularly potent vehicle of social criticism, spoofing the pretensions of the wealthy and presenting sympathetic portraits of the poor. Mack Sennett, one of the most influential directors of silent comedy, later recalled the themes of his films: "I especially liked the reduction of authority to absurdity, the notion that sex could be funny, and the bold insults hurled at Pretension."

Many films of the early silent era dealt with gender relations. Before 1905, as Kathy Peiss has argued, movie screens were filled with salacious sexual imagery and risqué humor, drawn from burlesque halls and vaudeville theaters. Early films offered many glimpses of women disrobing or of passionate kisses. As the movies' female audience grew, sexual titillation and voyeurism persisted. But an ever-increasing number of films dealt with the changing work and sexual roles of women in a more sophisticated manner. While D.W. Griffith's films presented an idealized picture of the frail Victorian child-woman, and showed an almost obsessive preoccupation with female honor and chastity, other silent movies presented quite different images of femininity. These included the exotic, sexually aggressive vamp; the athletic, energetic "serial queen"; the street-smart urban working gal, who repels the sexual advances of her lascivious boss; and cigarette-smoking, alcohol-drinking chorus girls or burlesque queens.

In the late 1910s and the 1920s, as Lary May has demonstrated, the movies began to shed their Victorian moralism, sentimentality, and reformism and increasingly expressed new themes: glamour, sophistication, exoticism, urbanity, and sex appeal. New kinds of movie stars appeared: the mysterious sex goddess, personified by Greta Garbo; the passionate, hot-blooded Latin lover, epitomized by Rudolph Valentino; and the flapper, first brought to the screen by Coleen Moore, with her bobbed hair, skimpy skirts, and incandescent vivacity. New genres also appeared: swashbuckling adventures; sophisticated sex comedies revolving around the issue of marital fidelity; romantic dramas examining the manners and morals of the well-bred and well-to-do; and tales of "flaming youth" and the new sexual freedom.

During the 1920s a sociologist named Herbert Blumer interviewed students and young workers to assess the impact of movies on their lives, and concluded that the effect was to reorient their lives away from ethnic and working-class communities toward a broader consumer culture. Observed one high-school student: "The daydreams instigated by the movies consist of clothes, ideas on furnishings and manners." Said an African American student: "The movies have often made me dissatisfied with my neighborhood because when I see a movie, the beautiful castle, palace ... and beautiful house, I wish my home was something like these." Hollywood not only expressed popular values, aspirations, and fantasies, it also promoted cultural change.

The movies as a cultural battleground

Reformers of the Progressive era took a highly ambivalent view of the movies. Some praised movies as a benign alternative to the saloon. Others viewed nickelodeons and movie theaters as breeding grounds of crime and sexual promiscuity. In 1907, the *Chicago Tribune* threw its editorial weight against the movies, declaring that they were "without a redeeming feature to warrant their existence … ministering to the lowest passions of childhood." That year, Chicago established the nation's first censorship board, to protect its population "against the evil influence of obscene and immoral representations." Also in 1907, and again in 1908, New York's mayor, under pressure from various religious and reform groups, temporarily closed down all of the city's nickelodeons and movie theaters.

Many middle-class vice crusaders regarded the movies with horror and struggled to regulate the new medium. A presidential study concluded that films encouraged "illicit lovemaking and iniquity." A Worcester, Massachusetts, newspaper described the city's movie theaters as centers of delinquent activity, and reported that female gang members "confessed that their early tendencies toward evil came from seeing moving pictures." Several bills were introduced in Congress calling for movie censorship.

The drive to censor films spread from Chicago to other municipalities and states, especially after a 1915 Supreme Court ruling that movies were not protected by the First Amendment because they "were a business pure and simple … not to be regarded as part of the press of the country or as organs of public opinion." Eager to combat the trend toward local censorship, movie manufacturers worked with moral reformers in New York to establish the voluntary National Board of Censorship of Motion Pictures in 1909, to review the movies' treatment of violence, drugs, prostitution, and, above all, sexual immorality (such as "over-passionate love scenes; stimulating close dancing; unnecessary bedroom scenes in negligee; excessively low-cut gowns; [and] undue or suggestive display of the person").

After World War I a series of sex scandals raised renewed threats of censorship or boycotts. William Desmond Taylor, a director, was found murdered under suspicious circumstances; actor Wallace Reid committed suicide amid allegations of drug addiction; and comedian Fatty Arbuckle was acquitted of rape and complicity in murder. To clean up Hollywood's image, the industry banned Arbuckle and a number of other individuals implicated in scandals, and appointed Will Hays, President Warren Harding's Postmaster General, to head their trade organization. Hays introduced a voluntary code of standards.

The rise of Hollywood and the arrival of sound

In cinema's earliest days, the film industry was based in the nation's theatrical center, New York, and most films were made in New York or New Jersey, although a few were shot in Chicago, Florida, and elsewhere. Beginning in 1908, however, a growing number of filmmakers located in southern California, drawn by cheap land and labor, the ready accessibility of varied scenery, and a climate ideal for year-round outdoor filming. Contrary to popular mythology, moviemakers did not move to Hollywood to escape the film trust; the first studio to move to Hollywood, Selig, was actually a trust member.

By the early 1920s, Hollywood had become the world's film capital. It produced virtually all films show in the United States and received 80 percent of the revenue from films shown abroad. During the 1920s Hollywood bolstered its position as world leader by recruiting many of Europe's most talented actors and actresses, such as Greta Garbo and Hedy Lamarr, directors such as Ernst Lubitsch and Josef von Sternberg, as well as camera operators, lighting technicians, and set designers. By the end of the decade, Hollywood claimed to be the nation's fifth largest industry, attracting 83 cents out of every dollar Americans spent on amusement.

Hollywood had also come to symbolize "the new morality" of the 1920s – a mixture of extravagance, glamour, hedonism, and fun. Where else but Hollywood would an actress like Gloria Swanson bathe in a solid gold bathtub, or a screen cowboy like Tom Mix have his named raised atop his house in six-foot-high letters?

During the 1920s, movie attendance soared. By the middle of the decade 50 million people a week went to the movies – the equivalent of half the nation's population. In Chicago in 1929, theaters had enough seats for half the city's population to attend a movie each day.

As attendance rose, the moviegoing experience underwent a profound change. During the twentieth century's first two decades, moviegoing tended to conform to class and ethnic divisions. Urban workers attended movie houses located in their own working-class and ethnic neighborhoods, where admission was extremely inexpensive (averaging just 7 cents during the 1910s), and a movie was often accompanied by an amateur talent show or a performance by a local ethnic troupe. These working-class theaters were rowdy, high-spirited centers of neighborhood sociability, where mothers brought their babies and audiences cheered, jeered, shouted, whistled, and stamped their feet.

The theaters patronized by the middle class were quite different. Late in the new century's first decade, theaters in downtown or middle-class neighborhoods became increasingly luxurious. At first many of these theaters were designed in the same styles as many other public buildings, but by around 1915 movie houses began feature French Renaissance, Egyptian, Moorish, and other exotic decors. The Strand Theater in Worcester, Massachusetts boasted having "red plush seats," "luxurious carpets," "rich velour curtains," "finely appointed toilet rooms," and a $15,000 organ. Unlike the working-class movie houses, which showed films continuously, these high-class theaters had specific show times and well-groomed, uniformed ushers to enforce standards of decorum.

During the late 1920s independent neighborhood theaters catering to a distinct working-class audience were bought up by regional and national chains. As a result, the moviegoing experience became more uniform, with working-class and middle-class theaters offering the same programs. Especially after the introduction of the "talkies," many working-class movie houses shut down, unable to meet the cost of converting to sound.

For decades, engineers had searched for a practical technology to add synchronized recorded sound to the movies. In the 1890s, Thomas Edison tried unsuccessfully to popularize the kinetophone, which combined a kinetoscope with a phonograph. In 1923 Lee De Forest, an American inventor, demonstrated the practicality of placing a soundtrack directly on a film strip, presenting a newsreel interview with President Calvin Coolidge and musical accompaniments to several films. But the film industry showed remarkably little interest in sound, despite the growing popularity of radio. Hollywood feared the high cost of converting to sound technology.

Warner Brothers, a struggling industry newcomer, turned to sound as a way to compete with its larger rivals. A prerecorded musical soundtrack eliminated the expense of live entertainment. In 1926, Warner Brothers released the film *Don Juan* – the first film with a synchronized film score – along with a program of talking shorts. The popularity of *The Jazz Singer*, which was released in 1927, erased any doubts about the popular appeal of sound, and within a year 300 theaters were wired for sound.

The arrival of sound produced a sharp upsurge in movie attendance, which jumped from 50 million a week in the mid-1920s to 110 million in 1929. But it also produced a number of fundamental transformations in the movies themselves. As Robert Ray has shown, sound made the movies more American. The words that Al Jolson used in *The Jazz Singer* to herald the arrival of sound in the movies – "You ain't heard nothing yet" – embodied the new slangy, vernacular tone of the talkies. Distinctive American accents and inflections quickly appeared on the screen, like James Cagney's New Yorkese or Gary Cooper's Western drawl. The introduction of sound also encouraged new film genres, like the musical, the gangster film, and comedies that relied on wit rather than slapstick.

In addition, the talkies dramatically changed the moviegoing experience, especially for the working class. Where many working-class audiences had provided silent films with a spoken dialogue, moviegoers were now expected to remain quiet. As one film historian has observed: "The talking audience for silent pictures became a silent audience for talking pictures." Moreover, the stage shows and other forms of live entertainment that had appeared in silent movie houses increasingly disappeared, replaced by newsreels and animated shorts.

Movies meet the Great Depression

In 1934 Will Hays, head of the Motion Picture Producers and Distributors Association, said that "No medium has contributed more greatly than the film to the maintenance of the national morale during a period featured by revolution, riot and political turmoil in other countries." During the Great Depression, Hollywood played a valuable psychological and ideological role, providing reassurance and hope to a demoralized nation. Even at the Depression's depths, 60 to 80 million Americans attended the movies each week, and in the face of doubt and despair films helped sustain national morale.

Although the movie industry considered itself Depression-proof, Hollywood was no more immune to the Depression's effects than any other industry. To finance the purchase of movie theaters and the conversion to sound, the studios had tripled their debts during the mid- and late 1920s to $410 million. As a result, the industry's very viability seemed in question. By 1933, movie attendance and industry revenues had fallen by 40 percent. To survive, the industry trimmed salaries and production costs, and closed the doors of a third of the nation's theaters. To boost attendance, theaters resorted to such gimmicks as lower admission prices (cut by as much as 25 cents), double bills, give-aways of free dishes, and Bank Night – in which customers who received a lucky number won a cash prize.

Why did Depression America go to the movies? Escapism is what most people assume. At the movies they could forget their troubles for a couple of hours. Depression films, one left-wing critic maintained, were a modern form of bread and circuses, distracting Americans from their problems, reinforcing older values, and dampening political radicalism. Yet movies were more than mere escapism. Most films of the Depression years were grounded in the social realities of the time. The most realistic were social problem films – like *I am a Fugitive from a Chain Gang* – "torn from the headlines," usually by Warner Brothers or Columbia Pictures. Yet even the most outrageously extravagant Busby Berkeley musicals – portraying chorus girls as flowers or mechanical wind-up dolls – were generally set against recognizable Depression backdrops.

The kinds of movies that Hollywood produced during the Depression underwent sharp changes as the public mood shifted. During the Depression's earliest years, a profound sense of despair was reflected in the kinds of characters Americans watched on the screen: a succession of tommy-gun-toting gangsters, haggard prostitutes, sleazy backroom politicians, cynical journalists, and shyster lawyers. The screen comedies released at the Depression's depths expressed an almost anarchistic disdain for traditional institutions and conventions. In the greatest comedies of the early Depression, the Marx Brothers spoofed everything from patriotism (in *Duck Soup*) to universities (in *Horse Feathers*); W.C. Fields ridiculed families and children; and Mae West used sexual innuendo and double entendres to make fun of the middle-class code of sexual propriety, with lines like "When a girl goes wrong, men go right after her."

The gangster pictures and sexually suggestive comedies of the early 1930s provoked outrage – and threats of boycotts – from many Protestant and Catholic religious groups. In 1934, Hollywood's producers' association responded by setting up a bureau (later known as the "Breen Office") to review every script that the major studios proposed to shoot and to screen every film before it was released to ensure that the picture did not violate the organization's "Code to Govern the Making of Talking, Synchronized and Silent Motion Pictures." The Production Code, as it is known, drafted by a Jesuit priest, Father Daniel Lord, had been originally adopted in 1930, but the producers had regarded it as a public relations device, not as a code of censorship.

But in 1933 the newly appointed apostolic delegate to the US Catholic Church, the Most Reverend Amleto Giovanni Cicognani, called on Catholics to launch "a united and vigorous campaign for the purification of the cinema, which has become a deadly menace to morals." Many Catholics responded by forming the Legion of Decency, which soon had 9 million members pledged to boycott films that the Legion's rating board condemned. Threatened by a realistic threat of boycotts, the producers decided to enforce the Production Code and placed one of their employees, Joseph I. Breen, in charge. The code prohibited nudity, profanity, white slavery, miscegenation, "excessive and lustful kissing," and "scenes of passion" that "stimulate the lower and baser element." It also forbade Hollywood from glorifying crime or adultery. To enforce the code, the Breen Office was empowered to grant or withhold a seal of approval, and without a seal, a movie could not be played in the major theater chains.

The Breen Office dramatically altered the character of films in the later 1930s. It had at least one positive effect: it led Hollywood to cast more actresses in roles as independent career women, instead of as mere sex objects. More negatively, it encouraged moviemakers to evade the harsher realities of Depression-era life and to shun controversial political and moral issues. It also contributed to what Maury Klein has called a "stylization of technique" as directors and screenwriters searched for subtle, creative, and often witty ways to treat sexuality and violence while avoiding censorship.

A renewed sense of optimism generated by the New Deal also contributed to the production of new kinds of films in the second half of the Depression decade. G-men, detectives, Western heroes and other defenders of law increasingly replaced gangsters. Realistic Warner Brothers exposés rapidly declined in number. Instead audiences enjoyed Frank Capra's comedies and dramas in which a "little man" stands up against corruption. The complex word-play of the Marx Brothers and Mae West increasingly gave way to a new comic genre – the screwball comedy. Movies like *It Happened One Night* or *My Man Godfrey*, which traced the antics of zany eccentrics, presented, in Pauline Kael's words, "Americans' idealized view of themselves – breezy, likable, sexy, gallant, and maybe just a little harebrained."

As Andrew Bergman has shown, the fantasy world of the movies played a critical social and psychological role for Depression-era Americans: in the face of economic disaster, it kept alive a belief in the possibility of individual success, portrayed a government capable of protecting its citizens from external threats, and sustained a vision of America as a classless society. Again and again, Hollywood repeated the same formulas: a poor boy from the slums uses crime as a perverted ladder of success; a back-row chorus girl rises to the lead through luck and pluck; a G-man restores law and order; a poor boy and a rich girl meet, go through wacky adventures, and fall in love. Out of these simple plots, Hollywood restored faith in individual initiative, in the efficacy of government, and in a common American identity transcending social class.

Wartime Hollywood

Beginning in September 1941, a Senate subcommittee launched an investigation into whether Hollywood had campaigned to bring the United States into World War II by inserting pro-British and pro-interventionist messages in its films. Isolationist Senator Gerald Nye charged Hollywood with producing "at least twenty pictures in the last year designed to drug the reason of the American people, set aflame their emotions, turn their hatred into a blaze, fill them with fear that Hitler will come over here and capture them." After reading a list of the names of studio executives – many of whom were Jewish – he condemned Hollywood as "a raging volcano of war fever."

While Hollywood did in fact release a few anti-Nazi films, such as *Confessions of a Nazi Spy*, what is remarkable in retrospect is how slowly Hollywood awoke to the fascist threat. Heavily dependent on the European market for revenue, Hollywood feared offending foreign audiences. Indeed, at the Nazi's request, Hollywood actually fired "non-Aryan" employees in its German business offices. Although the industry released a number of preparedness films (like *Sergeant York*), anti-fascist movies (such as *The Great Dictator*), and pro-British films (including *A Yank in the R.A.F.*) between 1939 and 1941, it did not release a single film advocating immediate American intervention in the war on the Allies' behalf before Pearl Harbor.

Richard R. Lingeman has described Hollywood's immediate reaction to America's entry into the war. The studios, he noted, quickly copyrighted topical movie titles like "Sunday in Hawaii," "Yellow Peril," and "V for Victory." Warner Brothers ordered a hasty rewrite of "Across the Pacific" which involved a Japanese plot to blow up Pearl Harbor, changing the setting to the Panama Canal. The use of searchlights at Hollywood premiers was prohibited, and Jack Warner painted a 20-foot arrow atop his studio, reading: "Lockheed – Thataway."

Hollywood's greatest contribution to the war effort was morale. Many of the movies produced during the war were patriotic rallying cries that affirmed a sense of national purpose. Combat films emphasized patriotism, group effort, and the value of individual sacrifices for a larger cause. They portrayed World War II as a people's war, typically featuring a group of men from diverse ethnic backgrounds who are thrown together, tested on the battlefield, and molded into a dedicated fighting unit. Many wartime films featured women characters playing an active role in the war by serving as combat nurses, riveters, welders, and long-suffering mothers who kept the home fires burning. Even cartoons, like Bugs Bunny "Nipping the Nips," contributed to morale.

Off the screen, leading actors and actresses led recruitment and bond drives and entertained the troops. Leading directors like Frank Capra, John Ford, and John Huston made documentaries to explain "why we fight" and to offer civilians an idea of what actual combat looked like. In less than a year, 12 percent of all film industry employees entered the armed forces, including Clark Gable, Henry Fonda, and Jimmy Stewart. By the war's end, one-quarter of Hollywood's male employees were in uniform.

Hollywood, like other industries, encountered many wartime problems. The government cut the amount of available film stock by 25 percent and restricted the money that could be spent on sets to $5,000 for each movie. Nevertheless, the war years proved to be highly profitable for the movie industry. Spurred by shortages of gasoline and tires, as well as the appeal of newsreels, the war boosted movie attendance to near-record levels of 90 million a week.

From the moment America entered the war, Hollywood feared that the industry would be subject to heavy-handed government censorship. But the government itself wanted no repeat of World War I, when the Committee on Public Information had whipped up anti-German hysteria and oversold the war as "a Crusade not merely to re-win the tomb of Christ, but to bring back to earth the rule of right, the peace, goodwill to men and gentleness he taught." Less than two weeks after Pearl Harbor, President Roosevelt declared that the movie industry could make "a very useful contribution" to the war effort. But, he went on, "The motion industry must remain free … I want no censorship."

Convinced that movies could contribute to national morale, but fearing outright censorship, the federal government established two agencies within the Office of War Information (OWI) in 1942 to supervise the film industry: the Bureau of Motion Pictures, which produced educational films and reviewed scripts voluntarily submitted by the studios, and the Bureau of Censorship, which oversaw film exports.

At the time that these agencies were founded, OWI officials were quite unhappy with Hollywood movies, which they considered "escapist and delusive." The movies, these officials believed, failed to accurately convey what the Allies were fighting for, grossly exaggerated the extent of Nazi and Japanese espionage and sabotage, portrayed the Allies in an offensive manner, and presented a false picture of the United States as a land of gangsters, labor strife, and racial conflict. A study of films issued in 1942 seemed to confirm the OWI concerns. It found that, of the films dealing with the war, roughly two-thirds were spy pictures or comedies or musicals about camp life – conveying a highly distorted picture of the conflict.

To encourage the industry to provide more acceptable films, the Bureau of Motion Pictures issued the Government Information Manual for the Motion Picture. This manual suggested that, before producing a film, moviemakers consider the question: "Will this picture help to win the war?" It also asked the studios to inject images of "people making small sacrifices for victory – making them voluntarily, cheerfully, and because of the people's own sense of responsibility." During its existence, the Bureau evaluated individual film scripts to assess how they depicted war aims, the American military, the enemy, the Allies, and the home front.

After the Bureau of Motion Pictures was abolished in the spring of 1943, government responsibility for monitoring the film industry shifted to the Office of Censorship. This agency prohibited the export of films that showed racial discrimination, depicted Americans as single-handedly winning the war, or which painted America's allies as imperialists.

Postwar Hollywood

The film industry changed radically after World War II, and this change altered the style and content of the films made in Hollywood. After experiencing boom years from 1939 to 1946, the film industry began a long period of decline. Within just seven years, attendance and box-office receipts fell to half their 1946 levels.

Part of the reason was external to the industry. Many veterans returning from World War II got married, started families, attended college on the GI Bill, and bought homes in the suburbs. All these activities took a toll on box-office receipts. Families with babies tended to listen to the radio rather than go to the movies; college students placed studying before seeing the latest film; and newlyweds purchasing homes, automobiles, appliances, and other commodities had less money to spend on movies.

Then, too, especially after 1950, television challenged and surpassed the movies as America's most popular entertainment form. In 1940 there were just 3,785 TV sets in the United States. Two decades later, 9 homes in every 10 had at least one TV set. For earlier Americans, clothing styles, speech patterns, and even moral attitudes and political points of view had been shaped by the movies. For post-World War II Americans, television largely took the movies' place as a dominant cultural influence. The new medium reached audiences far larger than those attracted by motion pictures, and it projected images right into families' living rooms.

Internal troubles also contributed to Hollywood's decline. Hollywood's founding generation – Harry Cohn, Samuel Goldwyn, Louis B. Mayer, Darryl Zanuck – retired or were forced out as new corporate owners, lacking movie experience, took over. The film companies had high profiles, glamour, undervalued stock, strategically located real estate,

and film libraries which television networks desperately needed. In short, they were perfect targets for corporate takeovers. The studios reduced production, sold off back lots,
and made an increasing number of pictures in Europe, where costs were lower.

Meanwhile, Hollywood's foreign market began to vanish. Hollywood had depended
on overseas markets for as much as 40 percent of its revenue. But in an effort to nur-
ture their own film industries and prevent an excessive outflow of dollars, Britain,
France, and Italy imposed stiff import tariffs and restrictive quotas on imported
American movies. With the decline in foreign markets, moviemaking became a much
riskier business.

Then an antitrust ruling separated the studios from their theater chains. In 1948,
the United States Supreme Court handed down its decision in the *Paramount* case,
which had been working its way through the courts for almost a decade. The court's
decree called for the major studios to divest themselves of their theater chains. In
addition to separating theater and producer-distributor companies, the court also
outlawed block booking, the fixing of admissions prices, unfair runs and clearances,
and discriminatory pricing and purchasing arrangements. With this decision, the
industry the moguls built – the vertically integrated studio – died. If the loss of foreign revenues shook the financial foundations of the industry, the end of block booking (a practice whereby the exhibitor is forced to take all of a company's pictures to
get any of that company's pictures) shattered the weakened buttress. Filmmaking had
become a real crap shoot.

One result of the *Paramount* decision was an increase in independent productions.
Yet despite a host of innovations and gimmicks – including 3-D, Cinerama, stereo-
phonic sound, and cinemascope – attendance continued to fall.

Hollywood also suffered from Congressional probes of communist influence in the
film industry. In the late 1930s, the House of Representatives established the
Un-American Activities Committee (HUAC) to combat subversive right-wing and
left-wing movements. Its history was less than distinguished. From the first it tended
to see subversive communists everywhere at work in American society. HUAC even
announced that the Boy Scouts were communist-infiltrated. During the late 1940s
and early 1950s HUAC picked up the tempo of its investigation, which it conducted
in well-publicized sessions. Twice during this period HUAC traveled to Hollywood
to investigate communist infiltration in the film industry.

HUAC first went to Hollywood in 1947. Although it didn't find the party line
preached in the movies, it did call a group of radical screenwriters and producers into
its sessions to testify. Asked if they were communists, the "Hollywood Ten" refused to
answer questions about their political beliefs. As Ring Lardner, Jr., one of the ten, said,
"I could answer … but if I did, I would hate myself in the morning." They believed
that the First Amendment protected them. In the politically charged late 1940s, however, their rights were not protected. Those who refused to divulge their political affiliations were tried for contempt of Congress, sent to prison for a year, and blacklisted.

HUAC went back to Hollywood in 1951. This time it called hundreds of witnesses
from both the political right and the political left. Conservatives told HUAC that
Hollywood was littered with "Commies." Walt Disney even recounted attempts to
have Mickey Mouse follow the party line. Of the radicals, some talked but most didn't.
To cooperate with HUAC entailed "naming names" – that is, informing on one's
friends and political acquaintances. Again, those who refused to name names found

themselves unemployed and unemployable. All told, about 250 directors, writers, and actors were blacklisted.

In 1948 writer Lillian Hellman denounced the industry's moral cowardice in scathing terms: "Naturally, men scared to make pictures about the American Negro, men who only in the last year allowed the word Jew to be spoken in a picture, who took more than ten years to make an anti-fascist picture, these are frightened men and you pick frightened men to frighten first. Judas goats, they'll lead the others to slaughter for you."

The HUAC hearings and blacklistings discouraged Hollywood from producing politically controversial films. Fear that a motion picture dealing with the life of Hiawatha might be regarded as communist propaganda led Monogram Studio to shelve the project. As the *New York Times* explained: "It was Hiawatha's efforts as a peacemaker among warring Indian tribes that gave Monogram particular concern. These it was decided might cause the picture to be regarded as a message for peace and therefore helpful to present communist designs." The hearings encouraged Hollywood to produce musicals, biblical epics, and other politically neutral films.

The HUAC hearings also convinced Hollywood producers to make 50 strongly anticommunist films between 1947 and 1954. Most were second-rate movies starring third-rate actors. The films assured Americans that communists were thoroughly bad people – who didn't have children, exhaled cigarette smoke too slowly, murdered their "friends," and went berserk when arrested. As one film historian has commented, the communists in these films even looked alike; most were "apt to be exceptionally haggard or disgracefully pudgy," and there was certainly "something terribly wrong with a woman if her slip straps showed through her blouse." If these films were bad civic lessons, they did have an impact. They seemed to confirm HUAC's position that communists were everywhere, that subversives lurked in every shadow.

It is ironic that at the same time that HUAC was conducting its investigations of communist subversion, moral censorship of the movies began to decline. In 1949, Vittorio de Sica's *The Bicycle Thief* became the first film to be successfully exhibited without a seal of approval. Despite its glimpses of a brothel and a boy urinating, this Italian film's neorealist portrait of a poor man's search for his stolen bicycle received strong editorial support from newspapers and was shown in many theaters.

In 1952, the Supreme Court reversed a 1915 decision and extended First Amendment protections of free speech to the movies. The landmark case overturned an effort by censors in New York State to ban Roberto Rossellini's film *The Miracle* on grounds of sacrilege. In addition, the court decreed that filmmakers could challenge censors' findings in court. The next year, Otto Preminger's sex comedy *The Moon Is Blue* became the first major American film to be released without the code's seal. Even though the film was condemned by the Legion of Decency for its use of the words "virgin" and "pregnant," efforts to boycott the film fizzled out and the film proved to be a box-office success. In 1966, the film industry abandoned the Production Code, replacing it with a film rating system which is still in force.

New directions in postwar film

During the 1940s, a new film genre – known as film noir – arose, which gave tangible expression to the psychic confusion of a nation that had won the largest war in history but faced even greater uncertainties in peacetime. Though film noir received its named from French film critics and was heavily influenced by German expressionist filmmaking techniques, it stands out as one of the most original and innovative American movie genres.

World War II had produced far-reaching changes in American life: it accelerated the mobility of the population, raised living standards, and profoundly altered race relations and the role of women. Film noir metaphorically addressed many anxieties and apprehensions: the disorientation of returning GIs, fear of nuclear weapons, paranoia generated by the early Cold War, and anxieties aroused by the changing role of women. Characterized by sexual insecurity, aberrant psychology, and nightmarish camera work, film noir depicted a world of threatening shadows and ambiguities – a world of obsession, alienation, corruption, deceit, blurred identity, paranoia, dementia, weak men, cold-blooded femmes fatales, and, inevitably, murder. Its style consisted of looming close-ups, oblique camera angles, and crowded compositions that produced a sense of entrapment. The films' narratives were rarely straightforward; they contained frequent flashbacks and voiceovers.

After the war, Hollywood's audience not only shrank, it also fragmented into distinct subgroups. An audience interested in serious social problem films expanded. During the postwar period Hollywood produced a growing number addressing such problems as ethnic and racial prejudice, anti-Semitism, the sufferings of maltreated mental patients, and problems of alcohol and drug addiction.

Although the early postwar period is often regarded as the golden age of the American family, the popular family melodramas of the 1940s and 1950s reveal a pattern of deeply troubled family relationships. These films depicted sexual frustration; anxious parents; cold, domineering mothers; alienated children; insensitive or fretful fathers; defiant adolescents; and loveless marriages. In part this obsession with the theme of marriage and family life "as a kind of hell" reflected a popularized form of psychoanalytic thought, which offered simplistic formulas to explain human behavior. Films of the early postwar period laboriously repeated the theme that sexual frustration inevitably led to neurosis, and that harsh, neglectful, or uncomprehending parents produce alienated children. It was a far cry from the soothing and funny fare available on TV.

According to many of the popular films of the period, the source of family woes lay in a lack of familial love. Love was treated as the answer to problems ranging from juvenile delinquency to schizophrenia. Adolescents in films like *Splendor in the Grass* are rebellious because their parents "won't listen." Husbands and wives drink too much or stray sexually because they cannot communicate adequately with their spouses. While many films of the early postwar era appear to offer a critical and ambivalent view of marriage and family life, their underlying message is hopeful. Even the most severe family problems can be resolved by love, understanding, and perseverance.

At the same time that it turned out serious social problem films about drugs and family life, Hollywood also produced movies that explored disturbing changes in the lives of American youth. Films such as *The Wild One* (1954), *Blackboard Jungle* (1955), and *Rebel Without a Cause* (1955) portrayed adolescents as budding criminals, emerging homosexuals, potential fascists, and pathological misfits – everything but perfectly normal kids. On close inspection, cultural critics concluded that something was indeed wrong with American youth, who, like Tony in *I Was a Teenage Werewolf* (1957), seemed closer to uncontrollable beasts than civilized adults. As Tony tells a psychiatrist, "I say things, I do things – I don't know why."

Many factors contributed to a belief in adolescent moral decline. J. Edgar Hoover, head of the FBI, linked a rise in juvenile delinquency to the decline in the influence of family, home, church, and local community institutions. Frederic Wertham, a psychiatrist, emphasized the pernicious influence of comic books. He believed that crime and horror comic books fostered racism, fascism, and sexism in their readers.

In fact, these fears were grossly overstated. During the late 1940s and 1950s, for example, juvenile delinquency was not increasing. But changes were taking place, and popular movies suggest some of the responses to these broader social transformations. In retrospect, it appears that the proliferation of juvenile delinquency films reflected adult anxieties over the growth of a new youth culture, with its distinctive forms of music (rock and roll), dress, and language, as well as a deep disdain for the world of conventional adulthood. Marlon Brando captured a new attitude when he responded to the question, "What are you rebelling against?" with the reply: "Whadda ya got?"

The growing popularity of science fiction thrillers also reflected the emergence of the youth market and the spread of a certain paranoid style during the Cold War years. Historian Richard Hofstadter defined the paranoid style in these terms:

> The distinguishing thing about the paranoid style is ... that its exponents see ... a "vast" or "gigantic" conspiracy as the motive force in historical events ... The paranoid spokesman sees the fate of this conspiracy in apocalyptic terms – he traffics in the birth and death of whole worlds, whole political orders, whole systems of human values.

As Nora Sayre has shown, science fiction films of the 1950s can be viewed as allegories of the Cold War, reflecting broader social concerns with domestic subversion, infiltration, and the pressures for conformity in a mass society. Unlike the cheerful, humorous, quasi-religious science fiction of the 1970s and 1980s, the films of the 1950s conveyed an atmosphere of paranoia and foreboding, and dealt with themes – like mind-control and the after-effects of atomic bomb tests – that tapped into deep-seated anxieties of the period.

The "new" Hollywood

As the 1960s began, few would have guessed that the decade would be one of the most socially conscious and stylistically innovative in Hollywood's history. Among the most popular films at the decade's start were Doris Day romantic comedies like *That Touch of Mink* (1962) and epic blockbusters like *The Longest Day* (1962), *Lawrence of Arabia* (1962), and *Cleopatra* (1963). Yet, as the decade progressed, Hollywood radically shifted focus and began to produce an increasing number of anti-establishment films, laced with social commentary, directed at the growing youth market.

By the early 1960s, an estimated 80 percent of the filmgoing population was between the ages of 16 and 25. At first, the major studios largely ignored this audience, leaving it the hands of smaller studios like American International Pictures, which produced a string of cheaply made horror movies, beach blanket movies – like

Bikini Beach (1964) and *How to Stuff a Wild Bikini* (1965) – and motorcycle gang pictures – like *The Wild Angels* (1966).

Two films released in 1967 – *Bonnie and Clyde* and *The Graduate* – awoke Hollywood to the size and influence of the youth audience. *Bonnie and Clyde*, the story of two Depression-era bank robbers, was advertised with the slogan: "They're young, they're in love, they kill people." Inspired by such French new wave pictures as *Breathless* (1960), the film aroused intense controversy for romanticizing gangsters and transforming them into social rebels. A celebration of youthful rebellion also appeared in *The Graduate*, which was the third-highest-grossing film up until this time. In this film, a young college graduate rejects a hypocritical society and the traditional values of his parents – and the promise of a career in "plastics" – and finds salvation in love.

A number of the most influential films of the late 1960s and early 1970s sought to revise older film genres – like the war film, the crime film, and the Western – and rewrite Hollywood's earlier versions of American history from a more critical perspective. Three major war films – *Little Big Man*, *Patton*, and *M*A*S*H* – reexamined the nineteenth-century Indian wars, World War II, and the Korean War in light of America's experience in Vietnam. *The Wild Bunch* (1969) and *McCabe and Mrs. Miller* (1971) offered radical reappraisals of the mythology of the American frontier. Francis Ford Coppola's *The Godfather* (1972) revised and enhanced the gangster genre by transforming it into a critical commentary on an immigrant family's pursuit of the American dream.

During the mid- and late 1970s, the mood of American films shifted sharply. Unlike the highly politicized films of the early part of the decade, the most popular films of the late 1970s and early 1980s were escapist blockbusters like *Star Wars* (1977), *Superman* (1978), and *Raiders of the Lost Ark* (1981) – featuring spectacular special effects, action, and simplistic conflicts between good and evil; inspirational tales of the indomitable human spirit, like *Rocky* (1976); or nostalgia for a more innocent past – like *Animal House* (1978) and *Grease* (1978). Glamorous outlaws like *Bonnie and Clyde* were replaced by law and order avengers like *Dirty Harry* and *Robocop*. Sports – long regarded as a sure box-office loser – became a major Hollywood obsession, with movies like *Hoosiers*, *Chariots of Fire*, *Karate Kid*, and *The Mighty Ducks* celebrating competitiveness and victory. Movies which offered a tragic or subversive perspectives on American society, like *The Godfather* or *Chinatown*, were replaced by more upbeat, undemanding films, and especially by comedies, featuring such actors as Dan Ackroyd, Chevy Chase, Eddie Murphy, and Bill Murray.

Critics partly blamed the trend toward what Mark Crispin Miller has called "deliberate anti-realism" upon economic changes within the film industry. In 1966, Gulf and Western Industries executed a takeover of Paramount, and the conglomerization of the film industry began. In 1967, United Artists merged with Transamerica Corporation; in 1969 Kinney Services acquired Warner Brothers. In one sense the takeovers were logical. Conglomerates wanted to acquire interests in businesses that serviced Americans' leisure needs. The heads of the conglomerates, however, had no idea how to make successful motion pictures. Too often they believed that successful movies could be mass-produced, that statisticians could discover a scientific method for making box-office hits.

A trend toward the creation of interlocking media companies, encompassing movies, magazines and newspapers, and books, accelerated in 1985 when the Department of Justice overturned the 1948 antitrust decree which had ended vertical integration within the film industry. As a result, many of the major studios were acquired by large media and entertainment corporations like Sony, which purchased Columbia Pictures, Time Warner (which owns *Time* magazine, Simon & Schuster publishers, and Warner Brothers), and Rupert Murdoch, whose holdings include HarperCollins publishers, the Fox television network, and 20th Century Fox. At the same time that these large entertainment conglomerates arose, many smaller independent producers, such as Lorimar and De Laurentiis, disappeared.

Nevertheless, important issues continued to be addressed through film. Many films focused on problems of romance, family, gender, and sexuality – aspects of life radically changed by the social transformations of the 1960s and early 1970s. Certainly, some films tried to evade the profound changes that had taken place in gender relations – like *An Officer and a Gentleman*, an old-fashioned screen romance, or *Flashdance*, an updated version of the Cinderella story, or *10* and *Splash*, which depicted male fantasies about relationships with beautiful, utterly compliant women. But many other popular films addressed such serious questions as the conflict between the family responsibilities and personal aspirations (for example, *Kramer v. Kramer*) or women's need to assert their independence (like *An Unmarried Woman*, *Desperately Seeking Susan*, and *Thelma and Louise*).

At a time when politicians and news journalists were neglecting racial and urban issues, movies like *Boyz in the Hood*, *Grand Canyon*, *Do the Right Thing*, and *Jungle Fever* focused on such problems as the racial gulf separating blacks and whites, the conditions in the nation's inner cities, the increasing number of poor single-parent families, police brutality, and urban violence.

Ironically, the most controversial issue of the 1960s and early 1970s, the Vietnam War, only began to be seriously examined on the screen in the late 1970s. Although many films of the late 1960s and early 1970s embodied the bitter aftertaste of the war, the conflict itself remained strikingly absent from the screen, as Hollywood, like the country as a whole, had difficulty adjusting to the grim legacy of a lost and troubling war. During the conflict, Hollywood produced only a single film dealing with Vietnam – John Wayne's *The Green Berets*. Modeled along the lines of such World War II combat epics as *The Sands of Iwo Jima* and earlier John Wayne Westerns like *The Alamo*, the film portrayed decent Americans struggling to defend an embattled outpost along the Laotian border nicknamed Dodge City.

Although America's active military participation in the Vietnam War ended in 1973, the controversy engendered by the war raged on long after the firing of the last shot. Much of the controversy centered on the returning veterans, who were shocked by the cold, hostile reception they received when they returned to the United States. In *First Blood* (1982), John Rambo captured their pain: "It wasn't my war – you asked me, I didn't ask you … and I did what I had to do to win …. Then I came back to the world and I see all those maggots at the airport, protesting me, spitting on me, calling me a baby- killer …."

During the 1970s and 1980s, the returning Vietnam War veteran loomed large in American popular culture. He was first portrayed as a dangerous killer, a deranged, ticking time-bomb that could explode at any time and in any place. He was Travis

Bickle in *Taxi Driver* (1976), a veteran wound so tight that he seemed perpetually on the verge of snapping. Or he was Colonel Kurtz in *Apocalypse Now* (1979), who adjusted to a mad war by going mad himself.

Not until the end of the 1970s did popular culture begin to treat the Vietnam War veteran as a victim of the war rather than a madman produced by the war. *Coming Home* (1978) and *The Deer Hunter* (1978) began the popular rehabilitation of the veteran, and such films as *Missing in Action* (1984) and *Rambo: First Blood II* (1985) transformed the veteran into a misunderstood hero.

Where some films, like the Rambo series, focused on the exploits of one-man armies or vigilantes armed to the teeth, who had been kept from winning the war because of government cowardice and betrayal, another group of Vietnam War films – like *Platoon*, *Casualties of War*, and *Born on the Fourth of July* – took quite a different view. Focusing on innocent, naive "grunts" – the ground troops who actually fought the war – these movies retold the story of the Vietnam War in terms of the soldiers' loss of idealism, the breakdown of unit cohesion, and the struggle to survive and sustain a sense of humanity and integrity in the midst of war.

Hollywood today

In a 1992 bestseller *Hollywood vs. America*, Michael Medved, co-host of public television's *Sneak Previews*, described Hollywood as a "poison factory," befouling America's moral atmosphere and assaulting the country's "most cherished values." Today's films, he argued, use their enormous capacity to influence opinion by glamorizing violence, maligning marriage, mocking authority, promoting sexual promiscuity, ridiculing religion, and bombarding viewers with an endless stream of profanity, gratuitous sex, and loutish forms of behavior. Where once the movies offered sentiment, elegance, and romance, now, Medved contended, ideologically motivated producers and directors promote their own divisive agenda: anti-religion, anti-family, anti-military.

In fact, the picture is more complicated than Medved suggests. As film critic David Denby has observed, abandonment of the Production Code in 1966 did indeed increase the amount of sex, violence, and profanity on the screen; but particularly in the 1980s, 1990s, and 2000s Hollywood has also increased the amount of family entertainment it offers, including feature-length cartoons like *WALL-E* and *Shrek* and children's fantasy movies including the Harry Potter and Lord of the Ring series. At the same time that some films merely exploited history as a backdrop for action and adventure, such as the Indiana Jones films, there has also been a revival of serious historical films like *Charlie Wilson's War* and *Hotel Rwanda*. Meanwhile, independent directors released a growing number of idiosyncratic and inexpensive films, like *Slumdog Millionaire*, while within Hollywood itself female moviemakers, like Sofia Coppola and Jane Campion, and African American filmmakers, like Spike Lee, have received an unprecedented opportunity to bring fresh viewpoints to the screen.

Nevertheless, as the movie industry enters its second century, many Americans worry about Hollywood's future. Medved is not alone in complaining that "they don't make movies like they used to." A basic problem facing today's Hollywood is the rapidly rising cost of making and marketing a movie: an average of $100 million today. The immense cost of producing movies has led the studios to seek guaranteed hits: blockbusters loaded with high-tech special effects, sequels, and remakes of earlier movies, foreign films, and even old TV shows.

Hollywood has also sought to cope with rising costs by focusing ever more intently on its core audiences. Annual ticket sales in the United States peaked in 2002 at $1.6 billion and fell to $1.3 billion in 2008, with the biggest drop occurring among adults. With the decline in the size of the adult audience, the single largest group of moviegoers now consists of teenage boys, who are particularly attracted to thrills, violence, and crude laughs. And since over half of Hollywood's profits are earned overseas, the industry has concentrated much of its energy on crude action films easily understood by an international audience.

For a century, the movie industry has been the American nation's most important purveyor of culture and entertainment to the masses, playing a critical role in the shift from Victorian to distinctively modern, consumer values; from a world of words to a visual culture; from a society rooted in islands of localities and ethnic groups to a commercialized mass culture. The movies taught Americans how to kiss, make love, conceive of gender roles, and understand their place in the world. Whether film will continue to serve as the nation's preeminent instrument of cultural expression – reflecting and also shaping values and cultural ideals – remains to be seen.

Part I
The Silent Era

Introduction
Intolerance *and the Rise of the Feature Film*

Intolerance (1916), the great film director D.W. Griffith's epic attack on bigotry throughout history, was American silent cinema's greatest artistic achievement and a ruinous box-office failure. Created in response to charges that Griffith's notorious *Birth of a Nation* (1915) was bigoted, as well as to protest efforts to censor that earlier epic, *Intolerance* interweaves four stories that illustrate "how hatred and intolerance, through all the ages, have battled against love and charity": the fall of Babylon, the crucifixion of Christ, the St. Bartholomew's Day Massacre of the French Huguenots in 1572, and the wrenching poverty and exploitation of the modern American urban worker. Initially, the silent epic attracted large crowds; soon, however, increasingly bewildered audiences shrank.

In a masterful display of film editing, director D.W. Griffith cuts among four distinct stories: a mountain girl's struggle to warn the Babylonian king Belshazzar of the imminent arrival of the Persian army; Christ's march toward Calvary; a French Protestant's effort to rescue his fiancée from French mercenaries intent on killing the Huguenots; and, in the modern story, labor strikers battling the state militia, crowded tenements, wretched slums, an unjust legal system, and intrusive social reformers. Linking these four stories is a recurring shot of Lillian Gish rocking a cradle, accompanied by lines from Walt Whitman:

> Out of the cradle endlessly rocking.
> Today as yesterday, endlessly rocking, ever bringing the same joys and sorrows.

A dramatic illustration of film's artistic possibilities, the picture cost at least $300,000 to make – more than three times the cost of *Birth of a Nation*. Much of this was spent on the grandiose Babylonian set, perhaps the most famous film set ever built. But in the end the film disappointed as spectacle and went unheard as message. Its plea for peace and tolerance was ignored as the nation crept closer to involvement in World War I.

Intolerance was only the most dramatic example of how rapidly the movies matured during their first two decades. As early as 1909, primitive films – drawing upon the conventions of vaudeville and featuring sight gags, simple skits, pranks and practical jokes, chases and rescues, and scenes of everyday life – began to give way to the modern feature film. The earliest films had been quite brief, usually involving a single shot, often viewed from a distance. Newer films were longer and more complex in structure. Drawing inspiration from the novel and the dramatic theater rather than vaudeville, these new films emphasized storytelling, and were likely to fix on individual psychology and personality. The new feature films offered a distinctive aesthetic and visual style as well: lighting, camera angles, editing, framing, and camera placement were designed to tell the story as clearly and unobtrusively as possible. To focus the viewers' attention on the film's narrative, directors kept camera angles at eye level and framed shots to keep action in the screen's center. Directors used dissolves and fade-outs to convey the passage of time, and cross-cutting to link chains of separate events. Styles of acting changed as well. Exaggerated pantomime increasingly gave way to more restrained forms of expression; emotions more and more were conveyed by facial gestures rather than by elaborate hand gestures.

D.W. Griffith contributed greatly to the creation of the modern narrative film. But in important respects his epic *Intolerance* departed from the emerging conventions of the classical Hollywood style. Indeed, the film's financial failure may have been due to its radical deviation from audiences' notions of what constituted a feature film. At a time when audiences expected movies to tell an entertaining story, Griffith's goal was to send a clear message. His film consisted of four separate allegories, featuring unnamed characters (like the "Mountain Girl" or the "Friendless One" or the "Dear One") at a time when viewers expected to see a unified narrative focusing on individual characters. This refusal to individualize his characters may have been a large reason for its failure to grip its viewers.

1

Silent Cinema as Social Criticism
Front Page Movies

Kay Sloan

Today, silent films are largely unwatched, with the notable exception of comedies starring Charlie Chaplin and Buster Keaton. Many contemporary viewers regard silent films with condescension: as over-acted, slow-paced, and excessively melodramatic. Today's audiences tend to dislike the lack of dialogue and color and are particularly put off by the subtitles that interrupt the films' flow. But silent movies were not simply a more primitive version of modern films. They embodied a different aesthetic and sensibility. Makers of silent films produced powerful visual images whose haunting beauty and lyricism exceed those found in most current Hollywood films. Equally important, many silent films were explicitly "political" in a way most contemporary films are not.

Although many people conceive of silent films as pictures of innocence – filled with gentlemanly tramps and virginal beauties – many early directors ripped their plots directly from the headlines of newspapers. As film historian Kay Sloan shows in the following essay, early cinema directly addressed many of the social problems raised by Progressive era reformers.

Sheiks, flappers, comic tramps, and vamps: silent film has left a legacy of bizarrely colorful images preserved in the popular mind by nostalgia. Yet in the early days of the primitive film industry, the cinema treated social problems in a way that was, ironically, as fantastic as the glamorous stars and tinsel world of Hollywood's later silver screen. The earliest audiences pushed their coins across box office windows to watch melodramas and comedies that often celebrated characters who literally animated the social and political dilemmas of the Progressive Era. The cinema turned these dilemmas into fairy tales of the day. Greedy corporate tycoons, villainous landlords, corrupt politicians, flamboyant suffragettes, and striking workers flickered across the bed sheets that sometimes sufficed for screens in hastily created movie houses just after the turn of the century.

Kay Sloan, "Front Page Movies," *The Loud Silents: Origins of the Social Problem Film* (Urbana: University of Illinois Press, 1988), pp. 1–16.

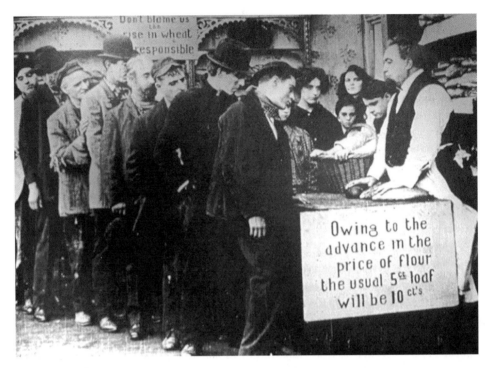

Figure 3 *A Corner in Wheat* (1909). American Mutoscope and Biograph Company. Directed by D.W. Griffith. Author's screenshot.

This is the story of that early silent cinema, a largely pre-corporate, inconsistently censored film industry that had its roots not in Hollywood but in the nation's inner cities. It is an important story both for the vision it provides of how entertainment can deliver social problems to the public, and for the historical portrait it paints of America just after the turn of the century. In the era before World War I, moviegoing often involved paying a nickel or a dime to watch a series of short one or two reelers in the cramped quarters of storefront theaters that populated the urban ghettoes. The elaborate movie "palace" was, for the most part, an anomaly; so was the feature film. Film companies were small business operations that might shoot several one-reel films every week in a makeshift studio. This was a time when the traditions of the cinema were in the process of formation, when both the subject matter and the form of film were in flux. Inventions rapidly became conventions that helped shore up a sense of social order, as a new art form began to link human desire with the needs of society.

In New York, Chicago, Boston, and in an obscure community called Hollywood out in California, small film companies often turned to the literary and political milieu of the muckrakers and the Progressives for storylines. The "muckraking" cinema cranked out stories that entertained primarily working class audiences who could afford the five or ten cent price of admission to the nickelodeons. There, seated on wooden folding chairs, moviegoers watched graphic portrayals of America's social problems, some of which were part of their everyday lives.

In 1910, Walter Fitch, a film critic for the *Moving Picture World*, one of the film industry's first trade journals, stepped back from the immediacy of the new medium – it was, indeed, a cinema in search of itself – to take a long look at its potential and its possibilities. Filmmakers, mused Fitch, "may play on every pipe in the great organ of humanity." The early cinema did indeed attempt to compose euphonious sounds from the cacophony of the era. With titles such as *Capital Versus Labor*, *The Suffragettes' Revenge*, *A Corner in Wheat*, *The Usurer's Grip*, *The Girl Strike Leader*, or *The Reform Candidate*, all released in the first fifteen years of the twentieth century, the cinema championed the cause of labor, lobbied against political "bosses," and often gave dignity to the struggles of the urban poor. Conversely, other films satirized suffragists, ridiculed labor organizers, and celebrated America's corporate leaders in anti-labor melodramas that the American Federation of Labor denounced and boycotted.

The period itself encompassed vast contradictions. While socialists such as Eugene Debs and Mother Jones fought for drastic changes in the nation's economic system, the new industrial leaders attempted paternalistic, philanthropic solutions to labor activism. At the same time that radicals pushed for fundamental changes in American life, middle class reformers lobbied for legislation on labor and women's rights that would offer moderate change within the existing structure. Progressive thinkers such as the economist Richard T. Ely and the sociologists Edward A. Ross and Thorstein Veblen condemned what they saw as the dynamics of inequality in America; their voices became part of the milieu of protest in which the movies were born. Others, like Louis D. Brandeis, later a Supreme Court justice, indicted the banking system he analyzed in *Other People's Money*, and successfully challenged corporate America in the courts. Muckraking journalists exposed the horrors of child labor and the corruption of political machinery in the nation's magazines and newspapers. Articles by such investigative journalists decried "the shame of the cities" and their failure to adequately meet the needs of their citizens. Upton Sinclair created a national furor by exposing unsanitary meat-packing conditions in his novel *The Jungle*; Frank Norris took on railroad tycoons in *The Octopus*. Lincoln Steffens's articles for *Everybody's Magazine*, with their prostitutes, gamblers, policemen "on the take," corporate tycoons, and greedy landlords, provided an array of stories that pointed to the need for social change.

It was a volatile, exciting world for the new lively entertainment form of the motion picture to enter. Conflicts that challenged the foundations of society found their way into the cinema as film companies seized on the news in the headlines for rich melodramatic and comic material. They also documented contemporary events in early newsreels. In an era long before the advent of television, motion pictures served as news reportage and propaganda at the same time that they revolutionized entertainment. Savvy political figures quickly learned to use the new medium to advertise themselves. In 1906, William Randolph Hearst made talking films of his campaign speeches to circulate in areas in which his personal travel was difficult. Performing a function similar to that of a modern television reporter, the filmmaker Siegmund Lubin released films in 1908 reporting the campaigns of the political rivals William Jennings Bryan and John W. Kern. But, though the films showing news events or national political campaigns served as important justifications for the existence of the often criticized new medium of the motion picture, the fictions of those actual conflicts told a richer story about the climate of the period. The fictionalization of conflicts allowed an injection of fantasy and ideology into the stories. Films interpreted the nation's headlines in dramatic visual images that at once persuaded and entertained.

The comedies, melodramas, and occasional westerns about labor conflict, tenement poverty, or political corruption reveal through fantasy an America torn with ideological conflict.

Often, special interest groups made their own motion pictures in collaboration with film industrialists. An important part of the process of translating the news involved opening the channels of filmmaking to groups advocating change. The earliest film audiences watched motion pictures made or sponsored by groups like the National Child Labor Committee, the National American Woman Suffrage Association, and even by individuals such as Upton Sinclair and the Progressive New York Governor, William Sulzer, who produced and starred in his own melodrama in 1914. Other Progressive activists joined them. For instance, the birth control activist Margaret Sanger made a melodrama to promote the basic civil liberties that she was repeatedly denied during the Progressive Era.

Conservatives as well as Progressives seized on the new medium as a way to dramatize their ideas. Organizations such as the National Association of Manufacturers and the Russell Sage Foundation made film melodramas to promote corporate paternalism. Such films circulated through the nation's movie houses as if they were no different from slapstick comedies, westerns, and historical dramas. Distributors offered such politically oriented films to exhibitors along with material produced solely for entertainment. Often, a film reviewer would suggest to exhibitors that a motion picture with a pro-labor message, for instance, or a plea for women's rights would be popular in areas where such ideas were already accepted. Essentially, the early audiences paid their nickels and dimes to see the political tracts of special interest groups on the same program as less controversial material.

Regardless of the ideological message, however, the vision that commercial film could serve as a vehicle for overt political causes seems startling – even revolutionary – today. For instance, Progressive woman suffragists made melodramas in collaboration with Hollywood film companies. Certainly it is difficult to imagine a modern day equivalent: the National Organization of Women collaborating with Twentieth Century Fox in the early 1980s to make a melodrama starring Meryl Streep or Jane Fonda promoting the Equal Rights Amendment might be such an event. By contemporary standards, such a film would be an utter aberration from Hollywood practices. Yet in the early twentieth century, such was the notion of what film might – and even should – be. Film became a vehicle for overtly presenting social problems to the public.

The rise of the feature length film during the World War I years contributed to the decline of the numerous early social problem films. Since demand for motion pictures dictated that the companies turn out films rapidly, it was crucial that story ideas be readily found. It was easier for filmmakers to take risks about controversial issues in an era when the companies were releasing, as one Hollywood veteran remembers, at least "one reel a week." When film companies turned out several short films a month, the production of a potentially controversial film was far less of an economic risk than it would be in the later age of the blockbuster. Even without the encouragement and participation of special interest groups, the young film companies made melodramas and comedies that exploited the issues splashed across the nation's headlines.

One of the most notorious of these films bore the innocent title of *Why?* Released in 1913, *Why?* shocked critics with its tale of corrupt elites and its vision of workers revolting against capitalism in America. The film's hero, a fiery-eyed immigrant with wild hair, dreamed of revenge against the wealthy classes who feasted while enslaved workers starved. The three parts of *Why?* contained episodes of capitalists and workers shooting it out with revolvers over child labor, corporate greed, and class inequality. In a scene that could have been scripted by Marx himself, the capitalists turn into sacks of gold when shot. Released by the American arm of the independent French company Eclair Films, *Why?* culminated with workers burning down Manhattan. The blazes, ironically, had been handpainted red by workers for the capitalist film company. The film ended with the Woolworth building still burning, violating one of the ideological tenets of the bourgeois narrative closure that flames, like western bad guys or melodramatic villains, have to die in the end. Instead of restoring responsibility and order, the film simply left its audience in a liminal world that granted power and legitimacy to unleashed desire. "Socialist doctrine!" cried one outraged reviewer.

Why?'s virtual celebration of anarchy frightened censors as well as critics. Early censors feared the political content of films as much as their occasional sexual content. The potential of the cinema to champion such organized violence disturbed Frederic C. Howe, the chairman of the National Board of Censorship of Motion Pictures. That organization had been formed by the filmmakers themselves in 1909 to discourage "immoral" or "lurid" material that had roused criticism from more traditional sectors of society. Howe feared the mounting success of radical, politically oriented moving pictures. He was a liberal reformer, but hardly a radical. Despite local outcries over the supposed "immorality" of the movies, Howe suggested that the political role of film was potentially as threatening to society as were its challenges to a Victorian moral code.

Particularly since the early films touched the sentiments of masses of people, including the millions of newly arrived immigrants to whom the English printed word was still a mystery, they elicited condemnation from those, like Howe, who feared the power of the motion picture over those in the ghetto. Motion pictures, noted one journalist in 1908, had become "both a clubhouse and an academy for the working-man." The class of people attending motion pictures, stated another observer delicately, "are not of the rich." At their outset, motion pictures found audiences primarily among the many Americans whose lives were dominated by the uncertainties of poverty and the cultural ruptures of immigration.

Thus Frederic Howe worried about the content of films in 1914. The films that "tended to excite class feeling or ... tend to bring discredit upon the agencies of the government," wrote Howe, could lead to a time "when the movie ... becomes the daily press of industrial groups, of classes, of Socialism, syndicalism, and radical opinion."

Howe's fears, of course, remained unfounded. The revolutionary content of *Why?* was an anomaly among the early social problem films. The young film companies themselves attempted to make their business more "respectable," and broaden the appeal of motion pictures to the middle classes. They made the social problem films as part of that process, with the notion that such films might be seen as "educational" and "uplifting."

It was a cinematic role encouraged by critics. In 1913, one film journalist suggested that the cinema might be a weapon "in the battle against child labor, white-slavery, labor-conflicts, and vice development." He suggested that film should take up the subjects headlined on the front pages of the nation's newspapers and "expose injustice, cruelty, and suffering in all their naked ugliness." This critic suggested that both the film industry's need for stories and America's pressing social problems might be settled if only the filmmakers would turn their attention to social issues. But the solution to such issues, he emphasized, must be calm, reasoned change, not the revolutionary message of a film like *Why?*

Such liberal film critics played an important role in channeling film into a vehicle for middle class reforms. They pointed out causes that might be taken up in melodrama. *The Moving Picture World*'s Louis Reeves Harrison promoted the role that film could play in pointing out the need for social reform, and he denounced what he called "the desire for power on the part of the ruling classes." Filmmakers, he urged, should pay attention to such inequities in corporate society. The cinema might act as a cultural watchdog, appealing for responsibility from all levels of society. One issue demanding treatment by the moving pictures suggested Harrison, was child labor – another was what he applauded as women's "broadening knowledge and experience." The expression of those issues could not only strengthen the nation, but the role of film in it.

In 1912, Harrison reminded filmmakers that the often denigrated cinema might serve as a tool for "uplifting" the masses. He offered a virtual litany of themes for the melodrama that expressed the interests of both the era's reformers and some early filmmakers:

> the social battle for justice to those who do the world's work, the adjustment of compensation to labor, the right of common people to liberty and the pursuit of happiness, the betterment of humanity through the prevention of crime rather than its cure, the prevention of infant mortality, and the prevention of hoggishness wherever theatrical trusts will permit, the self-conflict between material tendency and spiritual clarification, all these furnish subjects of widespread interest which the dramatist may handle with or without gloves.

The film industry increasingly addressed the issues suggested by Harrison. In 1914, one film director boasted that he got the "best points for [his] work from the newspapers," turning the turmoil of the era into comedy and melodrama.

Concerned that the cinema raised subversive questions, Howe neglected the important role it played in laying them to rest. *Why?*'s radical solution to class conflict was, not surprisingly, rare cinema. It represented the starkest challenge to the nation's economic powers – the wheat speculators, tenement owners, loan sharks, or captains of industry. More typically, the films dealt with social problems in a way that muted their critiques of economic or social injustice. They called for careful reforms or fatalistic surrenders to uncontrollable "natural" forces that doled out troubles and misfortunes. Such films proved that the radically new entertainment form of the cinema could act as a conservative force in the emerging industrial society.

For instance, the Thomas Edison Company's *The Usurer's Grip* was a modern-day fairy tale set in the tenements. Funded by the Russell Sage Foundation in 1912, the film warned audiences about unscrupulous moneylenders who thrived on the poverty stricken, hounding them further and further into financial desperation. The film's hero and heroine found themselves in mounting debt to a usurer, but they were saved at last by an understanding businessman who directed them to the loan division of the

Russell Sage Foundation. There they were rescued by the paternalism promoted by Sage's vision of benevolent capitalism. *The Usurer's Grip* was a self-serving advertisement for the Sage Foundation. Such early films precursed modern television advertising by blending entertainment with commercial messages. Through melodrama, the Edison Company and the Russell Sage Foundation advertised direct social reform and suggested that philanthropic measures might remedy urban poverty.

Increasingly, the early films moved from primitive one or two reelers exploiting class conflict to more sophisticated films with complicated plots. At times, they advocated specific reforms. Film began to shift from the sensationalism of muckraking issues into serious calls for reform through "enlightenment" – whether it be better management to assuage striking workers, calls for woman suffrage, the abolition of child labor, poor tenement conditions, and the illegality of birth control. Film industrialists tried to establish the middle-class nature of the cinema by allowing reform groups or special interest groups access to the medium. In 1912, the National Association of Manufacturers (NAM) collaborated with Thomas Edison's Company to make a propagandistic melodrama on factory safety called *The Crime of Carelessness*. It was written by the Progressive writer James Oppenheim, who was quickly earning a reputation as a writer of what the *New York Times* called "social films." His first film for the Edison Company, titled *Hope*, had dealt with the problem of tuberculosis. With *The Crime of Carelessness*, he turned to the more controversial issue of problems in the workplace. The film laid equal blame for hazardous working conditions on workers and negligent owners – but insidiously punished a careless worker for a factory fire. The problems of the workplace, then, might be resolved merely by responsibility on the part of individual employees. It was, wrote the *New York Times* critic, a "long and stirring drama," one of a line of Oppenheim's "social films." NAM's film, of course, did more than link industrial problems with careless workers. It also linked the interests of the film industry with those of the larger corporate interests represented by NAM.

A similar theme emerged in the Vitagraph Company's *Capital Versus Labor*, an expose of labor problems made in 1910. Punctuated by bloody scenes of rioting workers battling company- hired thugs, the film suggested that the strikers had legitimate grievances to air. But the workers alone were powerless to change their situation. The eventual "happy ending" came not through the organized protests or negotiations of labor unions, but through the intervention of the church. The violence in *Capital Versus Labor* continued until a minister finally calmed the mobs and convinced the greedy capitalist to compromise with his workers. The film thus revealed the futility of rioting in the streets while it still acknowledged the validity of the strikers' complaints. From such plots came a dual statement about workers in America: while the films granted them dignity and self-worth as individuals, it also rendered them and their organizations powerless. *The Crime of Carelessness* and *Capital Versus Labor* serve as examples of how workers might be portrayed as irresponsible individuals who are ultimately dependent on the good graces of their generous bosses.

Such films relied on the "happy ending," which provided audiences with continuity and faith in "the system." Even actual historical events were rewritten to accommodate that expectation. A 1915 melodrama on political corruption in New York City provides a telling example of how important the happy ending had become. *The Governor's Boss* took a political tragedy and transformed it into victory for the democratic process. The film was one of the most unusual melodramas made about political corruption for another reason: it actually starred an impeached governor of New York, William Sulzer.

Sulzer publicized his case against the Tammany Hall machine in 1915 with a melodrama written by James S. Barcus, a friend and political crony. He first took it to Broadway, where the play had a brief run of sixteen performances at the Garrick Theatre. Following the play's unsuccessful Broadway run, he turned to the cinema with the script. To heighten the realism of the film, Sulzer played himself in the starring role, but he took the unique opportunity that film provided to rewrite his own history with a happy ending. *The Governor's Boss* ended not with Sulzer's impeachment, but with the defeat of his opponents in court. Sulzer restored justice and democracy to New York City through the power of the cinema rather than the power of political office. Imagine Richard Nixon producing and starring in a cinematic version of Watergate in 1975 – with an ending in which he retained his grip on the presidency. Despite the vast differences between Sulzer and Nixon, the preposterous nature of the contemporary example is nevertheless a striking indication of just how unique this Progressive Era vision of film as political propaganda was.

Like the many previous melodramas calling for social change, *The Governor's Boss* restored democracy in such a way that rendered the film a less powerful statement against Tammany Hall. The *New York Times* critic found the ending so absurd that he sarcastically observed that "the Governor, his secretary, his daughter, and Virtue in general triumph." Even real occurrences took on fantastic proportions to assure a society in distress that its institutions worked for the good of all, despite the news broadcast in the nation's headlines.

The headlines were powerful material in a time when muckraking journalists and novelists like Ida Tarbell and Upton Sinclair constantly probed the underside of the "American Dream." Both Sinclair and Tarbell were among the era's crusaders who made their own films. Their cinematic efforts reflected a period in film history when the motion pictures were seen as a medium that might lie open to the public, particularly to those with a cause. Tarbell, who had condemned John L. Rockefeller when she exposed the ruthless practices of the Standard Oil Company in 1902, collaborated with Vitagraph Studios in 1914 as part of their series of photoplays scripted by "famous authors." Interestingly, she chose not a political subject but a historical play to dramatize, as part of a broader effort by the membership of the Authors' League of America to help less recognized writers. In 1913, Upton Sinclair ambitiously put his powerful expose of the meat packing industry, *The Jungle*, into five reels of a motion picture. At the same time, however, the issues that Tarbell and Sinclair were publicizing with their news articles and novels found their way into the cinema in ways that were less overtly political than *The Jungle*. Motion pictures took on the preoccupations of muckraking journalists and absorbed them into the ethos of individualism and the "virtue" that mended society in *The Governor's Boss*. In that process, they helped establish film as a respectable entertainment form, as they mediated the problems of society.

Many security minded reformers from the educated middle class saw that new function of film, and moved from their early position of unrelenting condemnation of the newly emerged entertainment form to an attempt to "re-form" it. These reformers realized that film had the capacity to solve problems, to suggest solutions that would contain disorder and push forward moderate change. Their motion pictures raised issues among masses of people that the printed word might not reach, as Walter Fitch had commented in 1910. Film critics such as Louis Reeves Harrison and his colleagues at the *Moving Picture World*, W. Stephen Bush and the Reverend E. Boudinot Stockton, all had long stressed the use of film to "uplift." Jane Addams turned from her call for censorship of the moving pictures ("debased" and "primitive" she had called them in 1909) to actually starring in a melodrama in 1913 titled *Votes for Women*. Filmmaking seemed to have become fashionable among liberal reformers.

In their collaboration with professional filmmakers, the reformers used some of the conventions rapidly developing in the film to serve their own purposes. Through the "happy ending," the films presented the possibility that change could take place without massive upheaval or disruption. Such purposes led reformers such as Jane Addams to move from initial condemnation of the motion picture to praise for its capacity to "uplift" or "educate." Film could serve the interests of the middle class and of the film industry by appealing to a broader audience by using virtuous calls for reform.

The reformist dramas provided a respectable mission for a cinema in search of itself. By 1915, the poet and film critic Vachel Lindsay could observe that "the motion picture goes almost as far as journalism into the social fabric in some ways, further in others." Whatever their political message, however, films penetrated the social fabric even further than did muckraking journalists by tapping fantasy as well as reality, animating and heightening the stories told in print. The cinema offered fantastic solutions that appealed to unconscious human desire at the same time that it raised problems of everyday life. Some of this process had been observed as early as 1915 during the height of the early silent film era. In the summer of that year, a portly, balding psychologist from Harvard discovered a diversion from Boston's humid afternoons. Professor Hugo Munsterberg became one of the cinema's most ardent devotees. Munsterberg's first movie experience, a somewhat risqué film called *Neptune's Daughter*, had been, by his own daughter's account, one of the most startling adventures of the professor's life. Settled in the anonymous darkness of a theater, he had watched a fascinating phenomenon unfold. On the movie screen before him, the actress Annette Kellerman danced in a costume that left little to the imagination. But what fascinated the professor even more than Kellerman were the actual illustrations of the nuances of human perception that he had studied and taught for years in the university. Munsterberg was captivated by the manner in which the camera appeared to virtually become the human eye, and in which it might also create a new vision of the world controlled by moral forces. He spent the rest of the summer of 1915 carefully studying the new art form, even securing for himself a personal tour of the Vitagraph Studios.

Part of Munsterberg's interest lay in interpreting how the cinema dwelled on human needs and how it could direct the emotions of audiences. In a treatise on the motion picture, *The Photoplay*, published by the psychologist shortly before he died in 1916, he laid the foundation for a sophisticated theory of film. One of the greatest attractions of the cinema, he suggested, was its "stirring up of desires together with their constant fulfillment."

More than a simple mirroring of visual perception, motion pictures became immensely popular with the masses in those formative years because, in part, they captured the enduring subtleties of human desire, with their tales of wistful longing for a better life. "The work of art," explained Munsterberg, "aims to keep both the demand and its fulfillment forever awake." The theater thus roused longing while it also left audiences with the "constant fulfillment" recognized by the psychologist. The popular culture emerging at the turn of the century acted as an agent of both social cohesion and the desire for change. That process emerges as the protest films addressed political and social subjects that held the capacity to rupture society.

Entertainment in itself involves a certain rupturing – a temporary suspension of belief in the outside world takes place along with a suspension of disbelief in the inner world constructed through entertainment. The melodrama of social protest suspended audiences between what they escaped from (their everyday lives) and what they escaped to (a more romantic version of the situation that structured those daily lives). By often resolving those situations in "happily ever after" endings, movies released their audiences from the grim cinematic creations of shabby tenement life, or sweatshop lines, into a world transformed, however briefly, into a realm where fantasy entered the tenement or sweatshop on the wings of romance or sudden wealth. If the melodramas refused to allow such interventions, they at least endowed their heroes and heroines with dignity.

A whole host of archetypal villains and victims danced in the flickering lights of the nickelodeons in a melodramatic exorcism of social wrongs. Such archetypes have never really left the motion picture – nor has the "happy ending," which restored faith in the enduring individual. In its early era of inventions, the cinema also set conventions. The primitive social problem films were the beginning of a long psychological trip into the present with which they are intimately joined. Like any pioneers, the early movies were original, but the trail they blazed into the American psyche became a familiar path marked with desires and frustrations – and so timeworn that we have taken its twists and turns for granted.

By the eve of World War I, most of the small film companies were gone, and with them the storefront nickelodeons and those primitive short films that raised social problems, much as the muckrakers did. Those formative years of the cinema, unique as they were, established the manner in which films continue to raise social issues while at the same time containing them in satisfactory bourgeois resolutions. America's dilemmas are in many ways similar to those faced by the country just after the turn of the century – overcrowding, sexual inequalities, political corruption, and corporate irresponsibility still find their way into a cinema that solves those problems in a private fashion, just as the early films did. But never again will the process be quite so blatant as in the silent social problem films.

Something was forgotten in the following decades, or lost in sentimentalized versions of the early period. In 1915, Vachel Lindsay expressed a thought that is poignant in retrospect. He dramatically claimed that film is a "new weapon of men, and the face of the whole earth changes." Lindsay, regrettably, was wrong. Much still remains to be explored and "remembered" from that era when "the whole earth changed" because of a new entertainment form.

In those one or two reelers are more than the origins of the social problem film. The films contain cultural signposts of paramount importance about how entertainment shapes the political issues affecting the lives of moviegoers. They are a reminder of the capacity of film to explore the problems of society and lessen their threat while still suggesting the need for change. When Stephen Crane's fictional Maggie attended her turn-of-the-century melodramas, she would leave "with raised spirits" after watching people like herself defeat those with power over them. Though such triumphs in the cinema were measured in terms of religious redemptions or acts of fate, they were still significant glimpses into class conflict in America. Within that complex role is buried an even deeper significance. The films also reveal a society struggling to maintain order in a period of terrific unrest – an order that allowed inequality and the essential powerlessness of the average American to continue.

Those days when the film industry was young reveal that the cinema reverberates through time itself. It goes beyond its specific era to illuminate the ongoing power of the motion picture to dramatize the needs and desires of its viewers through generations of archetypal characters and situations. Like H.G. Wells's heroes, one can travel into the past with the flick of a switch on a projection machine and discover America at the turn of the century. Unfortunately, however, such a cinematic "journey" can be as difficult as a ride on Wells's time machine: many of the films simply no longer exist, and can be known only through reviews or synopses. When silent films lost their commercial viability within several years after release, the film companies, eager for fast production and quick profits, carelessly discarded them. Often the companies themselves were too short-lived to maintain their films. The perishable silver nitrate stock on which the motion pictures were printed further reduced their chance for survival. As early as 1906, one critic recognized the danger of losing such valuable cultural artifacts as the new motion picture. "We often wonder where all the films that are made and used a few times go to," he wrote, "and the questions come up in our minds, again and again: Are the manufacturers aware that they are making history? Do they realize that in fifty or one hundred years the films now being made will be curiosities." Now, some eighty years later, one only wishes that filmmakers had listened to his admonition. The films that exist today are rare cultural documents.

Though the preserved film footage offers valuable insight into the climate of American cultural and political tensions, an understanding of their full impact must, ironically, rely heavily on original printed material. Controversy over the issues of social protest spilled over into the pages of early trade magazines such as the *Moving Picture World*, *Photography*, *Variety*, and *Photoplay*. Their reviews testify to the lively arguments over workers' rights, class conflict, political graft, and sexual politics that the films once delivered.

Such themes that the films repeatedly explored illustrate the larger dilemmas of society in dealing with injustices and inequalities. [These include] the class-bound nature of early melodrama and what the sociologist Edward A. Ross called "criminaloids" – those who grew wealthy by exploiting the poor. Such characters made ideal villains in films that ventured into the inner circles of the nation's corrupt elites .... [These also include] the "cinema of the submerged," particularly as D.W. Griffith defined it. There, a cinema made heroes and heroines out of those "submerged" in powerlessness. Tenement dwellers attempted to flee the ghetto and escaped prisoners tried to elude their captors in plots that pointed out the plight of the victims of economic or legal injustice. ....

[Early silent films also showed] ... working-class heroes [who] fought back against their employers. But the problem of "Capital Versus Labor," as the film of that title designated it, varied from visions of unruly "ferret-eyed workers" to cruel "fat cat" factory owners who exploited children and honest working people. White slavery ... was one of the most controversial topics ever sensationalized by the cinema. Taken alone, it was a euphemism for forced prostitution. The central concern of the explosive white slavery films and the melodramas on alcoholism and birth control was the preservation of the private sphere of the family.

The films about the woman suffrage movement … brought together a wide spectrum of propaganda for and against the movement. Caricatures of man-hating suffragettes paraded across movie screens as comedies ridiculed the notion of women voting. Suffragists themselves fought back with movie cameras, countering the comic attack with persuasive melodramas starring beautiful suffragist heroines. They elevated film into a significant political tool for their cause. The suffrage films, with their span of satire, newsreels, and melodramas, offer an opportunity to look at the tremendous range of political positions that the cinema took on a single subject.

The early risk-taking silent filmmakers saw their new medium as one that could both entertain and, in due course, instruct. They catered to the masses with a gamut of social commentary that reflected the traditional American belief that, once social wrongs were exposed to the people, the people would see to it that they were righted. More importantly, the companies catered to the masses to build their own business empires. Thus they were reformers who also sought a profit; with their sermons on social injustice and their faith in the individual, they became, quite unintentionally, America's newest street preachers, making movies that became indeed "loud silents."

2

Silent Cinema as Historical Mythmaker
The Birth of a Nation

Eric Niderost

Director D.W. Griffith's The Birth of a Nation *was the longest, costliest, and most popular American film of its day. Released in 1915 at a running time of nearly three hours, the film cost $100,000 to make, an enormous sum at the time. It became the first film shown in the White House, and was eventually seen by nearly 200,000,000 people. Not only was it the largest-grossing film of its day, it may have been the largest-grossing film of all time. For the film industry, then, it was pure gold, but the film also provided historical justification for segregation and disfranchisement. The movie inflamed racial tension and badly distorted a terrible and violent chapter in American history.*

The message embedded in the film was that Reconstruction, the period following the Civil War, was an unmitigated disaster, that African Americans could never be integrated into white society as equals, and that the violent actions of the Ku Klux Klan were justified because they were necessary to reestablish legitimate and honest government. To convey an impression of historical accuracy, Griffith incorporated cinematic reconstructions of famous historical scenes, such as the assassination of Abraham Lincoln. He also filled the film with scenes that played to racial prejudice, showing arrogant freedmen pushing whites off sidewalks and murdering blacks who remained loyal to their masters. Many of the film's characters were crude stereotypes: loyal house servants, deluded field hands, arrogant mulattoes lusting after Southern white women.

The early twentieth century marked the nadir of race relations in the United States. Lynching was widespread. Race riots directed against African Americans took place in many cities. African Americans in the South were relegated to separate schools and restaurants and denied the right to vote. Birth of a Nation *helped justify the denial of civil rights to African Americans. In this essay, Eric Niderost reviews what made the film so influential and why it aroused so much passion.*

Eric Niderost, "The Birth of a Nation," *American History Magazine* (October 2005), pp. 62, 64, 65, 66, 67, 78, 80. Reprinted with permission, American History Magazine, October 2005, © Copyright Weider History Group.

On July 4, 1914, director D.W. Griffith began work on a new movie called *The Clansman*, an epic about the Civil War and the subsequent agonies of Reconstruction. It was a major production, an epic in every sense of the word, with sets that seemingly filled every foot of his Fine Arts Studio in Hollywood, California.

Griffith was a curious figure who didn't conform to the popular image of a silent-film director. Unlike his contemporary Cecil B. DeMille, he eschewed the usual costume of rolled-up sleeves, jodhpurs, and riding boots, opting instead for a crisply tailored business suit complete with celluloid collar and immaculate tie. It was an outfit more in keeping with the boardroom than the cutting room, but it somehow reflected Griffith's reserved Victorian persona.

The Clansman, later retitled *The Birth of a Nation*, is still considered a landmark of the American cinema. The film has been praised for its technical virtuosity and damned for its demeaning and racist depiction of black Americans. *Birth* was a kind of rite of passage for American movies, marking a transition from crude infancy to a robust adolescence. Griffith and his cameraman Billy Bitzer used a dazzling array of techniques to propel the story forward. Moving, tracking, and panning shots gave new life to even static scenes. Crosscutting between two scenes built suspense, and the use of cameo profiles and close-ups gave the movie a new emotional intimacy.

Although Griffith did not invent these techniques, he used them in such brilliant and innovative ways that it seemed as if he had. The director was a master storyteller, and by 1914 he was at the height of his powers. Monumental in conception, epic in scope and narrative power, the movie influenced filmmakers for generations to come. *The Birth of a Nation* was pure Griffith, and every frame of celluloid bore his stamp.

David Wark Griffith, son of Jacob Wark Griffith, was born on January 22, 1875, in Floydsfork, later Crestwood, Ky. The older man, nicknamed Roaring Jake, was a veteran Confederate colonel who had once commanded the 1st Kentucky Cavalry during the Civil War. Roaring Jake filled young David's head with nostalgic tales of dashing, gray-clad cavaliers defending the antebellum way of life.

The Confederacy was no more, and slavery had been abolished, but by 1880 most of the civil rights that blacks had enjoyed immediately after the war had been taken away by newly reestablished white supremacist state governments. The Peculiar Institution, chattel slavery, had been replaced by a kind of serfdom in which black sharecroppers, debt-ridden and disenfranchised, were relegated to second-class citizenship.

Jacob Griffith died suddenly when David was only 10. The old colonel had been badly wounded in the war, and there was speculation that the injuries had been responsible – at least in part – for his demise. In any case, Roaring Jake's passing caused quite a commotion, and his deathbed scene was forever etched in young David's memory.

In later years, the director took great pains to hide his true self from the public, adopting a patrician reserve that exuded an air of mystery. But when he described his father's death, he also unintentionally revealed his own deeply cherished core beliefs. When Griffith entered his father's bedroom, he later recalled, he was met by a scene of grief and lamentation: "Four [older African Americans] were standing in the back at the foot of the bed weeping freely. I am quite sure they really loved him." The unconscious racism and implied unquestioning acceptance of black inferiority in that statement reflect Griffith's view of black–white relations. Thirty years later, those attitudes would find new expression in *The Birth of a Nation.*

As a young man, Griffith tried a variety of jobs but nursed a secret ambition to become a great playwright. Initially, he became an actor, traveling across the country and appearing in stage productions of varying quality. Finally one of his plays was produced in 1907. Titled *A Fool and a Girl*, it was an embarrassing flop.

Faced with near-destitution, Griffith turned to motion pictures as a source of income. The movies in the 1890s were cheap entertainment for the masses. Working-class people, many of them European immigrants crowded into urban slums, flocked to nickelodeons for a few minutes' escape from their daily toil. The early offerings were only about one reel long – that is, about 12 to 14 minutes. By 1910 more middle-class people were attending movies, but many still held a deeply rooted prejudice against them as cheap shows for cheap people.

Griffith shared these sentiments, at least at first, but then he began to see film in an entirely different light. He was among the first to grasp the potential of the movies – their as yet untapped power to educate as well as entertain. The fledgling movie actor soon joined the Biograph Company in New York City, where in addition to appearing in front of the camera he wrote film scenarios. When Biograph's leading director became ill, Griffith was hired as a replacement.

The Adventures of Dollie, released in the summer of 1908, was Griffith's first directorial effort. Within a few years, the helmsman had his own stock company, which included performers such as Lillian Gish, Mary Pickford, Blanche Sweet, Henry B. Walthall, and Lionel Barrymore. Eventually, however, Griffith broke from Biograph and formed a partnership with Harry and Roy Aitken of Mutual. The Aitkens would stay in their New York base, while Griffith would set up shop in Hollywood. He had done some filming on the West Coast before, but now the move would be more or less permanent. Many Biograph people followed Griffith, including Lillian Gish and cameraman Billy Bitzer, so there was no shortage of talent on hand.

All the pieces were falling into place; now what was needed was a subject worthy of Griffith's ambitions. A writer named Frank Woods introduced Griffith to a 1905 work titled *The Clansman*. It had achieved modest success as both a novel and stage play, and Woods was sure it would suit the screen. Griffith fully agreed and responded with alacrity. For him *The Clansman* was both inspired and inspiring, and it dealt with a subject close to his Southern roots.

The timing seemed right as well. The Civil War was very much in vogue, since the years 1911–15 marked the 50th anniversary of the bloody four-year conflict that had torn the nation asunder. More than 600,000 Americans had died in that self-inflicted holocaust, and millions had served in Northern and Southern armies. Many veterans were still alive, and in 1913 there had been a great reunion of some 50,000 of them, Union and Confederate, at Gettysburg.

The Clansman, Griffith thought, presented an accurate account of the Southern side of the story. The director was interested in the social, not political, effects of the Civil War and its immediate aftermath. In the film, Griffith makes clear that he is not in sympathy with states' rights and secession. After Lee surrenders to Grant, a title card speaks with seeming approval of Liberty and Union, one and inseparable, now and forever.

But Griffith the Southerner could recall the bitterness of Reconstruction through the tales told by his father and others. According to them, it was a time when Northern carpetbaggers descended on the prostrate South like a horde of ravenous wolves.

Worse yet, they destroyed the natural order of society by giving blacks the franchise and equality with whites. The result, so this view held, was a period of suffering and white subjugation, until the depredations were reversed by the glorious exploits of the Ku Klux Klan.

The Clansman was written by Thomas Dixon, a lawyer turned Baptist preacher from North Carolina who was incensed when he saw a revival of *Uncle Tom's Cabin* in 1901. To Dixon, *Uncle Tom's Cabin* was Northern propaganda that depicted blacks in a favorable light and was full of lies and calumnies about the antebellum South and, by implication, the turn-of-the-century South as well.

Dixon set out to answer these lies with his own version of the truth in his 1902 novel *The Leopard's Spots: A Romance of the White Man's Burden, 1865–1900.* The book was a success, encouraging Dixon to pen *The Clansman* in 1905. That same year, a stage version of *The Clansma*n appeared that was an amalgam of both works. The stage production enjoyed a successful road run, though box-office receipts were perhaps greater in the South, where it struck a responsive chord with white audiences. Dixon initially wanted $25,000 from the filmmakers for the movie rights, but then agreed to $2,000 up front and 25 percent of the gross.

In his works, Dixon expressed some then common views on Reconstruction. The preacher once noted, "my object is to teach the North, the young North, what it has never known – the awful suffering of the white man during the dreadful Reconstruction period." He went on to say that he "believed Almighty God anointed the white men of the South by their suffering … to demonstrate to the world that the white man must and shall be supreme." These were sentiments that D.W. Griffith endorsed as well.

The shooting schedule was a long one, lasting from July to November 1914. The first part of the film is highlighted by spectacular battle scenes, some of the best ever committed to celluloid. They were shot in the San Fernando Valley, between today's Warner Brothers Studio and Universal City.

The movie's plot revolves around two families, one Northern and one Southern. The Stoneman clan is headed by Congressman Austin Stoneman, a Northern abolitionist and Radical Republican who is loosely based on real-life Pennsylvania Senator Thaddeus Stevens. Stoneman has three children, sons Phil and Tod, and a vivacious daughter named Elsie, played by Lillian Gish.

When the film opens, Phil and Tod are seen visiting their old boarding school friends the Camerons, Southern gentry who live in Piedmont, SC. In the epic, life in the prewar South is depicted in an idyllic, moonlight-and-magnolias fashion, with paternalistic whites taking care of happy, carefree slaves.

Ben Cameron, nicknamed The Little Colonel, develops a romantic attachment to Northern Elsie, and she welcomes his attentions. In similar fashion, eldest Northern son Phil Stoneman falls in love with Southern belle Margaret Cameron. But these promising romances are cut short by the outbreak of the Civil War. Griffith is at his best in depicting both the horrors and heroism that war engenders. In the scenes portraying the Battle of Petersburg, Ben leads a heroic, if ultimately futile, assault against the Union lines. He is badly wounded and captured.

The war ends with the North triumphant, but then President Abraham Lincoln is assassinated. His death signals the start of Radical Reconstruction, and Congressman Stoneman is now a power in the land. He dispatches his henchman, the mulatto Silas Lynch, to Piedmont to establish carpetbagger rule and black supremacy. As the story continues, Southern whites are degraded, abused, and forced to acknowledge blacks as equals. Lawless blacks freely engage in pillage and rapine, while whiskey-swilling black politicians lustfully leer at white women and crudely scratch bare feet.

His soul tormented by the ruin he sees all around him, Ben Cameron is close to utter despair when he sees some white children don sheets and pretend to be ghosts. Their childish masquerade scares some black youngsters, providing Ben with the inspiration he needs to create the Ku Klux Klan.

The film builds to a powerful climax. When a former slave named Gus makes advances to another Cameron daughter, Flora, she loses her balance and falls off a cliff. The title card opines that Flora found sweeter the opal gate of death – that is, death was preferable to a possible rape or even a black man's embrace. Ben witnesses his sister's fall or leap (the action is ambiguous) and swears revenge.

The Klan then appears on screen, decked out in full white-sheeted regalia, as aveng-ing knights who track Gus down and give him a fair trial before lynching him. His lifeless corpse is dumped at Silas Lynch's door as a warning. The mulatto leader reacts, throwing off all restraints in a bid for ultimate power. His black militia ravish the land, and at one point trap some of the Cameron family and Northerner Phil Stoneman in a cabin that just happens to be the abode of two Union veterans. The Yankees wel-come the fugitives, and before long the former enemies of North and South are united again in common defense of their Aryan birthright.

Meanwhile, Silas Lynch tells Elsie he wants to marry her. Even the staunch aboli-tionist Congressman Stoneman recoils in horror at the thought of this race-mixing, this miscegenation, and the possibility of a black son-in-law. Lynch, however, is unde-terred, and proceeds with plans for a forced wedding.

In a series of exciting crosscuts and tracking shots, the Klan rides to the rescue in the nick of time. The Camerons are rescued from the black militia, and Silas Lynch's nefarious plans are foiled. The forces of black Reconstruction are defeated by the tri-umphant Klan. At film's end, Ben and Elsie are reunited, and peace, justice, and white supremacy are restored to the South.

After some sneak previews on January 1 and 2, 1915, the movie was scheduled to have its official premiere on February 8 in Los Angeles. The local chapter of the National Association for the Advancement of Colored People (NAACP) tried to get an injunction to stop the premiere, but the legal argument had too narrow a focus and failed to stop the screening. The NAACP, founded in 1909, was composed of both blacks and white liberals and actively campaigned for black rights.

The Los Angeles premiere was a triumph, but the picture's real test would be its New York opening in March. In 1915 Los Angeles was still considered a cultural backwater, but New York City was thought to be the cultural capital of the nation. No expense was spared for the film's Gotham debut. The Liberty Theatre, near Times Square, was leased for the premiere and its subsequent run. It was also announced that the top admission price would be $2, a steep tariff in an era when a first-run pic-ture ticket might cost 25 cents.

Everyone associated with the picture – now retitled *The Birth of a Nation* – knew they had won a censorship skirmish with the NAACP, but the civil rights organization was far from conceding defeat. In fact, the Los Angeles clash was only the first round. Thomas Dixon was impressed with the movie, and decided to pull some strings to ensure its ultimate success.

Dixon remembered an old college friend from his student days at Johns Hopkins University. The friend's name was Woodrow Wilson, and he just happened to be president of the United States. *The Clansman* author quickly penned a letter to the White House asking for a half-hour meeting with the president. It was granted, and Dixon did all he could to flatter Wilson – not as the nation's powerful chief executive but as a scholar and student of history and sociology.

The wily Dixon knew his schoolmate well. Wilson was an academic at heart and was willing to view this controversial motion picture. But there was a problem: Wilson was still in mourning for his first wife, and publicly attending a movie theater would be out of the question. The president suggested a solution to the dilemma: Why not have a special screening at the White House? This was more than even Dixon had expected, and arrangements were soon made.

The Birth of a Nation was shown to the president, the cabinet, and staff members on February 18, 1915. It was the first time a film was ever officially screened at the White House. Wilson was a Southerner, a man who endorsed Jim Crow segregation in Washington, DC, so the film's basic premise was one the president seemed to share, at least in part. The fact that many of the movie's title cards were excerpts from Wilson's own 1902 work, *History of the American People*, certainly didn't hurt.

Wilson was awed by the movie, commenting that it was like writing history with lightning, adding, "and my only regret is that it is all so terribly true." The president's ringing endorsement gave the picture a new credibility. Dixon's shrewd maneuver had paid off.

The NAACP tried to stop the upcoming New York premiere by appealing to the National Board of Censorship. The movie was shown to the entire board, some 125 people, and a few of the more liberal members – notably Chairman Frederic C. Howe – found the blatant racism disquieting. But the board as a whole was dazzled by the movie's sheer narrative power and sweeping spectacle. It was decided the film could be shown, though the board would withhold formal approval until a few strategic edits were made.

In an 11th-hour attempt to stop the premiere, the NAACP argued in court that the picture endangered the public peace. In other words, the inflammatory nature of the subject matter would cause racial tension, possibly even riots. The judge was unmoved; the premiere would go on as planned.

The March 3, 1915, opening was a personal and professional triumph for Griffith. Thousands of New Yorkers flocked to see the movie, in spite of the $2-a-seat ticket price and a running time of almost three hours. The NAACP picketed the Liberty Theatre, but they were virtually ignored by eager patrons waiting to be admitted. *The Birth of a Nation* played in New York for 10 months, during which an estimated 825,000 viewed the film.

Ten days after the premiere, social reformer and NAACP member Jane Addams blasted the film in an interview published by the *New York Post*. Addams, best known for her work among the urban poor and immigrant populations of Chicago, was a respected figure whose opinion mattered. She hated the racism she saw in the film, especially the pernicious caricature of the Negro race.

Unfortunately, the protests of Addams and others were drowned out by the swelling chorus of critical, and even academic, approval. "A new Epoch of art is reached," enthused the *New York Herald*, while the *New York Globe* was of the opinion that never before had such a combination of spectacle and tense drama been seen.

Griffith was genuinely hurt by the controversy. He loved Negroes, he claimed, and felt white Southerners had a special rapport with blacks and a unique understanding of their natures. To accuse him of prejudice against blacks "is like saying I am against children, as they were our children, whom we loved and cared for all our lives." The idea that blacks might have wanted a higher degree of human dignity and to be treated as adults, not children, seems never to have crossed his mind.

The major black roles in *The Birth of a Nation* are played by white actors. Their faces are covered with burnt cork, and there is some suggestion of whitened lips that harkens back to the popular minstrel shows of the 19th century. Griffith tried to side-step the issue by claiming he had given the matter careful consideration, but there was not going to be any black blood among the principals. The implication was that blacks lacked both the intelligence and talent to play a character of their own race.

It is true that Dixon's ranting, hysterical, almost foaming at the mouth racism is toned down in the movie. In his book, a black is a thick-lipped, flat nosed, spindle-shanked Negro, exuding his nauseous animal odor. Griffith's dreamy-eyed Victorian romanticism eliminated the viciousness, substituting a paternalism that was ultimately just as offensive. Griffith's South is a mythic one, rooted in his own nostalgic child-hood memories and in the pro-Southern scholarship prevalent at the time.

Griffith was a man of his time and place, sincere in his misguided beliefs. He may not have anticipated the storm of controversy that was about to break over his head, but he was smart enough to hedge his bets. In an obvious effort to disarm his critics, Griffith added a title card that firmly states, "This is an historical presentation of the Civil War and Reconstruction period, and is not meant to reflect on any race or people of today."

In Griffith's world there are two kinds of blacks. The first are described in the sub-titles as Faithful Souls, childlike Uncle Toms, who know their place and accept their natural inferiority. Happy and contented, eager to do ole massa's bidding, they can work 10 hours in the cotton fields and still dance and sing for de white folks at the end of the day. They know that racial equality will only lead to disaster. "Yo' northern low-down black trash!" a faithful Cameron maid declares when she sees a Northern black. "Don't try no airs on me!"

The other kind of black is the renegade, who refuses to accept his lot and dares to think he is as good as a white person. Denied the guidance of his betters, he soon falls into a life of laziness, vice, and crime. Griffith insisted that, appearances to the con-trary, carpetbagging Northerners, not renegade blacks like Silas Lynch, were the real villains of the story. In his view, scheming Northern politicians and carpetbaggers used the blacks as dupes to further their own ends. While white Southerners were distracted by black depredations, white Northerners moved in to secure both wealth and power behind the scenes.

Its efforts to ban the film having proved abortive, the NAACP decided to change tactics. It would try to get the most offensive scenes cut from existing release prints – a partial concession to the film's enormous popularity with white audiences as it opened across the country. Black leader W.E.B. Dubois entered the fray, writing a series of scathing attacks against *Birth*'s unvarnished racism, and the NAACP pub-lished a 47-page pamphlet entitled *Fighting a Vicious Film: Protest Against The Birth of a Nation*.

Matters came to a head in Boston, where Mayor James Curley convened a special meeting to determine if all showings of *The Birth of a Nation* should be banned. Curley was concerned about the possibility of violence: There had been threats to blow up the theater with dynamite. But, the mayor said, the gross black caricatures in the film were no different than the exaggerations one would see in productions of Shakespeare.

Defenders of the film came forward, but were drowned out by a chorus of hisses, boos and catcalls from civil rights advocates. D.W. Griffith himself was saluted with a loud and raucous round of boos when he tried to argue against censorship. Moorfield Storey, the white head of Boston's NAACP, challenged Griffith's claims of absolute historical accuracy. He asked the director if it was historic that a [henchman like Lynch] held a white woman in a room and demanded forced marriage!

Of course Storey was right. In spite of the film's historic set pieces – like the Lincoln assassination and Lee's surrender at Appomattox – many incidents were wholly fictitious. The Klan was not created by a man who watched some white children playing ghost. It was founded by a group of former Confederate officers in Tennessee, and in May 1866, famed cavalry general Nathan Bedford Forrest became their Grand Wizard. What began as a charitable organization that helped Confederate widows and orphans soon took a more sinister turn. Klansmen used intimidation, torture, and even murder against carpetbaggers and scalawags and to prevent newly enfranchised blacks from going to the polls. As violence in the name of the KKK increased, the original group disbanded in 1869, but loosely formed klaverns continued to operate throughout much of the South. Following a government crackdown on such groups, notably through the passage of the 14th and 15th Amendments, the Civil Rights Enforcement Act of 1870–71 and the Ku Klux Act of 1871, these groups, most of whose goals had been achieved anyway, withered.

Griffith knew that many of his plot details were fictional, but tried to deflect this criticism by inviting his adversary to come see the play. The director tried to shake hands with Storey, who recoiled with an icy "No, Sir!"

The stage was set for a confrontation. A few of the more offensive scenes were cut for Boston consumption, but many racist episodes still remained. Black activist and newspaper publisher William Monroe Trotter led some 200 African Americans to a place just outside the Tremont Theater, where *The Birth of a Nation* was playing to packed houses. The theater had hired Pinkerton detectives in anticipation of trouble, and they were soon joined by uniformed Boston police.

Trotter and a few followers entered the lobby, but when they tried to buy some tickets they were bluntly told, Sold out! It wasn't true, and Trotter knew it, so he repeated his request for a ticket. Again he was refused, but this time he was told to leave the theater. When he loudly protested against this blatant discrimination, the police acted to forcibly remove him. A scuffle broke out, and in the melee Trotter was hit by a policeman's billy club. Trotter and 10 other blacks were arrested and led away.

But other blacks and a few sympathetic whites had managed to sneak into the theater, where they caused an uproar by jeering during racist scenes and pelting the screen with eggs. Some of the protesters went a step further by detonating stink bombs that filled the auditorium with an acrid stench. After the movie ended, violence flared in the streets, with groups of blacks and whites battling it out until arrested by the police.

The New York and Boston screenings were only two of the battles in an increasingly acrimonious debate about the picture and its merits. When the NAACP appealed to local censorship boards or government officials, they met with varying responses. Usually the most blatantly racist scenes were cut, not because they were offensive, but because they might incite violence or race riot.

The movie was banned in a few places, including the entire state of Kansas (a restriction lifted in 1923). Picket lines and protests only sparked people's interest and curiosity and added to box-office receipts.

Blossoming from the burgeoning Nativist movement in the early 20th century, the KKK was reincarnated in 1915 by Atlanta businessman William J. Simmons. This version, which claimed some 5 million adherents by 1925, not only opposed black equality but was also anti-Catholic, anti-Semitic and anti-immigrant. Unfortunately, *The Birth of a Nation* became a recruiting tool for the revived Klan, which was certainly not Griffith's intention. Some have claimed that Griffith's epic sparked the resurgence of the Klan, since Klan recruiting propaganda was sometimes printed side by side with the movie's theater ads. The film's impact on that resurgence, though considerable, has been grossly exaggerated.

In spite of all the controversies, vilifications, and court battles, *The Birth of a Nation* was a critical and popular success, far and away the most profitable film of the silent era. After its initial run, it was rereleased in 1924, 1931, and 1938. If the rereleases are added to the totals, *Birth* earned somewhere between $13 and $18 million.

D.W. Griffith became a household name, lionized by press and public alike. *Birth*'s huge profits gave him a kind of creative independence, but he failed to change with the times. He continued making films – *Intolerance* in 1916, followed by, among others, *Orphans of the Storm*, *Way Down East*, and *Abraham Lincoln*. He directed his last movie, *The Struggle*, in 1931, in the early sound era. His peculiar brand of Victorian romanticism, however, had fallen out of favor by the late 1920s. While many of his later films were successes in one way or another, D.W. Griffith died in 1948 without having produced another motion picture that generated the kind of critical acclaim, box-office success, and controversy that *The Birth of a Nation* did.

3

The Revolt Against Victorianism
Douglas Fairbanks, Mary Pickford,
and the New Personality

Lary May

A profound shift in public discourse took place in the United States during the 1910s. In August 1913, a popular magazine announced that it was "Sex o'clock in America." A few months later, an article entitled "The Repeal of Reticence" declared that an "obsession with sex has set us all a-babbling about matters once excluded from the amenities of conversation" – subjects like birth control, divorce, prostitution, and venereal disease. Many developments associated with the 1920s – such as the appearance of the flapper, with her scanty attire, cosmetics, bare legs and arms, and bobbed hair, and a craze for lively and intimate dancing– actually began in the preceding decade. Meanwhile, the formalities of courtship gave way to a new custom, dating, and more and more young women worked side by side with men, as secretaries and store clerks, rather than as domestic servants, factory operatives, and teachers.

The movies played a critical role in promoting the revolution in morals and manners of the 1910s. In this essay, film historian Lary May describes how films in the teens began to shed their Victorian trappings and to celebrate glamour, the exotic, and pleasure.

At the point when Griffith's masterpieces infused Victorianism with moral passion, there arose from the ranks of his company two offspring who began to match the promise of the media to something dramatically new: a cultural reorientation. These disciples went far beyond their master in creating images for the modern era. Douglas Fairbanks and Mary Pickford became so popular that from 1914 until America's entry into World War I, they may have been more widely admired than their political counterparts, Woodrow Wilson and Theodore Roosevelt. "Doug" and "Mary" had risen to fame by becoming something truly new: movie stars. Pickford's films gained such acclaim that magazines voted her the "most popular girl in the world" and "America's Sweetheart." Yet the "Queen of Our People," as the *New Republic* called her, gained that love not by radiating pure womanhood, but by doing what seemed impossible, merging the virgin to the harlot, and moving beyond the spheres which had divided the sexes in the nineteenth century. At the same time, her weekly columns in the press and her screen roles depicted her as the modern working woman who supported suffrage and was emancipated morally as well. As the perfect parallel male, Fairbanks

Figure 4 Douglas Fairbanks in *The Black Pirate* (1926). United Artists. Directed by Albert Parker. Courtesy of Jerry Murbach, www.doctormacro1.info.

merged the cowboy to the athletic urbanite at a time when it appeared that the frontier might be gone. When they married in 1920, the circled closed. On the screen as in reality, their celebrity showed that leisure was not an extension of the past, but something dramatically different.

Where did this come from? What did it mean for the modern urbanite? In the beginning of Pickford's and Fairbanks's careers in 1914, it was by no means obvious that such a reorientation was possible. D.W. Griffith's great film, *The Birth of a Nation*, had not only given the art a tremendous dynamism, but it infused moviegoing with a sense of energy it would never lose. Nevertheless, Griffith's forward looking techniques were fused to a backward-looking ideal. The great director's work would continue to be popular until the twenties; but in 1914 new producers arose who realized that resistance to the modern age in the name of Victorianism was no longer viable. These film makers had to appeal to the special needs of an audience gathered after 1914. The "new" middle classes had now joined workers and small property owners, and together they confronted large organizations as a fact of life. Neither these viewers nor the film makers could return to the old ways. Still, as people who had inherited the Anglo-Saxon tradition of ascetic individualism, they were sensitive to the reformers' critique of modern life. The central question in their lives was how to find a morality appropriate to the corporate order, one that solved the difficult issues of work, family, and class status that had infused the politics of the era.

Generally we are accustomed to thinking that the vast cultural and economic changes of the era occurred separately, rather than in some dynamic relation. Yet for the movie audience created after 1914, these forces were vitally connected. Clues to this symbiosis can be gleaned from recent studies which show that the "new middle classes" were undergoing a major political reorientation. In contrast to the pre-1914 audience of workers and small property owners, these groups were not concerned with rolling back the clock to an entrepreneurial world. Rather, as employees and managers of large organizations, they followed the new nationalism of Theodore Roosevelt, believing that well-run corporations and professional organizations might serve the public interest. In this, the code of expertise and efficiency superseded earlier values of local control and individualism. Thus they were not so concerned with moral crusading or attacking large business concerns. In fact, although these people were heir to an Anglo-Saxon tradition, they were shedding the asceticism that demanded control over property, production, and oneself. Describing this change, one participant recalled,

> Our fathers' businesses were run by other men, brought from elsewhere. Our first families became absentee landlords of distant corporations rather than magnates of industry whose gates gaped for us, and if this brought economic evils with it, it at least ended the tyranny of business over the mind of youth.

The result brought a transformation in personal and social behavior. Vice crusaders' worries were not totally unfounded. Recent social historians have documented a measurable change, particularly among the urban middle classes. There was not just a shedding of Victorian norms, but an increase in the pursuit of pleasure. Dress reform, "exotic" dances, and the advent of sports were visible to observers; but there is also hard evidence to show a rise of consumer spending and sexual experimentation during the first two decades of the twentieth century. Contemporaries saw this shift manifested most dramatically in the home. The family seemed less concerned with self-denial and more geared toward self-indulgence. In the Victorian era, youth was something to master and shed, along with play, upon reaching maturity. But now adults seemed eager to bring these elements into their lives as well. As Henry Seidel Canby recalled,

> Self-expression for youth is supposed to have brought about the change in family life that came with the new generation. It was a cause, but an equally powerful one was self-expression for parents who wanted to stay young and live their own lives, while the boys and girls were sent off to camps and schools. Fathers and mothers in the earlier time put fatherhood and motherhood first.

The fact that the economic and cultural changes occurred simultaneously opens the possibility that the moral revolution was helping to ease some of the fears people had about the rise of big business. A previous generation of reformers had tried to master the new economy with the values of Victorians and small entrepreneurs. They saw that an organized work world thwarted the sense of freedom and autonomy found in the open marketplace; and the hierarchical order also disrupted the sexual and family roles of the past. People then used affluence to enjoy urban amusements formerly considered degraded. Yet to unleash consumption seemed to threaten the code of asceticism needed for success. Abundance might erode the work ethic, which rested on incentive. With so much at stake, how was this task with its dangers of class and sexual chaos accomplished? How could a new urban middle-class ideal be attained, one that might solve the problems of alienating work and social conflict? While few businessmen had solutions to these problems, and reformers tried to master them through state action and Victorian policing, those who had inherited the new order were pioneering new realms of democratic freedom in arenas outside conventional life.

Nowhere was this quest more evident than in the motion picture industry. Before 1908, vice crusaders had seen the movies as a dangerous example of mass culture. The movie theater was a place where people broke from the formalities of work and socializing institutions. In reforming amusements from 1908 to 1914, crusaders hoped that movies could help resist the ill effects of modern life. Paradoxically, *The Birth of a Nation* was both the culmination and collapse of this thrust. It clearly identified motion pictures and mass culture with a reinvigorated sense of individualism against the corrupt powers of the day. It also brought more affluent audiences into the movies. Yet the controversy surrounding the film cracked the consensus of film makers and the censorship board. Then, the expensive failure of Griffith's *Intolerance* signaled that the audiences he helped to generate were not drawn to the themes he cherished: attacking big business and restoring the entrepreneurial economy. Other producers now realized that with the Board in disarray and corporations here to stay, it was time to break away from the old Victorian patterns. In that quest, they would use the liberating aesthetics pioneered by the master, but merge them to new social themes.

One clear indicator of that change was the rise of the movie stars. The use of a featured player to attract audiences had been the custom on the Broadway stage, the nineteenth-century touring companies, vaudeville, melodrama and ethnic theaters catering to the workers. Such players radiated a sense of power and personal magnetism that towered over the story. Yet film makers in the period after reform rarely gave players featured billing. This was partially due to their efforts to cut costs; they did not want to spend money on a "name." More importantly, directors like Griffith saw their art as separate from the entertainment popular with the rich and the immigrants. As agents of a higher destiny, his characters subordinated themselves to the larger message of the plot. Consequently, when movie producers after 1914 began to draw featured players from Broadway, vaudeville, and ethnic theaters, it signaled a crack in a long-standing tradition. Audiences might see characters who did not just serve a higher ideal, but were unique and dynamic personalities. As they came into the movies, they carried with them the aura of upper and lower class styles that the bourgeois had previously avoided. Now marquee favorites might offer models for dealing with the questions of cultural mixing and sexual experimentation.

Running parallel to the rise of the star system was an alteration in the themes of film stories. An examination of the plots listed in the major trade journals from 1907 to 1919 reveals a subtle shift. In the period from 1908 to 1912, the newer photoplays made by the independents had Victorian themes made so popular by Griffith. Shortly thereafter, the Anglo-Saxon tradition began to be questioned. More plots revolved around characters who succumbed to sins that previously had been attributed to foreigners, villains, and aristocrats. Usually the hero or heroine overcame dangers such as drink, overspending, and sexual women, suggesting that the conscience of the old culture still prevailed. Starting around 1913, this began to change, first with the comedy genre. Formerly, the viewers had laughed when characters failed to meet Victorian standards; now they laughed at the Victorian standards themselves. Still none of these films mocking formal roles offered a viable alternative. Eventually, around 1914, the full implications of this questioning yielded a completely modern approach to family life, as well as a reformist style different from Victorians or Progressives of Griffith's ilk. ....

[T]here was little doubt that both sexes were attracted to something other than Victorianism. Precisely at this point of tension between past and present desires, two players emerged, Douglas Fairbanks and Mary Pickford, who offered a transformation of domestic assumptions. Between 1914 and 1918, they became the first major dramatic stars of the films; only Chaplin's popularity and audience appeal equaled theirs. Coming from Broadway, they brought the prestigious aura of the stage into a formerly immigrant entertainment. Each was also part comic who made fun of restraints while pointing to the future. In the process, they both shed their original names, a symbolic act of separation from the past which would become typical among stars. For these extremely talented figures, cosmopolitan fun and healthy beauty replaced the spiritual symbolism connected to … Griffith characters. Both on and off the screen, their films, success, books, columns, and writings showed their fans how to solve the era's major dilemmas.

This was no small task. In endless interviews, Fairbanks related his own struggle against the ropes binding him to the past. As he told it, he was born in Denver, Colorado, in 1883, and grew up in the heart of a culture that glorified the self-made man. His father was Charles Ulman, the scion of a prominent Pennsylvania family who helped found the American Bar Association and served in the Union Army as a Civil War officer. Shortly thereafter, he went west to become a noted industrialist in Denver, where he wrote speeches for Republican presidential candidate Benjamin Harrison. Yet for some unknown reason he deserted the family, and his wife then changed her two sons' names to Fairbanks. Douglas attended the Colorado School of Mines; but soon he left school for the lure of the Broadway stage. Quickly he became a star, and married Beth Sully, the daughter of a Wall Street banker. Fairbanks then worked in his father-in-law's firm and joined the high society of the New York rich, participating in the European tours and sports of those who had the means to spend lavishly.

In 1915 Fairbanks returned to showbusiness, joining Harry Aitkin's company and working with D.W. Griffith. Yet the great director was soon at odds with the energetic Fairbanks, and the star soon struck a favorable contract with Famous Players-Lasky. So popular would he become that by 1920 he could form his own company with Pickford and Chaplin, United Artists. Throughout this era, "Doug" made over twenty-eight films in which he usually had control over his plots, in order to guarantee that the spirit of the character would reflect his concerns. Typically, the smiling, energetic hero mirrored Fairbanks himself. He has luxury and urban comfort; but within his mind and soul he still wants to be self-made. Even though his cheerful persona suggested to audiences a sense of optimism and a feeling that everything would turn out all right, the typical Fairbanks film would find the hero loaded with the worries of modern middle-class existence.

Fairbanks best dramatized the character in *His Majesty the American* (1919). The story charts the life of a young urbanite who does not know who his father is. Behind the symbolic quest for identity lies the vision of an expanding frontier where the hero might be a cowboy. His New York apartment is filled with snowshoes, saddles, and cowboy hats, suggesting that he is ready to master savages and bandits. But he is trapped in an urban civilization where he is faced with office routine and no challenges. Seeking outlets for his restless energy, he rescues poor girls from vice dens and babies from fires. With no thrills left, he goes west. Next we see him sleeping in a luxury Pullman car. The Indians on the frontier are all tamed, and he is nothing but a tourist. So he goes to Mexico, hoping to find excitement in the Revolution, but it has been quelled. Back in the city, there is nothing left to conquer, for reforms have created order. In desperation, he goes to Europe and finds that his father was not a self-made man, but an aristocrat. Now Fairbanks puts down a rebellion against the nobles at precisely the time when revolutions were spreading across the continent. Here he finds an identity, and marries a princess.

Within this film we see some of the classic dilemmas of the Fairbanks genre. Who am I, what is an American, are questions that reverberate through the film. Usually the hero has a metaphorical name such as Andrew Jackson, Jr., Daniel Boone Brown, or Cassius Lee. He admires the "steel stamina and efficiency" of the symbolic fathers who built and rule the industrial system, like Charles Schwab, Andrew Carnegie, and Theodore Roosevelt. Yet at the same time he feels trapped in their creations. Unlike the small producers of a Griffith film, Fairbanks is not outside the corporate system. Rather, he is a manager, clerk, or employee in a large office. His egalitarian spirit is crushed by the capitalists above him, whom he admires, but can never equal. These same powerful people have taken his autonomy, and he feels like a helpless cog in the organization. So he dreams nostalgically of a western frontier that is gone. Every now and then a threat to the society erupts, bringing a challenge to the young hero who fears he is not up to the task.

Two central problems face the hero. One is his boredom at work, the other confronts him at leisure. As to the first, through humor, Fairbanks lightened the heaviness of sons trapped in the industrial creations of their fathers. Loyalty to the patriarch, in fact, inhibits rebellion. *Wild and Wooly* (1917) presents a modern urbanite dressed in a suit and tie who dreams of riding a horse across the deserts of Arizona. As the camera pulls backwards from his face, he appears seated in a luxurious New York estate where his father asks the butler to "tell the Comanche Indian we are wanted." Brown punches a time clock, and a caption explains that "his boundless energy is trapped at a desk in a button factory." *When Clouds Roll By* (1919) amplified the discontent by showing the hero entering an office where "all time and space is economized." As he falls asleep shuffling papers, his uncle, the boss, pronounces that the boy will add up to "nothing." The youth finds this all too true. He leaves work and confronts the overpowering city, where he loiters around Fifth Avenue, hoping to rub elbows with the rich. But at the Plaza Hotel, even the waiters echo his uncle and treat him like a "nobody."

Luxury poses the second problem. Initially, as an heir to the Protestant ethic, the hero fears that pleasure will endanger the frontier spirit. A typical Fairbanks film, *The*

Mollycoddle (1920), opens on the dissipation of a sheriff's son. His father had won the West, and he became effete and soft on the inherited wealth, gallivanting around Europe. Similarly, the hero of *When Clouds Roll By* works in an office during the day, but at night his nightmares are filled with monsters who feed him by force. In this film, even the inner life is corrupted for, stuffed with rich pastries, he is too fat to master his devilish pursuers. Others show the hero trying to recharge his boring life through cocaine, amusement parks, boxing matches, or the new women drawn to the bohemian life of New York's Greenwich Village. Often, these threatening activities were personified by non-whites. One dream sequence includes men dressed and masked in black toppling Liberty from her pedestal. And in interviews, Fairbanks talked of his fears of Asians and Negroes, whom he constantly wanted to dominate through physical battle. In other words, the softness of modern life might literally drown the hero and make him "no better than a Negro." ....

Today's readers might find it difficult to believe not only that [Mary] Pickford's popularity ran parallel with Doug's, but that she portrayed a heroine who complemented his cultural reorientations. Was she not the sweet little girl of Griffith's films, or the angelic youth of *Pollyanna* (1920) or *Sparrows* (1926)? True, these films show her persona to be little different from nineteenth-century stereotypes. Nevertheless, it is well to note that Pickford did not like her portrayal in Pollyanna, and thereafter deeply regretted conforming to the image of girlhood. One reason why she disdained that association was that, in the period from 1914 to 1918, when rising to unprecedented fame and becoming the most popular star in all film history, she did not fit that image at all. In fact, during these key years of her career, "Mary" played a female role which made a fundamental break from the past, and embodied many of the aspirations of women in her generation.

Precisely because Pickford attempted the impossible, she became the most popular star of the day. While Fairbanks questioned the male role, Pickford questioned the female role at work and in the family. Over and over again she portrayed women striving to be economically free and morally emancipated. No doubt because these films took place in real-life circumstances and seemed so convincing, publishers asked her to write weekly columns for women on how to deal with their own lives. Mary responded by continually backing women's suffrage and echoing the messages offered on the screen. Above all, she was a self-sufficient woman who hired female writers who were much like herself. Together they created the character of a heroine who pioneered new trails for women into the domains of men. Formerly, for example, the ideal of great wealth and upward mobility was reserved for males; but Pickford made the Horatio Alger aspiration viable for women. The press not only praised her work, but paid a great deal of attention to the star's salary – for it was the first time that such a publicly acclaimed "good girl" made so much money in the degraded, at least for women, marketplace. "Mary Pickford," wrote one typical enthusiast in 1914, "gets more money than the President ... nine million people would rather see her on the screen than Bryan, Wilson, Roosevelt and Vernon Castle. That is why they will have to pay her $50,000 a year in 1914 and double that in 1915." Indeed, she reached her peak when in 1920 she was the only woman to join Fairbanks, Chaplin, and Griffith to form United Artists, earning the incredible salary of one million dollars a year. Through it all, Pickford realized why she was constantly voted in newspaper polls the "most popular girl in the world":

I like to see my own sex achieve. My success has been due to the fact that women like the pictures in which I appear. I think I admire most in the world the girls who earn their own living. I am proud to be one of them.

It is no accident that the most noted stars of the era created their unique screen characters largely from their own lives. Like Chaplin, Fairbanks, and others, Pickford made the most of her origins. Pickford loved to tell the press how she was born Gladys Smith of Toronto, Canada, in 1893. On her father's side she was English Methodist, on her mother's she was Irish Catholic. The father ran a small grocery store, and insisted that the women stay dependent at home. Her mother and grandmother on both sides of the family guarded the domestic realm, forbidding drink or any suggestion of impropriety. Mary's grandmother in particular tried to cleanse prostitutes and convert them from sin. Yet when Mr. Smith died, the mother took the first step away from Victorianism by placing her two girls and a son on the stage, allowing them financial independence. Never did Mrs. Smith remarry; she cut her ties with the past by changing the family name to Pickford, a classier name giving status to their still unrespectable occupation. From the age of about ten onwards, Mary toured the country as a stage performer. But always Mrs. Smith trained Mary to stay clear of actresses who smoked, used bad language, or worked in studios which reeked with the scandal surrounding the Stanford White and Evelyn Nesbit affair. Mary's highest aspiration was to join David Belasco's company on Broadway. Yet reluctantly, out of financial desperation, she joined the recently cleansed movies in 1909.

In this realm of "scandal," Pickford was fortunate enough to join D.W. Griffith's company. But the films she made for the master cast her as a traditional Victorian heroine, giving little indication of her future. *Lena and the Geese* (1911), for example, featured her as a poor peasant girl whose love redeems a young man from his wasted life. When she discovers that she is in fact the long-lost child of a noble family, she accepts her true class status. A slight deviation from this melodramatic formula came in *The New York Hat* (1912). In that production she played an orphan whose guardian forbids her using her inheritance to buy a hat. The local minister, charmed by her vivacity, persuades the oppressive guardian to let her have some fun, and buy the bonnet. Following the success of these minor films, Pickford achieved her heart's desire: Belaseo brought her to Broadway. There she starred in *The Good Little Devil* (1913). As the play became a major hit, Pickford's public persona reflected the high life of New York City.

In the following years, as film makers brought established stars from Broadway, Adolph Zukor hired Pickford to star in a photoplay "completely separate," she recalled, "from what I had been doing .... They thought I was just another actress, but when I made *Tess of the Storm Country* that was really the beginning of my career." Now audiences saw a heroine who offered more than old femininity. In contrast to her work with Griffith, where she resisted the director's desire to mold her into genteel patterns, Pickford now took on a personality free of abstract ideals of purity. "Little Mary" was above all a person in her own right. No doubt her projection of a unique personality was because she was one of the premier performers of the day. On the screen her character displayed a whole range of emotions, while mixing drama with humor in an utterly convincing blend. Once audiences came to expect the Pickford image as something special, Pickford left standard roles where she had displayed predictable emotions in equally predictable situations. She then became a model of vitality, and a boundless force that could not be confined to one place or social station. As Pickford recalled of her struggle against the old melodramas that forced one into formalized and educational categories,

> I always tried to get laughter into my pictures. Make them laugh and make them cry and back to laughter. What do people go to the theater for? An emotional exercise, and no preachments. I don't believe in taking advantage of someone who comes to the theatre by teaching them a lesson. It's not my prerogative to teach anything.

Nevertheless, the quest for personal freedom had deep social implications. In the film that sparked the Pickford image for the next six years, *Tess of the Storm Country* (1914), the heroine is a rebellious, independent, and energetic Cumberland mountain girl whom we first see dancing a jig. She and her hunter father would live contentedly were it not for Mr. Graves, the sheriff, and the local elite. He takes away her father's livelihood by forbidding "poaching in the forest." At the same time, Graves's daughter has an illegitimate child with a lover who dies. To save herself from paternal "wrath," she gives the baby to the heroine, Tess. As Tess raises the infant, the town assumes it is hers. Graves, as the church elder, refuses to baptize the baby, so Tess marches to the altar and sprinkles sacramental water on the child herself. Continuing this rebellion, she leads the farmers and tradesmen in a successful fight against Graves's game laws. Only when the villain learns whose child Tess protects does he soften, allowing his daughter to raise his grandchild and apologizing to Tess. He now repeals the poaching ordinance, and blesses his son's marriage to Tess.

Pickford's spunky heroine who fought economic and domestic tyranny in the countryside was equally effective in the face of urban problems. *The Eternal Grind* (1916) opens on a rural American girl leaving for the city – an experience relevant to much of her audience. Although she is in quest of freedom, she finds that the only employment available for women is routine and menial. So she takes a job as a sewing-machine operator and soon becomes a "slave." Lording over the female workers is the boss. He exploits the laboring women and forbids his sons to mingle with them. Yet the dancing and gaiety of the working girls attracts one son, who then has an affair with the heroine's best friend. When the girl becomes pregnant, Mary insists that they marry, reinforced by a gun in her hand. But the lad's father forbids it. Meanwhile, the heroine has fallen in love with the other son, a social worker. Together they convince the father to give up his greedy ways, and he finally allows both marriages. Such love also inspires him to install labor-saving devices to improve the conditions for his workers.

Equally important, Pickford broke from the Victorian mode of purity. Half the star's appeal lay in her ability to confront the major social problems of her day, and resolve them on the personal level. But the other half was her vitality. For she expanded the perimeters of respectable female behavior far beyond their nineteenth-century coordinates. Unlike the serial queens who might look but never touch, Pickford rolled up her sleeves and plunged her hands into previously forbidden realms. Some films showed her as an outsider, fighting against the system. But in others, she was caught in it. These films portray her as a genteel girl stifled in a home with a work-obsessed father and a socialite, charity-worker mother. In response to her restlessness, the heroine looks down the class order for excitement. Reflecting the culture's persistent ambivalence, a common device was the kidnap. *Poor Little Peppina* (1916) and *Less Than the Dust* (1916) show her as an American girl snatched from her Victorian home by foreigners. This gives her an excuse for taking on a different personality without guilt. Growing up with gypsies, Italians, Hindus, or Indians she learns to wear their exotic clothes, assume a swarthy complexion, and participate in public festivals with both men and women. Another formula for breaking down barriers between the sexes was to cast Pickford as a foreigner herself. In *Amarilly of Clothesline Alley* (1918), *Madame Butterfly* (1915), or *Hulda of Holland* (1916), Mary is a real Irish, Japanese, or Dutch girl who mingles in saloons, dances in New York, or embodies exotic qualities of an Asian or European female, complete with bright clothes and a sensual personality. ....

After the War came the appropriate merging of their careers, when Pickford and Fairbanks divorced their spouses and married each other. As in their films, the modern home was not achieved without a struggle against confining norms of the past. Nevada's district attorney threatened to sue the couple for defying the state's residence laws; the Catholic bishop excommunicated Pickford, using the opportunity to preach against marital infidelity and separation; the Baptist minister who presided over their wedding was nearly censured for marrying a divorced man and woman; Pickford's former husband, Owen Moore, threatened to sue for adultery. Yet the criticism soon gave way to acclaim. Rather than encouraging divorce, their union appeared as the way to perfect wedlock. Neither saw divorce as an admirable thing. Yet they both felt it was the unfortunate price to pay for the domestic ideal. Pickford claimed that her former husband was an abusive drunkard, jealous of her success. Now, with Fairbanks, she had a marriage of equals. As they honeymooned in Europe, the press heralded the golden couple, and the huge crowds seemed to sanction their emancipation. Presumably, their breaks from the past had led to the happiness their films promised to millions.

During the next ten years their union was constantly in the public eye. Symbolic of the modern marriage they epitomized was their famous Hollywood estate, Pickfair. The home was now expanded far beyond the functional Victorian domicile. Modeled on a European chateau, Pickfair collected and refined elements of upper- and lower-class pleasures. It was a consumer's paradise that resembled an innocent doll's house more than a formidable, aristocratic mansion typical of the eastern elites. Swimming pools, gyms, fountains, and cultivated lawns supplied a private "vacation land." Inside, the couple decorated each room in the motif of a foreign country, so that movement from one part of the house to another provided exotic adventure. In this kingdom of eternal youth, Doug and Mary highlighted continual newness by dipping into their vast wardrobes of stylish clothes for each of the day's activities: work, sports, dining, dancing, and parties. It followed that whenever the two sat for photographs, their smiles radiated happiness. A typical reporter described the Pickfair life as "the most successful and famous marriage that the world has ever known," succeeding where "others failed." For neither Pickford nor Fairbanks envisaged the home as "the dumping ground for the cares of the day."

In the attention the press and fan magazines paid to their tastes, likes, and dislikes, the modern imagery of the star was fully born. On and off the screen, they were "Doug and Mary" – ordinary folk like you and me who were blessed by opportunity.

Yet as European royalty and the American rich visited Pickfair, and Doug and Mary emulated in small the styles formerly reserved for a Vanderbilt, Astor, or Rockefeller, they showed the aspiring urbanite that upward mobility could be expressed in this new realm of leisure even more than on the job itself. Instead of being resentful of the wealthy, they demonstrated how modern consumption allowed one to emulate the styles of the high and mighty. In real life, "Doug" was the smiling, youthful hero whom Mary described as "always on the jump." Fairbanks himself extolled "sunrises over sunsets, beginnings over endings," and never spoke of failure, death, or depressing things. Pickford recalled that he had an endless habit of writing "success" on scraps of paper – a code that he both lived and preached in self-improvement pamphlets for the boy scouts, as well as fan magazines. In his partner Mary he found the new woman with the old values. She participated in charity and orphanage work, yet radiated a modern consumer ideal. Together, their common touch appeared equal to any nobility.

The golden couple eventually divorced, and each went on to a third spouse. Yet in the period from 1914 to 1918 their importance as cultural reformers cannot be over-emphasized. Every major player before them suggested that the crisis of the age was not so much status decline or a search for order as it was the dissolution of the family values of the past. Unlike vice crusaders, and early film makers like Griffith, who had tried to hold on to traditional domesticity in the face of the forces that were tearing it apart, Pickford and Fairbanks pointed to the twentieth century. True, they rebelled against the constraints at work and the sexual roles of the past; but they showed how to resolve these potentially explosive issues in private ways. Instead of trying to contain the fruits of the corporate order within a Victorian framework, they tried to make high-level consumption a means for restoring family stability. The idea was not to resist the modern organization, or to question its rationality with counter-cultural values. Rather, they tried to find freedom in the realm of leisure, which would then offer an uneasy accommodation to the new order. By carrying her moral emancipation into the home, the new woman hoped that an expanded domestic realm might compensate for the inadequacies of public life, and strengthen relations between the sexes. In turn, men would think of success more in terms of the money that would provide the good life. Although there was no conspiracy of big business to foist this formula on the public, the movie industry had synthesized consumption to Progressive ends, which perfectly suited the needs of the emerging corporate era.

4

Primary Sources

Edison v. American Mutoscope Company

US Circuit Court of Appeals for the Southern District of New York, 1902

The first two decades of the twentieth century were a time of bitter struggles between the film trust, led by Thomas Alva Edison, and independent film producers. In this landmark 1902 decision, the US Circuit Court of Appeals for the Southern District of New York overturned Edison's claim that he held patent rights to the whole of motion picture technology.

The photographic reproduction of moving objects, the production from the negatives of a series of pictures representing the successive stages of motion, and the presentation of them by an exhibiting apparatus to the eye of the spectator in such rapid sequence as to blend them together, and give the effect of a single picture in which the objects are moving, had been accomplished long before Mr. Edison entered the field. The patent in suit pertains mainly to that branch of the art which consists of the production of suitable negatives. The introduction of instantaneous photography, by facilitating the taking of negatives with the necessary rapidity to secure what is termed "persistence of vision," led to the devising of cameras for using sensitized plates and bringing them successively into the fields of the lens, and later for using a continuously moving sensitized band or strip of paper to receive the successive exposures. The invention of the patent in suit was made by Mr. Edison in the summer of 1889. We shall consider only those references to the prior art which show the nearest approximation of it, and are the most valuable of those which have been introduced for the purpose of negativing the novelty of its claims.

The French patent to Du Cos, of 1864, describes a camera apparatus consisting of a battery of lenses placed together in parallel rows, and focused upon a sensitive plate; the lenses being caused to act in rapid succession, by means of a suitable shutter, to depict the successive stages of movement of the object to be photographed ....

The camera apparatus of M. Marey, described in the *Scientific American* of June, 1882, and used by him, mounted in a photographic gun, to produce a series of instantaneous photographs, showing the successive phases of motion of birds and animals, describes a single-lens camera and clock mechanism which actuates the several parts ....

It is apparent from the references considered that while Mr. Edison was not the first to devise a camera apparatus for taking negatives of objects in motion, and at a rate sufficiently high to result in persistence of vision, the prior art does not disclose the specific type of apparatus which is described in his patent. His apparatus is capable of using a single sensitized and flexible film of great length with a single lens camera, and of producing an indefinite number of negatives on such a film with a rapidity theretofore unknown. The Du Cos apparatus requires the use of a large number of lenses in succession, and both the lens and the sensitized surface are in continuous motion while the picture is being taken; whereas in the apparatus of the patent but a single lens is employed, which is always at rest, and the film is also at rest at the time when the negative is being taken. Nor is it provided with means for passing the sensitized surface across the camera lenses at the very high rate of speed, which is a feature, though not an essential feature, of the patented apparatus ....

The important question is whether the invention was in such sense a primary one as to authorize the claims based upon it. The general statements in the specification imply that Mr. Edison as the creator of the art to which the patent relates, and the descriptive parts are carefully framed to lay the foundation for generic claims which are not to be limited by importing into them any of the operative devices, except those which are indispensable to effect the functional results enumerated. It will be observed that neither the means for moving the film across the lens of the camera, nor for exposing successive portions of it to the operation of the lens, nor for giving it a continuous or intermittent motion, nor for doing these things at a high rate of speed, are specified in the claims otherwise than functionally. Any combination of means that will do these things at a high enough rate of speed to secure the result of persistence of vision, and which includes a stationary single lens and tape-like film, is covered by the claims.

It is obvious that Mr. Edison was not a pioneer, in the large sense of the term, or in the more limited sense in which he would have been if he had also invented the film. He was not the inventor of the film. He was not the first inventor of apparatus capable of producing suitable negatives, taken from practically a single point of view, in a single-line sequence, upon a film like his, and embodying the same general means for rotating drums and shutters for bringing the sensitized surface across the lens, and exposing successive portions of it in rapid succession. Du Cos anticipated him in this, notwithstanding he did not use the film. Neither was he the first inventor of apparatus capable of producing suitable negatives, anµ embodying means for passing a sensitized surface across a single-lens camera at a high rate of speed, and with an intermittent motion, and for exposing successive portions of the surfaces during the periods of rest. His claim for such an apparatus was rejected by the patent office, and he acquiesced in its rejection. He was anticipated in this by Marey, and Marey also anticipated him in photographing successive positions of the object in motion from the same point of view.

The predecessors of Edison invented apparatus, during a period of transition from plates to flexible paper film, and from paper film to celluloid film, which was capable of producing negatives suitable for reproduction in exhibiting machines. No new principle was to be discovered, or essentially new forms of machine invented, in order to make the improved photographic material available for that purpose. The early inventors had felt the need of such material, but, in the absence of its supply, had either contented themselves with such measure of practical success as was possible, or had allowed their plans to remain upon paper as indications of the forms of mechanical and optical apparatus which might be used when suitable photographic surfaces became available. They had not perfected the details of apparatus especially adapted for the employment of the film of the patent, and to do this required but a moderate amount of mechanical ingenuity. Undoubtedly Mr. Edison, by utilizing this film and perfecting the first apparatus for using it, met all the conditions necessary for commercial success. This, however, did not entitle him, under the patent laws, to a monopoly of all camera apparatus capable of utilizing the film. Nor did it entitle him to a monopoly of all apparatus employing a single camera.

"The Nickel Madness"

Barton W. Currie, *Harper's Weekly*, August 24, 1907

This article provides a vivid first-hand description of early movie theaters at a time when the movies were just beginning to become mass entertainment.

Crusades have been organized against these low-priced moving-picture theatres, and many conservators of the public morals have denounced them as vicious and demoralizing. Yet have they flourished amazingly, and carpenters are busy hammering them up in every big and little community in the country.

The first "nickelodeons," or "nickelet," or whatever it was originally called was merely an experiment, and the first experiment was made more than a year ago. There was nothing singularly novel in the idea, only the individualizing of the motion-picture machine. Before it had served merely as a "turn" in vaudeville. For a very modest sum the outfit could be housed in a narrow store or in a shack in the rear yard of a tenement, provided there was an available hallway and the space for a "front." These shacks and shops are packed with as many chairs as they will hold and the populace welcomed, or rather hailed, by a huge megaphone-horn and lurid placards. The price of admission and entertainment for from fifteen to twenty minutes is a coin of the smallest denomination in circulation west of the Rockies.

In some vaudeville houses you may watch a diversity of performances four hours for so humble a price as ten cents, provided you are willing to sit among the rafters. Yet the roof bleachers were never so profitable as the tiny show-places that have fostered the nickel madness.

Before the dog-days set in, licenses were being granted in Manhattan Borough alone at the rate of one a day for these little hurry-up-and-be-amused booths. They are categorized as "common shows," thanks to the Board of Aldermen. A special ordinance was passed to rate them under this heading. Thereby they were enabled to obtain a license for $25 for the first year, and $12.50 for the second year. The City Fathers did this before Anthony Comstock [the Purity Crusader] and others rose up and proclaimed against them. A full theatrical license costs $500.

An eloquent plea was made for these humble resorts by many "friends of the peepul." They offered harmless diversion for the poor. They were edifying, educational, and amusing. They were broadening. They revealed the universe to the unsophisticated. The variety of the skipping, dancing, flashing, and marching pictures was without limit. For five cents you were admitted to the realms of the prize ring; you might witness the celebration of a Pontifical mass in St. Peter's; Kaiser Wilhelm would prance before you, reviewing his Uhlans. Yes, and even more surprising, you were offered a modern conception of Washington crossing the Delaware "acted out by a trained group of actors." Under the persuasive force of such arguments, was it strange that the Aldermen befriended the nickelodeon man and gave impetus to the craze.

Three hundred licenses were issued within the past year in the Borough of Manhattan alone for common shows. Two hundred of these were for nickelets. They are becoming vastly popular in Brooklyn. They are springing up in the shady places of Queens, and down on Staten Island you will find them in the most unexpected bosky dells, or rising in little rakish shacks on the mosquito flats.

Already statisticians have been estimating how many men, women, and children in the metropolis are being thrilled daily by them. A conservative figure puts it at 200,000, though if I were to accept the total of the showmen the estimate would be nearer half a million. But like all statisticians, who reckon human beings with the same unemotional placidity with which they total beans and potatoes, the statistician I have quoted left out the babies. In a visit to a dozen of these moving-picture hutches I counted an average of ten babies to each theatre-et. Of course they were in their mothers' or the nurse-girls' arms. But they were there and you heard them. They did not disturb the show, as there were no counter-sounds, and many of them seemed profoundly absorbed in the moving pictures.

As a matter of fact, some mothers – and all nurse-girls – will tell you that the cinematograph has a peculiarly hypnotic or narcotic effect upon an infant predisposed to disturb the welkin. You will visit few of these places in Harlem where the doorways are not encumbered with go-carts and perambulators. Likewise they are prodigiously popular with the rising generation in frock and knickerbocker. For this reason they have been condemned by the morality crusaders. The chief argument against them was that they corrupted the young. Children of any size who could transport a nickel to the cashier's booth were welcomed. Furthermore, undesirables of many kinds haunted them. Pickpockets found them splendidly convenient, for the lights were always cut off when the picture-machine was focused on the canvas. There is no doubt about the fact that many rogues and miscreants obtained licenses and set up these little show-places merely as snares and traps. There were many who thought they had sufficient pull to defy decency in the choice of their slides. Proprietors were said to work hand in glove with lawbreakers. Some were accused of wanton designs to corrupt young girls. Police Commissioner Bingham denounced the nickel madness as pernicious, demoralizing, and a direct menace to the young.

But the Commissioner's denunciation was rather too sweeping. His detectives managed to suppress indecencies and immoralities. As for their being a harbor for pickpockets, is it not possible that even they visit these humble places for amusement? ...

But if you happen to be an outlaw you may learn many moral lessons from these brief moving-picture performances, for most of the slides offer you a quick flash of melodrama in which the villain and criminal are always getting the worst of it.

Pursuits of malefactors are by far the most popular of all nickel deliriums. You may see snatch-purses, burglars, and an infinite variety of criminals hunted by the police and the mob in almost any nickelet you have the curiosity to visit. The scenes of these thrilling chases occur in every quarter of the globe, from Cape Town to Medicine Hat.

The speed with which pursuer and pursued run is marvelous. Never are you cheated by a mere sprint or straightaway flight of a few blocks. The men who "fake" these moving pictures seem impelled by a moral obligation to give their patrons their full nickel's worth. I have seen dozens of these kinetoscope fugitives run at least forty miles before they collided with a fat woman carrying an umbrella, who promptly sat on them and held them for the puffing constabulary ....

The popularity of these cheap amusement-places with the new population of New York is not to be wondered at. The newly arrived immigrant from Transylvania can get as much enjoyment out of them as the native. The imagination is appealed to directly and without any circumlocution. The child whose intelligence has just awakened and the doddering old man seem to be on an equal footing in the stuffy little box-like theatres. The passer-by with an idle quarter of an hour on his hands has an opportunity to kill the time swiftly, if he is not above mingling with the hoi polloi. Likewise the student of sociology may get a few points that he could not obtain in a day's journey through the thronged streets of the East Side.

Of course the proprietors of the nickelets and nickelodeons make as much capital out of suggestiveness as possible, but it rarely goes beyond a hint or a lure. For instance, you will come to a little hole in the wall before which there is an ornate sign bearing the legend: FRESH FROM PARIS Very Naughty.

Should this catch the eye of a Comstock he would immediately enter the place to gather evidence. But he would never apply for a warrant. He would find a "very naughty" boy playing pranks on a Paris street – annoying blind men, tripping up gendarmes, and amusing himself by every antic the ingenuity of the Paris street gamin can conceive.

This fraud on the prurient, as it might be called, is very common, and it has led a great many people, who derive their impressions from a glance at externals, to conclude that these resorts are really a menace to morals. You will hear and see much worse in some high-priced theatres than in these moving- picture show-places.

In some of the crowded quarters of the city the nickelet is cropping up almost as thickly as the saloons, and if the nickel delirium continues to maintain its hold there will be, in a few years, more of these cheap amusement-places than saloons. Even now some of the saloon-keepers are complaining that they injure their trade.

Mutual Film Corp. v. Industrial Commission of Ohio

United States Supreme Court, 1915

This landmark Supreme Court decision, which denied motion pictures First Amendment protections of free speech, stood as the law for 37 years, providing legal sanction for public censorship.

In its discussion, counsel have gone into a very elaborate description of moving picture exhibitions and their many useful purposes as graphic expressions of opinion and sentiments, as exponents of policies, as teachers of science and history, as useful, interesting, amusing, educational, and moral. ... We may concede the praise. It is not questioned by the Ohio statute .... Films of a "moral, educational, or amusing and harmless character shall be passed and approved," are the words of the statute. No exhibition, therefore, or "campaign" of complainant will be prevented if its pictures have those qualities. Therefore, however missionary of opinion films are or may become, however educational or entertaining, there is no impediment to their value or effect in the Ohio statute. But they may be used for evil, and against that possibility the statute was enacted. Their power of amusement, and, it may be, education, the audiences they assemble, not of women alone nor of men alone, but together, not of adults only, but of children, make them the more insidious in corruption by a pretense of worthy purpose. Indeed we may go beyond that possibility. They take their attraction from the general interest, eager and wholesome it may be, in their subjects, but a prurient interest may be excited and appealed to. Besides, there are some things that should not have pictorial representation in public places and to all audiences. And not only the state of Ohio, but other states, have considered it to be in the interest of public morals and welfare to supervise moving picture exhibitions. We would have to shut our eyes to the facts of the world to regard the precaution unreasonable or the legislation to effect it mere wanton interference with personal liberty. ...

It cannot be put out of view that the exhibition of moving pictures is a business, pure and simple, originated and conducted for profit, like other spectacles, not to be regarded by the Ohio Constitution, we think, as part of the press of the country, or as organs of public opinion. They are mere representations of events, of ideas and sentiments published and known; vivid, useful, and entertaining, no doubt, but as we have said, capable of evil, having power for it, the greater because of their attractiveness and manner of exhibition. It is this capability and power, and it may be in experience of them that induced the state of Ohio, in addition to prescribing penalties for immoral exhibition, as it does in its Criminal Code, to require censorship before exhibition, as it does by the act under review. We cannot regard this as beyond the power of government. ...

The objection to the statute is that it furnishes no standard of what is educational, moral, amusing, or harmless, and hence leaves decision to arbitrary judgment, whim, and caprice; or, aside from those extremes, leaving it to the different views which might be entertained of the effect of the pictures, permitting the "personal equation" to enter, resulting "in unjust discrimination against some propaganda film," while others might be approved without question. But the statute by its provisions guards against such variant judgments, and its terms, like other general terms, get precision from the sense and experience of men, and become certain and useful guides in reasoning and conduct. The exact specification of the instances of their application would be impossible as the attempt would prove futile. Upon such sense and experience, therefore, the law properly relies .... If this were not so, the many administrative agencies created by the state and national governments would be denuded of their utility, and government in some of its most important exercises become impossible ....

FIGHTING A VICIOUS FILM: PROTEST AGAINST
THE BIRTH OF A NATION

Few films ever aroused as much controversy as D.W. Griffith's Birth of a Nation. *Critics denounced it as a gross distortion of American history that promoted racial strife. These two selections offer examples of the kinds of arguments raised against Griffith's epic.*

Boston Branch of the National Association for the Advancement of Colored People, 1915

In its advertisement we are told that *The Birth of a Nation* is founded on Thomas Dixon's novel *The Clansman*; that it is a war play "that worked the audience up into a frenzy"; that "it will make you hate."

In an interview with a Boston editor, Thomas Dixon said, "that one purpose of his play was to create a feeling of abhorrence in people, especially white women, against colored men"; "that he wished to have Negroes removed from the United States and that he hopes to help in the accomplishment of that purpose by *The Birth of a Nation*."

In furthering these purposes the producers of the film do not hesitate to resort to the meanest vilification of the Negro race, to pervert history, and to use the most subtle form of untruth – a half truth.

Well knowing that such a play would meet strong opposition in Boston, large sums of money were spent in the employment of Pinkerton detectives and policemen to intimidate citizens, and the managers of the theatre refused to sell tickets to colored people. To soften opposition, the impression was given that the president of the United States had endorsed the play and that George Foster Peabody and other distinguished people favored it. One method of working up support was to pass cards among the auditors asking them to endorse the play. These cards were circulated, signed and collected at the end of the first act and before the second act in which appear the foul and loathsome misrepresentations of colored people and the glorification of the hideous and murderous band of the Ku Klux Klan ....

Analysis by Francis Hackett

If history bore no relation to life, this motion picture could well be reviewed and applauded as a spectacle. As a spectacle it is stupendous. It lasts three hours, represents a staggering investment of time and money, reproduces entire battle scenes and complex historic events; amazes even when it wearies by its attempt to encompass the Civil War. But since history does bear on social behavior, *The Birth of a Nation* cannot be reviewed simply as a spectacle. It is more than a spectacle. It is an interpretation, the Rev. Thomas Dixon's interpretation, of the relations of the North and South and their bearing on the Negro ....

In *The Birth of a Nation* Mr. Dixon protests sanctimoniously that his drama "is not meant to reflect in any way on any race or people of today." And then he proceeds to give to the Negro a kind of malignity that is really a revelation of his own malignity.

Passing over the initial gibe at the Negro's smell, we early come to a negrophile senator whose mistress is a mulatto. As conceived by Mr. Dixon and as acted in the film, this mulatto is not only a minister to the senator's lust but a woman of inordinate passion, pride and savagery. Gloating as she does over the promise of "Negro equality," she is soon partnered by a male mulatto of similar brute characteristics. Having established this triple alliance between the "uncrowned king," his diabolic colored mistress and his diabolic colored ally, Mr. Dixon shows the revolting processes by which the white South is crushed "under the heel of the black South." "Sowing the wind," he calls it. On the one hand we have "the poor bruised heart" of the white South, on the other "the new citizens inflamed by the growing sense of power." We see Negroes shoving white men off the sidewalk, Negroes quitting work to dance, Negroes beating a crippled old white patriarch, Negroes slinging up "faithful colored servants" and flogging them till they drop, Negro courtesans guzzling champagne with the would-be head of the Black Empire, Negroes "drunk with wine and power," Negroes mocking their white masters in chains, Negroes "crazy with joy" and terrorizing all the whites in South Carolina. We see blacks flaunting placards demanding "equal marriage." We see the black leader demanding a "forced marriage" with an imprisoned and gagged white girl. And we see continually in the background the white Southerner in "agony of soul over the degradation and ruin of his people."

Encouraged by the black leader, we see Gus the renegade hover about another young white girl's home. To hoochy-coochy music we see the long pursuit of the innocent white girl by this lust-maddened Negro, and we see her fling herself to death from a precipice, carrying her honor through "the opal gates of death."

Having painted this insanely apprehensive picture of an unbridled, bestial, horrible race, relieved only by a few touches of low comedy, "the grim reaping begins." We see the operations of the Ku Klux Klan, "the organization that saved the South from the anarchy of black rule." We see Federals and Confederates uniting in a Holy War "in defense of their Aryan birthright," whatever that is. We see the Negroes driven back, beaten, killed. The drama winds up with a suggestion of Lincoln's solution – "back to Liberia" – and then, if you please, with a film representing Jesus Christ in "the halls of brotherly love."

My objection to this drama is based partly on the tendency of the pictures but mainly on the animus of the printed lines I have quoted. The effect of these lines, reinforced by adroit quotations from Woodrow Wilson and repeated assurances of impartiality and goodwill, is to arouse in the audience a strong sense of the evil possibilities of the Negro and the extreme propriety and godliness of the Ku Klux Klan. So strong is this impression that the audience invariably applauds the refusal of the white hero to shake hands with a Negro, and under the circumstances cannot be blamed. Mr. Dixon has identified the Negro with cruelty, superstition, insolence, and lust. ...

Whatever happened during Reconstruction, this film is aggressively vicious and defamatory. It is spiritual assassination. It degrades the censors that passed it and the white race that endures it.

Part II
Hollywood's Golden Age

Introduction
Backstage During the Great Depression: 42nd Street,
Gold Diggers of 1933, *and* Footlight Parade

Three Warner Brothers musicals that appeared in 1933 occupy a special place in the affections of moviegoers. With their astonishingly intricate examples of Busby Berkeley's choreography (which arranged women in the form of pinwheels and violins), their fast-talking chorus girls, smiling ingénues, tough troubled Broadway directors, and their good-natured glimpses of backstage life in the theater, these films have come to represent what the critic Pauline Kael has called "pure thirties."

These films helped form some of our society's most lasting cultural clichés. The basic plot of *42nd Street* – the tale of an untried chorus girl who becomes a star after the leading lady breaks her ankle – remains, even today, a vivid fantasy. The speech that director Warner Baxter uses to urge young Peggy Sawyer on has often been mimicked:

> Miss Sawyer, you listen to me ... and you listen hard. Two hundred people, 200 jobs, $200,000, five weeks of grind and blood and sweat depend upon you! ... You've got to go on and you've got to give and give and give! They've got to like you, got to. You understand? You can't fall down, you can't. Because your future's in it, my future and everything all of us have is staked on you. All right now, I'm through. But you keep your feet on the ground and your head on those shoulders of yours, and, Sawyer, you're going out a youngster, but you've got to come back a star!

To the casual viewer today, these backstage musical fantasies may appear to be nothing more than pure escapism. In fact, their appeal to Depression-era audiences went far deeper. The tone and message of these films are far more complex than the word "escapism" suggests.

Take, for example, the opening of *Gold Diggers*. Ginger Rogers and 60 chorus girls, wearing costumes made up of oversized silver dollars, sing "We're in the Money."

Figure 5   *Footlight Parade* (1933). Warner Bros. Directed by Lloyd Bacon. Courtesy of Jerry Murbach, www.doctormacro.info.

The actresses' costumes and the song's words – "we never read a headline about a breadline" – seem superficially to epitomize the flight into fantasy that characterizes the thirties backstage musical. In actuality, however, the opening sequence is anything but a simple musical escape from Depression realities. It concludes when local authorities arrive to shut down the rehearsal and repossess the actresses' costumes because the producer has failed to pay his bills,

On close examination, *42nd Street*, *Gold Diggers*, and *Footlight Parade* obliquely address broad political and economic issues and anxieties raised by the Great Depression. Their upbeat plots – in which talented newcomers rise to stardom and wealthy bluebloods marry common chorus girls – helped Depression-era Americans sustain a faith that class differences could be overcome and that, despite many obstacles, happiness and success would eventually prevail.

Yet alongside this upbeat vision of class healing and success is a more somber vision. The title sequence of *42nd Street* is filled with jarring images of violence and domestic abuse. The musical finale of *Gold Diggers* – "The Forgotten Man" – gained resonance from the 1932 "Bonus March" of more than 10,000 World War I veterans on Washington, demanding immediate payment of a bonus that they had been promised in exchange for service (due in 1945). Etta Moten, an African American, poignantly reminds viewers of this bitter episode, which concluded when federal troops led by Douglas MacArthur dispersing the veterans and destroying their encampment with tanks, tear gas, and bayonets:

> Remember my forgotten man;
> You put a rifle in his hand;
> You sent him far away;
> You shouted – Hip Hooray!
> But look at him today!

5

Depression America and its Films
Laughing Through Tears

Maury Klein

Hollywood offered Depression America much more than mere (escapism.) It helped main-
tain the nation's morale and preserve values. The fantasy world of the movies fulfilled a
critical psychological function for Depression-era Americans: in the face of economic dis-
aster, the movies kept alive a belief in the possibility of individual success. The movies also
portrayed a government capable of protecting its citizens from crime and injustice. And
the movies sustained a vision of a classless society. Again and again, Hollywood repeated
the same formulas: a poor boy from the slums uses crimes as a perverted ladder of success; a
back-row chorus girl rises to the lead through luck and pluck; a G-Man restores law and
order; a poor boy and rich girl meet, go through wacky adventures, and fall in love. Out of
these simple plots, Hollywood restored faith in individual initiative, in the efficacy of gov-
ernment, and in a common American identity transcending social class. In the following
selection, historian Maury Klein surveys Hollywood's response to the Great Depression.

Not even the Great Depression stopped Americans from going to the movies. In 1930 an estimated 110 million people trooped into theaters each week to forget their cares for an hour or two. Three years later, when the economy hit rock bottom, 60 to 80 million citizens still managed to scrounge the price of admission every week. Whatever else they sacrificed, Americans clung to this pleasure with a fervor that went beyond mere escapism. In its short lifetime, the motion picture industry had already assumed the role of dream factory, but hard times gave it a new dimension. Film became the fantasy life of a nation in pain.

On the eve of the stock market crash, movies had just learned to talk and the indus-try had emerged from an era of upheaval into one dominated by the major studios. The larger studios had evolved into models of vertical integration. Five of them – MGM, Twentieth Century Fox, Paramount, Warner Brothers, and RKO – owned chains of theaters which enabled them to control the process from shooting to show-ing. Three others, Universal, Columbia, and United Artists, produced, sold, and dis-tributed their films but depended on the big five for theaters in which to show them.

Maury Klein, "Laughing Through Tears," *American History Illustrated* (March 1983), pp. 12–21. Reprinted with permission, American History Magazine, March 1983, © Copyright Weider History Group.

As a whole the industry churned out upwards of 500 feature films a year, with the major studios each producing fifty or so. Together the eight major film companies accounted for about three-fourths of all feature films released and gathered about eighty-five percent of all rental income.

The financial squeeze of the Depression years strengthened the hold of the studio system, which continued to dominate (some said tyrannize) the industry for more than two decades. Movies, like music, sports, and breakfast cereal, had become big business, a product peddled in the vast national marketplace by shrewd entrepreneurs. Intent on reaping large profits, the movie moguls relied heavily on advertising and promotion, which put them in the curious position of using one form of illusion to sell another. Like most businessmen, they tacked wherever the economic winds blew. Pitched and heaved by the gales of depression, they trimmed their sails and steered the safest course possible.

In that sense the moguls followed the lead of the New Deal, which was itself less a revolution than a cautious, minimal response to a cataclysm. Their task was to divine the longings and ambitions of their audience, reduce their findings to a formula, and repeat the formula in film after film. As the mood of the public changed, so did the formulas that embodied it. Those who wonder how network television came to assume its dreary form can find the model from which it sprang in the movie industry of the thirties. Among the 5,000 feature films that rolled off the production line during the decade, there emerged certain distinct genres which – at their worst – meant that each new film was made, as Jeffrey Paine observed, "by the movie immediately preceding it."

The moguls rivaled politicians as barometers of public attitudes. Their films, like the mood of national politics, reflected the abrupt transition from the dark night of Hooverian bleakness to the dawn of Rooseveltian optimism. Prior to 1933, the motion picture industry intensified its attack on traditional middle class values begun a decade earlier. Studio heads were not social revolutionaries but merely opportunists who found a postwar generation weary of causes, bored with convention, and eager for a taste of the glamorous and the exotic. To these audiences the studios fed a steady diet of titillation; already they had discovered the market value of sex and violence.

The genres that emerged during the early 1930s clearly revealed how severe a blow economic collapse had dealt to traditional values and, paradoxically, how resilient those values were even in the worst of times. A good example was the gangster films, which burst on the scene with such classics as *Little Caesar* (1930), *The Public Enemy* (1931), *City Streets* (1931), and *Scarface* (1932). Sound gave the genre a new dimension of shock, with gunfire, screams, wailing sirens, screeching tires, and shattering glass, but the appeal went much deeper. In their own curious way the gangster films offered a twisted version of the Horatio Alger success story. The hero, usually an immigrant from them slums, pulled himself to the top by hard work before suffering his inevitable downfall. He lived and died by the rules: the difference was that the rules lay outside the law.

In these films law and government were impotent, inept, or simply absent. Unemployed viewers warmed to a hero who defied the society that had never given him a break, and who was tough enough to carve his own destiny. The gangster films embodied both the triumph of the individual and the failure of the social system.

Another genre, the shyster films, filled the screen with charming rogues who, their innocence blighted by bitter experience, marched down the avenue of good intentions to a new knowledge of how the whole dirty game was played. The shysters in movies

Figure 6   *Public Enemy* (1931). Warner Bros. Directed by William A. Wellman. Courtesy of Jerry Murbach, www.doctormacro.info.

like *The Front Page* (1931), *Scandal Sheet* (1931), *Lawyer Man* (1932), *The Mouthpiece* (1932), and *The Dark Horse* (1932) included not only lawyers but also politicians and journalists – cynics all, who had learned their lessons about corruption in the classroom of the big city.

For the shyster as well as for his client, the gangster, society was a fraud, politics was a sham, and the law was a joke or a vacuum, with the root of all evil somehow connected to that most enduring American theme: corruption. Against these forces, the forces of good seemed helpless. In *The Dark Horse*, a savvy politico was plucked from jail to manage a gubernatorial campaign for an idiot nominee. "He's the dumbest human being I ever saw," said the manager. "We're going to convince the voters that they're getting one of them. That's what voters want in these days of corruption and depression." The candidate won in a landslide after learning to answer all questions first "Yes," then "No."

One common theme bound the gangsters and shysters together. In an age of national paralysis, they were men who knew how to get things done, however deplorable their means. Their appeal lay mainly in the fact that they were both victims and men of action. So too with the comics. While sound rendered the rich genre of silent comedy extinct, it ushered in a new breed who demolished everything from the grandest institutions to the most ordinary of conventions. Borrowing heavily from their native soil, vaudeville, the new comedians mixed sight gags with verbal patter to create routines that were no less definitive trademarks than Charlie Chaplin's walk. Whether it was the Marx Brothers making shambles of every sacred cow from education to the state, or W.C. Fields lacerating the pretensions of the middle class family, the comics embodied the outrage of thousands embittered by a system that was not supposed to fail them, but had.

In *Duck Soup* (1933) the Marx Brothers lambasted politics, patriotism, the state, and war. Historian Robert Sklar has rightly called it "as thorough a satire on politics and patriotism as any film before *Dr. Strangelove*." A masterpiece of invention, it had the misfortune to be released shortly after Roosevelt took office and, in the new mood of hope, did poorly at the box office. "Even a small town knows when there is a flop," declared the manager of a Nebraska theater, while an Iowa manager was "afraid these boys are washed up." Benito Mussolini got the message; the film was banned in Italy. Afterward the Marx Brothers retreated to safer themes until, like Fields, they were reduced to a form of self parody by the decade's end.

As usual sex reared its alluring head, but the unique presence of Mae West gave it an unexpected twist toward comedy. Early Depression films like *Susan Lenox* (1931), *Safe in Hell* (1931), *Blonde Venus* (1932), and *Faithless* (1932) cast major stars as women forced to become prostitutes or mistresses of wealthy men. Unable to control their own destinies, they fell back on sex as their only bargaining chip and suffered the inevitable degradation and punishment It was the old recipe of titillation wrapped in a layer of moralism.

West discarded the image in favor to one that approached the battle of the sexes boldly and frankly. "Neither the sweet ingénue nor the glamour girl fit the depression years," recalled producer-director Adolph Zukor of Paramount Pictures. "Mae did. She was the strong, confident woman, always in command." In her first film, *She Done Him Wrong* (1933), West displayed the formula that wilted the flower of American manhood. As Andrew Bergman described it, "Her voice radiated irony, her eyes sized up potential lovers as though they were sides of beef, and her hips mesmerized a nation." The "fallen woman" tradition would never recover from her liberated spirit and unabashed appetite for pleasure. "Haven't you ever met a man who could make you happy?" Cary Grant asked her in the film. "Sure," West replied. "Lots of times."

Such frankness was too much for the watchdogs of morality. Hollywood filmmakers had been skating on thin ice since 1922 when they hired Will Hays, a prominent Republican and Presbyterian elder, to launder their excesses. When observant moralists protested that nothing had changed, the Hays office responded in 1930 with the Production Code, a curious document drafted by a Catholic professor and a prominent Catholic layman. Jack C. Ellis has observed that "Like the Ten Commandments, the Code's language was largely negative." Under twelve headings the code itemized the forbidden fruit of film, and a crazy-quilt garden it was. Nevertheless, complaints arose that it was being ignored. Outraged Catholics formed the Legion of Decency in 1934 and promised to boycott offending films.

The threat of lost revenue was enough to galvanize the moguls into creating their own enforcing mechanism. Joseph I. Breen, a Catholic journalist, was given the task of certifying every film with a code seal. Breen's authority was such that for two decades no major film was released without the seal. For moralists the victory was at best a Pyrrhic one. Ellis noted that "The reasons for the Code and the Seal were financial rather than moral," and that "it sapped creative energy at the source." Sklar agreed that "the code cut the movies off from many of the most important moral and social themes of the contemporary world."

The code's effects were predictable and far reaching. It reinforced the peculiar American tendency to substitute violence for sex. As Robert Warshow observed long ago, two of our most classic genres, the western and the gangster films, featured the gun as their central symbol. Not that sex vanished; it merely changed form. The leer replaced candor, and what could not be shown could be suggested in a dozen ways. Perhaps the most significant legacy of the code was that it nudged directors toward stylization of technique as they realized that serious themes could only be treated obliquely.

The trend toward stylization coincided with the upbeat mood generated by the election of Roosevelt and the onset of the New Deal. Impressed by the rising spirit of hope and the return of national pride, the studios discarded their attack on traditional values with unabashed speed and began pouring old wine into cheerful new bottles. Law and order returned not only to the streets but to the frontier as well. James Cagney signaled the change in *G-Men* (1935) by switching from gangster to federal agent. As an ad proclaimed, "HOLLYWOOD'S MOST FAMOUS BAD MAN JOINS THE G-MEN AND HALTS THE MARCH OF CRIME" Edward G. Robinson followed suit in *Bullets or Ballots* (1936), proving, as Robinson said, that "A good detective should be a tough guy, too." In most cases it was not cops who subdued the mob but the feds, who had the muscle to do what local authorities could not manage.

Early in the decade the popularity of westerns had languished to the point where studios did no more than churn out endless strings of grade B "oaters." With most of the old heroes like Tom Mix and William S. Hart gone, the genre seemed played out until several directors, inspired by the new national mood, discovered history. In such films as *The Plainsman* (1936), *The Texas Rangers* (1936), *Stagecoach* (1939), and *Drums Along the Mohawk* (1939), the western was reborn as the epic of "How the West Was Won." The old elements were still there – the violence, the oversimplification of good and evil, the hero as rugged individual – but now they were fused into larger, mythic themes of taming the frontier, curbing lawlessness, and forging a nation. That they took gross liberties with history did not affect their appeal at the box office.

Three other genres of the new vintage revealed its potency for myth making. The musical, creature of the new technology, was at first content to transfer theater revues to the screen but soon went beyond anything possible on a stage. In 1933 three Warner Brothers' blockbusters, *Gold Diggers of 1933*, *42nd Street*, and *Footlight Parade* created the new idiom. If these lavish pastries, with their extravagant staging by Busby Berkeley and others, seemed rampant escapism, they were in part reincarnations of Horatio Alger. All three featured success stories grounded in the Depression. Thanks to faith, hard work, and some luck, the kid(s) came through in each one, with some spectacular singing and dancing along the way. The timing was perfect to enthrall audiences starved for reaffirmation of the old verities. Later musicals lost this core of relevancy and, for all their glitz and glamour, seemed vapid by comparison. An Indiana theater manager thought he knew why, "The ensembles are well done," he said about *Gold Diggers of 1937*, "… but why expect musical numbers to hold up a weak, shallow, artificial story."

Another offspring of technical wizardry, the cartoon, came of age thanks to the unique genius of Walt Disney. As Sklar has pointed out, Disney's philosophy was as conservative as his techniques were innovative. The world of fantasy he created might lift one above the cares of ordinary life, but it was a world solidly grounded in the tradition of free enterprise, rugged individualism, and self-help. *Three Little Pigs*, released in May 1933 amid Roosevelt's first Hundred Days, became a runaway hit with its timely, upbeat theme song, "Who's Afraid of the Big Bad Wolf?" By the time of his first feature film, *Snow White and the Seven Dwarfs* (1937), Disney had won the nation's heart and firmed the moral boundaries of a fantasy world in which those who did not stick to the rules or trust the tried and true got burned.

A third genre, the screwball comedy, demonstrated brilliantly that one did not need cartoons to construct myth out of entertainment. The undisputed master of screwball was film director Frank Capra, who enchanted audiences with a string of hits: *Lady for a Day* (1933), *It Happened One Night* (1934), *Mr. Deeds Comes To Town* (1936), *Lost Horizon* (1937), *You Can't Take It With You*, and *Mr. Smith Goes to Washington* (1939), Capra's films were shrewdly topical, yet born of a vision intent on healing the wounds and divisions of a dispirited nation. Andrew Bergman called them "the masterwork of an idealist and door-to-door salesman."

The true screwball comedy featured wealthy eccentrics who stood the world on its ear with antics at once zany and larded with common sense. In *It Happened One Night* Capra reversed the premise: poor boy and bored rich girl met improbably, delighted in their differences and, through a series of wacky adventures, fell in love. The poor boy made good, the rich girl found true happiness, class divisions were healed, and all lived happily ever after. Capra made this formula work with his extraordinary warmth, humor, comic inventiveness, and eye for detail. The message of his films satisfied everyone's fantasies; the endearing charm of his characters made everyone wonder what the fuss had been about.

Capra's instinct for convincing audiences that his world was the way life should be lived was uncanny. To it he added topical relevance that fashioned mythical portraits of an America in which people longed to believe. The poor boy got the beautiful rich girl and climbed the social ladder; Mr. Deeds shrugged off a $20 million inheritance ("Twenty million! That's a lot, isn't it?"), used it to buy farms for the poor, and subdued the swells and slickers with his simplicity and goodness: Mr. Smith fought political corruption on behalf of the people and won. No one did more to build the national image than Capra. When later he harnessed his talent to the war effort, he said of audiences, "For two hours you've got 'em. Hitler can't keep 'em that long."

Capra's films, like the frontier epics, appealed directly to the craving for an earlier, simpler America where life had not yet been scrambled by the baffling complexities of war, industrialization, and depression. No one captured this mood more poignantly than Thornton Wilder in the play *Our Town* (1938). On screen the yearning for nostalgia gave immense popularity to a string of movies starring Will Rogers. An incomparable folk humorist, Rogers had made films since 1918 but did not blossom until the advent of sound, which brought the full warmth and wit of his personality to audiences. Playing himself in such films as *State Fair* (1933), *David Harum* (1934), and *Steamboat 'Round the Bend* (1935), Rogers invoked the mythical harmony of small town America (*David Harum* was set in Homeville), a place where the larger, uglier world never intruded beyond a point where Uncle Will could handle it. Such was

Rogers' popularity that two of his films were released after his untimely death in 1935. "He is," wrote one reviewer, "what Americans think other Americans are like."

Homeville was a warm, friendly place that had little to do with the world outside the theater. What almost no one seemed willing or able to do was look the Depression straight in the eye. Except for the bleak realism of Mervyn Leroy's *I Am a Fugitive from a Chain Gang* (1932), the topical films churned out by Warner Brothers failed to capture the searing pain of Depression life. Elsewhere, director King Vidor look an earnest but naive swipe at social statement in *Our Daily Bread* (1934), while John Ford's rendition of *The Grapes of Wrath* (1940) stayed carefully within the norms of traditional American myths and values. Pare Lorentz's two epic documentaries, *The Plow That Broke the Plains* (1936) and *The River* (1937), were self conscious hymns of affirmation.

"No medium has contributed more greatly than the film to the maintenance of the national morale during a period featured by revolution, riot and political turmoil in other countries," crowed Will Hays in 1934. "It has been the mission of the screen, without ignoring the serious social problems of the day, to reflect aspiration, optimism, and kindly humor in its entertainment."

Perhaps Hays was more right than he knew. Whatever else the films of the 1930s accomplished, the best of them displayed a brilliance of style and technique that has endured as a living legacy of the craft. Certainly they impressed today's generation of filmmakers, who seem capable of nothing more original than imitating or remaking their work.

6

The Depression's Human Toll
Gangsters and Fallen Women

Peter Roffman and Jim Purdy

The early Depression mood of despair was reflected on the screen through a succession of ruthless gangsters, haggard prostitutes, and hardened prison inmates. But as film historians Peter Roffman and Jim Purdy show, the appeal of these characters came of much more than fondness for outlaws at a time when the social order appeared to be breaking down. These figures also helped to preserve older cultural ideals during a period of upheaval.

The Gangster Cycle

Between the beginning of the Depression in 1930 and the early days of the Roosevelt administration in 1933, when confusion and desperation gripped much of the country, Hollywood momentarily floundered. Not only did the studios have to make the difficult transition to sound, they had to adjust to the rapidly changing tastes of a nation in upheaval. These two variables – sound and the Depression – created a whole new set of aesthetic demands requiring that the old Formula be placed within a new context. The studios at first experimented with extravagant musicals and photographed plays, but dwindling audience interest quickly prompted them to revert to action and melodrama. It didn't take too long to realize that the talkies required a greater surface realism. The romantic, ethereal fantasies of the twenties films sounded ridiculous when put into words: John Gilbert's passion may have been eloquently mirrored in his face and eyes, but when he attempted to express it verbally the emotions seemed silly and banal. Correspondingly, the hard facts of the Depression demanded a shift in subject matter. Latin lovers and college flappers now seemed rather remote, completely unrelated to the changed mood and the overriding preoccupation with social breakdown. The romantic ideals of the thirties had to be more firmly grounded in a topical context.

Peter Roffman and Jim Purdy, "Gangsters and Fallen Women," *The Hollywood Social Problem Film: Madness, Despair, and Politics from the Depression to the Fifties* (Bloomington: Indiana University Press, 1981), pp. 15–25. Reprinted with permission of Indiana University Press.

The films of the early Depression years reflect much of the desperation of the time, both in their initial groping for new character types and settings and in their eventual preoccupation with an amoral society and the inefficacy of once-sacred values. By late 1933, with the New Deal inspiring confidence, Hollywood had found its bearings. The studios were now secure with the new sound medium and had established the dramatic conventions expressive of new attitudes. New Deal confidence and Hays Office moralism removed much of the hard edge from the early thirties cycles, but the basic groundwork for the remainder of the decade had been laid and Hollywood could now proceed with greater self-assurance.

It was during this period that the social problem film emerged as an important genre. It did not immediately spring into existence with the arrival of a major social crisis but was rather the end product of a gradual evolution. Important stylistic and narrative motifs had to be developed before the talkies could begin self-consciously to analyze the issues of the day. First among these were character prototypes – the gangster, the fallen woman, the convict, and the shyster – and a contemporary setting – the alleyways, slums, and speakeasies of the big city. Shot in a racy but essentially realistic style, these early films are the archetypal Depression movies. Though they do not really constitute problem films in themselves, the gangster, fallen woman, and prison cycles metaphorically comment on the relationship between the individual and society, taking a highly cynical attitude toward social institutions. The hero must be tough and amoral in order to endure in a society crumbling under the weight of its own corruption and ineffectuality. Dramas lingering on images of a hostile urban environment and glorifying criminal heroes seethed with antisocial undertones. Then, by 1932–33, with these dramatic conventions firmly entrenched as part of popular culture, they could be readily extended into an overt discussion of modern society. The implied social criticism of these cycles quickly gave way to the exposés, commentaries, and inquiries of the problem film.

The most popular of the prototype cycles was the gangster movie. It reestablished the action movie as Hollywood's staple by grafting a realistic, fast-paced narrative style onto stories out of the headlines. For the first time, films went beyond mere talk and exploited the full possibilities of sound, utilizing the soundtrack to create a physical impact which increased dramatic tension. The screen exploded with "the terrifying splutter of the machine gun, the screaming of brakes and squealing of automobile tires." Furthermore, the gangsters were character types more familiar to audiences than the teacup sophisticates of the photographed plays. They spoke like truckdrivers (Bugs Raymond in *Quick Millions*, 1931), slum kids (Tommy Powers in *Public Enemy*, 1931), Italian immigrants (Rico in *Little Caesar*, 1930, and Tony Camonte in *Scarface*, 1932), and stockyard workers ("Slaughterhouse" in *The Secret Six*, 1931). And most important of all, the films adapted the Formula to make the gangster a contemporary hero. Stress was still placed on the individual, but his circumstances were made more appropriate to the times. Like the traditional Formula hero, the gangster hungers after personal success, but he is different in that he can no longer fulfill this goal within the bounds of society and must pursue it through crime. The old avenues of fulfillment had been circumvented by the Depression.

Rico (Edward G. Robinson) in *Little Caesar* demonstrates an absolute faith in the American Dream by carefully following Andrew Carnegie's step-by-step formula for success: he starts at the bottom and with a single-minded dedication works his way to the top, the whole time abstaining from such distractions as sex and alcohol and studying hard to learn the operation of his organization. Rico typifies the hardworking Puritan businessman, except that the corporation has been replaced by the gang and murder is Rico's main business tactic. Similarly, Tommy Powers of *Public Enemy* is a more cynical version of the early Douglas Fairbanks comic hero. Lewis Jacobs' description of the Fairbanks persona perfectly fits Jimmy Cagney's portrayal of Powers: "In all these films Fairbanks was the 'self-made man,' unbeatable and undismayed. Quick intelligence and indefatigable energy always won him success in terms of money and the girl." But the only area that can accommodate Powers' drive and energy is that of the corrupt underworld. So Tommy, the true thirties go-getter, turns to bootlegging to fulfill his potential.

Thus the traditional good guy whose success affirms society had been transformed into the good bad guy whose success questions society. The films demonstrate that in thirties America only crime pays. Tommy's virtuous older brother (Donald Cook) is ambitious but stays within the law and languishes as a frustrated trolley conductor, while Tommy graduates to stylish suits, fast cars, and luxury penthouses. This of course contradicts a basic moral tenet, and the films must therefore kill off their heroes to invalidate lawlessness as a route to success. But in trying to uphold society, the endings only reinforce the films' basic pessimism. The success drive either leads to frustration within the system or violent death outside it. The viewer is left with the choice between the bland existence of Tommy's brother and the exciting, doomed career of Tommy.

The Happy Ending has been temporarily turned topsy-turvy. The audience identifies with the evil gangster's aims and frustrations and is invited to laugh at the representatives of good. Tommy sneers that his brother is just a "ding-dong on the streetcar." The legal establishment is likewise hopelessly inept, something to beat. If the police manage to arrest a gangster, a mouthpiece lawyer is immediately able to secure his release. Newton (Lewis Stone), the lawyer-gangleader in *The Secret Six*, is able to clear Slaughterhouse (Wallace Beery) of murder by manipulating the jury with courtroom tricks and bribery. In *Scarface*, the manipulation becomes a running gag. Every time Tony Camonte (Paul Muni) is arrested, he uses the phrase "habeas corpus" as an open sesame for his automatic release. The gangster's downfall is usually the result of gangland rivalry or a tragic personal flaw, not police efficiency. Rico has already been toppled by his rivals and has turned to alcohol when the police kill him, while Tony Camonte is destroyed by his incestuous love for his sister.

Thus, Good is hardly triumphant, and the audience, which vicariously identifies with the gangster's flaunting of every accepted code of social behavior (e.g. Cagney mashing the grapefruit in Mae Clarke's face), has very mixed feelings about Evil being vanquished. Robert Warshow suggests that the films are emblematic of our deepest fears, that the gangster expresses "that part of the American psyche which rejects the qualities and the demands of modern life, which rejects 'Americanism' itself."

> At bottom, the gangster is doomed because he is under the obligation to succeed, not because the means he employs are unlawful. In the deeper layers of the modern consciousness, all means are unlawful, every attempt to succeed is an act of aggression, leaving one alone and guilty and defenseless among enemies: one is punished for Success. This is our intolerable dilemma: that failure is a kind of death and success is evil and dangerous, is – ultimately – impossible. The effect of the gangster film is to embody this

dilemma in the person of the gangster and resolve it by his death. The dilemma is resolved because it is his death, not ours. We are safe; for the moment, we can acquiesce in our failure, we can choose to fail.

Warshow's thesis that the success ethic and evil are one finds its most explicit expression in the films of writer-director Rowland Brown. His *Quick Millions* and *Blood Money* (1933) are the only gangster films to self-consciously connect the corruption of the gangster with that of society, to directly state that organized crime is just another form of business. In *Quick Millions*, Bugs Raymond (Spencer Tracy) succeeds by applying efficient business techniques to the rackets. He is the perfect corporate man, thinking up the plans for a protective organization and having others do the work while he collects the profits. His is less the world of machine guns and booze than of managerial manipulation. Likewise, Bill Bailey (George Bancroft) of *Blood Money* succeeds through his business acumen, making an excellent living by supplying bail money for members of the underworld. Bill's partner, nightclub owner Ruby Darling (Judith Anderson), combines legitimate business with more dubious enterprises, bluntly declaring that crime is a business like any other.

Brown continually emphasizes the many ties between the underworld and straight society, showing that the two are practically indistinguishable. Both Bugs and Bill have considerable contact with officials of law and government, who seem no less corrupt than the gangsters. Bugs avoids police harassment through either bribery or blackmail, keeping files on the illicit activities of various officials. Bill backs a conservative mayoralty candidate for the same reason that businessmen support particular politicians – because the candidate's election will be good for business: "The only difference between a liberal and a conservative is that a liberal recognizes the existence of vice and controls it while a conservative turns his back and pretends it doesn't exist." In Brown's chain gang exposé, *Hell's Highway* (1932), the equation is reversed to prove that business is just another form of crime. Legitimate businessmen and government officials prove to be more criminal than the convicts, overworking and underfeeding them in order to build a highway at the smallest cost for the greatest profit.

But except for the intimations of Brown's films, which were never as popular as the others of the series, social commentary in the gangster movies rarely moves beyond metaphor. They may tell us much about the attitudes of the times, but they can hardly be labeled social problem films. Economic breakdown is not an explicit issue within the films but rather an assumed backdrop for the action. Nor do the films make more than token attempts to analyze the social roots of criminality. Despite *Public Enemy*'s claim that its purpose is "to depict an environment rather than glorify the criminal," there is little dramatic or sociological connection between the film's early depiction of Tommy Powers' slum childhood and his later career as a racketeer. Similarly, the prefatory statement that *Scarface* "is an indictment against gang rule in America and the careless indifference of the government .... What are you going do about it?" has nothing to do with the actual drama. Rather than indict the criminal, the film glorifies his ingenuity. We laugh with Tony when his lawyer gets him out of jail and he proves himself invulnerable to the law. The only "analysis" of a social problem occurs when a newspaper editor makes a plea for martial law. The scene is completely gratuitous to the rest of the plot – we never see or hear from the editor again – and its reactionary law-and-order viewpoint is out of keeping with the film's mockery of authority. While the police do kill Tony, no connection is made between his death and the editorial. It turns out that the scene was indeed added to the film long after its completion in order to placate censorship pressure. Director Howard Hawks disclaimed it, stating that it was not part of the original script and was shot against his wishes by another director.

As the addition to *Scarface* indicates, these elements of overt social analysis are flimsy attempts to mask the films' antisocial implications. The producers' failure to effectively counter the glorification of violence and crime aroused a flurry of censorship activity which eventually killed the cycle. The censors understood that such glorification was central to the audience's experience of the films and the main reason for the gangster film's popularity in the early thirties.

Though the gangster of 1930–1932 disappeared from Hollywood films, his influence remained. The sound film was transformed by the biting dialogue, naturalistic characterizations, and fast-paced continuity of the cycle. Essential to the style and technique of the gangster films is the cynicism and topicality which verges on social criticism. Although the blatant glorification of criminal violence faded from the screen after 1932, the corrosiveness lingered on in other films. The individual's relation to society continued to be viewed with disaffection, but the reasons for such disaffection gradually emerged as central to the drama. Social criticism became a major motivating force behind the films, and society was now directly indicted for the plight of the hero.

The Fallen Woman Cycle

Another group of films popular during the pre-FDR Depression years was the "fallen woman" cycle. As with the gangster film, this cycle rarely deals with the Depression in terms of social problems, but nevertheless clearly reflects the situation. The films have three basic subjects, each one demonstrating a moral breakdown within society – the unwed mother, the mistress of a married man, and the prostitute. All the films attempt to shore up morals and reaffirm America's Puritan heritage, but the drastic plot twists necessary for this reaffirmation reveal the strains of the times.

Though the films allow for the fact that crime and sin are justifiable in times of social duress, they display a heavy-handed moralism foreign to the gangster cycle. Apparently a more sensitive issue than gangland racketeering, female sexuality requires a more complicated set of rationalizations and more severe forms of punishment. It is naturally accepted that crime is a positive expression of the energetic male's rugged individualism and there is no real need to explain why a gangster is a gangster. The fallen woman's fall, however, must be thoroughly explicated and is only acceptable as an extreme necessity, a last recourse which is never a positive experience so much as a tragic degradation.

First of all, the heroine loses her chastity only for the purest of motives, usually that of true love. In the early films of the cycle centering on the unwed mother, she and her lover are prevented from marriage through extenuating circumstances. He is either a well meaning, sincere fellow inadvertently separated from the heroine or a wealthy, irresponsible playboy who abandons her in her time of need. *Born to Lose* (1931), featuring Constance Bennett, "queen of the confession films," and her most frequent partner, Joel McCrea, is typical of this series. McCrea plays Barry Craig, a World War I aviator on leave, and Bennett, Doris Kendall, an off-duty nurse. With no time or opportunity to get married but still madly in love, they spend the night together. Afterwards, he returns to the front where he is soon reported missing and presumed dead while she finds herself pregnant, husbandless, and living in shame. *Common Clay* (1930), representative of the playboy seducer plot, has the pregnant serving girl (Constance Bennett) deserted by the wealthy heir (Lew Ayres), who bows to his family's class prejudice.

In these and similar films, the heroine struggles to legitimize her child. Either her lover relents and marries her or some adoring boob takes his place. *Born to Love*'s nurse weds British stuffed shirt Sir Wilfred Drake (Paul Cavanaugh) for the sake of the baby; the abandoned heroine of *Common Clay* goes to court to sue for support. In both cases, the heroine suffers harsh treatment but valiantly fights on to selflessly provide the baby with a father, financial security, and social approval. And even in those films where she manages to win both true love and the baby's wellbeing, this happens only after the heroine has languished in a trap which seems throughout to be inescapable.

The circumstances which force her to detour around the altar and head straight for bed are rarely economic. At a time when lack of money led to countless wedding postponements and made premarital sex a necessary alternative, when families were torn apart as members scattered over the country searching for work, the early confession films avoided explicitly linking the breakdown of socioeconomic structures with the strains on morality and personal relationships. Still, with their portrait of frustrated love, their stress on sacrifice for children and the struggle for security within a tragic set of circumstances, they reflect the instabilities of the times. The continual emphasis on the need to maintain the family seems a conscious effort to reaffirm traditional mores to reassure a shaky audience that the family unit is still the basis of American life.

This reaffirmation is strongly evident in the mistress films. The mistress character continually sacrifices her own happiness rather than have her lover break up his marriage and leave his children fatherless. In *Rockabye* (1932) the ubiquitous Ms. Bennett sends playwright Jake Pell (Joel McCrea) home to his estranged wife because Mrs. Pell is pregnant. When *Christopher Strong*'s (1933) mistress, aviatrix Cynthia Darlington (Katharine Hepburn) discovers her pregnancy, she crash dives to her death so that honorable Christopher (Colin Clive) will not have to abandon his family for her. In *Back Street* (1932), the most famous of the fallen woman weepies, Ray Schmidt (Irene Dunne) forgoes her desire to have children rather than disrupt her lover's family. She acquiescently lives out her years in their back street hideaway, fantasizing about the children she never had. The mistress is a martyr, valiantly surrendering personal satisfaction to uphold the sanctity of the family.

As the cycle developed and the Depression worsened, the fall of the heroine became ever more severe. By 1932, she was taking to the streets as a prostitute. The prostitute films best illustrate the relationship between moral and economic breakdown and hence provide the cycle's most direct, if still metaphoric, allusions to the Depression. The prostitute, like the gangster, must move outside a system that cannot accommodate her. Just as the gangster turns to crime to fulfill his success drive, so the prostitute takes to the streets to provide food for herself and her family.

Though the standard plot of these films finds the heroine beset by an economic crisis, only rarely is this crisis labeled as the Depression. It is because a husband or boyfriend suddenly becomes ill or abandons her that the heroine must quickly find some alternative means of support. Through various plot circumstances, she is unable to find work and has no choice but to use her one saleable commodity. Stranded and jobless in Panama, awaiting the return of her boyfriend, the heroine (Helen Twelvetrees) of *Panama Flo* (1932) reluctantly becomes involved in a world of crime and sin.

The title character (Greta Garbo) in *Susan Lennox: Her Fall and Rise* (1931) is also led into sin while searching for her missing lover. When she does find him, her ruined reputation prompts his rejection and, still alone, she is forced to take a number of progressively sleazy jobs which trade on her sex. Helen Faraday (Marlene Dietrich) in *Blonde Venus* (1932) becomes the mistress of a corrupt politician to pay for an expensive operation which will save her husband's life. When the cured but outraged husband casts her out, she kidnaps their son and flees across the country. The only way she can feed the boy while evading police is to become a prostitute.

The sole films to indicate any concrete relation between the heroine's prostitution and social circumstances are *The Easiest Way* (1931) and *Faithless* (1932). In the former, department store clerk Laura Murdock (Constance Bennett, again) is the daughter of an unemployed longshoreman. The film depicts a poverty-stricken environment, but the father's joblessness, it is made clear, is the result of his own laziness, not of any unemployment crisis. It is not society but her father's irresponsibility that has created Laura's revulsion for poverty and lust for the security and comfort of wealth. This leads her first to pose as a model for an ad agency (always the sign of a loose woman) and from there to become the mistress of agency president Willard Brockton (Adolphe Menjou). He keeps her in a luxurious apartment complete with lavish wardrobe and chauffeured limousine, all of which she accepts not necessarily because it is the only way (she has been employed in the department store) so much as the easiest way to get by.

In *Faithless*, Carol Morgan (Tallulah Bankhead) is a rich heiress wiped out by the Crash who becomes the mistress of a wealthy boor in order to maintain her lifestyle. Unable to tolerate his sadistic treatment she decides to fend for herself but cannot find a job and slips into poverty. Eventually she marries the penniless William Wade (Robert Montgomery), and when he is brutally beaten while looking for a job she must return to a life of sin in order to pay for his food and medicine. Carol rushes into the night, declaring "There isn't anything I won't do." For the first time in the series, the sacrifice the woman makes for her man is clearly the result of the Depression.

But even in those films where the Depression backdrop remains amorphous, the implications are clear. Prostitution can be presented only as a last recourse and it can only be a last recourse within a broken-down world where all normal means of survival are cut off. The weakened or missing male figure is clearly representative of a society no longer able to support those it is responsible for.

Like the gangster films, the prostitute pictures must undercut the antisocial implications of the thesis that crime or sin is the only option available for the heroine: The conventional morality must be upheld and the women punished. But whereas the gangster is allowed to wreak havoc and enjoy the good life until the very last shootout, the prostitute continually pays the price for her violation of the Puritan code. Her career is a series of ever more degrading acts and escalating anguish. Susan Lennox has to sleep with a circus owner for the right to work in his sleazy sideshow.

Later, stranded in the tropics, she is reduced to entertaining sailors in a cheap cafe-cum-brothel. Helen Faraday is forced to dress in rags and hide with her son in a New Orleans bordello. When the police finally catch up with her and take custody of the boy, she is left alone to languish with other tramps in an overcrowded flophouse. Noting the fact that all these women gradually proceed southward as their fortunes deteriorate, Andrew Bergman remarks "how accurately it demonstrates the really iron-clad moralism of the 'fallen woman' pictures. The heavy symbolism of deflowered women sweating off their sins in fetid tropics gave away Hollywood's assumptions about sin and its price."

Even when the prostitutes find their trade profitable, they remain unhappy and unfulfilled. Susan Lennox, Carol Morgan, and Helen Faraday suffer through periods of affluence as kept women and in the end shamefully submit themselves to their one true love. Though Carol and Helen have saved their husbands' lives, they must still plead for the male's forgiveness and depend on his generosity before they can be happy again. Susan Lennox must repeatedly try to convince her lover that she is not what she really seems despite the fact that his rejection has contributed to her compromised situation.

The films make paradoxical statements: the only way to survive is through sin, thus implying a condemnation of society; but as long as a woman is sinning she must be miserably unhappy, thus upholding the established social morality. Society cannot supply the economic means to support true love and family; prostitution provides the means yet excludes the possibilities of love and family. The paradox is resolved by having the heroine overcome her economic plight through sin and then reject the sin. Both Carol Morgan and Helen Faraday can repentantly return to their healthy and stable husbands only because they have sinned to save them.

This reaffirmation of moral values is obviously rather shaky. The films' final and illogical declaration that love is more important than wealth and can, after all, be achieved within society is about as believable as the gangster films' assertion that crime doesn't pay. Carol Morgan's final submission to docile Robert Montgomery completely contradicts the vitality and independence of the Tallulah Bankhead persona.

This paradox is played out on a more sophisticated level in *Blonde Venus*, the one film in the cycle with any lasting artistic merit. Director von Sternberg despised the film, his original story significantly rewritten by Paramount to follow the fallen women conventions. But although the movie in plot outline sounds very much like other anonymous potboilers of the cycle, there is a subversive subtext that points up the dilemma of Helen's and women's position in society. Helen's descent from family normality to cabaret singer/prostitute represents a quest for identity, so that her final return to the husband she now clearly resents indicates the impossibility of finding any satisfying sense of self. As wife-mother in the opening scenes, Dietrich is desexualized, reduced to knitting in an apron with her hair pinned back and her singing career frustrated. When she does return to the stage, it is her legs that get her the job and her sexual favors the attention and money of politician Nick Townsend (Cary Grant). Her attempts to combine career with motherhood are then thwarted by her husband and officialdom. She finally gives up trying to be a self-fulfilled woman, using sex only to manipulate her way to the top of Parisian night life. In her Montmartre night club, she mocks the notion of manhood and even takes on the male role as aggressor by wearing a tuxedo. But her life is empty: "Nothing means much to me now" – and her return to Faraday, on one level a positive assertion of motherly love as self-definition, also implies a return to the tepid domesticity of the beginning, an admission of failure and despair. According to Robin Wood:

> The film … can be taken as a classic statement of one of the radical tenets of Feminism: that true femininity cannot yet exist, since all available roles for women in society are determined by male dominance. Every myth of woman is exposed in the film, not celebrated. It also constitutes an astonishingly comprehensive analysis of the manifold forms of prostitution – from the home to the dollhouse – available to women within our culture.

Though *Blonde Venus* is the only one of these films that could be described as radical, there is nevertheless an inherent tension within the entire cycle indicative of a strained affirmation. The unhappy hookers and unwed mothers find eventual normality through contorted, last minute plot twists, with the heroine's final marriage to her love occurring only after she has endured countless indignities and years of suffering. In the mistress films, the family unit is upheld through tragedy: Cynthia Darlington's suicide and Ray Schmidt's lonely, childless aging. Despite the reassurances of the cycle, the most resonant images are those of suffering and degradation. Woman is a martyr and must endure pain no matter which course of action she takes. The films supplement the image of the individual and society established by the gangster film: the individual is an innocent victim entrapped by a broken-down society with few options open to him or her.

This strained affirmation was soon comically turned on its ear by Mae West. Through sarcastic slander she reveled in what the fallen woman film had to disguise and circumvent, completely reversing their moral deadliness by making sin a sheer delight and woman a strong, assertive individual who didn't need any man. She quite frankly boasted, "Goodness had nothing to do with it." And like the gangster, she became a central target for the Hays Office.

7

Depression Allegories
Gone with the Wind *and* The Grapes of Wrath *as Hollywood Histories of the Great Depression*

Thomas H. Pauly

The Great Depression produced far-reaching transformations in gender roles and family life. While many men, unable to adequately fulfill their breadwinning role, experienced profound feelings of shame and humiliation, many women assumed a new centrality within the family household. Despite the widespread belief among policymakers that jobs should be reserved for husbands and fathers, a growing number of women took on money-making roles outside the household and a leadership role within the home. Today, many members of the audience are repelled by Gone with the Wind*'s portrait of deferential household servants and docile, obsequious field hands. But for an earlier generation of viewers, it was Scarlett O'Hara's fierce independence and her steadfast determination to overcome impoverished circumstances that drew their admiration. Somewhat similarly, the cinematic adaptation of John Steinbeck's* The Grapes of Wrath *was both a powerful condemnation of the exploitation of migrant farm laborers and a poignant portrayal of a family's persistence in the face of hardship and loss. As film historian Thomas H. Pauly shows in this essay, two of the Depression's most popular films dealt metaphorically with the broad transformations that reshaped American life during the 1930s.*

Popular culture of the later Depression years was dominated by *Gone with the Wind* and *The Grapes of Wrath*. As novels these two creations topped the best-seller lists during 1936, 1937, and 1939. Interest in both works was then renewed in early 1940 – perhaps even reached its greatest peak – when both opened as movies within weeks of one another (*Gone with the Wind* on December 15, 1939, and *Grapes of Wrath* on January 24, 1940). Though both were tremendous box-office successes their critics responded to each quite differently. While the reviews of *Gone with the Wind* strove to top one another with accounts of all the gossip, glitter, and money involved in the making of *Gone with the Wind*, those discussing *The Grapes of Wrath* stressed the out-standing quality of the film itself. "No artificial make-up, no false sentiment, no glam-our stars mar the authentic documentary form of this provocative film," asserted Philip Hartung in his review of *The Grapes of Wrath* for *Commonweal*. Similarly Otis Ferguson was confident enough of the dissatisfaction *Gone with the Wind* would bring that he postponed going, but he opened his review, entitled "Show for the People": "The word that comes in most handily for *The Grapes of Wrath* is magnificent ... this

Figure 7   *The Grapes of Wrath* (1939). 20th Century Fox. Directed by John Ford. Courtesy of Jerry Murbach, www.doctormacro.info.

is the best that has no very near comparison to date." Despite the overwhelming critical preference for Ford's movie, however, it won only one Oscar (Best Director) in the 1940 balloting, whereas Selznick's extravaganza swept all the major awards in 1939 except one (Best Actor). Clearly the later film was the people's choice. At issue here was an intense, unacknowledged debate over what the age preferred in its movies. In an era fraught with intense sociological upheaval, *Gone with the Wind* seemed consciously intended to project its audience into a realm of sentiment and nostalgia beyond the confines of actual experience. As Lincoln Kirstein complained in the opening paragraph of his scathing review for *Films*:

> … history has rarely been told with even an approximation of truth in Hollywood because the few men in control there have no interest in the real forces behind historical movements and the new forces that every new epoch sets into motion. *Gone with the Wind* deserves our attention because it is an over-inflated example of the usual false movie approach to history.

Implicit in these remarks is a charge often leveled against the movies produced during this era. Critics and historians of the cinema repeatedly call attention to Hollywood's striking reluctance to address itself to the problems of the Depression. Nothing, they point out, could have been further from the bread lines and the deprivation photographed by Dorothea Lange than the social comedies of Lubitsch, the slapstick of the

Marx Brothers, and the polished dance routines of Fred Astaire and Ginger Rogers. Nonetheless as Andrew Bergman has asserted and then persuasively demonstrated in his book on films of the Depression, *We're in the Money*, people do not escape into something they cannot relate to. The movies were meaningful because they depicted things lost or things desired. "What is 'fantastic' in fantasy is an extension of something real." In other words the "dreams" the audience is said to have demanded – those for which they spent the little extra money they had – were not mere illusions or abstractions but exciting, imaginative articulations of their greatest hopes and fears – their deepest doubts and beliefs. On this score, *Gone with the Wind* possesses a significant measure of both historical validity and importance. The fact that it was far and away the most successful film of the decade probably had less to do with the glittering surface that so annoyed the critics than the common ground it shared with *The Grapes of Wrath*. Though it was less daring and less accomplished than Ford's work, as an artistic creation *Gone with the Wind* was similarly preoccupied with the problem of survival in the face of financial deprivation and social upheaval. Both movies also demonstrate a nostalgic longing for the agrarian way of life which is ruthlessly being replaced by the fearful new economic forces of capitalism and industrialization. By way of extension both reflect an intense concern for the devastating consequences of these conditions upon self-reliant individualism and family unity, two of America's most cherished beliefs. In each case, however, serious concern for these implications is dissipated into indulgent sentimentalism so that the audience's anxieties are alleviated rather than aggravated.

Even if the script had been available, *The Grapes of Wrath* dealt with issues that were too familiar and too painful to have been made during the early thirties. Yet in deciding to produce a movie of this controversial novel at the time he did, Darryl Zanuck was sufficiently concerned about the specter of the Depression that he decided to mute and even eliminate some of the more charged aspects of Steinbeck's social criticism. As Mel Gussow has explained, "For Zanuck, *The Grapes of Wrath* and *How Green Was My Valley* were not really social documents but family pictures of a very special kind: movies about families in stress." Thus the movie's emphasis falls upon the sentimental aspect of the conditions confronting the Joads. At the outset this takes the character of the loss of a home which deprives the family of its essential connection with the land. Tom's initial return assumes the character of a search for a place of refuge from the suffering and hostility he has been forced to endure in prison and on his truck ride. That everything has changed is made clear by his encounter with Casy; but the full impact of this upheaval is registered only when he beholds the vacant, crumbling house in which he was raised and hears Muley's distracted tale of how his reverence for the land has been desecrated. "My pa was born here," he insists: "We was all born on it and some of us got killed on it and some died on it. And that's what makes it ourn …." Equally striking in this regard is the later scene where Grampa asserts: "I ain't a-goin' to California! This here's my country. I b'long here. It ain't no good – but it's mine," and then underlines his points by distractedly gripping his native soil.

In dramatizing the intense suffering these people experience, these lines serve the more important function of locating its source. The former agrarian way of life predicated upon man's intimate attachment to the land has given way to an economy of industrialization, with its efficiency, practicality, and inhumanity. For Tom and his fellow farmers, there is no possibility of retaliation. The fury that drives Muley to take up a gun produces only frustration and helpless dejection because there is no enemy to shoot. The man on the caterpillar turns out to be his neighbor who is trapped by the same problem of survival. The machines that level their homes, like the foreclosures which are delivered in dark, sinister automobiles, cannot be associated with particular individuals; they are the weapons of a system devoid of both personality and humanity.

The Man:	Now don't go blaming me. It ain't my fault
Son:	Whose fault is it? …
The Man:	It ain't nobody. It's a company. He ain't anything but the manager…
Muley (bewildered):	Then who do we shoot?
The Man:	… Brother I don't know.

Deprived of the only home he has known, Tom Joad joins his family in their quest for a new one. However great may be their need for food and money, keeping the family together, Ma Joad makes clear, is the most pressing concern. She sees that nourishment involves the spirit as well, and in the face of the increasingly depersonalized world confronting her the shared concerns of the family offer the only remaining source of humanity. These become the basic issues by which the audience measures the significance of the ensuing trip to California. As Ford dramatizes them, the policemen who harass the Joads, the bosses who dictate to them, [and] the thugs who break up the dances and union gatherings are like the handbills that bring them to California, products of a sinister conspiracy beyond human control. They combine with the inhospitable landscape encountered to create an environment in which the family is unable to survive. Grampa and Gramma die before the destination is reached; Connie cannot stand up to the punishment inflicted upon him and flees: Casy is killed by the growers' hired guns; having avenged Casy's death Tom is forced to flee for his life.

The Grapes of Wrath, however, is more than a mere drama of defeat. The futility of individualism and the breakdown of the family furnish in the end a distinct source of optimism. Having witnessed the miserable living conditions in which the Joads have futilely struggled to endure – the filthy tent in the clapboard road camp, the concentration of starving people in Hooverville, the gloomy squalor of the cabin at the Keene ranch – the audience is now introduced to a utopia of cooperative socialism which has been as scrupulously sanitized of communism as it is of filth. In contrast to the derogatory view expressed earlier in the movie, working with the government is shown to offer a more valid prospect of salvation than fighting against the prevailing conditions at the Wheat Patch camp, the spirit of Tom's involvement with Casy is realized without the self defeating violence and killing. Here, as George Bluestone notes, the Joads find "a kind of miniature planned economy efficiently run, boasting modern sanitation, self government, cooperative living, and moderate prices." Here people work together with the same automatic efficacy as the flush toilets. Cleanliness nourishes kindness, the caretaker explains, with the serene wisdom of his kindly, confident manner (does he remind you of FDR?).

Even the language has been changed to accord with this new society: one finds here not a shelter, a house or a home but a "sanitary unit." Though this community has been conceived to accord with the depersonalized society outside its gates it has also incorporated a basic respect for human dignity. It is a world characterized by its Saturday dance with its democratic acceptance, its well controlled exclusion of the forces of anarchy, its ritualistic incorporation of the outdated family into a healthy new society – a new society which would actually be realized only two years later in the "comfortable" concentration camps for Japanese-Americans during World War II. Above all, the Wheat Patch camp episode affords a bridge to the "new" ending Zanuck was moved to write for his movie. As Tom and the Joad truck return to the outside world and strike out in different directions they have no idea where they are going but they all have renewed hope that they can find salvation just by being with "the people."

> Rich fellas come up an' they die an' their kids ain't no good an' they die out. But we keep a'coming. We're the people that live. Can't nobody wipe us out. Can't nobody lick us. We'll go on forever Pa. We're the people.

Such conviction, Zanuck concluded, was not to be thwarted by the "No Help Wanted" originally indicated in Nunnally Johnson's screenplay, so he gave them an open road – which appropriately enough leads off to nowhere.

The Grapes of Wrath is a fine movie but it is considerably flawed. Furthermore, for all its "documentary" technique, it is badly distorted history. Its depiction of the plight of the migrant worker contributes considerably less to our understanding of the conditions of the Depression than its suspicion of big business, its manifest agrarianism, and, above all, its sentimental concern for the breakdown of the family. Given the striking commercial success of the movie one cannot help wondering what it was the public went to see – an artistic masterpiece, a direct confrontation with the reality of the Depression, or its handling of the above concerns. Of the three the last was perhaps the most important for this was the one striking point of resemblance between it and the biggest box office movie of the decade. *Gone with the Wind* succeeded as well as it did in large part because it so effectively sublimated the audience's own response to the Depression. For them, the panoramic shot of the Confederate wounded littering the center of Atlanta was not a matter of fact but of feeling. All concern for the scene's historical authenticity simply vanished in the face of its dramatization of the sense of helplessness and devastation they themselves had experienced.

Amidst these circumstances, Scarlett's subsequent return to Tara bears a striking resemblance to Tom's homecoming in her quest for refuge from the adversities she has endured. Yet her expectation is shattered by the same scene of desolation that Tom discovered. For her, also, there is the same decaying ruin in place of the secure home she formerly knew. Tom's encounter with Muley seems almost a rerun of Scarlett's even more painful confrontation with her father, whose demented condition strikingly illustrates the magnitude of change resulting from the war's upheaval. As in *The Grapes of Wrath*, this breakdown in the integrity of the family is associated with the destruction of an agrarian way of life which strikes at the very core of Scarlett's emotional being. The burned soil of Tara that Scarlett grips in the concluding scene of Part I is fraught with the same significance which attended Grampa's similar gesture in *The Grapes of Wrath*.

Scarlett's response, however, marks an important point of difference. Unlike Tom Joad, who took to the road and sought to survive by working with his family, Scarlett resolves to be master of her destiny. Her moving declaration, "As God is my witness … I'll never be hungry again," pits her will against the prevailing conditions. Her determination is such that she not only antagonizes the remnants of her family but she also exploits them; having slapped Suellen she proceeds to steal her prospective husband Frank Kennedy. Nonetheless her actions are prompted by some of the same motives that carried the Joads to California.

In the characterization of Scarlett is to be found most of the complexity that *Gone with the Wind* possesses. As the reviewer of the *New York Times* observed, "Miss Leigh's Scarlett is the pivot of the picture." Were she merely a bitch or strong-willed feminist the appeal of this movie would have been considerably diminished. In order to appreciate the intense response she elicited from the audience one has to understand the particular way in which Scarlett's return to Tara and her subsequent commitment to rebuilding it qualifies her initial assertion of independence and results in a tragic misunderstanding that brings her downfall. In the opening scenes of the movie Scarlett wins the audience's sympathy for her determined spirit of rebellion. It is she who provides critical perspective on the glittering world of plantation society. Tara and Twelve Oaks with their surrounding profusion of flowers and lush background sweep of countryside are as magnificently attired as the people who congregate there and therefore are perfect settings for the featured scenes of dressing and undressing, posturing and strutting. The main function of women in this world is providing ornamental beauty. The illusion of grace and elegance they sustain is predicated upon a harsh standard of propriety a painfully tight corset. Parties become major moments in their lives in helping them to achieve their ordained goal of marriage, but their area of decision is limited to the choice of a dress or hat. Since the threat of a rival is the only war they can be expected to understand they are all herded off to bedrooms to freshen their appearance and restore their frail energies while the men debate the future of the South. Given the stifling confinement of this role, Scarlett balks. Like the other women she entertains a vision of marriage and consciously attends to her appearance, but unlike them she is determined to act on her wishes. Thus while her rivals retire according to the convention of the submissive female, she slips downstairs to confront Ashley in the belief that he will not be able to resist her assault.

The war which preempts Scarlett's fight for Ashley dramatically affirms these and all the other deficiencies of this society but as a "lost cause" it also forces Scarlett to determine her highest priorities. At first she displays only a selfish interest; its tragedy is for her a source of gain in relieving her of an unwanted husband. However, the flames of Atlanta which occasion a nightmare of emotion as they destroy the Old South illuminate a new romantic potential in Scarlett's deepening relationship with Rhett. During their flight, their affair of convenience predicated upon the same spirited but pragmatic individualism which alienates them both from plantation society achieves a new level of interdependency in the intense feelings they exchange and share. Having been stripped of her gentility, her vanity, and finally her self confidence, Scarlett is reduced to her greatest moment of need. At this point Rhett's selfishness which reveals itself to have been basically an emotional shield also gives way. For the first time both reach out for something greater than themselves. The result however is not a common understanding. Rhett proposes a marriage and a new future only to discover that Scarlett prefers to retreat to the past. Survival, she has come to believe, lies in the red earth of Tara. Rejected, Rhett goes off to fight for the cause. Thus the situation which brought Rhett and Scarlett together propels them along separate paths in search of ideals which ironically the war is at that moment destroying. Though they survive to marry one another, the decisions forced by the war constitute an insurmountable breach which the conclusion of the movie simply reaffirms as Rhett goes off to Charleston in search of "the calm dignity life can have when it's lived by gentle folks – the genial grace of days that are gone," while Scarlett heeds her father's words calling her back to Tara.

In his concerted effort to reproduce the novel as thoroughly as possible Selznick felt that the increased emphasis he accorded to Tara was one of the few points of departure. "I felt," he explained in one of his memos, "that the one thing that was really open to us was to stress the Tara thought more than Miss Mitchell did." For him, Scarlett's character was grounded in Tara, in agrarianism, and the family just as the identity of the Joads was. Yet, in according it much the same meaning, he dramatized its tragic consequence quite differently. Scarlett's vow never to be hungry again as she grips the burned soil of Tara at the end of Part I moves the audience with its stirring determination, but this vow is severely qualified by the scene's logic. Quite simply Tara or "terra " cannot provide the nourishment she requires. The turnip she ravenously devours and then vomits is strikingly emblematic of Tara's true value. In the first place the fact that the earth is red is an obvious signal that the soil sustains crops with great difficulty. Without the slaves and strong willed owners Tara is not even capable of generating enough capital to pay its taxes. The main reason for Scarlett's determination to return to Tara, however, transcends all these considerations. Tara is home – its essence is to be found more in the echoing sound of her father's voice and the heart tugging strains of Max Steiner's music. For her, Tara is the sphere of her father's influence, a refuge where matters were firmly under control and she was treated with tolerance and indulgence. Yet this is equally foolish for she discovers that her father has been broken by the war and now relies on her for the consolation she has expected him to provide. Nowhere are the disadvantages of Tara revealed more dramatically than in the buckboard visit of Jonas Wilkerson, whose association with the new economic forces supplanting agrarianism recalls the nameless men of *The Grapes of Wrath* in their sinister cars.

Since money has become the only source of power Scarlett must seek beyond Tara for survival. Scarlett appears to marry Frank Kennedy to pay the taxes on Tara but she obviously sees that he is associated with the prospering forces of industrialization. Consequently, in becoming his wife she really becomes a businesswoman. These conflicting allegiances to Tara and to her lumber mill place Scarlett in the paradoxical position of shunning the role of wife and mother in order to uphold her passionate commitment to family and the home. Her identification with business and its ruthless practices now loses her the audience's sympathy, yet because she never understands the character and consequences of what she is doing she proves more tragic than villainous. Her determined quest for the greatest margin of profit is not to be understood as her predominant aim. Much more essential is her desire that Tara be rebuilt. To do so is not only to eliminate the desperate state of poverty to which she had been reduced but also to restore the spiritual strength of her family home. Only the audience, however, comprehends the hidden cost. Frank becomes her lackey and her marriage no more than a working partnership. She herself becomes a social pariah. Most important, Scarlett begins to die from emotional starvation as her business absorbs her energies without providing any of the attention and compassion she has always craved. The sorrow she drowns with liquor following Kennedy's death is neither anguish nor a pained sense of confinement – it is a strange lack of feeling.

Once again Rhett comes to offer her salvation. Despite his manifest contempt for propriety, Rhett's invasion of her privacy and his cynical proposal of marriage are joyfully welcomed because they offer Scarlett an opportunity to escape her business and enjoy her own home. Unfortunately the seeds of her undoing have already been sown. The self reliant determination of her struggles has rendered her temperamentally incapable of filling the role of the devoted wife she would like to be. Rhett's gifts – the house and even Bonnie – all simply deprive her of the thing she needs most – a challenge. For this she returns to Ashley, whose embodiment of the devoted husband she must destroy in order to win. Her visit with the dying Melanie causes her finally to realize this, as well as the fact that Rhett is a much worthier ideal. Sensing her folly, she rushes home to find that he has indeed become unreachable. As a mother without a child, a wife without a husband, Scarlett is left by Selznick at the end of the picture turning to a home she can inhabit only in her dreams. The famous concluding line of the novel, "tomorrow is another day," is almost drowned out in the movie by the emotionally charged flashback scene of Tara with Gerald O'Hara's words echoing in the background. Thus Scarlett stands at the end a strong willed individualist in possession of all the wealth the audience could imagine, yet no better off than they because of her inability to realize her impossible dream of a happy home and a loving family.

At the height of the Depression thirteen million workers were unemployed. People who had enjoyed marked prosperity during the twenties suddenly found themselves struggling just to stay alive. Equally troubling was their inability to comprehend the reasons for this devastating reversal. As Leo Gurko has observed, "The decade of the thirties was uniquely one in which time outran consciousness ... the misery of the country was equaled only by its bewilderment." The absence of checks and balances in the market place which was supposed to provide the ordinary citizen with opportunity seemed only to be making the rich richer and the poor poorer. Everywhere, big business seemed to be prospering. The general lack of knowledge about those who ran it or how it operated simply added to the pervasive belief that these companies were somehow profiting at the expense of the suffering individual. Similarly frustrating was the helplessness and loss of dignity caused by unemployment. No longer was the working man able to fill his expected role as head of the household. Either he could not support his family or he was forced to strike out on his own in order to do so. Consequently his traditional source of consolation now only contributed to his distress. In the cities where these problems were most acute the idea of "getting back to the land" seemed to offer a ready made solution. As Broadus Mitchell explains:

> In the cities unemployment emphasized crowding, squalor and cold; the bread lines were visual reproaches. In the country on the other hand was ample room. Further, in the cities workers won bread by an indirect process which for some reason had broken down. But life in the rural setting was held to be synonymous with raising family food. The thing was simple, direct, individually and socially wholesome.

This solution, of course, turned out to be most impractical. Yet it reveals the direction in which the people's anxieties were working. Coming at the end of the

Depression as they did, *Gone with the Wind* and *The Grapes of Wrath* appealed to viewers who had lived through this ordeal. Both succeeded in large measure because they so effectively tapped the emotional wellsprings of this urban audience which was their chief patron. Repeatedly, the viewer found himself confronting these same troubling issues; but they were presented in such a way that he was reassured that everything would work out just as he hoped it would. At the same time, neither could have been as compelling had this sentimentality not been treated with a subtlety and understanding notably lacking in similar films like *Our Daily Bread*.

8

African Americans
on the Silver Screen
The Evolution of Black Film

Thomas R. Cripps

Since the movies' beginning, African Americans have played a critical but largely neglected role in film production and acting. In this essay, historian Thomas R. Cripps chronicles the African American experience in film, from the 1890s until World War II, including the extraordinary efforts to establish independent black film production. He also examines the struggle of black performers, filmmakers, and civil rights organizations like the National Association for the Advancement of Colored People to challenge the stereotypes found in Hollywood films.

From the very beginning of American cinema in the 1890s, Afro-Americans appeared on the screen. One might argue that these early films were not truly black because their function, more or less, was to tell whites about the black curiosa on the periphery of their culture. Early topical vignettes in Thomas Edison's films included watermelon-eating contests, Negroes leading parades, black soldiers in Cuba, reenactments of campaigns against guerrillas in the Philippines, and fragments of anthropological ephemera such as West Indian women dancing, coaling ships, or bathing babies. There were occasional bits, such as Biograph's *A Bucket of Cream Ale* (1904), which was drawn from a vaudeville routine in which a "Dutchman" is hit in the face with a growler of beer tossed by his black-faced maid. In a small way these films attained a range of black imagery that has gone remarkably unnoticed. In their day, the films were black only in the sense that they thrust a heretofore invisible image upon general American viewers. Their roots emerged from a faddish popular anthropology that had been a fountainhead of European exploration in Africa, complete with rival expeditions in search of the sources of the Nile, voyages to polar icecaps, attempts by the U.S. Department of the Interior to collect Indian lore, and even whitewater adventures down the Colorado River. Therefore many early black figures on the screen were no more than the subjects of a quest for the legendary, the curious, and the bizarre, through darkest Africa and Carib isle. Along with stray vaudeville routines and gag shots, occasional faithfully recorded visual records appeared, such as

Thomas R. Cripps, "The Evolution of Black Film," *Black Film as Genre* (Bloomington: Indiana University Press, 1978), pp. 13–15, 17, 19–24, 26–31, 33–8. Reprinted with permission of Indiana University Press.

that of Theodore Roosevelt's journey to Africa and *The Military Drill of the Kikuyu Tribes and Other Native Ceremonies* (1914). In another vein, cameramen pursued the black heavyweight champion Jack Johnson, either to record his frequent breaches of racial etiquette or to document his hoped-for eventual defeat.

But if early films, lacking as they were in black sources, point of view, or advocacy, whetted black appetites, they hardly could have satisfied them. In fact, within a dozen years of their beginnings, the early black appearances were snuffed out by a renewed fascination with the Civil War era brought on by the approach of its Golden Anniversary. During these early years, amidst the stereotyped crapshooters, chicken thieves, and coon shows that the screen inherited from Southern popular literature, movies also offered, in addition to reportorial film of exotic locales, Edwin S. Porter's *Uncle Tom's Cabin* (1903), with its wisp of Abolitionism and a flurry of authentic cakewalking. A genuine bit of "rubberlegs" dancing in Biograph's *The Fights of Nations* (1907) was another example of occasional deviations from Southern metaphor. But after 1910 the celebration of the Civil War removed almost all authentic depiction of black Americans from the nation's screens, the semi-centennial serving as an inspiration to put aside realism in favor of romantic nostalgia as a model for presenting Negroes on film.

In a movie world populated by Afro-Americans who embraced slavery, loved the Union but not the principle of Abolition, expressed their deepest humanity through loyal service to white masters, and counted the master class, its families, and fortunes above their own, there could not have been a genuinely black film. The movie slaves either served the white cause in such films as *A Slave's Devotion* (1913), *Old Mammy's Charge* (1914), *The Littlest Rebel* (1914), *His Trust* (1911), *His Trust Fulfilled* (1911), and *Old Mammy's Secret Code* (1913), or they at least stood by passively, lending atmosphere to the Southern setting in *The Empty Sleeve* (1914), *Days of War* (ca. 1914), *For the Cause of the South* (1914), *A Fair Rebel* (1914), *The Soldier Brothers of Susannah* (1912), and literally hundreds more.

Coincident with these social forces, the editorial techniques of filmmaking had been growing more sophisticated. In 1915 D.W. Griffith, a sentimental Southerner with a feel for Victorian melodrama and a keen visual sense, synthesized nearly a decade's observation and practice into a film of unprecedented three-hour length, *The Birth of a Nation* – and sold it through the grandest publicity campaign ever given a motion picture. The film was an illiberal racial tract that celebrated Southern slavery, the fortitude of the Ku Klux Klan, and the fealty of "good Negroes."

The national Negro leadership, just beginning to enjoy the fruits of a quarter-century of experiment (and tinkering with various Afro-American Leagues, the National Negro Business League, the Niagara Movement, and the like), came together in the National Association for the Advancement of Colored People. Its urbane bourgeois members, including many whites, felt singularly offended by the hoary Southern metaphors signified by Griffith's imagery. Unfortunately for the future of black film, they countered with censorship rather than filmmaking, resulting in a briefly successful campaign that unwittingly had the long-range effect of driving all but the most comic black roles from the screen.

During the year following *The Birth of a Nation*, black genre film began in earnest. Although newspaper stories hinted of a few early attempts in the Middle West – notably those of Bill Foster – the first truly genuinely black film companies were those organized by Emmett J. Scott and the brothers George and Noble Johnson. Scott's group promised more, but perhaps because it came first, suffered the more resounding failure. Scott, a former Texas newspaperman and Booker T. Washington's secretary at Tuskegee Institute for almost twenty years, looked to filmmaking as a first step to his independence after the death of the authoritarian Washington in 1915. At first Scott, together with the NAACP, pursued an impossible course, making Lincoln's Dream, a film graced with the scholarly credentials of historian Albert Bushnell Hart, written by a veteran scriptwriter, financed by matching funds from the NAACP and Universal Pictures, and showcased in a prestigious premiere. Unfortunately, Carl Laemmle of Universal, the prospective "angel," backed off. When the NAACP was paralyzed by a resulting internal debate, Scott was forced to take up negotiations with a small and greedy Chicago firm.

The resulting *Birth of a Race* (1919) suffered from the absence of a strong black voice in defense of a film concept, scattered and often deferred shooting schedules and locations ranging from Chicago to Tampa, and a theme and plot that shifted its emphasis from a biblical to a pacifist idea conditioned by the coming of World War I. After almost three years of shooting and cutting, most of the black elements had been pushed aside by presumably more timely and universal themes. Despite a glittering opening in Chicago and a few additional bookings, the film dropped from sight and Scott gave up cultivating prospective black middle-class investors in a film project.

Nevertheless, the project attracted the attention of the Johnsons: George, then a postman in Omaha, and Noble, a Universal contract player. In 1916, together with black investors from Los Angeles and a white cameraman, Harry Gant, they had set out to make motion pictures with a black point of view. Like most of the black middle class in the 1920s, they embraced the American success myth brought to light by Horatio Alger. Between 1916 and 1922, the Johnsons' Lincoln Motion Picture Company averaged almost one film per year, each filled with individualist heroes, who promised blacks the hope of success and the conquest of despair. *By Right of Birth* (1921) was an anatomy of the genteel black upper class of Los Angeles. It starred Clarence Brooks, who later appeared in John Ford's *Arrowsmith* (1931), and Anita Thompson, a tall, stylish actress from the cast of *Runnin' Wild*, a black revue.

Another Lincoln film, *The Realization of a Negro's Ambition* (ca. 1917) recast the Horatio Alger legend in black terms. *The Trooper of Troop K* (ca. 1920) recounted the yarn of the rough western loner, played by Noble Johnson, who, carrying a pure heart under his saddle dust and army blues, proves his goodness and wins the girl after fighting in a reenactment of a famous cavalry battle with Mexican marauders in the Southwest.

The marketing efforts of both the Birth of a Race Company and the Lincoln Motion Picture Company revealed the hazards of distributing movies outside established Hollywood channels. Hollywood had become an oligopoly that controlled almost all aspects of American filmmaking. All Independent companies, whether "B" producers on Hollywood's "poverty row," Yiddish moviemakers in Manhattan, or race movie makers, suffered from both a lack of capital and outlets for sufficient distribution. Their finished films generally ran only in small, second-run "grind" houses which owed no scheduling obligations to the large theater chains that were the backbone of Hollywood profits. At both ends of the production line, the economic structure threatened independent filmmakers with either loss of control or actual extinction. The Johnsons' inventive but eventually unsuccessful solution employed a string of black newspapermen, who both plugged their movies and acted as bookers.

Rather than holding out the promise of another stride toward a black genre, the next stage of black filmmaking revealed a negative aspect of making race movies. The Ebony Motion Picture of Chicago, like a number of other small white companies, produced films for black audiences behind a facade of black managers. But apparently their white "angels" and Southern white writer, Leslie T. Peacock, insisted on films like *A Black Sherlock Holmes* (ca. 1918) that were mirror images of white movies. Ebony's *Spying the Spy* (1919), for example, employed a talented black comedian in the role of an American spy in pursuit of a stereotyped German agent; the film's climax was an orgy of editorial effects which played upon the old-fashioned notion of the Afro-American fear of ghosts. While many blacks had migrated to cities, surprisingly, little of urban black life appeared on the screen. Furthermore, interest in foreign exotica had declined into a cycle of Edgar Rice Burroughs's *Tarzan* with its African supernumeraries. Revived by the coming of sound, blackface roles persisted.

Before 1925, strong black roles were brought to the screen by corps of black Hollywood regulars in a handful of films that touched some unconscious truth about American racial life. Madame Sul-te-Wan, Onest Conley, Carolynne Snowden, Nathan Curry, Zach Williams, Raymond Turner, and boxers Sam Baker and George Godfrey brought conviction to these few roles. Noble Johnson typified their accomplishment and captivity by white Hollywood. His career spanned from World War I with Lubin to a job as the Indian hothead, Red Shirt, in John Ford's *She Wore a Yellow Ribbon* (1949). Because his work with the Lincoln Motion Picture Company competed with the movies produced by his white employer, Universal Pictures, Johnson was asked to give up his work at Lincoln. Thereafter, through World War I not only did he continue as a stock heavy in Universal's various "B" western series, *Red Feather*, *Red Ace*, and *Bull's Eye*, but went on to appear as scores of Indians, Latins, Asians, and primitive tribesmen in such movies as *Robinson Crusoe* (1917), *Leopard Woman* (1920), *Kismet* (1920), *The Four Horsemen of the Apocalypse* (1921) (in which he was one of the mounted plagues), *The Ten Commandments* (1923), *Flaming Frontier* (1926), *Aloma of the South Seas* (1926), *Ben Hur* (1927), and *Lady of the Harem* (1926). In some years he appeared in a half dozen or more pictures, ranging from major "epics" to routine "programmers."

The other source of strong black characterizations appeared in white movies in an indirect, muted way that barely hinted at the fact that American society had begun to deal with a new Negro who had migrated to Northern cities. In 1916 Bert Williams, the distinguished black comedian of the Ziegfeld Follies, appeared in *Fish* and *A Natural Born Gambler*, two movies that used blackface routines in a fresh way. In the former Williams was a gangling country boy, who tries to sell a fish as it grows stale. In *A Natural Born Gambler* he presides over the card table at his fraternal lodge while contriving to elude the white police. In the same period, Vitagraph made two parodies of white boxers whose fear of Jack Johnson formed the basis of comedy – *Some White Hope* (1915) and *The Night I Fought Jack Johnson* (1913). A black confidante far shrewder and more knowing than the Civil War cycle maids appeared in *Hoodoo Ann* (1916). Aggressive and even derisive black women appeared in Cecil B. DeMille's *Manslaughter* (1922). Several children's series that set the mood for the debut of Hal

Roach's egalitarian *Our Gang* began in the late 1910s. The variety of black roles expanded to include French and American soldiers, wise old boxing trainers, horse trainers, and a number of servants who resembled Tonto. the Lone Ranger's sidekick, more than they did Rastus, the antebellum butler.

Despite their contribution to the wearing away of old icons that had symbolized the former inferior status of Afro-Americans, these deviations from ancient norms spoke little of the "new Negro" who was already celebrated in Northeastern literary circles. If white moviemakers understandably failed to take into account the changed circumstances of urban blacks, their black counterparts also failed to fill the existing void. Nor did a growing number of black critics suggest new images to replace the outdated ones, except for a vague plea for presenting "positive," meaning middle-class, characters on the screen.

But the condition of the "new Negro" was not that clear-cut. As Afro-Americans moved from Southern farms to Northern cities, they fell prey to oppressive forces from outside the group. Their plight may be likened to that of the Germans, described in an essay by Erich Kahler (1974). In the Middle Ages, Germans, like blacks, spoke a language built upon linguistic traditions from outside the group; lived in rural regions and disdained the city or found it alien; embraced millennial ideals rather than small victories; and chose in-group stratification as a means of preserving the group, despite anarchic forces pressing from the outside. Moreover, in the face of these external forces, whether Frankish kings in Paris, Italian *condottieri* in the pay of the Pope, or Magyar invaders, the Germans often responded with in-group aggression.

The wide gulf between white movies and black aspirations may be seen in a fragmentary glance at some of D.W. Griffith's 192 films. After the release of *The Birth of a Nation*, Griffith went on to make several masterpieces, such as *Intolerance* (1916), *Broken Blossoms* (1919), *Way Down East* (1920), and *Orphans of the Storm* (1921). Like most of his works, these films commented on social issues from the safe vantage point of the past or foreign locales. In the mid-1920s, however, Griffith addressed himself to modern times.

Here Griffith's racial vision, like that of most of his white countrymen, was unable to distinguish rural blacks from the new urban Negro. The black characters in *One Exciting Night* (1922) were strikingly off the mark. The central character, an improbable detective, was a "Kaffir, the dark terror of the bootleg gang." The remaining black roles were played by blackfaced whites as traditional servile flunkies, who trailed through the plot. A year later, in *The White Rose* (1923), Griffith attempted to return to Southern ground, but his critics leapt upon him for his "mawkish sickening sentimentality" and his "jumbled and pointless plot." According to them, he seemed a "genius out of touch with the world." Next he began *His Darker Self* (1924), another blackface picture starring Al Jolson, who eventually deserted the project. Still later Griffith made an unsatisfying and fruitless appearance on the set of Universal's *Topsy and Eva* (1927), an exploitation spinoff from that studio's successful *Uncle Tom's Cabin*. In every case these were "white" movies, retailing Negroes almost as an in-group joke.

At last in the mid-1920s black critics on black newspapers, among them Lester Walton of the *New York Age*, Romeo Daugherty of the *Amsterdam News*, J.A. Rogers, and D. Ireland Thomas, began to develop a common vision. A few white papers also developed a racial sensitivity, in particular, *Variety* crowed in glee when the Ku Klux

Klan muddled a filmmaking project. When promoters gave a preview of a racist tract called *Free and Equal* (1925), *Variety* howled: "it is not only old fashioned but so crudely done that the Sunday night audience laughed it practically out of the theater."

But neither Griffith nor the press provided the fairest gauge of Hollywood's inability to deal with black themes. Rather, it was the mixed response that blacks gave to the best and most well-meaning Hollywood movie, Universal's *Uncle Tom's Cabin*. In 1926 Carl Laemmle started the project by signing Charles Gilpin, the most distinguished black actor of his day, to play Tom. However, Gilpin was soon replaced by James Lowe, who gave one of the finest black cinema performances in a faithful rendering of the spirit of Harriet Beecher Stowe's novel.

Unfortunately for Laemmle, black critics and audiences alike split in their judgment of the film that had been aimed at a "crossover" audience of blacks and whites, who would like either its abolitionism or its nostalgia. But no amount of mere preaching on the subject of race satisfied those blacks who looked to film as a medium for communicating to a black audience.

Nevertheless, in comparison with the films of the early 1920s, blacks saw in *Uncle Tom's Cabin* a new Hollywood that seemed to promise a fair representation of black characters, liberal progress, and cause for hope. One producer promised a movie of the new Broadway hit, *Porgy* (1927); John M. Stahl put a serious black love scene in *In Old Kentucky* (1927); William Wellman's hopeful *Beggars of Life* featured a fine role by Edgar "Blue" Washington; DeMille's *Old Ironsides* (1926) carried a crew that included strong black roles, as did Alan Crosland's *The Sea Beast* (1926); and Monta Bell's *Man, Woman, and Sin* (1927) established its urban milieu with neat vignettes of black city life.

In the absence of movies that spoke directly to black concerns, a kind of black underground grew outside the major studios, Although largely white-owned, it nonetheless attempted to reach the black audience that was untouched by Hollywood. Strapped by poor distribution channels, paltry budgets, amateurish actors, technical failings, and untrained crews, these production companies were somehow able to release films for black audiences throughout the silent era. Their films reached beyond mere representation of Negroes on the screen to depict Afro-Americans as a presence in American life.

Most of these race movie makers felt an obligation to present blacks as icons of virtue and honor. One case in point, the Douglass Company of New Jersey, used war film heroism "to show the better side of 'Negro life'" and to "inspire in the Negro a desire to climb higher." They also adapted films from the works of popular Negro authors, such as Paul Laurence Dunbar's *The Scapegoat* (1917). Another Douglass project, *The Colored American Winning His Suit* (1916), followed the career of the Negro hero who was "getting ahead." Other companies turned War Department films into *From Harlem to the Rhine* (ca. 1918), *Our Hell Fighters Return* (1919), and other compilations showing black troops in combat.

By the early 1920s the *New York Age* headlined that COLORED MOTION PICTURES ARE IN GREAT DEMAND. The filmmakers were undaunted by any topic; the whole black world was their stage, and their regional roots gave a varied flavor to the black experience they recorded on film. This excitement stirred still other prospective producers to grind out glossy prospectuses that promised great black films which would never be made. Their known films included the Norman Company's all-black westerns shot in the famous all-black town of Boley, Oklahoma, starring the New York actress Anita Bush. The Cotton Blossom Company and the Lone Star Company made similar pictures in San Antonio. Dr. A. Porter Davis made *The Lure of a Woman* (1921), the first film produced in Kansas City.

After 1922, the Renaissance Company made black newsreels. White producers like Ben Strasser and Robert Levy (whose Reol Company made a movie from Dunbar's *Sport of the Gods* [1921]) joined the ranks of race movie makers. War movies persisted as a genre. Among these, Sidney P. Dones's *Injustice* (1920) was a wartime tale of Negroes and the Red Cross; two others, *Democracy, Or a Fight for Right* (1919) and *Loyal Hearts* (1919), "a smashing Virile Story of Our Race Heroes," were released by the Democracy Photoplay Corporation.

The most dogged of the race movie makers was Oscar Micheaux. Micheaux, a young black who had been a homesteader on the Dakota prairie, survived nearly twenty-five years in a desperately cutthroat business, turning out approximately two dozen movies in Chicago, New York, and New Jersey. As early as 1919, Micheaux tried unsuccessfully to link up with the Lincoln Company, a union that failed because the Johnsons considered him an upstart, a mountebank, and an untrustworthy hustler, ironically all traits that would help him achieve success.

Micheaux's production style gave texture to black genre films even if his work was not noted for its excellence of cinematic technique. To make up for a lack of technical expertise his black and white casts and crews exhibited a fellowship that blended the ideals of African tribal communities with the like values of a typical John Ford stock company of the 1940s. Ford's people shared the dust, cursed the heat, and passed the whiskey bottle together, thereby giving an unmistakable Ford quality to their films, Micheaux never shot a film in the desert, but his companies, by sharing poverty, late paychecks, and shabby working conditions, somehow managed to give a generic texture to their films.

In like manner, Micheaux's shooting in idle and antique studios in Chicago, Fort Lee, and the Bronx; the jarring effect of the uneven talents of his actors; his use of unsung, underemployed white cameramen abandoned by the drift of filmmaking to Hollywood; and his shoestring operation which reflected the cast's own lives, all lent the enterprise an aura of outlawry. By merely finishing a film, Micheaux's company was like the legendary tricksters of black folklore, who win the game against the system. Thus the low pay, borrowed equipment, and nagging debtors helped define the character of the completed movie.

The difference between Micheaux and the other producers of the black genre can be compared to the difference between Orson Welles and Irving Thalberg. Welles was the outsider, flippant and contemptuous of established custom; Thalberg was the middle-class company man, loyal to MGM until his dying day, who succeeded by not offending either boss or audience. Micheaux, like Welles, had the gall to be opinionated in the presence of more experienced filmmakers, Welles once described his studio facilities as the finest Erector set a boy could ever hope for. Like Welles from his vantage point outside the system, Micheaux may have experienced a similar feeling of raw, fey power over the conventional filmmaking regime.

Motion pictures gave Micheaux the power to say, however amateurishly, what no other Negro film maker even thought of saying. He filmed the unnameable, arcane, disturbing things that set black against black. When others sought only uplifting and positive images, Micheaux searched for ironies.

A recurring theme appeared in his work from his very first film in 1919, the auto-biographical *The Homesteader* recounted the story of a farm boy torn between rural values and urban glitter, a vehicle later used by Richard Wright in *Native Son* and Ralph Ellison in The *Invisible Man*. In this film, the conflict between the values of Southern black migrants to the city and the urbane sensibility that had scant room for enthusiastic religion, filiopietism, and the pride of land ownership was examined.

Save for his densely packed polemic against jackleg preachers, *Body and Soul*, Oscar Micheaux's silent films are lost. But surviving reviews indicate that Micheaux was capable of an arrogant variety of themes, each one bringing some corner of Negro life to the screen. Indeed, he explored even white life as it impinged upon blacks – a rarity in race movies, His movies formed an anatomy of black filmmaking by the breadth of their topicality. In *Within Our Gates* (1920), Micheaux reconstructed an anti-Semitic lynching he had witnessed in Atlanta. *The Brute* (1925) starred black boxer Sam Langford. *The Symbol of the Unconquered* (1921) indicted the Ku Klux Klan at the height of its Middle Western revival.

Birthright (1924) adapted T.S. Stribling's novel about the racism that blighted the life of a black Harvard graduate. *The Spider's Web* (1927) dramatized the ghetto's love-hate affair with the infamous gambling system, the numbers game. With the release of *The Conjure Woman* (1926) and *The House Behind the Cedars* (1927), Micheaux revealed his most unabashed nerve by persuading the distinguished black novelist Charles Waddell Chesnutt not only to sell the movie rights to two of his books for a few dollars, but also to tolerate Micheaux's heavy-handed rewriting.

Sadly, only *Body and Soul*, the lone survivor of Micheaux's early films, reveals the quality of his silent work. Although flawed by censors' efforts, *Body and Soul* made use of the young and marginally employed football player, singer, budding actor, and preacher's son, Paul Robeson, to make a strong case against venal preachers. This film helped make Micheaux a central figure in black genre film, if for no other reason than he willingly, even sensationally, assaulted black problems. In addition, he brought black fiction to the screen, criticized American racial custom, and made his own migratory life an allegory for the black experience in the twentieth century.

Parallel to Micheaux's career in the 1920s, another variant of black genre film producers emerged: the company rich in white capital, technical capacity, and leadership, with a self-conscious ambition to present films that reflected the lives of its Negro audiences, Unlike their competitors who ground out shabby black mimics of white life, this enterprising group of easterners kept a keen ear tuned to black circles and a sharp eye on box office trends as sensors of black taste, In the early 1920s the best of them, theater owner Robert Levy, a backer of the Lafayette Players black theatre group, founded Reol as a studio that intended to produce such films as Chesnutt's *The Marrow of Tradition*.

Still another white force was the owner whose theater gradually had turned "colored" and who subsequently made films for the new audiences. On the eve of sound film, such a group, led by David Starkman and a white studio crew, united behind Sherman "Uncle Dud" Dudley, a black vaudevillian and impresario from Washington. The resulting Colored Players Company produced its first film by July 1926, *A Prince of His Race*, a melodrama on the theme of the black bourgeois fear of lost status. By the end of the year they released a black version of the old temperance tract, *Ten Nights in a Bar Room*, starring Charles Gilpin. Far from a rehash, the brief film used its all-black cast to achieve a certain poignancy, as though the actors themselves were making a special plea to urban blacks, warning them against urban vices in a manner reminiscent of Micheaux.

In 1928 the Colored Players Company achieved its finest hour with *The Scar of Shame*, which, in the wrong hands, might have become no more than a sentimental "women's picture." In style, mood, and theme, however, the Colored Players' film brought a sophisticated close to the silent film era. Scriptwriter David Starkman, two Italian collaborators, director Frank Perugini and cameraman Al Ligouri, and black stars Lucia Lynn Moses, Harry Henderson, Lawrence Chenault, and Pearl McCormick combined efforts to produce a wistful satire on the color caste system that stratified urban black society. The completed film went beyond its premise by adding a commentary on the American success myth. Perhaps because authors can most successfully romanticize or satirize what they know from a distance, as in Samuel Taylor Coleridge's *Xanadu*, J.M.W. Turner's painting of a shimmering man-o'-war in the tow of a steam tug, or J.R.R. Tolkien's Middle Earth, the largely white Colored Players sympathetically exposed an anomaly in black life – Negroes, the victims of racial discrimination, sometimes stratified into fraternities, professions, marriages, and even churches along lines denoted by skin color.

The boom of the 1920s ended sadly for Afro-Americans. The Great Depression proved a shattering experience, hitting blacks sooner and more severely than it did whites. Even the Republican party cast them aside in Herbert Hoover's so-called "lily white" convention of 1928.

And yet the sound film era began at the same time, holding out the promise of revolutionary change for blacks in Hollywood. MGM and Fox stumbled over each other trying to exploit sound film through the use of Negro themes and motifs. These studios were so successful that their work instigated the gradual turning away of black film audiences from race movies, toward Hollywood.

Although Christie Comedies had once used Spencer Williams as a writer, for the first time Hollywood producers really made use of black consultants, MGM's *Hallelujah!* benefited from the counsel of Harold Garrison, the studio bootblack, and James Weldon Johnson of the NAACP, Fox's *Hearts in Dixie*, like the MGM film, brought black religion, tragedy, music, and emotion to the screen with the help of Clarence Muse and other blacks on the set.

Immediately a rash of musical shorts emerged from the studios, The worst of them, such as Christie's comedies, were based on Octavus Roy Cohen's old *Saturday Evening Post* dialect stories, The best of them used black performers in ways that allowed them to influence the ambience of the films. Aubrey Lyles and Flournoy Miller, the comedy team from the original *Shuffle Along* revue of 1921, the dancing Covans, the Hall Johnson Choir, baritone Jules Bledsoe, Duke Ellington, and many others were signed by Hollywood studios.

The best of these appeared early in the decade. Louis Armstrong and Cab Calloway infused a strong jazz beat into *I'll Be Glad When You're Dead, You Rascal You* (1932), *Minnie the Moocher* (1932), *Rhapsody in Black and Blue* (1932), and *Jitterbug Party* (1935). Eubie Blake and Noble Sissie enlivened *Pie Pie Blackbird* (ca. 1932). The Nicholas Brothers brought their jazz acrobatics to *Barbershop Blues*

(1933) and *The Black Network* (1936). Jimmy Mordecai, one of the greatest jazz dancers, did a stylized, moody rendering of Southern folk life in *Yamacraw* (1930), These films continued until World War II, when Lena Horne, Teddy Wilson, Albert Ammons, and Pete Johnson did a musical fantasy of the disinherited, *Boogie Woogie Dream* (1944).

The most balanced combinations of mood, lighting, music, black social themes, and theatrical elements were offered in Duke Ellington's *Symphony in Black* (1935) and *Black and Tan* (1929). *Symphony* was scored in four movements with stylized bits of black history cut to match the beat of work songs, chants, and fervent religious moods. The film's ending featured Billie Holiday and Earl "Snakehips" Tucker in an urban scene that symbolized Negro migration from Africa, to the South, to Harlem, to modern times. Almost ritual in form, the film demonstrated the possibilities of black art emerging from a Hollywood factory. In like manner *Black and Tan* recreated a similar ambience but stressed plot more than music by focusing on Ellington's woman, who, despite poor health, dances so that he might finish his composition; but she dies on the dance floor, a martyr to black music, Both films were effectively heightened by chiaroscuro lighting of a quality that seldom graced feature movies.

A few musical films made outside Hollywood provided still more promising avenues of black expression within the context of a medium dominated by whites. The best single case is Dudley Murphy's *The St. Louis Blues* (1928). Its gritty black mood emanated from the musical contributions of W.C. Handy, Jimmy Mordecai, J. Rosamond Johnson, and Bessie Smith. It was as though Murphy served only as a neutral vehicle which carried the black imagery to the screen.

Five years later, another combination of cinematically inexperienced blacks joined Murphy to produce a unique film version of Eugene O'Neill's *The Emperor Jones* (1933). O'Neill's play mixed psychological depth with racial grotesques through the treatment of a black hero, who aimed beyond traditionally accepted black channels of endeavor. Murphy's film became an instrument through which white writers and black musicians and performers combined to construct a black film. Paul Robeson, Fredi Washington, and Frank Wilson starred in the black roles and Rosamond Johnson scored the music, using traditional black themes, motifs, and styles.

Many Hollywood movies that followed treated Negroes with awareness if not sensibility, with politesse if not equality, and affection if not understanding. Nevertheless, these films of the depression years amounted to a quantum jump from the old-fashioned racial metaphors of the previous decade. These gestures toward a liberalized cinema promised enough to attract larger black audiences into 1930s movie palaces. As a result, during the Great Depression, producers of race movies lost ground to their Hollywood adversaries. The black press, motivated by increased studio and theater advertising and loyalty to black actors, cheered the trend, In contrast to the Hollywood product, race movie makers appeared more than ever as inept, erratic mavericks.

The trendy black images ranged broadly, if not deeply, Lewis Milestone's *Hallelujah, I'm a Bum* (1933) featured a black hobo among its down-and-outers. A cycle of exposes of horrible prison conditions featured black prisoners. Etta Moten and Ivie Anderson sang important songs in *Gold Diggers of 1933, Flying Down to Rio* (1933), and *A Day at the Races* (1937). Louis Armstrong and Martha Raye's raucous interracial number in *Artists and Models* (1937) shocked southern censors, Stepin Fetchit, the arch foe of the black bourgeoisie, worked steadily, though with ever narrowing range. Following a trend set by MGM's *Trader Horn* (1931), the worst painted-savage stereotypes faded from major movies, although they continued to survive in the "B" pictures shot on the back lots of "poverty row." A few movies depicted the South in unflattering terms and its Negroes as less than happy with their lot. Among these were *Cabin in the Cotton* (1932), *I Am a Fugitive From a Chain Gang* (1932), *Slave Ship*, *Jezebel* (1938), and *The Little Foxes* (1941). Black boon companions grew more humane in *Dirigible* (1931), *Broadway Bill* (1934), O'Shaughnessy's *Boy* (1937), *Prestige* (1932), *The Count of Monte Cristo* (1934), and especially *Massacre* (1934), A few genuinely fine roles appeared: Clarence Brooks's Haitian doctor in John Ford's *Arrowsmith*, Fredi Washington's wistful mulattoes in *Imitation of Life* (1934) and *One Mile from Heaven* (1937), Muse's angry rebel and Daniel Haynes's big-house butler in *So Red the Rose*, Hattie McDaniel's prickly servants in *Alice Adams* (1935), *The Mad Miss Manton* (1938), and *Gone with the Wind* (1939), and Clinton Rosamond's outraged father in *Golden Boy* (1939).

A sample taken from twenty months at mid-decade reveals the broad sweep of change in Hollywood Negro roles during the New Deal. Despite the changing times, some traditional roles persisted, Old Southern legends were faithfully served by Bill Robinson's dancing servants in *The Little Colonel* (1935) and *The Littlest Rebel*, along with nostalgic relics such as Edward Sutherland's *Mississippi* (1935). Stepin Fetchit's career reached high gear in a string of Fox's celebrations of rural folk life such as *Steam Boat Round the Bend* (1935), *David Harum* (1934), *Judge Priest* (1934), and *The County Chairman* (1934), *Bullets or Ballots* (1936), and *Hooray for Love* (1935) brought Negroes into urban contexts through Louise Beavers's "numbers' queen" and Bill Robinson's street dandy. John Ford's *The Prisoner of Shark Island* (1936) depicted black soldiers as well as slaves. A few Broadway successes brought strong black roles to Hollywood intact, among them Edward Thompson's "Slim" in *The Petrified Forest* (1936), Leigh Whipper's "Crooks" in John Steinbeck's *Of Mice and Men* (1939), and Rex Ingram's "De Lawd" and "Hezdrel" roles in Marc Connelly's fable of black folk religion, *The Green Pastures* (a less than total success among black critics). Universal's remake of *Showboat* (1936) brought "Joe" to the screen in the person of Paul Robeson. And Fritz Lang and Mervyn LeRoy made indictments of lynching – *Fury* (1936) and *They Won't Forget* (1937) – although each was weakened by placing blacks on the periphery rather than depicting them as victims of mobs.

Black critics and audiences waffled. On the one hand they were happy to see more blacks on the screen, but on the other, they fretted over Hollywood's superficiality and its ignorance of black life. David O. Selznick's *Gone With the Wind* grew into the media event most symptomatic of black division over the merits of a Hollywood movie. Nominally a film version of Margaret Mitchell's overweight novel of the South during Reconstruction, the movie quickly developed a split personality. Selznick was torn between the conflicting goals of wishing to accommodate to liberal political trends by having (according to a memorandum) "the Negroes come out decidedly on the right side of the ledger," at the same time that he was striving for historicity and genuine Southern ambience.

To achieve this all but impossible ambition, Selznick hired experts – Atlanta architect, artist, and antiquarian Wilbur G, Kurtz and Susan Myrick of the *Macon Telegraph* – to authenticate details of regional atmosphere and racial etiquette. They saved the film from countless errors of manner, accents, and clichés, such as warning the company against having the slaves rise in song; in the latter episode, they worked in cooperation with Hall Johnson, the black choirmaster. From the North, writers Sidney Howard, Ben Hecht, O.H.P. Garrett, and F. Scott Fitzgerald, in deference to modern tastes, elided references to the Ku Klux Klan and depictions of the Yankee army as marauders and looters. The hoped-for result, Selznick felt, would be that authentic black maids, mammies, and field hands were considerably more humanized than those appearing in earlier Southern genre films.

Despite its brilliance as a work of popular art, *Gone With the Wind* inspired both black praise and calumny, revealing a still unsatisfied hunger for a black genre cinema. On one side many urban blacks agreed with a *Pittsburgh Courier* critic who found that "much of it was distasteful to the Negro race." On the other, Bill Chase of the *Amsterdam News* responded with exaggerated disbelief. "Ye gads, what's happening to Hollywood?" he wrote. Several writers focused on the black acting, especially that of Hattie McDaniel, who made mammy "more than a servant" and won an Oscar. She tipped still more black opinion in favor of the movie.

This is not to say *Gone With the Wind* revolutionized Hollywood into a center of black genre filmmaking. Yet the film stood astride two epochs. In the period between the wars, black roles had slowly moved away from tradition. With the coming of World War II, the liberal drift became part of the rhetoric of Allied war aims.

Gone With the Wind admirably expressed the tension between the two poles of racial ideals – tradition and change – with the result that on the eve of World War II, Afro-Americans responded to cinema in two distinct ways, both of them new departures from convention, They tempered their customary cynical view of Hollywood with a renewed faith in their own ability to change Hollywood through social and political pressure....

9

Primary Sources

THE INTRODUCTION OF SOUND

The introduction of sound into the film industry is a tale filled with myths. According to the traditional Hollywood legend, the financially strapped Warner Brothers turned to sound in a desperate gamble to save the company. More recently, film historian Douglas Gomery has shown that the coming of sound in fact reflected calculated corporate decisions about the potential profits to be reaped from introducing the new technology. These primary sources give some sense of the public reaction to the arrival of the talkies.

"Pictures That Talk"

Photoplay, 1924

And now the motion pictures really talk. It has been almost twenty years since Thomas A. Edison first tried to accomplish this, but it has remained for Dr. Lee De Forest to bring the "talkies" to their present stage of advancement.

Mr. Edison's first attempt was made by the simple process of playing stock cylinder records on a phonograph and having the actors sing, or pretend to sing, with the record, while the camera photographed the lip movement. By this method synchronization was impossible. Sometimes the singer would be so far ahead or behind the record that the result would be laughable.

Edison knew this would never do, so he finally invented the "kinetophone." Again, he used the phonograph, but he obtained better results by making the phonograph record at the same time as the motion picture negative. This gave perfect synchronization in the taking of the pictures, but two operators were needed for the projection – one for the film in the booth and the other, back stage, to run the phonograph.

Sometimes the results were good. More often were not. But, nevertheless, these pictures had quite a vogue and drew great audiences all over the country. Edison was not satisfied, but he never was able to get perfect synchronization, nor were any of the dozen others who tried.

About this time Lee De Forest, then a young electrical engineer in the West, was experimenting with wireless, or radio, as it is now called. Out of this came the "audion," which is now a part of every radio set and which makes broadcasting and receiving possible. Three years ago De Forest became interested in motion pictures and began his experiments to make them talk. He realized that synchronization and audibility were essential. After three years he has worked out his "Phonofilm." He has synchronized the picture and the voice by photographing the sound on the same strip of film with the action and at the same time. Instead of the voice being phonographed, it is radioed from the speaker's lips, by sound waves, to the camera. There these sound waves are converted into light waves and photographed on the left side of the film.

All of this is accomplished with any standard motion picture camera, to which has been added an attachment for photographing sound. The negative thus produced is developed in the usual manner and prints made exactly similar to the prints of any other motion picture.

In projecting the De Forest Phonofilms, an inexpensive attachment is necessary, which fits on any stand projection machine. In this attachment is a tiny incandescent lamp. As the film passes this light, the lines made by the voice become "flickers" or light waves. These light waves are picked up by the infinitesimal wires and converted into sound waves again. Other larger wires take the sound waves into the amplifier, from which they are carried from the projection room by ordinary wires back-stage, amplified again, and thrown on the screen in precise synchronization with the action of the scene ....

Review of Don Juan

Mordaunt Hall, *The New York Times*, 1926

A marvelous new device known as the vitaphone, which synchronizes sound with motion pictures, stirred a distinguished audience in Warners' Theatre to unusual enthusiasm at his initial presentation last Thursday evening. The natural reproduction of voices, the tonal qualities of musical instruments and the timing of the sound to the movements of the lips of singers and the actions of musicians was almost uncanny ....

The future of this new contrivance is boundless, for inhabitants of small and remote places will have the opportunity of listening to and seeing grand opera as it is given in New York, and through the picturing of the vocalists and small grounds and small groups of musicians, or instrumental choirs of orchestras, the vitaphone will give its patrons an excellent idea of a singer's acting and an intelligent conception of the efforts of musicians and their instruments ....

"Silence is Golden"

Aldous Huxley, *Golden Book Magazine*, 1930

I have just been, for the first time, to see and hear a picture talk. "A little late in the day," my up-to-date readers will remark, with a patronizing and contemptuous smile. "This is 1930; there isn't much news in talkies now. But better late than never."

Better late than never? Ah, no! There, my friends, you're wrong. This is one of those cases where it is most decidedly better never than late, better never than early, better never than on the stroke of time ....

The explanation of my firm resolve never, if I can help it, to be reintroduced will be found in the following simple narrative of what I saw and heard in that fetid hall on the Boulevard des Italiens, where the latest and most frightful creation saving device for the production of standardized amusement had been installed.

We entered the hall halfway through the performance of a series of music-hall turns – not substantial ones, of course, but the two-dimensional images of turns with artificial voices. There were no travel films, nothing in the Natural History line, none of those fascinating Events of the Week – lady mayoresses launching battleships, Japanese earthquakes, hundred-to-one outsiders winning races, revolutionaries on the march in Nicaragua – which are always the greatest and often the sole attractions in the programs of our cinema. Nothing but disembodied entertainers, gesticulating flatly on the screen and making gramophone-like noises as they did so. Some sort of comedian was performing as we entered. But he soon vanished to give place to somebody's celebrated jazz band – not merely audible in all its loud vulgarity of brassy guffaw and caterwauling sentiment, but also visible in a series of apocalyptic close-ups of the individual performers. A beneficent Providence has dimmed my powers of sight so that at a distance of more than four or five yards I am blissfully unaware of the full horror of the average human countenance. At the cinema, however, there is no escape. Magnified up to Brobdingnagian proportions, the human countenance smiles its six-foot smiles, opens and shuts its thirty-two-inch eyes, registers soulfulness or grief, libido or whimsicality, with every square centimeter of its several roods of pallid mooniness. Nothing short of total blindness can preserve one from the spectacle. The jazz players were forced upon me; I regarded them with a fascinated horror. It was the first time, I suddenly realized, that I had ever clearly seen a jazz band. The spectacle was positively terrifying.

The performers belonged to two contrasted races. There were the dark and polished young Hebrews, whose souls were in those mournfully sagging, seasickishly undulating melodies of mother love and nostalgia and yammering amorousness and clotted sensuality which have been the characteristically Jewish contributions to modern popular music. And there were the chubby young Nordics, with Aryan faces transformed by the strange plastic forces of the North American environment into the likeness of very large uncooked muffins or the unveiled posteriors of babes. (The more sympathetic Red Indian type of Nordic-American face was completely absent from this particular assemblage of jazz players.) Gigantically enlarged, these personages appeared one after another on the screen, each singing or playing his instrument and at the same time registering the emotions appropriate to the musical circumstances. The spectacle, I repeat, was really terrifying. For the first time, I felt grateful for the defect of vision which had preserved me from an earlier acquaintance with such aspects of modern life. And at the same time I wished that I could become, for the occasion, a little hard of hearing. For if good music has charms to soothe the savage breast, bad music has no less powerful spells for filling the mildest breast with rage, the happiest with horror and disgust. Oh, those mammy songs, those love longings, those loud hilarities; How was it possible that human emotions intrinsically decent could be so ignobly parodied? I felt like a man who, having asked for wine, is offered a brimming bowl of hogwash. And not even fresh hogwash. Rancid hogwash, decaying hogwash. For there was a horrible tang of putrefaction in all that music. Those yearnings for "Mammy of Mine" and "My Baby," for "Dixie" and the "Land Where Skies Are Blue" and "Dreams Come True," for "Granny" and "Tennessee and You" – they were all a necrophily. The Mammy after whom the black young Hebrews and the blond young muffin-faces so fetchingly yearned was an ancient Gorgonzola cheese; the Baby of their tremulously gargled desire was a leg of mutton after a month in warm storage; Granny had been dead for weeks; and as for Dixie and Tennessee and Dream Land – they were odoriferous with the least artificial of manures.

When, after what seemed hours, the jazz band concluded its dreadful performances, I sighed in thankfulness. But the thankfulness was premature. For the film which followed was hardly less distressing. It was the story of the child of a cantor in a synagogue, afflicted, to his father's justifiable fury, with an itch for jazz. This itch, assisted by the cantor's boot, sends him out into the world, where, in due course and thanks to My Baby, his dreams come tree-ue, and he is employed as a jazz singer on the music-hall stage. Promoted from the provinces to Broadway, the jazz singer takes the opportunity to revisit the home of his childhood. But the cantor will have nothing to do with him, absolutely nothing, in spite of his success, in spite, too, of his moving eloquence. "You yourself always taught me," says the son pathetically, "that the voice of music was the voice of God." Vox jazz vox Dei – the truth is new and beautiful. But stern old Poppa's heart refuses to be melted. Even Mammy of Mine is unable to patch up a reconciliation. The singer is reduced to going out once more into the night – and from the night back to his music hall.

The crisis of the drama arrives when, the cantor being mortally sick and unable to fulfill his functions at the synagogue, Mammy of Mine and the Friends of his Childhood implore the young man to come and sing the atonement service in his father's place. Unhappily, this religious function is booked to take place at the same hour as that other act of worship vulgarly known as the First Night. There ensues a terrific struggle, worthy of the pen of a Racine or a Dryden, between love and honor. Love for Mammy of Mine draws the jazz singer toward the synagogue; but love for My Baby draws the cantor's son toward the theater, where she, as principal Star, is serving the deity no less acceptably with her legs and smile than he with his voice. Honor also calls from either side; for honor demands that he should serve the God of his fathers at the synagogue, but it also demands that he should serve the jazz-voiced god of his adoption at the theater. Some very eloquent captions appear at this point. With the air of a Seventeenth Century hero, the jazz singer protests that he must put his career before even his love. The nature of the dilemma has changed, it will be seen, since Dryden's day. In the old dramas it was love that had to be sacrificed to painful duty. In the modern instance the sacrifice is at the shrine of what William James called "the Bitch Goddess Success." Love is to be abandoned for the stern pursuit of any sort of newspaper notoriety and dollars.

In the end the singer makes the best of both worlds – satisfies Mammy of Mine and even Poor Poppa by singing at the synagogue and, on the following evening, scores a terrific success at the postponed first night of My Baby's revue. The film concludes with a scene in the theater, with Mammy of Mine in the stalls (Poor Poppa is by this time safely under ground), and the son, with My Baby in the background, warbling down at her the most nauseatingly luscious, the most penetratingly vulgar mammy song that it has ever been my lot to hear. My flesh crept as the loud speaker poured out those sodden words, that greasy, sagging melody. I felt ashamed of myself for listening to such things, for even being a member of the species to which such things are addressed. But I derived a little comfort from the reflection that a species which has allowed all its instincts and emotions to degenerate and putrefy in such a way must be pretty near either its violent conclusion or else its radical transformation and reform.

FILM CENSORSHIP

During the 1920s pressure to censor the movies grew. In 1922 alone, 22 state legislatures considered bills to impose state and local censorship. Hollywood responded by establishing a trade organization in 1922 known as the Motion Picture Producers and Distributors of America, with Will H. Hays (Postmaster General under President Warren Harding) as president. Hays's call for "self-regulation" to forestall outside censorship, and The Don'ts and Be Carefuls, adopted in 1927 along with the Production Code of 1930, represented important steps toward industry self-censorship. Nevertheless, criticism of the industry mounted, and by 1932 some 40 religious and educational groups had called for censorship. Unlike Protestant religious groups, which were fragmented, the Catholic church was unified in its demand that the industry recognize its moral responsibilities to the public. The threat of movie boycotts by the Catholic Legion of Decency led the industry's trade association in 1934 to establish the Production Code Administration Office, headed by Joseph Breen, to regulate films.

The Sins of Hollywood, 1922

The Sins of Hollywood: An Expose of Movie Vice was a book written by Ed Roberts, former editor of *Photoplay*, and published in May 1922 by the Hollywood Publishing Company.

To the Public:
The sins of Hollywood are facts – Not Fiction!

The stories in this volume are true stories – the people are real people –

Most of those involved in the events reported herein are today occupying high places in motion pictures – popular idols – applauded, lauded and showered with gold by millions of men, women and children – especially the women and children!

To the boys and girls of this land these mock heroes and heroines have been pictured and painted, for box office purposes, as the living symbols of all the virtues –

An avalanche of propaganda by screen and press has imbued them with every ennobling trait.

Privately they have lived, and are still living, lives of wild debauchery.

In more than one case licentiousness and incest have been the only rungs in the ladders on which they have climbed to fame and fortune!

Unfaithfully and cruelly indifferent to the worship of the youth of the land, they have led or are leading such lives as may, any day, precipitate yet another nation-wide scandal and again shatter the ideals, the dreams, the castles, the faith of our boys and girls!

It is for these reasons that the Sins of Hollywood are given to the public –

That a great medium of national expression may be purified – taken from the hands of those who have misused it – that the childish faith of our boys and girls may again be made sacred!

Fully eighty percent of those engaged in motion pictures are high-grade citizens – self-respecting and respected:

In foolish fear of injuring the industry, Hollywood has permitted less than one per cent of its population to stain its name.

The facts reported in these stories have long been an open book to the organized producers – No need to tell them – they knew!

They knew of the horde of creatures of easy morals who have hovered about the industry and set the standard of price – decided what good, clean women would have to pay – have to give – in order to succeed –

They knew of the macqueraux – of the scum that constituted the camp followers of their great stars. They knew of the wantonness of their leading women –

They knew about the yachting parties – the wild orgies at road houses and private homes –

They knew about Vernon and its wild life – Tia Juana and its mad, drunken revels –

They knew about the "kept" women – and the "kept" men –

They knew about the prominent people among them who were living in illicit relationship –

There was a time at one studio when every star, male and female, was carrying on an open liaison – The producer could not help knowing it.

Eight months before the crash that culminated in the Arbuckle cataclysm they knew the kind of parties Roscoe was giving – and some of them were glad to participate in them –

They knew conditions – knew about the "hop" and the "dope" – but they took the stand that it was "none of our business" –

Their business was piling up advance deposits from theater owners and manipulating the motion picture stock market.

They frowned on all attempts to speak the truth –

Any publication that attempted to reveal the real conditions – to cleanse the festering sores – was quickly pounced upon as an "enemy of the industry" – A subsidized trade press helped in this work!

Any attempt to bring about reform was called "hurting the industry."

It was the lapses and laxities of the producer that precipitated the censorship agitation – that led a nauseated nation, determined to cleanse the Augean stables of the screen, into the dangerous notion of censorship – almost fatally imperiling two sacred principles of democracy – freedom of speech and freedom of the press!

They have made "box office" capital of everything – Nothing has been too vile to exploit –

They created the male vamp –

Nothing was sacred – nothing was personal – if it had publicity possibilities ....

If the screen is to be "cleaned-up," the sores must be cut open – the pus and corruption removed – This always hurts! But it is the only known way!

"The Don'ts and Be Carefuls"

Motion Picture Producers and Distributors of America, 1927

Resolved, That those things which are included in the following list shall not appear in pictures produced by the members of this Association, irrespective of the manner in which they are treated.

1. Pointed profanity – by either title or lip – this includes the words "God," "Lord," "Jesus," "Christ" (unless they be used reverently in connection with proper religious ceremonies), "hell," "damn," "Gawd," and every other profane and vulgar expression however it may be spelled;
2. Any licentious or suggestive nudity – in fact or in silhouette; and any lecherous or licentious notice thereof by other characters in the picture;
3. The illegal traffic in drugs;
4. Any inference of sex perversion;
5. White slavery;
6. Miscegenation (sex relationships between the white and black races);
7. Sex hygiene and venereal diseases;
8. Scenes of actual childbirth – in fact or in silhouette;
9. Children's sex organs;
10. Ridicule of the clergy;
11. Willful offense to any nation, race or creed;

And be it further resolved, That special care be exercised in the manner in which the following subjects are treated, to the end that vulgarity and suggestiveness be eliminated and that good taste may be emphasized:

1. The use of the flag;
2. International relations (avoiding picturizing in an unfavorable light another country's religion, history, institutions, prominent people, and citizenry);
3. Arson;
4. The use of firearms;
5. Theft, robbery, safe-cracking, and dynamiting of trains, mines, buildings, etc. (having in mind the effect which a too-detailed description of these may have upon the moron);
6. Brutality and possible gruesomeness;
7. Techniques of committing murder by whatever method;
8. Methods of smuggling;
9. Third-degree methods;
10. Actual hangings or electrocutions as legal punishment for crime;
11. Sympathy for criminals;
12. Attitude toward public characters and institutions;
13. Sedition;
14. Apparent cruelty to children and animals;
15. Branding of people or animals;

16. The sale of women, or of a woman selling her virtue;
17. Rape or attempted rape;
18. First-night scenes;
19. Man and woman in bed together;
20. Deliberate seduction of girls;
21. The institution of marriage;
22. Surgical operations;
23. The use of drugs;
24. Titles or scenes having to do with law enforcement or law-enforcing officers;
25. Excessive or lustful kissing, particularly when one character or the other is a "heavy."

The Motion Picture Production Code of 1930

First Section

GENERAL PRINCIPLES

I. Theatrical motion pictures, that is, pictures intended for the theatre as distinct from pictures intended for churches, schools, lecture halls, educational movements, social reform movements, etc., are primarily to be regarded as *Entertainment*. Mankind has always recognized the importance of entertainment and its value in rebuilding the bodies and souls of human beings.

But it has always recognized that entertainment can be of a character *harmful* to the human race, and, in consequence, has clearly distinguished between:

Entertainment which tends to improve the race, or, at least, to recreate and rebuild human beings exhausted with the realities of life; and

Entertainment which tends to degrade human beings, or to lower their standards of life and living.

Hence the *moral importance* of entertainment is something which has been universally recognized. It enters intimately into the lives of men and women and affects them closely; it occupies their minds and affections during leisure hours, and ultimately touches the whole of their lives. A man may be judged by his standard of entertainment as easily as by the standard of his work.

So *correct entertainment raises* the whole standard of a nation.

Wrong entertainment lowers the whole living condition and moral ideals of a race.

NOTE, for example, the healthy reactions to healthful moral sports like baseball, golf; the unhealthy reactions to sports like cockfighting, bullfighting, bearbaiting, etc. Note, too, the effect on a nation of gladiatorial combats, the obscene plays of Roman times, etc.

II. Motion pictures are very important as *Art*.

Though a new art, possibly a combination art, it has the same object as the other arts, the presentation of human thoughts, emotions and experiences, in terms of an appeal to the soul thru the senses.

Here, as in entertainment:

Art *enters intimately* into the lives of human beings.

Art can be *morally good*, lifting men to higher levels. This has been done thru good music, great painting, authentic fiction, poetry, drama.

Art can be morally evil in its effects. This is the case clearly enough with unclean art, indecent books, suggestive drama. The effect on the lives of men and women is obvious.

NOTE: It has often been argued that art in itself is unmoral, neither good nor bad. This is perhaps time of the *thing* which is music, painting, poetry, etc. But the thing is the *product* of some person's mind, and that mind was either good or bad morally when it produced the thing. And the thing has its *effect* upon those who come into contact with it. In both these ways, as a product and the cause of definite effects, it has a deep moral significance and an unmistakable moral quality.

HENCE: The motion pictures which are the most popular of modern arts for the masses, have their moral quality from the minds which produce them and from their effects on the moral lives and reactions of their audiences. This gives them a most important morality.

1) They *reproduce* the morality of the men who use the pictures as a medium for the expression of their ideas and ideals;

2) They *affect* the moral standards of those who thru the screen take in these ideas and ideals. In the case of the motion pictures, this effect may be particularly emphasized because no art has so quick and so widespread an appeal to the masses. It has become in an incredibly short period, *the art of the multitudes.*

III.   The motion picture has special *Moral obligations*:

A) Most arts appeal to the mature. This art appeals at once to every class – mature, immature, developed, undeveloped, law-abiding, criminal. Music has its grades for different classes; so has literature and drama. This art of the motion picture, combining as it does the two fundamental appeals of looking at a picture and listening to a story, at once reaches every class of society.

B) Because of the mobility of a film and the ease of picture distribution, and because of the possibility of duplicating positives in large quantities, this art *reaches places* unpenetrated by other forms of art.

C) Because of these two facts, it is difficult to produce films intended for only *certain classes of people*. The exhibitor's theatres are for the masses, for the cultivated and the rude, mature and immature, self-restrained and inflammatory, young and old, law-respecting and criminal. Films, unlike books and music, can with difficulty be confined to certain selected groups.

D) The latitude given to film material cannot, in consequence, be as wide as the latitude given to *book material*. In addition:

(a) A book describes; a film vividly presents.

(b) A book reaches the mind thru words merely; a film reaches the eyes and ears thru the reproduction of actual events.

(c) The reaction of a reader to a book depends largely on the keenness of the reader; the reaction to a film depends on the vividness of presentation.

E) This is also true when comparing the film with the newspapers. Newspapers present by description, films by actual presentation. Newspapers are after the fact and present things that have taken place; the film gives the events in the process of enactment and with apparent reality of life.

F) Everything possible in a *play is* not possible in a film.

(a) Because of the larger audience of the film, and its consequently mixed character. Psychologically, the larger the audience, the lower the moral mass resistance to suggestion.

(b) Because thru light, enlargement of character presentation, scenic emphasis, etc., the screen story is brought closer to the audience than the play.

(c) The enthusiasm for and interest in the film *actors* and *actresses*, developed beyond anything of the sort in history, makes the audience largely sympathetic toward the characters they portray and the stories in which they figure. Hence they are more ready to confuse the actor and character, and they are most receptive of the emotions and ideals portrayed and presented by their favorite stars.

G) Small communities, remote from sophistication and from the hardening process which often takes place in the ethical and moral standards of larger cities, are easily and readily reached by any sort of film.

H) The grandeur of mass meetings, large action, spectacular features, etc., affects and arouses more intensely the emotional side of the audience.

IN GENERAL: The mobility, popularity, accessibility, emotional appeal, vividness, straight-forward presentation of fact in the films makes for intimate contact on a larger audience and greater emotional appeal. Hence the larger moral responsibilities of the motion pictures.

Second Section

WORKING PRINCIPLES

I.   No picture should lower the moral standards of those who see it. This is done:

(a) When evil is made to appear *attractive*, and good is made to appear *unattractive*.

(b) When the *sympathy* of the audience is thrown on the side of crime, wrong-doing, evil, sin. The same thing is true of a film that would throw sympathy against goodness, honor, innocence, purity, honesty.

NOTE: *Sympathy with a person who sins, is* not the same as sympathy with the sin or crime of which he is guilty. We may feel sorry for the plight of the murderer or even understand the circumstances which led him to his crime; we may not feel sympathy with the wrong which he has done.

The presentation of evil is often essential for art, or fiction, or drama. This in itself is not wrong, provided:

(a) That evil is *not presented alluringly*. Even if later on the evil is condemned or punished, it must not be allowed to appear so attractive that the emotions are drawn to desire or approve so strongly that later they forget the condemnation and remember only the apparent joy of the sin.

(b) That thruout the presentation, *evil and good are not confused* and that evil is always recognized clearly as evil.

(c) That in the end the audience feels that *evil is wrong* and *good is right*.

II.   Law, natural or divine, must not be belittled, ridiculed, nor must a sentiment be created against it.

A) The *presentation of crimes* against the law, human or divine, is often necessary for the carrying out of the plot. But the presentation must not throw sympathy with the criminal as against the law, nor with the crime as against those who punish it.

B) The *courts* of the land should not be presented as unjust.

III.   As far as possible, life should not be misrepresented, at least not in such a way as to place in the mind of youth false values on life.

NOTE: This subject is touched just in passing. The attention of the producers is called, however, to the magnificent possibilities of the screen for character development, the building of right ideals, the inculcation in story-form of right principles. If motion pictures consistently held up high types of character, presented stories that would affect lives for the better, they could become the greatest natural force for the improvement of mankind.

PRINCIPLES OF PLOT

In accordance with the general principles laid down:

1) No plot or theme should definitely side *with evil and against good.*

2) Comedies and farces *should not make fun* of good, innocence, morality or justice.

3) No plot should be constructed as to leave the question of right or *wrong in doubt or fogged.*

4) No plot should by its treatment *throw the sympathy* of the audience with sin, crime, wrong-doing or evil.

5) No plot should present evil *alluringly.*

Serious Film Drama

I.   As stated in the general principles, *sin and evil* enter into the story of human beings, and hence in themselves are dramatic material.

II.   In the use of this material, it must be distinguished between *sin* which by its very nature *repels* and *sin* which by its very nature *attracts.*

   (a) In the first class comes murder, most theft, most legal crimes, lying, hypocrisy, cruelty, etc.

   (b) In the second class come sex sins, sins and crimes of apparent heroism, such as banditry, daring thefts, leadership in evil, organized crime, revenge, etc.

   A) The first class needs little care in handling, as sins and crimes of this class naturally are unattractive. The audience instinctively condemns and is repelled. Hence the one objective must be to avoid the *hardening* of the audiences, especially of those who are young and impressionable, to the thought and the fact of crime. People can become accustomed even to murder, cruelty, brutality and repellent crimes.

   B) The second class needs real care in handling, as the response of human natures to their appeal is obvious. This is treated more fully below.

III.   A careful distinction can be made between films intended for *general distribution* and films in~ended for use in theatres restricted to a *limited audience.* Themes and plots quite appropriate for the latter would be altogether out of place and dangerous in the former.

NOTE: In general, the practice of using a general theatre and limiting the patronage during the showing of a certain film to "adults only" is not completely satisfactory and is only partially effective. However, maturer minds may easily understand and accept without harm subject matter in plots which does younger people positive harm.

HENCE: If there should be created a special type of theatre, catering exclusively to an adult audience, for plays of this character (plays with problem themes, difficult discussions and maturer treatment) it would seem to afford an outlet, which does not now exist, for pictures unsuitable for general distribution but permissible for exhibitions to a restricted audience.

PLOT MATERIAL

1) *The triangle* that is, the love of a third party by one already married, needs careful handling, if marriage, the sanctity of the home, and sex morality are not to be imperiled.

2) *Adultery* as a subject should be avoided:

(a) It is *never a* fit subject for *comedy*. Thru comedy of this sort, ridicule is thrown on the essential relationships of home and family and marriage, and illicit relationships are made to seem permissible, and either delightful or daring.

(b) Sometimes adultery must be counted on as material occurring in serious drama.

In this case:

(1) It should not appear to be justified;

(2) It should not be used to weaken respect for marriage;

(3) It should not be presented as attractive or alluring.

3) *Seduction and rape* are difficult subjects and bad material from the viewpoint of the general audience in the theatre.

(a) They should never be introduced as subject matter unless absolutely essential to the plot.

(b) They should *never* be treated as comedy.

(c) Where essential to the plot, they must not be more than *suggested*.

(d) Even the struggles preceding rape should not be shown.

(e) The *methods* by which seduction, essential to the plot, is attained should not be explicit or represented in detail where there is likelihood of arousing wrongful emotions on the part of the audience.

4) *Scenes of passion* are sometimes necessary for the plot. However:

(a) They should appear only where necessary and *not* as an added stimulus to the emotions of the audience.

(b) *When not essential to the plot* they should not occur.

(c) They must *not* be *explicit* in action nor vivid in method, e.g. by handling of the body, by lustful and prolonged kissing, by evidently lustful embraces, by positions which strongly arouse passions.

(d) In general, where essential to the plot, scenes of passion should *not* be presented in such a way as to *arouse or excite the passions of the ordinary spectator.*

5) *Sexual immorality* is sometimes necessary for the plot. It is subject to the following:

GENERAL PRINCIPLES – regarding plots dealing with sex, passion, and incidents relating to them: All legislators have recognized clearly that there are in normal human beings emotions which react naturally and spontaneously to the presentation of certain definite manifestations of sex and passion.

(a) The presentation of scenes, episodes, plots, etc., which are deliberately meant to excite these manifestations on the part of the audience is always wrong, is subversive to the interest of society, and a peril to the human race.

(b) Sex and passion exist and consequently must *sometimes enter* into the stories which deal with human beings.

(1) *Pure love*, the love of a man for a woman permitted by the law of God and man, is the rightful subject of plots. The passion arising from this love is not the subject for plots.

(2) *Impure love* the love of man and woman forbidden by human and divine law, must be presented in such a way that:

a) It is clearly known by the audience to be wrong;

b) Its presentation does not excite sexual reactions, mental or physical, in an ordinary audience;

c) It is not treated as matter for comedy.

HENCE: *Even within the limits of pure love* certain facts have been universally regarded by lawmakers as outside the limits of safe presentation. These are the manifestations of passion and the sacred intimacies of private life:

(1) Either before marriage in the courtship of decent people;

(2) Or after marriage, as is perfectly clear.

In the case of pure love, the difficulty is not so much about what details are permitted for presentation. This is perfectly clear in most cases. The difficulty concerns itself with the tact, delicacy, and general regard for propriety manifested in their presentation.

But in the case of impure love the love which society has always regarded as wrong and which has been banned by divine law, the following are important:

(1) It must not be the subject of comedy or farce or treated as the material for laughter;

(2) It must not be presented as attractive and beautiful;

(3) It must not be presented in such a way as to arouse passion or morbid curiosity on the part of the audience;

(4) It must not be made to seem right and permissible;

(5) In general, it must not be detailed in method or manner.

6) *The presentation of murder* is often necessary for the carrying out of the plot. However:

(a) Frequent presentation of *murder* tends to lessen regard for the sacredness of life.

(b) *Brutal killings* should not be presented in detail.

(c) *Killings for revenge* should not be justified, i.e., the hero should not take justice into his own hands in such a way as to make his killing seem justified. This does not refer to killings in self-defense.

(d) *Dueling* should not be presented as right or just.

7) *Crimes against the law* naturally occur in the course of film stories. However:

(a) *Criminals* should not be made heroes, even if they are historical criminals.

(b) *Law and justice* must not by the treatment they receive from criminals be made to seem wrong or ridiculous.

(c) *Methods of committing crime* e.g., burglary, should not be so explicit as to teach the audience how crime can be committed; that is, the film should not serve as a possible school in crime methods for those who seeing the methods might use them.

(d) Crime need *not always be punished* as long as the audience is made to know that it is wrong.

DETAILS OF PLOT, EPISODE, AND TREATMENT

Vulgarity

Vulgarity may be carefully distinguished from obscenity. Vulgarity is the treatment of low, disgusting, unpleasant subjects which decent society considers outlawed from normal conversation.

Vulgarity in the motion pictures is limited in precisely the same way as in decent groups of men and women by the dictates of good taste and civilized usage, and by the effect of shock, scandal, and harm on those coming in contact with this vulgarity.

(1) *Oaths* should never be used as a comedy element. Where required by the plot, the less offensive oaths may be permitted.

(2) *Vulgar expressions* come under the same treatment as vulgarity in general. Where women and children are to see the film, vulgar expressions (and oaths) should be cut to the absolute essentials required by the situation.

(3) The name of *Jesus Christ* should never be used except in reverence.

Obscenity

Obscenity is concerned with immorality, but has the additional connotation of being common, vulgar and coarse.

(1) *Obscenity in fact*, that is, in spoken word, gesture, episode, plot, is against divine and human law, and hence altogether outside the range of subject matter or treatment.

(2) Obscenity should *not be suggested* by gesture, manner, etc.

(3) An obscene reference, even if it is expected to be understandable to only the more sophisticated part of the audience, should not be introduced.

(4) *Obscene language* is treated as all obscenity.

Costume

GENERAL PRINCIPLES

(1) The effect of nudity or semi-nudity upon the normal man or woman, and much more upon the young person, has been honestly recognized by all lawmakers and moralists.

(2) Hence the fact that the nude or semi-nude body may be *beautiful* does not make its use in the films moral. For in addition to its beauty, the effects of the nude or semi-nude body on the normal individual must be taken into consideration.

(3) Nudity or semi-nudity used simply to put a "punch" into a picture comes under the head of immoral actions as treated above. It is immoral in its effect upon the average audience.

(4) Nudity or semi-nudity is sometimes apparently necessary for the plot. *Nudity is never permitted*. Semi-nudity may be permitted under conditions.

PARTICULAR PRINCIPLES

(1) *The more intimate parts of the human body* are male and female organs and the breasts of a woman.

    (a) They should *never be uncovered.*

    (b) They should not *be covered with* transparent *or translucent* material.

    (c) They should not be clearly and unmistakably *outlined* by the garment.

(2) *The less intimate parts of the body* the legs, arms, shoulders and back, are less certain of causing reactions on the part of the audience.

    Hence:

    (a) Exposure necessary *for the plot* or action is permitted.

    (b) Exposure *for the sake of exposure* or the "punch" is wrong.

    (c) *Scenes of undressing should* be avoided. When necessary for the plot, they should be kept within the limits of decency. When not necessary for the plot, they are to be avoided, as their effect on the ordinary spectator is harmful.

    (d) *The manner or treatment of exposure* should not be suggestive or indecent.

    (e) The following is important in connection with *dancing costumes*:

1. Dancing costumes cut to permit *grace* or freedom of movement, provided they remain within the limits of decency indicated are permissible.

2. Dancing costumes cut to *permit indecent actions* or movements or to make possible during the dance indecent exposure, are wrong, especially when permitting:

    a) Movements of the breasts;

    b) Movements or sexual suggestions of the intimate parts of the body;

    c) Suggestion of nudity.

Dancing

(1) Dancing in general is recognized as an *art* and a *beautiful* form of expressing human emotion.

(2) Obscene dances are those:

    (a) Which suggest or represent sexual actions, whether performed solo or with two or more;

    (b) Which are designed to excite an audience, to arouse passions, or to cause physical excitement.

HENCE: Dances of the type known as "Kooch," or "Can-Can," since they violate decency in these two ways, are wrong. Dances with movements of the breasts, excessive body movement while the feet remain stationary, the so-called "belly dances" – these dances are immoral, obscene, and hence altogether wrong.

Locations

Certain places are so closely and thoroly associated with sexual life or with sexual sin that their use must be carefully limited.

(1) *Brothels and houses of ill-fame* no matter of what country, are *not* proper locations for drama. They suggest to the average person at once sex sin, or they excite an unwholesome and morbid curiosity in the minds of youth.

    IN GENERAL: They are dangerous and bad dramatic locations.

(2) *Bedrooms.* In themselves they are perfectly innocent. Their suggestion may be kept innocent. However, under certain situations they are bad dramatic locations.

    (a) Their use in a comedy or farce (on the principle of the so-called bedroom farce) is wrong, because they suggest sex laxity and obscenity.

(b)In serious drama, their use should, where sex is suggested, be confined to absolute essentials, in accordance with the principles laid down above.

Religion

(1) No film or episode in a film should be allowed to *throw ridicule on* any religious faith honestly maintained.

(2) *Ministers of religion* in their characters of ministers should not be used in comedy, as villains, or as unpleasant persons.

NOTE: The reason for this is not that there are not such ministers of religion, but because the attitude toward them tends to be an attitude toward religion in general. Religion is lowered in the minds of the audience because it lowers their respect for the ministers.

(3) *Ceremonies* of any definite religion should be supervised by someone thoroly conversant with that religion.

PARTICULAR APPLICATIONS

I.   *Crimes against the law:*

These shall never be presented in such a way as to throw sympathy with the crime as against law and justice or to inspire others with a desire for imitation:

The treatment of crimes against the law must not:

a. Teach methods of crime.

b. Inspire potential criminals with a desire for imitation.

c. Make criminals seem heroic and justified.

1. MURDER

a. *The technique of murder must* be presented in a way that will *not* inspire imitation.

b. *Brutal killings* are not to be presented in detail.

c. *Revenge* in modern times shall not be justified. In lands and ages of less developed civilization and moral principles, revenge may sometimes be presented. This would be the case especially in places where no law exists to cover the crime because of which revenge is committed.

2. METHODS OF CRIME shall not be explicitly presented.

a. *Theft robbery safe-cracking* and *dynamiting* of trains, mines, buildings, etc., should not be detailed in method.

b. *Arson* must be subject to the same safeguards.

c. *The use of firearms* should be restricted to essentials.

d. *Methods of smuggling* should not be presented.

3. ILLEGAL DRUG TRAFFIC must never be presented.

Because of its evil consequences, the drug traffic should never be presented in any form. The existence of the trade should not be brought to the attention of audiences.

4. THE USE OF LIQUOR in American life, when not required by the plot or for proper characterization, should not be shown.

The use of liquor should never be *excessively* presented even in picturing countries where its use is legal. In scenes from American life, the necessities of plot and proper characterization alone justify its use. And in this case, it should be shown with moderation.

II. *Sex*

The sanctity of the institution of marriage and the home shall be upheld. Pictures shall not infer that low forms of sex relationship are the accepted or common thing.

1. ADULTERY, sometimes necessary plot material, must not be explicitly treated, or justified, or presented attractively. Out of regard for the sanctity of marriage and the home, the *triangle* that is, the love of a third party for one already married, needs careful handling. The treatment should not throw sympathy against marriage as an institution.

2. SCENES OF PASSION must be treated with an honest acknowledgment of human nature and its normal reactions. Many scenes cannot be presented without arousing dangerous emotions on the part of the immature, the young or the criminal classes.

    a. They should not be introduced when not essential to the plot.

    b. Excessive and lustful kissing, lustful embraces, suggestive postures and gestures, are not to be shown.

    c. In general, passion should be so treated that these scenes do not stimulate the lower and baser element.

3. SEDUCTION OR RAPE

    a. They should never be more than suggested, and only when essential for the plot, and even then never shown by explicit method.

    b. They are never the proper subject for comedy.

4. SEX PERVERSION or any inference to it is forbidden.

5. WHITE SLAVERY shall not be treated.

6. MISCEGENATION (sex relationship between the white and black races) is forbidden.

7. SEX HYGIENE AND VENEREAL DISEASES are not subjects for motion pictures.

8. SCENES OF ACTUAL CHILDBIRTH, in fact or in silhouette, are never to be presented.

9. CHILDREN'S SEX ORGANS are never to be exposed ....

Part III
Wartime Hollywood

Introduction
Hollywood's World War II Combat Films

Ninety million Americans went to the movies every week during World War II. The shows began with a newsreel. The audience might see Hitler dancing a jig. Or a battleship engulfed in flames. Or Roosevelt meeting with Winston Churchill, Joseph Stalin, or some other national leader. A cartoon followed, perhaps Bugs Bunny "Nipping the Nips." Then came the main attraction, with Errol Flynn spitting grenade pins out of his mouth or John Wayne using a bulldozer to push an enemy tank off a cliff.

Many of our deepest images of war's glory and ugliness come from World War II combat films. They helped shape our very conceptions of courage, patriotism, and teamwork. Their images remain firmly etched in our imagination: Axis troops torturing and mutilating prisoners; heavily outnumbered American GIs fending off enemy forces; a corporal telling a young marine, "Nothing wrong with praying. There are no atheists in foxholes."

In comparison to Hollywood's efforts to promote public support for the war effort during World War I, the movies of World War II were relatively subtle and restrained. Many films made during World War I depicted imagined enemy atrocities – for example wicked German soldiers ravishing innocent Belgium women. Hollywood's World War II produced a more diverse response, ranging from films like *Mission to Moscow*, presenting America's Soviet allies in a positive light, to *Casablanca*, with its portrait of a Rick Blaine's gradual shift from self-centered detachment to active involvement in the Allied cause.

Of the many kinds of films that Hollywood produced during World War II to rally the public behind the war effort, perhaps the most distinctive was the combat film. Such films as *Air Force*, *Destination Tokyo*, *Flying Tigers*, *Guadalcanal Diary*, *Objective, Burma!*, *Thirty Seconds Over Tokyo*, and *Wake Island* gave viewers on the home front a vicarious sense of participating in the war. Employing an almost documentary style, these films helped bring the war home. But these war films did much more: they helped educate viewers in the reasons why Americans fought by depicting "democracy

Figure 8 *Objective Burma!* (1945). Warner Bros. Directed by Raoul Walsh. Courtesy of Jerry Murbach, www.doctormacro.info.

in action." Apart from offering a sense of wartime crisis, these films are allegories of a democratic nation at war.

Typically, these films focus on a small group of men involved in a life-or-death mission: struggling valiantly to hold an island or to attack a target deep behind enemy lines. Thus, the film *Air Force* tells the story of a single B-17 Flying Fortress; *Wake Island* is the tale of the small group of marines and civilians who struggle to hold off a much larger force of attacking Japanese; and *Destination Tokyo* depicts a single submarine's efforts to enter Tokyo Bay in preparation for Jimmy Doolittle's raid on Tokyo in 1942. By centering on a single isolated group, Hollywood was able to reveal the human meaning of war to individuals with whom the audience could identify.

Invariably, this small group is a microcosm of the American melting-pot, made up of Catholics, Protestants, and Jews, men from diverse ethnic groups, and distinct personality types. *Objective, Burma!* has, for example, a Hennessy, a Miggleori, a Neguesco. The group's very composition signifies that this was a democratic war, a people's war – drawing upon every segment of society.

Although these groups are usually commanded by a strong leader, success ultimately depends on the men's ability to operate as a team, balancing individual acts of heroism with professionalism and mutual cooperation. In *Thirty Seconds Over Tokyo*, the story of Jimmy Doolittle's bombing raid, each man has a critically important role, whether he is a mechanic, a navigator, a bombardier, a pilot. Individualism and cooperation – both were necessary, according to these films, to preserve American freedoms.

The key crises in these films' plots tend to come not from the threats posed by enemy forces – which the men face with remarkable stoicism – but rather, as Robert B. Ray has noted, from the arrival of an outsider – a coward, a malcontent, a reckless loner – who threatens group cohesion and the men's ability to concentrate on the task at hand. The plot ultimately turns on whether this outsider can be successfully integrated into the group and become a contributing member of the team. In one of the most famous examples, in the film *Wake Island*, a selfish civilian contractor, who initially refuses to obey air-raid warnings, ultimately joins a marine commander in a foxhole in a desperate attempt to stave off a Japanese attack.

Much more than mere entertainment, the combat films of World War II were veritable civic lessons that taught Americans that winning the war required for the country to live up to its democratic values.

10

Casablanca as Propaganda
You Must Remember This: The Case of Hal Wallis' Casablanca

Randy Roberts

Even viewers who have no interest in classic Hollywood cinema and who hate black and white films love Casablanca. *Its appeal works on multiple levels. First, there are the stars: Humphrey Bogart, playing Rick Blaine, an expatriate nightclub owner with a mysterious past, whose surface cynicism cannot completely disguise how soft-hearted he is underneath; and Ingrid Bergman, Rick's former lover, torn between her love for him and her obligations to her husband, a leader of the anti-Nazi resistance. Then there is the dialogue, filled with classic one-liners; the camerawork, which, while shot in a studio, gives the impression that the film was shot on site; and a script that combines humor, suspense, patriotism, and romance. In addition, there are the film's profoundly moving themes – the notion of sacrificing ones personal happiness for a higher cause and the triumph of duty over cynicism and righteous-ness over evil.*

But Casablanca *is much more than a story of reluctant heroism and lost love rekindled. The most famous romantic melodrama in Hollywood history, the film was also a potent piece of political propaganda. In this essay, historian Randy Roberts examines the film's political messages.*

*C*asablanca haunts the imagination. Fifty years after it was made it still seems fresh. Unlike so many other World War II films that had one eye on the box office and the other on the need to boost wartime morale, *Casablanca* has not gone stale with age. If a scene or two seems a touch campy to us today, the film as a whole can still call forth deep emotions. Watching the film, we are apt to laugh at the same jokes, be aroused by the same appeals for patriotism, and sense the same demands for sacrifice that moved audiences a half-century ago. How can one not smile when Captain Louis Renault (Claude Rains) questions Richard Blaine (Humphrey Bogart) about why he left America and came to *Casablanca*:

> *Renault*: I have often speculated on why you don't return to America. Did you abscond with the church funds? Did you run off with a senator's wife? I like to think you killed a man. It's the romantic in me.
> *Rick*: It was a combination of the three.
> *Renault*: And what in heaven's name brought you to Casablanca?

Figure 9   *Casablanca* (1942). Warner Bros. Directed by Michael Curtiz. Courtesy of Jerry Murbach, www.doctormacro.info.

> *Rick*:   My health. I came to Casablanca for the waters.
> *Renault*: Waters? What waters? We're in the desert.
> *Rick*:   I was misinformed.

The producers of *Casablanca*, however, hoped that their film would educate as well as entertain its viewers. From the first day of production, *Casablanca* was consciously designed to aid America's war effort. To be sure, Warner Bros., the studio that made the *Casablanca*, planned to make money from the film, but it also wanted the film to dramatically show the battle between good and evil that had so recently engulfed the world. In short, the movie mixed propaganda with entertainment, patriotism with laughter and romance, and became a document for America at a particular time. Today, a viewer can passively watch *Casablanca* and be thoroughly entertained, but the same viewer can also subject the film to a more critical analysis and as a result be entertained and learn something about Hollywood, America, and the world in the early months of World War II.

The history of the making of *Casablanca* is almost as interesting as the film itself. It started when Murray Burnett, a New York high school vocational teacher, took a trip to Europe in 1938. Although Burnett visited Europe a full year before the outbreak of the European phase of World War II, he saw everywhere signs of an impending conflict. German dictator Adolf Hitler was on the move, and had been for several years. Since 1936, his armies had reoccupied the Rhineland, forced an anschluss (reunion) with Austria, and overrun Czechoslovakia. Frightened by Hitler's anti-Semitic and fascist doctrines, many German, Austrian, and Czech Jews, as well as liberal and radical Catholics and Protestants, fled their homelands. Burnett witnessed the sad exodus of the refugees. At one point on his trip, Burnett sat in a cafe on France's Mediterranean coast listening to a black American piano player entertain the cafe's patrons and to refugees discuss the best route out of Europe. Many of the refugees, Burnett noted, were en route to Casablanca in French Morocco, from where they hoped to board a plane to Lisbon and then another to the United States.

It was a dramatic story, and Burnett dabbled in drama. In 1940 he teamed with Joan Allison, and the two wrote a play about an American who runs a cafe in Casablanca. Entitled *Everyone Comes to Rick's*, the play centers on Richard Blaine, the disillusioned cafe owner, and a woman torn between loyalty for her heroic husband and her love for Rick. Although the play generated modest interest among several New York producers, it had problems that kept it from being produced. Failing in New York, Burnett and Allison turned to Hollywood. On December 8, 1941, the day after the Japanese attack on Pearl Harbor and the United States' entry into World War II, *Everyone Comes to Rick's* reached the desk of Warner Bros.' story analyst Steven Karnot. He thought the story had possibilities and sent it to Hal Wallis, Warner Bros.' leading producer. Wallis was intrigued by the story's mixture of romance and sacrifice, cynicism and idealism. In addition, the story was set in Casablanca, an exotic setting that reminded him of *Algiers*, the successful 1938 film which featured Charles Boyer and Hedy Lamarr. Although Wallis recognized that Burnett and Allison's story had serious problems, he was confident that he could correct the troubled areas and turn the story into a profitable movie. Within a few months, Wallis had purchased the rights to *Everyone Comes to Rick's* and renamed the story *Casablanca* to underscore its exotic setting and identify it in the public mind with *Algiers*.

During the next eight months, a team of Hollywood screenwriters labored to solve the play's problems and turn it into a patriotic romance. To be sure, improvements were made: the central characters and issues were more clearly defined and the dialogue was polished until almost every line and scene became memorable. But the story remained essentially unchanged.

Summary of *Casablanca*

Casablanca is set in early December 1941. As the film opens, a narrator informs the viewers that with the start of World War II many Europeans

> turned hopefully, or desperately, toward the freedom of the Americas. Lisbon became the great embarkation point. But not everyone could get to Lisbon directly; and so, a tortuous, roundabout refugee trail sprang up. Paris to Marseilles, across the Mediterranean to Oran, then by train, or auto, or foot, across the rim of Africa to Casablanca in French Morocco. Here, the fortunate ones through money, or influence, or luck, might obtain exit visas and scurry to Lisbon, and from Lisbon to the New World. But the others had to wait in Casablanca, and wait, and wait, and wait.

Into this world of waiting and intrigue comes Victor Laszlo (Paul Henreid), the leader of the Czech underground and symbol of the resistance to Nazi domination of Europe, and his beautiful wife Ilsa (Ingrid Bergman). They too are struggling to obtain passage to Lisbon. In fact, they are scheduled to meet the black marketeer Ugarte (Peter Lorre) who had killed two Nazi couriers and secured two letters of transit signed by General de Gaulle. Unfortunately for Laszlo and Ilsa, Ugarte is killed before he can sell the letters of transit to them, but not before he gave them to American Rick Blaine (Humphrey Bogart) for safe keeping.

Rick is a man of mystery. Little is known of his past. Apparently he was once something of an idealist and an anti-fascist. In 1935 he had been involved in supplying guns to Ethiopia, and in 1936 he had fought in Spain on the Loyalists' side. But now he is committed only to his own neutrality. As he says several times in the film, "I stick my neck out for nobody." Rick is a man without a country. Some unknown reason prevents him from returning to the United States, and when asked his nationality, he replies, "I'm a drunkard." To which Captain Louis Renault (Claude Rains), the prefect of the police in *Casablanca*, adds, "That makes Rick a citizen of the world." Rick, then, is a cold cynic, jealous of his own neutrality and interested only in the affairs of his own cafe. The mystery is what changed Rick from an active idealist to a drunken cynic.

Ilsa provides the answer. Before the war she and Rick had been lovers in Paris, but when Rick had been forced to flee that city, Ilsa had not joined him at the railroad station. When Ilsa and Laszlo show up at Rick's Cafe American, the pain of those memories sweeps over Rick, making him bitter and angry. He vows never to give the letters of transit to Laszlo and Ilsa. But slowly Rick's anger and cynicism melt away. He and Ilsa meet, she explains why she couldn't leave Paris with him, and the two profess their love for each other. They also hatch a plan to get Laszlo out of Casablanca while they remain behind.

All goes according to plan until they reach the airport. This time Rick forces Ilsa to leave without him. Similar to Ilsa's motives in Paris, Rick's is motivated by idealism and sacrifice. Always a citizen of the world, he has joined the world's fight against fascism. "Where I'm going," he tells Ilsa, "you can't follow. What I've got to do, you can't be any part of. Ilsa, I'm no good at being noble, but it doesn't take much to see that the problems of three little people don't amount to a hill of beans in this crazy world." The film ends with Rick and Renault, another cynic who has suddenly been converted to idealism, striking off for a Free French garrison in Brazaville.

A Critical Examination of *Casablanca*

Casablanca is a wonderful film, but it is also a propaganda document. The film premiered on Thanksgiving Day, November 26, 1942, only nineteen days after the United States had landed forces at Casablanca in Morocco and, along with Great Britain, in Algeria. It was the first direct American blow against the Nazis and it thrilled Americans. Casablanca dominated the headlines. The day after the nationwide release of *Casablanca*, the city was once again in the news. On that day, January 24, 1943, it was announced that American President Franklin Roosevelt, British Prime Minister Winston Churchill, and Soviet Premier Joseph Stalin had met secretly earlier in the month to formulate a joint war plan to fight Germany. The American public learned that Roosevelt's headquarters had been codenamed "Rick's Place." Certainly, the publicity surrounding the Allied invasion of North Africa and the Casablanca

Conference generated interest in the film *Casablanca*. But the military and political activity did more than simply guarantee financial success; it gave the film an almost mythic quality. Rick became the symbol of America, and his transition from isolationism to involvement underscored America's similar transition.

Critical thinking involves asking questions. If we consider *Casablanca* as a wartime document, what can it tell us about Hollywood, America, and the world during the early months of World War II?

What biases or underlying assumptions animate the film?

A film is a collaborative product. Before considering the message of any film, it is important to recognize that a film is the result of the labor of many people, from the producer, director, writers, and actors to the photographers, gaffers, and grips to the editor, music coordinator, and publicists. At no time was this more true than during the Studio Era, a period in the history of Hollywood that started toward the end of World War I, reached its full maturity during the 1930s, and achieved its high point during World War II.

Casablanca was made at Warner Bros., a studio known for a certain style. "Warners' pictures," said one film historian, "were blunt and tough and fast. Their mise-en-scene was flat and cold; their individual cadences were clipped." Warners' leading actors and actresses – James Cagney, Humphrey Bogart, Edward G. Robinson, George Raft, Paul Muni, John Garfield, Bette Davis, Joan Blondell – were also noted for their tough, raw style. They were urban types, often cynical, sometimes mean, and never stupid. They might die at the end of film, but they were not rubes or suckers. Warner Bros. did not shy away from making pictures with social messages. *Little Caesar, I Am a Fugitive from a Chain Gang, Dr. Ehrlich's Magic Bullet*, and *Angels with Dirty Faces* explored some of the social problems that plagued America during the Depression. And Warner Bros. was the first major studio to make films that emphasized the threat of Adolf Hitler. *Confessions of a Nazi Spy* and *Sergeant York* attempted to warn America of the threat posed by Hitler and German militarism. America, the films suggested, did have a stake in European affairs, and wars were often the result of a real clash between good and evil.

The head of production for Warner Bros. was Jack Warner, an outspoken and irreverent mogul who rubbed almost everyone the wrong way. He told vulgar jokes, dressed in flashy clothes, and seemed to delight in embarrassing people. His own nephew once called him "an endearing personality – treacherous, hedonistic, and a tyrant." But as a Roosevelt Democrat, Jack Warner was also perhaps the most liberal of the studio heads, and he was certainly patriotic. He was commissioned as a lieutenant colonel during World War II. From the first, Warner and the other people who worked on *Casablanca* intended that the film would have a pro-war message.

The original play was anti-Nazi but not really pro-war. To tighten the political theme of the picture, Hal Wallis, the film's producer, hired screenwriter Howard Koch to work on the script. Just as anyone who wants to fully understand the biases woven into *Casablanca* has to understand Warner Bros. and Jack Warner, that person should also ask questions about the background and political beliefs of Howard Koch. Like many other screenwriters, Koch came to Hollywood after writing for Broadway and radio. He gained national attention as the man who adapted H.G. Wells' *The War of the Worlds* for Orson Welles' famous 1938 broadcast. But his best work was done in message films. Although he never joined the Communist party, Koch was a political radical who was active in several liberal causes. (During the politically repressive period that followed World War II, Koch was blacklisted in Hollywood.)

Koch gave Rick his political conscience. In the play *Everybody Comes to Rick's*, Rick lacks a defined political philosophy. In *Casablanca* his anti-fascist credentials are impeccable. He had fought against fascism in Ethiopia and Spain and, although he professes his neutrality, it is clear that he will eventually resume the struggle against fascism. Most importantly, Rick sees the folly of America's prewar isolationism. In one exchange with his friend and employee Sam, the black piano player, Rick asks, "Sam, if it's December 1941 in Casablanca, what time is it in New York? I bet they're asleep in New York. I'll bet they're asleep all over America." The point of the exchange could not have been lost on American audiences in 1942 and 1943. Trapped in its isolationism, America was asleep in early December 1941. Pearl Harbor provided an unpleasant wake-up call.

Questioning the biases of the people who made *Casablanca* provides several clues of the nature of the film. Even if you had not seen the film, you could predict that it would be patriotic, politically liberal, and interventionist. You could predict that it would follow fairly closely President Roosevelt's own view of the conflict.

How was the film received when it premiered in 1942?

One of the pitfalls of historical – or critical – thinking is presentism. We have a tendency to read our present values into past events. What we think of *Casablanca* or internationalism or even World War II is partially conditioned by our feelings toward the international events – from the Cold War to the Vietnam War to the remarkable international changes of the recent years – that have shaped our own lives. To avoid presentism, historians try to reconstruct how an event was received and interpreted at the time that it occurred. To fully understand the impact and importance of *Casablanca* we have to examine what was written and said about the film in late 1942 and early 1943.

Reviews provide an important clue to how audiences reacted to *Casablanca*. The *New York Times'* reviewer commented that the film "makes the spine tingle and the heart take a leap." Other reviewers agreed that the *Casablanca* was a remarkably good film: "a crackling, timely melodrama" (*New York Morning Telegraph*); "today's headlines translated into arresting drama" (*New York Mirror*); "smashing ... moving ... superior" (*New York Herald Tribune*). The Hollywood trade journals echoed the dailies' opinions, emphasizing the film's timeliness as well as its suspense, drama, and entertainment qualities. The review in the *Hollywood Reporter* epitomized the favorable reception of *Casablanca*: "Here is a drama that lifts you right out of your seats .... The picture has exceptional merits as absorbing entertainment, reflecting the fine craftsmanship of all who had hands in its making."

A technically near-perfect film, to be sure, but how was *Casablanca* judged as an example of propaganda? To answer this question we have to leave the published reviews in newspapers and trade journals and look elsewhere. As you might expect, the United States government was quite interested in the content of movies. The average ticket sales in America each week during World War II ranged between eighty and ninety million, or two-thirds of the country's population. Movies were the nation's leading entertainment outlet, and as such, they exerted an awesome power to influence and mold public opinion. In fact, two months before the Japanese attack on Pearl Harbor, Senator Gerald P. Nye, the isolationist from North Dakota, had charged that Hollywood was making films designed to pull the United States into the European war. A special subcommittee of the Committee on Interstate Commerce looked into Nye's charges. Although the subcommittee issued no report when it adjourned on September 26, 1941, it did suggest that Hollywood was at least partially guilty of the charge.

After Pearl Harbor, the Roosevelt administration quickly enlisted Hollywood in America's war effort. The Office of War Information (OWI), which coordinated the country's wartime information and propaganda activities, established the Bureau of Motion Pictures (BMP) to watch over the film industry. Although the BMP did not have direct control over the film industry, it did exert a powerful influence in Hollywood. In its *Government Informational Manual for the Motion Picture Industry*, the BMP asked every producer to consider one central question: "Will this picture help win the war?" The BMP reviewed every film made during the war. Its reports evaluate the contribution – or lack of contribution – that each film made to the war effort.

The BMP report on *Casablanca* assesses the movie's effectiveness as propaganda. "From the standpoint of the war information program," noted the BMP report, "*Casablanca* is a very good picture about the enemy, those whose lives the enemy has wrecked and those underground agents who fight him unremittingly on his own ground." More specifically, the report detailed how *Casablanca* aided America's fight against Germany: the film portrays evil, arrogant Nazis who disregard "human life and dignity" and who create "chaos and misery" throughout Europe; the film demonstrates "the spirit of the underground movement" and suggests that not all of the French people are cooperating with the Nazis; the film presents the United States as "the haven of the oppressed and homeless" and as the defender of democracy and freedom; and the film shows the need to sacrifice "personal desire" to defeat fascism. In short, *Casablanca* presents the BMP's slant on the United States, its enemy, and its allies as well as underscoring the reasons America is in the war.

The reviews of *Casablanca* and the BMP report on the film illustrate the need for the critical historian to return to the primary sources to understand how an event – in this case a movie – was greeted. The critical thinker is aware that his or her reactions to an older film or event from history may be different from how the film or event was originally perceived. The critical thinker, therefore, attempts to overcome this natural presentism by examining primary sources.

Could Ilsa have stayed with Rick?

Legends swirl around *Casablanca*. The most famous legends involve the script, which was still not finished when filming started at the end of May, 1942. One Hollywood legend holds that problems with the script forced director Michael Curtiz to shoot the film, from first scene to last, in the same order as the scenes appeared in the finished movie. This legend is utterly fantastic. No movie is filmed in such a fashion. To do so would involve tying up several sound stages – the most precious commodity at any studio – as well as paying all the actors and actresses and renting all the needed props and equipment for the duration of the filming. No studio could afford that wasteful luxury.

Script problems gave rise to an even more intriguing legend, that until nearly the end of the shooting it had yet to be decided whether Ilsa would leave *Casablanca* with her husband Victor Laszlo or stay behind with her true love Rick. One variation of the legend holds that the screenwriters wrote two different endings; another variation claims that both endings were actually shot. Indeed, Ingrid Bergman has said that for most of the production period she had no idea who she would end up with in the film's final scene. At one point, she told the writers, "You must tell me because after all there is a little bit of difference in acting toward a man that you love and another man for whom you may just feel pity or affection." "Well," the writers replied, "don't give too much of anything. Play it in between ...."

Clearly *Casablanca* suggests that Ilsa loves Rick but only respects Laszlo. Several times in the film Laszlo professes his love for Ilsa, and each time she deflects his comments. In one scene Laszlo says, "I love you very much, Ilsa." She replies, "Your secret will be safe with me." Later in the film, when Laszlo realizes that Ilsa had been in love with Rick in Paris, he tells her again, "I love you very much, my dear." "Yes, yes I know," she responds. In contrast to her guarded responses with her husband, she freely confesses her love for Rick. Toward the end of the film, Ilsa tells Rick, "The day you left Paris, if you knew what I went through! If you knew how much I loved you, how much I still love you! ... I know I'll never have the strength to leave you again .... I can't fight it anymore. I ran away once. I can't do it again .... I wish I didn't love you so much."

But in the end, Ilsa does leave Rick. Could the film have ended otherwise? Could the scriptwriters have discovered a way to have Laszlo leave without his wife? The question may at first seem trivial and not of any critical significance. But it is not, for its answer illuminates an important aspect of Hollywood and the movies during the 1930s and 1940s. The answer also demonstrates that Hollywood legends, like so many other good stories, should not be taken at face value.

To begin with, although the film differed in many details from the play, *Casablanca* was faithful to the intent of *Everybody Comes to Rick's*. In the play, Rick moves from moody isolationist to passionate patriot. For a higher ideal, he convinces Ilsa to leave Casablanca with Laszlo. He sacrifices his personal desire for the good of a more important cause, the battle against fascism. In none of the drafts of *Casablanca* is there any hint that Ilsa would not leave with Laszlo. Legends are nice, but at no time did the screenwriters consider altering the core of the play's ending.

Even if the screenwriters wanted to change the story and invent a pat Hollywood ending, they would have faced powerful opposition. Throughout the 1930s and 1940s, one of the most influential voices in [the] movie industry was that of Joseph Ignatius Breen, head of the Motion Picture Producers and Distributors Association (MPPDA). Breen's job was to make sure that every Hollywood release was good, clean, wholesome, family entertainment. The mop Breen used to keep movies clean was the Motion Picture Production Code, which clearly stated the dos and don'ts of moviemaking. Almost everything about *Casablanca* attracted Breen's attention. Raised in a devout Catholic family and a former student at the Jesuit St. Joseph's College, Breen was not likely to approve any script or give the Code's blessing to any movie where the hero and heroine had an adulterous love affair. It just couldn't happen, not as long as Breen exerted any power in Hollywood.

The Code was quite specific on such matters. Article II of the Code states, "The sanctity of the institution of marriage and the home shall be upheld. Pictures shall not infer that low forms of sex relationship are the accepted or common thing." And in Article II (1), the Code further notes, "Adultery, sometimes necessary plot material, must not be explicitly treated, or justified, or presented attractively." In short, the producers of *Casablanca* had better dance delicately around the relationship between Ilsa and Rick. One slip, one overly suggestive comment or scene, could doom the film to perdition.

Breen pored over the script of *Casablanca*, searching for anything that might offend American tastes – or what he judged to be American tastes. (Remember, in *Gone With the Wind*, Breen objected to the use of the word "damn" in the film's last scene.) He demanded that Renault's character – or at least, dialogue – be cleaned up. Captain Renault, the prefect of police who exchanges visas for sexual favors, upset Breen. Early in the script submitted to Breen, an aide informs Renault that several "visa difficulties" have come up. When Renault discovers that two beautiful women are having "problems," he muses, "Which one?" Then with a sigh, he says to aide, "Ten years ago there would have been no problem. Oh, well, tell the dark one to wait in my private office and we'll go into her visa matter thoroughly … And it wouldn't hurt to have the other one leave her address and phone number." Such suggestive comments were far too direct, Breen decided. They had to be toned down considerably. Hal Wallis, the film's producer, argued that Renault's exploitative nature was important to the film because in the end when Renault joins the anti-fascist cause it proved that even the self-admitted "poor corrupt officer" was not beyond political redemption. Using the rule of "compensating moral values," Breen allowed Renault to keep a few of his less blatantly suggestive lines.

As for Ilsa and Rick, Breen was less tolerant. Not only could Ilsa not remain with Rick, the film could not suggest, even obliquely, that the two had a sexual reunion in Casablanca. Ilsa and Rick's affair in Paris could be explained: Ilsa thought Laszlo was dead and that she was therefore single. But in Casablanca, Laszlo is quite alive and Ilsa is indisputably married. Breen insisted that, when Ilsa and Rick meet alone in Rick's private quarters and she reaffirms her love, the set contain no bed or couch, "or anything whatever suggestive of a sex affair." In addition, Breen insisted that the scene be shot differently. As originally written, there was a time shift in the middle of the scene. "The action ends," commented one authority on the film, "with her declaration of love and resumes as she is telling Rick why she originally left him." After reading the script, Breen commented, "The present material seems to contain a suggestion of a sex affair which would be unacceptable if it came through in the finished picture. We believe this could possibly be corrected by replacing the fade out on page 135, with a dissolve …." This solution, used in the film, prohibited the audience from imagining that Rick and Ilsa resumed their Paris affair. In *Casablanca*, their love was pure and idealized, not physical.

The question of why Ilsa didn't remain with Rick thus leads into a larger discussion of the morals and politics of the motion picture industry. It involves Joseph Breen, MPPDA, and the regulation of movies, and it touches on censorship in American arts and society. Only by critically thinking about what you read and see will you be able to move beyond passive consumption to active engagement with the subject and the issues it raises.

11

Bureau of Motion Pictures Report: *Casablanca*

Feature Review
Casablanca   95 minutes
Warner Bros.   WB   Feb., 1943 (Sched.)
Screenplay by Julius and Philip Epstein and Howard Koch, from play by Murray
Burnett and Joan Alison
Hal Wallis   (A)
  Major: III B (United Nations – Conquered Nations) Drama
  Minor: II C 3 (Enemy - Military) Drama

Nelson Poynter	Warner Bros	October 26, 1942
Dorothy Jones	"	"
Marjorie Thorsch	"	"
Lillian Bergquist	"	"
Lillian Bergquist	"	October 28, 1942

From the standpoint of the war information program, CASABLANCA is a very good
picture about the enemy, those whose lives the enemy has wrecked and those underground agents who fight him unremittingly on his own ground. The war content is
dramatically effective. Many excellent points are scored:

(1) The film presents an excellent picture of the spirit of the underground movement.
Victor Laszlo, a Czech patriot, has fought fascism by printing the truth about it in
illegal newspapers in Prague and Paris. He has suffered in a concentration camp, from
which he finally escaped. Unintimidated by his experiences he plans to continue his
work. In *Casablanca*, a Norwegian anti-Nazi says: "The underground is well organized here as everywhere." We learn that people of all nationalities meet secretly everywhere, despite the danger, planning the destruction of the oppressor. Their courage,
determination and self-sacrifice should make Americans proud of these underground
allies.
(2) Some of the chaos and misery which fascism and the war has brought are graphically illustrated. Refugees of all nationalities are crowded into *Casablanca*. A few have
money, but it goes quickly. They attempt to sell their jewels, but the market is flooded.

Some refugees are reduced to stealing; women sell themselves; others bribe corrupt officials who in turn doublecross them. There are pickpockets, murderers, Black Markets in visas. Personal honor and dignity have departed; degradation and treachery have taken their place. This is part of what fascism has brought in its wake. Another facet of Nazi aggression is shown in scenes which depict the Nazi march into Paris. A sense of the honor and confusion of the French population is very well projected.

(3) It is shown that personal desire must be subordinated to the task of defeating fascism. To Laszlo and the other underground workers, the defeat of fascism is of paramount importance. The heroine and the man she loves sacrifice their personal happiness in order that each may carry on the fight in the most effective manner. They realize that they cannot steal happiness with the rest of the world enslaved.

(4) It is brought out that many French are by no means cooperating wholeheartedly with the Nazis. Renault, the French Prefect of Police, tells Rick that he "goes the way the wind blows. He is cynical and not above taking bribes. Yet, when Rick, the American hero murders Strasser, Renault not only allows him to escape, but goes with him to the nearest Free French garrison. Then again, the French people in Rick's cafe, led by Laszlo, the Czech patriot, courageously sing the Marseillaise to drown out the song of their conquerors. Here is illustrated the love and pride of the French in their country, conquered though it is. We feel that it will rise again.

(5) America is shown as the haven of the oppressed and homeless. Refugees want to come to the United States because here they are assured of freedom, democratic privileges and immunity from fear. The love and esteem with which this country is regarded by oppressed peoples should make audiences aware of their responsibilities as Americans to uphold this reputation and fight fascism with all that is in them.

(6) Some of the scope of our present conflict is brought out. It is established that Rick, the American cafe owner, fought for the loyalists in the Spanish Civil War, and for democracy as far back as 1935 and 1936, when he smuggled guns for the Ethiopians. Points like these aid audiences in understanding that our war did not commence with Pearl Harbor, but that the roots of aggression reach far back.

(7) The film presents a good portrayal of the typical Nazi. In the arrogant Major Strasser, with his contempt for anything not German, his disregard for human life and dignity, his determination that all peoples shall bow to the Third Reich, we get a picture of the Nazi outlook. These are the kind of men who would enslave the world.

12

John Wayne and Wartime Hollywood
John Wayne Goes to War

Randy Roberts

John Wayne – 30 years after his death he remains one of the most recognizable stars in the history of Hollywood. Every day, somewhere, one of his films runs on television, and thousands of Americans can mimic his one-of-a-kind walk and familiar, halting cadence. His films present American history as a series of morality plays – cowboys versus Indians on the open plains, Americans versus Japanese and Nazis during World War II, Americans versus communists during the Cold War. It was "Us" versus "Them," defenders of truth, justice, and the American way versus the ruthless, the godless, and the greedy. Ironically, Wayne gained international fame and his iconic image during World War II, a conflict in which he did not enlist as a combatant but rather remained comfortable in Hollywood making movies. In the following essay, Randy Roberts examines John Wayne and Hollywood during the opening years of World War II.

December 7, 1941. The news reached Hollywood at 11:26 on a calm Sunday morning. The Japanese had attacked American naval and air bases in Honolulu. A few people refused to believe the news. It seemed impossible, almost like another "War of the Worlds" broadcast, and they waited for the soothing voice of an announcer to tell them that it was only make believe. Everything about the day clashed with the brutal facts. The weather was perfect, even for a city where ideal weather was the norm. A cool night breeze blew off the desert from the northeast, but by 11:00 it was already in the low 70s. For the Hollywood elite, many of whom had gone to their vacation retreats in Malibu, Palm Springs, or the High Sierras, golf and swimming, not war, was on the day's agenda. Before the news reached Los Angeles, harmony reigned. Only the day before, the UCLA Bruins and the USC Trojans had played to a 7–7 tie, and that very morning a *Los Angeles Times* headline announced "FINAL PEACE MOVE SEEN."

The attack stunned Los Angeles. Responses varied. Some followed normal schedules. Thousands turned up at the "little world championship" football game and watched the undefeated Hollywood Bears, led by Kenny Washington and Woody Strode, defeat the Columbus Bulls. During the game, news updates reminded the spectators that the Bears' victory would probably not be remembered as the day's most important event. In another part of town, several hundred spectators watched Paramount Studio's baseball team defeat an "all-Jap aggregation." After the game, the FBI took the Japanese team into custody. The attack, however, disrupted most schedules. Golfers finished the holes they were playing and returned to the clubhouse. Gossips ended their conversations about Harry Warner's new granddaughter or the removal of Eddie Albert's tonsils or the anti aircraft men who had set up shop at Hollywood Park, and turned to more urgent topics. Thousands simply got into their automobiles – tanks full and rubber treads still good – and drove aimlessly through the city, leading to traffic jams in downtown Los Angeles and Hollywood.

Soon the rumors started to ricochet like bullets.

Air defense men had known the attack was imminent. Two squadrons of airplanes – that's thirty planes – had been sighted over the California coast. Japanese airplanes had reconnoitered the Bay area. Bombed the Golden Gate Bridge. Pearl Harbor was only a stepping stone. California was next. There would be an uprising of Japanese Americans. Sabotage was certain. Moved to action by the rumors as well as sound precaution, policemen went on 12-hour shifts and sent extra security guards to dams, bridges, and power stations. Most others waited for FDR's announcement that the United States was now at war.

Hollywood and the entertainment industry responded to the attack with sincere feelings of patriotism mixed with an equally sincere desire to cash in on the event. Studios abandoned a few films already in production with poorly timed themes or poorly chosen titles – the musicals *Pearl Harbor Pearl* and *I'll Take Manila* and the comedy *Absent Without Leave*, about a GI who goes AWOL. Just as quickly studios secured the copyrights for more promising titles – *Sunday in Hawaii, Wings Over the Pacific, Bombing of Honolulu, Remember Pearl Harbor, Yellow Peril, Yellow Menace, My Four Years in Japan,* and *V for Victory.* Tin Pan Alley produced topical songs within days of the attack. Although none muscled onto the Hit Parade, such songs as "Let's Put the Axe to the Axis," "We're Going to Find the Follow Who Is Yellow and Beat Him Red, White and Blue," "They're Gonna Be Playin' Taps on the Japs," "The Sun Will Soon Be Setting for the Land of the Rising Sun," "To Be Specific, It's Our Pacific," "When Those Little Yellow Bellies Meet the Cohens and the Kelleys," and "You're a Sap, Mr. Jap" expressed the angry mood of the country. The Metropolitan Opera Company, sensing that Americans did not want to see a sympathetic portrayal of any Japanese, dropped their production of *Madame Butterfly.* The Greenwich Village Savoyards followed the Met's lofty example and dumped their production of *The Mikado.*

While Tin Pan Alley turned out their topical tunes and opera companies pruned their repertoires, Americans huddled close to their radios. On Monday morning and Tuesday night F.D.R. delivered his impassioned war speeches before Congress. For a few days, America – and particularly the West Coast – moved through a fog of air raid alarms, blackouts, and tense expectations.

They listened as America's foreign commentators broke the news that Germany and Italy had declared war on the United States. They listened to the news that the Germans had sunk two British ships and that the Japanese had followed up Pearl Harbor with attacks in the Philippines, Hong Kong, Wake Island, Guam, and other Pacific strongholds.

Hollywood moaned that the war was a killer at the box office. Certainly flights of parochialism were the standard Hollywood reaction to any event. In 1935 when

Mussolini's troops stormed into Ethiopia and the world focused on the League of Nations, a Hollywood producer asked a friend, "Have you heard any late news?" Yes, the friend replied hotly, "Italy just banned Marie Antoinette!" This episode of tunnel vision was surpassed in 1939 when Italy ruthlessly invaded Albania. Louella Parsons, Hollywood's leading gossip writer, began her column that week: "The deadly dullness of the past week was lifted today when Darryl Zanuck announced he had bought all rights to *The Bluebird* for Shirley Temple."

By mid-December Hollywood spokesmen complained that Americans were too interested in the war to go to the movies. Attempting to demonstrate that Hollywood was concerned with other events, *Variety* observed that the war had also hurt Christmas shopping, but clearly the box office crisis overshadowed all other concerns. The *Wolf Man's Variety* advertisement announced "Listen to That Box Office Howl!" but the only noise was the studio's howl of financial pain. The same was true for *The Great Dictator, Sergeant York, Citizen Kane*, and the season's other top pictures. Amidst considerable hand wringing, Hollywood leaders speculated on the long-term impact of the war on the industry.

John Wayne shared the industry's general concern, although his worries focused more specifically on the effect the war would have on his own career. After years of struggle with bad scripts and tight budgets, by late 1941 he was moving closer to the fringes of stardom. The reviews he had received for *Stagecoach* and *The Long Voyage Home* had pushed his career to a new level. Republic's head Herbert Yates responded by searching for better scripts, assigning first-line directors, and increasing the budgets for Wayne films. *The Dark Command*, Wayne's first film for Republic under the contract his new agent had negotiated for him, reflected Wayne's new status. Yates allocated $700,000 for the film – more than any previous Republic project – and hired Raoul Walsh to direct it. He also arranged for Claire Trevor and Walter Pidgeon to star in the film with Wayne. And less than four months before the attack on Pearl Harbor, Wayne had finished his work on Cecil B. DeMille's *Reap the Wild Wind*, which Paramount had scheduled for a March 1942 release.

New agents, new contracts, better directors, better films – at the age of thirty-four Duke was a player in Hollywood. But he was not yet a major star. In late December 1941, *Variety* issued its annual review of the stars. It set down clearly where an actor or actress stood in the complicated Hollywood pecking order. At the Summit of the hierarchy were the performers whose pictures earned the most money for the year: Gary Cooper, Abbott and Costello, Clark Gable, Mickey Rooney, Bob Hope, Charlie Chaplin, Dorothy Lamour, Spencer Tracy, Jack Benny, and Bing Crosby. They had helped make 1941 the best year ever for domestic box office receipts.

Next came the individual studio reports. The stars and featured performers of the individual studios were listed and briefly discussed. The major studios controlled the major talent. MGM led the pack; its stars included Gable, Rooney, Tracy, Robert Taylor, Lana Turner, James Stewart, Hedy Lamarr, Judy Garland, Myrna Loy, William Powell, Joan Crawford, Nelson Eddy, Jeanette MacDonald, Greta Garbo, Norma Shearer, the Marx Brothers, and a host of other leading performers. If the other studios could not match MGM, they could all boast of their proven box-office attractions. Warner Brothers, king of the gangster genre, had James Cagney, Humphrey Bogart, Edward G. Robinson, John Garfield, and George Raft, as well as Erroll Flynn, Bette Davis, Merle Oberon, and Ronald Reagan. Twentieth Century Fox had a group of attractive leading men and women which included Tyrone Power, Betty Grable, Gene Tierney, Henry Fonda, Randolph Scott, Maureen O'Hara, and Linda Darnell. Paramount had its comedians – Hope, Crosby, and Benny – as well as Lamour, Claudette Colbert, Veronica Lake, Paulette Goddard, Fred MacMurray, and Ray Milland. RKO featured Ginger Rogers, Orson Welles, Cary Grant, Carole Lombard, Ronald Coleman, and Gloria Swanson. Universal had a great year in 1941 thanks to the success of Abbott and Costello. And Columbia featured Peter Lorre, Boris Karloff, Fay Wray, and the recently acquired Rita Hayworth.

At the bottom of the hierarchy were the smaller studios and their performers. There dwelled Monogram. "No pretenses. No ambitious production. Just bread and butter," noted *Variety*. Its older cowboy and action stars – Jack LaRue, Buck Jones, Tim McCoy, and Bela Lugosi – kept the studio afloat. Finally came Republic. *Variety* listed Gene Autry and John Wayne as Republic's "two corking box-office assets." Wayne's reputation derived from his "loanout" status. Like Monogram, Republic produced films for theaters outside of the major distribution circles, and a star like Wayne who was used by the major studios gave prestige to the Poverty Row studio.

Wayne, always a clear-thinking realist, knew where he stood in the Hollywood hierarchy. He was a star in the third- and fourth-run theaters in the South and Southwest, in areas with more cattle than people. His success following *Stagecoach* introduced him to the first- and second-run palaces of the East, Midwest, and West. At the end of 1941 he was nowhere near the summit of the hierarchy, far from the status of such leading men as Clark Gable, Robert Taylor, Tyrone Power, Cary Grant, Gary Cooper, or Henry Fonda. But Wayne was ambitious, and no one in the industry had his capacity for work. The facts were indisputable: his reputation was growing but not yet firmly established, and he was a thirty-four-year-old leading man. If he enlisted, would his fragile reputation survive two, three, four years in the service? How many years did he have left as a leading man? Enlistment, in the final analysis, would probably end his career.

While Wayne pondered his future and prepared for his next picture, other Hollywood stars put their careers on hold and their lives on the line. Pearl Harbor aroused deep emotions in Hollywood. During the next four years journalists and politicians would accuse the film industry of being cynical, opportunistic, greedy, and worse. The charges were often accurate. But in late 1941 and early 1942 scores of actors, directors, producers, and technicians enlisted out of a deep sense of patriotism. Like millions of other Americans, they were shocked by the Japanese attack and wanted to help win the war.

Henry Fonda, one of Duke's boon companions on vacations to Mexico, felt the pull of patriotism. He was thirty-seven – three years older than Wayne – and had a wife and three children. For all practical purposes, he was exempt from the draft. But he had a baby face, and he did not want the wives and mothers of soldiers and sailors to see him on the screen and ask, "Why isn't he out there?" Besides, as he told his wife, "this is my country and I want to be where it's happening. I don't want to be in a fake war in a studio or on location …. I want to be on a real ocean not the back lot. I want to be with real sailors and not extras." After he finished *The Ox-Bow Incident*, the film in which he was then starring, Fonda drove to the Naval Headquarters in Los Angeles and enlisted. No screen photographers were present; his press agent had not tipped off any reporters. Fonda wanted it simple, no different than other Americans.

John Ford, the man Duke admired the most, also felt the pull. During the late 1930s he had followed with growing uneasiness the spread of fascism in Europe. When

Ford's leading writer Dudley Nichols sent him a wire of congratulations for winning the 1940 Academy Award for his direction of *The Grapes of Wrath*, Ford wrote back, "awards for pictures are a trivial thing to be concerned with at times like these." That spring he organized the Naval Field Photographic Reserve unit, which Washington officially recognized. The forty-six-year-old Ford was ordered to report to Washington for active duty in the month before Pearl Harbor. Immediately and without publicity he left Hollywood. He left the money, the fame, the career, the glamour.

When the Japanese attacked Pearl Harbor, Ford was eating lunch at the eighteenth-century Alexandria, Virginia, home of Admiral William Pickens. He watched the Admiral take the urgent phone call. He saw the blood drain from his face. After they heard the news, Pickens' wife, Darrielle, showed Ford a scar on their home where a Revolutionary War musket ball had torn through a wall. "I never let them plaster over the hole," she said. Throughout the war and for the rest of his life Ford would remember the story. He wanted to be part of that tradition.

Tradition and patriotism pulled Jimmy Stewart into the war. Stewart's grandfather had fought for the union during the Civil War. Stewart's father had fought in the Spanish–American War and World War I. In February 1941, Stewart attempted to enlist in the Army Air Corps but was rejected because his 147 pounds was ten pounds too light for his six-feet four-inch frame. He went on a diet of candy, beer, and bananas. In a month he had put on the ten pounds, and he was sworn into the Army. He left his $1,500-a-week movie salary for a private's wages.

Other leading men and Hollywood personalities also felt the pull. Wayne's fellow star at Republic, Gene Autry, joined the Army Air Corps. Robert Montgomery enlisted in the Navy. Tyrone Power joined the Marines. William Holden went into the Army. After the death of his wife Carole Lombard in January 1942, Clark Gable also enlisted in the Army. David Niven, Laurence Olivier, and Patrick Knowles returned to their native Britain and enlisted. Ronald Reagan, Sterling Hayden, Burgess Meredith, and Gilbert Roland all signed up. So too did directors Frank Capra, William Wyler, Anatole Litvak, John Huston, and William Keighley; producers Hal Roach, Jack Warner, Gene Markey, and Darryl E. Zanuck; writers Garson Kanin and Budd Schulberg; cameraman Gregg Toland; and thousands of other Hollywood workers. By October 1942 over 2,700 – or 12 percent – of the men and women in the film industry had entered the armed forces. Some, like Fonda and Stewart, enlisted quietly and without fanfare. Others like Reagan and Zanuck and Gable made the process of enlistment and service an act of Hollywood. But quietly or loudly they did serve.

In 1941 professional baseball players were the only men who received as much attention and adulation as Hollywood stars. When the war started they laid down their bats and picked up service issue weapons. Joe DiMaggio, Hank Greenberg, Bob Feller, Ted Williams, Bill Dickey, Peewee Reese, and most of the other baseball legends from the 1930s entered the service. More than 4,000 of the roughly 5,700 players in the major and minor leagues served in the armed forces during the war. Some were killed or seriously injured during the conflict. Others experienced the loss of crucial skills because of a lack of practice. And even the players who returned to the big leagues after the war lost several years from a career which at best was painfully short.

Even America's popular comic book heroes enlisted in the war effort. Joe Palooka and Snuffy Smith joined the Army; Mickey Flynn enlisted in the Coast Guard; Dick Tracy received a commission in naval intelligence. Batman, Robin, the Flash, Plastic

Man, Captain America, Captain Marvel, the Green Lantern, the Spirit – the cream of the super heroes – fought Germans and Japanese in the pages of thousands of comic books. The only important super hero who did not enlist was Superman – and he stayed at home for a very good reason. His creators, Jerry Siegel and Joe Schuster, reasoned that Nazis and Japs would be no match for the Man of Steel, and with real Americans fighting and dying in the war it might denigrate their efforts if Superman defeated the Axis. To keep Superman out of the war but still show his patriotism, Siegel and Schuster had Clark Kent – a.k.a. Superman – declared 4-F. Superman's famed X-ray vision malfunctioned during his preinduction physical; instead of reading the eye chart in front of him, Superman accidentally looked through the wall and focused on the one in the next room. Shazam-4-F. Instead of fighting abroad, Superman battled Fifth Columnist activities in the States.

Movie stars and baseball stars, superheroes and boxing champions – they took their place with millions of other less famous Americans. More than any other war in America's history, World War II was a popular, democratic war. In the five years between December 1941 and December 1946, 16.3 million Americans entered the armed forces. All males between the ages of 18 and 64 had to register for the draft, although the upper age limit for service was set at 44 and later lowered to 38. One out of every six American men wore a uniform during the war. The wealthy fought alongside the poor, the single beside married men with children. Unlike the Vietnam War, relatively few men tried to avoid military service. For a man in his twenties or thirties not in uniform, the central question was, "Why not?"

It was a question John Wayne had to face for the next four years. Wayne's case was not a matter of draft dodging. Although by late 1941 Wayne's marriage was falling apart and his visits to his home and children were becoming more infrequent, he was technically married and had four children. This, coupled with his age, meant that he was not a prime candidate for the draft. And in February 1942 General Lewis B. Hershey, Director of Selective Service, called the motion picture industry "an activity essential in certain instances to the national health, safety and interest, and in other instances to war production." In accordance with his statement, he instructed Selective Service officials in California to grant deferments to men vital to the industry. Although Hershey's order was not meant as a blanket deferment, and although the Screen Actors Guild announced that it did not want any privileged status, the California draft board was liberal in its application of the ruling. Many Washington and California officials argued that Gary Cooper was more valuable to the war effort as Sergeant York – a role he played in the top money grosser in 1941 which oozed patriotism – than as Sergeant Cooper.

The most visible Hollywood commodity in need of protection during the war was the leading man. Out of sincere feelings of patriotism or the fear of being branded as a slacker, many of Hollywood's youngest and most famous leading men enlisted. The shortage created a ticklish problem for studio public relation staffs. Leading men were supposed to project youth, sexuality, virility, and strength. But a movie star projecting those traits on the screen during the war faced the painful question, "Why isn't he in the army?" As *Daily Variety* commented, "No more he-man build up of young men as in the past, for these might kick back unpleasant reverberations. If the build up is too mighty, [the] public may want to know if he's that good why isn't he in the Army shooting Japs and Nazis. This is a particularly touchy phase and p-r has to be subtle about it." The irony of the situation was best expressed by an agent who told a producer about his latest discovery: "I've got a great prospect for you – a young guy with a double hernia."

A leading man during the war needed a good profile and an adequate voice, but more importantly he had to be either over forty, married with two or more children, or 4-F. Gary Cooper, Bing Crosby, James Cagney, John Garfield, Don Ameche, and Joel McCrea all "had a brood at home to call [them] 'pop'." Warner Baxter, Neil Hamilton, and Nils Aster – all forty to fifty – led the new crop of "semi-romantic" leading men. Sonny Nuts, the handsome, ex-Yale football player who starred in the hit *So Proudly We Hail* was safely classified as 4-F. John Wayne's draft status was a family present.

Like other actors with two or more children, he could have enlisted. Like his friends Henry Fonda or John Ford, he could have placed his concern for his nation above his concern for his family, status, and career. There were some aspects of his life that Wayne never spoke to the press about; some that he rarely ever even spoke to his family or closest friends about. His decision not to enlist was a part of his life that he did not discuss. Pilar Wayne, whom Duke met and married a decade after the war, said that the guilt he suffered over his failure to enlist influenced the rest of his life. Mary St. John, who worked at Republic during the war and became Wayne's personal secretary after the war, agreed. She recalled that Wayne suffered "terrible guilt and embarrassment" because of his war record. The fact that his brother Robert served in the Navy only exasperated Wayne's sensitivity. His mother, who always openly favored Robert, was not above reminding Wayne that Robert, and not Duke, had served his country during the great crisis. On the screen, Wayne was the quintessential man of action, one who took matters into his own powerful hands and fought for what he believed. Never had the chasm between what he projected on the screen and his personal actions been so great.

Throughout 1942 and 1943, as he made one picture after another and as his reputation as a leading man soared, Wayne flirted with the idea of enlistment. He was particularly concerned about his stature in Ford's eyes, and he suspected that Ford had little respect for Celluloid soldiers. His suspicion was dead right. In early October 1941, shortly after he went on active duty, Ford wrote his wife that Wayne and Ward Bond's frivolous activities were meaningless in a world spinning toward total war. "They don't count. Their time will come." Three months after Pearl Harbor, Ford again mentioned Wayne in a letter to his wife. In a letter soaked in contempt, he remarked that he was "delighted" to hear about Wayne and Bond sitting up all night on a mountain top listening through earphones for signs that the Japanese were attacking California: "Ah well – such heroism shall not go unrewarded – it will live in the annals of time."

A pattern developed in Wayne's letters to Ford during the first two years of the war. Again and again, Wayne told Ford that he wanted to enlist – planned to enlist – as soon as he finished just one or two pictures. In the spring of 1942, Wayne inquired if he could get in Ford's unit, and if Ford would want him. If that option were closed, what would Ford suggest? Should he try the Marines? Plaintively, Wayne insisted that he was not drunk and that he hated to ask for favors, adding, "But for Christ's sake, you can suggest can't you?" A year later, Wayne was still considering enlistment in his letters to Ford. After he finished one more film he would be free: "Outside of that [film] Barkus [*sic*] is ready, anxious, and willin'."

But Barkus never did enlist. Toward the end of his life, Wayne told Dan Ford, John Ford's grandson, that his wife Josie had prevented him from joining Ford's outfit. According to his story, OSS head and Ford's superior William Donovan had sent a letter to Wayne explaining when Duke could join the Field Photographic Unit, but Josie never gave him the letter. He also confessed that he considered enlisting as a private, but rejected the idea. How, he pondered, could he fight alongside seventeen- and eighteen-year-old boys who had been reared on his movies? For them, he said, "I was America." In the end he concluded that he could best serve his country by making movies and going on an occasional USO tour.

The problem with any discussion of Wayne's "war record" is that it depends too much on statements made by Duke and others long after the war ended. Did his wife hide Donovan's letter? There is no such letter in Donovan's public and private papers. Did he believe that he was such an American institution by 1942 that he could not enlist as a private? This statement is difficult to take at face value when one considers that Gable, Power, Fonda, and Stewart – far more important stars than Wayne – were willing to share a foxhole or a cockpit or a ship deck with 17- and 18-year-old American soldiers or sailors. Did, in fact, Wayne try to enlist? Catalina Lawrence, a script supervisor at Republic during the war who sometimes doubled as Wayne's secretary, remembers writing letters for Wayne attempting to get him in the service. "He felt so bad," she recalled, "especially after Robert was drafted into the Navy. Duke wanted to get in, but he just never could."

The closest one can come to the truth is Wayne's Selective Service record, and even here there are a few problems. The government has destroyed full individual records; all letters between Wayne and his draft board have long since been turned into ashes in official government incinerators. The skeleton of Wayne's record, however, remains. When the war started, Marion Mitchell Morrison – Selective Service Serial Number 2815, Order Number 1619 – was classified. 3-A, "deferred for dependency reasons." A commutation of that classification was requested and granted on November 17, 1943. Local draft boards periodically reviewed all classifications, and depending on their needs the government changed some classifications. To maintain a deferment or obtain a different deferment, a person or his employer had to file an official request. After returning the initial Selective Service Questionnaire, Wayne never personally filed a deferment claim, but a series of claims were filed "by another." Although the records have been destroyed, Republic Pictures almost certainly filed the claims. After Republic's leading money earner Gene Autry enlisted in 1942, studio president Herbert Yates was determined to keep Wayne out of uniform and in front of the camera. Therefore, in April 1944 another deferment claim was filed and granted reclassifying Wayne 2-A, "deferred in support of national health, safety, or interest." A month later Wayne was once again reclassified. With the war in Europe and the Pacific reaching a critical stage, Duke received a I-A classification, "available for military service." This reclassification generated a series of new deferment claims, and on May 5, 1945, Wayne was once again classified 2-A. His last classification came after the war when he received a 4-A deferment on the basis of his age.

At any time during the war Wayne could have appealed his classification. At no time did he file an appeal. Always an active man, the war years were particularly frantic for Wayne. With his career bolting forward, he worked at four different studios and starred in thirteen pictures. In addition, he divorced his first wife, met and married his second wife, and led an active social life. When he was not working, the absence of a uniform gnawed into Wayne's self-respect and sense of manhood. It was then that he wrote Ford that "Barkus was ready." But then would come another movie, another delay, another link in a chain of delays that stretched from Pearl Harbor to Hiroshima.

Perhaps in his own mind his single-minded pursuit of his career meshed with his sense of patriotism. If so, Wayne was not the only person in Hollywood who expressed such beliefs. In March 1942, shortly after the premiere of *Reap the Wild Wind*, Wayne attended a luncheon for the Associated Motion Picture Advertisers. Cecil B. DeMille addressed the audience on the subject of the role Hollywood should play in the war. DeMille, his voice charged with moral urgency, remarked, "The job of motion pictures is to help bring home a full realization of the crisis and of the deadly peril that lurks in internal squabbles. Ours is the task of holding high and ever visible the values that everyone is fighting for. I don't mean flag waving, but giving the embattled world sharp glimpses of the way of life that we've got to hang on to in spite of everything." In DeMille's mind, the civilians who worked in the motion picture industry had a job and a duty every bit as important to the war effort as the American Marines fighting on Pacific islands or American sailors battling the Germans on the Atlantic. Victory demanded unity and dedication by all Americans at home and abroad, civilian and military.

The Roosevelt administration agreed with DeMille. Only weeks after the war began, F.D.R. announced that Hollywood had an important role to play in the war effort: "The American motion picture is one of our most effective media in informing and entertaining our citizens. The motion picture must remain free in so far as national security will permit." Unlike steel, automobiles, and other vital American industries, which were heavily controlled by the government during the war, the controls on the film industry were comparatively light. Although several of F.D.R.'s advisors counseled him to take over Hollywood production, he believed that the industry leaders would perform their duty better if they remained in charge. But the subtext of Roosevelt's message to Hollywood was clear. The studio heads could continue to make money, but their product had to serve the war effort. They had to combine propaganda within the entertainment. If they did not, then the government would take over the industry.

Washington's liaison with Hollywood was Lowell Mellett, a former editor of the *Washington Daily News* who had the good looks of an older Hollywood character actor. After considerable bureaucratic reorganization in June 1942, Mellett was placed in charge of the Bureau of Motion Pictures (BMP), which was nominally under the Domestic Branch of the Office of War Information (OWI). While Mellett, dubbed the "white rabbit" for his less than forceful character, administered the BMP from his Washington office, the bureau's Hollywood office was run by Nelson Poynter. A close friend of Mellett's as well as a newspaper man, the dark-haired, frail-looking Poynter had unassailable New Deal and interventionist credentials but lacked even basic knowledge of Hollywood and film making. Nevertheless, F.D.R. charged the team of Mellett and Poynter with making sure Hollywood produced the kind of pictures deemed important to the war effort.

If he were uncertain about the process of making pictures, Poynter was very explicit about what kind of films he expected Hollywood to produce. From his tiny office in

Hollywood, Poynter and his small staff compiled a blueprint to guide the motion picture industry's wartime behavior. Officially titled *The Government Informational Manual for the Motion Picture Industry*, it set down the official – and ideological – government line. The central question every producer, director, and writer should ask was "Will this picture help win the war?" Every film should contribute to that end by presenting America's effort and cause, its allies and friends, in the most generous possible terms. The manual emphasized that the United States was engaged in nothing less than "a people's war" to create a "new world" where want and fear were banished and freedom of religion and speech were a birthright. Social democratic and liberal internationalist in its intent, the manual was designed to move Hollywood toward its ideological position.

In practical terms, *The Government Informational Manual for the Motion Picture Industry* codified a long list of "dos" and "don'ts" for Hollywood. Whenever possible, for example, films should "show people making small sacrifices for victory" – "bringing their own sugar when invited out to dinner, carrying their own parcels when shopping, travelling on planes or trains with light luggage, uncomplainingly giving up seats to servicemen or others travelling on war priorities." Americans on the home front should be portrayed as happy, busy, productive, rationing, loving patriots, planting victory gardens, taking public transportation even when they could afford to drive, and generally pitching in to win the war. Heading the list of "don'ts" was disunity on the home front or the battlefront. America was not to be presented as divided by any racial, class, or gender issue. Scenes of strikes or labor conflict critical of labor were frowned upon; plots which suggested that the United States was anything less than a paradise for black Americans were verboten; and resorts to ethnic or religious bigotry were censored. Similarly, the allies of the United States had to be presented as paragons of national virtue. Hollywood was instructed to use its magic to manufacture a classless Britain, an efficient and incorruptible China, and a democratic Russia. Noting the irony of Hollywood's whitewash of the Soviet Union, *Variety* commented, "War has put Hollywood's traditional conception of the Muscovites through the wringer, and they have come out shaved, washed, sober, good to their families, Rotarians, brother Elks, and 33rd Degree Mason."

During the war, John Wayne starred in movies which fit comfortably within the parameters defined by Mellett, Poynter, and the BMP. To be sure, the producers of the Wayne films occasionally clashed with the BMP, but the conflicts were usually caused by the BMP's narrow ideological interpretation of individual scenes or insistence that a specific propaganda message appear in the film's dialogue. In a larger sense, *The Government Information Manual for the Motion Picture Industry* described an America – if not a world – that Wayne already held dear. Perhaps the physical world of Hollywood was closer to the ideal presented by the BMP than any other American community. The motion picture industry was populated by WASPs and immigrants, Catholics and Jews, whites and blacks, men and women. A communist might write a screenplay which a liberal would produce and a reactionary direct, but for a time all three would be unified by a common bond – the movie. In Hollywood some of the highest paid stars were women, and a few blacks – very few – earned incomes higher than Southern cotton planters. And nowhere in America was the Horatio Alger ideal of rags to riches so religiously enshrined. Hollywood was an industry that literally manufactured modern American folk heroes. It was America's "last frontier." It was the crossroads where luck, looks, and talent intersected. And in a strange way, it was the America described in the pages of the BMP official manual. Of course Wayne believed in its message. He was its message.

John Wayne's wartime movies portrayed the BMP's message even before the bureau was created and the manual written. During the first four months of 1942, as American forces experienced painful losses in the Pacific and the Atlantic, Wayne made two pictures – *The Spoilers* and *In Old California*. Both films have similar plots. *The Spoilers*, based on the Rex Beach novel, is set in Nome in 1900 during the Alaskan Gold Rush, centers on a claim-jumping scheme, and features a love triangle between Wayne, a society woman, and a dance-hall girl. During the course of the film, Wayne thwarts the claim-jumping scheme as he discovers that the society woman is heartless and the dance-hall girl has a heart as pure as a Klondike nugget. *In Old California* is set in Sacramento in 1848–1849 during the California gold rush, features a land grabbing scheme, and highlights a love triangle between Wayne, a society woman, and a dance-hall girl. By the end of the film, not only does Wayne foil the land grabbing scheme and discover that the society woman is heartless and the dance-hall girl has a heart as pure as a nugget from Sutter's Mill, but he also saves the entire region from a particularly nasty typhoid epidemic.

The message of both films was also similar: defend your property with every fiber of your being. Neither film expresses any sympathy for men who traffic in appeasement or legal niceties. In *The Spoilers* two prospectors announce in a saloon that they were "just working along kinda peaceful like" when at least twenty claim-jumpers forced them off their stake. What could we do, they ask. "Ya still have five fingers on your gun hand, ain't ya," comes the immediate reply. All at the bar nod in agreement to the sage advice. Even the sexual innuendo revolves around claim-jumping and force. Crooked gold commissioner Alexander McNamara (Randolph Scott) plans to jump both Roy Glennister's (John Wayne) Midas Gold Mine and his woman, Cherry Malotte (Marlene Dietrich). He tells Cherry that he might "move into [Glennister's] territory." "Could be tough going," Cherry cautions. "But worth it," McNamara replies. Glennister's use of brutal force defeats both forms of aggression. In one of the longest fist fights in film history, Glennister outlasts McNamara. Force – not the impotent and even dishonest representatives of the law – proves the only solution to aggression.

The same conclusion is expressed in *In Old California*. When the good but timid citizens of Sacramento are attacked, Tom Craig (John Wayne), the otherwise peace-loving town pharmacist, asks, "Doesn't anybody fight back around here?" "Angry men defending their home," he asserts, can never be defeated. And, of course, they do triumph. Lead by the forceful Craig, "the people" overcome both the land grabbers and the typhoid epidemic. For Americans embroiled in a war to prevent land-grabbing aggression, the message of *The Spoilers* and *In Old California* – both released in the dark month of May 1942 – reinforced official government statements about the causes of the war.

In Old California was little more than an inexpensive Republic formula picture. Without John Wayne, wrote the *New York Times* reviewer Bosley Crowther, the picture "would be down with the usual run of strays." *The Spoilers*, however, received favorable reviews. "The he men are back," noted the *New York Times*. "John Wayne is ... virile," commented *Variety*. "John Wayne is a valuable piece of property," was the judgment of the *Chicago Tribune*. The acting characteristics which Wayne had spent a decade perfecting – the sideways glance and smile at his female lead, the tight-lipped, shark-eyed stare at his evil rival – found worthy recipients in *The Spoilers*. Dietrich's seething sexuality and Scott's oily villainy contrasted nicely with Wayne's cocky masculinity.

Wayne was maturing as an actor, and he knew it. On the set he was more self-confident. He was occasionally rude and impatient with Scott, who took a more artistic approach to his craft than Wayne. Scott, a Southerner with courtly manner, disliked Duke. On and off the set of *The Spoilers*, Dietrich occupied Wayne's attentions. The affair which had begun when Wayne and Dietrich were starring together in *Seven Sinners* had not yet run its passionate course. On and off the set they were constantly together. They dined at Ciros, the Brown Derby, Mocambo, and the Trocadero, Hollywood's trendiest restaurants. They went to sporting events and on weekend hunting and fishing trips together. Dietrich "was the most intriguing woman I've ever known," Wayne later told his wife Pilar. She shared her bedroom and ideas with Duke. And this combination of sexual and intellectual stimulation bolstered Wayne's belief in himself.

At Republic Pictures, Herbert Yates was not as interested in Wayne's emotional and intellectual growth as in his burgeoning box office power. Paramount released *Reap the Wild Wind* in March 1942, and it opened in the first-run theaters and music halls throughout the country. Respected *New York Times* reviewer Bosley Crowther saw the Technicolor epic in Radio City Music Hall. Always a generous reviewer for DeMille's films, he was particularly lavish in his praise for *Reap the Wild Wind*. It was "the essence of all [DeMille's] experience, the apogee of his art and as jam-full a motion picture as has ever played two hours upon a screen. It definitely marks a DeMille stone," Crowther wrote. The review, and others like it, echoed like gold coins in Yates's mind. *Reap the Wild Wind* was a hit – reviewers compared it with that other breezy film, *Gone With the Wind* – and John Wayne was one of its stars, even if he was killed in the movie by a giant squid and therefore failed to win the heroine. And Wayne belonged to Yates and Republic. If Yates had been unimpressed by Duke's success in *Stagecoach* and *The Long Voyage Home*, he now fully understood the worth of his star attraction.

With profits and the war in mind, Yates put Wayne into his first war film. If it were not for the fact that *Flying Tigers* was a shameless rip off of *Only Angels Have Wings*, the film might be considered as the prototype for World War II combat films. It possessed everything but originality, a point that did not cause serious concern for an action-oriented studio like Republic. Howard Hawks' *Only Angels Have Wings* (1939) contained all the motifs that film scholar Robert B. Ray has labeled as basic to Hollywood's World War II combat films: "the male group directed by a strong leader, the outsider who must prove himself by courageous individual action, the necessity for stoicism in the face of danger and death, the premium placed on professionalism, and the threat posed by women."

Only Angels Have Wings centers on a group of pilots in a South American jungle contracted to deliver the mail over a range of dangerous, stalactite mountains of unearthly appearance. In this group of flying mercenaries is a brave leader called "Pappy" who emphasizes teamwork, a man branded as a coward who has to prove his courage to win acceptance, a woman who threatens to destroy the chummy fraternity atmosphere, and pilots who share a common Hemingwayesque code of life and language. They speak with their actions, resist expressing emotions, and demonstrate their dependency and even love in such nonverbal ways as asking for a cigarette or a match.

Flying Tigers contains all the same elements.

This time the mercenary pilots are part of Colonel Claire Lee Chennault's "American Volunteer Group," flying against the Japanese for China on the eve of Pearl Harbor. Once again, the leader stresses the value of teamwork and is called "Pappy" by his men. Once again, there is a suspected coward who must prove himself, a flamboyant individualist who on the surface seems to only care about himself, and a woman who threatens the harmony and effectiveness of the male unit. There is even the same language of cigarettes and matches and painful grimaces when talk turns to matters of the heart. The similarities of plot and structure are so striking that Ray commented that "Hawks should have sued for plagiarism."

But for all the similarities – and there were many – there was a major difference. *Flying Tigers* went into production shortly after Pearl Harbor during America's darkest months in the Pacific War and dealt with the most urgent topic in the world: the war. It was filmed from May to July 1942, months that saw the Japanese take Corregidor and the United States win the Battles of Coral Sea and Midway. *Flying Tigers* capitalized on the national mood. At a moment when the nation demanded a hero, Republic responded with John Wayne. At a time when the Americans longed for good news from the Pacific, *Flying Tigers* recounted the heroics of Chennault's "American Volunteer Group." During a crisis when the country wanted to believe the best of its allies and the worst of its enemies, the film presented Chinese straight from the pages of Pearl S. Buck's *The Good Earth* and automaton Japanese fresh from hell. In addition, the film touched the rawest of American nerves – Pearl Harbor. F.D.R.'s full war speech is replayed in the film, and the climactic scene occurs after the Japanese attack on Pearl Harbor.

The film was an ideal vehicle for Wayne. The role of the solid, quiet leader around whom all the action and all the other parts revolved played to Duke's strengths. Increasingly in his recent films he was developing a palpable screen presence. Without talking, often without moving, he dominated a scene. In one scene, for example, the pilots listen to F.D.R.'s war speech on the radio. Slowly the camera moves in for a close-up on Wayne, who stands silent, listening to the message, a cigarette in his left hand. During the entire message, Wayne never moves. His eyes and mouth do not change expression. The only movement is the smoke drifting upward from Wayne's unsmoked cigarette. At the end of the speech, he takes a deep breath and walks off screen. Roosevelt had said it all; Wayne could only have added a trite cliché. Duke played the scene with controlled passion and complete sincerity. It is a powerful scene which underscored Wayne's screen presence.

Republic believed *Flying Tigers* conveyed the message advocated by the Office of War Information's Bureau of Motion Pictures. The film emphasized teamwork. Woody Jason (John Carroll) tells his fellow mercenaries early in the film that he is in China for the $600 a month and the $500 bonus for every Japanese plane he shoots down: "This is not our home. It's not our fight. It's a business. And, boy, I hope business is good." "It's every man for himself, isn't it," he asks just before he bums a cigarette from one man and a match from another. But by the end of the film Woody sacrifices his life in a suicide mission to save Jim "Pappy" Gordon (John Wayne). After Pearl Harbor, he realizes that China is as important as his "home street." Scenes that emphasize the importance of non-flying personnel and mechanics similarly stress the themes of teamwork and cooperation. And if that did not provide enough propaganda content, *Flying Tigers* is filled with good-hearted, loyal Chinese and cold, ruthless Japanese.

Government officials, however, had mixed reactions to the film. Harry B. Price, a government consultant on China, noted that although the film was generally of a high caliber, it left "much to be desired from the standpoint of an adequate portrayal of our Allies, the Chinese." Like so many other Hollywood films, wrote Price, *Flying Tigers* presented the Chinese as "likable, but slightly ludicrous," and there is "little in the picture to suggest that the Chinese people are human beings just as varied and many sided in their natures as Americans." In addition, the film did not explore Chennault's tactical innovations. The Bureau of Motion Picture staffer who reviewed *Flying Tigers* agreed with Price's assessment. Marjorie Thorson complained that the film's glorification of individual heroics muted its theme of teamwork and cooperation, that the Chinese are presented as harmless and slightly incompetent people, and that the major issues of the war are not discussed. She notes that although there are Chinese nurses and doctors in the movie, only American nurses are shown changing bandages and "the final decision in any matter of a flier's health is left to the non-professional American squadron leader ... just being an American presumably qualifies him to make medical decisions over the head of the trained Chinese." Even worse, "no Chinese men are shown fighting." Altogether," she concluded, the "picture attempts a great deal more than it accomplishes."

Official complaints often demonstrated an ignorance both of film making and the war. Members of the "American Volunteer Group" charged that *Flying Tigers* was "unbelievably bad" because it contained several factual errors and employed two former members of the AVG as technical advisors who had been dishonorably discharged for being "suspected of perversion." Contentions that film makers distort history by focusing on the individual or the small group at the expense of historical reality reveal a deep misunderstanding of the industry. As for *Flying Tigers'* treatment of Chiang Kai-shek and the Chinese, blindly generous is the best description. Divided by warlordism and civil war, plagued by corruption and inefficiency, Chiang's Kuomintang government dismissed "aggressive action" against the Japanese before Pearl Harbor and after December 7, 1941, left any serious fighting to the United States. As one American military official noted in late 1941, "The general idea in the United States that China has fought Japan to a standstill and has had many glorious victories is a delusion." If *Flying Tigers'* portrayal of the Chinese is historically inaccurate, it was closer to reality than the line adopted by the BMP. And the assertion in the film that Americans provided the combat muscle in the war did reflect actual conditions.

The entire debate was irrelevant at Republic. Yates was not interested in the veracity of *Flying Tigers*; Republic was a bottom line studio, and its only concern was ticket sales. From its first preview, the film exceeded Republic's usual modest expectations. The *Hollywood Reporter* announced, "*Flying Tigers* marks an all-time production high for Republic. It is a smashing, stirring, significant film. It will be a record grosser in all engagements, and no theater in the land should hesitate about proudly showing it." *Variety* agreed: "In *Flying Tigers*, Republic has its best picture."

Even though the film was released late in the year, *Flying Tigers* became one of 1942's leading box office successes and the only picture in the top twenty not produced in one of the major studios.

No one at Republic had to search for the reason. It was John Wayne. If Republic executives needed confirmation, they found it in every major review. *Hollywood Reporter*: "John Wayne is at his peak ....."; *Variety*: "John Wayne matches his best performance ....."; *New York Times*: "Mr. Wayne is the sort of fellow who inspires confidence ..... ." Republic had a hit and a star. Yates was now convinced. So was the rest of the industry. And during the next three years of war, Wayne would reconfirm again and again his star status as his name alone came to guarantee box-office success.

Now more than ever, Yates was determined to keep Wayne. Shortly after the release of *Flying Tigers* the film's producer, Edmund Grainger, and director, David Miller, entered the armed service. Neither would make another picture until the late 1940s. Wayne believed that he too should enlist. Yates refused to release Wayne. The loss of Gene Autry, whose contract to make eight straight pictures for Republic had to be shelved when the singing cowboy enlisted in the Army air service, devastated Yates. He told Wayne that he would sue him for breach of contract if Duke enlisted. Furthermore, Yates announced, if Wayne enlisted he would make certain that Duke would never work for Republic or any other studio again. Although Yates's threat violated government policy – every person in uniform was guaranteed their civilian job once the war ended – Wayne did not press the issue. He feared poverty and unemployment, and perhaps more, he feared losing the status he had achieved and sinking into obscurity. Always a man haunted by the ghosts of his own insecurity, he stayed out of uniform, secure in his home at Republic.

Wayne's home was Republic, but his contract allowed him to make pictures for other studios. With the scarcity of leading men becoming more pressing every month, Duke was never in greater demand. It was an ideal situation for Wayne. He was a man who never made peace with inactivity. He loved his work and he hated the time between pictures. Mary St. John, who worked as Wayne's personal secretary for over twenty-five years, said that part of his problem was that he had no hobbies, nothing to do to fill the empty days. His daughter Aissa commented that he "was a slave to his energy." On location he always awoke by four thirty or five a.m., and even when he was not working on a picture he was up at dawn. "He never slept late. Ever," Aissa remembered. Once up, and wired by his morning coffee, he was ready for work, and when there was no work, he simply had to endure long periods of restless rest. And in 1942, such stretches were intolerable. His home life was empty, his marriage almost over, many of his friends in uniform. When he worked, his life had structure and purpose. When he was not working, he had time to mull over the irony that without serving a day in the armed forces he was becoming a World War II hero. It was during these periods that he penned "Barkus" letters to Ford.

Throughout 1942 Duke worked at a hectic pace. *The Spoilers* was shot in January and February, *In Old California* in March and April, and *Flying Tigers* in May, June, and July. While *Flying Tigers* was in post-production, Wayne moved on to other films. Between the end of July and September he starred in *Reunion in France* for MGM, and in September and October he starred in *Pittsburgh*, another Universal film with Marlene Dietrich and Randolph Scott. Both *Reunion in France* and *Pittsburgh* were released in December. In one year Wayne had made five films, all released that same year. In addition, *Lady for the Night* and *Reap the Wild Wind* had also premiered in 1942. There were few empty periods.

Like *Flying Tigers*, *Reunion in France* and *Pittsburgh* were war films. *Reunion in France*, however, was a peculiar sort of war film, the product of MGM's odd but predictable slant on life. MGM, noted Warner Brothers' executive Milton Spalding, "was a studio of white telephones." Quality – or at least the illusion of quality – mattered, and studio head Louis B. Mayer spent money to obtain it. As a result, at MGM nothing was what it seemed, everything was idealized. Reality never entered the MGM lot. Women especially had to look perfect. Cameramen "had to photograph the movie queens and make them look damn good," said MGM director George Cukor. If such MGM women as Greta Garbo, Joan Crawford, Jean Harlow, Norma Shearer, Lana Turner, Greer Garson, and Myrna Loy had individual styles, they all shared a common glamour and elegance. Regardless of the role they were called on to play, they always projected beauty and glamour.

After Pearl Harbor and the start of the war, Hollywood wags exchanged jokes about how the conflict would be portrayed at MGM. "The Japs may take California but they'll never get in to see Louis B. Mayer," quipped one wit. When an industry personality remarked that the United States needed a positive slogan that articulated what the country was fighting for, a less earnest listener replied, "Lana Turner." There was a truth in both jokes. As long as Louis B. Mayer called the shots at MGM, only movies that presented a highly stylized version of World War II would be made. And as long as Mayer approved all projects, MGM would fight a war to make the world safe for Lana.

Reunion in France brought America face to face with the stark glamour of war. The film centers on the trials and clothes of Michele de la Becque (Joan Crawford), a wealthy French socialite who loses her mansion and carefree life when the Germans invade France in 1940. With the swiftness of the Nazi blitzkrieg, her comfortable, insulated world is shattered. Her industrialist fiancé turns collaborationist, her wealth is confiscated, and she is forced to work for her former dressmaker – a job that pays poorly but allows her to remain the best-dressed woman in Paris – to pay her bills. Resisting Nazi domination, she befriends Pat Talbot (John Wayne), an American RAF Eagle Squadron flier who has been shot down and wounded behind enemy lines, and helps him escape. The film ends with Michele's reunion with her fiancé, who turns out to be a resistance fighter in collaborationist clothing. Far from helping Germany, the industrialist had been sending the Nazis faulty war materials to foil their efforts to dominate Europe.

The BMP reacted angrily to MGM's sanitized version of the war. "If there were ever a perfect argument for OWI reading of scripts before they are shot, this picture is it," wrote BMP staffer Marjorie Thorson in her review of the film. The picture failed the war effort on a number of counts. Count one: the film presented the Gestapo as "cruel, suspicious, and sadistic" but contained a favorable portrayal of all other Germans. The German military governor of Paris is depicted as a courtly, sweet, and charming older gentleman, an echo of a European aristocracy of decency and integrity. Furthermore, the German soldiers were disciplined and polite. Count two: the film suggests that any greedy, opportunistic collaborationist may really be an upstanding, patriotic member of the French Resistance. "It is a well known fact," the reviewer reported, "that many of the great French industrialists were pro-fascist long before the present war began; that they helped the Nazis conquer France; that they are now reaping the blood-stained rewards of their betrayal." Count three: the film shows nothing of the misery that the Germans have brought to the French people. MGM portrays a France that "falls with great elegance. Everyone we see is beautifully gowned, comfortably housed, and apparently well fed." Nazi occupation of Paris, the film insinuates, only means that the swastika hangs on the railroad stations and dumpy German women get the first crack at the latest Parisian fashions. Count four: the film misses the chance to contrast Nazi and democratic ideologies. Beyond the heroine saying that democracy is not dead and will live again in France, the film fails to explore the vital issue. In the context of the film, democracy suggests only that thin French women will someday reclaim their own fashions.

The serious charges led to the final verdict: *Reunion in France* "is a very poorly conceived picture. It misrepresents France, the French underground, the Nazis. Far more serious, it unintentionally gives aid and comfort to the enemy in the peace offensive that will surely, and perhaps soon, be launched." That was the crux of the matter. The Office of War Information predicted a German peace offensive in January 1943, and it believed *Reunion in France* would work to the benefit of the Germans. At the time when the Office of War Information was pressing the BMP to get producers to seriously discuss the issues of the war in their films, MGM suggested that the war was between fat German and thin French women with fashion hanging neatly pressed in the balance. Reviewing the film, the Office of War Information's Bureau of Intelligence commented, "the most striking feature of France as shown in the picture is a genius for designing and wearing women's clothes .... The preservation of this genius from the bad taste of the Germans is the big issue."

Newspaper reviews agreed with the government's assessment. One review commented that Joan Crawford behaves in the film "like nobody except an MGM movie star," and the *New York Times* found Wayne "totally unconvincing as an American flyer." Most reviews emphasized that the war was a serious affair and should not be used as an MGM costume drama. The reviews, however, did not kill *Reunion in France* at the box office. It was one of MGM's top fifteen grossers for 1943. Once again, Wayne had demonstrated his worth. The message in Hollywood was clear: even a bad Wayne film made money.

Wayne's last film of 1942 was his most ambitious attempt to aid the war effort. As originally. planned by agent Charles K. Feldman, *Pittsburgh*, like *The Spoilers*, was to be a vehicle for three of his clients – Dietrich, Wayne, and Scott. But it soon turned into a tribute to the industrial home front. Associate Producer Robert Fellows worked closely with the BMP to ensure that the film conveyed the government's exact propaganda message. It focuses on the Markham-Evans Coal Company, and its heroes are industrialists and workers in the coal and steel industries. In the film, Wayne plays the flawed hero Charles "Pittsburgh" Markham, a man who rose from the depths of a coal mine to the ownership of the Company. In a role that Wayne was to develop more fully in such films as *Red River, Hondo, The Sea Chase, The Searchers*, and *The Man Who Shot Liberty Valance*, he portrays a man obsessed, driven by his own inner demons. Pittsburgh willingly uses anything and anyone to acquire power. On his way to the top, he abandons the woman who loves him (Marlene Dietrich) and his trusted partner (Randolph Scott). But the same ruthlessness that allowed him to rise in the coal business leads to his downfall, causing him to lose his wife, his company, and his self-worth.

World War II provides a rebirth for Pittsburgh. Once again, he rises from the mines to manage the company. Only this time he works for his nation, not himself. He is redeemed by submerging his own ego into his nation's crusade for a better world.

When Nelson Poynter and his BMP staff previewed *Pittsburgh* at Universal Studios on December 1, 1942, they were delighted. The picture was a preachy epic of coal and steel that appealed to the BMP's wordy sense of effective propaganda. It contained long semi-documentary sections of the coal and steel industries, and it rarely said anything visually that could be put into flat dialogue. But there was no mistaking its message: every American – soldier and industrial worker alike – can and should contribute to the war effort; victory would only result if "all the people" work and fight as one. The BMP applauded the results. "*Pittsburgh* succeeds in making many excellent contributions to the war information program," noted the BMP review of the film. In fact, much of the dialogue "appears to have been culled directly from the OWI Manual of Information for the picture industry ...." Nevertheless, the picture was "highly commended for an earnest and very successful contribution to the war effort." As far as the BMP was concerned, *Pittsburgh* was "one of the best pictures to emerge to date dealing with our vital production front ...."

Poynter, who had worked so closely with Bob Fellows on *Pittsburgh*, thought he had scored a real coup. Often ignored by the more important producers, Poynter actually believed that *Pittsburgh* was a good film and that his contributions to the film had been significant. As soon as he saw the final cut, he shot off a series of letters complimenting everyone involved with the movie including himself. "Magnificent .... It shows what can be done if the creative unit sets out to help interpret the war and at the same time put on a helluva good show," he wrote Fellows, Faldman, and several Universal executives. Poynter wrote Lowell Mellett, his BMP superior in Washington, telling him to see *Pittsburgh* and to take other Office of War Information and War Production Board people with him.

Mellett went, but he did not share Poynter's enthusiasm. "The propaganda sticks out disturbingly," Mellett responded to Poynter. Most newspaper reviewers shared Mellett's opinion. "This business of instructing and informing intrudes at times at the expense of the entertaining," noted the *Motion Picture Herald*, but the film "yields realistic results when not hampered by dialogue freighted with purpose." From West Coast to East, the reviews were the same. *Pittsburgh* was not exactly a bad film, but it was certainly "not in the inspired class," or, more to the point, it was "routine entertainment at best." In a New York theater, a cartoon entitled *Point Rationing*, which explained the use of the new rationing book, drew a more positive review than *Pittsburgh*.

The critical and financial failures of *Pittsburgh* reinforced the belief in Hollywood that if F.D.R. and alphabet agencies could get America out of the Depression, they certainly could not make a hit movie. The resistance against Poynter and his staff that was present in the industry from the beginning stiffened even more in the months after the release of *Pittsburgh*. Hollywood was right. The BMP was not film literate. Both Mellett and Poynter were newspaper men who thought in terms of words. They wanted dialogue that sounded like it was straight off an editorial page. As far as they were concerned, if a movie did not use dialogue to present the government's message, then the message was not delivered. They had difficulty thinking visually. The major studio executives realized the government approach toward propaganda would mean death at the box office. They were willing to make propaganda pictures that served the interest of the country, but they wanted to make them in their own way.

No film better demonstrates Washington's lack of understanding of movies than *Casablanca*. The classic film ran into trouble in Washington. Various sections of the Office of War Information were disappointed by the movie. Most were upset with Rick's (Humphrey Bogart's) cynicism. Others were dissatisfied with the treatment of the French, the Germans, and the North Africans And the last line – "This could be the beginning of a beautiful friendship" – well, as far as the OWI was concerned, it said nothing about the Atlantic Charter or why the United Nations were fighting Fascism. As film historians Gregory D. Black and Clayton R. Koppes observed, Washington "Was not content to let meaning emerge from the interaction of the characters and the overall story line ... it would have preferred a two-paragraph sermonette explaining Nazi aggression and the justice of the Allied cause."

The battle between Washington and Hollywood would drag into 1943 and would last in a more limited way for the rest of the war. It was a war fought by studio heads and producers, not actors, and as in the larger war, Wayne avoided the conflict. But his hectic activity of 1942 had begun to undermine his health. On January 21, 1943, he collapsed on a movie set and was rushed to the hospital. Doctors told him he had influenza and needed rest. That was the bad news. The good news was that his collapse was reported in the *New York Times*. Duke was a star.

13

The Woman's Film
When Women Wept

Jeanine Basinger

During the 1930s and 1940s, when women dominated the moviegoing audience, many of Hollywood's most popular movies dealt with key issues in women's personal lives. Known as the "woman's film," and featuring such stars as Joan Crawford, Bette Davis, and Barbara Stanwyck, these movies looked at love triangles, unwed motherhood, illicit affairs, and the tangled relations between mothers and daughters. Often criticized for reinforcing conventional values – above all, the notion that women could only find happiness in love, marriage, and motherhood – these highly moralistic, melodramatic films, Jeanine Basinger argues, were not simply escapist fantasies. They were subtly subversive. If, on the one hand, these films implied that a woman could not combine a career and a happy family life, they also offered women a glimpse of a world outside the home, where they did not sacrifice their independence for marriage, housekeeping, and childrearing. Not only did these pictures depict women with successful careers – as journalists, pilots, car company presidents, and restaurateurs – but they also offered distinctly unflattering portraits of weak-willed, untrustworthy, easily manipulable men; neglectful, work-obsessed husbands; and heartless abusers who toy with and discard women. Far from being simply schlock or instruments of female oppression, these films voiced women's anger and frustration and portrayed a world in which women's lives and emotions occupied center stage.

What suffering! What sighing! What kitsch! The woman's film, the domain of triangles and unwed mothers and powerful females, has passed away. But the genre intrigues again for what it reveals about the frustrations of women a few decades back.

Whatever happened to Stella Dallas? And Kitty Foyle? Or Alice Adams, Lydia Bailey, Vergie Winters, Nora Prentiss, Lilly Turner, Martha Ivers, Sadie McKee, Thelma Jordan, Mildred Pierce, Flaxy Martin, Harriet Craig, Claudell Inglish, Serena Blandish, and countless others? Those ladies all seem to have left town, and all we know for sure is that Alice doesn't live here any more. Whatever happened to all those put-upon females from Hollywood's past? In short, whatever happened to the "women's film"?

Unlike such popular Hollywood genres as the gangster film, screwball comedy, or Western, the woman's film is not often revived in museums or college classrooms. The average audience's idea of it has been shaped by spoofs on television and send-ups in the theater. From the vantage point of satire, women's films are a series of inter-changeable productions called *Imogene Davis* or *Maude Crawford* or *Irene Baker* or *Loretta Lewis* – the kind of films that were shot in three weeks on leftover sets.

On that basis, it's not hard to create your own "woman's film" skit. Imagine the satiric scenario for *Lurene Dishe*: "She was born in a town too small to hold her and clawed her way to the big town." Or, "She might be bad or she might be good, but you'll think she's good when she's bad." The story opens up in a shabby roadside diner. (If a diner set is not available, the scene could shift to a dime store. Or a mani-cure parlor. Or a burlesque house.)

Though the woman's film has always been an easy target for satire, the films them-selves were hardly ever a laughing matter. (They *might* be comedies, in which case they would star Rosalind Russell, but there would be a bitter edge to the story.) It's fair to say that many women's films were superficial, sentimental, badly made, and just plain awful, but they were no more so than any other genre. The best of the gangster films justify the worst of them, and this is true of the woman's film, also. Most were not only well made and directed, but solidly written, ambitious, and even profound in their observations. The women's films were almost always lavishly produced. Today they are intriguing for what they reveal about women's roles in society, and about how women with brains and drives tried to find a position in a world which decreed that they should remain powerless. Although the worst of the women's films might be dubbed soap opera, the best of them form a hard core of fine melodrama. They deserved to be revived and respected, and, like other genres, taken on their own terms.

What really was the woman's film? Basically, it was a film in which the woman, not the man, was the central figure. The story line concerns her struggle to sort out the problems of her life. Love versus career. Bad love versus good love. Love versus duty. Love versus the demands of motherhood.

Like other genres, the woman's film had its own conventions, familiar plot con-structions, recurring characters, and, obviously, the woman. She was either evil or good. If she was evil, she did awful things to other people, shoved them off cliffs, poisoned their mushrooms, or shot them in the head. In addition, the evil woman was a husband stealer, not above running off with her sister's man. She was naughty because she manipulated men instead of accepting them as her master. It was usually explained that she was just "born that way," but whatever her motivations, she was bad news. The good, on the other hand, was good. But she wasn't that good. How else could there be a story?

In the woman's films, there was also the man. Men in pictures about women tended to be a lackluster group, often weak, shallow, unreliable, caddish. They gambled, drank, and ran off with other women (usually the evil ones who would eventually poison their mushrooms). Their lack of strength was compensated for by the woman's abundance of it. Over and over again, the woman's film established the dilemma of the strong woman tied down to a weak man who wrecked her life as he destroyed his own. The hope for women in these films was seldom liberation, but to meet *the better man* and find him to be strong, reliable, honest, even fatherly.

Joan Crawford's *Mannequin* (1938) illustrates this right man–wrong man concept in a light–dark motif common to the genre. Crawford is a factory worker who lives in the slums, and dreams of a better life. She marries her handsome lover, played by Alan Curtis, whose weakness is indicated by his dilettantish mustache. While she struggles

Figure 10 *Mildred Pierce* (1945). Warner Bros. Directed by Michael Curtiz. Courtesy of Jerry Murbach, www.doctormacro.info.

to make their living, he lounges around and gets into trouble. They seem to live eternally in shadows, and Crawford's mother warns her it will always be this way as the two of them peel potatoes over a hot stove on a stifling summer night. Later, Crawford ditches Curtis and meets Spencer Tracy, who is not only kind and fatherly, but also lonely and loaded. They are always seen in sunlight, and Crawford begins wearing peasant clothes and humming around the house. But Crawford is a stronger presence on the screen than Spencer Tracy, and when the crisis comes, it is *she* who saves *him* from financial disaster by her generosity and wit. They end up in each other's arms, but it is really Joan Crawford who is the hero.

Other familiar characters in the genre included, besides the woman and the man, the *other* woman and the *other* man. There was also a warped family circle, with fathers, mothers, brothers, sisters, cousins, uncles, aunts – all locked into living with each other under severe duress. The family circle provided the leading lady with a group of critics who hung on the sidelines and predicted disasters which surely did occur. There were children, of course, hers, his, theirs, and nobody's. And, for the woman, there usually was a reliable friend, probably an older woman who warned the heroine of what was in store for her.

One of the most interesting characters indigenous to the genre was the sexless male. Usually an older man, possibly European, he offered the woman security and luxury (but not necessarily marriage). It would be understood that he did not require sex from her. For the unhappy wife in the audience, this situation offered the dream life of being cared for in the highest style with nothing asked for in return. Metaphorically, the character might stand for a hidden desire for liberation. Riches without sexual enslavement. Or perhaps he represented the parental figure in disguise, reflecting some women's desire to remain well-cared-for little girls. Hence, the no sex pattern.

The plot conventions of these films worked many twists, ramifications, convolutions, and reversals on several basic themes: the triangle, the unwed mother (or sacrificial mother), the evil unleashed, the rise to power.

The triangle provided many plot variations. The heroine could love two men, one good for her and one bad. A steady, reliable suitor usually waited in the wings for the leading lady. Perhaps he represented for the women in the audience the man they felt they should have married, the guy who now owned the box factory where their husband worked.

Sometimes two women loved the same man, and he would be unable to make up his mind between them. They might be sisters, or even, as in *The Dark Mirror* and *A Stolen Life*, twin sisters at that. How to choose between the two women who were identical was indeed a problem. Many women's films presented the triangle in which the heroine was the woman on the outside, doomed to watching the man she loved be mistreated by her best friend. Bette Davis found herself more than once living outside of happiness, as in *The Old Maid*, *Old Acquaintance*, or *Jezebel*.

With a lifetime of taking in washing or sewing facing them, women loved stories about triangles and how to resolve them. Particularly triangles like the one in *Housewife*, in which Ann Dvorak, in aprons, outwits Bette Davis, in mink, for the affections of her own husband, George Brent. One thirties title summed it up … *Wife vs. Secretary*.

Unwed mother pictures were almost as popular. Since a large part of any woman's life was the acceptance of the role of mother, films jerked tears mercilessly over the fate of the mother of an illegitimate child. Or the mother forced to give up her child. Or the mother whose child, legal or otherwise, dies. Several generations wept over the hackneyed plot of *Madame X*, made in 1915, and remade successfully in 1920, 1929, 1937, 1960, and 1966.

Sympathetic explanations were always offered for unwed motherhood. Typically the woman was yearning for *more* out of her life, when a man would come along who seemed to offer just that. In *To Each His Own* (1946), Olivia de Havilland is a small-town beauty who dreams of excitement. A barnstorming pilot comes to town, and it turns out that flying too high with some guy in the sky is her idea of something to do. The pilot is soon killed in World War I, leaving de Havilland in a familiar predicament. De Havilland is sympathetic because she's lovely, intelligent, and misled by her own romantic dreams. Therefore, she is readily accepted and understood by the women in the audience. Besides, she spends the rest of her life both getting rich *and* suffering over having her child raised by others. This enabled the audience to envy her, judge her, and pity her all in one sitting.

The evil-unleashed plot allowed women a release for whatever pent-up rage or desire for power they felt. Many stars played evil women with no loss of their own popularity because a relationship was established between onscreen anger that unleashed the evil and the anger the audience felt. These films constituted a vicarious revolution for women who could not or would not revolt in life.

The rise-to-power film constituted the core of women's films. As Molly Haskell has pointed out, many Hollywood films were constructed around mature, intelligent actresses. Since the entire story of the film concerned them, they had to *do* something to keep the story moving. They couldn't just stand there and wear clothes. So they went to work. They ran businesses and wrote books. They became famous concert pianists and mayors of cities. They were newspaper women, lawyers, doctors, detectives. They painted, sculpted, sang and danced. They worked in factories and waited on tables. They flew airplanes and drove fast cars. Above all, they earned their own livings; they rose to power.

And then they paid for it. The true woman's film has to be dark, laced with moods, complexities, and no easy happy endings. Sometimes it has no happy ending at all. The plot usually reflected the conventional wisdom that the woman who rose to power either economic or sexual, was going to be an unhappy woman. Feminists today love to dispute the rise-to-power film and the ambivalence of the typical ending, in which the woman is destroyed or gives it all up and returns to home and hearth, or embraces true love. Did the message of the last five minutes of the film outweigh the eighty-five minutes that went before, in which the woman proved she could do more than be a housewife?

The early audiences felt reassured by the endings in which the women they admired on screen told them that what they had was better than what they had just enjoyed watching. Those audiences knew their fate. The woman's film allowed them both escape from their trap and a reassurance that the trap was really what they should settle for. But the actresses who appeared in these films had not settled for that trap.

Joan Crawford, Bette Davis, Rosalind Russell, Barbara Stanwyck, Ginger Rogers, Loretta Young, Irene Dunne. Most of them understood the issues raised in these films. With few exceptions, they had pulled themselves up from nowhere to become film stars, without benefit of education, family connections, money, or a man to lean on.

In the thirties, these stars were remarkably frank when they talked in interviews about their hard-won careers. They stood beside their swimming pools and looked very satisfied, and although the magazines liked to play up the stars' tragedies such as floundering marriages and thwarted desires for motherhood, who really thought they were hurting? They either did not have children at all, had them in small numbers, late in life, or had plenty of help to raise the ones they did have. Helen Twelvetrees flatly told a reporter, "Today motherhood is not enough." Joan Blondell gave an interview on the set to talk "about her new baby," who was, significantly, back home with a nurse. Ginger Rogers offered, "I'd love to have a baby. Of course I could, naturally, adopt one. I read in recent article that a certain star's last baby cost her exactly $150,000 – because of her having to be out of production for so long. Time is very valuable to a movie star ...." (Rogers, in fact, never had or adopted a child.) Whatever happened, they did not give up their work for marriage and motherhood. If the personal lives of the stars of the woman's film were turned into screenplays, the last five minutes would remain true to the other 85: the stars rose to power – and asked for increases.

At its best, the woman's film contradicts itself as it unfolds. *Mildred Pierce* hints openly to its audience that a life of dependency on men was a lousy deal, even if it seems to sell that dependency. Joan Crawford's performance in *Mildred Pierce* is an intense, restrained piece of acting that reflects an intelligent woman's desperation. Mildred, no matter how much she glamorizes herself, will always feel like a waitress deep inside. She is so angry it takes all her energy just to keep a grip on herself. As her penance for having ended up a tycoon, she overindulges her only daughter.

The cold glitter laid over the sets and costumes of *Mildred Pierce* gives the audience a sense of the success dream turned to stone. It is a downbeat film in which the meant-to-be-happy ending is unconvincing, as Mildred walks out into the morning sunshine with her first husband. He, after all, is the no-account jerk she had to start baking pies to support in the first place. Poor Mildred, damp and desperate on a foggy night, with not much to look forward to except selling her pies and cakes. Even if she doesn't have to bake them herself any more, what kind of progress has she made?

Another Crawford picture, *Daisy Kenyon*, is the story of three people (the triangle motif) who are using each other and being used. Crawford plays an unmarried career woman having an affair with a married man. In her precarious situation, she is hanging on as best she can, fighting for her identity. ("I have to fight for everything. Fight to stay happy. I've just got my work, and you've even messed that up," she tells her lover.) The lover, played superbly by Dana Andrews, is the successful American male. But in his personal life, his lack of success is quickly established in searing quarrels both with Crawford and with his wife at home.

The third character in the *Daisy Kenyon* triangle, played by Henry Fonda, is the man Daisy marries in an attempt to free herself from Andrews. He is a rootless, confused army veteran who marries her to satisfy his own needs. "You're using me," Daisy accuses. "Yes," he replies, "aren't you using me?"

Daisy Kenyon takes the conventions of the woman's picture and lays their hidden meanings bare. Andrews's character is the sort of man women often dream of marrying – wildly successful in business, rich and powerful, a man who provides his wife with the sort of lifestyle that American mothers have long promised their daughters if they played their cards right. Yet, in the dream, the man is tenderhearted and loving. He remembers birthdays and brings home flowers and candy to cheer up the little woman after Junior has fallen out of the car on his head. Needless to say, he loves his kids and spends plenty of time with them, at the circus, baseball games, boy scouts, and shopping trips to buy things for mom.

In *Daisy Kenyon* – no dream film – the successful businessman is seen for what he often really is, ruthless, unscrupulous, manipulative, and totally uninterested in his wife and kids. "You see them just five minutes a day," wails Andrews's wife, "just enough to spoil them." In some women's pictures, the gentle poetic man is offered as a poorer, though more suitable, alternative to the powerful businessman, but Fonda instead is saddled with his own problems. Daisy herself is confused about what she wants out of life. She just hangs on grimly, and finally is forced to choose between the two men.

Women's films presented women characters who struggled to get on their own two feet. Then when they got on them, they struggled to forge ahead. And struggled some more to get on top. After they got on top, they struggled with themselves and their guilts. Finally, society overcame them. They went down struggling, found "true love," and prepared to resume life's struggle in a state that was acceptable to society.

But today's women no longer have to accept a lifestyle as preordained by the rules of the game. The right of women to struggle has been established. The myth has been penetrated. The woman's film of the thirties and forties has died out, is seldom revived, and has become a subject for television variety show mockery.

With this change in society, will a new kind of "woman's film" emerge? More films featuring stories about women are scheduled to be released this year [1977] than at any other time in the past decade. Being prepared for release are *Julia*, based on Lillian Hellman's account of one woman shielding another from Nazi persecution; *Looking for Mr. Goodbar*, featuring Diane Keaton in the greatest female self-destruction role since *Anna Karenina*; and *The Turning Point*, in which Anne Bancroft and Shirley MacLaine play two aging ballerinas. Already reaping critical success is Robert Altman's *Three Women*, based on "a dream" – Robert Altman's dream, that is – and presenting three women whose identities merge and blur.

The new woman's film, if there is to be such a thing, will have to deal with life from a woman's perspective. It will have to take into account the sudden opportunities and problems that are facing many women and that are causing some to question who and what they are. The huge mass of women, however, aren't likely to identify their own lives with those of liberated women on the screen. But that won't matter. What they can identify with – or at least learn from – will be the struggle of the new woman not to be somebody in a man's world but, instead, to be herself.

14

Primary Sources

US Senate Subcommittee Hearings on Motion Picture and Radio Propaganda, 1941

In 1941, a US Senate subcommittee held hearings to investigate charges that the motion picture industry was manipulating movies in an effort to drag America into war in Europe. The investigation came to an abrupt end with the Japanese attack on Pearl Harbor.

[Senator Gerald Nye]
At the outset, I should like to point out that no contention can validly be raised that any investigation of propaganda in the movies, amounts to censorship of freedom of speech or freedom of the press. The fact is, and the law is, that the movies are not part of the press of this country, and are not protected by the first amendment to our Constitution ....

I entertain no desire for moving-picture censorship .... I do hope, however, that the industry will largely recognize the obligation it owes our country and its people ....

Mr. Chairman, I am sure that you and members of your committee are quite aware of the determined effort that has been put forth to convey to the public that the investigation asked is the result of a desire to serve the un-American, narrow cause of anti-Semitism ....

I bitterly resist, Mr. Chairman, this effort to misrepresent our purpose and to prejudice the public mind and your mind by dragging this racial issue to the front. I will not consent to its being used to cover the tracks of those who have been pushing our country on the way to war with their propaganda intended to inflame the American mind with hatred for one foreign cause and magnified respect and glorification for another foreign cause, until we shall come to feel that wars elsewhere in the world are really after all our wars ....

Those primarily responsible for the propaganda pictures are born abroad. They came to our land and took citizenship here entertaining violent animosities toward certain causes abroad. Quite natural is their feeling and desire to aid those who are at war against the causes which so naturally antagonize them. If they lose sight of what some Americans might call the first interests of America in times like these, I can excuse them. But their prejudices by no means necessitate our closing our eyes to these interests and refraining from any undertaking to correct their error ....

If the anti-Semitic issue is now raised for the moment, it is raised by those of the Jewish faith ... not by me, not by this committee ....

[Senator D. Worth Clark]
[The motion picture studios] declare that this [investigation] is an attempt to restrain the right of the motion-picture screen to present the problems of contemporary life without restraint from the Government ....

I am willing and eager to meet these gentlemen on that ground. There are a great many naive souls who think that speech is free so long as political authority, particularly the Government, does not shackle it. They overlook the fact that there can be such a thing, particularly in our day, as the denial of speech when one individual or small collection of individuals can band together and get control of the instruments of speech and deny them to everybody but themselves ....

Today a hitherto unknown politician or newspaper columnist can go on the radio and in one night talk to four, five, or ten million people ....

It comes down to this: That the man who owns that machine now exercises over the freedom of discussion a power which no government could ever exercise. To interfere with a man's speech the Government has to pass oppressive laws, organize a ruthless constabulary, must hound men and prosecute them and put them in jail and incur the difficulties of opposition and the freedom of revolution. But the man who owns the radio machine can cut off from discussion those who disagree with him by the simple expedient of saying "No." And who is this man? He is not a public official; he is not elected to office; he is not an authorized public censor; he is not chosen by the people. He is just a businessman who by virtue of his acquisitive talents has gotten possession of this little microphone.

Now, the same thing is true of the moving-picture machine, save that the moving-picture machine is even more powerful than the microphone. Any man or any group of men who can get control of the screen can reach every week in this country an audience of 80,000,000 people. If there is a great debate before the Nation involving its economic life or even its liberties, no man can get a syllable in the sound pictures save by the grace of the men who control the sound pictures. And I here formally and deliberately charge that a handful of men have gotten possession of both the radio microphone and the moving-picture screen, beside which all other forms of discussion are antique and feeble, and that men and women in America discussing the great problems of America can use these machines or not only by the grace of this small oligarchy ....

There are 17,000 moving-picture theaters in the United States. They do not belong to a handful of men, of course, but the pictures that appear on the screens of those theaters are produced by a handful of men and that handful of men can open or close those 17,000 theaters to ideas at their sweet will. They hold the power of life and death over those motion-picture houses because by their block-booking system, blind-selling system, and other devices they can close almost any house that they please on any day and at any time.

At the present time they have opened those 17,000 theaters to the idea of war, to the glorification of war, to the glorification of England's imperialism, to the hatred of the people of Germany and now of France, to the hatred of those in America who disagree with them. Does anyone see a pictorial representation of life in Russia under "Bloody Joe" Stalin? They do not. In other words, they are turning these 17,000 theaters into 17,000 daily and nightly mass meetings for war ....

Dozens of pictures, great features – costing some of them hundreds of thousands of dollars, some of them millions of dollars – are used to infect the minds of their audiences with hatred, to inflame them, to arouse their emotions, and make them clamor for war. And not one word on the side of the argument against war is heard .... Unless they are restrained, unless the people of this country are warned about them, they will plunge the country into war ....

[Harry M. Warner, President of Warner Brothers Pictures, Inc.]
The charges against my company and myself are untrue ....

I am opposed to nazi-ism. I abhor and detest every principle and practice of the Nazi movement. To me, nazi-ism typifies the very opposite of the kind of life every decent man, woman, and child wants to live. I believe nazi-ism is a world revolution whose ultimate objective is to destroy our democracy, wipe out all religion, and enslave our people – just as Germany has destroyed and enslaved Poland, Belgium, Holland, France, and all the other countries. I am ready to give myself and all my personal resources to aid in the defeat of the Nazi menace to the American people ....

Shortly after Hitler came to power in Germany I became convinced that Hitlerism was an evil force designed to destroy free people, whether they were Catholics, Protestants, or Jews. I claim no credit as a prophet. Many appraised the Nazis in their true role, from the very day of Hitler's rise to power.

I have always been in accord with President Roosevelt's foreign policy. In September 1939, when the Second World War began, I believed, and I believe today, that the world struggle for freedom was in its final stage. I said publicly then, and I say today, that the freedom which this country fought England to obtain, we may have to fight with England to retain.

I am unequivocally in favor of giving England and her allies all supplies which our country can spare. I also support the President's doctrine of freedom of the seas, as recently explained to the public by him.

Frankly, I am not certain whether or not this country should enter the war in its own defense at the present time. The President knows the world situation and our country's problems better than any other man. I would follow his recommendation concerning a declaration of war.

If Hitler should be the victor abroad, the United States would be faced with a Nazi-dominated world. I believe – and I am sure that the subcommittee shares my feeling – that this would be a catastrophe for our country. I want to avoid such a catastrophe, as I know you do.

I have given my views to you frankly and honestly. They reduce themselves to my previous statement: I am opposed to nazi-ism. I abhor and detest every principle and practice of the Nazi movement. I am not alone in feeling this. I am sure that the overwhelming majority of our people and our Congress share the same views.

While I am opposed to nazi-ism, I deny that the pictures produced by my company are "propaganda," as has been alleged. Senator Nye has said that our picture *Sergeant York* is designed to create war hysteria. Senator Clark has added *Confessions of a Nazi Spy* to the isolationist blacklist. John T. Flynn, in turn, has added *Underground*. These witnesses have not seen these pictures, so I cannot imagine how they can judge them. On the other hand, millions of average citizens have paid to see these pictures. They have enjoyed wide popularity and have been profitable to our company. In short, these pictures have been judged by the public and the judgment has been favorable.

Sergeant York is a factual portrait of the life of one of the great heroes of the last war. If that is propaganda, we plead guilty. *Confessions of a Nazi Spy* is a factual portrayal of a Nazi spy ring that actually operated in New York City. If that is propaganda, we plead guilty.

So it is with each of our pictures dealing with the world situation or with the national defense. These pictures are prepared on the basis of factual happenings and they were not twisted to serve any ulterior purpose.

In truth, the only sin of which Warner Bros. is guilty is that of accurately recording on the screen the world as it is or as it has been. Unfortunately, we cannot change the facts in the world today ....

I have no apology to make to the committee for the fact that for many years Warner Bros. has been attempting to record history in the making. We discovered early in our career that our patrons wanted to see accurate stories of the world in which they lived. I know that I have shown to the satisfaction of the impartial observer that Warner Bros., long before there was a Nazi Germany, had been making pictures on topical subjects. It was only natural, therefore, with the new political movement, however horrible it may be, that we should make some pictures concerning the Nazis. It was equally logical that we should produce motion pictures concerning national defense ....

If Warner Bros. had produced no pictures concerning the Nazi movement, our public would have had good reason to criticize. We would have been living in a dream world. Today 70 percent of the nonfiction books published deal with the Nazi menace. Today 10 percent of the fiction novels are anti-Nazi in theme. Today 10 percent of all material submitted to us for consideration is anti-Nazi in character. Today the newspapers and radio devote a good portion of their facilities to describing nazi-ism. Today there is a war involving all hemispheres except our own and touching the lives of all of us ....

Part IV
Postwar Hollywood

Introduction
Double Indemnity *and Film Noir*

During the mid-1940s a new film genre appeared that would exert enormous influence on the shape of postwar American movies. Called "film noir" by French critics, this genre depicted a disturbing world – a world of treachery, entrapment, mistaken identity, psychopathology, greed, lust, betrayal, and finally murder. Dimly lit, set in nightmarish locations, these films featured a cast of amoral or corrupt characters: drifters, patsies, cold-blooded femmes fatales, and sinister widows. Film noir drew upon the characters and plots of the gangster movies and hard-boiled detective fiction of the 1930s. But in style and tone, these films were unlike anything Hollywood had ever produced before. They were much more cynical and pessimistic than classical Hollywood films, their characters were more corrupt, their tone much more fatalistic. It was no wonder that French critics used the term "noir" to describe their tone.

Nor was it an accident that many of these films were directed by European émigrés who had fled Hitler's Germany, among them Fritz Lang, Otto Preminger, and Billy Wilder. Well versed in the traditions of German expressionist filmmaking, these directors brought a new visual style to the American screen, characterized by looming shadows, oblique camera angles, and stark contrasts of darkness and light. This style also reflected wartime necessity, which limited availability of bright set lighting. Along with their keen visual sense, these directors brought a host of stylistic innovations such as voiceover narration, interior monologues, and flashbacks. The profound sense of alienation, pessimism, and paranoia in their films clearly gave tangible expression to their awareness of the horrors of European fascism.

The appeal of film noir to the mass audience indicates that these directors were also able to tap into broader cultural concerns. Film noir was much more realistic than the films of the Depression era. The public had grown increasingly weary of movies that sought to raise morale and reinforce traditional values. It craved a more gritty view of American society. Film noir offered such realism. Set in everyday locations, it offered an honest, if harsh, view of American life, a view that captured the seedy, sleazy

Figure 11 *Double Indemnity* (1944). Paramount Pictures. Directed by Billy Wilder. Courtesy of Jerry Murbach, www.doctormacro.info.

underside of life. Film noir also gave symbolic expression to a deep current of anxiety and apprehensions that pervaded American society during World War II and the early postwar era. Outwardly optimistic, American society was in fact beset by profound fears. Film noir belonged to a time of public confusion in an unsettled world: the disorientation of returning GIs, insecurity about the future, radical redefinitions in women's roles, cold war paranoia, and fears of nuclear annihilation.

Billy Wilder's 1944 classic *Double Indemnity* epitomizes what is meant by film noir. The film tells the story of Phyllis Dietrichson (Barbara Stanwyck), a scheming, seductive platinum blond, who lures a weak-willed insurance salesman, Walter Neff (Fred MacMurray) into a scheme to murder her husband and collect on the double indemnity clause in his life insurance policy. Based on James M. Cain's tawdry novella, the story is set along the southern California coast, a restless, rootless, unstable society. It was, in film critic Richard Schickel's words, a land of "gas stations and roadside restaurants ... small hopes and pinched dreams, which modest as they were, often enough ended in foreclosure." This was a world of strangers, where old customs had been disrupted and traditional values subverted, and egos set free from traditional moorings. Despite the bright California sun, it is a place of hopelessness and death.

Double Indemnity helped establish many of the themes and stylistic devices that characterized many of the most influential postwar films. The city is depicted – not as an escape from small-town provinciality or as an oasis of affluence where Fred Astaire and Ginger Rogers put on the Ritz – but as a place of menace, malevolence, and temptation. Gender relations are represented as highly fraught: passionate and seductive, yet often adversarial and antagonistic. Lies, betrayals, jealousy, obsession, sexual restlessness, and deceit are portrayed as a normal part of interpersonal interactions.

Heavily influenced by Freudian psychoanalysis, film noir exhibits a psychological sophistication far greater than anything that had previously appeared in Hollywood film. These films explore characters' motivations, mental states, and irrational drives. Psychopathology and psychological perversion are omnipresent. Many characters in these films are psychologically flawed, and those who appear to be wholly innocent run the risk of being victimized.

Perhaps the most important theme to run through film noir is the notion of inevitability. The title of the classic film noir *The Postman Always Rings Twice* sums up this theme: although one might temporarily elude the consequences of one's actions, eventually one will be caught. Fate occupies a particularly important place in film noir. Characters are stalked and terrorized. The past inexorably haunts the present. Characters inescapably succumb to their weaknesses. We often think of the postwar era as a time of optimism fueled by economic prosperity, but film noir reveals the underside of the era: its anxieties, its paranoia, and, in the wake of the Holocaust, the concentration camp, and the dawn of the atomic age, its doubts about the essential goodness of human nature.

15

The Red Scare in Hollywood
HUAC and the End of an Era

Peter Roffman and Jim Purdy

Twice – in 1947 and 1951 – the House Un-American Activities Committee investigated (HUAC)
communist infiltration of the movie industry. Members of the committee contended that
communists in Hollywood had inserted pro-Soviet messages in films and portrayed the
United States in a critical manner. Although there was virtually no evidence to support
those allegations, a few hundred people in Hollywood had been members of the Communist
Party or of so-called "front" organizations during the 1930s. Committee members knew
that investigations of Hollywood would attract far more public attention than similar
investigations of unions, the armed forces, or the State Department. The aim of many
committee members was to undermine and discredit liberalism.

The committee investigations took place at a time when the atmosphere in Hollywood
was charged with fear, anxiety, paranoia, and hatred. Box-office receipts were in steep
decline, the studios were racked by labor unrest, and the actors' and screenwriters' guilds
were deeply divided between left- and right-wingers. In the end, several hundred screen-
writers and performers were blacklisted for failing to clear their names. In this essay, film
historians Peter Roffman and Jim Purdy examine the impact of the House Un-American
Activities Committee's investigations into the film industry.

The Black List

Conservative elements have always attacked liberalism by associating it with the
extreme left, seeing in many progressive social welfare programs the dangerous seeds
of communism. Throughout the thirties, enemies of New Deal liberalism conducted
a campaign to so discredit Roosevelt, but the overall viability of the New Deal's programs and the immense personal appeal of the President overrode such attacks. Then,
with Roosevelt's death and the advent of the Cold War, this right wing thesis found a
sympathetic audience. Given a veneer of credibility by international events (the

Peter Roffman and Jim Purdy, "The Red Scare in Hollywood," *The Hollywood Social Problem Film: Madness,*
Despair, and Politics from the Depression to the Fifties (Bloomington: Indiana University Press, 1981),
pp. 284–93. Reprinted with permission of Indiana University Press.

imperialist postures of Stalin, the rise of Red China) and a series of domestic spy scandals (especially the case involving New Dealer Alger Hiss), the "Red scare" snow-balled into a major political movement. First the House Un-American Activities Committee in the late forties and then Senator Joseph McCarthy in the early fifties aroused the public to the "danger" in its midst. Any form of social protest became suspect – to have signed an anti-fascist petition or merely to have been in the presence of a "known" radical was enough to have many people fired from their jobs, slandered and ostracized by the community. All major institutions, from the federal government to the universities, the Army, and the mass media, came under severe scrutiny. In many industries there existed illegal blacklists of supposed Communists who were considered unemployable. That the Red-hunters could never find proof of a substantial Communist threat to the United States and that the American Communist Party was a completely legal political organization until the Communist Control Act of 1954 were irrelevant.

Among the earliest targets of HUAC was the movie industry, an industry with a high public profile and therefore a source of maximum publicity for the Committee and its work. The Hollywood blacklist is now almost as big a legend as the stars and movies of the period. It is a sorry tale of political repression, of individuals unfairly tormented and careers often ruined, of an industry which far too readily surrendered any semblance of its political independence. The initial hearings were called for October 1947 as an "investigation of Communism in motion pictures," but the tone of the proceedings quickly established that the Committee was not so much interested in the subversive content of movies as in the political affiliations and activities of the people who made the movies.

At first, the industry protested. Nineteen of the forty-one witnesses subpoenaed declared their intention to be "unfriendly" and refused to answer questions concerning their political beliefs. A group of Hollywood liberals, including Bogart, Bacall, Danny Kaye, John Huston, Gene Kelly, and William Wyler, formed the Committee for the First Amendment, while Eric Johnston, prestigious president of the Motion Picture Association of America, defended the movies' right to freedom of speech.

The hearings quickly dashed liberal hopes. Friendly witnesses such as Jack Warner, L.B. Mayer, Walt Disney, Leo McCarey, Sam Wood, Robert Taylor, Adolphe Menjou, Ronald Reagan, George Murphy, and Gary Cooper were allowed, as *Daily Variety* reported, to "read prepared statements, use notes and ramble widely in offering testimony of strong nature without supporting evidence." The "unfriendlies," on the other hand, were prohibited in all but two cases from making statements so that their protests had to be shouted out over Chairman Parnell Thomas's rulings. The spectacle of the "unfriendly" witnesses vociferously challenging the Committee's legal authority and their refusal to answer any questions boomeranged, creating much adverse publicity. After calling only eleven of the unfriendlies, the Committee abruptly called off the hearings and charged ten of the eleven – the Hollywood Ten – with contempt of Congress. Parnell Thomas ended the hearings by warning the industry to "set about immediately to clean its own house and not wait for public opinion to do so."

Protest quickly gave way to expediency as industry personnel began to worry about their careers. The Committee for the First Amendment disintegrated, with such luminaries as Bogart and Bacall referring to their participation as a "mistake." Within a month, industry heads held the infamous summit meeting at the Waldorf Astoria and issued the "Waldorf Statement," a tacit agreement to form a blacklist: the industry would not reemploy the Ten or any other members of a party advocating the overthrow of the United States government. Eric Johnston declared:

> We are frank to recognize that such a policy involves dangers and risks. There is the danger of hurting innocent people. There is the risk of creating an atmosphere of fear. Creative work at its best cannot be carried on in an atmosphere of fear. We will guard against this danger, this risk, this fear.

But of course, just such an atmosphere was created. In 1950, the Supreme Court upheld the contempt charges against the Hollywood Ten, sending them to prison for a year and paving the way for a new set of HUAC hearings in 1951. This time there was no pretense of investigating Communist propaganda in the movies. Nor was there any protest.

The victim of the blacklist was caught, no matter what course of action he took, in an impossible dilemma. Merely being named at the hearings set off a relentless chain of events even though membership in the Party or signing an anti fascist petition represented no transgression of the law.

Once named, the individual was automatically labeled as suspect and found himself on the blacklist. Since the individual had done nothing illegal his accusers required no documented evidence of his transgression and he had no legal recourse to defend himself. When actually called before HUAC, the accused had but two choices, neither of them particularly palatable. First, he could cooperate, confessing to left-wing political affiliations and naming any people engaged in similar activities. By so doing, the individual generally cleared himself and saved his career, but he also lent validity to the Committee and helped perpetuate the investigation by supplying more names and forcing more individuals to face the same predicament. The other alternative was to defy the Committee and thus destroy one's career. The witness could refuse to testify under the First Amendment and face a jail sentence for contempt or he could invoke the Fifth Amendment, refusing to testify on the grounds of self-incrimination. The latter tactic failed to save the witness from blacklisting since, in Representative Morgan M. Moulder's words, any "refusal to testify so consistently leaves a strong inference that you are still an ardent follower of the Communist Party and its purpose." Either way, then, whether confessing to a "crime" that was no crime or refusing to confess on the basis of constitutional rights, the individual was "guilty" and yet without legal recourse.

Over two hundred individuals within the movie industry were named by HUAC, and countless others were judged by the studios and pressure groups as "guilty" by association. Many submitted to the Committee's demands and to other clearance procedures (such as studio loyalty tests) in order to salvage their careers, while many others refused to yield and paid the price. Virtually everyone else within the industry proceeded with extreme caution lest they grant the Committee or any right-wing zealot the slightest grounds for criticism. The very last thing those still employed dared do was stand up for their former coworkers, since such action would only blacklist them to the same limbo.

Movies and Communism: From *Mission to Moscow* to *Big Jim McLain*

Not surprisingly, the 1947 Committee and its successors failed to establish that Communist propaganda had ever been injected into the Hollywood film. A thorough study undertaken by Dorothy Jones failed to uncover any fragments of Marxism in the movies and even Robert Vaughn, himself an anti-Communist, concedes in his book *Only Victims*:

> At no time during the Thomas, Wood, or subsequent investigations of Hollywood film content was the Committee ever able to establish conclusively that Communist Party dogma managed to find its way to the American people via the American screen.

As we have discussed, Hollywood throughout the thirties had taken a strong anti-Communist line, viciously caricaturing leftists as villainous agitators or lazy, cowardly bums. About the only examples of Marxist propaganda the Committee members or witnesses were able to unearth were preposterous: single lines of dialogue as innocuous as "Share and share alike – that's democracy" – spoken by down-and-out college roommates who decide to pool their resources in *Tender Comrade* (1943, written by Dalton Trumbo). Clifford Odets' *None but the Lonely Heart* (1944) was damned by Mrs. Lela Rogers (Ginger's mother) because among other reasons, the *Hollywood Reporter* had said that it was "moody and somber throughout in the Russian manner."

The main basis for HUAC's claims was the series of wartime propaganda films that glorified America's Russian allies. And even here the Committee failed to unearth any real threat: Ayn Rand felt MGM's *Song of Russia* was propagandistic because it presented Russia in a positive light by showing Soviet children laughing and playing. That these films were the expression of the official foreign policy of the time was no defense, since that policy, the product of Roosevelt's "Communist-influenced" New Deal, was itself suspect. In fact, when Jack Warner took the stand, the Committee members were less interested in the film *Mission to Moscow* than in getting Warner to incriminate FDR by admitting that the President personally requested the movie be made.

Mission to Moscow was the only film that could really be said to conform to the official Communist line. While the other wartime films about Russia set out to improve the Russian image in America, *Mission* also took a direct look at the internal policies of the Soviet Union. Based on Ambassador Joseph Davies' book, the film dramatizes Davies' experiences in Russia during the late thirties, where FDR had sent him to assess the Soviets' willingness to fight. In the film, Davies (Walter Huston) first learns that we're all alike, that Soviets are no different from Americans. A factory foreman explains that he has worked hard and studied to get ahead and that the factory operates on a capitalist-like profit motive system to ensure "the most good for the most people." Davies replies, "It's the same in our country." Also, Mrs. Davies, upon visiting a cosmetic factory, inquires, "Isn't this against Soviet principles?" to which she is answered, "Women all over the world like to look feminine. Beauty is no luxury." Then, the ambassador comes to his most important discovery – that the purge trials and secret police repression are necessities in a country threatened by sabotage. He does not even mind his own embassy being bugged since he has nothing to hide: "Perhaps counterespionage is a matter of self-preservation."

The film's main thrust is to demonstrate how truly anti fascist the Soviets are, and how those aligned against them are pro-Nazi. The Nazi–Soviet pact is justified as a stalling tactic, a means of buying time to prepare for a war Stalin knew was inevitable all along. Internal sabotage is pinned on the Nazis. At the purge trials, Davies learns that Trotsky, along with Bukharin and Radek, was involved with the Germans and Japanese in a plot to overthrow the government. The film naively accepts the Stalinist version of the trials as gospel, something that even the real Davies had trouble believing. Stalin (Manart Kippen) himself is portrayed as a wise, affable grandfather figure, who along with Roosevelt and Churchill is the only world leader to foresee the dangers of Nazi Germany. Yet, when Davies returns to America and tries to arouse support for Russia, he is confronted with the wrath of isolationists who see no danger in Hitler ("We got a coupla' oceans, ain't we?") but are violently opposed to Stalin. The film thus attacks anti-Communists and isolationists as pro-fascists. Though the Warners could hardly be accused of Bolshevism and *Mission* would never have been made if not for the war cause, any film which supported Stalin was wide open for attack. To paraphrase Alistair Cooke, the film was judged in one era for what it represented in another.

As ever, hypersensitive to such controversy and "advised" by Chairman Thomas to produce films which attack communism, the studio readily complied with an entire cycle of anti-Red pictures. Just as the wartime propaganda films had been a complete reversal in attitude from the thirties anti-Communist movies, so the postwar cycle performed political flip-flop from the war pictures. Within weeks of the 1947 hearings, MGM released its 1939 anti-Communist satire, *Ninotchka*, in which cold commissar Greta Garbo is seduced by captivating capitalist Melvyn Douglas. Then, in May 1948, Twentieth Century Fox released *Iron Curtain*. The other studios soon followed suit. Except for the modest success of *Iron Curtain* (it was number two at the New York box office for the month of May), none of these films were particularly popular. Yet despite a cool public response, Hollywood relentlessly pursued the anti-Communist theme and when it appeared to be waning throughout 1950–51, the second HUAC hearings produced another even greater, flurry of movie Red-baiting. Dorothy Jones estimates that there were between thirty-five and forty films released between 1948 and 1954 attacking communism and the Soviet Union. This perseverance with a political issue in the face of poor box office is unprecedented in Hollywood history and indicates the degree of paranoia felt by the studios during the period.

The cycle itself followed the tradition of the World War II features, translating the ideological conflict between capitalism and communism into the most simplistic form of morality play. As [film critic] Pauline Kael, among others, has pointed out, if we were not told that the villains were Communists, we could easily mistake them for Nazis:

> the filmgoer who saw the anti-Nazi films of ten years ago will have no trouble recognizing the characters, just as ten years ago he could have detected (under the Nazi black shirts) psychopathic killers, trigger-happy cattle rustlers, and the screen villain of earliest vintage – the man who will foreclose the mortgage if he doesn't get the girl. The Soviet creatures of the night are direct descendants of the early film archetype, the bad man.

Again, the films closely conform to genre conventions, the majority of them indistinguishable from *Confessions of a Nazi Spy.* Films such as *Iron Curtain, Walk a Crooked Mile* (1948), *I Was a Communist for the FBI* (1951), *Walk East on Beacon* (1952), and *Big Jim McLain* (1952) are generally shot in the same documentary style, with the same authoritative narrator who tells us that this is based on a real case, and the familiar plot of the investigator-hero uncovering a scheme by nefarious foreigners to overthrow the country. The other most common story line, seen in *Sofia* (1948), *The Red Danube* (1949), *Never Let Me Go* (1953), *Man on a Tightrope* (1953), and *Night People* (1954), is borrowed from *Escape* (1940) and dramatizes the attempts of the protagonists to flee from repressive Iron Curtain countries to the freedom of America. One genre which the World War II propagandists had failed to use was science fiction. In *Red Planet Mars* (1952), both the Martians and God help destroy the atheistic Soviet regime.

Like the Nazis, the Communists are condemned on character traits more than ideology. Party members are almost always severely disturbed – some are blood-hungry killers (Arnold in *I Married a Communist* [also known as *The Woman on Pier 13*], 1949); others are mad scientists (*Whip Hand*, 1951); the women, if not nymphomaniacs (Mollie in *The Red Menace*, 1949, and Christine in *I Married a Communist*), are frigid and repressed (*Walk East on Beacon*). One of the most dramatically deranged Communists is Yvonne (Betty Lou Gerson) in *The Red Menace*, who bursts forth in a demented tirade about the revolution when questioned by the authorities. The leaders are either hysterical fanatics like Vanning in *I Married a Communist* or shysters. Generally the Party elite live, as Karel Reisz points out, "in large, luxurious flats with suspect modernistic furniture (but the larder is always a photographic darkroom) and large libraries, eat off silver plates and openly look forward to the age of caviar for the commissar." As one character in *Walk East on Beacon* enthuses, "Someday we won't have to worry about dough. A commissar gets everything for free – everything!"

Just as Hollywood never dealt with the fascist ideology, so the political and economic principles of communism are never really explicated. They receive token expression in crudely distilled comments and speeches. "Man is state – state is man. Someone upstairs says something and that's that," intones a Party intellectual in *I Married a Communist.*

The Communist Party doesn't seem to stand for anything, only against sacred American principles such as God, motherhood, and true love. It is continually in conflict with members of the Catholic Church, including a priest in *I Was a Communist*, a cardinal in *Guilty of Treason* (1949), and a Mother Superior in *The Red Danube*. In *My Son John* (1952), John Jefferson (Robert Walker) betrays both God and his mother when he swears on the Bible that he is not a Communist, while Mollie, an amoral floozy in *The Red Menace*, turns her back on Father O'Leary for the truth "as laid down by Marx, Engels, Lenin, and Stalin." In other films, the Party boss is continually warning romantically inclined members: "Love! Why don't you call it what it is – emotion!" (*I Married a Communist*). According to Karel Reisz, the following lines of dialogue occur with minor variations in four of the films:

PARTY GIRL: (in love and therefore deviating) Don't worry about my private life.
PARTY BOSS: You have no private life.

Nor is human life very sacred to the Communists. Party members are expendable, expected to give themselves up to the police in order to protect more important compatriots. In *Iron Curtain*, one imprisoned unfortunate is consoled: "Don't be too unhappy, Keith. We'll name a city after you when we take over." The faithful are even expected to kill those close to them when the leaders so demand: a brother is ordered to murder his sister in *Whip Hand* and a husband his wife in *Conspirator* (1950). Whole sections of the population are equally dispensable. In *Whip Hand*, the "Commies" talk of germ warfare, and in *Big Jim McLain*, they plan to poison the waterfront as a strike tactic. In the latter film, John Wayne, with his customary political insight, explains to a spy the difference between Americans and Communists:

> I wanted to hit you one punch, just one full-thrown right hand. But now I can't do it. Because you're too small. That's the difference between you and us, I guess. We don't hit the little guy. We believe in fair play and all that sort of thing.

If the Soviet Union represents the evils of totalitarianism, of course America is the land of freedom and goodness. But though our society is basically sound, the films warn that it is still vulnerable and locates the source of that vulnerability in America's innocence. The country is so free and open that people have become too trusting, taking everyone including the Communists, at their word. Idealistic dupes are seduced into the Party ranks by phony front organizations such as the anti fascist group in *I Was a Communist for the FBI* which really raises funds for Party activities. Blacks, Jews, and other minorities are lured into the Party through its platform of racial equality only to discover that the leaders are in fact vicious racists seeking new members to manipulate in their quest for world power. A student who has won a trip to Russia returns home brainwashed in *Big Jim McLain* while to John Jefferson communism is like a contagious disease: he begins attending meetings for intellectual stimulation and before he knows it he's being enticed into spying for the Party.

When the innocents discover the truth (the cabbie in *Walk East on Beacon* describes it as "like waking up married to a woman you hate") they soon realize that the Communists are much more ruthless than expected and will kill anyone who tries to desert. Such a fate befalls the protagonists in *I Married a Communist* and *My Son John*, as well as minor characters in *The Red Menace*. *I Was a Communist for the FBI* even implies that this is what happened to such important figures as Trotsky and Masaryk. Many other innocents choose suicide either to avoid corruption (the ballerina in *The Red Danube*) or to free themselves from the living death of Party membership (the Jewish poet in *The Red Menace* and the army officer in *Conspirator*). So great is their sin that the only way the Communists can redeem themselves is through martyrdom. These films echo the common sentiment of "innocence betrayed" propounded by such writers as Leslie Fiedler, who saw the liberals of the New Deal as culpable because they had allowed themselves to be used by the Communists. Just as the liberals have been betrayed, so they have betrayed their countrymen. FDR, under the influence of New Deal "Reds" like Alger Hiss, "sold us out" at Yalta.

To combat any further chance of betrayal, the films offer a vigilant anti-intellectualism. In films such as *My Son John* and *Big Jim McLain*, the parents of the fallen youths argue for a return to the old values. John's father (Dean Jagger) is meant to represent the ideal American: a Legionnaire, staunch churchgoer, and small-town schoolteacher who gives lessons in "simple down-to-earth" morality and Americanism. He scorns his son's university education, his important Washington job, and his relations with intellectuals and professors. Mr. Jefferson relies on the Bible and patriotic platitudes for enlightenment and mistrusts any open debate which deviates from these narrow principles. In short, the heroic American patriarch is a right-wing bigot who frequently bursts into song: "If you don't like your Uncle Sammy / Then go back to your home o'er the sea." Mr. Lester, the father in *Big Jim McLain*, reveres the values of hard work and religious faith which have allowed him to "retire on my pension and live free in the sun." He too sees his son's communism as a repudiation of America and God.

 Like HUAC, these films rely on their own internal logic which betrays a tendency toward the very totalitarianism that they are supposedly combating. Any of the beliefs and freedoms which fail to conform precisely to the values of the American right are held up as suspect, as the means by which the Communists infiltrate and poison the country. So, although America is glorified as the land of freedom where everyone can speak and think for himself, the threat of communism is simultaneously located in that very exercise of free thought. This logic is succinctly captured in *Big Jim McLain*. After he breaks up the Communist spy ring, Big Jim does not take the criminals to court where they would be tried as spies under normal procedures, but subpoenas them to appear before HUAC. By thus misrepresenting HUAC's role, the film is able to attack Constitutional freedom. The Communists are guilty of espionage, but by invoking the Fifth Amendment, they elude the Committee's investigations and go free to continue their evil work. By conforming to the principles of the Constitution, HUAC cannot do justice to the traitors and the country remains unprotected. According to McLain, America's freedom is both glorious and dangerous: "There are lot of wonderful things written into our Constitution that were meant for honest, decent citizens. I resent the fact that it can be used an abused by the very people who want to destroy it." In short, to preserve our freedom we must relinquish it. Loyalty to motherhood and HUAC must be as absolute as loyalty to the Party.

16

The Morality of Informing
Ambivalence and On the Waterfront

Kenneth R. Hey

The most suspenseful moment at the 1999 Academy Awards ceremony was not whether Saving Private Ryan *would win the Oscar for Best Picture. It was how Hollywood would respond to a lifetime achievement award for Elia Kazan, the director of such acclaimed movies as* On the Waterfront. *Kazan, who had been born in Istanbul, helped bring a new style of acting to the screen, one in which male actors revealed their characters' psychology, emotions, and psychoses. In 1952, Kazan was summoned before the House Un-American Activities Committee and asked to name the names of those who he knew had been members of the Communist Party in the mid-1930s. Kazan initially declined to answer, but later relented, evoking scorn from some former colleagues.*

Few films of the Cold War era are more powerful than On the Waterfront. *Ostensibly the story of racketeering within a longshoreman's union, the film metaphorically addresses one of the central issues of the McCarthy era: the morality of informing. The film also features one of the screen's greatest performances: the young Marlon Brando's stirring portrayal of Terry Malloy, the inarticulate, alienated tough and former prize fighter, who "could have been a contender."*

The study of film in American culture poses some interesting challenges to the person using an interdisciplinary method. First, as an historical document, film has contextual connections with the contemporary world. The people who make a film bring to the project their own interests and attitudes, and these various perspectives, when added to the collaborative process, forge a product which resonates in some way with society. Second, as a work of art, film requires textual analysis similar to drama, photography, painting, and music. But as an aesthetic object which combines different artistic media into a single experience, film requires an analytical method which considers all contributing disciplines. Finally, as an art historical object, film stands at the intersection of ongoing traditions in the medium's own history and of theoretical interests alive at the time the film is made. To single out one feature of the film (e.g., its historical context or a self-contained meaning in the text) is to sacrifice

Reproduced by permission of *Film & History: An Interdisciplinary Journal of Film and Television Studies*.

Figure 12   *On the Waterfront* (1954). Columbia Pictures. Directed by Elia Kazan. Courtesy of Jerry Murbach, www.doctormacro.info.

the film for something less. To avoid examining the relative contributions of all the major participants is to miss the unique feature of this collaborative art form.

As an example of the collaborative film process and as an object of cultural significance, *On the Waterfront* (1954) has few competitors. Bringing together some of the best and most innovative artists in their respective media, the film was an attempt to weave together the threads of two contemporary events with the strands of aesthetic themes derived from several different artistic media. Unlike many intriguing films which lose their appeal as society changes, this … film continues to evince the intended moral outrage from viewers ignorant of its historical background and to receive harsh criticism from detractors aware of the film's origins.

On the Waterfront tells of Terry Malloy (played by Marlon Brando) who begins as an ignorant and complacent member of a corrupt gang that controls the longshoreman's union. Terry previously boxed professionally for the mob and obediently took "a dive" so the mobsters could win big on the opponent. He now contents himself with a "cushy" dock job and a "little extra change on the side." The mob, headed by Johnny Friendly (played by Lee J. Cobb) with the assistance of Terry's brother, Charley "the Gent" (played by Rod Steiger), applies "muscle" discipline where necessary: when a dissident member breaks the "D and D" rule ("Deaf and Dumb") and talks to the Crime Commission, the mobsters have him killed. Edie Doyle (played by Eva Marie Saint), the sister of the film's first murder victim Joey Doyle, tries to unravel the mystery of union corruption, hoping to uncover the identity of her brother's murderer. Joined by Father Barry (played by Karl Malden), she soon concentrates her attentions on Terry, whose basic philosophy ("Do it to him before he does it to you") clashes with the Christian morality ("Aren't we all part of each other") she has absorbed at a convent school. Terry's indifference to Edie's pleas eventually leads to the murder of "Kayo" Dugan (played by Pat Henning) whose violent death extracts an emotional eulogy from Father Barry. After the mob kills Charley for protecting his brother, the younger Malloy seeks revenge. Father Barry convinces Terry to vent his anger in open testimony before the State Waterfront Crime Commission. But the impersonality of formal testimony fails to appease Terry's desire for vengeance, and he confronts Johnny Friendly directly. Although he loses the ensuing fist fight, he seems to win a "battle" by circumventing Friendly's authority and personally leading the men back to work.

The following study will seek to explain how and why *On the Waterfront* came to be. As a method of explaining the film's origins and meaning, each collaborator's career, point of view and major interests will be discussed briefly and fitted into the evolving product. When all of the artists' efforts are considered as part of the whole, a single theme predominates: ambivalence. The film argues openly that injustice can be remedied through existing political institutions: but it grafts onto this basic liberal position the suggestion that individuals are frequently casualties of the conflict between right and wrong in society and that the individual's response to the clash of absolute moral standards is ambivalent. In the film, the "thesis" of evil (Johnny Friendly) is confronted by its "antithesis" of good (Father Barry and Christian morality); the new "synthesis" (Terry Malloy) miraculously fuses selfishness and selflessness, but as an individual staggering beneath the burden of moral decisions he remains unconvinced of the rightness of either extreme.

The idea for a waterfront drama came from a person who had nothing to do with the final product. In 1949 Arthur Miller flushed with the success of two Broadway plays (*All My Sons*, 1947; *Death of a Salesman*, 1949) directed his considerable talent toward the social struggle then being waged on the Brooklyn docks. His play *The Bottom of the River* (also titled *The Hook*) told of the misadventures of Peter Panto who in the late 1930s tried to organize dissident longshoremen in Brooklyn's Red Hook district. According to the longshoremen with whom Miller talked, mobsters feared Panto's rapid rise to popularity and had him killed dumping his body in the East River. In 1951 when the first script was finished Miller contacted colleague Elia Kazan, suggesting that they work jointly on the film.

Kazan after completing his studies at the Yale School of Drama in 1932 had joined both the innovative Group Theatre and the energetic Communist Party but his radical fervor soon waned and he severed Party affiliations because of a conflict over artists' prerogatives and freedoms. From his 1930s experiences in dramatic art and radical politics Kazan developed an aesthetic theory which favored optimistic realism and assumed a political posture "left of center and to the right of the Communist Party." A deft creator of dramatic tension on stage Kazan usually directed Broadway plays that projected his liberal ideas. From his work on the Group Theatre's *Golden Boy* to his direction of Tennessee Williams' *A Streetcar Named Desire* (play 1947; film 1951) and of Arthur Miller's *All My Sons* and *Death of a Salesman*, Kazan had helped shape studies of inhuman exploitation, bestial degradation, and aimless materialism, as well as statements concerning moral responsibility. But the pessimism which often infused

these social dramas was not wholly suited to the optimism of a scrapping and successful immigrant like Kazan. In *On the Waterfront* he would resurrect Clifford Odets'
"golden boy" and make his own original golden warrior, Terry Malloy, rise from his
beating and depose momentarily his corrupt adversary. Kazan would also revive
Tennessee Williams' characters from *A Streetcar Named Desire*. In the play Kazan had
directed Vivien Leigh to play Blanche DuBois as "an ambivalent figure who is attracted
to the harshness and vulgarity" surrounding her at the same time she fears and rejects
it. For the waterfront drama, Kazan would transfer the character ambivalence to Terry
Malloy converting Blanche DuBois into an effective Edie Doyle and the befuddled
Mitch into a forceful Father Barry (both played by Karl Malden). Stanley Kowalski and
Terry Malloy (both played by Marlon Brando) would share several characteristics – an
inability to express themselves clearly, an incapacity to control or even comprehend
their situations and actions, and a vulnerability which belies a certain sensitivity. But
unlike Kowalski, Terry Malloy would be permitted to grow and change. Kowalski's
bestial drives mixed with brute strength would give way under persistent moral preach-
ings to Malloy's survival instincts tempered with human indecisiveness.

Kazan's successful Group Theatre experiences, his fleeting glance at radical politics,
his personal rise from immigrant boy to Broadway's "gray-haired" wonder and his early
Hollywood popularity (*A Tree Grows in Brooklyn*, 1945; *Boomerang* and *Gentleman's
Agreement*, both 1947) led him to believe in the value of his own work and in the real
possibility of reform. But Kazan stopped short of naive idealism. When confronted
with large, historical forces, the individual becomes a victim who may, despite a heroic
character, flinch and recoil as did Emiliano Zapata when offered the reins of the Mexican
government (*Viva Zapata!*, 1952). Thus by the time Arthur Miller contacted Kazan
about a waterfront film the two Broadway collaborators had shared several artistic
experiences but Miller's clearly defined goods and evils so evident in *All My Sons* did
not blend well with Kazan's admixture of optimism and moral ambivalence.

Despite this difference in perspective the two authors collected Miller's completed
script and headed west to seek financial backing. After feelers to Kazan's studio,
Twentieth Century-Fox, proved unsuccessful, the two appealed to Harry Cohn,
president of Columbia Pictures. Cohn, who showed interest in the project, contacted
Roy Brewer, whose advice on labor affairs Cohn considered essential. Brewer headed
several Hollywood unions and served on the Motion Picture Alliance for the
Preservation of American Ideals, an organization of conservative filmmakers who
fought communism in Hollywood by aiding the House Committee on Un-American
Activities (HUAC). He supplied union workers and projectionists for films he considered politically acceptable and made it impossible for filmmakers disdainful of HUAC
to secure a crew in Hollywood. Cohn and Brewer suggested that the authors convert
the waterfront mobsters into communists. When Miller and Kazan refused Brewer
retorted that the creators were dishonest, immoral, and un-American. The power
behind this hardline position must have seemed ominous to Kazan in 1952 when he
received a subpoena from the House Committee on Un-American Activities to testify
concerning his knowledge of communist activities in the 1930s.

According to Kazan *On the Waterfront* was "partly affected" by his two appearances
before the celebrated House Committee on January 14 and April 9, 1952. "I went
through that thing," he later admitted, "and it was painful and difficult and not the
thing I'm proudest of in my life but it's also not something I'm ashamed of." No

doubt Kazan confronted his unfortunate role as friendly witness with the perspective that he was trapped between two opposing and irreconcilable forces of evil, neither of which deserved his allegiance. However, he also must have seen that the federal government and the strong pro-HUAC sentiment lodged in Hollywood could destroy his career. The general "good" he perceived in the exposure and criticism of the American Communist Party's activities could be easily fused with the individual "good" of his personal success. "It is my obligation as a citizen," he told the committee, "to tell everything." Like "golden boy" Joe Bonaparte, Willy Loman, and even Blanche DuBois, Kazan saw himself as another victim of social and political forces which corrupt even the most honorable intentions. With the committee as audience Kazan read a carefully prepared statement which contained three clearly framed sections. First, he admitted and repudiated membership in the Communist Party. "I was a member of the Communist Party from some time in the summer of 1934 until the late winter or early spring of 1936 when I severed all connection with it permanently .... I had had enough anyway. I had had a taste of police state living and I did not like it." Second, he explained the depth of his complicity by describing his mission and by listing people with whom he had worked.

> For the approximately nineteen months of my membership, I was assigned to a "unit" composed of those party members who were like myself members of the Group Theatre acting company .... What we were asked to do was four-fold: 1) to educate ourselves in Marxist and party doctrine; 2) to help the party get a foothold in the Actors Equity Association; 3) to support various "front organizations" of the party; 4) to try to capture the Group Theatre and make it a communist mouthpiece.

All the people Kazan named had previously been named and thus he did not actually lengthen the HUAC list. But he gave legitimacy to the Committee's witch hunt, and – not insignificantly – insured his future employment in Hollywood.

In the third section of his dramatic presentation, Kazan defended his career since leaving the Party and tried to show that his artistic activities were in no way un-American. "After I left the party in 1936 except for making a two-reel documentary film mentioned above in 1937 [*The People of the Cumberlands*], I was never active in any organization since listed as subversive." In characterizing his artistic efforts since 1936 Kazan described *Death of a Salesman* as a story which "shows the frustrations of the life of a salesman and contains implicit criticism of his materialistic standards": he called *Viva Zapata!* "an anti-communist picture." He labored to show how even the most critical works were essentially American in intent, purpose, and effect. Depicting himself as a staunch defender of democracy, Kazan asserted that concern for the social problems of the 1930s had drawn him to the Communist Party, but that the Party's preoccupation with political subversion had actually harmed real social reform.

Prior to his second appearance before the House committee Kazan wrote a lengthy letter to the editor of *The Saturday Review*, defending the anti-communist message of *Viva Zapata!* In explicating the democratic theory behind the film's action Kazan described Zapata (played by Marlon Brando) as "no communist; he was that opposite phenomenon, a man of individual conscience." The true reformer was an individualist who fought for the same ends as did the Communist Party but consulted his conscience rather than ideology when making political decisions. Kazan submitted his entire letter to the House committee as part of his formal statement. In the same issue of

The Saturday Review, Norman Cousins delineated the essential differences between a communist and a liberal. "A Communist, although he pretends to be independent, always takes his order from above; a liberal makes up his own mind. A Communist because he takes orders from above is sometimes trapped by an overnight change in Party policy; a liberal can change his mind but he does so slowly, painfully, and by his own volition." Three days after testifying Kazan purchased advertising space in the amusement section of *The New York Times*. In the two-column, page-long "Statement," Kazan defended his actions before the committee and called upon other liberals to come forward. "Secrecy," he wrote, "serves the communists." In May 1952, Clifford Odets, whom Kazan had named as a former member of the Communist Party, appeared before the Committee and reiterated the emerging liberal theme. "One must pick one's way very carefully through the images of liberalism or leftism today," he told the subcommittee, "or one must remain silent." Odets, Kazan, and others like them had evidently changed their minds "slowly, painfully, and by [their] own volition" because they chose, as Terry Malloy would choose, not to remain silent.

Yielding to political hysteria on the right did not appeal to all liberals. Kazan's performance before the committee incensed his associate, Arthur Miller, and the two embarked on an artistic duel which lasted into the 1960s. Miller fired the first round with *The Crucible* (1953), an apparent study of witchcraft in Puritan Salem. According to Miller, "the witch hunt was a perverse manifestation of the panic which set in among all classes when the balance began to turn away from communal unity and toward greater individual freedom." Miller tried to link the Salem witch-hunts with Washington red-baiting. While hoping to avoid spurious connections between witchcraft and communism he did seek to explore hysterical and oppressive responses to individual acts of conscience. Kazan's return volley in the artistic duel, *On the Waterfront*, made mobster control over the waterfront analogous to Communist Party control over the individual. But the film did not confuse communism per se with gangster racketeering; it sought to explore two forms of oppression. Miller and Kazan, the liberal duelists, were firing at each other by firing in opposite directions. Standing back to back Kazan fired at the political left while Miller fired at the right.

Kazan's role as a friendly witness before the House Committee on Un-American Activities and Miller's efforts to capture the "witch-hunt" in dramatic form left undeveloped their ideas for a film on waterfront crime. After testifying Kazan contacted author Budd Schulberg. Son of a famous Hollywood producer B.P. Schulberg, the young writer had grown up surrounded by famous people and great wealth. After graduating from Dartmouth College, he returned to his hometown, wrote extra dialogue for various studios and released his first novel, *What Makes Sammy Run?* (1941). This searing critique of money-hungry executives in the film industry not only singed the coats of all capitalists, it also avenged his father's premature ouster from Paramount Studios. His second novel, *The Harder They Fall* (1947), updated and expanded Odets' *Golden Boy*, detailing the moral failings of comfortable and dependent employees of a corrupt boxing syndicate. Schulberg followed this cynical blast at complacent self-interest with *The Disenchanted* (1950), a partially autobiographical novel which simultaneously traced the demise of Manley Halliday (known to be F. Scott Fitzgerald) during the filming of *Love on Ice* (Walter Wanger's *Winter Carnival*) and the slow disenchantment of a fresh young screenwriter (Shep/ Schulberg) with 1930s socialist thought.

In each of these novels Schulberg created a powerful character whose success depended upon pitiable humans who cowered before the very force that exploited them. While exploring the curious dynamics of social structure which propelled the most vicious hoodlums to the top, the three works recorded the slow and agonizing incapacitation of a lone victim struggling to maintain dignity in a hostile environment. From his first novel, which condemned ambitious Hollywood capitalists, to his third, which followed the demise of an "artist" in Hollywood's film factory, Schulberg sketched a debased and graceless society which protected and rewarded the powerful for trouncing upon the weak.

Shortly after his third novel appeared on the market Schulberg's attention was diverted to the New York waterfront. In 1949 Joseph Curtis, an aspiring film producer with Hollywood connections, had founded Monticello Film Corporation for the sole purpose of converting to celluloid Malcolm Johnson's *New York Sun* articles on union corruption. In 1950, the articles which won Johnson a Pulitzer Prize appeared in book form. With this popular momentum Curtis convinced Robert Siodmak to direct the film and asked Schulberg to write the script. Despite his original hesitancy to return to an industry he had lacerated mercilessly in his fiction, Schulberg agreed. Measuring the distance between successful people and social rebels, Schulberg explained his fascination with the film's subject matter. "The epic scale of the corruption and violence intrigued me. Only a few blocks from Sardi's and Shor's and other places where itinerant social philosophers assemble to discuss the problems of the day, guys who said 'no' to industrial-feudalism were getting clobbered and killed." Invigorated by the importance and scale of the project, Schulberg investigated, planned, and finished *Crime on the Waterfront* by the spring of 1951, but due to grievous errors in the financial planning, the script was languishing in production limbo when the House Committee on Un-American Activities summoned the author to Washington.

As a disillusioned ex-member of the Communist Party, Schulberg chose to obey the subpoena. Testifying on May 23, 1951, he admitted Party membership, explained Party methods of controlling dissident writer-members, and named former associates. He argued that the limited choices available to the 1930s reformer matched with the urgent need to do something made Party membership seem reasonable. "I joined," he told the committee, "because at the time I felt that the political issues that they seemed to be in favor of, mostly I recall the opposition to the Nazi and Mussolini and a feeling that something should he done about it, those things attracted me, and there were some others too." He separated offenders into those who joined the Party to advance basically humanitarian causes and those who wished to manipulate the humanists to advance totalitarian ends. Ideological fanatics within the Party exploited socially credible writers who sought to study society's ills. Irritated over the Party's attempts to regulate his own writing, Schulberg left the organization. In his testimony, he contended there were communists and innocent communist dupes, and the "innocent" were really solid democrats fighting for legitimate causes.

In 1952, with the Curtis project still in financial trouble, the rights to *Crime on the Waterfront* reverted to Schulberg. Shortly thereafter, Kazan, who was interested in making a film on corrupt judicial processes in an eastern city, contacted Schulberg. Because they had both been involved in aborted film projects concerned with waterfront crime, they quickly agreed to develop a realistic story based on mobster control of longshore unions. Drawing upon personal investigations, two previously completed scripts, and Johnson's *Crime on the Waterfront*, the two collaborators familiarized themselves with the details of waterfront conditions.

From 1946 to 1951, the docks in New York and New Jersey were rampant with illegal activities. Attempts at reform, as demonstrated by the ill-fated effort of Peter Panto, proved fruitless. After a wildcat strike in 1945 focused national attention on the waterfront William F. Warren, the workers' popular leader, reportedly fell and hurt himself on the job, and before reappearing on the docks, made a public "confession" that he had been "a dupe" of the Communist Party. In 1948 a second major strike reached its peak soon after the New York Anti-Crime Commission subpoenaed mobster John M. Dunn who while awaiting execution in prison promised to name the man known as "Mr. Big" – called "Mr. Upstairs" in the film. While most workers assumed "Mr. Big" to be financier millionaire William "Big Bill" McCormick, dockworker speculation thought New York City's Mayor William O'Dwyer better suited the description. But Dunn reneged on his threat, the strike was settled with force, the Anti-Crime Commission recessed, and Mayor O'Dwyer ran for reelection.

By November 1952, when Kazan and Schulberg started writing their story, the New Jersey harbor, the specific location for the film, was the setting of frequent assaults, firebombings, beatings, and mobster activities. With the year coming to a close, the New York State Crime Commission (the Commission in the film) made known its findings. With a sweep of media sensationalism, the Commission charged the obvious: the docks were battlefields for entrenched corruption. Workers were forced to take extortionary loans for guaranteed work and illegal strikes were called to extract larger fees from shippers. Union leaders abused elections, bookkeeping practices and pension systems; and shippers to insure against loss remained silent. Drawing upon this vast cityscape of corruption Kazan and Schulberg ran through eight different scripts, each of which exposed illegal activities on the New York waterfront while providing the authors an opportunity to explain their position on analogous contemporary events of seemingly greater national significance.

The themes which emanated from Kazan's and Schulberg's HUAC testimonies – the beguiled innocent manipulated for unwholesome purposes; individual responsibility to the democratic whole; preference for individual morality over ideological fanaticism – were literary in nature and religious in tone and they helped the authors shape the raw material of waterfront crime. Likewise the testimonial ceremony, which included confessing anti-social activities, identifying associates and theories responsible for those misguided endeavors, and recommending more desirable ways of expressing social concern, suggested dramatic form. The three stages of their testimony became the three major steps of Terry Malloy's conversion. The first segment of the film exposes Malloy's associations with the corrupt gang; a second segment depicts his discovery of corruption as well as the depths of his own guilt; the final segment shows him battling for his own "rights."

Each segment has a ritualized scene which summarizes the action. The "shape-up" scene discloses the dehumanizing conditions fostered by union corruption. A union leader throws "brass checks" on the ground where longshoremen wrestle to retrieve their guarantee of one day's work. Terry, shown separated from the central scramble, is given a "cushy" job as a reward for setting up Joey Doyle for "the knock-off." A "martyrdom" scene in the middle of the film includes Father Barry's oration over the dead body of "Kayo" Dugan. The "waterfront priest" pleads with the men to come forward and speak because silence only serves the mobsters. A "testimonial" scene at the Crime Commission hearings completes the trilogy. The legal institutions receive reinforcement and Terry confesses to society his complicity. The state's principal investigator thanks Terry profusely, explaining that his actions "have made it possible for decent people to work the docks again." This speech echoes the one Representative Francis E. Walter addressed to Kazan after his HUAC appearance: "Mr. Kazan, we appreciate your cooperation with our committee. It is only through the assistance of people such as you that we have been able to make the progress that has been made in bringing the attention of the American people to the machinations of this Communist conspiracy for world domination." In the film, confession and reassurance release Terry from his past transgression and enable him to reclaim his "rights."

The first two ritual scenes – the shape-up and the martyrdom – were borrowed from Johnson's *Crime on the Waterfront.* The prize-winning reporter for the *New York Sun* characterized the longshore working conditions "as not befitting the dignity of a human being," a theme consistent with the testimonies and previous creations of both Schulberg and Kazan. The city's district attorney claimed that the abject conditions on the docks were "a direct result of the shape-up system." Johnson's description of the typical dockside call for workers – the morning shape-up – was to fit neatly into the Kazan–Schulberg script:

> The scene is any pier along New York's waterfront. At a designated hour, the longshoremen gather in a semicircle at the entrance to the pier. They are the men who load and unload the ships. They are looking for jobs and as they stand there in a semicircle their eyes are fastened on one man. He is the hiring stevedore and he stands alone, surveying the waiting men. At this crucial moment he possesses the power of economic life or death over them and the men know it. Their faces betray that knowledge in tense anxiety, eagerness, and fear. They know that the hiring boss, a union man like themselves can accept them or reject them at will .... Now the hiring boss moves among them, choosing the man he wants, passing over others. He nods or points to the favored ones or calls out their names, indicating that they are hired. For those accepted, relief and joy. The pinched faces of the others reflect bleak disappointment, despair. Still they linger. Others will wander off inconsolately to wait another chance.

The potency of this scene in the film results from camera positioning. When Big Mac (played by James Westerfield) blows his whistle to call the workers the camera stands behind him permitting his large figure to obscure the huddled longshoremen. During the scramble for tags the camera is low to the ground capturing facial expressions; character movement is downward and the camera seems to press the viewer against the dirty dockside surface. When Edie, who has come to the "shape-up" to study the causes of union corruption, tries to retrieve a tag for her father, she comes in contact with Terry Malloy. He overpowers her and recovers the contested tag for his friend, suggesting that muscle prevails on the docks. But when Terry learns that his female adversary is the sister of the kid whom he "set-up for the knockoff," his "conscience" convinces him to surrender the tag to her. Thus the conflict between muscle and morality is established. During this encounter, the camera first frames Edie and Terry's contest in the foreground with the longshoremen's struggle in the background. When the scramble gives way to moral considerations the camera changes position, isolating their conversation and making a special case within the generally demeaning environment. The moral "conscience" which Edie embodies alters the situation. For the scene as a whole the camera presents the viewer with the facts of the story (a sense of viewing a "real" event in the workers' daily lives), the filmmakers' opinion about the story (Mac and his associates have the power; the workers are oppressed and unorganized), and Terry's special relationship to the depicted waterfront conditions. Through camera positioning the scene establishes conflicts to be explored as the film progresses.

To Kazan and Schulberg the discipline within the communist "unit" of the 1930s depended upon similar insults to personal dignity. "The typical Communist scene of crawling and apologizing and admitting the error of my ways," as Kazan described the practice degraded human intelligence, and the film's "shape-up" scene was intended to capture such dehumanization. After Mac throws the last tags on the ground exasperation leads to pushing which eventually leads to chaos. In the film, this central expository scene attempts to highlight the hopelessness and futility of longshoremen in a place "which ain't part of America."

Johnson's portrait of waterfront conditions also contained a model for the film's moral catalyst, Father Barry. As associate director of the St. Xavier School (Manhattan), Rev. John M. Corridan, the "waterfront priest," delivered sermons, held meetings, contributed advice to troubled longshoremen, and exhorted the dock workers to strike and rebel. On the violent New Jersey docks where the film was actually shot. Corridan delivered a virulent attack on union corruption. His sermon, "A Catholic Looks at the Waterfront" was reproduced in Johnson's book:

> You want to know what's wrong with the waterfront? It's love of a buck …. Christ also said "If you do it to the least of mine, you do it to me." Christ is in the shape-up …. He stands in the shape-up knowing that all won't get work and maybe He won't …. Some people think the Crucifixion took place only on Calvary …. What does Christ think of the man who picks up a longshoreman's brass check and takes 20 per cent interest at the end of the week? Christ goes to a union meeting … [and] sees a few with $150 suits and diamond rings on their fingers.

As his words make clear, Corridan applied the moral teachings of Christ to waterfront unionism, and this unadorned social gospel reinforced the dualism between brutality and innocence which had figured prominently in previous works by Kazan and Schulberg. Because of the familiar set of visual symbols attached to Christian mythology as well as the moral authority and political safety of such a conservative institution, the filmmakers expanded and made essential Father Barry's role in convincing Terry Malloy to testify.

The filmmakers, both former members of the Communist Party, used Father Barry's funeral oration to air their rejuvenated ideology and to challenge silent liberals to speak out against past totalitarian activities. The emotional speech introduces the idea of shared guilt and encourages action to combat and defeat the mobsters. As the shrill accusations resound through the ship's hold, the forces of chaos (the "mugs" who throw cans and tomatoes) are silenced (Malloy punches Tillio on the chin). With the camera searching high overhead to find Friendly and Charley, it is obvious that the power relationships have not changed. But the men begin to realize that their silence only serves their oppressors.

While Father Barry speaks, the shadow of a cross-like form rises on the wall behind him. After the speech Dugan's body ascends from the worker's hell (the lower depths of the ship) accompanied by Father Barry and Pops, two saintly escorts for the workingman's martyr. The men stand with their hats off, unified at least momentarily by this ritual. Whereas the shape-up belittled the workers, this affirmative scene "resurrects" their self-image. The action of the men at the shape-up was downward to the ground; here it is upward toward the sources of oppression.

A "testimonial" session with the Crime Commission, the third ritual scene in the film, completes the film's structural argument. Corruption and human indignity exposed in the shape-up and then condemned over a martyr's body are finally made public before a tribunal which seeks to punish those responsible. In the Commission hearing room mobsters, newspapermen, commissioners, and interested citizens have a designated place in a physically ordered environment where legal processes are conducted in the open for all to see. Unlike the dreary alleys and dingy asylums of waterfront criminals, the brightly lighted and crowded room encourages photographers and reporters to publish what they hear. Investigators doggedly pursue the illegality hidden behind unions without accounting books and without elections. The degraded competition between workers in the shape-up has become a fair and open contest between equal adversaries made possible by a legal system which insures individual rights. Totalitarian irreverence is supplanted by democratic dignity.

17

Science Fiction as Social Commentary

The Age of Conspiracy and Conformity: Invasion of the Body Snatchers *(1956)*

Stuart Samuels

Cold War era science fiction films were not merely popular entertainment directed at the burgeoning youth audience. These films dealt metaphorically with many of the era's preoccupations: the infiltration of foreign ideologies into the United States; the threats to individuality posed by the forces of conformity; anxieties over "group think" – the tendency of groups to achieve consensus without weighing alternatives; the soullessness and emotionlessness of mass society. In this essay, Stuart Samuels examines the paranoia of the early Cold War years and the way it was expressed in science fiction films.

"If art reflects life, it does so with special mirrors." (Bertolt Brecht)

In what way can a seemingly absurd science fiction/horror film, *Invasion of the Body Snatchers*, give us insight into the history and culture of America in the mid-1950s? How is a film about people being taken over by giant seed pods "reflective" of this critical period in our history?

Films relate to ideological positions in two ways. First, they reflect, embody, reveal, mirror, symbolize existing ideologies by reproducing (consciously or unconsciously) the myths, ideas, concepts, beliefs, images of an historical period in both the film content and film form (technique). Secondly, films produce their own ideology, their own unique expression of reality. Films can do this by reinforcing a specific ideology or undercutting it.

All films are therefore ideological and political insomuch as they are determined by the ideology which produces them. Fictional characters are only prototypes of social roles and social attitudes; every film speaks to some norm. Some behaviors are deemed appropriate, others not. Some acts are condemned, others applauded. Certain characters are depicted as heroic, others as cowardly. Film is one of the products, one of the languages, through which the world communicates itself to itself. Films embody beliefs, not by a mystic communion with the national soul, but because they contain the values, fears, myths, assumptions, point of view of the culture in which they are produced.

While films relate to ideology, they also relate to specific historical and social events, most obviously when the content of a film deals directly with a subject that is identifiable in its own period. In the 1950s, for example, such films as *I Was a Communist for the FBI* (1951) and *My Son John* (1952) spoke to a society increasingly concerned with the nature of the internal communist threat. Similarly, in the previous decade such films as *The Best Years of Our Lives* (1946) attempted to analyze some of the problems and confusions of the immediate post-World War II period and *The Snake Pit* (1948) addressed a society trying to deal with the tremendous increase in the hospital treatment of the mentally ill. As far back as Griffith's *Intolerance* (1916), which relayed a pacifist message to a nation struggling to stay out of war, films have reflected society's attempts to come to grips with contemporary problems.

Film "reflects" an agreed-upon perception of social reality, acceptable and appropriate to the society in question. Thus, in the 1950s when a conspiracy theory of politics was a widely accepted way of explaining behavior (being duped), action (being subversive), and effect (conspiracy), one would expect the films of the period to "reflect" this preoccupation with conspiracy. But *Invasion of the Body Snatchers* is not about McCarthyism. It is about giant seed pods taking over people's bodies. Indirectly, however, it is a statement about the collective paranoia and the issue of conformity widely discussed in the period.

The idea for the film came from Walter Wanger, the producer, who had read Jack Finney's novel of the same name in serial form in *Collier's Magazine* in 1955. Wanger suggested the project to his friend Don Siegel, who in turn assigned Daniel Manwaring to produce a screenplay from Finney's book.

The story of the film is contained within a "framing" device – a seemingly insane man, Miles Bennell (Kevin McCarthy), telling a bizarre story to a doctor and a policeman. In flashback we see Bennell's tale – of giant seed pods taking over the minds and bodies of the people of Santa Mira, a small town in California, where Bennell was the local doctor. Returning home after a medical convention, Miles finds the pretty little town and its peaceful inhabitants in the grip of a "mass hysteria." People seem obsessed by the conviction that relatives and friends are not really themselves, that they have been changed. Despite the outward calm of Santa Mira, there is a creeping contagion of fear and paranoia, of wives not knowing their husbands, children fleeing from parents.

Miles's friend Becky (Dana Wynter) struggles against this delusion, tends to dismiss it as improbable, but nevertheless finds her own Uncle Ira slightly changed: "There's no emotion in him. None. Just the pretense of it." The improbable becomes real when Miles's friend Jack calls him to report something fantastic: a semi-human body, without features, has been found on Jack's billiard table. From this point on events move rapidly. The unformed body is clearly growing into an exact duplicate of Jack, and in the greenhouse Miles stumbles upon giant seed pods, each containing a half-formed body. In Becky's basement Miles finds still another embryonic shape – this time a model of Becky herself. Now Miles believes the fantastic stories, and determines to escape and warn the world of this danger.

But escape is not simple. The town of Santa Mira has nearly been taken over by the pods, who while the inhabitants sleep form themselves into precise replicas of human beings – even-tempered, peaceful, but soulless automatons. Miles is terrified and drags Becky from her bedroom, to flee in his auto. But the town has now mobilized against them; the pod-people cannot allow the story to be told, and the "people" of Santa Mira organize to catch Miles and Becky. In a desperate escape attempt, they flee over the mountains, pursued by those who had once been their friends and neighbors.

The horror mounts when, in a tunnel, Becky succumbs to the pods. She falls asleep and soon her mind and body are taken over, cell by cell. In a moment of utmost panic, Miles looks into her eyes and realizes the awful truth. Continuing on alone, he comes to a highway where he makes wild attempts to flag down motorists who are terrified by his insane behavior. Eventually, he is picked up by the police, who naturally consider him mad, and is taken to a hospital for medical examination. The doctors agree that he is psychotic, but then fate intervenes. An intern reports an accident to a truck from Santa Mira, and in a casual aside, he tells how the driver of the wreck had to be dug out from under a pile of strange giant seed pods. The truth dawns on the police inspector, who orders the roads to Santa Mira closed, and in the final shot tells his assistant to "call the FBI."

The political, social, and intellectual atmosphere of the era that created *Invasion* must be understood in light of several preoccupations: the "Red Menace," which crystallized around the activities of Senator Joseph McCarthy and the somewhat less spectacular blacklisting of figures in the communications and entertainment industry, who were seen as a nefarious, subversive element undermining the entire fabric of American society; learning to cope with the consequences of a modern, urban, technologically bureaucratized society; and the pervasive fear of atomic annihilation. All these factors undermined the traditional American myth of individual action. The experience of the Depression, the rise and threat of totalitarianism, the loss of American insularity, the growth of technocracy all in one form or another challenged the integrity of the individual. It is therefore not surprising to note that film genres like science fiction or horror films proliferated in the 1950s. The central themes of these films show a preoccupation with depersonalization and dehumanization. Moreover, as Susan Sontag has suggested, it is by no means coincidental that at a time when the moviegoing public had for over ten years been living under the constant threat of instant atomic annihilation films of the 1950s should be concerned with the confrontation of death. As Sontag expressed it: "We live[d] under continued threat of two equally fearful, but seemingly opposed destinies: unremitting banality and inconceivable terror." On the surface there existed a complacency that disguised a deep fear of violence, but conformity silenced the cries of pain and feelings of fear.

In response to the threats of social banality and universal annihilation, three concepts dominated the decade: (1) conformity, (2) paranoia, (3) alienation. Each concept had its keywords. Conformity: "silent generation," "status seekers," "lonely crowds," "organization men," "end of ideology," "hidden persuaders." Paranoia: "red decade," "dupes," "front organization," "blacklisting," "un-Americanism," "fifth column," "fellow travelers," "pinkos." Alienation: "outsiders," "beats," "loners," "inner-directed men," "rebels." For the most part, the decade celebrated a suburbanized, bureaucratized, complacent, secure, conformist, consensus society in opposition to an alienated, disturbed, chaotic, insecure, individualistic, rebel society. Each of those three concepts dominating the 1950s finds obvious expression in *Invasion of the Body Snatchers*. First – conformity.

During the 1950s a concern for respectability, a need for security and compliance with the system became necessary prerequisites for participation in the reward structure of an increasingly affluent society. Conformism had replaced individuality as the principal ingredient for success. This standard extended to all aspects of life. Tract-built, identical, tidy little boxlike ranch houses on uniform fifty-foot plots bulldozed to complete flatness were the rage. Conformity dictated city planning in the form of Levittowns, the same way it silenced political dissidents in Congress. Creativity meant do-it-yourself painting-by-numbers. One created great artistic masterpieces by following directions.

The concern with conformity grew out of a need to escape from confusion, fear, worry, tension, and a growing sense of insecurity. It was accentuated by a sense of rootlessness and increased mobility. Consensus mentality offered a refuge in an anxious and confusing world. It represented an attempt to shift the burden of individual responsibility for one's fate to an impersonal monolithic whole. Excessive conformity, as in the 1950s, was a salve to smooth over obvious conflict and turmoil. A country that emerged from war victorious around the globe feared internal subversion at home; a society powered by a new technology and a new structure (corporate bureaucracy) feared a loss of personal identity. In the White House was a person whose great appeal was that he represented a politics of consensus, classlessness, and conformism – Eisenhower.

By the time *Invasion* was released (May, 1956) the intensity of the drive for consensus politics had diminished – the Korean War had ended, McCarthy had been censored, Stalin was dead, the spirit of Geneva had thawed the Cold War, the imminent threat of atomic annihilation had subsided, witch hunting had lost its appeal, and the threat of internal subversion had lessened. But the context of fear was still active. The political reality might not seem as frightening, but the mindset of the period was always ready at any moment to raise its repressive head. To many people, the fact that the enemy appeared less threatening only meant that he was better at concealing his subversion and that the eternal vigilance of good Americans had to be even more effective.

David Riesman's *The Lonely Crowd* (1955) spoke of a society obsessed by conformity. His now-famous formulation about inner-directed and other-directed men focuses on the same conflicts outlined by Siegel in Invasion. Miles Bennell is "inner-directed" – a self-reliant individualist who has internalized adult authority, and judged himself and others by these internalized self-disciplined standards of behavior. The "pods" are "other-directed" beings whose behavior is completely conditioned by the example of their peers. While inner-directed individuals like Miles felt concern and guilt about violating their inner ideals – in fact were driven by them – the other-directed pods had no inner ideals to violate. Their morality came from the compulsion to be in harmony with the crowd. Their guilt developed in direct proportion to how far they deviated from group consensus. The other-directed pods were uncritical conformists. It was no coincidence that the most popular adult drug of the 1950s was not alcohol or aspirin, pot or cocaine but Miltown and Thorazine – tranquilizers.

The second basic concept in 1950s America, the natural corollary to the drive toward conformity, was the notion of conspiracy. Conformity is based on the idea that there is a clear-cut division between them and us. In periods of overt conflict, like wars or economic crises, the division between the good and the bad is obvious. But in periods of confusion, the identification of enemies becomes more problematic. Covert expressions of subversion are more common than overt challenges; the enemy – whether real or imagined – attacks through subversion and conspiracy rather than war. In the 1950s subversion seemed to be everywhere. Appearances were deceptive;

to many, nothing was what it appeared to be. Schools named after American heroes like Jefferson, Lincoln, Walt Whitman, Henry George were rumored to be fronts for communists, calls for free speech were seen as pleas for communism, and racial unrest as being fomented by party activists. To many, taking the Fifth Amendment in order not to incriminate oneself was just another way of disguising one's political treason.

Threats to social order in the 1950s were not so much associated with personal violence as with an indefinable, insidious, fiendishly cold undermining of the normal. Conspiracy theories feed off the idea of the normal being deceptive. In *Invasion*, the pods, the alien invaders, take on the appearance of normal people. It becomes physically impossible to tell the difference between the aliens and the normals. In *Invasion* all forms of normalcy are inverted. Friends are not friends, "Uncle Ira" is not Uncle Ira, the police do not protect, sleep is not revivifying, telephones are no longer a way of calling for help but a device to tell the pod-people where the remaining non-pod-people are. Even the name of the town is paradoxical. Mira in Spanish means "to look," but the people of Santa Mira refuse to look; they stare blankly into the unknown.

A patina of normalcy hides a deep-seated violence. A man holds a giant seed pod and calmly asks his wife, "Shall I put this in with the baby?" "Yes," she replies, "then there'll be no more crying." In another scene, what appears to be a quiet Sunday morning gathering in the town square turns out to be a collection point where fleets of trucks filled with pods quietly dispense these "vegetables" to people who carry them to their cars and buses, ready to spread the invasion to neighboring towns. It is during a typical home barbeque among friends that Miles finds the pods in his greenhouse.

At the end of the film, when all avenues of help seemed closed, Miles and Becky, hiding in an abandoned cave, hear sweet, loving music – a Brahms lullaby. Miles decides that such beauty and feeling could not possibly be the singing of unemotional pods. He scrambles off to find out where this music is coming from only to discover that its source is a radio in a large truck being loaded by robot-like people with seed pods destined for far-off towns. The familiar is fraught with danger. It is no wonder that Miles comes to the edge of madness, no wonder that he treats people with a paranoid suspicion. Paranoia becomes the logical alternative to podlike conformism.

Finally, conformism and conspiracy signaled a new age of personal alienation.

From the very beginning of our history, one of the most persistent myths about American society has been the myth of natural harmony. The idea is derived from the notion made popular by Adam Smith and John Locke that there is a natural and harmonious relationship between the desires of individuals and the demands of social necessity, that individuals who act out of self-interest will automatically move the society as a whole in the direction of natural perfection. At the heart of this notion was the belief that nothing in the system prevented people from achieving their own individual goals, and that the traditional barriers of class, religion, and geography were absent in the American experience. The concept of natural harmony is further based on the belief of abundance. Individual failure had to be due to personal shortcomings because a society of abundance offered opportunity to anyone capable of grasping it – conflict was not built into the system. People were basically good. Solutions were always within grasp. Control was inevitable. Progress was assured.

This underlying belief in natural harmony was one of the casualties of the post-1945 world. In the 1930s American films had portrayed people ordering their environment. "The people," the Mr. Smiths, the Mr. Deeds, the Shirley Temples, and the Andy

Hardys, saw to it that control and harmony were restored. Individual "good acts" reinforced "social good" in the desire to control life. In the 1940s the theme of conquest, control, and restoration of the natural was the underlining statement of war films. Commitments to courage, self-sacrifice, and heroism were shown instead of Senate filibusters, talks with Judge Hardy, or faith in "the people." Depictions of failure, helplessness, and feelings of inadequacy were introduced as muted themes in the postwar films. Although we had won the war, conquered the Depression, and tamed nature by splitting the atom, things seemed out of control in the 1950s as conflict emerged between the desire for personal autonomy and the pressures for collective conformity. Individual acts of heroism were suspect. Group work and group think were the ideals. Success was measured by how much individuals submerged themselves into some larger mass (society, bureaucracy) over which they had little individual control. The rewards of status, popularity, and acceptance came with conformity to the group. In the films of the period, people who did not sacrifice individual desires for general social needs were fated to die, commit suicide, be outcast, or simply go mad.

Popular books like Riesman's *The Lonely Crowd*, William Whyte's *The Organization Man*, and Vance Packard's *The Status Seekers* showed how the traditional model of the hardworking, rugged individualist was being rejected for a world of the group – big universities, big suburbs, big business, and big media. Such harmony as existed resulted from the artificial ordering to an agreed upon surface norm. After the scarcity of the Depression came the affluence of the 1950s – complete with its never-ending routine of conspicuous consumption. Out of the victory for democracy and freedom came a society more standardized, less free, more conformist, and less personal. Out of splitting the atom came the threat of instant annihilation.

The mid-1950s films portrayed people trying desperately to ward off failure in the face of overwhelming destructive forces of nature (horror films), technology (science fiction films), and human imperfection (film noir). There were films about people being taken over or reincarnated: *The Search for Bridie Murphy* (1956), *I've Lived Before* (1956), *Back from the Dead* (1957), *The Undead* (1957), *Vertigo* (1956), *Donovan's Brain* (1953); about individuals in conflict with their societies: *High Noon* (1952), *The Phenix City Story* (1955), *No Place to Hide* (1956), *Not of this Earth* (1957); about superior forces beyond man's control: *Them* (1954), *Tarantula* (1956), *The Beast from 20,000 Fathoms* (1953), *This Island Earth* (1955), *Earth versus the Flying Saucers* (1956); about the apocalypse: *20,000 Leagues Under the Sea* (1954), *On the Beach* (1959), *The Thing* (1951). In these films, the world seemed menacing, fluid, chaotic, impersonal, composed of forces which one seldom understood, and certainly never controlled. Fear is centered on the unknown, unseen terrors that lurk beneath the surface normality.

Invasion's podism is depicted as a malignant evil, as a state of mind where there is no feeling, no free will, no moral choice, no anger, no tears, no passion, no emotion. Human sensibility is dead. The only instinct left is the instinct to survive. Podism meant being "reborn into an untroubled world, where everyone's the same." "There is no need for love or emotion. Love, ambition, desire, faith without them, life is so simple." A metaphor for communism? Perhaps! But, more directly, podism spoke to a society becoming more massified, more technological, more standardized.

The motto of the pods was "no more love, no more beauty, no more pain." Emotionless, impersonal, regimented, they became technological monsters. But they were not the irrational creatures of blood lust and power – they were just nonhuman. They became tranquil and obedient. They spoke to the fear of the 1950s – not the fear of violence, but the fear of losing one's humanity. As Susan Sontag argued, "the dark secret behind human nature used to be the upsurge of the animal – as in *King Kong* (1933). The threat to man, his availability to dehumanization, lay in his own animality. Now the danger is understood to reside in man's ability to be turned into a machine." The body is preserved, but the person is entirely reconstituted as the automated replica of an "alien" power.

The attraction of becoming a pod in the 1950s was all too real. But although dangling the carrot of conformity, *Invasion* opts ultimately for the stick of painful individuality. The possibility of moral uncertainty was the price we must pay for continued freedom. As Miles says: "Only when we have to fight to stay human do we realize how precious our humanity is." Podism, an existence without pain or fear or emotion, is seen as no existence at all. The fear of man becoming a machinelike organism, losing his humanity, was centered around the ambiguous dual legacy of an increasingly technological civilization. The atomic bomb was both a testament to man's increased control over his universe and a clear symbol of man's fallibility. *Invasion* mirrors this duality. It praises the possibility of a society without pain, yet it raises the spectre of a society without feeling. Security at what price? – the price of freedom and individualism. The rise of technology at what cost? – the cost of humanness itself. Although *Invasion* is ambiguous on this issue, demonstrating the positive effects of "podism" at the same time as condemning its consequences, this confusion, this ambiguity, is very much at the heart of the American cultural issues of the period – the internal conflict between the urge for conformity and the painful need for individuality, between an antiheroic loner and an institutionalized, bureaucratized system of mindless automated pods.

In his struggle to remain his own master, Miles fights against control by first falling back on the traditional notions inherited from the past. He appeals to friends – only to be betrayed. He appeals to the law – only to be pursued by it. He appeals to the system – only to be trapped by it. He appeals to love – only to be disappointed by losing it. All betray him. All become his enemy. Not because they are corrupt, or evil, but because they have become pods, because they have given up their individuality, their ability to choose.

If there is a 1950s vision of historical reality in *Invasion*, there is also a system of film technique designed to reinforce this vision. The language and technique of *Invasion* come out of the social reality of the period and speak directly to that context.

One of the major themes of life in the 1950s was the feeling of constraint – people feeling enclosed within boundaries. People were cut off from options, limited in their choices. There was a closing down of dissent, a shrinking of personal freedom. Silence became the acceptable response to oppression.

Invasion is a film about constraints. It is the story of a man whose ability to make sense of the world decreases and diminishes to the point of madness and frenzy. The film's action takes place within enclosed physical spaces and the physical spaces in the film induce a sense of isolation and constraint. The sleepy California town of Santa Mira is surrounded by hills. When Miles tries to escape he must run up a series of ladderlike stairs to flee the pod-people and reach the open highway that separates the town from the outside world. Miles and Becky are constantly running – in and out of small rooms, darkened cellars illuminated only by matches, large but empty night-clubs, miniature greenhouses, closets, low-ceilinged dens, abandoned caves. The giant seed pods are found in basements, closets, car trunks, greenhouses. The main actors are claustrophobically framed by doorways and windows photographed from low angles, and spend much of their time running down and up endless stairs, into locked doors, and beneath towering trees. The narrative structure of *Invasion* resembles a series of self-contained Chinese boxes and is designed to tighten the tension of the story at every step. Though Miles returns from his convention on a sunny morning and the film ends in a confused mixture of daylight and darkness, the main section of the film takes place in darkness – at night.

The whole film is enclosed within a framing device of prologue and epilogue. Siegel's original version had not included this frame, but the addition of a prologue and epilogue, making the film narrative appear as an extended flashback, has the unin-tended effect of constricting the narrative – itself contained in a rigidly enclosed time frame – even further. Within this framing device, Siegel also uses the technique of repeating a situation at the end of the film that mirrors a sequence presented at the beginning. In the final flashback episode, Siegel has Miles running in panic down the road and being pursued by a whole town of pod-people. This scene mirrors the open-ing scene when we see little Jimmy Grimaldi running down the road being pursued by his "podized" mother.

The effect of these devices is to keep the narrative tight in order to heighten tension and suspense. The use of flashback, prologue and epilogue, repeated scenes, interplay of lightness and darkness, all keep the narrative constrained within a carefully defined filmic space. The unbelievable tension is released only in the epilogue, when Miles finally finds someone who believes his story. The ending is not about the FBI's ability to counteract the threat of the pods but about the fact that Miles has finally made contact with another human – and that he is not alone. The film is more about being an alien, an outsider, an individualist, than about the "invasion" by aliens. When Dr. Bassett and his staff finally believe Miles's story, the enclosing ring of constraint is broken, and Miles collapses, relaxing for the first time in the film, knowing that at least he has been saved from a horror worse than death – the loss of identity. The final line – "Call the F.B.I." – is the signal that he is not alone and acts as an affirmative answer to the shout heard at the opening of the film – "I'm not insane." Up to the point when the doctor finally believes Miles's story, the film is actually about a man going insane.

Time is also a constant constraint on humanity, and Siegel emphasizes the fact that time is running out for Miles. The whole film is not only a race against madness, but also against time – of time slipping away. Time in *Invasion* is circumscribed by the fact that sleep is a danger. Miles needs to escape Santa Mira before he falls asleep. He takes pills, splashes his and Becky's face in a constant battle to stay awake. Sleep is not com-fort and safety but the instrument of death.

Siegel uses a whole arsenal of filmic techniques to reinforce the feelings of enclo-sure, isolation, and time running out. His shot set-ups focus on isolated action. People are photographed in isolation standing beneath street lamps, in doorways, alone at crowded railway stations. A background of black velvet darkness and a direct artificial light are used to highlight objects which in isolation take on an "evil clarity." In the film, objects are always illuminated, people's faces are not. Shadows dominate peo-ple's space and obscure personality. Diagonal and horizontal lines pierce bodies.

Darkness is combined with a landscape of enclosure to increase the feeling of fear. There is a stressed relationship between darkness and danger, light and safety. Those who wish to remain free of the pods must not only keep awake, but must constantly keep themselves in direct light. For example, when Miles discovers Becky's pod-like double in the basement of her home, he hurries upstairs into her darkened bedroom and carries her out of the dark house into his car which is parked directly beneath a bright street lamp.

Tension in the film is not only created by lighting techniques and camera setups, but most significantly by the contrast in how the actors play their roles. Miles is frenzied, harried, hard-driving, always running. The robot-like, affectless pod people stare out at the camera with vacant eyes, openly unemotional, unbelievably calm, rational, logical. They appear to be normal, and Miles appears to be insane; however, the reverse is true. The pods' blank expression, emotionless eyes mask their essential nature.

The whole film texture is based on the internal contrast between normal and alien. The hot dog stands, used-car lots, small office buildings, friendly cops, sleepy town square, and neighborhood gas stations only create the illusion of normalcy played against mounting terror.

The mise-en-scène, lighting, acting styles, physical presence, props, and Carmen Dragon's unrelenting, spine-chilling musical score keep the audience in a constant state of tension. The same is true of the constant introjection of siren sounds, cuckoo clocks, screams in the middle of the night, and the use of distorting lenses, claustrophobic close-ups, juxtaposed long shots, and low-angled shots that establish a mood of vague disquiet. All help to create a basic tension between the normal and the fearful, the familiar and the sinister, and to result in a film designed to give the audience a sense of isolation, suspense, and feeling of constraint.

Historians will debate the actual nature of the 1950s for a long time. But through the films of a period we can see how a particular society treated the period, viewed it, experienced it, and symbolized it. Few products reveal so sharply as the science fiction/horror films of the 1950s the wishes, the hopes, the fears, the inner stresses and tensions of the period. Directly or indirectly, *Invasion* deals with the fear of annihilation brought on by the existence of the A-bomb, the pervasive feeling of paranoia engendered by an increasing sense that something was wrong, an increasing fear of dehumanization focused around an increased massification of American life, a deep-seated expression of social, sexual, and political frustration resulting from an ever-widening gap between personal expectation and social reality, and a widespread push for conformity as an acceptable strategy to deal with the confusion and growing insecurity of the period. It is a film that can be used by historians, sociologists, and psychologists to delineate these problems and demonstrate the way American society experienced and symbolized this crucial decade.

18

The Western as Cold War Film
Gunfighters and Green Berets: The Magnificent Seven and the Myth of Counter-Insurgency

Richard Slotkin

For much of the twentieth century, the Western dominated American film. About a quarter of all the movies released between 1926 and 1967 were Westerns. Although the Western's popularity has declined in recent years, as recently as 1990 and 1992 two Westerns – Dances with Wolves *and* Unforgiven *– won the Academy Award for Best Picture.*

There are many reasons why Westerns proved so popular. Metaphorically, the Western addressed some of the most profound issues in American society: the conquest of a continent, migration, cultural conflict, crime and punishment, and the role of violence in the spread of American civilization. The Western also helped to define a certain ideal of masculinity: the western hero was laconic, loyal, tough, and firmly committed to his own code of honor.

At various times Westerns have taken diverse forms. Some, often featuring figures like Jesse James, celebrate the Western outlaw, who is viewed as resisting the expanding power of banks and corporations. Others, like High Noon *and* Shane, *honor the western hero as a defender of law and order. A few, like* Broken Arrow, *criticize the mistreatment of the original inhabitants of the West, Native Americans. In this essay, Richard Slotkin analyzes the political ideologies that Westerns expressed during the Cold War era.*

In this study, I want to account for the Western's special role in the culture of the American 1950s and '60s, and to interpret the genre's effect on ideological discourse, by looking closely at a single film, John Sturges' *The Magnificent Seven* (1960). The film was an epic rendition of the traditional "gunfighter" Western, but it was also a seminal film of the new subgenre of "Mexico Westerns" – and although it predates our military intervention, it was also in many respects the first "Vietnam Western." Before we can interpret the special uses to which Sturges put the language of the

Figure 13 *The Magnificent Seven* (1960). United Artists. Directed by John Sturges. Courtesy of Jerry Murbach, www.doctormacro.info.

genre, however, we need to review the genre's history and its relation to the development of American myth and ideology.

Myths are stories drawn from a society's history, which have acquired through persistent usage the power of symbolizing that society's ideology and dramatizing its moral consciousness, with all of the complexities and contradictions that consciousness may contain, Mythic versions of history transform accepted "facts" into ideological imperatives for belief and action, The myths of Custer's Last Stand, the Alamo, and Pearl Harbor are all based on historical events, but we use them as symbols and metaphors, interpreting crises different in character and time according to these mythic models, and deriving from the models sanctioned scenarios of political response,

The Myth of the Frontier is one of our oldest myths, expressed in a body of literature, folklore, ritual, historiography and polemics produced over a period of three centuries, Its symbols and concerns shaped the most prevalent genres of both nineteenth-century literary fiction and twentieth-century movies. The myth celebrates the conquest and subjugation of a natural wilderness by entrepreneurial individualists, who took heroic risks and so achieved windfall profits and explosive growth at prodigious speeds,

Violence is central to both the historical development of the frontier and its mythic representation, The Anglo-American colonies grew by displacing Amerindian societies and enslaving Africans to advance the fortunes of white colonists, As a result, the Indian war became a characteristic episode of each phase of westward expansion; the conflict of cultural and racial antagonists became the central dramatic structure of the Frontier Myth, providing the symbolic reference points for describing and evaluating other kinds of conflict, such as those between different generation or classes of settlers.

In the myth, both material and moral progress depend on success in violent enterprises. Conquest of the natural wilderness makes Americans "better off," but the struggle against the Indians and over the analogous classes of "savages" within civil society makes the American a "better man." The moral problem, and its triumphant solution, is embodied in the Frontier's mythic heroes: the scouts and Indian fighters of popular history and literature, "living legends" like Daniel Boone and literary myths like James Fenimore Cooper's Hawkeye. Their fables teach the necessity of racial solidarity against a common enemy, which cements a social compact that is otherwise imperiled by the ideology of self-interest. These figures stand on the border between savagery and civilization; they are "the men who know Indians," and in many ways their values and habits of thought mirror those of the savage enemy. Because of this mirroring effect, the moral warfare of savagery and civilization is, for the heroes, a spiritual or psychological struggle, which they win by learning to discipline or suppress the savage or "dark" side of their own human nature. Thus they are mediators of a double kind, who can teach civilized men how to defeat savagery on its native grounds: the natural wilderness, and the wilderness of the human soul.

By the time movie-makers took up the subject, the West – as the Frontier had already become a thoroughly mythologized space, defined by an elaborate system of cultural illusions and ideological formulae. In 1903, when Porter's *The Great Train Robbery* became the first Western and the pattern-setter for the development of narrative cinema, the Myth of the Frontier had become the dominant formula of American historiography and geopolitics. Frederick Jackson Turner's "Frontier Hypothesis" explained all of American history as the consequence of frontier experiences; Theodore Roosevelt, the philosopher John Fiske, and the Social Darwinist spokesmen for Manifest Destiny extended the metaphor into a model of world race history and used it to justify America's assumption of world power.

From 1903 to 1929 the silent Western developed distinctive generic patterns in its handling of Frontier stories. This development was interrupted by the advent of sound and the Depression; beginning in 1931 the genre went into a nine-year eclipse, during which few feature-length Westerns were produced. But in 1939 the Western experienced a "renaissance," which inaugurated a 30-year period in which Westerns were the most consistently popular form of action movie, with both audiences and producers, in the theater and in the new medium of television. These Westerns were resolutely "historical" in their references, and they succeeded in establishing a powerful association between the imagery of the West and the idea of a heroic age of American progressive enterprise. The pastoral and wilderness imagery of the Western invested these fables of power and achievement with an aura of natural innocence. The narrative structure of the Western story, however, insisted that whatever the nominal historical setting, violence was the necessary and justified determinant of the outcome. Every variety of Western has its characteristic form of violent resolution: the cavalry Western has its Indian massacre or charge into battle, the gunfighter or town-tamer movie has its climactic shoot-out in the street, the outlaw movie has its disastrous last robbery or assassination, the romantic Western has its bullet-riddled rescue scene. Moreover, because the Western has been seen as a representation of American history, the genre's insistence on the necessity of violence amounts to a statement about the nature of history and of politics.

By the Korean War, the symbolic language of the Western had been developed by its practitioners to a level of high sophistication and formal economy. Narrative formulae and characterizations were so well understood as to constitute a kind of media folklore; and in this form they invited all sorts of virtuosi and allegorical play with forbidden or difficult subjects: coexistence, civil rights, homosexuality, psychoanalysis. But because the genre's material had been so heavily encoded as referring to history and politics, this artistic play was actually quite serious as both a reflection of and an influence on the ideologies of Cold War liberalism and conservatism in the years preceding the Vietnam War.

One of the most important subgenres of the Western had been the so-called "Cult of the Outlaw," derived from Henry King's epic version of *Jesse James* in 1939. These films had taken a Depression era view of the outlaw as social bandit, rooting his outlawry in an experience of social oppression at the hands of corporate tyrants (railroads) or military despots (Reconstruction officers). Outlaw Westerns embodied the most explicitly populist reading of the West, and functioned as vehicles for social and political criticism.

Starting in 1950, however, with Henry King's *The Gunfighter*, the outlaw character was reduced to the simple elements of his screen persona: his loneliness and alienation, his living outside the law, and his skill with a gun. In place of the elaborately narrated social motives of outlawry, the gunfighter appeared as a man almost entirely lacking in a past, or in the social motives that drove the outlaw. This tendency reached its most extreme development in Clint Eastwood's Westerns of the early '70s, in which the hero is so abstracted from history of any kind that he is called "The Man with No Name."

The ideological significance of the shift from outlaw to gunfighter can be seen in the contrast between King's *Jesse James* and George Stevens' *Shane* (1953). King's movie spends most of its narrative describing and analyzing the outlaw's response to oppression and injustice, and relates these concerns to the life of the outlaw's community, showing how Jesse emerges from the heart of that community, serves it, then goes too far and is cast out of it. The hero of *Shane* is also a skilled fighter who assists small farmers against a tyrannical proprietor. But Shane arrives from outside, and his past is concealed. His style, manners and speech mark him as an aristocrat of some kind, and the deference with which he is treated is due to both his air of refinement and his skill with a gun. He is the only character in the movie who never acts (or hesitates to act) from self-interested motives. But because Shane's motives for helping the farmers are unique, and arise from no visible history or social background, they appear to be expressions of his nature, signs of a chivalric nobility which is independent of history, like the attributes of a "higher race." Shane is never part of the community, and his superior values are not seen as belonging to that community. He is an aristocrat of violence, an alien from a more glamorous world, who is better than those he helps and is not accountable to those for whom he sacrifices himself.

Shane's popularity was exploited in a wave of Westerns that developed the figure of the gunfighter as chivalric rescuer. In order to get new stories out of well-used material, these films queried the romantic idealism of Shane, played variations on the opposition of economic and chivalric motives for violence, and raised new issues out of the original problem of the hero's proper elation to the erotic life and the cash nexus. A more naturalistic version of the gunfighter appeared, in which the hero begins as a mercenary professional, and experiences a kind of "conversion" to the chivalric ideal in the course of the action. The means to this conversion is usually the love of a woman who promises both the fulfillment of romantic desire and reconciliation with a social code that demands self-sacrifice. One of the earliest and most spectacular exercises in this vein was also the first of the "Mexico Westerns," *Vera Cruz* (1954), directed by Robert Aldrich and starring Burt Lancaster and Gary Cooper. The film drew criticism for its lavish and humorous display of cynical and self-interested motives in both hero and heavy. But its strong association of heroic competence with mercenary pragmatism set the pattern for future "adult" Western.

Which brings us to *The Magnificent Seven*, which tells the story of a group of American gunfighters – professionals and technicians of violence, rugged individualists all – who go into Mexico to aid a peasant village against a predatory warlord or bandit who controls their region. Before Kennedy took office, before the Special Forces landed in Saigon, movie-makers had begun to imaginatively explore and test out the mythological and ideological premises that lay behind the counterinsurgency of the New Frontier. The movie is a complex reflecting mechanism, not simply a device for propagating Cold War values. By combining the political concerns of the new Cold War with the traditional terms of the Western, *Magnificent Seven* frames a vision which on the one hand rationalizes and justifies counter-insurgency, but which also exposes the contradictions and weaknesses of that ideology, and the military practices the policy begot.

John Sturges' *The Magnificent Seven* was released several months before Kennedy's inauguration, and had begun production long before the 1960 presidential campaign. Obviously, we are not dealing with a case of direct influence (unless the film influenced the President). Rather, film and President share a common set of ideological premises, a common mythology, and a common conception of heroic style.

Sturges' film was officially an American remake of Akira Kurosawa's *Seven Samurai* – a film which itself owed a great deal to American Westerns, and which had enjoyed both commercial success and critical prestige during its run in the States. *The Magnificent Seven* was successful in ways that go beyond its considerable box office: it became the basis of imitation and a rich source of popular icons. The musical score by Elmer Bernstein became the Marlboro cigarette theme-song, and thus part of one of the major advertising triumphs of the era, which ended by identifying the whole West as "Marlboro country." Yul Brynner and Eli Wallach revived and redirected their flagging careers from the film's success. Supporting player Steve McQueen emerged immediately as a major star, to be followed by others of the Seven: Horst Buchholz, James Coburn, Robert Vaughn and Charles Bronson. Several sequels and innumerable imitations of the film have been made in both Europe and the United States over the last 25 years, in the combat and science fiction genres as well as the Western, many starring one or more of the original players.

A poor Mexican village is being raided and tyrannized by Calvera (Wallach), a brutal and complex villain who acts like a bandit, but speaks the language of paternal authority – "I am a father to these men; they depend on me" – to justify his rape of the village. Driven at last to resist, the villagers send a delegation to the United States to buy guns, but they discover that in the US, guns are expensive while "men are cheap." Apparently the end of the wild west phase of the frontier has thrown a lot of gunfighters into unemployment. The peasants show their amenability to moderniza-tion by the speed with which they learn to think like capitalists, and take advantage of the situation. They decide to hire an American mercenary.

The peasants' decision is aided by a moral drama to which they are an audience. The town drunk has died – an Indian named "Old Sam" – and the town's bigots will not let him be buried in Boot Hill. True to the canons of the outlaw and the Indian-centered Westerns of the '40s and early '50s, the film invokes a kind of pastoral nos-talgia as the basis for a critique of American social hypocrisy. But the scene also invokes current history, specifically the civil rights battles of the previous five years, some of which concerned the integration of southern military graveyards.

At this point two gunfighters step forward, drive the hearse to the cemetery, stand off the bullies, and bury the Indian. These are Chris and Vin (Brynner and McQueen) – Chris is a solemn, black-clad figure, Vin a laid-back, easy man with a Mark Twain style, full of folk-sayings, irony and tall tales. It is not clear why they do it; not a word is said about integration or racism, nor do they accept money, though both are out of funds, It appears that the sight of injustice, and of an important job undone, is more than they can resist: ask not what your country can do for you, but what you can do for your country.

Old Sam's funeral highlights the central importance of racial imagery in the adapta-tion of Kurosawa's film to American and Western-movie terms. *Seven Samurai's* nar-rative counterpoints two kinds of conflict: the tactical struggle of the samurai to save the peasants from the bandits, and the class conflict between the values and practices of the fading military aristocracy and the peasantry. The ideological tradition of the Frontier Myth, even in its most sophisticated historiographical formulations, had always insisted on American exceptionalism and our exemptions from the class con-flicts of the Old World. The gestures toward the mythic representation of class con-flicts made during the Depression were very tentative; even in the "outlaw" Westerns of 1939–50, the oppressed farmers are seen as a mistreated interest group rather than a peasantry. Now, in 1960, the only way the American producers can imagine American engagement with the issues of class raised by *Seven Samurai* is to identify class with race, and project the conflict beyond the borders, into the Third World.

The contrasting motives that impel gunfighters and peasants are presented as the signs of both class and racial difference. The peasants try to persuade Chris to help them by using a naive and inconsistent mixture of crass materialism ("We can pay you well") and a sentimental appeal to his sympathies. In fact, the money they offer is inadequate by Chris' professional and American standards, and Chris has already demonstrated his contempt for mere sentiment by dismissing the effusive praise an eastern "drummer" offers for his burial of Old Sam. The American's moral choices are determined by a mix of motives more complex and "sophisticated" than the Mexican peasants can imagine. Accessibility to the appeal of human sympathy and the needs of the weak is balanced and offset by the hard-headed materialism and tactical pragmatism of the mercenary, and the pride of the professional man of arms, for whom violence is a calling, a discipline and an art. What tips Chris' balance is his discovery that the little bag of coins and the gold watch the Mexicans offer are their sole possessions. He squares his chivalric sympathies with professional hard-headedness by saying, "I have been offered a lot for my services before, but never everything."

Chris then recruits six other gunfighters, through an elaborate series of tests and rituals. The narrative thus makes clear that the force that must aid the Mexicans is an elite one, carefully chosen by means that are technically and morally sophisticated, But the group which is put together is designed to emphasize the range and variety of skills and motives that compose such a killer elite, The common denominator is tough-mindedness and professionalism; the test for this is adherence to the formulas of self-interest. The good work of saving the Third World is not to be undertaken in the sentimental or idealistic spirit of romantic missionaries; it is to be firmly based in realism and a sense of self-interest, the implication being that pure idealism is too rare and perishable a quality to sustain a long twilight struggle.

There is only one pure mercenary in the crowd, however – Chris' oldest friend, Harry, who refuses to believe that there is not some hidden treasure Chris is angling for. For the rest, professionalism (as an ideal and a social status) weighs equally with cash values: Vin joins up because he is out of money, and must choose between killing for low wages or clerking in a store – "good, steady work," one of the Mexicans tells him. But Vin despises that kind of work, and the loss of status and dignity that it suggests, and he paradoxically demonstrates his contempt for the Mexican's values by immediately enlisting in the villagers' cause. The maintenance of professional status outweighs the peasant (actually, the bourgeois) considerations of cash value and security.

From the first, then, we see that the differences between Mexicans and Americans have both a racial and a class aspect: the Americans are a white aristocracy or elite, whose caste-mark is their capacity for effective violence; the Mexicans are non-white peasants, technologically and militarily incompetent. Professionalism is thus a metonymy of the class and ethnic superiority of Americans to Mexicans. As more gunfighters are recruited, this definition is developed and extended. The most professional of the crew, Reb (James Coburn), is like a Zen master gunfighter; he joins because he sees an occasion to test himself and exercise his skills, and this compensates for the low pay – professionalism here is a form of religious discipline or calling. Lee (Robert Vaughn) is the neurotic gunfighter, who joins up to get away from his past, and from the vengeful Johnson brothers – professionalism is the last virtue of a failure, the last strength of the psychically damaged. The youngest and least competent of the gunfighters, Chico or "The Kid" (Horst Buchholz), is a child of Mexican peons (who may have been killed by bandits or gringo gunfighters), who wants desperately to be one of the elite – professionalism is the means to Americanization, higher status, self-transformation. This theme is emphasized by the role of Bernardo Riley (Bronson), the child of a Mexican mother and an Irish father, whose identity is split between pride in his status as American killer-professional, and nostalgia for the maternal and familial values represented by Mexico.

In these seven, Sturges gives us a sampling of the major types of gunfighter developed by the movies in the preceding decade: the wild kid, the crazed neurotic, the aristocratic loner, the folksy populist, the ethnic outsider seeking acceptance. By multiplying heroes in this way, Sturges enlarges a form that had canonically focused on the single gunfighter. He gives us a platoon of lonely men, whose motives map the range of heroic motives, and even take in a range of ethnic possibilities: Reb is a

Southerner, Chris a Cajun, Riley is Irish and Mexican, Chico is Mexican. In effect, Sturges has merged the conventions of the Western and the combat movie – the adventure of the lonely man blends with the adventure of the representative platoon. Although these men are gunfighters, the form of their recruitment and association suggests that they are also commandos, or Green Berets.

Once in the village, the gunfighters begin to train the Mexicans in self-defense. As in the combat film, there is comic contrast between the incompetence and innocence of the peons (recruits) and the expertise and professionalism of the gunfighters (sergeants), There is also ethnic tension and mutual suspicion: the farmers hide their wives and daughters, and otherwise show their distrust, until action proves the worth of the gunfighters. Likewise, the gunfighters maintain a professional reserve; they will help only as long as the peasants keep their bargain and obey orders. They keep reminding themselves that it is a canon of their professional code not to get emotionally involved with their work. Each party modifies the other, however. Association with the tribal life of the village softens the gunfighters, specifically by evoking paternal feelings. The key figure here is Riley, who becomes a father-figure to a group of children, and who will be killed at the end because of that. For Riley, acceptance of the children means accepting the part of himself that is Mexican, but he does this in a style that affirms his own higher paternalism – the paternalism of violence – even while he denies it. When the children ask to go with him, because they despise the cowardice of their peasant fathers, Riley spanks them, and orders them to believe that their fathers are not cowards because they cannot fight, that it takes more courage to be a good father and breadwinner than to be a gunfighter.

This nominal ideology, however, is undercut by the film's entire structure, which shows frame by frame that the gunfighter is both technically and morally superior to the farmer. This clash of nominal and actual ideology is brought to full articulation in a scene late in the film, in which the gunfighters, questioned by Chico, voice their code in a formal chorus, The gunfighters begin to get sentimental about the village and its families; lonely technocrats dreaming of a lost pastoral. But Chico breaks into the mood, reminding them that "you owe everything to the gun." No false pastoral for Chico, he knows the dark side of peon life all too well. Chico's question provokes the gunfighters to think things over, and each answers him in turn, at first emphasizing the emptiness of their life – "Home? None, Wife? None, Kids? None." Then Chris and the others chime in, and the balance shifts towards the pride and power of their calling – "Places tied down to? None, Men you step aside for? None." Although the passage is meant to underline the ideological premise that the solid family life and working-class virtues of the Mexicans are morally superior to gunfighting, it becomes a paean to rugged individualism. The audience's emotional response is voiced by Chico, the peon who would be a gunfighter: "This is the kind of arithmetic I like!"

Thus the film's visual and stylistic apparatus valorizes the gunfighter ethic of violence, mobility and individualism at the expense of the farmer values, the peon values. The gunfighters are "good paternalists," whose order conforms to the Camelot slogan, which described the ideal world order as one in which "the strong are just, and the weak are protected." But the movie is consciously ironic in its deployment of this chivalric/paternalistic structure, because the most eloquent spokesman in the movie for paternalistic ideology, the most eloquent sloganeer for the party of order, is none other than Calvera the bandit.

The characterization of Calvera is very different from Kurosawa's bandit chief. The latter is virtually an abstraction of evil ferocity; Calvera has complexity and irony, and sardonic humor of a kind that has great appeal on the screen. There is even a kind of perverse innocence in his belief that all men, and especially all thieves and professional mercenaries, can be trusted to act on a rational calculation of self-interest. When he first arrives to rape the village, he says he must do so because he is "a father to his men," who depend on him; and he praises the village for its old-fashioned piety and hard work. He has a mouth full of cynical proverbs: "If God did not mean them to be sheared, he would not have made them sheep."

He is more than a simple bandit, then. The movie's imagery links him to figures like Villa and Zapata, who (in their movie biographies) are transformed from horseback bandits to social revolutionaries. If Calvera looks like Villa or Zapata, he talks like Porfirio Diaz or General Huerta, cynically mouthing paternalistic slogans and religious pieties while he "taxes" the village, Clearly he is more accurately described as a "warlord" than as a bandit, but since we cannot limit Calvera's type specifically to either the revolutionary left or the patriarchal right, he becomes an abstraction of the tyrannical potential inherent in the "extremes." This paradoxical combination makes Calvera the perfect enemy: the enemy counterinsurgency always sought and never found, the enemy who is native, but more hated by the people than the alien Americans, who represents simultaneously the principle of excessive order (tyranny) and excessive disorder (banditry, revolution), who embodies two "extremes," leaving the center to the Americans.

Calvera is a savage parody of paternalism, but as such, he also offers a critique – implied and stated – of the character and motives of the Americans. Like them, he is a professional, which is to say a man whose actions are motivated by pure pragmatism, self-interest and an advanced understanding of weapons and tactics. This parallel is perceived by every Mexican, from Calvera to Chico to the townspeople themselves, When Calvera appeals to the understanding of self-interest and pragmatism common to all professionals, he expects the Seven to understand, and is mystified when they persist in acting "unprofessionally," "We are in the same business," Calvera says. They are thieves – why do they pretend to be policemen?

The parallel becomes sharper as the plot moves toward its climax. After Calvera's first attack is repulsed, the villagers realize that they will have to fight to the death against the outraged bandit. A party of appeasement arises, and Chris suppresses it by demanding that the peasants choose now between fighting and surrender. He holds a kind of false plebiscite right there in Sotero's bar; and when those present (some of whom are intimidated by his glare) choose to fight, he tells them that they are now committed, and if anyone backs off or tries to get out of it, Chris will shoot him. Chris deals with Sotero and the Mexican fathers as Riley deals with the children: he "spanks" and disciplines them coercively, replacing their authority with his own in everything but name; he asserts that this paternalistic coercion will make them free and independent adult men.

The paradox in Chris's response to Sotero mirrors the contradiction on which the Green Beret approach to counter-insurgency foundered. At the center of the counter-insurgency ideology was the assumption of American superiority, not merely at the level of technology and technique, but at the level of political culture, consciousness and commitment. According to [Larry E.] Cable's study, between 1956 and

1962 American counter-insurgency doctrine held that "the organic and unsponsored insurgency was not a viable possibility." It was "the American political shibboleth that insurgency could not be organic," but must absolutely depend upon an external sponsor," not only for the material of war, but for political will, for the motivation that initiates and sustains purposeful political action over a period of years and decades.

This belief blinded policy-makers not only to the political character of the North Vietnamese regime, but also to the existence of an indigenous political culture in the South. If the native political culture was null, it followed that the American task would be to supply something in the place of nothing: to inscribe the forms of national organization on the "blank slate" of a pre-nationalist culture. Like Fenimore Cooper's Hawkeye, the Green Beret "knows Indians" and mirrors their qualities, but his mission (after all) is not to vindicate and protect their culture, but to discredit, transform, and replace it with a "more civilized" model. Thus the various programs of "reform" and "nation-building" tended to become programs of Americanization. Since there was in fact a strong and intractable political culture in Vietnam, however, Americanization of the war served only to alienate the people it was intended to protect, and to allow the Communists to identify themselves with the defense of the indigenous culture.

At the moment when Chris asserts his dominance, the narrative of *Magnificent Seven* departs radically from the plot of Kurosawa's *Seven Samurai*. The samurai and villagers achieve a kind of comradeship, and their solidarity is never broken. But the gunfighters dictate to the villagers; and the villagers betray the Seven to Calvera. For at least some in the village, Chris and Calvera are morally equivalent, and Calvera is in some ways preferable – or at least, he seems the more powerful and inescapable of the two, This moral equivalency is voiced again by Calvera, who says that "A thief who robs from a thief is pardoned for a thousand years … I pardon you." He allows them to live, and returns their guns to them, in return for their promise to leave Mexico. His reasons are thoroughly professional – he recognizes that the Seven probably have friends in the States who would avenge them. Calvera doesn't want gringo trouble; he's won his point, proven the enterprise futile, He expects men of similar professional expertise to recognize the facts and bow to them in a rational and disinterested spirit.

Calvera's version of a "Geneva settlement" offers the gunfighters peace at the expense of their honor, and it is clear that they are humiliated by his terms. But Chris' behavior, and his discussion with the most mercenary of the gunfighters (Harry), confirms Calvera's assertion that the arrangement is rational and in perfect accord with the code of more or less enlightened self-interest by which the professional, modern man determines his actions. Indeed, Calvera's treaty is just the sort of pragmatic stick-and-carrot deal which President Johnson offered the North Vietnamese in his speech at Johns Hopkins in April 1965. The logic behind the offer derived from the deterrent aspect of counter-insurgency doctrine which aimed at deterring future guerrilla wars by demonstrating a will to impose "excessively high" costs on the enemy.

The Seven are "magnificent" because they follow the imperatives of pride and "honor," rather than the ethic of rational self-interest. Rational self-interest, as a principle of action, is rendered morally questionable by its association with Calvera. At work here is an ideological double-standard, which sees Americans and their (non-white) enemies as governed by fundamentally different motives and standards, What is sanity and reason for the enemy is madness and dishonor for us; what is "selfless idealism" in the Seven would appear as irrational fanaticism in an enemy. Moreover, it is clear that the American chivalric standard is the higher of the two: carrots and sticks appeal only to a lower order of moral intelligence. Americans ask not what their country can do for them (nor fear what it may do to them), but ask what they can do for their country.

The decision of the Seven to return to the village heightens the distinction between hapless Mexicans and powerful Americans. The gunfighters will go back and redeem the village in spite of the villagers' betrayal, in the teeth of evidence that the village polity does not fully sustain them, and that its culture is alien to them. Their motives are again mixed: Chris, Vin and Riley have learned to care about the little people of the town; Chico wants to vindicate his race. The common denominator is that their reasons are personal: they will finish the fight to resolve moral dilemmas which arise more from their character as Americans and professionals than from any real tie to the village. They return because their feelings of affection for the village and their desire for symbolic vindication now coincide precisely; there is no choice between making love and making war – pragmatically, they have become the same thing.

Again, the movie reads accurately the mix of values in the political ideology of the Green Beret moment in foreign affairs. More than this, it predicts the direction in which that ideology would move: from an assertion that Vietnam must be defended for material reasons of national interest, to the assertion that the war is necessary as a "symbol" of American determination, down to the strident and pathetic demands of Nixon and Kissinger that the war must be continued and extended – through bloody infantry assaults on symbolic targets, through signals in the form of massive bombing campaigns – to prevent our being perceived as "a pitiful helpless giant."

In the movie, what follows this shift is a massacre scene which, had it been filmed a few years later, would have raised echoes of My Lai: the Seven stage a commando-style attack on the village, in which bandits and townsfolk are completely intermingled, yet so expert is their technique that they never kill any townspeople, they only and precisely kill bandits. The mythical "surgical strike," so central to the fantasies of military scenario-makers, and the counter-insurgency fantasy of killing the guerrillas without harming any of the peasants, are visualized here. But the literal representation of the attack as an extermination of the bandits is offset by the visual impression that this is indeed an attack on the village which has betrayed them. The contrast with Kurosawa's movie throws this point into high relief: Kurosawa's samurai are never outside the village, and in the last attack samurai and peasants fight as comrades. Sturges goes out of his way to show that in the crisis the peasants are helpless, dependent on the violent incursion of the Americans outside – and on the chivalric caritas of men who owe them nothing, except perhaps contempt. Only when the Americans have begun their act of self-sacrifice do the peasants join them.

The surviving gunfighters do not remain in the village after their triumph, however. Only Chico stays behind, to marry a local girl – the film's only bit of sexual romance. The Americans help this world, but literally have no interest in it; they are not hewers of wood and drawers of water, but professionals. This ending also fulfills in fantasy the scenario of counter-insurgency, which envisioned the victorious Green Berets – like Washington after the Revolution – declining the mantle of imperial rule. With the old colonial power gone, and the new Communist takeover defeated, the Green Berets could safely turn power back to the natives, or rather to a new class of Americanized leaders – that elusive "Third Force" envisioned by policy-makers, that would be neither communist nor reactionary, neither peasant nor landlord. The war done, the Americans leave the scene, either to go back home or, like the Lone Ranger, to ride on to similar adventures in yet another imperiled town ....

19

Popular Culture in the Age of White Flight
Film Noir, Disneyland, and the Cold War (Sub)Urban Imaginary

Eric Avila

The characteristics of film noir are almost comfortingly familiar: skewed framing, chiaro-scuro lighting, deep shadows, oblique lines, ominous silhouettes, alienated heroes, and deadly women. Film noir is a world of flashbacks and voiceovers, a place where the worst usually happens, criminals hold the upper hand, and paranoia, isolation, and despair are the order of the day (and night). But, as Eric Avila reminds us, it is a particular urban world. Classic film noir is set in a post-World War II urban environment. It suggests that cities house and foster social and cultural evils, from robbery and murder to alienation and shift-ing gender balances. Using film noir and Disneyland as opposite poles, he demonstrates how Americans culturally constructed the meaning of cities and suburbs in postwar America.

This article takes popular cultural expressions as a window onto the transformation of the American city after World War II. First, it considers the film genre known as film noir as evidence of a larger perception of social disorder that ensued within the context of the centralized, modern city, which peaked at the turn of the century. Second, it turns to Disneyland as the archetypal example of a postwar suburban order, one that promised to deliver a respite from the racial and sexual upheaval that characterized the culture of industrial urbanism. Together, film noir and Disneyland illuminate the meanings assigned to the structural transformation of the mid-century American city and reveal the cultural underpinnings of a grass-roots conservatism that prized white suburban homeowner-ship. Ultimately, this article emphasizes the interplay of structure and culture, demon-strating the linkage between how cities are imagined and how they are made.

Urban life in the United States underwent a dramatic transformation toward the middle of the twentieth century. To the extent that one can think of the history of the American city as a series of successive but overlapping paradigms, the 1930s marked the beginnings of a transition from the modern, industrial, centralized city, which emerged around the turn of the century, to the postwar, decentralized urban region. The shifting concentration of public resources and private capital, coupled with federal incentives toward suburban home ownership among broader segments of the population, accelerated the pattern of decentralized urbanization in postwar

Eric Avila, "Popular Culture in the Age of White Flight," *Journal of Urban History*, vol. 31, no. 1 (2004), pp. 3–22.

America and decimated the economic and social life of the inner city. The regional biases of such development were manifest in the postwar ascendance of the Sun Belt, which cradled a compelling vision of the suburban good life, whereas an "urban crisis" took shape within the Rust Belt cities of the industrial Northeast.

This transition accompanied a profound reconfiguration of social relations. In the second half of the twentieth century, after a wave of labor strikes during the mid-1940s, class gradually subsided as the discursive basis of social conflict, whereas racial and gendered divisions assumed greater prominence.

What role the spatial transformation of American society at midcentury played in this development, however, requires additional exploration. The postwar suburban boom created a space, literally and figuratively, for reinstating racial and sexual barriers that weakened within an ascendant urban liberalism that reached its zenith during the 1930s and 1940s. As the racially exclusive patterns of postwar suburbanization facilitated the "blackening" of American inner cities, white flight reflected and reinforced the racial resegregation of the United States. And whereas the modern city incorporated women into public life – as workers and consumers – postwar suburbanization placed greater demands on women to return to the private sphere to resume their traditional responsibilities as mothers and wives. Creating a space for a return to normalcy, the postwar suburban boom offered a setting in which to restore traditional divisions between the races and the sexes.

Urban historians, geographers, and sociologists have measured and mapped the political, economic, and social transition from the modern industrial city to the decentralized urban region, but the cultural corollary to this process has been overlooked. White flight during the postwar period necessitated the formation of a new cultural order, one that marked an exchange of the heterogeneous, anonymous, promiscuous spaces of the centralized city for the contained, segregated, homogeneous experiences of the decentralized urban region. This article explores that transformation through the lens of popular culture, considering the mid-1940s debut of film noir as a popular genre of film and the successive opening of Disneyland in 1955. Both cultural productions posited a critique of the modern city and its typical pattern of social relations, and both arrived alongside the heightened thrust of postwar suburbanization. If film noir situated its indictment of the racial and sexual promiscuity within the spatial context of the modern city, Disneyland offered a suburban antithesis, modeling a new sociospatial order that took shape along the fringes of the urban core. The juxtaposition of film noir and Disneyland within their historical context illustrates a key cultural tension between a reinvigorated suspicion of urban modernity, on one hand, and a suburban retreat from the black city and its disordered culture, on the other. This tension underscored the post-World War II construction of a white suburban ethos and encompassed the political unconscious of a "silent majority" still in its formative years.

The Modern City, its New Mass Culture, and their Midcentury Decline

Not too long ago, a generation of historians discovered the culture of the modern city as a rich field of historical inquiry and illustrated how diverse groups of Americans collectively experienced the transition to urban modernity through a burgeoning set of cultural institutions. In world's fairs, expositions, movie palaces, amusement parks, spectator sports, and night clubs, urban Americans reveled in the "new mass culture" that electrified the landscape of the American city at the turn of the century. As the preeminent metropolis of the nineteenth century, New York City dominated this discussion as the city's cultural institutions facilitated the transition from a Victorian social order, with its strict separation of classes, races, and sexes, to a new cultural order, one that promoted a promiscuous set of interactions among a motley crowd of urban strangers. In New York City, as well as in its urban counterparts at the turn of the century, the crowded venues of the new mass culture reflected the ways in which urban Americans negotiated the perils and pleasures the modern city.

The vitality of the new mass culture, however, rested in no small part on the economic fortunes of the great industrial centers of the Northeast and Midwest, but such fortunes began to contract toward the middle of the twentieth century. The Great Depression crippled the urban economies of New York City, Philadelphia, Detroit, and Chicago, but perhaps more than any other singular event, World War II undermined the hegemony of urban industrial society and culture by initiating the deconcentration of public resources and private capital. Beginning in the early 1940s, the federal government actively promoted industrial decentralization as a strategy to protect a burgeoning military-industrial infrastructure from the event of an air attack. When the Chrysler Warren Tank Plant took advantage of federal incentives to open on an undeveloped tract of land some fifteen miles north of downtown Detroit in 1941, for example, it augmented the suburban model of postwar industrial development that weakened the economic vitality of traditional urban centers.

The urban crisis initiated during the war years was as much social as it was economic. World War II unleashed a wave of racial violence in the nation's cities, demonstrating the level of discomfort that accompanied the sudden diversification of urban society. The great migration of African Americans from the rural South to wartime centers of employment in the Northeast, Midwest, and Far West "blackened" the face of American cities considerably and aroused hostility from local whites, whose sense of entitlement to defense jobs rested on an entrenched conviction of white supremacy. On June 6, 1944, for example, ten thousand white workers at Cincinnati's Wright aircraft engine plant staged a wildcat strike to protest the integration of the machine shop. Race riots exploded in cities elsewhere. The year 1943 delivered a moment of intense racial violence for the nation's cities, as race riots erupted in New York City, Detroit, and Los Angeles, where the infamous Zoot Suit Riots between white sailors and Chicano youth demonstrated the extent to which other racial groups besides African Americans were implicated within wartime racial tensions.

As American cities festered with racial violence during the war years, an emergent pattern of suburbanization materialized during and after World War II and offered a setting removed from such tensions. Again, the federal government played no small part in this development. Housing policy under the New Deal administration set the stage for the postwar suburban boom and offered incentives to industrialists and aspiring home owners to abandon the nation's urban centers. In particular, the creation of the Homeowners Loan Corporation, the Federal Housing Administration, and, later, the Veterans Administration stimulated the national market for housing construction by shifting the focus of urban development away from the inner city and toward the suburbs. But, as historians have demonstrated, the discriminatory measures built into federal housing policy created the basis for the racial resegregation of postwar America. The urbanization of African Americans throughout and beyond the war years coincided with the largest phase of mass suburbanization in American history, in which millions of Americans who qualified themselves or were qualified as white realized their dream of suburban home ownership. Generally, excluded from the greatest mass-based opportunity for wealth accumulation in American history, African Americans and other minority groups largely remained concentrated within decaying cores of urban poverty. The racial dimensions of the postwar urban crisis thus gave rise to "chocolate cities and vanilla suburbs," which became the dominant paradigm of race and space after World War II.

As a generation of white Americans pursued their dreams of home ownership in the suburbs and as the face of the American city blackened considerably in the aftermath of that exodus, it is not difficult to understand how the culture of industrial urbanism entered a period of decline. Reports of the demise of the new mass culture circulated throughout the networks of public discourse in postwar America, and not surprisingly race emerged as a primary explanation for this development. For example, though Coney Island at the turn of the century reigned as the capital of modern urban culture, the *New York Times* reported in 1962 "Coney Island Slump Grows Worse," drawing attention to the postwar plight of the amusement park. Amidst the many reasons cited for Coney Island's decline, "concessionaire after concessionaire" agreed "the growing influx of Negro visitors [to the park] discouraged some white persons to the area." Three years later, Steeplechase Park, the first of Coney Island's great amusement parks, became the last, closing its doors forever.

Chicago's Riverview Park experienced a similar fate. Once billed as the world's largest amusement park, Riverview stood on 140 acres of land on the city's northwest region. Whereas Riverview enticed an ethnically diverse array of pleasure seekers throughout its sixty-four-year popularity, the amusement park could not withstand the changing demographics that ensued in the era of racial desegregation. By the 1960s, Riverview entered a period of rapid decline, and on October 3, 1967, Riverview closed its doors forever. The *Chicago Tribune* explained that the park's "natural defenses began to crumble. Racial tension ran rampant inside the park."

Amusement parks were not the only genre of popular amusement that fell by the wayside. Urban baseball parks that grew alongside amusement parks encountered similar difficulties during the postwar period. Philadelphia's Shibe Park, for example, once hailed as the crown jewel of ballparks, lost much of its appeal among baseball fans during the 1950s. In 1970, Bob Carpenter, owner of the Philadelphia Phillies, removed his team from its inner-city locale, convinced that baseball was "no longer a paying proposition" at Shibe Park and that its location in "an undesirable neighborhood" meant that white baseball fans "would not come to a black neighborhood" to see a ball game. Similarly, in the aftermath Walter O'Malley's infamous decision to move the Dodgers from Brooklyn to Los Angeles, one disappointed fan pointed to Brooklyn's changing racial profile to explain O'Malley's decision: "I guess O'Malley was like everybody else, as long as you're not my neighbor, it was okay. But once [blacks] started to live in the neighborhood, it was time to move out."

Clearly, a complex interplay of factors contributed to the decline of these cultural landmarks, but in the era of desegregation, a perception emerged that black urbanization facilitated a retreat from the modern city and its culture among a white public.

Such a perception informed the tenor of American popular culture as far back as the early postwar period. Take, for example, that body of American film that critics and historians have identified as film noir. Coined by French film critics in the late 1940s, film noir describes a cycle of American filmmaking roughly spanning the ten years following the end of World War II. Defined as a genre, a mood, a sensibility, and a movement, film noir eludes precise definition but includes a diverse array of crime dramas ranging from individual case studies of murder and criminal deviance to more general treatments of gangsters and organized crime.

Historical assessments of film noir tend to emphasize the experience of the war and its effects on the nation's psyche, but when viewed through the lens of urban history, the genre reveals some striking perceptions about the American city and its culture at midcentury. One of film noir's defining characteristics, after all, is its use of the modern city as setting and subject. Unlike the gleaming spires of the *Wizard of Oz*, however, the noir city exposed the seedy side of urban life. Noir's dark urban vision resonated throughout its titles: *Dark City, City of Fear, The Naked City*, and *Cry of the City*. The noir vision of urban life drew on a representational tradition in Western culture. In contrast to the Enlightenment view of the Western city as the summit of social progress, film noir emphasized the social and psychological consequences of urban modernity. Based initially on the writings of Dashiell Hammett, Raymond Chandler, and James Cain, and with striking parallels to the paintings of Reginald Marsh, George Bellows, and Edward Hopper, noir's erotic portrait of an urban wasteland intonated a deep ambivalence toward the midcentury American metropolis. By the 1940s, as the postwar urban crisis took shape, film noir translated the literary and artistic visions of urban malaise into a more popular cinematic discourse that paralleled the midcentury fate of the American city.

Film noir targeted those urban spaces that best conveyed its vision of urban malaise. The tenement, for example, is a recurrent noir setting, identified as an appropriate milieu for noir's gallery of urban deviants. Its peeling walls, dingy lighting, and rickety stairs frame the encounters between prostitutes and their johns in *Act of Violence* and hide the monstrous fetishes of child molesters in *M*. Film noir featured other spaces of the modern city in its blighted urban landscape. Desolate train stations and abandoned warehouses, vacant streetcars and late-night diners, deserted alleys and empty sewers, seedy nightclubs and tawdry amusement parks: these were the landmarks of film noir and they symbolized of the brand of industrial urbanism that entered a period of decline at the outset of the postwar period.

Noir's portrait of urban life focused on the social disorder that ensued within the spatial context of the modern city. In particular, as film historians have demonstrated, noir emphasized the degraded state of sexual relations at the outset of the postwar period. Similar to African Americans, women entered urban public life in unprecedented numbers in the early 1940s, as the female workforce in the United States rose from eleven million to nearly twenty million during the war years. But the very public profile of "Rosie the Riveter," particularly within the nation's cities, aroused animosity toward women who abandoned traditional social roles. As men returned from the war front to resume the routines of work and family, film noir channeled such animosities into its alluring yet disturbing portrait of a new breed of public woman – sassy, conniving, and out to undermine masculine authority through her many misdeeds. The femme fatale resurfaced with a vengeance in American culture vis-à-vis film noir, but the urban context in which she debuted underscored the dangers of a promiscuous urban world where the gendered divisions between public and private life dissolved. Film noir saw the ascendance of such actors as Joan Crawford, Barbara Stanwyck, and Veronica Lake, who perfected the image of the public woman and modeled a clear contempt for the traditional role of women as guardians of the private sphere.

Noir's urban vision of sexual disorder had a racial corollary as well. By the mid-1940s, amidst the blackening of American cities, film noir – translated from French as "black film" – offered a recurring portrait of the promiscuous mixing of the races. Film noir dramatized a larger discourse of race that likened the denigrated condition of blackness to white criminality. In this capacity, film noir echoed a larger discursive affinity between white deviance and black identity. For example, the National Association of Real Estate Board issued *Fundamentals of Real Estate Practice* in 1943, which advised real estate agents to be wary of those living on the margins of respect-ability:

> The prospective buyer might be a bootlegger who could cause considerable annoyance to his neighbors, a madam who had a number of call girls on her string, a gangster who wants a screen for his activities by living in a better neighborhood, a colored man of means who was giving his children a college education and thought they were entitled to live among whites....

No matter what the motive or character of the would-be purchaser, if the deal would instigate a form of blight, then certainly the well-meaning broker must work against its consummation.

Within the discourse of real estate industry at midcentury, race and deviance went hand in hand. In their marketing of a suburban alternative to urban blight, real estate agents likened blacks to the city's deviants: bootleggers, madams, call girls, and gang-sters. But within their definition of "blight," the racial distinctions between black people and white deviants disappear. To real estate agents and presumably their white clientele, blacks are akin to the white criminals who reside within the noir city: all are equally undesirable as neighbors.

Film noir deploys a similar discourse. In the noir city, white criminality and black identity are mutually constitutive. The morally corrupt white folks who inhabit the noir city, for example, often are viewed alongside black service workers – servants, custodi-ans, garage attendants, shoe shine boys, Pullman porters, and jazz musicians – suggest-ing their ease within the city's black underworld. In *Double Indemnity*, for example, arguably the quintessential film noir, Walter Neff depends on a colored woman to look after him. After he executes his plans for murder, he relies on the black janitor of his apartment building for an airtight alibi. Throughout his many crimes, Neff's whiteness is compromised by his conspicuous position alongside African Americans. Moreover, noir's innovative and masterful use of light and shadow reinforced the symbolic black-ening of white deviants. Darkness pervades the noir screen, always encroaching on the sources of light within the frame. Noir's deviants often are mired in blackened cine-matic compositions as if to illuminate their corrupt souls. Throughout *He Walked by Night*, for example, the face of a violent psychopath, never seen in its totality, is marred by dark shadows, reinforcing the black connotations of white criminality.

As film noir coincided with a general retreat from the blackening spaces of industrial urbanism, the genre honed in on those spaces that sanctioned racial and ethnic transgression. The nightclub and its exotic music offer a quintessential noir setting where the boundaries between whiteness and blackness blur. In *Criss Cross*, Steve Thompson wanders through downtown Los Angeles, stumbling into "the old club," where he is hypnotized by the haunting music of Esy Morales and his Rhumba Band. There, Thompson reignites a relationship with an old flame that leads him to his demise. In *D.O.A.*, as Frank Bigelow sacrifices his engagement by swinging with "jive crazy" women in a San Francisco nightclub, the camera focuses tightly on the black face of a trumpeter, reinforcing the racialized milieu of urban nightlife. And in *T-Men*, as two undercover agents from the treasury department venture into a Chinatown nightclub to pursue a mob moll who fancies silk kimonos and fastens tiger lilies to her hair, a vaguely Asian music enhances the mood of mystery and danger. The nightclub, a prominent cultural institution of the Swing Era that sanctioned racial intermingling, figured prominently with noir's portrait of urban malaise.

Ultimately, film noir identified a crisis of white masculinity at the outset of the postwar period, but the spatial context of that crisis demands an awareness of how filmmakers and their audiences at midcentury shared a perception of the modern city as a detriment to traditional models of social order. Noir's parade of "weak men," rendered so memorably by the acting of Fred MacMurray, Robert Mitchum, and Burt Lancaster, underscored the destabilization of the white male identity within the topsy-turvy world of the modern city. Duped by conniving women at every turn and mired within the shadows of the black city, noir's white male anti-heroes met their demise within the culture of urban modernity. As many Americans craved some semblance of normalcy after the social turmoil of depression and war, and as they satisfied that yearning by removing themselves, physically, from the racialized spaces of the new mass culture, film noir prefigured the need for a "new" new mass culture, one that offered an alternative to the modern city and its degraded culture.

Disneyland and the "New" New Mass Culture of Postwar America

Recent scholarship emphasizes the degree to which black urbanization and white suburbanization belonged to a larger set of social, economic, and political processes that enabled the transition from the centralized metropolis to the decentralized urban region. For this reason, popular culture in the age of white flight included a suburban antithesis to its noir vision of urban life. If film noir dramatized the degraded condition of the black city, Disneyland premiered the cultural mythography of suburban whiteness. Arguably the preeminent cultural impresario of postwar America, Walt Disney took deliberate steps to model his theme park as the very antithesis of its New York predecessor, Coney Island. In its proximity to freeways, its highly disciplined ordering of space, its validation of patriarchy and the nuclear family, and its thematic emphasis on racial distinctions, Disneyland provided a spatial articulation of a new suburban ethos that millions of Americans adopted in their claim to home ownership after World War II.

Disney's decision to locate his new theme park in Orange County, California, underscores the significance of that region to the shifting basis of cultural capital in postwar America. Whereas Detroit suffered the most severe effects of the postwar urban crisis, Orange County profited handsomely from the westward migration of federal defense expenditures during the cold war. In the decades following World War II, the region sheltered the development of a vast military industrial complex that for decades provided Orange County's main source of income. The growth of a regional defense industry, in turn, spurred suburban development, as ranchers turned property developers and real estate speculators marketed affordable, suburban tract housing units for an expanding middle-class population. Orange County's expansion during the postwar period was nothing short of spectacular. While in 1940, 130,760 people made their homes in Orange County, that total reached nearly 1.5 million by 1970.

The very newness of Orange County's suburban communities created a cultural space for the resurrection of traditional social values that seemed to dissipate within the promiscuous spaces of the noir city. Removed from Southern California's dominant urban center and far distant from the cosmopolitan culture of eastern cities, Orange County fostered a distinctive political identity that increasingly appealed to groups of Americans disaffected from decades of New Deal liberalism. In a region sustained by a militarized economy, a staunch nationalism and a rigid defense of the American way took shape against the presence of un-American outsiders, whereas the privatized nature of suburban growth in the region nurtured a homegrown appreciation for the values of privacy, individualism, and property rights. The region's remarkable social homogeneity, moreover, coddled an antipathy toward the expansion of a collectivist welfare state and a repudiation of federal interventions on behalf of civil rights activists and other special interest groups. By the 1960s, Orange County sheltered a conservative populism that catapulted New Right ideologues such as Ronald Reagan into California's and ultimately, the nation's, highest public office. With 72 percent of its electorate voting for Reagan in California's 1966 gubernatorial election, Orange County first emerged as "Reagan Country" toward the end of the postwar period.

Orange County sustained a political culture amenable for not only Reagan's postwar metamorphosis from a crusader for the New Deal to an ideologue of the New Right but also Walt Disney's foray into other cultural enterprises besides filmmaking. In fact, as if to underscore the ideological affinities between the two men, Reagan "starred" at the opening ceremonies of Disneyland held on June 17, 1955. Both Reagan and Disney emerged as men of their time, embracing a set of values that resonated with an expanding middle class who sought refuge from the disordered culture of the modern city within the well-ordered landscapes of suburbia. Not unlike Reagan, Disney underwent a political transformation during the cold war, in which his hostility grew toward those groups whose gains during an era of New Deal reform threatened to undermine the postwar prospects for resurrecting the American way: intellectuals, racial and ethnic groups, labor unions, and, most of all, Communists. After an embittering experience with labor unions during the war years and at the height of cold war anxiety, Disney retreated into a vision of a homogeneous WASP folk who for him embodied the traditional values of hard work, rugged individualism, tightly knit families, and traditional gender roles. Such values inspired the basis for not only a spate of Disney films including *Davy Crockett, Swiss Family Robinson,* and *Pollyanna* but also the creation of Disneyland.

As postwar Americans withdrew from the racialized spaces of the modern city, Disney labored to create a cultural alternative to its noir culture. The war years left Walt Disney Productions in financial disarray, prompting company executives to seek alternate venues in which to market Disney products.

Following his foray into television, Disney began to think seriously about the creation of an amusement park, and he expressed the "need for something new" but admitted that he "didn't know what it was." He was clear, however, about his aversion toward that paragon of urban industrial culture: Coney Island. The showman once remarked that Coney Island and its generation of amusement parks were "dirty, phony places run by tough looking people." After visiting a dilapidated Coney Island in the course of planning Disneyland in the mid-1950s, Disney recoiled from "its tawdry rides and hostile employees." Subsequent admirers of Disneyland affirmed Disney's indictment of Coney Island. *New York Times* reporter Gladwin Hill asserted that Disneyland marked a departure from "the traditionally raucous and ofttimes shoddy amusement park," delighting in the fact that Disneyland eliminated the "ballyhoo men to assault [the visitor's] ears with exhortations to test his strength, skill, courage, digestion or gawk at freaks or cootch dancers."

Disney repudiated the slick cynicism of the noir city and sought to restore the innocence and wonder that seemed lost on generations of urban Americans. Raised by a strict father who cautioned against the "corruptive influences of a big city," Disney remained suspicious of modern urban culture throughout his life. His disdain for New York City, for example, became public after the success of Disneyland. When asked by a reporter to consider New York as the site for a second theme park, he dismissed that suggestion in large part because he doubted the capacity of New Yorkers to embrace the Disney worldview. "He said that audience is not responsive," recalled Disneyland's chief architect and Disney's close associate, John Hench, "that city is different." Hench also elaborated on Disney's conviction that urban modernity preyed on the moral conscience of Americans:

> In modern cities you have to defend yourself constantly and you go counter to everything that we've learned from the past. You tend to isolate yourself from other people you tend to be less aware. You tend to be more withdrawn. This is counter life, you really die a little .... I think we need something to counteract what modern society – cities – have done to U.S.

Having to "defend yourself constantly" became a hallmark experience of the noir city, especially at places like Coney Island, where women, particularly unescorted women, were forced into a defensive posture against the unwanted advances of lustful men. As Kathy Peiss discovered in her study of working women and popular amusements in New York at the turn of the century, the typical shopgirl at Coney Island was "keen and knowing, ever on the defensive ... she distrusts cavaliers not of her own station."

Disney deplored modernity's sacrifice of innocent virtue. The average citizen, he once remarked, "is a victim of civilization whose ideal is the unbotherable, poker-faced man and the attractive, unruffled woman." Disney's revulsion toward the poker-faced man and the unruffled woman echoed earlier cultural anxieties about "confidence men" and "painted women" in antebellum America. Much like the trickster figure of various folk cultures, the confidence man was the seducer who preyed on the naïveté of the strangers, particularly women, for self-aggrandizement. The confidence man, however, unlike the trickster, owed his existence to the modern city in the first half of the nineteenth century, where individuals could lay claim to new and higher social status through deceit and manipulation. In her study of middle-class culture in nineteenth-century America, Karen Haltunnen located cultural anxieties about confidence men and painted women within the rapid expansion of the city and its ambiguous social milieu. "Hypocrisy," the art of deceit and manipulation mastered by the confidence man, "paid off in an urban environment." Though removed from the historical context in which middle-class moralists denounced the rise of confidence men and painted women, Disney, in his critique of phony amusement parks, poker-faced men, and unruffled women, shared a similar antipathy toward the hypocrisy and deception that defined social relations in the urban world of strangers.

To combat the dissonance and heterosociality of the noir city, Disneyland presented a counterculture of visual order, spatial regimentation, and social homogeneity. Reacting against what Disney criticized as the "diffuse, unintegrated layout" of Coney Island, the park's designers sought to maximize control over the movement of the crowd through the meticulous organization of space. Whereas Coney Island had multiple entrances and exits, Disneyland offered only one path by which visitors could come and go. Upon entering the park, visitors began their day in Main Street, USA, a central corridor built as a replication of a small-town commercial thoroughfare that channeled pedestrians toward the central hub of the park, "from which the other lands radiate out like spokes in a wheel" – Tomorrowland, Fantasyland, Frontierland, and Adventureland. The spatial organization of Disneyland reflected the designers' intentions to direct the continual movement of people with as little indecision as possible. "Each land is easy to enter and easy to exit," asserted one Disney official in a speech to the Urban Land Institute, a national organization of urban developers, "because everything leads back to the central hub again. The result is a revelation to anyone who has ever experienced the disorientation and confusion built into world's fairs and other expositions."

Disneyland's location alongside the Interstate 5 freeway, moreover, underscored the degree to which park designers situated Disneyland within the burgeoning spatial order of the postwar urban region. As Southern California garnered state and federal monies toward highway construction during the 1950s, freeways increasingly dictated regional patterns of development. Following the advice of the Stanford Research Institute – a think tank promoting industrial development in California – Disney strategically situated his theme park alongside the proposed route of Santa Ana freeway and built what was the largest parking lot in the nation at the time. So vital was the freeway to the success of Disneyland that it earned a permanent place inside the park. Among the thirteen original attractions included in the park's opening in 1955, the Autopia Ride in Tomorrowland was a "real model freeway," not unlike the "motorways of the world of tomorrow" that highlighted the "Futurama" exhibit of the 1939 New York World's Fair. Situated between a rocket-ship ride and the "Voyage to the Moon" attraction, the Autopia Ride demonstrated Disney's optimistic vision of the future and how freeways constituted an integral part of that vision. Like almost every other attraction within the park, and very much unlike the titillating sensations of Coney Island rides, the Autopia Ride had a didactic function, "constructed to acquaint youngsters with traffic conditions on the highways of tomorrow."

The location and layout of Disneyland reflected a larger spatial culture that took shape within the myriad suburban communities that sprouted across the terrain of the decentralized urban region. Lakewood, for example, emerged alongside Disneyland in the early 1950s, and it reflected the intense preoccupation with order that followed the heyday of the noir city. Like the designers of Disneyland, the builders of Lakewood positioned their development in between the proposed routes for two major freeways and incorporated the principles of efficiency, uniformity, and predictability into its design. Typical of postwar suburban development, Lakewood was built on the grid system, a fraction of a larger grid on which Southern California's decentralized urban region took shape. At the center of Lakewood's grid stood Lakewood Center, an outdoor pedestrian mall featuring one hundred retail shops and a major department store. Similar to the way in which the designers of Disneyland organized space to exert maximum control over the vision and movement of the crowd, the architects of Lakewood Center implemented a rigid spatial order to create a self-contained environment dedicated wholly to consumption.

Lakewood also implemented a set of innovations in municipal government that effected a more homogeneous social environment. In 1954, the developers of Lakewood struck a deal with the county of Los Angeles. For minimal costs, Los Angeles County would provide vital services (fire, police, library) to Lakewood, which incorporated as an independent municipality. Contracting services from county government without submitting to its authority, the citizens of Lakewood escaped the burden of supporting county government and enjoyed a greater degree of control over the social composition of their community. "Local control" became a mantra among suburban Southern Californians, whose widespread use of the Lakewood Plan minimized the kind of racial heterogeneity that characterized the modern city and its culture. Given the degree to which the Lakewood Plan effected racial segregation within the context of Southern California's increasingly diverse urban region, one policy expert concluded, "The Lakewood Plan cities were essentially white political movements."

If the Lakewood Plan enforced a literal distance between white and nonwhite people within the postwar urban region, Disneyland underscored that development by asserting a figurative distinction between suburban whiteness and racial otherness. Race and racial difference figured prominently among Disneyland's many themes. Frontierland, for example, described by publicity materials as "a land of hostile Indians and straight shooting pioneers," featured Indians among its main attractions. There one also could find Aunt Jemima's Pancake House, a recreation of a southern plantation where an African American woman, dressed as "Aunt Jemima did ... on the plantation ... was on hand everyday to welcome visitors warmly." Aside from featuring a southern mammie, Disneyland included other stereotypes of African Americans. Adventureland, for example, beckoned visitors to "the sound of native chants and tom-tom drums," where the Jungle Cruise attraction featured "wild animals and native savages [that] attack your craft as it cruises through their jungle privacy."

The racial dimensions of the Disneyland experience surfaced not only in those places of the park where images of blacks and Indians prevailed but also where such images did not appear. Main Street, USA, promoted as "everybody's hometown," and "the heartline of America," reiterated Disney's populist idealization of a WASP folk. Richard Hofstadter noted in the *Age of Reform* the latent xenophobia within the populist sensibility, which, although seeking to maintain "the primary contacts of country and village life" also cherished a vision of "an ethnically more homogeneous nation." That vision guided the design of Main Street, USA, where the absence of mammies, Indians, and savages reified Disney's racialized and deeply nostalgic vision of the American "folk." The exclusion of African Americans and their history from the representational landscape of Main Street was most glaring in the "Great Moments with Mr. Lincoln" exhibit, which debuted in Disneyland in 1966. The "Audio Animatronic" Lincoln recited a speech designed to elicit patriotic sentimentality, although making no mention of such divisive conflicts as slavery or the Civil War.

The point here is not to elicit scorn or indignation but rather to understand such racialized representations within their spatial and historical context. White Americans have long maintained a fascination with race and its representation in popular culture, but the contours of race relations had changed significantly in postwar America. After World War II, which brought unprecedented levels of racial cohabitation in American cities, a new generation of white Americans, or at least those who qualified themselves as such, looked to the decentralized urban region as a place that could maintain separate and not necessarily equal communities. In the aftermath of the Supreme Court's 1948 ruling against racially restrictive covenants in *Shelley v. Kraemer*, and amidst an explosion of civil rights activism, cultural stereotypes of nonwhite racial groups affirmed the racial distinctions that seemed to dissipate within the politically charged climate of a nascent civil rights era. Disneyland, removed from the "darker" shades of the inner city in Orange County yet permeated with representations of racial difference, provided a space where white Southern Californians could reaffirm their whiteness against the fictions of the racial other. Given the battles that Southern California's white home owners subsequently waged against such public initiatives as fair housing, busing, and affirmative action, it is not difficult to comprehend how Disneyland's racial representations prefigured the racial underpinnings of a white suburban identity.

If the presence of Aunt Jemima at Disneyland signaled the subordinate position of blacks within Disney's vision of social order, it also symbolized the subservient position of women in that order as well. Disney land's delineation of a social order appropriate to the tastes and values of an expanding suburban middle class included an emphasis on patriarchal social relations and the centrality of the nuclear family. Suburbanization provided a setting in which postwar Americans could confront their anxieties about the changing position of women in American society, seeking comfort in cultural representations of domesticated housewives and stable nuclear families. Disney's effort to position the "typical family of four" at the center of the Disneyland experience signaled yet another departure from amusement parks of Coney Island's generation. The *New York Times*, for example, described Disneyland "not as a place where anyone would casually go to take a roller coaster ride or buy a hot dog, but as the goal of a family adventure."

Paradoxically, it was in that section of the theme park touted as a "show world of the future" where park designers chose to insert a traditional vision of gender roles. Tomorrowland featured as its centerpiece the "Monsanto House of the Future," which invited park visitors to preview "how the typical American family of four will live in ten years from now." When the house opened to the public on June 12, 1957, models Helen Bernhart and John Marion acted the part of the model couple at home. Photographs depicted the husband relaxing in the "psychiatric chair," which afforded "therapeutic relief after a hard day at the office," with his aproned wife standing in the "Atoms for Living Kitchen." Adhering to the reigning vision family life in postwar America, the interior space of the House of the Future was divided according to the individual needs of family members. The home's cruciform plan ensured "added privacy for various family activities," separating the children's room from the master bedroom. A step-saver kitchen opened onto the family dining room, an arrangement "convenient and perfect for party entertainment." As postwar Americans looked to suburban home ownership as means of restoring some sense of normalcy, Disneyland's House of the Future depicted a futuristic setting where women could return to traditional gender roles.

Moreover, the emphasis on domesticity and private life at Disneyland signaled a shifting cultural focus away from the urban spaces of working-class culture and toward the suburban spaces of middle-class home ownership. In the modern city of the nineteenth and early twentieth centuries, private life belonged to those privileged enough to enjoy the comforts of a townhouse, a carriage, or a private club, whereas the city's working class crowded within the congested spaces of tenements houses, streetcars, and entertainment venues. In the postwar urban region, as greater numbers of Americans attained suburban home ownership through a generous set of public policies, the focus of American popular culture, as Disneyland demonstrated, gradually shifted away from the public venues of the noir city to the private spaces of the home. Thus the park's emphasis on familial domesticity reflected not only a desire to return to traditional gender roles but also a more general valorization of private life that appealed to growing numbers of Americans who entered, or at least aspired to, the ranks of the middle class after World War II.

Disneyland is a complex cultural phenomenon, and there are other aspects of the theme park that underscore its significance to the transformation of urban culture and society at midcentury. Nonetheless, when viewed comparatively alongside simultaneous cultural developments, the theme park illustrates a broader cultural transformation that accompanied the changing configuration of the postwar American city. In its spatial organization, as well as in its thematic emphases, Disneyland asserted a repudiation of the noir sensibility that captivated the American public at the outset of the postwar period. By the mid-1950s, as the heyday of film noir began to wane, a new set of film genres won favor with the public – science fiction, musicals, westerns – that not only upheld traditional models of social order but also delivered the kind of happy endings that were absent from film noir. Disneyland appeared at this cultural moment, delivering its own happy ending to the midcentury transformation of urban life, at least for those who acquired the privileges and comforts of suburban home ownership. As film noir rendered its obituary for the modern city and its new mass culture, Disneyland heralded a new spatial culture that stressed order without complexity, pleasure without danger, and sociability without diversity.

The new suburban cultural order exhibited in film noir and at Disneyland also included other cultural institutions. Television's ascendance as a dominant cultural medium during the 1950s lowered the curtain on the grand movie palaces of the nation's inner cities and rendered the experience of going out on the town an inconvenient waste of time. Suburban shopping malls similarly offered a car-friendly alternative to the downtown department store, where the dire shortage of parking repelled a generation of Americans increasingly wedded to their automobiles. Freeways emerged on top of defunct streetcar lines, introducing a more privatized means of moving rapidly through urban space. The interior settings of the "new" new mass culture provided that very refuge that film noir dramatized a necessity for. Its disciplined, contained, and detached spaces removed consumers from the public realm of decaying cities and modeled idealizations of a new cultural order that captivated a new generation of home owners eager to create their own suburban retreat from the noir city.

These idealizations, moreover, delivered more than mere entertainment. They also provided a blueprint for a nascent political subjectivity that surfaced in places like Southern California during the 1960s, where a new conservative idealism took shape that aimed to restore traditional patterns of racial and gendered relations. No one better personified that new subjectivity than Ronald Reagan, who championed such principles as property rights, private enterprise, law and order, family values, and small government in his political metamorphosis from New Deal Democrat to New Right Republican. Well-attuned to the dawning sensibilities of an expanding suburban public, and affiliating himself with the spectacles of the "new" new mass culture Reagan fashioned a new political agenda by channeling the values hovering within the larger culture. Film noir, fixated on the disordered culture of the black city, corroborated Reagan's claim in the aftermath of Los Angeles' Watts riots that the urban "jungle is waiting to take over" white suburban communities, whereas Disneyland modeled the very order that his core constituency aspired to. Both cultural productions articulated a deep-seated hostility to urban modernity, both stressed a return to traditional patterns of social order, and both pandered to the political aspirations of an emerging silent majority that retreated from the public culture of the noir city into the private realm of suburban home ownership.

Popular culture in the age of white flight thus exposed the linkages between structure and culture during the post-World War II period. Disneyland, like film noir, owed its existence to the very real transformations that wrought new patterns of urban life in postwar America. Disneyland's calculated proximity to new freeways and its suburban location underscored the park's anticipation of accelerated patterns of decentralized development, whereas film noir refilled its techniques of on-location shooting to capture an authentic portrait of urban malaise. In their vital relationship to the postwar transformation of the American city – and it is well to remember that that process happened not simply through the collusion of unseen, abstract social forces but rather through the very conscious efforts of developers, planners, policy makers, and home owners – film noir and Disneyland codified the anxieties and ambitions, as well as the perceptions and assumptions, widely shared by a public who abandoned their cities for suburban jobs and housing. Their relationship to the postwar emergence of "chocolate cities and vanilla suburbs" was neither incidental nor merely reflective. In modeling popular aspirations toward a new sociospatial order, popular culture in the age of white flight thus enabled the very realization of that order.

The cultural history of the American city illuminates how previous generations of Americans have imagined city form, social order, and the proper relations between the two. Urban imaginings are indeed slippery subjects for the historian to grasp, but popular idealizations of urban life often shape the very real process of making cities. Daniel Burnham's White City, for example, which debuted so triumphantly at Chicago's Columbian Exposition in 1893, inspired a generation of urban planners who brought the classical imagery of the Beaux Arts style to bear on the landscape of the American city at the turn of the century. And for better or for worse, few can doubt the impact of Disneyland.

20

Primary Sources

United States v. Paramount Pictures, Inc. (1947)

In its 1947 Paramount antitrust ruling, the US Supreme Court deprived the major Hollywood studios of their guaranteed domestic market.

We have no doubt that moving pictures, like newspapers and radio, are included in the press whose freedom is guaranteed by the First Amendment …. The main contest is over the cream of the exhibition business – that of the first-run theatres …. The question here is not what the public will see or if the public will be permitted to see certain features. It is clear that under the existing system the public will be denied access to none. If the public cannot see the features on the first-run, it may do so on the second, third, fourth, or later run. The central problem presented by these cases is which exhibitors get the highly profitable first-run business ….

The controversy over monopoly relates to monopoly in exhibition and more particularly monopoly in the first-run phase of the exhibition business.

The five majors in 1945 had interests in somewhat over 17 percent of the theatres in the United States – 3,137 out of 18,076. Those theatres paid 45 percent of the total domestic film rental received by all eight defendants.

In the 92 cities of the country with populations over 100,000 at least 70 per cent of all the first-run theatres are affiliated with one or more of the five majors …. In 38 of those cities there are no independent first-run theatres ….

The District Court … found that the five majors … "do not and cannot collectively or individually, have a monopoly of exhibition." The District Court also found that where a single defendant owns all of the first-run theatres in a town, there is no sufficient proof that the acquisition was for the purpose of creating a monopoly. It found rather that such consequence resulted from the inertness of competitors, their lack of financial ability to build theatres comparable to those of the five majors, or the preference of the public for the best equipped theatres ….

The District court … did find an attempt to monopolize in the fixing of prices, the granting of unreasonable clearances, block booking, and other unlawful restraints of trade ….

HEARINGS REGARDING THE COMMUNIST INFILTRATION OF THE MOTION PICTURE INDUSTRY

US House of Representatives Committee on Un-American Activities, 1947

In 1947, the House Un-American Activities Committee conducted its first investigation of communist infiltration in the film industry. It called a group of radical screen writers and producers to testify about their political beliefs.

[Hon. J. Parnell Thomas (chairman) presiding]
The committee is well aware of the magnitude of the subject which it is investigating. The motion-picture business represents an investment of billions of dollars. It represents employment for thousands of workers, ranging from unskilled laborers to high-salaried actors and executives. And even more important, the motion picture industry represents what is probably the largest single vehicle of entertainment for the American public – over 85,000,000 persons attend the movies each week.

However, it is the very magnitude of the scope of the motion-picture industry which makes this investigation so necessary. We all recognize, certainly, the tremendous effect which moving pictures have on their mass audiences, far removed from the Hollywood sets. We all recognize that what the citizen sees and hears in his neighborhood movie house carries a powerful impact on his thoughts and behavior.

With such vast influence over the lives of American citizens as the motion picture industry exerts, it is not unnatural – in fact, it is very logical – that subversive and undemocratic forces should attempt to use this medium for un-American purposes.

US House of Representatives Committee on Un-American Activities, 1951

In 1951, HUAC went back to Hollywood and called hundreds of witnesses from both the political right and political left.

Testimony of Larry Parks, Accompanied by his Counsel, Louis Mandel

MR. TAVENNER (HUAC Counsel): Mr. Parks, when and where were you born?
MR. PARKS: I was born in Kansas on a farm. I moved when I was quite small to Illinois. I attended the high school in Joliet, Ill., and I also attended and graduated from the University of Illinois, where I majored in chemistry and minored in physics. I sometimes wonder how I got in my present line of work ....
MR. TAVENNER: Now, what is your present occupation?
MR. PARKS: Actor ....
MR. TAVENNER: You understand that we desire to learn the true extent, past and present, of Communist infiltration into the theater field in Hollywood, and the committee asks your cooperation in developing such information. There has been considerable

testimony taken before this committee regarding a number of organizations in Hollywood, such as the Actors' Laboratory; Actors' Laboratory Theater; Associated Film Audiences – Hollywood Branch; Citizens' Committee for Motion Picture Strikers; Film Audiences for Democracy or Associated Film Audiences; Hollywood Anti-Nazi League or Hollywood League Against Nazism; Hollywood Independent Citizens' Committee of the Arts, Sciences, and Professions; Hollywood League for Democratic Action; Hollywood Motion-Picture Democratic Committee; Hollywood Peace Forum; Hollywood Theater Alliance; Hollywood Writers' Mobilization; Motion Picture Artists' Committee; People's Educational Center, Los Angeles; Mooney Defense Committee – Hollywood Unit; Progressive Citizens of America; Hollywood Committee of the Arts, Sciences, and Professions; Council of the PCA; Southern California Chapter of the PCA; Workers School of Los Angeles.

Have you been connected or affiliated in any way with any of those organizations?

MR. PARKS: I have ....

MR. TAVENNER: Will you tell the committee whether or not in your experience in Hollywood and as a member of these organizations to which you have testified there were to your knowledge Communists in these various organizations which I have referred to, particularly those that you were a member of?

MR. PARKS: I think I can say "Yes" to that.

MR. TAVENNER: Well, who were these Communists?

MR. PARKS: There were people in the Actors' Lab, for instance – this, in my opinion, was not a Communist organization in any sense of the word. As in any organization, it has all colors of political philosophy ....

MR. TAVENNER: Well, were there Communists attached to these other organizations which you say you were a member of?

MR. PARKS: This I'm not familiar with. I don't know. I don't know who else was a member of them besides myself.

MR. TAVENNER: Your answer is because you do not recall who were members of these other organizations?

MR. PARKS: I think that is the gist of my answer; yes ....

MR. TAVENNER: Well, what was your opportunity to know and to observe the fact that there were Communists in [the Actors' Laboratory]?

MR. PARKS: May I answer this fully and in my own way?

MR. TAVENNER: I would like for you to ....

MR. PARKS: I am not a Communist. I would like to point out that in my opinion there is a great difference between – and not a subtle difference – between being a Communist, a member of the Communist Party, say in 1941, 10 years ago, and being a Communist in 1951. To my mind this is a great difference and not a subtle one ....

As I say, I am not a Communist. I was a member of the Communist Party when I was a much younger man, 10 years ago. I was a member of the Communist Party ....

Being a member of the Communist Party fulfilled certain needs of a young man that was liberal in thought, idealistic, who was for the underprivileged, the underdog. I felt that it fulfilled these particular needs. I think that being a Communist in 1951 in this particular situation is an entirely different kettle of fish when this is a great power that is trying to take over the world. This is the difference ....

MR. TAVENNER: In other words, you didn't realize that the purpose and object of the Communist Party was to take over segments of the world in 1941, but you do realize that that is true in 1951? Is that the point you are making?

MR. PARKS: Well, I would like to say this: That this is in no way an apology for anything that I have done, you see, because I feel I have done nothing wrong ever. Question of judgment? This is debatable. I feel that as far as I am concerned that in

1941, as far as I knew it, the purposes as I knew them fulfilled ... certain idealism, certain being for the underdog, which I am today this very minute ....

I wasn't particularly interested in it after I did become a member. I attended very few meetings, and I drifted away from it the same way that ... I drifted into it. To the best of my recollection, I petered out about the latter part of 1944 or 1945.

REPRESENTATIVE CHARLES E: POTIER (HUAC Committee Member). Who would call these meetings together? ...

MR. PARKS: I would prefer not to mention names under these circumstances ....

REPRESENTATIVE JOHN S: WOOD (HUAC Committee Chairman). Mr. Parks, in what way do you feel it would be injurious, then, to them to divulge their identities, when you expressed the opinion that at no time did they do wrong?

MR. PARKS: This brings up many questions on a personal basis, Mr. Congressman, as an actor .... One of the reasons is that as an actor my activity is dependent a great deal on the public. To be called before this committee at your request has a certain inference, a certain innuendo that you are not loyal to this country. This is not true. I am speaking for myself. This is not true. But the inference and the innuendo is there as far as the public is concerned ....

MR. WOOD: Don't you feel the public is entitled to know about [communist infiltration of the motion picture industry]?

MR. PARKS: I certainly do, and I am opening myself wide open to any question that you can ask me. I will answer as honestly as I know how. And at this particular time, as I say, the industry is – it's like taking a pot shot at a wounded animal, because the industry is not in as good a shape today as it has been, economically I'm speaking. It has been pretty tough on it. And, as I say, this is a great industry, and I don't say this only because it has been kind to me. It has a very important job to do to entertain people, in certain respects to call attention to certain evils, but mainly to entertain, and in this I feel that they have done a great job. Always when our country has needed help, the industry has been in the forefront of that help ....

On the question of naming names, it is my honest opinion that the few people that I could name, these names would not be of service to the committee at all. I am sure that you know who they are. These people I feel honestly are like myself, and I feel I have done nothing wrong. Question of judgment? Yes, perhaps. And I also feel that this is not – to be asked to name names like this is not – in the way of American justice as we know it, that we as Americans have all been brought up, that it is a bad thing to force a man to do this. I have been brought up that way. I am sure all of you have.

And it seems to me that this is not the American way of doing things – to force a man who is under oath and who has opened himself as wide as possible to the committee – and it hasn't been easy to do this – to force a man to do this is not American justice ....

My people have a long heritage in this country. They fought in the Revolutionary War to make this country, to create this Government, of which this committee is a part ....

I don't think I would be here today if I weren't a star, because you know as well as I, even better, that I know nothing that I believe would be of great service to this country. I think my career has been ruined because of this, and I would appreciate not having to – don't present me with the choice of either being in contempt of this committee and going to jail or forcing me to really crawl through the mud to be an informer, for what purpose? I don't think this is a choice at all. I don't think this is really sportsmanlike. I don't think this is American. I don't think this is American justice. I think to do something like this is more akin to what happened under Hitler, and what is happening in Russia today.

I don't think this is American justice for an innocent mistake in judgement, if it was
that, with the intention behind it only of making this country a better place in which
to live. I think it is not befitting for this committee to force me to make this kind of
choice ....

THE MIRACLE DECISION

Joseph Burstyn, Inc. v. Wilson, Commissioner of Education of New York, et al. (1952)

The Italian film The Miracle *had been banned in New York for "blasphemy." In this
landmark decision, the Supreme Court extended to the movies First Amendment protections of freedom of speech.*

The issue here is the constitutionality, under the First and Fourteenth Amendments,
of a New York statute which permits the banning of motion picture films on the
ground that they are "sacrilegious" ....

Appellant is a corporation engaged in the business of distributing motion pictures.
It owns the exclusive rights to distribute throughout the United States a film produced in Italy entitled "The Miracle." On November 30, 1950, the motion picture
division of the New York education department ... issued ... a license authorizing
exhibition of "The Miracle," with English subtitles ....

The New York State Board of Regents, which by statute is made the head of the
education department, received "hundreds of letters, telegrams, post cards, affidavits,
and other communications" both protesting against and defending the public exhibition of "The Miracle." The Chancellor of the Board of Regents requested three members of the Board to view the picture and to make a report to the entire Board. After
viewing the film, this committee reported ... that in its opinion there was basis for the
claim that the picture was "sacrilegious" .... On February 16, 1951, the Regents,
after viewing "The Miracle," determined that it was "sacrilegious" and ... ordered the
Commissioner of Education to rescind appellant's license to exhibit the picture ....

After the Mutual decision [1915], the present case is the first to present squarely to
us the question of whether motion pictures are within the ambit of protection which
the First Amendment, through the Fourteenth, secures to any form of "speech" or
"the press."

It cannot be doubted that motion pictures are a significant medium for the communication of ideas. They may affect public attitudes and behavior in a variety of
ways, ranging from direct espousal of a political or social doctrine to the subtle shaping of thought which characterizes all artistic expression. The importance of motion
pictures as an organ of public opinion is not lessened by the fact that they are designed
to entertain as well as to inform. As was said [in 1948] ...

The line between the informing and the entertaining is too elusive for the protection of that basic right [a free press]. Everyone is familiar with instances of propaganda through fiction. What is one man's amusement, teaches another's doctrine.

It is urged that motion pictures do not fall within the First Amendment's aegis
because their production, distribution, and exhibition is a large-scale business conducted

for private profit. We cannot agree. That books, newspapers, and magazines are published and sold for profit does not prevent them from being a form of expression whose liberty is safeguarded by the First Amendment. We fail to see why operation for profit should have any different effect in the case of motion pictures.

It is further urged that motion pictures possess a greater capacity for evil, particularly among the youth of a community, than other modes of expression. Even if one were to accept this hypothesis, it does not follow that motion pictures should be disqualified from First Amendment protection. If there be capacity for evil it may be relevant in determining the permissible scope of community control, but it does not authorize substantially unbridled censorship such as we have here ....

It is not the business of government in our nation to suppress real or imagined attacks upon a particular religious doctrine, whether they appear in publications, speeches, or motion pictures.

Since the term "sacrilegious" is the sole standard under attack here, it is not necessary for us to decide, for example, whether a state may censor motion pictures under a clearly drawn statute designed and applied to prevent the showing of obscene films. That is a very different question from the one now before us. We hold only that under the First and Fourteenth Amendments a state may not ban a film on the basis of a censor's conclusion that it is "sacrilegious".

Part V

Hollywood and the Tumultuous 1960s

Introduction
Bonnie and Clyde

Few films have ever aroused such intense controversy. The *New York Times* called it immoral: "a cheap piece of boldfaced slapstick comedy that treats the hideous depredations of that sleazy moronic pair as though they were as full of fun and frolic as the jazz-age cut-ups in *Thoroughly Modern Millie*." But many others responded much more positively. *Bonnie and Clyde* dress styles became the rage. A song, "The Ballad of Bonnie and Clyde," climbed to the top of the pop charts.

Set in Texas in 1931, the film tells the story of the Barrow Gang, a group of Depression-era bank robbers. The film portrays the gang's leaders, Bonnie Parker and Clyde Barrow, as sensitive young people – "drifters, nobodies, yearning to be any kind of somebodies." They are depicted as latter-day Robin Hoods, who rob banks – not their customers – and only kill reluctantly, when forced to. In real life, they were small-time criminals, who held up gas stations and grocery stores as well as banks. Their largest haul was about $1,500 and they killed 13 people – including two Texas highway patrolmen whom they shot from an ambush.

As played by Warren Beatty, Clyde Barrow is a sympathetic figure, cocky and reckless, who suffers from sexual impotence. In actuality, he was a vicious, sadistic killer. He was described at the time as "a shifty-eyed young Texas thug," "a snake-eyed murderer who killed without giving his victims a chance to draw." The film also treats Bonnie with compassion, depicting her as a sensitive figure who describes the gang's exploits in poetry. The real-life Bonnie Parker was a married Dallas waitress who killed three people.

Of course, the film's appeal does not lie in any claims of historical accuracy. Rather, the film successfully transforms Bonnie and Clyde into folk heroes, into rebels who might serve as precursors of the counterculture of the late 1960s. They are treated as underdogs who attack symbols of the establishment, defend the poor, and are ultimately gunned by lawmen who riddle them over and over with bullets from ambush when they stop to help a driver change his tire. The movie's advertising slogan – "They're young, they're in love, they kill people" – expressed the spirit of youthful rebellion that characterized the counterculture.

21

A Shifting Sensibility
Dr. Strangelove: *Nightmare Comedy and the Ideology of Liberal Consensus*

Charles Maland

Dr. Strangelove struck America like a bolt of lightning on a dark night. It threw a flash of light on the country's foreign policy and called into question stock beliefs and assumptions about the nature of the Cold War and the prospects of nuclear war. In the following essay, Charles Maland discusses an irreverent film that lingered on the minds and troubled the conscience of many Americans.

*D*r. Strangelove, or How I Learned to Stop Worrying and Love the Bomb (Stanley Kubrick, 1964) is one of the most fascinating and important American films of the 1960s. As a sensitive artistic response to its age, the film presents a moral protest of revulsion against the dominant cultural paradigm in America – what Geoffrey Hodgson has termed the Ideology of Liberal Consensus. Appearing at roughly the same time as other works critical of the dominant paradigm – *Catch-22* is a good literary example of the stance – *Dr. Strangelove* presented an adversary view of society which was to become much more widely shared among some Americans in the late 1960s. This essay will examine the Ideology of Liberal Consensus, demonstrate how *Dr. Strangelove* serves as a response to it (especially to its approach to nuclear strategy and weapons), and look at how American culture responded to its radical reassessment of the American nuclear policy in the early 1960s.

The American consensus to which *Dr. Strangelove* responds was rooted in the late 1930s and in the war years. When Americans in the late 1930s began to feel more threatened by the rise of foreign totalitarianism than by the economic insecurities fostered by the stock market crash, a previously fragmented American culture began to unify. A common system of belief began to form, a paradigm solidified during World War II, when American effort was directed toward defeating the Axis powers. Fueled by the success of the war effort and the economic prosperity fostered by the war, this paradigm continued to dominate American social and political life through the early 1960s.

Charles Maland, "*Dr. Strangelove*: Nightmare Comedy and the Ideology of Liberal Consensus," *American Quarterly*, 31 (1979), pp. 697–717.

The 1950s are commonly remembered as an age of conformity typified by the man in the gray flannel suit, the move to suburbia, and the blandness of the Eisenhower administration. There were, of course, currents running counter to the American consensus in the 1950s – C. Wright Mills challenging the power elite and the era's "crackpot realism"; James Dean smoldering with sensitive, quiet rebellion; the Beats rejecting the propriety and complacency of the era – yet most people remained happy with America and its possibilities. Much more than a passing mood or a vague reaction to events, this paradigm – the Ideology of Liberal Consensus – took on an intellectual coherence of its own. According to Geoffrey Hodgson, the ideology contained two cornerstone assumptions: that the structure of American society was basically sound, and that communism was a clear danger to the survival of the United States and its allies. From these two beliefs evolved a widely accepted view of America. That view argued its position in roughly this fashion: the American economic system has developed, softening the inequities and brutalities of an earlier capitalism, becoming more democratic, and offering abundance to a wider portion of the population than ever before. The key to both democracy and abundance is production and technological advance; economic growth provides the opportunity to meet social needs, to defuse class conflict, and to bring blue-collar workers into the middle class. Social problems are thus less explosive and can be solved rationally. It is necessary only to locate each problem, design a program to attack it, and provide the experts and technological know-how necessary to solve the problem.

The only threat to this domestic harmony, the argument continued, is the specter of Communism. The "Free World," led by the United States, must brace itself for a long struggle against Communism and willingly support a strong defense system, for power is the only language that the Communists can understand. If America accepts this responsibility to fight Communism, while also proclaiming the virtues of American economic, social, and political democracy to the rest of the world, the country will remain strong and sound. Hodgson sums up the paradigm well when he writes: "Confident to the verge of complacency about the perfectibility of American society, anxious to the point of paranoia about the threat of Communism – those were the two faces of the consensus mood.

These two assumptions guided our national leadership as it attempted to forge social policy in an era of nuclear weapons. After the Soviet Union announced in the fall of 1949 that it had successfully exploded an atomic bomb, President Truman on January 31, 1950 ordered the Atomic Energy Commission to go ahead with the development of a hydrogen bomb. By late 1952 the United States had detonated its first hydrogen bomb, 700 times more powerful than the atomic bomb dropped on Hiroshima. Less than a year later, on August 8, 1953, the Soviets announced that they, too, had a hydrogen bomb. The arms race was on.

About the time that Sputnik was successfully launched in 1957 – leading to national fears about the quality of American science and education – some American intellectuals began to refine a new area of inquiry: nuclear strategy. Recognizing that nuclear weapons were a reality, the nuclear strategists felt it important to think systematically about their role in our defense policy. Henry Kissinger's *Nuclear War and Foreign Policy* (1957), one of the first such books, argued that the use of tactical nuclear weapons must be considered by decision makers. More widely known was the work of Herman Kahn, whose *On Thermonuclear War* (1960) and *Thinking About the*

Unthinkable (1962) presented his speculations on nuclear war and strategy, most of which stemmed from his work for the RAND Corporation during the 1950s. Kahn was willing to indulge in any speculation about nuclear war, including such topics as the estimated genetic consequences of worldwide doses of radioactive fallout, the desirable characteristics of a deterrent (it should be frightening, inexorable, persuasive, cheap, non-accident prone, and controllable), and the huge likelihood of vomiting in postwar fallout shelters.

Though the professed intent of the nuclear strategists was to encourage a rational approach to foreign policy in a nuclear age, the mass media seemed intent on making the public believe that thermonuclear war might be acceptable, even tolerable. A few examples illustrate that some mass magazines believed that nuclear war would not really be that bad. *U.S. News and World Report* carried a cover article, "If Bombs Do Fall," which told readers that plans were underway to allow people to write checks on their bank accounts even if the bank were destroyed by nuclear attack. The same issue contained a side story about how well survivors of the Japanese bombings were doing. *Life* magazine placed a man in a reddish fallout costume on its cover along with the headline, "How You Can Survive Fallout. 97 out of 100 Can Be Saved." Besides advising that the best cure for radiation sickness "is to take hot tea or a solution of baking soda," *Life* ran an advertisement for a fully-stocked, prefabricated fallout shelter for only $700. The accompanying picture showed a happy family of five living comfortably in their shelter. I.F. Stone suggested in response to this kind of writing that the media seemed determined to convince the American public that thermonuclear warfare was "almost as safe as ivory soap is pure." While all this was going on, a RAND corporation study released in August 1961 estimated that a 3000 megaton attack on American cities would kill 80 percent of the population.

This paradoxical, bizarre treatment of the nuclear threat can be explained in part as an attempt by journalists to relieve anxiety during a time when the Cold War was intensifying. A number of events from 1960 to 1963 encouraged this freeze in the Cold War. Gary Powers, piloting a U-2 surveillance plane, was shot down over the Soviet Union in May 1960. In 1961, the Bay of Pigs fiasco occurred in May, President Kennedy announced a national fallout shelter campaign on television in July, and in August, the Berlin Wall was erected and the Soviet Union announced that they were resuming atmospheric testing of nuclear weapons. Worst of all, the Cuban Missile Crisis of October 1962 carried the world to the brink of nuclear war, thrusting the dangers of nuclear confrontation to the forefront of the public imagination. Though the crisis seemed to be resolved in favor of the United States, for several days nuclear war seemed imminent.

One result of this intensification was to erode the confidence of some Americans in the wisdom of American nuclear policy, Though there had been a small tradition of dissent regarding American nuclear policy in the 1950s – led by people like J. Robert Oppenheimer, Linus Pauling, Bertrand Russell, and C. Wright Mills, and groups like SANE (the National Committee for a Sane Nuclear Policy) – these people were clearly a minority, prophets crying in the wilderness. But Edmund Wilson's warning in 1963 that our spending on nuclear weapons may be one of mankind's final acts, and H. Stuart Hughes' impassioned challenge to deterrence strategy and his support of disarmament in the same year, were both symptomatic of a growing dissatisfaction of some Americans with the federal government's nuclear policy. Judged from another perspective, outside the assumptions of the Ideology of Liberal Consensus, the threat posed by the Soviet Union did not at all warrant the use of nuclear weapons. In the same vein, the realities of America itself – as the defenders of the Civil Rights movement were pointing out – did not live up to the rhetoric about the harmonious American democracy so prevalent in the 1950s. By 1962 and 1963, when *Dr. Strangelove* was being planned and produced, the Ideology of Liberal Consensus seemed increasingly vulnerable. In fact, it is not unfair to say that an adversary culture opposed to the hypocrisies and inconsistencies of the dominant paradigm was beginning to form.

Stanley Kubrick, director of *Dr. Strangelove*, played a part in extending that adversary culture. Born in 1928 to a middle-class Bronx family, Kubrick was from an early age interested in chess and photography. It is not hard to move from his fascination with chess, with the analytical abilities it requires and sharpens, to the fascination with technology and the difficulties men have in controlling it which Kubrick displays in *Dr. Strangelove* and *2001: A Space Odyssey*. Photography became a pastime when Kubrick received a camera at age thirteen, and a profession when Look magazine hired him at age eighteen as a still photographer. From there Kubrick became interested in filmmaking and made a short documentary on middleweight boxer Walter Cartier called *Day for the Fight* (1950). He followed this with a second documentary for RKO, *Flying Padre* (1951), after which he made his first feature film, *Fear and Desire* (1953). From then on Kubrick was immersed in making feature films.

In his mature work Kubrick has returned constantly to one of the gravest dilemmas of modern industrial society: the gap between man's scientific and technological skill and his social, political, and moral ineptitude. In Kubrick's world view, modern man has made scientific and technological advances inconceivable to previous generations but lacks the wisdom either to perceive how the new gadgetry might be used in constructive ways or, more fundamentally, to ask whether the "advance" might not cause more harm than good. Kubrick first faced this problem squarely in *Dr. Strangelove*.

Kubrick's films before 1963 do hint at interests which he was to develop more fully in *Dr. Strangelove*. *The Killing* shows a group of men working toward a common purpose under intense pressure and severe time limitations. *Paths of Glory* – one of a handful of classic anti-war films in the American cinema – vents its anger at the stupidity of military leaders, their callous disregard for other human lives, and their own lust for power. Released in 1957 in the midst of the Cold War, *Paths* was a courageous film made slightly more palatable for audiences because of its setting and situation – World War One and the evils of French military leaders.

It is not totally surprising, then, that Kubrick should make a film about military and civilian leaders trying to cope with accidental nuclear war. Actually, Kubrick had developed an interest in the Cold War and nuclear strategy as a concerned citizen in the late 1950s, even before he thought of doing a film on the subject. In an essay on *Dr. Strangelove* published in mid-1963, a half year before the release of the film, Kubrick wrote: "I was very interested in what was going to happen, and started reading a lot of books about four years ago. I have a library of about 70 or 80 books written by various technical people on the subject and I began to subscribe to the military magazines, the *Air Force* magazine, and to follow the U.S. naval proceedings." One of the magazines he subscribed to was the *Bulletin of the Atomic Scientist*, which regularly published articles by atomic scientists (Oppenheimer, Edward Teller, and Leo Szilard) and nuclear strategists (Kahn, Bernard Brodie, and Thomas Schelling). The more he read on the subject, the more he became engrossed in the complexities of nuclear strategy and the enormity of the nuclear threat.

> I was struck by the paradoxes of every variation of the problem from one extreme to the other – from the paradoxes of unilateral disarmament to the first strike. And it seemed to me that, aside from the fact that I was terribly interested myself, it was very important to deal with this problem dramatically because it's the only social problem where there's absolutely no chance for people to learn anything from experience. So it seemed to me that this was eminently a problem, a topic to be dealt with dramatically.

As his readings continued, Kubrick began to feel "a great desire to do something about the nuclear nightmare." From this desire came a decision to make a film on the subject. In preparation, he talked with both Thomas Schelling and Herman Kahn, gradually coming to believe that a psychotic general could engage in what Kahn termed "unauthorized behavior" and send bombers to Russia.

Kubrick found the literary work upon which his film was based almost by accident. When he requested some relevant readings from the Institute of Strategic Studies, the head of the Institute, Alastair Buchan, suggested Peter George's *Red Alert*, a serious suspense thriller about an accidental nuclear attack. The book contained such an interesting premise concerning accidental nuclear war that even a nuclear strategist like Schelling could write of it that "the sheer ingenuity of the scheme … exceeds in thoughtfulness any fiction available on how war might start." Kubrick, likewise impressed with the involving story and convincing premise, purchased rights to the novel.

However, when author and screenwriter started to construct the screenplay, they began to run into problems, which Kubrick describes in an interview with Joseph Celmis:

> I started work on the screenplay with every intention of making the film a serious treatment of the problem of accidental nuclear war. As I kept trying to imagine the way in which things would really happen, ideas kept coming to me which I would discard because they were so ludicrous I kept saying to myself: "I can't do this. People will laugh." But after a month or so I began to realize that all the things I was throwing out were the things which were most truthful.

 By trying to make the film a serious drama, Kubrick was accepting the framework of the dominant paradigm, accepting Cold War premises and creating the gripping story within these premises. This was the approach of *Red Alert* as well as of *Fail Safe*, a popular film of late 1964 adapted from the Burdick and Wheeler novel. But after studying closely the assumptions of the Cold War and the nuclear impasse, Kubrick was moving outside the dominant paradigm. Kubrick's fumbling attempts to construct a screenplay provide an example of what Gene Wise, expanding on Thomas Kuhn, has called a "paradigm revolution" in the making: a dramatic moment when accepted understandings of the world no longer make sense and new ones are needed.

Kubrick describes in an interview how he resolved his difficulties with the screenplay: "It occurred to me I was approaching the project in the wrong way. The only way to tell the story was as a black comedy, or better, a nightmare comedy, where the things you laugh at most are really the heart of the paradoxical postures that make a nuclear war possible." After deciding to use ⟨nightmare comedy⟩ in approaching his subject, Kubrick hired Terry Southern to help with the screenplay. This decision connects Kubrick to the black humor novelists of the early 1960s. Writers like Southern, Joseph Heller (*Catch-22*), Kurt Vonnegut (*Mother Night*), and Thomas Pyncheon (*V* and *The Crying of Lot 49*) shared with Kubrick the assumption of a culture gone mad, and responded to it with a similar mixture of horror and humor. Morris Dickstein's comment that "black humor is pitched at the breaking point where moral anguish explodes into a mixture of comedy and terror, where things are so bad you might as well laugh," describes quite accurately the way Kubrick came to feel about the arms race and nuclear strategy.

The premise and plot of the film are, paradoxically, quite realistic and suspenseful, which in part accounts for why the nightmare comedy succeeds. At the opening of the film an actor tells us that the Russians have built a Doomsday device which will automatically detonate if a nuclear weapon is dropped on the Soviet Union, destroying all human life on the planet – a case of deterrence strategy carried to the absurd. A paranoid anti-Communist Air Force general, unaware of the Russian's ultimate weapon, orders a fleet of airborne SAC B-52s to their Russian targets. The President of the United States finds out, but soon learns that the jets cannot be recalled because only the general knows the recall code. Moving quickly into action, the President discusses the problem with his advisors, calls the Russian Premier, and assists the Russians in their attempts to shoot down the B-52s. Finally, all the planes are recalled but one, which drops its bombs on a secondary target, setting off the Russian retaliatory Doomsday device. *Dr. Strangelove* concludes in apocalypse.

After the narrator's initial mention of a Doomsday device, Kubrick subtly begins his nightmare comedy by suggesting that man's warlike tendencies and his sexual urges stem from similar aggressive instincts. He does this by showing an airborne B-52 coupling with a refueling plane in mid-air, while the sound track plays a popular love song, "Try a Little Tenderness." The connection between sexual and military aggression continues throughout the film, as when an otherwise nude beauty in a *Playboy* centerfold has her buttocks covered with a copy of *Foreign Affairs*, but it is most evident in the names given the characters by the screenwriters. Jack D. Ripper, the deranged SAC general, recalls the sex murderer who terrorized London during the late 1880s. The name of Army strategist Buck Turgidson is also suggestive: his first name is slang for a virile male and his last name suggests both bombast and an adjective meaning "swollen." Major King Kong, pilot of the B-52, reminds viewers of the simple-minded beast who fell in love with a beautiful blonde. Group Captain Lionel Mandrake's last name is also the word for a plant reputedly known for inducing conception in women, while both names of President Merkin Muffley allude to female genitals. Appropriately, Ripper and Turgidson are hawks, while Muffley is a dove. Other names – Dr. Strangelove, the Soviet Ambassador DeSadesky, and Premier Dmitri Kissov – carry similar associations. These sexual allusions permeate the film, providing one level of the film's nightmare comedy.

More important than these sexual allusions, however, is *Dr. Strangelove's* frontal assault on the Ideology of Liberal Consensus. Above all else, *Dr. Strangelove* uses nightmare comedy to satirize four dimensions of the Cold War consensus: anti-Communist paranoia; the culture's inability to realize the enormity of nuclear war; various nuclear strategies; and the blind faith modern man places in technological progress.

The critique of American anti-Communist paranoia is presented primarily through General Ripper, played by Sterling Hayden. Kubrick portrays Ripper as an obsessed member of the radical right. Convinced that the Communist conspiracy has not only infiltrated our country but also, through fluoridation, contaminated our water, Ripper decides to take action by sending the B-52s to bomb Russia. Cutting off all communication to the outside world, he then orders his men to fight anyone attempting to capture the base.

The most grimly ominous character in the film, Ripper dominates its action in the first half, and Kubrick underlines this action stylistically, often shooting Ripper from a low camera angle. But Ripper's words also characterize his paranoia. Kubrick once agreed that whereas *2001* develops its focus visually, *Dr. Strangelove* does so much more through its dialogue. Early in the film, Ripper reveals his fears to Mandrake (Peter Sellers, in one of his three roles):

> Mandrake, have you ever seen a Communist drink a glass of water? Vodka, that's what they drink, isn't it? Never water – on no account will a Commie ever drink water, and not without good reason … Mandrake, water is the source of all life: seven-tenths of this earth's surface is water. Why, do you realize that 70 percent of you is water? And as human beings, you and I need fresh, pure water to replenish our precious bodily fluids …. Have you never wondered why I drink only distilled water or rain water and only pure grain alcohol? … Have you ever heard of a thing called fluoridation? Do you realize that fluoridation is the most monstrously conceived and dangerous Communist plot we've ever had to face?

Later Ripper mentions that fluoridation began in 1946, the same year as the postwar international Communist conspiracy. By portraying this paranoid officer willing to obliterate the world because of fluoridation Kubrick lays bare the irrational American fear of Communism as one source of the cultural malaise of the early 1960s.

The second object of attack through satire – the failure to realize how nuclear weapons have changed the nature of war – is carried out primarily on one of General Ripper's B-52s. The pilot of the plane, Major King Kong (Slim Pickens), gives evidence of outmoded notions about war in his pep talk to the crew after they have received the "go" code:

> Now look boys – I ain't much of a hand at makin' speeches … I got a fair idea of the personal emotions that some of you fellas may be thinking. Heck. I reckon you wouldn't even be human bein's if you didn't have some pretty strong feelin's about nuclear combat. But I want yall to remember one thing. The folks back home is a-countin on you and, by golly, we ain't about to let 'em down. I'll tell you something else: if this thing turns out to be half as important as I figger it just might be, I'd say you're all in line for some important promotions and personal citations when this thing's over with. And that goes for everyone of you, regardless of yer race, color, or yer creed.

Such a pep talk might be appropriate for a World War II film – in fact, most films about that war contained some such scene – but Kong's blindness to what he is being asked to do is almost complete. The fact that Kong wears a cowboy hat while making the speech, connecting him to the frontier heritage, and that "When Johnny Comes Marching Home" – a patriotic American war tune – plays on the soundtrack in the background, reinforces the conception of Kong as a dangerous anachronism.

To drive this point home, Kubrick has Kong go through the contents of a survival kit. It includes, among other items, a pistol, nine packs of chewing gum, several pairs of nylon stockings, a miniature combination Bible and Russian phrase book, and, of course, an issue of prophylactics. Besides parodying what every soldier shot down over enemy territory might need, the scene reasserts that Kong is fighting another war at another time, never having realized that if his bomber goes down after dropping its atomic load, the crew will not have to worry much about survival, to say nothing of survival kits. Kubrick, perhaps responding to the media articles which made light of the nuclear threat, attacks the shortsightedness of those who think nuclear war may not actually be that bad.

National strategies also come under attack. Here the satire is particularly pointed; the various strategic positions taken by characters in the War Room correspond quite closely to positions taken by military and civilian strategists. General Turgidson (George C. Scott) is a "hardliner." His position is even more severe than that of John Foster Dulles, who announced the policy of "massive retaliation" in 1954. Turgidson secretly favors a first-strike policy – he would like to see the U.S. obliterate the Russians offensively. After learning that the planes have been accidentally sent to their Russian targets, Turgidson urges the President to intensify the attack with even more planes:

> T: It is necessary now to make a choice, to choose between two admittedly regrettable but nevertheless distinguishable postwar environments. One, where you got twenty million people killed and the other where you got 110 million people killed.
> M: (Shocked) You're talking about mass murder, general, not war.
> T: I'm not saying we wouldn't get our hair mussed. But I do say no more than ten to twenty million killed, tops – depending on the breaks.
> M: (Angrily) I will not go down in history as the greatest mass murderer since Adolf Hitler.
> T: Perhaps it might be better, Mr. President, if you were more concerned with the American people than with your image in the history books.

Scott delivers these lines with zestful enthusiasm, and his animated features suggest that he can hardly wait for the annihilation to begin. In rhetoric distressingly similar to the arguments occurring occasionally in the journals, Turgidson advises "total commitment," sacrificing a "few lives" for what he believes would be a more secure and satisfactory "post-war environment."

President Muffley's position is the most reasonable of any in the War Room. He is neither a fanatic nor a warmonger. Unfortunately, he's also nearly totally ineffectual as he tries to implement his goal: attempting to avoid catastrophe at all costs through communication with the Soviets. Peter Sellers plays this role with a bald wig, in part to differentiate himself visually from his other two roles, in part to remind audiences of Adlai Stevenson, the quintessential liberal of the 1950s, twice-unsuccessful candidate for the Presidency. When Muffley negotiates with Premier Kissov over the hot line to Moscow, he appears ridiculous. After Kissov says Muffley should call the People's Central Air Defense Headquarters at Omsk, Muffley asks, "Listen, do you happen to have the phone number on you, Dmitri? … What? … I see, just ask for Omsk information." Muffley argues with Kissov about who is sorrier about the mistake, insisting that he can be just as sorry as Dmitri. Such small talk amidst the enormity of the crisis is ludicrous.

By appearing both ridiculous and ineffectual, Muffley furthers Kubrick's nightmare comedy. For if the person who has the most rational strategy (and who also happens to be the commander in chief) is unable to control nuclear weapons and his military advisors, citizens really have something to worry about.

Although Dr. Strangelove does not speak until the last third of the film, the creators seem to have taken a great deal of care in creating Strangelove as a composite of a number of pundits in the new "science" of nuclear strategy. As a physicist involved in weapons research and development, he invites comparisons to Edward Teller. Not only was Teller involved in the creation of the atomic bomb, but he was also a strong anti-Communist who pushed hard for the development of the much more powerful hydrogen bomb in 1949 and 1950. In his background, accent, and some of his dialogue, Strangelove suggests Henry Kissinger. Like Kissinger, Strangelove came from Germany in the 1930s and still speaks with a German accent. With his wavy dark hair and sunglasses, he also bears a physical resemblance to Kissinger. Even his definition of deterrence – "the art of producing in the mind of the enemy the fear to attack you" – sounds remarkably like the definition Kissinger offered in his *Nuclear Weapons and Foreign Policy* (1957). Finally, Herman Kahn plays a part in the Strangelove composite, primarily as related to the Doomsday device. Strangelove tells the President that he recently commissioned a study by the Bland corporation (Kahn worked for RAND) to examine the possibility of a Doomsday device. The study found the device technologically feasible; it would be hooked to a computer and programmed to detonate under certain prescribed circumstances. However, Strangelove found the machine impractical as a deterrent because it would go off even if an attack was accidental. All these details are similarly discussed in Kahn's *On Thermonuclear War*, with Kahn similarly concluding that though the device would contain most of the characteristics of a deterrent, it would not meet the final characteristics of being controllable. As a mixture of Teller, Kissinger, Kahn, and probably a number of others (Werner Von Braun is another possibility), Strangelove becomes a significant symbol. Essentially, he is the coldly speculating mind, not unlike one of Nathaniel Hawthorne's calculating and obsessed scientists. Like them, Strangelove is devoid of fellow feeling. He proves this near the end of the film: even after the American B-52 gets through to bomb its target, Strangelove has ideas. He offers a plan to take all military and political leaders (along with attractive women at a ratio of ten women to one man) into a mine shaft in an effort to survive the virulent radioactivity produced by the Doomsday device. Clearly, none of the strategic postures presented by Kubrick – Turgidson's militarism, Muffley's tender-minded rationality, or Strangelove's constant speculations – are able to control the inexorable march of nuclear holocaust.

Although *2001* is more famous for its exploration of technology, Kubrick shows a fascination with machines in *Dr. Strangelove*. Most prominent is the simulation of the B-52 cockpit, which Kubrick – after the Air Force denied him any assistance in making the film – had built from an unauthorized photograph he discovered in an aviation magazine. Throughout the B-52 scenes, Kubrick keeps viewer interest by alternating close-ups of various panel controls with shots of crew members expertly carrying out their orders. Besides those in the B-52, many other machines – telephones, radios, the electronic wall chart in the War Room – play important parts in the film.

Kubrick develops his attitude toward technology in *Dr. Strangelove* by making use of both machines of destruction and machines of communication; the problem in the film is that while people handle the machines of destruction with great alacrity, the more neutral machines of communication are either ineffectual or turned toward destructive purposes. Through a misuse of radio codes, Ripper sends the B-52s on their destructive mission; DeSadesky uses a camera to take pictures of the War Room, presumably for purposes of intelligence. When people try to use the neutral machines to prevent destruction, however, they prove to be ineffective. During President Muffley's call to Kissov, for example, social amenities and small talk hinder attempts to stop the B-52s, as does the slowness of the process. Likewise, when Mandrake tries to call the President after he has discovered the recall code, he cannot because he does not have a dime for the pay phone.

Though people can't use neutral machines effectively, they handle the machines of destruction with deadly efficiency. This includes not only the conventional weaponry at the Air Force base, where Army infantry and artillery attempt to take over the base, but also, more distressingly the nuclear weapons. The whole crew of the B-52 expertly manipulate their machines, even after the explosion of an anti-aircraft missile damages the plane. Kong, to the dismay of the audience, shows great ingenuity in repairing damaged circuits in time to open the bomb doors over the target. Kubrick is not really suggesting that machines are dominating men. Rather, he seems to perceive a human death instinct. Arising from a nearsighted rationality, this death instinct leads man first to create machines, then to use them for destroying human life. In questioning the "progress" inherent in technology, Kubrick was challenging a fundamental assumption of the dominant paradigm. This challenge to technology – both to the stress on technique in society and to the increasing importance of machines in modern life – was to become a dominant theme in the late 1960s, important in several works of social criticism during that era, including Theodore Roszak's *The Making of A Counter Culture* (1969), Lewis Mumford's *The Myth of the Machine: The Pentagon of Power* (1969), and Philip Slater's *The Pursuit of Loneliness* (1970).

The film's final scene underlines Kubrick's attack on the Ideology of Liberal Consensus. Mushroom clouds billow on the screen, filling the sky, exuding both an awesome power and a perverse beauty. Simultaneously, a light, sentimental love song from the late 1940s – Vera Lynn's "We'll Meet Again" – provides a contrasting aural message in an excellent use of film irony. Its opening lines are: "We'll meet again, don't know where, don't know when, but I know we'll meet again some sunny day." If we go on with the world view of the postwar era, Kubrick ironically suggests, we will never meet again, because there will be no one left on earth. Retaining the conflict between image and sound throughout the final credit sequence, Kubrick hopes to prod his viewers to reflect on all that they have seen.

Taken as a whole, *Dr. Strangelove* fundamentally challenges the Ideology of Liberal Consensus by attacking anti-Communist paranoia, American adherence to outmoded notions of heroism, various nuclear strategies, and faith in social salvation through technological expertise. The Cold War foreign policy so strongly supported by Americans in the late 1940s and 1950s rested on the belief that America was a fundamentally just society threatened only by the germs of "Godless Communism." *Dr. Strangelove*, though it certainly does nothing to imply that the Soviet leaders are any wiser than their American counterparts, suggests that no nation-state has a monopoly on foolishness and that the backstage strategies of military and political leaders are simply exercises in paranoia. The nightmare comedy presented a disturbing and deeply wrought challenge to America in 1963 and 1964.

The film would not be so important were it not so uncharacteristic in the way it treated the Cold War. The House Un-American Activities Committee investigated Hollywood in two waves, once in 1947 (resulting in the infamous Hollywood Ten trials) and later in the early 1950s. Hollywood responded not by fighting government interference – as it had in the mid-Thirties censorship controversies – but by cooperating, blacklisting people who were suspected of leftist affiliations in the Thirties and making a spate of films which overtly or covertly supported the dominant paradigm.

The paradigm was overtly supported by a good number of anti-Communist melodramas from the late 1940s and early 1950s, of which *My Son John* (1952) may be the most famous example. These films were most popular between 1940 and 1953: in 1952 alone, twelve of them were released. Films about World War II, portraying the Nazis or the Japanese as villains, tended also to divide the world into good (the Allies) and evil (the Axis powers) and thus to support the dominant paradigm. Here Kubrick's anti-war *Paths of Glory* (1957) was clearly an anomaly. Even science fiction films, like *The Thing* (1951) or *War of the Worlds* (1952), by using threats from outer space as a metaphor of the Communist threat, covertly supported this conventional way of looking at and understanding the world. More directly related to *Dr. Strangelove* are a series of films through the 1950s and into the 1960s dealing with the bomb and especially with the Strategic Air Command.

Dr. Strangelove seems all the more amazing when one contrasts its iconoclasm and sharp satire with *Above and Beyond* (1952), *Strategic Air Command* (1957), *Bombers B-52* (1957), *A Gathering of Eagles* (1963), and *Fail Safe* (1964). The first of these films concerns the story of Paul Tibbetts, commander of the group which actually dropped the first atomic bombs on Hiroshima and Nagasaki. Much of the story concerns Mrs. Tibbetts' gradual acceptance of her husband's secret yet important work. *Strategic Air Command* follows much the same vein. In it a major league baseball star and former World War II pilot, played by Jimmy Stewart, gives up the last years of his prime to return to active duty. Stewart's wife, at first upset at her husband's decision, realizes that it is necessary for the peace and well-being of the nation. Produced in the same year, *Bombers B-52* concerns a sergeant who resists the temptation to take a higher paying civilian job, and thus retains his wonderful existence as an enlisted man.

Both *A Gathering of Eagles* and *Fail Safe* were released about the time of *Dr. Strangelove*, yet their approaches to their subjects are light years from that of *Strangelove*. General Curtis LeMay, commander of SAC, took a personal concern in *A Gathering of Eagles*: he stressed the need to explain how many safeguards had been created to prevent accidental war. The film concerns a young colonel who takes over an SAC wing that has failed a surprise alert and gradually trains his men so they are ever ready to go to war if the necessity arises. LeMay was pleased with the film, judging it "the closest any of the Air Force films ever came to showing the true picture of what the military was all about."

Fail Safe, released less than a year after *Dr. Strangelove*, first seemed quite similar to *Dr. Strangelove* in that in both films, nuclear weapons are detonated by accident. But *Fail Safe* does nothing to suggest, as *Strangelove* does, that national policy is ridiculous. Instead it portrays the President (Henry Fonda) as a responsible and competent man caught in a tragic, yet controllable circumstance. His decision to obliterate New York City in exchange for the accidental destruction of Moscow prevents the destruction of the world and is powerfully rendered without a touch of irony: in the final moments, we see freeze frames of people on New York streets just before the bomb explodes. Despite its powerful cinematic ending, the film is, as Julian Smith has suggested, "a morally and intellectually dangerous film because it simplifies and romanticizes the issues of national responsibility."

All these films present a common respect for national and military leaders. Though bad apples may show up occasionally, though accidents may cause some difficulties, each film ends with control being reestablished, the viewer reassured that the American way is the best course and that the military is doing the best job possible to shield us from the Communist menace. None hint, as does *Dr. Strangelove,* that we may need protection against ourselves.

A look at how reviewers and the public responded to *Dr. Strangelove* can give us some indication of how Kubrick's adversary views were accepted. Since a feature film most often must reinforce the cultural values and attitudes of its viewers if it expects to be popular, it is understandable that neither critics nor the public were swept away by the film. Though few critics of mass magazines or political journals panned the film, a number of them, thinking within the bounds of the dominant paradigm, came up with strange interpretations. The critic for the right-wing *National Review,* for example, suggested that *Dr. Strangelove*'s theme was that all ideology should be abandoned. He went on to defend American ideology "with its roots thrust deep in Greek political thought," closing curiously with a hope that Kubrick might make a film criticizing Stalinism. *Saturday Review*'s Hollis Alpert gave a generally favorable review, concluding with these comments: "No one thinks our ingeniously destructive world-destroying bombs are a laughing matter. Certainly director Kubrick doesn't. But on some fairly safe planet out of view, maybe this is the way they would view our predicament." Alpert seems to miss Kubrick's point. No one accepting the dominant paradigm would see nuclear weapons as a laughing matter, but Kubrick, after studying the arms race, the Cold War, and the idea of deterrence carefully, realized the insanity of the situation and found that the only way he could possibly approach the material was through the satirical thrust of nightmare comedy. By having his audience laugh at the situation, he hoped not that they would realize its seriousness but rather that they would perceive its absurdity. Alpert, evidently, misunderstood the social rhetoric.

Two observers who thought highly of the film were Stanley Kauffmann and Lewis Mumford. Writing for *The New Republic,* Kauffmann – a critic notoriously harsh on most American films – thought *Dr. Strangelove* the best American film in fifteen years. The film showed "how mankind, its reflexes scored in its nervous system and its mind entangled in orthodoxies, insisted on destroying itself."

22

Films of the Late 1960s and Early 1970s

From Counterculture to Counterrevolution, 1967–1971

Michael Ryan and Douglas Kelner

The late 1960s represented one of Hollywood's most creative periods, as filmmakers experimented with new narrative and stylistic techniques and used film to present search-ing reexaminations of American values and history. Many of the most popular films of the era were explicitly political, and questioned the American dream and America's role in the world. In sharp contrast, during the early 1970s there occurred a strong reaction against many of the values glorified in the films of the late 1960s. Movies that sympa-thized with outlaws and rebels were replaced by films featuring law-and-order avengers. Sports movies, previously a largely unpopular genre, gained large audiences with their celebration of competitiveness and victory. The most striking development was the rise of the blockbuster, typically featuring cartoon-like characters, spectacular special effects, and escapist, roller-coaster ride plots.

In the late 1960s many Hollywood films, responding to social movements mobi-lized around the issues of civil rights, poverty, feminism, and militarism that were cresting at that time, articulated critiques of American values and institutions. They transcoded [expressed] a growing sense of alienation from the dominant myths and ideals of U.S. society. Film served as both an instrument of social criticism and a vehi-cle for presenting favorable representations of alternative values and institutions. "New Hollywood" films like *The Graduate, Bonnie and Clyde, Midnight Cowboy*, and *Easy Rider* were important not only for their social content. Some subverted the tra-ditional narrative and cinematic representational codes of Hollywood filmmaking. Many employed a disjunctive editing that undermined passive viewing (*The Graduate, Point Blank*), used experimental camera techniques as thematic correlates (*Midnight Cowboy*), mixed genres like slapstick and tragedy (*Bonnie and Clyde*), employed color as an ironic or critical rather than expressive correlate of meaning (*They Shoot Horses, Don't They?*), broke down the classical narrative patterns that had dominated the

Michael Ryan and Douglas Kelner, "From Counterculture to Counterrevolution, 1967–1971," *Camera Politica: The Politics and Ideology of Contemporary Hollywood Film* (Bloomington: Indiana University Press, 1990), pp. 17–19, 20–1, 23–4, 26–7, 37–42, 44–6. Reprinted with permission of Indiana University Press.

1950s and early 1960s (*Little Big Man*), introduced camera and editing techniques derived from television that significantly altered the pace and format of film (*M*A*S*H*), and underlined the mixture of blithe cynicism, complacent naïveté, and strained optimism that characterized the Cold War period (in some respects, a "Restoration Period" in Hollywood).

These films provided audiences with a new set of representations for constructing the world, new figures of action, thought, and feeling for positing alternative phenomenal and social realities, sometimes apart from, sometimes within the interstices of the dominant social reality construction. These alternative representations and figures were as important as the new institutions and laws brought into being by the direct actions of blacks, students, and women in the streets and legislatures during the period. Even though the social movements themselves could be repressed or contravened, those new figures of social understanding and behavior would become a permanent part of American culture. Perhaps the most important of these representations was that of the self or subject in rebellion against conservative authority and social conformity. It was the figure that marked the end of the fifties ideal of functional selflessness. Related representations included that of the "Establishment" as a set of outdated conservative values, of the police as an enemy rather than a friend, of the patriarchal family as an institution for the oppression of women, of the liberal ideal of consensus as a cloak for white racial domination, of the government as the slave of economic interests, especially war industry interests, of foreign policy as a form of neoimperialism, of Third World liberation struggles as heroic, of the value of subjective experiences related to mysticism and drugs, of the importance of the preservation of nature, of sexuality as a rich terrain of possibility rather than as an evil to be repressed, and of capitalism as a form of enslavement instead of a realm of freedom. This transformation of the dominant representations which determined how the commonly held sense of social reality was constructed would have lasting, indeed permanent effects. It would be impossible to return unquestioningly to the imposed discipline of the fifties or to restore the conservative order of sexual and moral propriety that prevailed prior to the sixties. A radical alternative culture came into being, one immune to the sort of McCarthyite repression that had silenced the radical culture of the twenties and thirties, because the new radicalism was as critical of the Soviet Union as it was of the United States. And that meant that the impunity with which the business-government class had acted, especially overseas, could no longer be assumed without opposition. Resistance had become a staple of American culture.

Alienation and Rebellion

The major movements of the sixties were the black struggle for civil rights, the struggle against the Vietnam War, the feminist movement, and the New Left student movement. The sixties were also characterized by a high level of disaffection on the part of white middle-class youth from the values and ideals of fifties America, the world of suburban houses, corporate jobs, "straight" dress and behavior, sexual repression, and social conformity. These alienated and rebellious youths took to the roads, dropped out of school, started communes, grew long hair, listened to rock music, took drugs, and engaged in the creation of alternative lifestyles to those associated with the bourgeois "Establishment."

We will begin our consideration of the sixties by looking at the phenomenon of alienation from and rejection of the "American Dream."

The American ideology which came to be rejected by so many during this period consisted of a set of codes for understanding the world and living in it that derived from American institutions and helped reproduce and legitimate them. Those codes provided an essentially metaphoric version of U.S. history and society. A metaphoric representation is one which replaces a real version of events or an accurate account of social reality with an elevated ideal. An understanding of the phenomenon of alienation from and rebellion against such ideals is therefore inseparable from an understanding of the representational strategies used to undermine such ideological idealizations.

Crucial among these representations is the individualist male hero, the ideal of the just American war, a righteous vision of U.S. history, and the frontier myth of expanding possibilities for achievement and wealth that are available to all. Many revisionist films criticize the myth of the traditional American hero through reconstructive representations that clash with the hitherto prevalent Hollywood conventions. For example, in *Little Big Man*, one of the most popular films of 1970, General Custer is portrayed as a megalomaniacal butcher who deserved his fate. The critical representational strategy of the film consists of adopting the position of the Native Americans and of depicting the U.S. soldiers from outside as the enemy. At a time when domestic opposition to the Vietnam War was on the rise, a number of satiric and tragic films like *M*A*S*H* and *Johnny Got His Gun* departed from the tradition of the just American war by representing war as something stupid and inhumane. The mythic representation of the frontier is undermined in films like *Soldier Blue* and *McCabe and Mrs. Miller*, which depict it as brutal. And the traditional representation of the ladder of individual success open to all talents is revised in critical films like *Midnight Cowboy* and *They Shoot Horses, Don't They?* – a film based, like *Johnny*, on a Depression-era novel. The revival of thirties leftism is also signaled by three critical films by directors from the heyday of the social problem film – Dassin's *Uptight*, Biberman's *Slaves*, and Polonsky's *Tell Them Willie Boy Is Here* – all of whom had been blacklisted.

The development of new narrative strategies in a number of these films is inseparable from their critiques of the major tenets of the American imaginary. The theme of individual success, like that of the great American patriotic tradition, is based in a narrative form. It is a story that entails a character, a plot, and a conclusion. Similarly, American history is a narrative with good and bad characters projected over actual events that moves from a happy beginning (the Founding Fathers) to an even happier conclusion (the present, or if that doesn't work, the future). The frequent use of discontinuous, reflexive, and interrupted narratives in these films is thus not only a playful formal device. It gets at the heart of the American imaginary, inasmuch as that is based in narratives (of individual success, of American history, and so on) ....

The Graduate (1967), one of the first alienation films, is the story of a college graduate who rejects his parents' upper-class career track, has an affair with a much older woman, and finally flees with her daughter. Images of immersion in water suggest the claustrophobia of the bourgeois world, the cloying sense of its hypocrisy and emptiness, which many young people of the time were experiencing. And the career advice Ben (Dustin Hoffman) receives – "Plastics" – sums up what many young people of the era thought of the fifties world of their parents and of the career imperatives of the American Dream – that they were crass and artificial. Directed by Mike Nichols, *The Graduate* was a key alienation film of the period and was also the biggest box-office success of the late sixties. It was innovative in style, relying on imported French New Wave techniques – jump cuts, long takes with handheld cameras, tight close-ups – to render the experience of alienation from the American ideal of material success. Though weighted down by Christian imagery (Ben uses a cross to fight for his beloved Elaine) and a traditionalist romantic conclusion, the film nonetheless expanded the lexicon of the American cinema through editing and music primarily. In the credit sequence, Ben's air of passivity as he is carried along an airport conveyor belt while a loudspeaker issues recorded instructions is reinforced by Simon and Garfunkel's song "The Sound of Silence." The music and the imagery suggest he is a cipher in a world of mass conformity and social control, the mode of being alienated young people claimed a technological and technocratic society was imposing on them. The film's critique is also executed through editing. Nonrealist transitions permit Ben to walk out of one space (his parents' outdoor pool) and into another quite different one (the hotel room where he carries on his affair), thus establishing contiguous links that suggest the interchangeability of upper-class luxury and cynical adultery. The [challenge to the ideal of] bourgeois success is realized fully at the end when the escaping young couple ride a common bus to freedom and leave behind their parents' wealth.

In the other great rebellion film of 1967, *Bonnie and Clyde*, the story of two young Depression-era outlaws who are ultimately murdered by the police, images of imprisonment and confinement (the bars of a bed which represent the constraints a young woman feels in her working-class world) are juxtaposed to images of the open fields of nature to establish a simple trajectory of escape. Contrasts in visual texture and tempo code the escape as one from confinement and fragmentation to openness and continuity. Throughout the film, images of open fields, single tone colors, an expansive camera frame for exterior shots, and jaunty banjo music suggest liberation from the tight focus shots in small-town settings. While the young rebels are associated with brown earth, blue sky, freedom of movement, and dynamic music, the figures of Establishment authority are represented negatively in association with bleak, white-washed prison settings and images of urban confinement. The film thus evokes the romanticism that was prevalent in the late sixties, which counterposed nature as a realm of freedom and equality to the authoritarianism of the Establishment ....

Yet both *The Graduate* and *Bonnie and Clyde* evidence the limitations of the sixties version of alienated white middle-class rebellion. The alternatives posed to bourgeois conformity frequently took the form of a search for more personal, self-fulfilling experiences. The self ("doing one's own thing") became a criterion of authenticity, and in many ways this representation cohered perfectly with traditional American individualism ....

Alienation from the "American Dream" assumed its most striking form during the period in the hippie counterculture. Founded on the values of a return to nature, of the virtue of preindustrial social forms like the commune, of the need to liberate oneself from "straight" behavior, especially regarding sexuality, of the ideal of a simple and more authentic life experience, usually gained with the aid of drugs, the counterculture seemed for a time to be in the process of constituting a genuine and permanent alternative to bourgeois life. But the effort was itself dependent on a well-fueled capitalist economy, which began to fizzle out in 1970, and dropping out soon gave way to caving in. Law school followed a quick shave and haircut for many former hippies.

Easy Rider (1968) was produced by Bert Schneider and Bob Rafelson's BBS company, which also was responsible for other alienation classics of the time like *Five Easy Pieces* (1970) and *The Last Picture Show* (1971). The story of two motorcycle-riding hippies who travel from Los Angeles to New Orleans to sell drugs and who are murdered by rural rednecks in the end, the film turned a small budget into a large profit and helped launch the "New Hollywood" of more "personal" and artistic independent films. It is in this film that the ambivalent ideology of sixties individualism is most evident. Such individualism is usually male and highly narcissistic. Consequently, the ride into nature which the bikers undertake is both a metaphor for the escape from urban oppression into the freedom of self-discovery and a synecdoche for male narcissistic regression to a warm, comforting maternal environment in the face of the constraints of modern mass life (signaled by the metal structures that seem to be devouring the bikers in a scene just before their death). Women are noticeably marginalized in the film; they appear as compliant sexual partners, prostitutes, or devoted wives. Moreover, although the hippie quest permits a critique of small-town southern provincialism, it is also essentially aimed toward an ideal of freedom that is highly traditional. Indeed, it recalls the Jeffersonian yeoman ideal of small rural capitalism. For example, at one point the bikers are compared to cowboys shoeing a horse in a medium shot which includes both within the frame. In a certain sense, the bikers' ride is as much into the past as it is into the heartland ....

While hippie romanticism can be conservative, it also helped spawn the ecology movement, legislation to protect the environment, and the rediscovery of natural agriculture and foods. In its benign progressive forms, the counterculture became a culture of alternative values based in nature that led eventually to such important later social movements as the antinuclear campaigns of the late seventies and Greenpeace. In light of the value of "nature," some of the more negative aspects of conservative capitalist life came into focus – toxic waste, pollution, etc. – and became objects of social opposition. Thus, hippie romanticism was not univocal. Even though its inflection in *Easy Rider* is male, individualist and narcissistic, it also gave rise to a mental health movement which questioned the prevailing definitions of psychological normality, emphasized the psychological costs of living in a capitalist society, and promoted ideals of self-expression as a way of gaining mental health. The very important Subjective psychology movement of the seventies (the so-called "culture of narcissism") derives from the counterculture's emphasis on expressivity. Although it was often limited to white professionals, that movement pointed toward the necessity of a focus on issues of mental health in any progressive vision of social reconstruction.

We have concentrated on films celebrating the values of alienation and rebellion, but many films of the era cast both the counterculture and the new hip rebelliousness in a somewhat more critical light. Richard Lester's *Petulia* (1968) and Paul Mazursky's *Bob and Carol and Ted and Alice* (1970), for example, criticized the alternative lifestyles of the new sexual revolution. And films like *Panic in Needle Park* (1971) and Arthur Penn's *Alice's Restaurant* (1969) depicted the countercultural use of drugs negatively. Penn's film also suggested the fragility of the communal experience. By 1971, the dark side of the counterculture would be revealed for many in *Gimme Shelter*, the film of the Rolling Stones concert at Altamont which culminated in violent death. Film itself contributed to the standardization of the counterculture. The "capturing" of the experience of Woodstock, the major commercial "happening" of the late sixties, in a film of 1970 was also a freezing of the supposed spontaneity of the occasion. What could be filmed and commercialized was to a certain extent already inimical to the countercultural rejection of bourgeois values in favor of more noncommercial and natural ideals. To be "counter" cultural was to place oneself at odds with the mainstream of American culture, and while taking advantage of so commercial a form as the rock concert or the rock movie could help spread the countercultural message, it also necessarily contradicted the essential values of the counterculture ....

The Hollywood Counterrevolution

The struggles and movements of the sixties began to provoke a conservative backlash by the early seventies. Polls indicated a change during this period toward more "conservatism" and toward more concern with material self-satisfaction. Whereas only 1% of the people listed national unity as a major concern in 1959, the figure had risen to 15% by 1971. Adults also registered a reduced sense of integration into the social structure, more anxiety accompanied by an increased search for intimacy, an increased concern about an uncertain future, and a move to less social, more personal and individuated integration and well-being. There seems to be a relation between the new conservatism and the onset of the first major economic recession of the period at the same time. But the social struggles of the sixties also took their toll, giving rise to a countertendency desirous of unity, order, and peace. The demolition in the sixties of the cultural representations essential to the traditional order seemed to lead to a search for alternative forms of representational security and ego-integrity. But the sixties' assault on traditional values also provoked a reassertion of exaggerated versions of conservative ideals. The fearful retreat from the public world of disharmony and conflict was accompanied by a resuscitation of security-providing patriarchal representations. One finds evidence of the turn to personalism in the great popularity of *Love Story* (the top-grossing picture of 1970) and of the desire for patriarchal unity in the success of right-wing police dramas like *The French Connection*, the Oscar winner in 1971, and *Dirty Harry* (1971), one of the most notorious films of the period.

Conservative films had been made during the late sixties. But on the whole, conservatives were then on the defensive, and the terrain of social struggle was determined by the insurgent liberal and radical social forces. The killing of student radicals at Kent State and Jackson State by National Guardsmen and police in 1971 marked a turning point in the limits of conservative tolerance for social revolt. By 1972, the Nixon counterrevolution was in full force, and the Nixon administration successfully mobilized conservative sentiments against young radicals, minorities, and feminists in the 1972 election by painting liberal Democrat George McGovern as the candidate of the three A's – abortion, acid, and amnesty for draft resisters. A meaner, more cynical discourse began to emerge as the dominant mode of Hollywood film. In 1971 alone, *The French Connection*, *Dirty Harry*, and *Straw Dogs* articulate an anti-liberal value system that portrays human life as predatory and animalistic, a jungle without altruism.

At stake in Peckinpah's *Straw Dogs* is the law of the patriarchal family. In the late sixties, women were striking out for independence from male law in the home, and sexuality, long a secure domain of male power, became problematic. *Straw Dogs* sets the tone for the antifeminist counterrevolution of the seventies. The woman in the film is depicted as a treacherous sex kitten who betrays her "wimpy" husband, David, and entices men who finally rape her, an act she is portrayed as enjoying. In the final segment of the film, the same men attack their house, and she attempts to join them but is prevented from doing so by her husband, who is eventually transformed into a warrior who ultimately kills the attackers. His ascent to true manhood is associated with learning that liberal civility and law are useless against brute force and that women need to be disciplined if they are not to go astray. At one point he calls out to his attackers that what they are doing is against the law, but of course his plea is ineffective. The local constable, whose ineffectuality is signaled by his lame arm, ultimately hands power over to David, telling him he is "the law here now." The benediction seems also to apply to the domestic sphere. David immediately tells his wife, "Do as you're told," and smiles beatifically. In the end, he separates out from her altogether and rides off into the night with another man, a sign of the homosocial origins of misogyny.

Peckinpah's style earnestly expresses the ideal of male redemption through violence. The color tones suggest a dark nature of instinct and passion, and the violence has all the frenzy of a sexual encounter; indeed this is a telling feature for understanding its origins. *Straw Dogs* opens with a shot of children playing against gravestones, a scene reminiscent of the juxtaposition of innocence and violence that opens *The Wild Bunch* – children tormenting a scorpion with ants, then setting it on fire. Even the innocent harbor bestial desires and violent instincts, the film suggests. *Straw Dogs*, therefore, concerns regression, the falling back upon a supposedly more basic or natural reality of violence when social order breaks down. Yet the film can also be said to undermine or deconstruct its own premises.

David is educated in the process of the film. He learns to be violent, to regress from civility to bestiality, and to be a "man." The film presents this metaphorically as a recognition of primordial realities (through the metaphors of primitive hunting devices), but it depicts the regression as a process of training or socialization, a random, contingent, and metonymic process, in other words. The constable's benediction is the most telling evidence of the initiatory or artificially induced character of David's learning experience. Moreover, his relation to his wife is characterized by a mixture of fear and dependence that situates his aggressive domination of her and his ultimate flight into the night with another man as further evidence of the social origins of this particular male "nature." In the penultimate scene, David is about to be overwhelmed by one of the aggressors. He lies on his back, with the other man on top, an explicitly "feminine" pose. He is passive and helpless, and his wife has to save him with a shotgun blast. She stands at the top of the stairs, he at the bottom, a curious literal denial of all the film figuratively asserts. The passive male's rage against woman is in fact an anger against dependence, against the possibility of being "on the bottom," that is linked to fears of passivity in regard to other men in a competitive male world. Violence permits an escape from those feelings, as well as an overthrowing of female power and potential independence. What is really regressed to is an earlier stage of psychic development when women have power over men as their primary caretakers. That power must be purged in order for the man to acquire a patriarchally defined male identity. But male anxiety is not limited to an abreaction of earlier experiences of female power, a metaphor of a narcissistic, atemporal simultaneity or fusion. It also concerns female sexuality. When David's wife almost leaves to join the other men, she displays the origin of male sexual anxiety in a female sexuality which is not ultimately beholden to male power, which, like the literal metonymic associations that trouble self-idealizing metaphors, can "go astray." Violence also cures this threat to impropriety.

The other major conservative films of 1971 – *Dirty Harry* and *The French Connection* – were crime dramas. These "law and order" thrillers transcoded discourse of the campaign against crime and drugs waged by Nixon and Agnew in the early seventies. They are also vehicles for conservative counterattacks against the liberalism that many conservatives blamed for the crisis in domestic order brought about by the sixties. Both films contest the liberal theories of criminal justice, exemplified in the *Miranda* decision, that gave more rights to criminal suspects and curtailed the powers of the police. In this vision, liberal criminal justice is unjust because it prevents good cops from doing their job, and it lets criminals go free to commit more crimes. Cops are portrayed as heroes whose zeal to protect the innocent and society is misinterpreted as brutality by liberals. Like *Straw Dogs* and *Clockwork Orange*, these films portray conservatism as a regression to primary process thinking, to a privileging of force and instinct over civil procedure. Unsublimated drives such as competition and domination are presented as more fundamental than such liberal civil modes as negotiation, mediation, and cooperation – all connective or metonymic ways of proceeding which encroach upon the firmly boundaried identities that conservative metaphors establish.

In *The French Connection*, a tough cop named Popeye Doyle (Gene Hackman) manages to crack a heroin smuggling operation, but all the criminals are let go in the end for lack of evidence. The suggestion is that liberals are responsible for the failure of the system, while the individualist cop is a better solution. The film is metaphoric to the extent that it presumes certain axioms that are not open to negotiation; the narrative obliges the audience to agree with the premises of the film because there are no spaces where reflection is possible. The cop reacts instinctively to the "problem" of crime (which, significantly, has not yet been committed), and the audience is given little time to do anything but react with equal rapidity to his actions, thus assuming guilt without judicial process. This is made clear in the famous chase scene. The subjective camera lodged in Popeye's car identifies the audience with his point of view in a way that works against reflection on the motivations and consequences of his actions. The audience's desires are manipulated into supporting a restoration of order or the achievement of the goal of catching the criminal, no matter what the cost in life or liberty (and Popeye almost does harm a number of people during the chase). When he finally does kill the hit man (unnecessarily; he could just as easily have wounded the disarmed man), the audience is prepared to desire the release of tension that ensues. Police brutality is thus legitimated stylistically.

A more overt and articulated statement against the sixties in general and against liberal criminal justice in particular is made in Don Siegel's *Dirty Harry*. Liberalism in crime prevention is outrightly condemned, and the evil figure in the film is a fanatical and "effeminate" killer named Scorpio who is associated with peace symbols, long hair, and other countercultural paraphernalia. The rhetorical procedure of this film is to position the audience as being knowledgeable of the criminal's guilt, then to show liberals letting him go after Harry has risked his life to capture him. When Scorpio kills again, the audience knows that Harry's only choice is to sidestep the liberal criminal system and use force. The style of the film is designed to produce both repulsion and idealization (two conjoined attitudes that reappear in a number of conservative films). It mixes naturalistic representations of violence and brutality (a raped adolescent girl being removed from a hole in the ground where she has been allowed to suffocate) with monumentalizing celebrations of white male individualist power (Harry standing alone against the sky overlooking the city like a Hobbesian sovereign). The representational mix is significant because such metaphoric idealization (which establishes Harry's higher meaning as a savior while separating him from the mass) is often a means of turning away from or denying something threatening or repulsive. In this case, the idealization is of extremely "male" traits such as aggressivity, toughness, lack of affect, and individualism. What is repulsive is "feminine" or, worse, indeterminate. Scorpio is associated with gays ("My, that's a big one," he remarks of Harry's gun, after Harry has mistaken a gay for Scorpio), and he is depicted as whining, weak, and very unmanly." What this suggests is that male-defined ideals of conservative law and order are bound up with the representational dynamics that construct male sexual identity. Metaphoric male idealization comes down to an insecurity in males over the determinacy of sexual identity, over being a "man" and not being confused with a "woman," an insecurity associated with representational patterns that are metonymic, that is, that break down male boundaries and male identity by establishing empathetic connections with people or differential relations between supposedly hermetic [separate] realms. Because Scorpio represents such a breakdown, he must be eliminated ....

Dirty Harry was not a significantly popular film, at least in regard to box office receipts. Its sequels would fare much better. Our audience survey also suggests that it wasn't successful in winning large segments of the population over to its viewpoint: 77% of our sample felt Harry's methods were the wrong way to deal with crime, and 73% felt that the D.A. represented necessary constitutional protections as opposed to unnecessary red tape. While 40% perceived Harry as a rebel against American society, a significant 68% characterized him as a reactionary. It may be important as well that nearly 30% of our sample had not seen the film, though some of these no-views may be due to the age of the film. While our survey suggests that many viewers rejected the film's vision of the world, we should also note that in our oral interviews we encountered a number of people who fully held the position of the film, and in a number of cases where people disagreed with the solution to crime, they nonetheless confessed to buying in temporarily to the action format and the plot premises of the film. This splitting of the ego between a reserved judgment and participation in the spectacle characterizes a number of audience response patterns to different films. It suggests that the popularity of right-wing films is not necessarily a testament to the prevalence of right-wing opinions in the film audiences. But it also points to the possibility of false consciousness and of unconscious influences. It is noteworthy, for example, that 79% of those polled also supported stronger punishment for criminals.

French Connection and *Dirty Harry* are reactionary films, yet they also contain immanent critiques of American society. To be able to proclaim their right-wing solutions, they must inadvertently describe a disintegrating society which is incapable of finding real solutions to its fundamental problems of economic, political, and social inequality. The films depict the failure of liberal solutions to the problems of crime and poverty generated by capitalism. More accurately than liberal films, they portray the real exercise of force that underlies seemingly apolitical problems like crime. Right-wing films in certain ways portray the harsh truth of a society which must rely on authoritarian and repressive police force, generally directed overwhelmingly at minorities, in order to avoid coming undone as a result of its structural imbalances ....

23

Reaffirming Traditional Values
The Blue Collar Ethnic in Bicentennial America: Rocky

Daniel J. Leab

Years after it first appeared, Rocky *remains one of the most popular films made during the 1970s. In this essay, the historian Daniel J. Leab locates the film in the context in which it was originally made, and shows how it reflected shifting cultural attitudes toward race, class, and ethnicity, and a broad cultural impulse to reaffirm traditional values that took place in the middle and late 1970s.*

The very foundations of the American Dream had been severely shaken during the first half of the 1970s: the Watergate crisis had resulted in the resignation of a President of the United States and criminal prosecution of high-ranking federal officials; the armed forces had been defeated in combat by an Asian people; the Arab oil embargo forced recognition that the United States no longer enjoyed unlimited natural resources; the economy floundered between the seemingly irreconcilable forces of increasing unemployment and inflation; a vocal and alien counterculture had challenged successfully various traditional values; "crime-in-the-streets" as well as rioting in the inner city and on campus threatened permanent damage to domestic tranquility; various minority groups through escalating, sometimes violent, demands seemed to have irreparably rent the fabric of American society. So dour, indeed, did everyday American life appear that in 1974 a positive and hopeful assessment of the United States in the 1970s characterized the decade thus far as "the age of the rip-off."

Suddenly, in 1976, with the celebration of the two hundredth anniversary of the Declaration of Independence and the creation of the United States, the nation's mood changed perceptibly. Bicentennial America, almost overnight, put behind it Watergate, Vietnam, stagflation, and many other problems. The media – which for so long had highlighted the negative side of American life – now spoke of "the ongoing resilience of what used to be called The American Dream." Even *U.S. News and World Report*, well known for its weekly prophecies of doom and analyses of the various malaises troubling the United States, now unabashedly declared that "nowhere on earth … do the hopes for the future appear more exciting than they do in the U.S., rich in spirit … power … and people." A German observer of the American scene found that concern over America's problems had given way, at least for the moment, to celebration of the bicentennial.

Rocky is an integral if somewhat unusual part of that bicentennial binge. Set in the white ethnic working-class slums of South Philadelphia, *Rocky* deals with such unappetizing aspects of current life in the United States as organized crime, professional boxing, media exploitation, and the hard-scrabble world of the working-class, blue-collar ethnic. Yet, even though dealing with the underside of contemporary America, *Rocky* is a celebration of the American Dream. Movie critic Frank Rich perceptively analyzed the film's wide appeal when he described *Rocky* as a "fairy tale" that "tapped the popular spirit of the present: ... the old-fashioned, Bi-Centennial vision of America."

At first glance the film's eponymous protagonist seems an unusual hero for bicentennial America. Rocky Balboa (Sylvester Stallone) – self-styled "The Italian Stallion" – is a dim-witted, fourth-rate, thirty-year-old club fighter of no particular distinction, except perhaps for the fact (of which he proudly boasts) that in ten years of fighting his nose has never been broken. Professional boxing has netted him nothing. He earns his keep working as a muscle man for Gazzo, a loan shark. Rocky's life is bleak. He seems to have no future. He lives alone, in squalor. Drunks, bums, and seedy layabouts line the streets of his rundown Philadelphia neighborhood. His friends and acquaintances are corrupt, moronic, or venal. Avuncular advice to a young teenage girl about "hanging out" at night "with them coconuts on the corner [older boys]" earns Rocky a derisive "Screw you, Creepo!!!"

Whatever the drawbacks of Rocky's world, the film makes clear in that peculiar cinematic shorthand so well understood by movie audiences all over the world, that although he may he a bum, he is a bum with heart. Rocky (to use one reviewer's exaggerated but apt words) is presented as "an innocent ... an earth child from the streets of a slum." He likes animals: his confidantes are two pet turtles named Cuff and Link. He cares about people: on a cold night he takes a drunkard out of the gutter and carries him into the corner saloon. He is not mean: even though ordered to break the thumb of one of Gazzo's clients, Rocky refrains from so doing.

Happenstance lifts Rocky out of his nether world. A bicentennial world heavyweight championship match has been scheduled for Philadelphia. A few weeks before the match, the contender is injured and the champion, Apollo Creed (Carl Weathers playing a nasty caricature of Muhammad Ali), decides that rather than scrap the intricate and profitable arrangements that already have been made, he will fight a "local boy." Creed chooses Rocky, in part because Rocky seems easily beatable, and in part because the champion believes that the "Italian Stallion" nickname should make good media copy and help maintain interest in the fight. A surprised Rocky is offered 150,000 dollars and a chance at the title. He accepts and trains to win. On the eve of the fight Rocky recognizes that he has been deceiving himself, but he resolves to prove his worth nevertheless by going the distance with Creed. And in a bruising, gritty, fifteen-round brawl Rocky does just that – even managing to knock down the champion several times. The decision goes to Creed, but Rocky has won personally, having proven that he is not "just another bum from the neighborhood."

As important as the title match for Rocky's growth in self-esteem is his romantic involvement with Adrian (Talia Shire), his friend Paulie's (Burt Young) painfully shy spinster sister. Adrian works in the pet shop that Rocky frequents. However, their first date comes about at the instigation of Paulie, who virtually orders Rocky to ask out Adrian and forces her to accept. Initially she appears on screen as an unattractive, mousey, withdrawn drudge who forlornly lives with and looks after her brother. But then Rocky takes her out, takes down her hair, takes off her glasses, and takes her to bed. As their romance blossoms she becomes a new person in the best traditions of Hollywood's Golden Age. And by the end of the film she has become a graceful, attractive, spirited young woman. After an argument with Paulie about his attempts to use Rocky, she moves out of her brother's home and in with the fighter. This concession to modern mores notwithstanding, the relationship between Rocky and Adrian is presented as sentimental and uplifting. In an age of sexually blatant movies, Rocky's love scenes are discreet: the sexual overtones are there, but only romance is made explicit; nudity and copulation are left to the audience's imagination.

Rocky's story is essentially the work of Sylvester Stallone. He began writing it in the early spring of 1975. He was in his late twenties and after six years of brash effort seemed to have failed as an actor. His one big part had been in *The Lords of Flatbush*, a 1974 artistic success/commercial flop. The majority of his roles had been small and/or forgettable in movies like *The Prisoner of Second Avenue* (1975), *Capone* (1975), and *Death Race 2000* (1975). He also had tried writing movie and television scripts but won little recognition – the major exception being a credit he earned for "additional dialogue" on *The Lords of Flatbush*.

Stallone got the idea for *Rocky* after watching the March, 1975, title bout between Muhammad Ali and Chuck Wepner for the heavyweight championship. Wepner, "a guy on the skids" known as "the Bayonne Bleeder," not only managed to knock Ali down, but also (unlike most of the champion's previous opponents) almost went the distance – the fight being stopped nineteen seconds from the end of the fifteenth and final round. Stallone and Gene Kirkwood, a "fledgling producer" (to use *Newsweek's* description) had been discussing various movie possibilities before the Ali–Wepner match. Inspired by the fight, Stallone in three and a half days of almost nonstop effort drafted the screenplay that became *Rocky*. An interesting sidelight to current movie-making is Stallone's comment that this "script was about 122 pages long and went to more than 330 or 340 pages of revisions and we barely altered it from the original concept." Kirkwood interested the independent producing team of Robert Chartoff and Irwin Winkler in Stallone's script. They in turn offered it to United Artists, who ultimately agreed to undertake the production. Shooting began in December, 1975.

Stallone was determined to play Rocky. The producers recognized the quality of the script but wanted a name star for the title role. They offered Stallone well over $100,000 to sell the script and "to bow out." He refused, even though, as Kirkwood recalls, Stallone was "hard up for bucks": he had a bank balance of $106, a pregnant wife, and few other foreseeable prospects. Stallone later recalled telling his wife "if you don't mind going out in the backyard and eating grass, I'd rather burn this script than sell it to another actor." She agreed, but the need to eat grass never arose. Stallone played Rocky. He won critical acclaim as well as Oscar nominations for his script and his performance – placing him in very select company, as only Orson Welles and Charlie Chaplin had received these dual nominations before.

Stallone made good media copy, and understandably he received far more publicity than anyone else connected with the film. However, as critic James Monaco pointed out, "while *Rocky* has been advertised as the protean conception of its star-writer, director John Avildsen's contributions are essential to its success and should not be overlooked." Avildsen has a flair for the kind of working-class milieu portrayed in

Rocky. Indeed, he first came to prominence in 1970 as director and photographer of *Joe*, whose central character was also lower class – albeit very different from the good-natured Rocky. Joe was a foul-mouthed, beer-drinking, hippie-hating factory worker, who joined with an upper-middle-class "friend" to murder some Greenwich Village "drop outs." The film's phenomenal box-office success stemmed in part from Avildsen's ability to present Joe so realistically and dramatically that there were "recorded incidents of kids shouting 'We'll get you, Joe!' at the screen." Joe's success enabled Avildsen to escape making exploitation pictures such as *Turn On To Love*, and in the next few years he directed a variety of films, including the 1973 Paramount release *Save the Tiger*, whose star, Jack Lemmon, won the Oscar for Best Actor.

Avildsen, noted for his economy and speed, shot *Rocky* in twenty-eight days (two under schedule) and did not overspend his budget. Critical response to Avildsen's direction of *Rocky* varied considerably. Pauline Kael found his approach to be "strictly-from-hunger." Andrew Sarris asserted that Avildsen provided "no glow, no aura for his hero." *Newsweek*'s Janet Maslin, on the other hand, maintained that the film had been "crisply directed." In *Time*, Richard Schickel argued that in *Rocky* the director showed a "stronger naturalistic gift than in *Joe* or *Save the Tiger*."

Certainly the film benefited from Avildsen's ability to capture the gritty atmosphere of South Philadelphia's garbage-strewn, joyless streets and seedy, worn, row houses. English critic Tom Milne waxed rhapsodic over Avildsen's ability to film the "extraordinary nocturnal landscapes of strangely dislocated urban geometry ... in which the human figures seem both estranged and yet as much a natural part of the scene as the tenuously impermanent structures themselves." Milne argued that Avildsen and his cameraman had turned the Philadelphia exteriors "into something very close to a series of Magritte paintings." Amidst all the justified praise for Stallone, it should be remembered that Avildsen won an Academy Award for his direction of *Rocky*.

Both the much-publicized genesis of the film and Stallone's insistence on playing Rocky had Horatio Alger overtones that appealed to bicentennial America. But the production of the film reflects no sentiment, only the hard-headed economic realities of the American movie industry in the 1970s. Chartoff and Winkler are not producers in the traditional sense; they are "packagers" and as such part of what the film journalist Axel Madsen has dubbed "the New Hollywood." They do not work with any one studio. They put packages together and then look to the studios for financing. As Chartoff has explained: "We go to Warner's and say 'Look, we have such and such a project that so and so is interested in ... ; the whole thing can be made for so and so much money ....'" If Warner's is not interested, "United Artists, Columbia, or any of the other majors then look at it and say yes or no, sometimes no ... or yes, if we can bring it down to such a figure." Chartoff, a theatrical lawyer, and Winkler, a television agent, met "by accident," became one of the first independent producing teams in Hollywood in the mid-1960s, and prior to *Rocky* had produced eighteen movies, including such interesting ones as *Point Blank* (released by MGM in 1967) and such clinkers as the Charles Bronson melodrama *Breakout* (distributed by Columbia in 1975).

After *Rocky* had proved itself, the head of West Coast production for United Artists gloated over "the excitement" provoked both by the film and by Stallone. But when Chartoff and Winkler initially sought approval from United Artists to meet Stallone's demand that he himself play Rocky, the company set some hard conditions. The film's budget was cut almost in half to one million dollars; Stallone was to be paid a minimal salary of twenty thousand dollars (albeit also a percentage of the possible profits); Chartoff and Winkler had to guarantee to make up any budget overruns. Just before the film was released, Winkler told an interviewer "everyone sacrificed for potential profits. We hope it pays off – we think it will ...."

And it did, probably far beyond his expectations. Financially the film turned out to be a bonanza, "one of the biggest movie winners of all time," according to *Newsweek*. Its one-million-dollar budget was very modest in terms of 1975–76 feature film production, "peanuts in today's movie world," to use critic David Sterritt's clichéd but apt description. By the end of April, 1977 – five months after the film had been released – *Rocky* had grossed over fifty million dollars in the United States and Canada. And in August, 1977, *Variety* estimated that thus far *Rocky* had grossed over one hundred million dollars in the United States and Canada, and that the film still had considerable earning potential in those markets. *Rocky* had proved to be one of the highest grossing films ever made, on a par in terms of impact and drawing power with films like *Gone With the Wind* (1939), *The Sound of Music* (1965), and *Jaws* (1975).

Critically, *Rocky* also scored a major triumph – albeit one less overwhelming than its box-office success. Film reviewers used words like "schmaltz" and "cliché" in discussing *Rocky*, and there was criticism of some aspects of the film in most reviews, but overall, few reviewers failed to respond positively to it. Even the toughminded and unsentimental Pauline Kael found much to praise in *Rocky*, and although alert to its shortcomings she described the film as "engaging" and "emotionally effective." Vincent Canby of the *New York Times* was a notable exception to the generally favorable critical response; he found the film lacking in verve, seemingly fraudulent, and he thought it "never quite measured up." But his comments had little effect. *Rocky* won a wide variety of awards, including ten Oscar nominations and three Academy Awards (Best Director, Best Picture, and Best Editing).

To what can one attribute *Rocky*'s extraordinary commercial success and generally favorable critical reception? An extensive, hard-hitting, intelligent publicity campaign played a significant role. A seemingly untiring Stallone, for example, made himself available for interview after interview by representatives from every branch of the media. Indeed, so ubiquitous was Stallone that one commentator claimed that *Rocky*'s creator "has granted more interviews in recent months than any American short of Lillian Carter." The *Variety* review of *Rocky*, written almost a month before the film went into release, noted that "the p.r. juggernaut is already at high speed." Vincent Canby in his *New York Times* review expressed uneasiness and displeasure at "the sort of high-powered publicity ... that's been attending the birth of *Rocky* ...." The extent of this high-powered publicity campaign is emphasized by the many echoes of Canby's attitude among reviewers. A trade journalist examining the selling of the film found that "whether rave, pan, or ... 'no opinion,' review after review of Rocky tore into the crescendo of advance comment. ...."

Hype alone, however, cannot account for the wildly enthusiastic response that many movie audiences afforded the film. They cheered Rocky, booed Creed, and at the end of the film, with tears in their eyes, applauded the credits. Critic Roger Greenspan reported that "the two times I saw *Rocky* people in the audience stood up and cheered at the end." Another reviewer detailed the reactions of an "Italian friend" at a screening of the film: "when the 'Italian Stallion' landed a savage right hook on the ... chin of Apollo Creed ... my friend let out a 'Whoop' as if he had a week's salary riding on the punch." Frank Rich expressed amazement at the number of usually blasé New York City moviegoers who after seeing *Rocky* left "the theater beaming and boisterous, as if they won a door prize rather than parted with the price of a first-run movie ticket, and they volunteer ecstatic opinions of the film to the people waiting on line for the next show."

Viewing *Rocky* was an emotion-charged experience for many American moviegoers. The film touched "a live nerve with the public," as Frank Rich put it. American audiences, influenced by the bicentennial's strong emphasis on the validity of the American Dream, had lost interest in downbeat themes, in bleak reality, in attacks on old-fashioned values – all subjects which as films of one sort or another had recently done well at the box office. Stallone rather perceptively touched on the changing interests of moviegoers in one of his many interviews: "I believe the country as a whole is beginning to break out of this … anti-everything syndrome … this nihilistic, Hemingwayistic attitude that everything in the end must wither and die …."

In discussing *Rocky*'s appeal (as well as its positive outlook) reviewers and other commentators referred over and over again to the optimistic, idealistic, sentimental, 1930s movies of director Frank Capra. Even Avildsen announced that he was fond of the comparison: "Capra's my idol. I love the emotionalism and idealism in what he was doing …." Capra himself said about *Rocky*: "Boy, that's a picture I wish I had made." But "Capra-corn" as evidenced by such films as *Mr. Deeds Goes to Town* (1936) or *Mr. Smith Goes to Washington* (1939) will not and should not serve as a point of reference for *Rocky*. In the Capra productions, as film historian Richard Griffith has astutely pointed out, "a messianic innocent, not unlike the classic simpleton of literature … pits himself against the forces of entrenched greed … his gallant integrity in the face of temptation calls forth the good will of the 'little people' and through combined protest, he triumphs." Rocky may be an innocent, but he is not messianic, and the "little people" he associates with are not the middle class on which Capra dotes. It is not surprising that Capra, when discussing his films at an AFI seminar in 1971, declared that Ralph Nader "would make a perfect Capra hero." And Rocky certainly is not a Nader type.

Just as *Rocky* owed little to the Capra films, so too did it owe little to previous Hollywood treatments of boxing. These in the main had concentrated on exposing the ills of "the fight game." But Rocky had none of the bleak cynicism of *Champion* (1949), the oppressive social consciousness of *Golden Boy* (1939), the vicious corruption of *The Harder They Fall* (1956), or the sleazy hopelessness of *The Set-Up* (1949). However, Rocky does not exist in a vacuum. It does owe something to the ingratiating style of *Somebody Up There Likes Me*, the enthusiastic 1956 screen biography of one-time middle-weight champion Rocky Graziano. And Rocky's love story obviously owes something to *Marty*, the poignant 1955 film about two lonely people who expect never to find love, but come together. In one respect, however, Rocky is almost unique, and that is its working-class perspective.

As James Monaco has pointed out, "the intellectual, middle class establishment has always felt quite comfortable with films whose subjects were workers …." But *Rocky* is not presented from a middle-class point of view; the film speaks for the working class, albeit as columnist Pete Hamill acidly commented: "nobody calls it the working class any more … the bureaucratic, sociological phrase is white lower-middle class," sometimes referred to as "the ethnics." Rocky obviously was palatable to the American middle class, but its success rests on the film's appeal to the white ethnic American (once succinctly described by a magazine writer as "perhaps the most alienated person" in the United States). *Rocky* endorsed the ethnic's prejudices, deferred to his fantasies, and highlighted his lifestyle.

The film's treatment of blacks accords with the racial attitudes that, in the view of many social scientists, govern the thinking of the white ethnic American. Their conventional wisdom holds that these white ethnics believe that they have "paid the costs" of American society's attempts to redress black grievances, that "the poorest, least secure, least educated, and least tolerant" in the white community believe they have been sacrificed by a liberal elite anxious to ensure "responsible social change." And, it is argued, the ethnics bitterly resent this attempt at change. Thus, a sociologist surveying the attitudes of a group of blue-collar workers about contemporary America in the early 1970s argues that except for the Vietnam war "the most explosive issue was the demand for black equality." And in this context he quotes as representative a carpenter who angrily declared, "I realize that something has to be done for the black bastards, but I sure as hell don't want them living next to me. I don't care to work with them either."

Rocky plays on these old prejudices and new fears. The film's racism is not overtly stated, but if not explicit, it is still vividly (and visually) implicit. At one point in the film Rocky is shown training in the meat-packing plant where Paulie works. He is training for the fight with Creed by using a carcass of beef as a punching bag, hitting the carcass until his hands are blood red from the juice of the meat. A local television station has sent a crew to film this unusual method of training. The reporter is an arrogantly glib, fashionably dressed, light-skinned black woman, who oozes condescension and contempt during her dealings with Rocky (and Paulie). In many ways she is an unpleasant burlesque of the female reporters found on television newscasts across the country. One can, of course, attribute her presence in the film to a hostility to television news programming or to the women's liberation movement. But one must also ask why a black woman, why that particular kind of arrogant black woman, who patronizes Rocky and Paulie. Here we must remember the words of a literary critic in dealing with another movie genre: "everything in a film is there because somebody wanted it there, although it is often hard to know why or even who that somebody was."

That "somebody" must also claim credit for the nasty, smarmy depiction of Apollo Creed. In public Creed acts the clown, satirizing traditional American values. He enters the arena for his fight with Rocky to the tune of "Yankee Doodle Dandy," and he prances around the ring in an elaborate Uncle Sam costume before stripping to star-spangled trunks. If publicly Creed mocks the bicentennial, privately he expresses contempt for the American Dream and views public belief in it as one more means of making money. Explaining his choice of Rocky as a substitute for the injured challenger, a mocking Creed says "I'm sentimental, and lots of people in this country are just as sentimental." The articulate, well-groomed, business-minded Creed stands in obvious contrast to Rocky – so much so that as Andrew Sarris points out, the "Italian Stallion" becomes "the most romanticized Great White Hope in screen history." Nor, despite over a decade of black heavyweight champions, should the White Hope feeling be ignored. Ali, for example, in his autobiography touches on "the racial issue" in boxing and asks "who put it there and who keeps it there." His answer is given by a veteran reporter who tells him, "they want your ass whipped in public, knocked down, ripped, stomped, clubbed, pulverized, and not just by anybody, but by a real Great White Hope."

The makers of *Rocky* had a feel for ethnic America. Somber authenticity marks the film's settings indoors and out. The home of Paulie and Adrian, for example, is in a row house with a tiny front yard in a decayed inner-city neighborhood. The furniture is neat but worn, the rooms are small, the lamps are chintzy, the living room is dominated by an old television set. The outdoor Christmas decorations, or lack of them, on various houses are just right for South Philadelphia, or Hamtramck, or Corona, or anyone of a hundred ethnic neighborhoods.

Paulie is presented as "pathetically brutish" (to use Judith Crist's apt phrase). A picture of him in uniform on the mantel hints at his only and temporary escape from the neighborhood. Paulie desperately wants to get away from the meatpacking plant and almost pleadingly asks Rocky for an introduction to Gazzo the loan shark. Paulie feels he could certainly do as good a job for Gazzo as Rocky. Michael Novak has commented that one of the reasons for "the new ethnicity" is the "suppressed anger" of the white lower-middle class. In a remarkable scene Paulie lets loose that anger, and stalking around his home strikes out wildly, viciously, forcefully with a baseball bat. He smashes doors, furniture, walls, as he rants against the dead-endedness of his life. Paulie, in Stallone's words, is "a symbol of the blue collar, disenfranchised, left-out mentality, a man who feels life has given him an unfair amount of cheap shots ...."

But in the final analysis neither racism nor reality brought people to the box office in such large numbers. *Rocky* succeeded because of its mythic qualities which neatly dovetailed with the imagery that had been sold by the bicentennial. The sociologist Andrew Greeley has argued that "ethnicity has become almost fashionable." But it was not that fashion which sold *Rocky*. The movie, as Frank Rich said, "can hold its own with Cinderella," as it sets forth that a bum can become a real contender overnight, that riches can come from nowhere, that hard work and the will to make good can still succeed in the United States, that "a shy and unattractive heroine can blossom into a worldly beauty by getting contact lenses and losing her virginity," and that happy endings still exist. And it is to such myths that *Rocky*'s audiences responded so enthusiastically.

Historian William Hughes contends that the feature film does not just "reveal popular attitudes," but "like other forms of cultural expression, can reveal more than they intend." *Rocky* is an excellent manifestation of this "covert-overt" approach to looking at feature films. On the surface it is a "fairy tale," and quite an ingratiating one at that. But *Rocky* also provides strong clues to the public mood in the United States in the mid-1970s. *Rocky* could do this because as a French commentator on American film points out, "the freedom of the Hollywood director is not measured by what he can openly do within the system, but rather by what he can imply about American society in general." John Avildsen wove Stallone's story into a richly textured film, shot through with social implications, reactionary as some of them may be.

The film itself and the public's response to it speak volumes about how Americans saw themselves in 1976. Rocky captured the mood of bicentennial America, a mood which saw the reaffirmation of many traditional values, including racial prejudices that seemed rejuvenated by the economic and social pressures of the 1970s. *Rocky* also highlighted America's changing attitude toward the white lower-middle class and toward ethnic blue-collar America. Stallone hit at the core of the matter in his comments on audience response to the film: "when they're cheering for Rocky, they're cheering for themselves."

24

Presenting African Americans on Film
The Rise and Fall of Sidney Poitier

Aram Goudsouzian

Sidney Poitier was one of the first successful black movie stars to step outside of negative racial stereotypes. Later in his career essentially integrationist roles – he often played opposite to white actors and actresses – brought him censure from black militants and their white admirers. But he never deviated in any major way from the roles that defined his integrity.

"Why Does White America Love Sidney Poitier So?" asked a *New York Times* headline in September of 1967. It was a good question. Earlier that year, an imprint of the actor's hands and feet had joined Hollywood's elite at the famous forecourt of Grauman's Chinese Theater. Now, two of his films – *To Sir, With Love* and *In the Heat of the Night* – were trading the top spot back and forth in box-office surveys. Poitier was the highest paid actor in Hollywood, and a Gallup poll found that he headed a list of stars – including Julie Andrews, Steve McQueen, Elizabeth Taylor, and Paul Newman – whose name could sell an otherwise unknown movie. He was a confirmed superstar, the first black actor to reach such heights.

But the article underneath that headline was no celebration of the actor's feats. Clifford Mason, a black playwright and drama critic, argued that Poitier constantly played an "antiseptic, one-dimensional hero." His roles were "merely contrivances, completely lacking in artistic merit." Mason criticized Poitier for soothing white consciences during an era of black political stridency. He rejected the notion that "the Negro is best served by being a black version of the man in the gray flannel suit, taking on white problems and a white man's sense of what's wrong with the world." *To Sir, With Love*, Mason went on, "had the all-time Hollywood reversal act. Instead of putting a love interest into a story that had none, they took it out." *In the Heat of the Night* exhibited "the same old Sidney Poitier syndrome: a good guy in a totally white world, with no wife, no sweetheart, no woman to love or kiss, helping the white man solve the white man's problem." Poitier did not reflect dignity or manhood; his passive sterility precluded it. He was a tool of the white establishment – in Mason's cruelest words, a "showcase nigger."

The essay joined a critical chorus denouncing Poitier as a passive attendant to his white co-stars, a neutered accomplice to stereotypes of black sexuality, and a too-perfect symbol of black martyrdom. The showers of scorn provided an ironic juxtaposition to Poitier's escalating mainstream appeal. In December of 1967 Columbia Pictures released *Guess Who's Coming to Dinner*, the actor's third blockbuster movie of the year. It showcased the same icon as the other two films: an educated, articulate, dignified black man who teaches and befriends whites. It also imposed the same limitations – he shows no sexual passion, lets white characters determine the scope of their relationship, and displays little connection to the issues that dominated the lives of most African Americans. *Guess Who's Coming to Dinner* became Poitier's most popular film ever, and it inspired the most critical abuse.

The contradictory reaction spoke to Poitier's unique position in American film history. He was the only black actor consistently to win lead roles in movies from the late 1950s to the late 1960s, the era of nonviolent mass protest that began with the Montgomery bus boycott and ended with the assassination of the Reverend Martin Luther King, Jr. The integrationist themes of his films helped win the hearts and minds of Americans during this quest for black equality. Like other Hollywood stars, Poitier constructed a lasting screen image – in his case, a mannered, humane, intelligent advocate of interracial cooperation.

Unlike other stars, Poitier had an image wrapped in rapidly shifting political realities. By the time of *Guess Who's Coming to Dinner*, America had reached a crossroads both in black politics and in black film representations. Urban riots, the emergent popularity of black radicals, and King's assassination suggested that the foundation of liberal political consensus underneath Poitier's career was crumbling. Yet the black rebellion that rejected Poitier simultaneously provoked fear among political moderates. Soothed by his restrained dignity, hordes of Americans flocked to his films, celebrating Hollywood's sole representative of the civil rights movement with one last, great hurrah.

The poor, nearly illiterate Bahamian child whose rise to screen exemplar of black middle-class polish is a remarkable story in its own right. Poitier grew up on Cat Island, a thin strip on the western edge of the Bahamas, unfettered by physical or racial boundaries. Very few whites lived on the island, and until he was old enough to help his parents and six older siblings with their small tomato farm, he roamed the island, swam the ocean, and daydreamed. By the time he was eleven, the Great Depression had ravaged the tomato market. His family sailed for the capital city of Nassau, moving into a crowded neighborhood of Out Island migrants called Over-the-Hill. They joined the large black underclass that serviced British colonial administrators and wealthy American tourists. After four years receiving only the most rudimentary of educations, working a few World War II-era construction projects, and sinking into petty crime and idle mischief, Poitier left Nassau for his older brother's house in Miami.

The headstrong, impulsive teenager collided with Southern racial codes. The Bahamian racial system never assumed social deference on the part of blacks, and Jim Crow grated on Poitier. After a three-month stay that included threats from the Ku Klux Klan (after he delivered a package to a white woman's front door) and a Miami sheriff (after he hitchhiked in a white neighborhood), he left for New York City. Fifteen and friendless in the booming metropolis, he further floundered. He slept in pay toilets and on the roof of the Brill Building, worked as a dishwasher by night and wandered the city by day, suffered through loneliness and withered in the harsh winter. He even joined the Army for an unsatisfying one-year stint at a Long Island psychiatric hospital. He considered returning to Nassau until he stumbled across an audition for the American Negro Theater (ANT).

At Poitier's original audition, ANT co-founder Frederick O'Neal – a giant with a withering glare and intimidating goatee – berated him for his slow, heavily accented reading. The rejection somehow galvanized the directionless youth. He trained himself by devouring newspapers and imitating the voices on the radio. He returned to ANT six months later for a second audition and joined its School of Drama. By then Broadway producer Douglas Wildberg had bought the ANT play *Anna Lucasta*, exposing black actors to more commercial success and opening doors for the younger actors such as Poitier. A quick study who enjoyed the sense of self-worth and camaraderie acting afforded him, Poitier capitalized on these opportunities, appearing on Broadway for an all-black, ill-fated 1947 production of *Lysistrata* before joining a touring cast of *Anna Lucasta*. He saw the country and honed his acting chops, and then returned to New York City in 1949. After a brief spell of unemployment, he landed a role in his first film, the Twentieth Century Fox production *No Way Out*.

A cycle of "message movies" addressing racial prejudice had begun in 1949 with *Home of the Brave*, *Lost Boundaries*, *Pinky*, and *Intruder in the Dust*. After the sacrifices of African Americans in World War II, blacks were beginning to be included in the democratic tradition. *No Way Out*, released in 1950, took the message movie genre to new lengths, presenting Poitier in the central role as a sympathetic medical intern who fends off a fanatical white racist. Building off the scattered positive minor characters of the World War II era and the themes of the message movies, *No Way Out* contradicted the historical burden of blacks on screen: docile slaves, pancake-flipping mammies, grinning song-and-dance men, and comic Stepin Fetchit types. Poitier's middle-class iconography (he played a doctor who has a family, and tries to defuse a race riot) suggested that at least some white Americans were willing to consider blacks as more complete, three-dimensional characters, not consigned to dancing or inanity. Poitier reinforced this perception in his next project, when in 1951 he played a virtuous South African priest in the film adaptation of Alan Paton's novel *Cry, the Beloved Country*.

He received fine reviews for both performances, and in other circumstances, he might have been on the cusp of stardom. But over the next three years, he appeared only in supporting roles in two minor films. It was the era of the blacklist, following HUAC's second Hollywood visit in four years. Already in the midst of crisis following the 1947 *Paramount* decision, the suburban migration and baby boom, and the impending threat of television, studios shunned pictures with liberal social messages – including nearly all films with racial themes – out of fear of negative publicity. Poitier hurt his own prospects by traveling in America's most radical social circles, joining the small circle of black artists and intellectuals who openly admired Paul Robeson, the famous black performer vilified by the mainstream for his Communist Party ties. The anti-Communist watchdog Counterattack later reported that during the early 1950s, Poitier spent "considerable time sponsoring, entertaining at, and otherwise supporting Communist front causes," including the Committee for the Negro in the Arts. Though he had no direct connection to organized radical politics, he had associated his talents with allegedly subversive plays and events.

Poitier's breakthrough role came in 1955, with *Blackboard Jungle*. The picture features violent scenes in an urban high school, sparking vigorous media debates over its accuracy. Cities and small towns throughout the United States banned or cut scenes from the film. Senator Estes Kefauver's subcommittee on juvenile delinquency investigated the film industry, paying particular attention to *Blackboard Jungle*. Months later Italian ambassador Clare Boothe Luce ignited an international controversy when she boycotted the picture at the Venice Film Festival. The furor centered around the explicit violence, but Poitier's cool menace lent an added subtext of black anger. His character does aid the white hero played by Glenn Ford at film's end, however, a pattern he would recreate in 1957 in his next major role, *Edge of the City*. Nevertheless, Poitier carried a reputation as a Hollywood maverick. Both for *Blackboard Jungle* and the live television version of *Edge of the City* (entitled *A Man is Ten Feet Tall*), lawyers implored Poitier to sign a loyalty oath denouncing his radical mentors Paul Robeson and Canada Lee. At risk to his career, he refused.

In the late 1950s, Poitier was not yet typecast into the staid middle-class image that characterized both his first films and his most popular pictures from the 1960s. Like his friend Harry Belafonte, who captained a fervent but short-lived Calypso Craze, Poitier conveyed elements of black exoticism: in 1957 a Mau Mau terrorist in *Something of Value*, and a cocksure slave in *Band of Angels*, the following year an African diplomat married to the steamy Eartha Kitt in *Mark of the Hawk* and a robust West Indian in *Virgin Island*. He also used his celebrity for political ends, speaking in Washington at the 1957 Prayer Pilgrimage and in New York City at a 1959 rally celebrating the fifth anniversary of the decision in *Brown v. Board of Education*. Columnists tied his films to the civil rights movement. Black newspapers constantly celebrated his demand to portray a positive black image, Dorothy Masters of the *New York Daily News* implied a connection between the actor and the ministers of the Montgomery bus boycott, and Barry Gray of the *New York Post* equated the hardships faced by the Little Rock Nine with his struggle to rise from poverty.

But Poitier's burgeoning notoriety caused complications. The legendary independent producer Samuel Goldwyn manipulated him into participation in *Porgy and Bess*, despite the actor's public dismissal of the Gershwin folk opera depicting the crap-shooting, razor-toting, dialect-speaking denizens of Catfish Row. His character Porgy, moreover, is an emasculated cripple. After one of Poitier's agents mistakenly promised him for the project, Goldwyn threatened legal action if Poitier instead accepted a role in the Stanley Kramer film *The Defiant Ones*, a story of a black and a white fugitive chained together. Poitier in 1959 compromised his image in *Porgy and Bess*, but the previous year's film *The Defiant Ones* had proved a career boon by providing him with his first star role in a commercially successful picture. Yet even that film revealed the limitations of the white liberal perspective that governed most Poitier films. James Baldwin reported that the movie's final scene, when Poitier leaps off a train to tend Tony Curtis and await certain capture, inspired tears and hosannas among white audiences. But black audiences howled: "Get back on the train, you fool!"

The actor left the entanglements of Hollywood for a six-month run on stage in *A Raisin in the Sun*, a milestone for blacks on Broadway. Lorraine Hansberry's play – with the black director Lloyd Richards, a predominantly black cast including Claudia McNeil and Ruby Dee, and Poitier as Walter Lee Younger – explores the struggles of a working-class black family through a riveting, emotional drama. The winner of the

1959 Drama Critics Circle Award, the play inspired heartfelt laughter, teary catharsis, and proclamations that it was not a "Negro play," but about people "who happened to be Negroes." This interpretation (or misinterpretation) spoke to the pervasiveness of black stereotypes on stage and screen, and *A Raisin in the Sun*'s ability to transcend them. The play and its 1961 film adaptation, the publicity from *Porgy and Bess*, Poitier's Academy Award nomination for *The Defiant Ones*, and his upcoming roles in the 1960 release *All the Young Men* and *Paris Blues* in 1961 generated countless media profiles of him. Always, he presented a humble yet thoughtful image, speaking eloquently on the necessity of including blacks in the American democratic tradition and emphasizing his own childhood poverty, work ethic, and middle-class ideology.

By the early 1960s, as the Greensboro sit-ins launched an era of continued nonviolent direct action in the South, Poitier had become an important representative of black America. He played a valuable fundraising role for civil rights organizations, attended the 1963 March on Washington, and even joined Belafonte on a dangerous 1964 mission to deliver money to civil rights workers in Greenville, Mississippi. He also spoke often on race and Hollywood. "Except for the coffee boy, I am the only Negro on the set," he told the House Labor Committee in 1962, "I have made 17 pictures, but it is no joy to me that I am used as an example to prove they really don't discriminate." As an additional frustration, he seemed unable to launch his career to the next level. Plans for his own production company, an opportunity to direct, and numerous film projects all failed to materialize.

His breakthrough came in the most unlikely of films, a 1963 low-budget production entitled *Lilies of the Field*. It featured Poitier as an itinerant handyman who builds a church for five German nuns, and its sweet message and endearing hero charmed audiences. The film made Poitier rich, as he negotiated one of the first deals that awarded an actor a percentage of the gross. And in 1964, the same year of the Civil Rights Act and Martin Luther King, Jr.'s Nobel Peace Prize, Poitier won the Academy Award for Best Actor. "It has been a long journey," he told the audience.

The Oscar opened opportunities. In 1964 Poitier had already filmed *The Long Ships*, roundly considered his most execrable movie, but he now chose roles that reinforced the proper, buttoned-down image he had exhibited in the 1962 film *Pressure Point*, when he played a psychiatrist. He was a journalist in both *The Bedford Incident* and *A Patch of Blue*, both of them appearing in 1965, and next year a volunteer at a crisis center in *The Slender Thread*. In each case, he embodied reason and virtue, warning crazed sea captains against Cold War paranoia, befriending a blind girl tormented by an abusive mother, and counseling a woman on the brink of suicide. Each, in its own way, served as an advertisement for racial integration. Like the civil rights demonstrators in Birmingham, Selma, and throughout the South, Poitier's characters embodied nonviolence and love for fellow man. The pictures were generally successful, capturing a broad middle-class audience.

Yet Poitier increasingly inspired groans among many intellectuals and black critics, who anticipated the nation's shifting racial climate. The media took note that for both *The Bedford Incident* and *The Slender Thread*, Poitier played roles not specifically designated for black actors. This was another milestone, but some regarded Poitier's acceptance of these roles as an abandonment of black identity. Moreover, he continued to play the sacrificial lamb: dying in a baling hook fight in *Edge of the City*, falling into an elephant pit in *Something of Value*, jumping off the train in *The Defiant Ones*, and so on.

In each case, his suffering enlightens his white co-star. Finally, Poitier rarely played the romantic lead typical of handsome Hollywood stars. In most every movie, he was in an all-male setting, married to a prim housewife à la Ruby Dee, or explicitly (and creatively) desexualized. His lust for a mulatto woman was written out of *Band of Angels,* and his Moorish villain takes a bizarre oath of celibacy in *The Long Ships.* In *A Patch of Blue,* he finally kisses a white girl but she is blind.

It was unfair to lay the burden entirely at the actor's feet. The bulk of the criticism stemmed from his being the film industry's sole black leading man. "We don't make race films," went a common adage. "We make Sidney Poitier films." But by 1967, as ghettos erupted in riots and radical voices such as Stokely Carmichael and H. Rap Brown became media darlings, either a revamping of Poitier's image or his fadeout from Hollywood might have been predicted. Instead, three films intensified every aspect of the Sidney Poitier stereotype, prompted the criticisms of intellectuals and black radicals, and – perhaps most remarkably – boosted Poitier's popularity even higher.

To Sir, With Love opened first, and it provided a soothing balm on national wounds of racial fracture and urban discontent. In a reversal of *Blackboard Jungle,* and an apt illustration of Poitier's career arc, he now played the new teacher sent to tame rowdy students – this time, in London's East End. After floundering at first, he throws out his books and teaches the students about practical issues they will face upon graduation, all the while injecting lessons of manners, tolerance, and nonviolence. The classroom abruptly transforms from clamorous to captivated. By the end, the students brim with excitement over finding jobs, and Poitier decides to remain a teacher. With a splash of Mod style and the debut of pop star Lulu, it became a sleeper hit that summer.

Appearing almost simultaneously in theaters was *In the Heat of the Night.* Poitier played a proud Philadelphia detective thrust into aiding an arrogant Southern sheriff played by Rod Steiger. The actual murder mystery is secondary to the tense relationship between the two outstanding actors. Poitier proves his detective skill and wins grudging acceptance of his status from the racist sheriff. They develop a prickly understanding. When an aristocratic cotton magnate slaps Poitier, he slaps back, and Steiger remains impassive. Later Steiger saves Poitier when the black detective is surrounded by armed vigilantes. After Poitier solves the case, Steiger walks him to the train station and tells him to "Take care, you hear." With those final words, a human connection is established.

September 1967, when audiences swarmed to the two pictures, *Variety* called "Sidney Poitier Month." *In the Heat of the Night* proved instantly successful, and *To Sir, With Love* recovered from an unambitious marketing campaign to surge atop box-office surveys well into October. After a summer of bloody riots, the middle class appreciated Poitier's restrained black superhero. The substantial, even disproportionately large black audience supported Poitier's films because there were no alternatives with blacks in lead roles. Also, his integrationist values still served some good. *Variety* called him "The Useful Negro." "Poitier on the screen," it surmised, "is the only Negro which myriads of Americans feel they know and understand."

That was a heavy burden. Since his first acting job, Poitier had accepted the responsibility of presenting a positive black image, both on screen and in print. But this position of solitary racial spokesman tore at him. As the keynote speaker for the 1967 conference of the Southern Christian Leadership Conference, reporters peppered him with questions about the summer riots. He exploded. "There are many aspects of my personality that you can explore very constructively," he seethed. "But you sit here and ask me such one-dimensional questions about a very tiny area of our lives. You ask me questions that continually fall within the Negroness of my life." He also called Hollywood "a hostile community" that sacrificed complete black depictions for broader appeal. But in the wake of his fantastic success, he insisted on playing the noble hero. "I'm the only one," he argued. "I represent 10,000,000 people in this country and millions more in Africa; I'm the only one for these people to identify with on the screen." He carefully chose his roles, and insisted that "if the fabric of society were different I would scream to high heaven to play villains and to deal with different images of Negro life that would be more dimensional. But I'll be damned if I do that at this stage of the game."

Poitier's persistent typecasting and isolation nettled some veteran critics. Stephen Farber called him "the suburban audience's dream of a well-adjusted Negro." Pauline Kael added that he "has been playing the ideal boy-next-door-who-happens-to-be-black for so long that he's always the same." In both *In the Heat of the Night* and *To Sir, With Love*, Poitier was less a real person than a vehicle through which whites question their belief system. He restrains himself from intimacy with an admiring white teacher in *To Sir, With Love*. He bathes in isolated righteousness during *In the Heat of the Night*.

Then came *Guess Who's Coming to Dinner*. The picture carried the Poitier arche-type to its logical end – and beyond. His character is not just a doctor: he has taught at Yale Medical School and the London School of Tropical Medicine, served as the assistant director of the World Health Organization, and been featured in *Commonweal*. He falls in love with a white woman – the daughter of a liberal San Francisco newspa-per publisher and his equally liberal wife – and arrives at their doorstep seeking her parents' blessing. The audience identifies with the father, played by Spencer Tracy, who must decide whether he can abide by the racial liberalism he has so long preached. As director and producer Stanley Kramer himself said, "The film is an adventure into the ludicrous – the characters so perfect that the only conceivable objection to this marriage could be ludicrously enough, the pigmentation of a man's skin."

But in its mission to expunge him of the slightest shard of negative black cultural stereotype, the picture strips Poitier of his humanity. His racial colorblindness, which even five years earlier would have made him a progressive, seems outdated by 1968. It is dramatic only in opposition to the obsolete political stance of the other black characters, his parents and a sassy maid. Moreover, only Spencer Tracy's approval car-ries any weight; Poitier even informs her parents that he will not marry their daughter if they disapprove. Finally, Poitier displays a debasing sexual priggishness, almost con-sciously avoiding physical contact with his fiancée, covering his bare chest with a towel when the maid enters his room, and refusing to sleep with his fiancée until they are married. He kisses her only once, briefly, during a cab ride. But even that scene is com-promised: the camera captures the moment through the cab driver's rear view mirror.

The picture disgusted an increasingly assertive segment of the population. "Even George Wallace would like that nigger," grumbled H. Rap Brown. College students lambasted Kramer when he traveled to campuses defending his picture. The theater critic Lindsay Patterson called the film "a perfect example in Hollywood's escapism, blithely disregarding the genuine and maybe altogether unendurable problems to be encountered in a mainland interracial marriage" Even mainstream publications ridiculed the outdated political message and subject. *Newsweek* wrote: "When this film was conceived several years ago, the problems of love among the comfortable middle classes may have still seemed more dramatic than the passions of ghetto blacks, but it was ill-conceived even then." "Now," the magazine concluded, "it seems an absolute antique."

Yet the film presented a message of racial integration that captured a broad segment of the population, illustrated by its box-office dominance in the winter of 1968. The film's massive appeal suggested that the majority of the American people, at least theoretically, embraced liberal racial attitudes. James Baldwin hated the movie, but presciently forecast its implications: "*Guess Who's Coming to Dinner* may prove, in some bizarre way, to be a milestone, because it is really quite impossible to go any further in that particular direction. Next time, the kissing will have to start." And as removed as the picture seemed from the emergent black ethic seeking racial confrontation and fixed on the problems of the urban poor, it still rankled the nation's staunchest white conservatives. A number of southern theaters endured Ku Klux Klan protests and cut out the interracial kiss scene. The picture's popularity, combined with the scathing attacks from each end of the political spectrum, illuminated the inability of Americans in 1968 to achieve any sort of consensus on racial politics. When that consensus disintegrated, so did Poitier's status of Hollywood leading man.

On April 4, 1968, just as the box-office momentum of *Guess Who's Coming to Dinner* began to wane, Martin Luther King, Jr. was assassinated. As the nation confronted racial uncertainty, the entertainment world struggled to respond appropriately. Columbia called back all copies of *Guess Who's Coming to Dinner* and edited out a scene where Poitier's fiancée asks the maid to "guess who's coming to dinner." "The Reverend Martin Luther King Jr.!" she sasses back. Poitier, Diahann Carroll, Sammy Davis Jr., and Louis Armstrong announced that out of respect for Dr. King, they could no longer participate in the upcoming Academy Awards.

The board of directors of the Academy of Motion Picture Arts and Sciences quickly agreed to postpone the ceremony for two days, and the black performers reconsidered. In the shadow of King's death, the ceremony included musings on entertainment's role in race relations. Hollywood equated Poitier with the King legacy; when he rose to present the award for Best Actress, he received the evening's biggest ovation. The Academy president Gregory Peck declared of the Poitier films: "One measure of Dr. King's influence on the society in which we live is that of the five films nominated for best picture of the year, two dealt with the subject of understanding between the races." Those films were *In the Heat of the Night* (which won the award) and *Guess Who's Coming to Dinner*. Peck called for more films "which celebrate the dignity of man, whatever his race or color or creed." Rod Steiger ended his acceptance speech for Best Actor with the words, "We Shall Overcome."

But King's death represented the end of an era of nonviolent protest for racial integration, and it was the hinge upon which Poitier's career turned. Two years later, the *New York Times* was asking, "is Sidney Poitier obsolete?" It explained: "The terrible thing about being a political point of view and a social symbol is that time, even before age, may suddenly overtake you" Poitier's responses to changing racial sensibilities appeared calculated and lame. His role in 1969 of black radical in *The Lost Man* was unconvincing and politically ambiguous. His reprise of his character from *In the Heat of the Night – They Call Me Mister Tibbs!* in 1970 and the next year *The Organization* – lacked the racial friction of the original, turning his character into a banal supercop.

In *Brother John*, also in 1971, the first project of his production company, he starred as a mystic archangel in what seemed a clumsy exercise in self-deification.

The shifting winds of black politics had sucked Poitier into a curious trap: unable to portray his trademark virtuous emblem of dignity, and unconvincing in a departure from that image. The times demanded a calculated reversal of the Poitier stereotype, embodied in a new generation of black films – *Shaft*, *Super Fly*, *Sweet Sweetback's Baadasssss Song* – that celebrated a novel black hero who uses violence, sleeps with white women, and dresses and speaks in urban styles. For an audience frustrated with the slow pace of racial progress, the new film icon offered blacks an emotional satisfaction that Poitier's characters could never approach.

Poitier never disappeared from Hollywood. In fact, he remained at the forefront of black progress in the film industry. In 1969 he founded, along with Paul Newman and Barbra Streisand, the First Artists Production Company to finance production and distribution of films they would each star in and produce. In 1972 he directed his first film, the western *Buck and the Preacher*. He directed and co-starred in a trio of successful comedies, *Uptown Saturday Night* in 1974, *Let's Do It Again* in 1975, and *A Piece of the Action* two years later. He addressed the conditions that he had complained about to the House Labor Committee a decade earlier, hiring black actors, writers, and technicians. But for many in the younger generation, Poitier seemed a relic, an apologetic accommodationist constructed by white liberals and stripped of black autonomy. Few remembered just how important, and just how controversial, Sidney Poitier had once been.

25

Coming to Terms
with the Vietnam War
A Sacred Mission: Oliver Stone and Vietnam

Randy Roberts and David Welky

From John Wayne's The Green Berets *(1968) to today, more than a hundred film-makers have addressed the war in Vietnam. From Michael Cimino and Francis Ford Coppola to Sylvester Stallone and Chuck Norris, from box-office hits to art-house flops, the war has provided a way to address a history of social and political issues. No film-maker has been more absorbed in the war and its meaning than Oliver Stone. In such films as* Platoon *(1986),* Born on the Fourth of July *(1989),* JFK *(1991),* Heaven and Earth *(1993), and* Nixon *(1995), he has addressed the elements of American culture and politics that led to the war, the nature of the conflict, and the human price of the engagement. For Stone, a Vietnam veteran, the war was the central American experience in the second half of the twentieth century. Understanding the war, then, became essential to understanding modern American history. In the following essay Randy Roberts and David Welky explore Stone's efforts to get to the heart of the Vietnam experience.*

"*To me the '60s were very hard – my parents got divorced, I went to Vietnam.*"

"*If it's a movie worth making, you should make it. If you can convey that passion, it should all be open. Anything is permitted.*"

"*Vietnam is not over, although some people say it is. Vietnam is a state of mind that continues all over the world – as long as m[a]n in his quest for power interferes in the affairs of other men*"

"*Part of me is scared, and wants to say, let's pull back, let's make a film that is understandable to everyone, that's sweeter, that the whole country can believe in, like Forrest Gump.*" (Oliver Stone)

In September 1967, Oliver Stone departed the United States on a transport bound for Vietnam. Behind him he left his life – an unhappy childhood; frustrating, lonely years at Hill School and Yale; a long, rejected novel manuscript. He might have been

Randy Roberts and David Welky, "A Sacred Mission: Oliver Stone and Vietnam," in Robert Brent Toplin, ed., *Oliver Stone's USA: Film, History, and Controversy* (Lawrence: University Press of Kansas, 2000), pp. 66–90.

Ernest Hemingway heading for Italy, or Joseph Conrad bound for the sea. Perhaps his mind was already tracking film images, imagining what might have been and what would be. Perhaps Vietnam was more of an escape than a mission. Whatever the case, the country would soon take hold of him, and it would occupy his thoughts and his creativity for much of the next thirty years. Few artists would delve so completely into the nature, texture, and causes of the Vietnam War. Fewer still would produce such a dazzling body of work. And at the heart of it all would be biography – Stone's and America's.

For Oliver Stone, exploring Vietnam would become a sacred mission. As a young man, he served two tours in the country – one as a civilian, the other as a soldier. These experiences changed him and set his artistic agenda. For the next twenty-five years he would return repeatedly to Vietnam for inspiration. The conflict became his touchstone; it provided him with both an avenue for personal exploration and a tool for understanding larger historical questions.

In a series of brilliant films about America and Vietnam, Stone moved from auto-biographical observations about the nature of war, to a sociological analysis of the American culture that led to the war, to historical investigation of the political causes and course of the war. In the process, Stone became the most influential historian of America's role in Vietnam. But to understand Stone's position, one has to come to terms with Stone himself.

Considering his career as a writer and director of powerful films that deal with war, it is perhaps not surprising that, had it not been for World War II, Oliver Stone's parents would never have met. Louis Stone, Oliver's father, was a Wall Street stock-broker and the scion of a wealthy family. He met Jacqueline Goddet, a poor nineteen-year-old beauty, shortly after V-E Day, while he was serving as a financial officer for General Eisenhower in Paris. After some initial hesitation, Jacqueline wed Louis in November 1945. By the time the couple returned to New York City, Jacqueline was pregnant with what would be their only child. William Oliver Stone was born on September 15, 1946.

The future critic of the establishment grew up within its comfortable embrace. Despite being prone to making poor financial decisions, his father generally proved to be a good provider, enabling Oliver to lead, by his own admission, "a sheltered existence." Oliver lived in a large townhouse complete with a nanny and a butler, dressed stylishly, studied piano, and listened to classical music and Broadway show tunes. After finishing eighth grade at Manhattan's Trinity School, his parents shipped him to the exclusive Hill School, an all-boys academy in Pottstown, Pennsylvania. Oliver knew that Hill was the first step that would probably lead to Yale and Wall Street, the path his father had taken.

Oliver's childhood was pampered, but hardly happy. Both his parents were distant. His mother seemed more interested in New York's party scene than in him, and his father was a "dark and pessimistic" man who had a hard time expressing his emotions. Oliver's closest family may have been his grandparents in France. As a youth, he spent his summers in Europe, raptly listening to his grandfather tell stories about the Great War and happily playing army with his cousins on the battlefields where millions of men had lost their lives. He passed summer days writing plays, many about war, that willing locals performed.

But the carefree summers ended, and he faced the unappealing prospect of return-ing to the States and school. Although he was intellectually curious and fascinated with American and European history, he was uncomfortable at Hill. A self-proclaimed "outsider," he made few friends, chafed under the strict discipline of the boarding school, and resented its efforts to impose a rigid "orthodoxy" upon him. Like many adolescents, Oliver was extremely "self-conscious," living in constant fear of being ridiculed by fellow students. Burdened with feelings of isolation, he pursued his interest in writing, primarily as a means of "retreat[ing] from reality."

His family life got even lonelier. In 1962, when he was fifteen, the headmaster of Hill called him to his office to inform him that his parents were separating. The news shocked him; he had failed or refused to see any signs of discord in his parents' relationship. In fact, the split surprised few others. Louis had had a string of affairs, and Jacqueline, fully aware of her husband's philandering, coped by partying, popping uppers, and, finally, taking lovers of her own. By the early 1960s, the Stones' marriage existed solely on paper. Now, when Oliver most needed attention, his parents reinforced his sense of isolation by refusing to visit him. Oliver wanted to take a leave from school, but his father would not hear of it, claiming that he was too busy at work to attend to anyone else. Jacqueline was even more remote – she left for Europe, expressing no interest in seeing her son. Oliver received another shock when he learned that Jacqueline's free-spending habits had driven the family into debt. Louis moved, with Oliver's possessions, from their spacious town house to a cramped hotel room. Oliver was devastated. His parents' actions taught him that "adults were dangerous" and "not to be trusted."

Abandoned by his parents, he accepted the grind at Hill. Unsure of his future, he struggled through his last tedious years of high school. World events seemed remote. Certainly, he did not see his destiny in the assassination of President Kennedy. Raised a staunch Republican by his conservative father (Oliver voted for Barry Goldwater in 1964), he has only vague memories of being "on a lunch break or something" when he heard of the president's death. Although he was never a "Kennedy lover when he was alive," Stone was shocked by the crime, but no more than others. He was not burdened with concerns for America's future, only "stunned" that "a young, handsome president could be killed like that." He fully accepted the Warren Commission's finding that Kennedy had been killed by Lee Harvey Oswald alone.

Personal concerns were more pressing. In accordance with his father's wishes, in 1964 he enrolled at Yale. He quickly realized that college would be more of "the same crap" that Hill had been. Even more than before, he desperately searched for meaning in his life, longing to break out of the constricting East Coast conservative mold that his father had crammed him into. Books provided a means of escape. He devoured Joseph Conrad's writings and was especially drawn to *Lord Jim*, with Conrad's dark view of human nature and his lush depictions of the exotic Orient. The idea of living in a primitive land, unsullied by civilization, consumed him, and he began inquiring about possibilities for overseas employment. After several rejections, he was finally accepted by the Free Pacific Institute in Taiwan, a church-based organization that operated a number of schools. The Institute offered him a position as an English teacher at a school in Cholon, the Chinese suburb of Saigon. In 1965, he dropped out of Yale and headed for Vietnam.

Saigon, with its gambling, drugs, and prostitution, was no Yale. It "was like Dodge City." Hookers stalked busy street corners, drunks spilled out from numerous bars, and guns and violence were common. The hot sun and the nearby ocean lent a sense of romance to the chaotic scene. Stone felt alive. After the suffocating depths of Hill

School and Yale, Saigon was like coming up for air. He plunged into his new job, working hard and living a spartan life, but loving it all.

But an immediate, itchy restlessness persisted. Travel had gotten into his blood, and he wanted to see more of the world. He quit his teaching position after two semesters and joined the merchant marine, where he passed his days cleaning toilets and engine rooms. After a long voyage from Vietnam to Oregon, the nineteen-year-old Stone drifted south to Mexico to write a novel. The manuscript, which he called "A Child's Night Dream," grew into a 1,400-page stream-of-consciousness look at the psyche of a bright, troubled youth. The largely autobiographical story followed the protagonist through his experiences in Asia and the merchant marine. Stone worked furiously through much of 1966 at what he thought was a literary masterpiece, eventually feeling confident enough to return to New York City and the harsh judgment of his father, who desperately wanted his son to return to Yale and a buttoned-down life. Stone finally gave in and reenrolled, but unenthusiastically. "Night Dream" continued to occupy his thoughts and his energy. He worked on his novel at a punishing pace, skipping classes and writing about ten hours every day. Not surprisingly, his return to Yale was brief and inglorious. He was expelled but, undaunted, returned to New York to finish his book. The incredible effort he poured into the novel only made it more painful when publishers panned the manuscript. Frustrated, he threw hundreds of pages into the East River and decided to take a drastic step. He would visit Vietnam again, this time as a soldier.

Because he was a well-educated white male, the army offered Stone a position at Officer Candidate School. He refused and requested infantry duty. His decision to go to war appears rash but actually stemmed from a number of factors. To be sure, he had been hurt by the series of personal and literary rejections. But he was equally upset by the grand literary pretensions he had harbored. In a sense, his decision to enlist was an act of atonement for his perceived character flaws; he yearned to "obliterate" the ego he had created and, after a long bout with individualism, become an "anonymous" grunt. Though he often considered suicide, he could not bring himself to "pull the trigger." Instead, he resolved to let someone else pull it for him on a battlefield.

But perhaps more than anything else, Stone went to Vietnam simply because he believed in the war. Like many other Americans who grew up during the 1950s, he had learned to "fear Russians and hate Communism." He fully believed that communism needed to be stopped in order to preserve American democracy, and he felt it was his duty to fight. His father had served during World War II, his grandfather during World War I. Now it was his turn to serve his country and, by doing so, to announce that he was "a man." Imbued with both pathos and patriotism, Private Bill Stone (he opted to enlist using his first name, fearing that "Oliver" was too effeminate) left for Vietnam on September 14, 1967, and was assigned to the second platoon of Bravo Company, Third Battalion, 25th Infantry, stationed near the Cambodian border.

Naive optimism and idealism soon crumbled under the weight of reality. Vietnam was not the same place it had been in 1965. By 1967, many Vietnamese had gone from loving to loathing the occupying Americans. Corruption ran rampant as noncombatants lived high, far behind the lines, and unscrupulous sergeants stole supplies to sell on the black market. Stone quickly discovered that Vietnam was not a people's conflict but a politicians' war fought by the poorest Vietnamese and Americans. Just as disconcerting for him were the unexpected attitudes of his new comrades in arms, who made it clear to him that he was as "expendable" as a piece of "raw meat." Very quickly he realized that enlisting had been "a terrible mistake" and that he was "in deep." One of his only pleasures was writing long, introspective letters to his grandmother, Adele Goddet, in France.

Stone was given little time to adjust to his new surroundings. After only a week, he found himself on point in a night ambush. He struggled through nearly a week of field duty without confronting the enemy. His greatest adversaries were the incessant swarms of mosquitoes that kept him awake at night, the spiders that crawled in his shirt, and the fifty pounds of equipment on his back that nearly overwhelmed him as he humped through the jungle. One night he fell asleep during his watch, waking to discover that the Vietcong (VC) were practically on top of the platoon. "Scared shitless" and numbed with fear, he forgot his training and silently stared. A comrade opened fire on the oncoming troops, jolting Stone out of his stupor. He pulled the trigger, but had forgotten to take the safety off his M-16. Eventually, he regained his bearings and the platoon beat back the VC approach, but not before at least one American was severely wounded. Stone received a flesh wound in the neck during the melee and was briefly out of action.

His first taste of battle improved his combat sense. It also, despite his mistake during the ambush, put him more at ease with the other members of the platoon. He could not, however, completely fit in. The differences in background between him and the other grunts were obvious. He enjoyed classical music and serious literature, while they favored Hank Williams and Motown, hard liquor and serious drugs. One of Stone's comrades later recalled that he was "a quiet person who kept to himself." At first, he did not drink, spending his leisure hours writing stories of his experiences. Slowly, however, the war changed him. As his tour dragged on, he felt himself becoming disconnected from his civilized roots and becoming a "jungle animal," operating less on reason than "instinct." Increasingly, he sided with the progressive element of the platoon, who preferred Motown and drugs to the country music and alcohol that fueled the platoon's other faction. Stone's association with this group, composed mostly of lower-class blacks and whites from small towns, expanded his horizons and exposed him to the social injustice and prejudice of American life.

Then came 1968. There was nothing happy about Stone's new year. On January 1, he and 700 other U.S. soldiers were attacked by some 2,000 VC troops at Firebase Burt. The enemy lobbed mortars into the American entrenchment before beginning a ground assault at one in the morning. The American perimeter collapsed, and Stone's platoon was thrown into the counterattack. The VC inched forward, taking bunker after bunker, and the battle quickly devolved into brutal hand-to-hand combat. But the fighting came to an abrupt close when American planes dropped bombs directly on the American position, killing friend and foe without discrimination. The incident embittered Stone. As he watched bulldozers push lifeless Vietnamese bodies into a mass grave, he wondered if the American force had been no more than bait, a dab of honey designed to lure the antlike VC army into the open.

But Stone had little time to ponder. Just two weeks later, Bravo Company was hit again, this time while on patrol a few miles from Firebase Burt. Bravo's third platoon stumbled into a VC bunker complex and got pinned down. The first platoon faced a similar predicament. It was up to Stone and the second platoon to extricate the men from the morass. But Stone's jungle instincts let him down; he got caught in a trip-wire explosion and received shrapnel in his leg and his rear. Medics shot him full of morphine, packed him on a stretcher, and loaded him on a helicopter. Bravo Company took about thirty casualties without inflicting any. Stone's rehabilitation kept him off the field during the Tet Offensive, which further devastated Bravo. By the time he returned to duty, he barely recognized anyone in his largely reconstructed platoon.

After another brief stint on combat duty, he was transferred to a military police auxiliary battalion in Saigon, where he guarded barracks and trolled for miscreants. The new duty bored Stone, and he numbed the tedium with drugs. The jungle beckoned. He wanted to get back into the heat of battle and got his wish after brawling with a rear-duty sergeant. In order to avoid having his tour extended as punishment, Stone opted in April 1968 to volunteer for the First Cavalry Division's reconnaissance and minesweeping detail.

The transfer proved portentous for his later career. While in the First Cavalry, Stone met a large black man from a small town in Tennessee who would later become the basis for "King" in *Platoon*. He also met a half-Spanish, half-Apache sergeant named Juan Angel Elias, who fascinated him. Elias, recalls Stone, "was like a rock star in the body of a soldier." Rather than terrify, the compassionate Elias inspired his men. He was a heavy drug user who was loathed by the lifers and juicers. Stone stayed close to Elias, learning how to rely on his senses, not his intellect, during combat. For the first time, Stone believed that it was possible to be both a good soldier and a good person.

By now, Stone had become a veteran, a fact he demonstrated in August 1968 when the platoon got pinned down by a North Vietnamese Army (NVA) soldier with a machine gun in a foxhole. With his fellow soldiers trapped under a hail of bullets, Stone lost contact with reality and functioned on pure instinct. With reckless abandon, he charged the bunker and, while on the run, lobbed a grenade directly into the hole, thus buying time for the platoon to be rescued. He is still at a loss to explain what happened to him. "Something went crazy in my head," he explains. "I flipped out." He received the Bronze Star for his heroism/confusion.

As the war dragged on, Stone sensed a loss of basic humanity. Yet another transfer brought him under the influence of Platoon Sergeant Barnes. Barnes had become something of an army legend. He had been wounded six or seven times, and one shot over the eye had left a large, sickle-shaped scar down the left side of his face. A passionate soldier, he volunteered to return to combat after every wound. In contrast to Elias, Barnes was "a very frightening man" with a "cold stare" that grunts felt "all the way down to [their] balls." Stone and the other awestruck soldiers were terrified yet intrigued by the grizzled warrior. From Barnes, Stone learned how to suppress his emotions, kill, and become a disciplined, mechanized soldier. Death came to concern him no more than life, and his sense of right and wrong eroded. He burned villages on "a steady basis." He watched uncaringly as frustrated U.S. troops sprayed mosquito repellent on their feet to make them sore so they could avoid marching and as they committed random acts of violence against Vietnamese civilians. He coolly stood by as one soldier, who would become "Bunny" in *Platoon*, bashed an old woman's head in with his rifle butt. In one village, Stone lost control and began shooting at an old man's feet because "he wouldn't stop smiling" at him. He could not, however, bring himself to kill the old man. Finally, he was shaken out of his complacency when he witnessed two U.S. soldiers raping a young village girl. He broke up the incident and decided that it was time to reassert his humanity. Looking at the world around him, he noticed the natural beauty of Vietnam. He purchased a 35mm Pentax and took the first of hundreds of snapshots of the country. For the first time, he thought of the war in visual terms.

Stone received his discharge orders in late November 1968. In fifteen months, he had earned a Bronze Star and a Purple Heart with an Oak Leaf Cluster for his multiple wounds. Yet even now there was sadness. Just before he was shipped home, he learned that Sergeant Elias had been killed, possibly by an errant American grenade. Stone was eager to leave the heat, insects, fatigue, jungle rot, and frustration behind, but he was still uncertain about his future. He thought that the war was "rotten and corrupt" and lacked "moral purpose" and integrity, but he did not feel that he could challenge the system. Burned out and drugged up, the twenty-two-year-old private returned to the United States with no immediate plans.

He was not prepared to return to New York – his father's New York, a city of commerce, commitment, and respectability. So, without even letting his parents know that he had come back from the war, he fled to Mexico. He found the experience unsatisfying and headed north after only a few days. But his homecoming would not be a happy one. American authorities busted Stone at the border for carrying two ounces of Vietnamese marijuana and threw him into a federal jail in San Diego. He faced the unpleasant prospect of five to twenty years behind bars. It was two weeks before prison officials allowed him to call his dad, but once Louis put up $2,500 for his son's defense, the public attorney suddenly took an interest in Stone's case, and he was soon released. The experience convinced him that nobody in America cared about Vietnam veterans and served to further radicalize him. Having seen injustice abroad, conditions in the prison alerted him to injustice at home. The jail was as horrible as those in Saigon. Inmates were stuffed "in every fucking nook and cranny"; and 5,000 prisoners, mostly young blacks and Hispanics, had to sleep on the floor.

Life outside of prison was not much better. Stone returned to New York and life with his father. Louis, however, complained about Oliver's drug use and ghetto speech. Further, Oliver felt estranged from his old acquaintances. His friends had avoided the war, and most of his Vietnam buddies went back to the small, southern towns they came from. Americans' lack of interest in the war, their "mass indifference," stung him. Nobody wanted to hear his stories of Vietnam's horrors; they were much more interested in "the business of making money." Even the antiwar movement troubled and disgusted him. He felt that it was not really serious about becoming "militarized and politicized" in order to force a peace and served only as a means for pampered college students to blow off steam.

Deciding that he would never be at peace with himself until he had written about Vietnam, Stone began writing a screenplay called *Break*, a story that moved on a symbolic level but contained characters that would later become Rhah, King, Bunny, Lehner, Barnes, and Elias in *Platoon*. After working slavishly on the script, he sent it to Jim Morrison of the Doors, whom he envisioned as the star. Though he never heard back from the singer, the experience convinced him that he could be a filmmaker. He was accepted at New York University's film school and studied under Martin Scorsese, who believed that, despite his penchant for cinematic excess, Stone showed potential as a filmmaker. He was particularly impressed with his student's first film, *Last Year in Vietnam*, a touching appraisal of the trials and tribulations of a Vietnam vet coming home. But Stone did not blend well with the other students. He was older than most and a loner by nature, leading many to believe that he was arrogant. Similarly, he found himself unable to participate in NYU's political scene. While other students marched, Stone advocated "a fucking revolution." He wanted to push beyond "bullshit meetings and conferences" and called for an armed march on Washington.

Stone's marriage in 1971 to Najwa Sarkis, a Lebanese woman who worked for the Moroccan Mission to the United Nations, seemed to calm him a bit. She made enough to support them both and encouraged him to work on writing screenplays. He completed his degree in September 1971 and began to bounce from job to job. While he wrote screenplays, he earned money as a Xerox boy for a copy pool, a messenger, and a cabdriver. By mid-1976, he had written eleven scripts and even directed one, *Seizure*, on a shoestring budget in Canada but failed to attract much critical or popular attention. It seemed he was going nowhere at a frantic pace. His marriage fell apart, he quit one job after another, and success continued to elude him. As America celebrated its bicentennial, Oliver Stone was a marginally employed twenty-five-year-old living in a cheap apartment in New York City.

Had Stone been a movie character, he would have been *Taxi Driver*'s Travis Bickle. He had lost all faith in the government, largely due to the trauma of Watergate. Oddly, he admired Nixon, whose toughness, conservatism, and emotionlessness reminded him of his father, but the scandal destroyed any respect he may have had for the president. Watergate also convinced him that the government was "a lie" and "hammered home the point" that it had "lied to us about Ho Chi Minh and it lied to us about the Vietnam War." His depression was magnified when his grandmother died in 1976. Instead of adding to his rootlessness, however, her death inspired Stone to rededicate himself to making something of his life. Armed with this newfound conviction, he turned once again to Vietnam – the real Vietnam this time, not a symbolic one. In a few weeks of furious typing he produced the screenplay for *Platoon*.

Stone started shopping *Platoon* around Hollywood and attracted the attention of Stan Kamen of the William Morris Agency. Encouraged, he moved to Los Angeles, but no studio expressed interest in the film. The writing, however, was powerful enough that Columbia Pictures hired him to write a treatment of Billy Hayes's autobiography, *Midnight Express*. His screenplay won an Academy Award for best adapted screenplay of 1978 and brought more opportunities his way, including an offer from producer Marty Bergman (*Serpico, Dog Day Afternoon*) to write a screenplay for Ron Kovic's book, *Born on the Fourth of July*. Al Pacino was set to star, and William Friedkin was to direct. The releases of *The Deer Hunter* and *Coming Home*, however, threatened to overload the market for Vietnam films, and *Born*'s funding fell through three days before shooting was to begin.

But work was now easier to find. Stone wrote and directed *The Hand* (1981), a low-budget thriller starring Michael Caine, and produced an early version of the script for *Conan the Barbarian* (1982). In Hollywood, he was earning a reputation for writing violent, right-wing screenplays, a charge that gained strength from his scripts for *Scarface* (1983), *Year of the Dragon* (1985), and *8 Million Ways to Die* (1986). He resented the stereotype and found inspiration in Warren Beatty's *Reds*, a film that proved to him that a Hollywood movie could be both big-budget and leftist. Then, in 1984, Dino DeLaurentis agreed to finance *Platoon*. Once again, however, funding fell through at the last moment. It was not until after the surprise success of *Salvador* (1986), which did well on video despite being underpromoted, that he received solid backing for *Platoon*, and then only by Hemdale, a British-based operation.

Part of Stone's problem with getting the funding for *Platoon* had to do with Hollywood's suspicion that Vietnam War films were both too controversial and too economically risky. This notion began to take form while Stone himself was still serving in Vietnam. In 1967, John Wayne filmed *The Green Berets* at Fort Benning, Georgia. Released in 1968 after the Tet Offensive, the hawkish, pro-American film provoked a violent left-wing critical response. "Unspeakable … stupid … rotten … false, vile and insane," commented Renata Adler in the *New York Times*. "Immoral … racist," agreed Michael Korda in *Glamour*. "Childishly sleazy," added Frank Mararella in *Cinema Magazine*. Although the film found its audience and made money, Hollywood producers who did not have Wayne's clout with moviegoers decided that the war was simply too hot.

For the next decade, filmmakers treated the war as little more than a reference or a source of inspiration. The WAR – that bloody, passionate creature sitting in America's living room – was not mentioned. Then came the first tentative steps. In 1978, *Coming Home* and *The Deer Hunter* explored the mentality of soldiers returning from the war, with mixed critical and financial results. The same year, *Go Tell the Spartans*, a fine film, was all but ignored. In 1979, Francis Ford Coppola released *Apocalypse Now*, a film buried beneath so much myth and symbol that critics read it as both hawkish and dovish. Its profound ambivalence – or perhaps its psychological complexity – may have penetrated to the heart of war's darkness, but it failed to say much about the everyday nature of combat.

During the Reagan era, Hollywood retrieved, dusted off, and modestly updated stock war-film materials. Once again, combat became a heroic enterprise, corrupted only by politicians. The *Rambo* films and the *Missing in Action* series captured the big bucks. Americans wanted to watch winners, not agonize over what happened or why it happened. They desired action, not introspection; results, not meaning. They wanted heroes for their next wars, not victims of lost crusades.

But Oliver Stone had his own agenda, which smacked against the political currents of Hollywood and Washington. Much of *Platoon* is an echo, not only to the themes of *Apocalypse Now* but also to the antiwar literature of World War I. Sergeant Barnes, the scarred figure from both Stone's own tour in Vietnam and *Platoon*, recalls Hemingway's injured hero Jake Barnes in *The Sun Also Rises*. And the use of Charlie Sheen as not only the protagonist but also the narrative guide serves the same purpose as Martin Sheen did in *Apocalypse Now*. The twin references announced that *Platoon* would explore both coming of age and the futility of modern war.

The strength of *Platoon* emerged from Stone's passion for and his palpable understanding of the subject. Like Hemingway, war was the defining experience in his life. He enlisted, he fought, he killed, he was injured; he believed, he questioned, he lost faith. He suffered the full range of emotions, entertained the gamut of thoughts. And when he turned to the subject, it was not like Francis Ford Coppola, Sylvester Stallone, or Chuck Norris, filmmakers and actors who embraced the war as a commercial vehicle rather than a biographical necessity. Stone, unlike others who depicted Vietnam on-screen, viewed the war as the central event not only in his life but also in the "soul" of America "and the world."

From the beginning of the *Platoon* project, he insisted on absolute realism. Anything less than fidelity would have betrayed his memory and experiences, although the U.S. Department of Defense refused to cooperate on the film because it believed that it was a "totally unrealistic" depiction of the war. Stone maintained that the film was not about larger issues; it was about "boys in the field." To ensure that his actors were as knowledgeable and competent as the real men of Bravo Company, he imposed a rigorous, two-week-long boot camp in the Philippine jungles under the dictatorial supervision of Captain Dale Dye, a twenty-year marine and a Vietnam veteran. Captain Dye subjected the cast to long marches with sixty-pound packs, cold army rations, and uncomfortable nights in foxholes, punctuated by sudden bursts of explosions to guarantee that no one would sleep. By the time filming began, the actors had the "tired, don't-give-a-damn attitude" that Stone had hoped to achieve. In a short time, Stone and Dye had made soldiers out of actors.

To maintain faith with his past, Stone set *Platoon* in a real time and a real place – his time, his place. The film details the activities of 25th Bravo Company, operating near the Cambodian border, in 1967. The film's central character, Chris Taylor (Charlie Sheen), views the war from a perspective similar to Stone's. Like Stone, Taylor is a white, upper-middle-class kid who went to Vietnam to escape from the boredom and rigors of civilized life. His experiences in Vietnam mirror Stone's – one reason why the film is so realistic and personal.

The film's initial impression of Vietnam focuses on the landscape, perhaps the overriding presence in the film. It is, in the fullest sense, a world without vision, a land of eight-foot elephant grass, overgrown virginal forests, and lush jungles. It is a landscape that one needs a machete to hack through. Much of the tension of the film originates in its confining setting; danger always seems to threaten from behind the next tree.

Daily discomforts add to the tension. Stone's Vietnam is a place where a grunt cannot relax. Mosquitoes swarm, ants bite, and leeches cling. Insects maintain a perpetual hum in the background, constantly reminding the viewer and the soldier of their presence. The product of a wealthy family, Chris finds it difficult to adjust to Vietnam's fatal environment; he staggers under the weight of his pack, gags at the sight of a dead body, and attracts the ants and leeches like a magnet. Making matters worse, night seems to conspire with the harsh environment to deny rest to the weary Americans. Bombs explode, flares light up the sky, ambushers lurk everywhere. "You never really sleep," observes Chris in a voice-over, as his year-long tour of Vietnam assumes the dimensions of an 8,760-hour day.

The language in *Platoon* is similarly authentic. Fresh soldiers are "cherries" and "newbies"; Vietnam is "the Nam," and America is "the world"; pot smokers are "heads" that meet in the "underworld." The film is also littered with obscenities, as Stone refused to pull any verbal punches. The music the soldiers listen to and the words they use reflect Stone's own experiences. The use of Motown hits like "Tracks of My Tears" alongside country classics like "Okie from Muskogee" adds to the realistic aura and helps to divide the platoon into two hostile camps – the "heads" and the "juicers" – just as it was in Stone's platoon. They are his people, "guys nobody really cares about" from small towns and villages, "the bottom of the barrel," the undereducated and the uneducated.

It is in the realistic portrayal of the platoon itself that the film departs most radically from the traditional war genre. The classic World War II film upholds the ideal of the melting pot: out of many, one. Multiethnic, multi-religious, and multiregional, the platoon is a smorgasbord of Italians, Poles, and Irish; Protestants, Jews, and Catholics; Brooklyn sharpies, southern Rebs, and midwestern rubes. Yet they all pull together toward a common goal. No such comfortable – and comforting – arrangement is present in *Platoon*. Stone observed a clear "moral division" in his platoon when he served in Vietnam, and Bravo's cinematic counterpart is faithful to Stone's memory. On a symbolic level, the film centers on the two sergeants, Elias and Barnes. For Barnes, all civilians are potential Vietcong and are liable to ruthless treatment. Elias, however, takes a more compassionate "hearts and minds" approach to the war. He wants to save Vietnam; Barnes merely wants to destroy the country.

But the platoon is split over more than war aims. Unlike traditional war films, Stone shows how race divided soldiers in Vietnam. In the base camp, African Americans are usually by themselves, shunted off to one side. Black soldiers are aware that they are being treated unfairly. One complains that they have to take extra turns on ambush patrol because of racial "politics," and another objects to "always being fucked by the rich." They are not, however, passive victims. Junior, a black grunt, for example, is not afraid to order Chris around. "Hey, white boy!" he shouts, before encouraging him to dig a foxhole with a little more enthusiasm. The only place blacks and whites can comfortably coexist is in the underworld, where, supervised by Sergeant Elias, they dance together in a drug-induced haze to the sounds of Smokey Robinson. In 1967, a year that saw vicious race riots in Detroit and other cities and heard former Student Nonviolent Coordinating Committee chairman Stokely Carmichael call for a black revolution, race was as much of an issue in Vietnam as it was in America. Stone, unlike other filmmakers, brought this reality to the screen. By doing so, he added a deeper, more nuanced understanding of America.

Despite their divisions, soldiers have to pull together when they are in combat. It is in these sequences that Stone achieves the greatest sense of realism in the film. Stone's war is the grunt's war, a war without maps, red and blue arrows, or a grand design. Men fight because they are attacked, not for any lofty goal or territorial objective, and battles often end as inconclusively as they begin. In such contests, "winning" loses any elevated meaning; soldiers fight to survive. Period.

The mise-en-scène of the battle sequences underscores Stone's idea of combat. His camera work captures Karl von Clausewitz's notion of the "fog of war." The camera becomes Chris's eyes – jerking back and forth, seeing nothing distinctly, and blindly reacting to threats both perceived and real. Violence erupts suddenly and brutally, often without warning or meaning. Death and injury are neither noble nor ignoble, they just are. The best answer to the suffering and violence is given early in the film by Barnes. In true Hemingway fashion, he clamps his hand over a screaming, dying man and demands that he "take the pain."

Premiering in New York and Los Angeles in December 1986, *Platoon* created an international sensation and propelled Stone into the forefront of American directors. *Time* proclaimed that Stone's effort portrayed "Viet Nam as It Really Was," and the *New York Times*'s Vincent Canby called the film "a succession of found moments" – that is, it had rediscovered the lost reality of the war. More importantly for Hollywood and Oliver Stone, *Platoon* was a massive commercial success as well. Made for a paltry $6.5 million, the film grossed $136 million in U.S. box office receipts. Video sales pushed the total gross to a staggering $250 million. For now, Stone believed that he had exorcised the demons of Vietnam, and he looked forward to new projects. Having suddenly become a famous director, he planned to move to a lighter subject for his next film. In 1987, he remarked that he "would love to do a comedy."

Had Oliver Stone been Francis Ford Coppola or even Sylvester Stallone, perhaps he could have jumped genres and made a quick transition to another project. But the whole point of *Platoon* was that it was not just a film project; it was Stone – his biography, his vision, his nightmare. He could no more set Vietnam aside than Hemingway could forget his war or Ahab abandon his whale. *Platoon* had not ended his dialogue with America about the war; it had only started it.

After *Platoon*, Stone made two movies, *Wall Street* and *Talk Radio*, before returning to Vietnam with a version of Ron Kovic's autobiography, *Born on the Fourth of July*. He had been interested in the project since 1980, but there was no money in Hollywood for a film about a paraplegic Vietnam veteran who discovers that all his country's cherished ideals are false and that the war in Vietnam was a sham. In a Hollywood marked by escape and fantasy, and a Washington following in lockstep, Kovic and Stone were as warmly embraced as repo men. They were pounding on the door, trying to get inside to claim their America, but nobody was at home. The financial success of *Platoon*, however, gave Stone the sledge he needed to break down the door.

Born on the Fourth of July centers on America's fatal flaw, the culture that conditions and indoctrinates young men to go to war. It is a brutal culture, life-hating, joy-denying, pleasure-destroying. In the film, Stone labors to subvert that culture, and by casting Tom Cruise in the lead, he moved far in that direction. By the mid-1980s, Cruise had become America's smile, the charming good-bad boy of *Top Gun* and *Risky Business*. Stone took Cruise's chiseled good looks and spit-shined image and caked them with mud. "Tom had the classical facial structure of an athlete," noted Stone. "He's the kid off a Wheaties box. I wanted to yank the kid off that box and mess with his image – take him to the dark side."

Seldom in the American cinema has the dark side initially seemed so benign. The opening sequences of the film are infused with a soft, golden light, and falling autumn leaves create a snow-globe effect. Everything about Kovic's Massapequa has a Norman Rockwell familiarity – small town and safe streets, boys playing war in the woods and men mouthing platitudes about the need to serve, rippling flags and firecrackers on the Fourth of July, baseball games and Yankee caps, wrestling matches and first loves. Kovic is his mother's "little Yankee Doodle Boy," born on the Fourth of July and raised with loving care. Yet something is out of whack in his comfortable, middle-class America. A parading World War II veteran flinches at the sound of an exploding fire-cracker, a coach's quest for victory borders on obsession, a mother's religious faith merges into zealotry. Kovic is taught not only to be upright, courteous, reverent, and clean but also that winning is everything, God hates quitters, communists are banging on our doors, and Uncle Sam needs you. As America's perfect son, he moves naturally from the Boy Scouts to the marines.

For Kovic and Stone, the culture of winning, violence, and unquestioning loyalty was America's dark side. It was a culture that despised softness and sensitivity and created a god out of John Wayne – in the book, Kovic writes that he resented having to give his "dead dick for John Wayne." These forces – family, community, school – imbued Kovic and Stone with a cold war mentality and the idea that manliness could be found only on a battlefield. The power of the culture makes Kovic's disillusion-ment all the more wrenching. After being wounded and returning home, he blames his country for making him go to Vietnam. "They told us to go," he cries, implicating the faceless establishment for perpetrating an immoral war.

Kovic's story also shows how easily this dark side can be foisted onto the next generation. As he rides through a crowd during a Fourth of July parade, his eyes come to rest on a boy who looks much as he once did. The child's Yankees cap and his toy gun suggest that little has changed since his own youth. By exposing America's dark side, Stone pushes his analysis of Vietnam beyond that presented in *Platoon*. Unlike *Platoon*, which made no effort to explain the larger issues behind the war, *Born on the Fourth of July* suggests that Vietnam, and war in general, are a product of America's own moral deficiencies, a theme that he would further explore in later films.

Kovic's and Stone's disillusionment is fueled by outrage, because they believed that they had been duped by their country's martial culture. The film implies that only the true believers, boys like Kovic born on the Fourth of July, evinced a willingness to fight and die for their country. Most of Kovic's high school classmates cannot understand why he wants to enlist; they do not feel particularly threatened by communists, and they are not moved by any overwhelming impulse to be "part of history." They seek only normal lives and a chance to prosper financially. When Kovic returns from Vietnam in a wheelchair, his friends have moved on with their lives. They are husbands, fathers, budding entrepreneurs, as distant as people can be from what he experienced on the other side of the world. Perhaps even more than his injuries, his friends' apathy gnaws at him. While he is consumed with the war, they could not care less. A hospital orderly tells him, "You can take your Vietnam and shove it up your ass." "They don't give a shit about the war," his friend Stevie adds. Even his mother switches the television station to *Laugh In* when a story about a Vietnam War protest comes on the news.

Stone shared Kovic's attitude toward America and his desire to shake his sleeping countrymen. The messages of *Born on the Fourth of July* are don't forget and get involved. America fought and lost the wrong war in the wrong place at the wrong time. It was a needless, senseless war, the product of a military culture and blind ideological faith. And unless Americans begin to question that culture and that faith, it will happen again. On this point, Stone and Kovic are products of the late 1960s and early 1970s political radicalization. Conservatives argue that protest movements had no effect. Stone disagreed. "That's why making *Born* was a particular thrill, 'cause it was flying in the face of that shit," he said. "People were outraged, I'd get letters saying … there was no protest, no hatred, why are you bringing up all this divisiveness? But I remember the late '60s as a very rough time …. A lot of people can't face their past, you know."

Stone felt so strongly about the message of the film that he allowed it to interrupt the narrative flow. Most of the film deals with Kovic's coming to terms with the forces that shaped him, a struggle that is largely internal and intellectual. The film ends, however, with sketchy scenes of Kovic's political activism, and the manipulation of historical footage to put Cruise/Kovic at the 1972 Republican Convention contrasts sharply with the camera work of the rest of the film. But the transition from internal search to external activism – personal to political – is the message of *Born on the Fourth of July.*

Stone's concern for America's involvement in the war runs even deeper, however. It was not enough for the director just to show the impact of the war on an individual – on Ron Kovic, Chris Taylor, or Oliver Stone. It was not enough just to be the cinematic Hemingway of the Vietnam War. Stone wanted to be the war's historian as well.

As a historian of the war, Stone moves on two levels: personal and political. *Platoon* and *Born on the Fourth of July* are primarily personal statements, though the political lurks beneath the surface. Both films were huge critical and commercial successes (*Born on the Fourth of July* was nominated for eight Academy Awards and won four, including an Oscar for Stone for best director).

Heaven and Earth (1994) is also largely a personal film of self-discovery, although it too has a historical and political message. The war, Stone says, was not only, or even mostly, about the United States. The overwhelming majority of people who were killed in the war were Vietnamese, and most of them were civilians. It was their land that was destroyed, their economy that was shattered, and their culture that was threatened with ruin. Stone commented that he made the film for two reasons – first, to explore the themes of Buddhist spirituality, reverence for ancestors, and respect for the land, and second, to respond to, in part, the blind militarism and mindless revisionism of the Vietnam War as typified by a certain odious brand of thinking that has snaked its way into our culture over the past decade or so, in which the conflict is refought in comic-book style by American superheroes, with a brand new ending … we win! Within the moronic context of these ideas, hundreds of nameless, faceless, Vietnamese are blithely and casually shot, stabbed, and blown to smithereens, utterly without the benefit of human consideration. Entire villages are triumphantly laid to waste, with not one microsecond of thought or care given to those inside the little bamboo hamlets being napalmed. Who were they?

In his attempt to give "the reverse angle" of the war, Stone succeeds. He depicts Phang Thy Le Ly Hayslip's world in loving detail, from the agricultural cycle to the serene beauty of the land to the peaceful stability of village and religious life. Seldom has a commercial filmmaker devoted so much attention to the undramatic nature of a third-world culture. When Stone finally turns his attention to Americans, he portrays them as rich, barbaric invaders. They intrude into the Vietnamese civil war, overlay it with an alien ideological meaning, then take it over, destroying or corrupting everything they touch. They disrupt nature by destroying entire villages, defoliating forests, and severing the rice cycle. American forces turn Le Ly's "most beautiful village on earth" into a scene from Dante's *Inferno*. Culturally, American capitalism corrupts the country, sending villagers to cities and bases where they become pimps, prostitutes, and black marketeers. Drawing not only on Le Ly's memoirs but also on his own experiences as an MP, Stone is at his best when showing American GIs at their worst.

Stone even contends that Americans are at their worst when they are trying to be at their best. In one scene, South Vietnamese soldiers – American allies – use honey donated by the United States and angry ants to torture Le Ly. On a metaphoric level, Stone uses Steve Jones (Tommy Lee Jones) as the representative American. A twisted, misguided killer, Steve attempts to atone for his own sins by showering Le Ly with gifts and by taking her out of her natural environment and dropping her in the United States. But just as the relationship between the United States and the Republic of South Vietnam rotted, so the unnatural union of Steve and Le Ly turns exploitive and violent. Steve's suicide reinforces Stone's view of the results of the American mission in Vietnam.

Heaven and Earth differed from *Platoon* and *Born on the Fourth of July* in its public reception. Expensive to make, it failed miserably at the box office. Production costs exceeded the combined costs of *Platoon* and *Born on the Fourth of July*, but *Heaven and Earth* grossed only $6 million in the United States. Although it was critically applauded – one reviewer called it "Stone's ultimate war film" – it failed to reach the audience the director intended it for. It had a message for all Rambo-cheering, Reagan-voting Americans, but few people paid it even passing attention.

After the success of *Born on the Fourth of July* and before the debacle of *Heaven and Earth*, Stone moved on to new topics. Instead of fulfilling his dream of making a comedy, he decided to catalogue the life of his musical hero, Jim Morrison. But even before *The Doors* was completed, he had laid the foundations for a bold return to the Vietnam genre. By the late 1970s, he had decided that the assassination of John F. Kennedy had drastically altered the course of the war and America's future, but it was not until 1988, when book publisher Ellen Ray gave him a copy of Jim Garrison's *On the Trail of the Assassins* in an elevator in Havana, that he became convinced that Lee Harvey Oswald had not acted alone. Stone devoured Garrison's work, buying the rights to the book with his own money. He then immersed himself in the "serious research" required of any historian. He read every book on JFK and the assassination that he could lay his hands on and, along with screenwriter Zachary Sklar and Vietnam coproducer A. Kitman Ho, conducted over 200 interviews with conspiracy theorists and other people with knowledge of the case.

Stone's conception of the film soon outgrew the mere circumstances of the assassination. "The central historical question" that courses through the movie centers on neither Jim Garrison nor the identity of the president's killers. Instead, Stone used the murder as a means of exploring the event that was central to both his and, he believed, his nation's life – Vietnam. In this way, he was building on issues he had explored in his previous films. *Platoon* was an autobiographical study that showed how the everyday horrors of the war affected a young man. *Born on the Fourth of July* carried the war home by examining how indifference, misunderstanding, and the perverted nature of American life affected Ron Kovic's life. But now, Stone cast an even wider net. *JFK* is a biography of America since World War II, with Vietnam serving as the defining event for the period.

Stone begins *JFK* by rehabilitating the slain president's image. A narrator informs the viewer that Kennedy represented "change and upheaval" in American government. We see Kennedy as he wanted to be seen, making conciliatory speeches toward the Soviets and frolicking with his family. Most importantly, we learn that Kennedy, through no fault of his own, found himself "embroiled" in a war in Southeast Asia. After the assassination, a stricken black maid, perhaps the mother of a grunt, sobs as she tells a reporter what "a fine man" Kennedy was. Meanwhile, Guy Banister (Ed Asner) cheers the killing, ripping Kennedy for letting the "niggers vote." Those who supported and those who objected to Kennedy are neatly delineated. Stone seems intent on transforming Kennedy into the stained-glass hero that the Vietnam War never had.

Vietnam barely ripples the surface of the first half of the film. As New Orleans district attorney Jim Garrison (Kevin Costner) initially becomes obsessed with the assassination, there is little indication that the war plays a pivotal role in anything. Instead, the war appears, as it did in the mid-1960s, as background noise – always present, but rarely commented on. A brief clip shows Lyndon Johnson declaring his intent to vigorously prosecute the war. Another quick mention informs us that Johnson is asking for more money and more men to fight the war.

As Garrison unearths more information, however, Vietnam becomes increasingly central to the story. The pivotal scene comes when Garrison travels to Washington, D.C., to meet "Mr. X" (Donald Sutherland). Mr. X gives him the broader perspective that the DA could never have unearthed on his own. Mr. X cannot tell Garrison who killed Kennedy, although he suggests that top government officials were involved – when he refers to "the perpetrators" and calls the killing a "coup d' etat," Stone flashes images of LBJ. He can, however, give Garrison information on the more important issue – why "they" killed Kennedy. Kennedy had irritated powerful militarists with his refusal to invade Cuba and his decision to eliminate the CIA's power to conduct covert activities during peacetime. The central issue, however, was Vietnam. Kennedy wanted to pull out of Vietnam by 1965, a decision clearly unacceptable to the military and the big arms dealers, who stood to make a killing if the killing continued. Somehow, these forces colluded, perhaps in combination with others, to remove the offending executive and replace him with the more hawkish Johnson, who was "personally committed" to Vietnam. Once Kennedy was out of the way, the war could start "for real." Kennedy's murder and the continuation of the war marked the final triumph of the military-industrial complex, a powerful junta that could run roughshod over any elected official. The personalized war Stone presented in *Platoon* had thus grown into a critical event that marked a decisive shift in the power structure of the United States.

JFK was a mortar lobbed at the establishment, and it set off a firestorm of controversy. Many critics ignored Stone's central thesis, seizing instead on the idea that he had proposed a "grand conspiracy" involving the CIA, FBI, elements of the military, anti-Castro Cubans, New Orleans homosexuals, the Dallas police department, and God only knows who else. Others blasted Stone for lionizing Garrison, who had, in real life, used some questionable methods (including truth serum and questioning hypnotized subjects) to gather his evidence, and for presenting speculation and composite figures as factual. Indeed, *JFK* attains the highest level of realism in any of Stone's films. As in *Platoon*, the camera acts as an eye, as fallible as any human's. The camera jerks as we see something out of the corner of our eye. Did we really see what we thought was there? Stone never provides an answer. Further, Stone has mastered the technique (first seen in the 1972 Republican Convention scene in *Born on the Fourth of July*) of combining documentary and new footage into a seamless unity. His realistic approach went too far for many of his detractors, one of whom referred to *JFK* as "the cinematic equivalent of rape."

Stone responded to the furor surrounding his film. He was willing to give way on most issues. He freely admitted that *JFK* was intended as "entertainment" and that he had taken "dramatic license" with the facts. *JFK* was not supposed to tell the truth about the assassination; Stone simply wanted to present a "paradigm of possibilities" that would point out the shortcomings of the Warren Commission's report. He noted where he had fictionalized or created composite characters and agreed that he had made his Garrison "better" than the real person. He was even willing to negotiate his portrayal of Kennedy. Stone was aware of Kennedy's faults – the pattern of "sex" and "drug use" that marked his life, his "stealing the election in '60," and his penchant for saying "one thing to the public" and doing "another thing behind their backs." In his defense, Stone correctly maintained that three hours was insufficient time to fully develop Kennedy's character and that, in any case, there was "a larger issue at stake."

On the "larger issue," however, Stone would not budge. He continued to insist that, had Kennedy lived, he would have ended the Vietnam War. Stone firmly believed that Kennedy had been reevaluating Vietnam and the cold war throughout 1963. Citing national security memoranda and statements made by Robert McNamara, Kennedy's secretary of defense, Stone claimed that Kennedy was only waiting to be reelected before withdrawing from Southeast Asia. Instead, he was murdered, thus putting "an abrupt end to a period of innocence and great idealism."

Though passionately and eloquently argued, Stone's position, however ardently held, does not stand up to scrutiny. There was, in fact, little to suggest that Kennedy wanted to end either Vietnam or the cold war, unless it was on America's terms. The conciliatory speeches that Stone quotes were anomalous. Even the speech he was to give in Dallas on November 22, 1963, took a hardline stance on communism. McNamara may have believed that Kennedy would have pulled out of Vietnam (even though he wrote to Kennedy in October 1963 that the "security of South Vietnam" was "vital to United States security"), but Kennedy advisers McGeorge Bundy and Robert Kennedy did not. Only three weeks before he was killed, Kennedy approved the overthrow of South Vietnam's president, Ngo Dinh Diem, on the grounds that a new government was needed to save South Vietnam from communism. Kennedy's National Security Memorandum (NSAM) 263, which Stone cites, did call for the withdrawal of 1,000 U.S. troops, but this was merely giving notice to Diem that the United States was not pleased with his corrupt regime. At no point did Kennedy plan to abandon Vietnam. Lyndon Johnson's NSAM 273, which Stone claimed was a radical departure from Kennedy's position, was nothing of the sort. In fact, the document appears in *The Pentagon Papers* as an "Order by Johnson Reaffirming Kennedy's Policy on Vietnam" and stated that the United States' "objectives" remained identical to those stated by Kennedy.

If Stone has been flexible on other issues, why does he remain so steadfast in his assertion that Kennedy would have ended the Vietnam War? To do otherwise would be to undermine all that he has done in the last twenty years. In his films, he has constructed an explanation for an unexplainable war, reducing a complex swirl of ideology and global politics to a simple cause-and-effect relationship. Further, his theory supports his contention that the war had "no moral purpose." In *JFK*, Vietnam resulted from the cowardly murder by a group of vicious, power-hungry warmongers of a benevolent "king" who was trying to bring peace to the world. A more despicable beginning could hardly be imagined, tainting the war with evil before it even began in earnest. Finally, placing Kennedy's death within the context of Vietnam gives Stone and other veterans a hero in a war without acknowledged heroes. Kennedy represents the only hope that America could escape from the clutches of "the Beast" that has held the reins of power since 1963. If Kennedy did not offer hope in the 1960s, what chance is there that any future leader would be inclined to give power back to the people?

In showing how a corrupted American society created Vietnam, Stone returned to the theme of *Born on the Fourth of July*. In earlier films, he showed how a culture of violence, manifested in both public and private institutions, caused one young man to go to war. *JFK* maintains the same image of America but makes a quantum leap in interpretation. Instead of exploring the effects of this culture on one person, he demonstrates how one manifestation of violence affected the course of the entire nation. Whereas Chris Taylor and Ron Kovic may have been naive individuals with no direct relation to viewers, the events in *JFK*, with Vietnam as its centerpiece, implicate all Americans who remain complacent and refuse to challenge the system.

Having, for the first time, explored the origins of the Vietnam War and situated it within a particular view of how American history operates, Stone was prepared to show how the war ended. Although it is impossible to say what he will do in the future, it may be that *Nixon* will mark Stone's final cinematic statement on the war. Although *Nixon* lacks some of the stridency of his earlier films, it reinforces the themes posited by Stone's other Vietnam War films. Instead of merely discussing the end of the war, he continues his bold explorations of the conflict's impact on both American and global history.

Even while he was president, Richard Nixon had intrigued Stone. Stone saw his father in the blunt and withdrawn executive, and the shame of Watergate helped turn Stone into a critic of America. Nixon, along with Kennedy, "shaped the era in which [he] grew up," and Stone eagerly plunged into the task of bringing the story of "the dominant figure in the latter part of this century" to the screen. Again, as with *JFK*, he engaged in the basic research required of any historian. He read "everything there was" on the ex-president and spoke with many of the people who would be portrayed on-screen. Stone also listened to some of Nixon's presidential tapes that had not yet been released to the public. Still smarting from critics' accusations that he had created characters and evidence for *JFK*, Stone released an advance copy of the script for *Nixon*, complete with hundreds of footnotes listing books, interviews, tapes, and oral histories.

At over three hours, *Nixon* is a lengthy yet compelling portrait of a complex politician. Stone's Nixon (Anthony Hopkins) is a master of detail, yet prone to confusion; a caring yet cold person; a man with a bold vision of the future who is haunted by the past. Nixon's greatest demon is the memory of JFK. Nixon resents Kennedy as only a hardscrabble, self-made man can resent a person who has been handed everything. At the same time, he maintains that he and the man from Massachusetts were like "brothers." Not content to merely expose this contradiction, Stone digs deep to explore the roots of Nixon's guilt, suggesting that he was indirectly responsible for Kennedy's death. Nixon, he says, was in charge of a program called "Track Two," a covert program to assassinate Fidel Castro, and may also have been involved in the Bay of Pigs in some way. By participating in this effort, Nixon unwittingly helped create the culture of violence that, as detailed in *JFK*, led to Kennedy's death and, as seen in *Born on the Fourth of July*, inspired Ron Kovic and others to go to war.

Although there is no evidence that Nixon knew of the plot to kill Kennedy, Stone shows him near the scene of the crime and explicitly links Kennedy's death to the Vietnam War. In the film, we see Nixon in Dallas in November 1963, meeting with a group of far-right businessmen headed by Jack Jones (Larry Hagman). As Nixon uncomfortably banters with high-class prostitutes, Jones and others urge Nixon to run for president in 1964. The wealthy businessmen are displeased with how Kennedy is handling Vietnam and promise Nixon "a shit-pot" of money and a victory in the South in exchange for a more militant foreign policy. Nixon demurs, claiming that Kennedy is unbeatable. But what if, one of the extremists asks, Kennedy does not run in 1964? Nixon is unnerved by the implications of this statement and beats a hasty retreat. Although he was clearly not responsible for Kennedy's death, Nixon's association with the forces that killed the president haunted him. Stone beautifully captures this mood by drenching the White House in a stormy, almost gothic atmosphere. In a very real sense, *Nixon* assumed the quality of a horror film.

Besides deepening his explanation of the causes of the war, Stone continues to expand his vision of how the war affected the world. *JFK* treats Vietnam as an event of national importance. *Nixon*, however, goes beyond this, and shows how the war played a critical role in the development of the global cold war. At times, *Nixon* seems to prosecute the war solely to salve his own bruised masculinity; he refuses to be pushed around by a smaller country. But, for the first time, we also see how Vietnam was but one aspect of a larger scene; Nixon refuses to back down in the face of a communist alliance. When he is in control of events, Nixon realizes that he has to continue to vigorously prosecute the war in order to gain concessions from the Soviets and the Chinese. He is successful in this endeavor. Stone shows Nixon's success in his meetings with Mao Zedong and Leonid Brezhnev. But, he argues, simply demonstrating Vietnam's importance in international politics does not make it a worthwhile war. Instead, Vietnam is reduced to a mere pawn in a global game. In January 1968, Private Stone's platoon acted as human bait to draw out a larger Vietnamese force. Other Vietnam veterans served the same purpose, only their job was to lure the world's major communist countries into negotiations with the United States. In Stone's view, the war was a chess game with one king and many pawns.

Finally, the Vietnam War comes to a close. It does not, however, reach either a glorious end or a satisfying resolution. After learning that the North Vietnamese are prepared to sign a treaty, an exhilarated Nixon calls a press conference to announce the conclusion of a successful war. He believes that he has finally negotiated a "peace with honor" and is prepared to join the country in celebration. But the press conference quickly turns hostile. One reporter challenges the president, claiming that the last several years of the war accomplished nothing, that the terms Nixon got were little different from those offered in 1968. As the president stammers, reporters bombard him with questions. Much to his surprise, they are less interested in the end of the war than in the breaking Watergate scandal. Vietnam has become a footnote in the history of the cold war. For Nixon and America, the war did not end so much as just fade away. There were no parades, no celebrations, and, for Stone and others, no closure. This stands as the final insult for a generation of soldiers and forced at least one to begin writing about his experiences. The lack of closure in 1973 led Stone to follow a twenty-year-long path to find redemption. In ending the war on-screen, Stone has taken us to the beginning of his own life as a filmmaker.

In a 1991 *Rolling Stone* interview, journalist David Breskin asked Oliver Stone if he felt like a great artist. "I never doubted it, from day one," Stone replied. "When I was eighteen, I just felt like I had a call …. And living up to that call has been the hardest part." From the first, Vietnam was an integral part of that calling. As a nineteen-year-old, he began a long, sprawling manuscript entitled "A Child's Night Dream." As a twenty-three-year-old film student at NYU, his first picture was entitled *Last Year in Vietnam*. At the age of forty, his first great commercial success as a director was *Platoon*. The circle closed eleven years later when *A Child's Night Dream*, heavily edited and slimmed down, was published by St. Martin's Press. The link between the nineteen-year-old would-be Hemingway and the fifty-one-year-old established artist was a passion for America's involvement in Vietnam – why we went, how we fought, what were the results and the implications.

In the process of becoming an artist, Stone also became the most successful and controversial historian of the war. For him, the past had an irresistible pattern, one woven with lost opportunities, conspiracies, fallen heroes, personal biographies, and impersonal forces. "I'm looking for a very difficult pattern in our history," he said. "What I see in 1963, with Kennedy's murder at high noon in Dallas, to 1974, with Nixon's removal, is a pattern." It is a pattern of promise and betrayal, vision and death, from John and Robert Kennedy to Martin Luther King, Jr., and Richard Nixon. "These four men came from different political perspectives, but they were pushing the envelope, trying to lead America to new levels. We posit that, in some way, they pissed off what we call 'the Beast,' the Beast being a force (or forces) greater than the presidency."

Stone's burden is to be history's witness. For him, the past is a very real, painful, and unresolved phenomenon. Like William Faulkner, he believes that "the past is never dead." In fact, "it's not even past." But Stone's view of history contains inherent problems. It indicts an entire culture but suggests that members of that culture can make a lasting difference. For example, in *Born on the Fourth of July*, Stone contends that a martial culture packed Ron Kovic off to Vietnam, but in *JFK* he argues that Kennedy would have ended the war and that his promise died with him. But on a higher level, Stone realizes that the duty of the historian is to keep the past alive. It is the tension between his desire to teach and entertain and his desire to be taken seriously as an arbiter of the past that makes Stone such a controversial figure. Always reluctant to accept the work of popular historians (which Stone certainly is), academics have resisted embracing his vision of the past. And yet, his Vietnam films seem to have touched a nerve in the American public. To his credit, as his fame has grown, he has consistently adopted more sophisticated methods of exploring the past. Beginning in 1986 with an insulated, autobiographical view of history, Stone has expanded his analysis to incorporate the broader themes and movements that lay behind his own experience in Vietnam. In doing this, he uses the methods of a professional historian, going so far as to issue footnotes to accompany his work. Still, Stone remains true to his vision above all else; the details must be subservient to the big picture, the facts must support the conclusion. As Stone wrote, "Elie Wiesel reminds us that survivors are all charged with a sacred mission: to serve as witnesses and teachers of what they suffered, thereby preventing such catastrophes from occurring again." It is this goal, this quest for relevance, that drives Oliver Stone's pursuit of the past, separates his work from that of academic historians, and forces Americans to decide which is more important: a truthful rendition of the facts, or facts rendered in such a way as to illustrate the truth.

26

Primary Sources

The Hollywood Rating System, 1968

In 1968, the film industry found a successful way to balance artistic independence with public demands that the movies exercise moral responsibility, The new rating system offered moviegoers an indication of the appropriate audience for a particular film.

This Code is designed to keep in close harmony with the mores, culture, the moral sense and change in our society,
   The objectives of the Code are:

1. To encourage artistic expression by expanding creative freedom,
2. To assure that the freedom which encourages the artist remains responsible and sensitive to the standards of the larger society.

Censorship is an odious enterprise, We oppose censorship and classification by governments because they are alien to the American tradition of freedom.

Much of this nation's strength and purpose is drawn from the premise that the humblest of citizens has the freedom of his own choice, Censorship destroys this freedom of choice.

It is within this framework that the Motion Picture Association continues to recognize its obligation to the society of which it is an integral part.

In our society parents are the arbiters of family conduct. Parents have the primary responsibility to guide their children in the kinds of lives they lead, the character they build, the books they read, and the movies and other entertainment to which they are exposed.

The creators of motion pictures undertake a responsibility to make available pertinent information about their pictures which will assist parents to fulfill their responsibilities.

But this alone is not enough, In further recognition of our obligation to the public, and most especially to parents, we have extended the Code operation to include a nation-wide voluntary film rating program which has as its prime objective a sensitive concern for children, Motion Pictures will be reviewed by a Code and Rating Administration which, when it reviews a motion picture as to its conformity with the standards of the Code, will issue ratings, It is our intent that all motion pictures exhibited in the United States will carry a rating. These rating are:

(G) SUGGESTED FOR GENERAL AUDIENCES
This category includes motion pictures that in the opinion of the Code and Rating Administration would be acceptable for all audiences, without consideration of age.

(M) SUGGESTED FOR MATURE AUDIENCES – ADULTS & MATURE YOUNG PEOPLE
This category includes motion pictures that in the opinion of the Code and Rating Administration, because of their theme, content and treatment, might require more mature judgment by viewers, and about which parents should exercise their discretion.

(R) RESTRICTED – PERSONS UNDER 16 NOT ADMIITED UNLESS ACCOMPANIED BY PARENTS OR ADULT GUARDIAN
This category includes motion pictures that in the opinion of the Code and Rating Administration, because of their theme, content or treatment, should not be presented to persons under 16 unless accompanied by a parent or adult guardian.

(X) PERSONS UNDER 16 NOT ADMIITED
This category includes motion pictures submitted to the Code and Rating Administration which in the opinion of the Code and Rating Administration are rated (X) because of the treatment of sex, violence, crime or profanity. Pictures rated (X) do not qualify for a Code Seal. Pictures rated (X) should not be presented to persons under 16.

The program contemplates that any distributors outside the membership of the Association who choose not to submit their motion pictures to the Code and Rating Administration will self-apply the (X) rating.

The ratings and their meanings will be conveyed by advertising; by displays at the theaters; and in other ways. Thus, audiences, especially parents, will be alerted to the theme, content, and treatment of movies, Therefore, parents can determine whether a particular picture is one which children should see at the discretion of the parent; or only when accompanied by a parent; or should not see.

We believe self-restraint, self-regulation, to be in the American tradition. The results of self-discipline are always imperfect because that is the nature of all things mortal. But this Code, and its administration, will make clear that freedom of expression does not mean toleration of license ....

Standards for Production
In furtherance of the objectives of the Code to accord with the mores, the c
and the moral sense of our society, the principles stated above and the following
standards will govern the Administrator in his consideration of motion pictures
submitted for Code approval:

–   The basic dignity and value of human life shall be respected and upheld. Restraint
    shall be exercised in portraying the taking of life.
–   Evil, sin, crime and wrong-doing shall not be justified.
–   Special restraint shall be exercised in portraying criminal or anti-social activities in
    which minors participate or are involved.
–   Detailed and protracted acts of brutality, cruelty, physical violence, torture and
    abuse shall not be presented.
–   Indecent or undue exposure of the human body shall not be presented.
–   Illicit sex relationships shall not be justified. Intimate sex scenes violating common
    standards of decency shall not be portrayed.
–   Restraint and care shall be exercised in presentations dealing with sex aberrations.
–   Obscene speech, gestures or movements shall not be presented. Undue profanity
    shall not be permitted.
–   Religion shall not be demeaned.
–   Words or symbols contemptuous of racial, religious or national groups, shall not
    be used so as to incite bigotry or hatred.
–   Excessive cruelty to animals shall not be portrayed and animals shall not be treated
    inhumanely.

Part VI
Hollywood in Our Time

Introduction
A Changing Hollywood

In the late 1960s and early 1970s, Hollywood released a series of landmark movies that radically revised old genres, offered graphically realistic portraits of American society, and presented revisionist perspectives on the American past. In 1969, films like *Easy Rider*, a countercultural tale of the travels of two bikers and drug couriers, and *Midnight Cowboy*, the story of a petty con man and a prospective gigolo, overwhelmed more conventional mainstream films like *Paint Your Wagon*, a Western musical, and *The Love Bug*, a Disney film about the adventures of a Volkswagen Beetle with a mind of its own. But by the mid-1970s, movies emphasizing alienation and laced with anti-authority themes gave way to films that were quite different. The mass audience craved action, gags, special effects, and plots that resembled roller coasters. Crowd-pleasing blockbusters, like *Jaws* and the *Star Wars* and *Indiana Jones* adventures, proliferated. Glamorous outlaws were replaced by a new breed of action hero, played by such stars as Sylvester Stallone, Jean Claude Van Damme, Clint Eastwood, Steven Segal, and Arnold Schwarzenegger.

Supplanting films that offered a probing look at the nature of American society, like *The Godfather* and *Chinatown*, were those promising fun, escape, and reassurance, not provocation. In marked contrast to films like *To Sir, With Love*, which depicted a teacher as a role model and source of inspiration, films like *Ferris Bueller's Day Off*, *Fast Times at Ridgemont High*, and Rodney Dangerfield's *Back to School* treated teachers as insensitive, affected, boring, and out of touch. Sports movies, perennial box-office losers, suddenly flourished. In a society increasingly preoccupied with competitiveness, sports movies like *Rocky*, *Breaking Away*, *Raging Bull*, *Karate Kid*, *The Natural*, *Bull Durham*, *Chariots of Fire*, and *Personal Best* expressed a fascination with victory and winning. In a period of rapidly rising divorce rates and a heightened public awareness of child abuse and domestic violence, a growing number of films dealt with family relationships. Many films, like such Academy Award winners as *Terms of Endearment*, *On Golden Pond*, and *Rain Man*, affirmed the importance of family ties. The desire for strong

Figure 14   Photograph of the real-life bank robbers Bonnie Parker and Clyde Barrow. Courtesy of the FBI.

family ties sometimes took metaphorical form, as in the blockbuster *ET: The Extra-Terrestrial*, which not only depicted an alien's yearning to return home, but also a boy's longing for the return of his own father, who has abandoned his wife and children.

At the same time, the structure of the movie industry underwent profound change, as the major studios became part of integrated entertainment conglomerates, sometimes including theme parks and magazines and other print media. A corporate preoccupation with return on investment led to an increase in sequels, special effects, and spin-offs of television shows, as well as more and more product tie-ins.

Of all the changes that have taken place in the movie industry, perhaps the most important has been the growth of home video – video cassettes, DVDs, video on demand, and other new technologies – that has rendered film-watching an increasingly private activity. Meanwhile, growing competition from the internet has led film makers to try to create the kind of immersive experiences, involving computer animation and intricate soundtracks, which personal computers can't yet match.

Still, it would be a mistake to be too pessimistic about film's future. African Americans, Asian Americans, and Latinos have made significant strides on screen and off. The digital revolution has meant that independent filmmakers have access to kinds of equipment that were wholly inaccessible a generation ago. Moviegoers have become increasingly receptive to documentaries. Alongside today's blockbusters is a host of smaller, quirkier, more idiosyncratic films that expose us to alternate sensibilities, introduce us to views of American society from different perspectives, challenge our values and presuppositions, dramatize life in its full complexity. Today, as in the past, movies retain the capacity to expand and transform our knowledge about the world around us. Movies may never again occupy the central place in our cultural imagination that they did from the 1910s to the 1980s, yet they continue to be the most important common reference point in a society in which a mass culture has given way to one that targets narrow niches and markets.

27

Feminism and Recent American Film

Gendering Expectations: Genre and Allegory in Readings of Thelma and Louise

Aspasia Kotsopoulos

In the end Thelma and Louise seem trapped, mistreated by men, lied to, beat up, falsely judged, and discarded. They are victims with no way out except to hold hands, push the pedal to the metal, and speed toward the abyss. The film is a social document of the 1980s. Released in 1991, the year when Anita Hill was accused of attempting to "bring down" a male Supreme Court nominee and there was a bubbling backlash against the feminist movement, Thelma and Louise *took stock of where women stood in American society. It is a bleak picture of life in a patriarchal society, an examination of exactly how much the feminist movement had achieved. It also raises questions concerning how much Hollywood has contributed to that patriarchal straitjacket. In the following essay Aspasia Kotsopoulos discusses the place that* Thelma and Louise *occupies in American society and Hollywood history.*

Reflecting on the vociferous attention her film received, screenwriter Callie Khouri says that the social climate into which *Thelma and Louise* (1991) was released largely explains the furor around it. This was the year of the Anita Hill/Clarence Thomas case, which drew public attention to the issue of sexual harassment in the workplace. In the American media and in politics, women's issues were constantly under scrutiny. "There was such a backlash around the Equal Rights Amendment and the bill on abortion," remembers Khouri. "The atmosphere became so hysterical, like men imagined that women were going to be storming their bathrooms!" 'Against this background of hysteria and backlash, *Thelma and Louise* emerges as testimony – a document of the times that effectively crystallizes the gender wars of that era.

In her book *Backlash: The Undeclared War Against American Women*, which documents the antifeminist backlash of the '80s, Susan Faludi describes this cultural phenomenon as a flaring up of hostility towards feminism, occurring in periods in which women are seen as making – either real or imagined – headway towards autonomy. *Backlash* suggests just how much definitions of femininity have become contested in

Aspasia Kotsopoulos, "Gendering Expectations: Genre and Allegory," in "Readings of *Thelma and Louise*," *Left History*, 8 (2003), pp. 10–33.

the last two decades. Mia Carter points out that the backlash against *Thelma and Louise* during its reception was indicative of male critics' anxiety about feminism and their inability to accept that "things have changed," that "women, whether Khouri's mythological heroines or those among *Thelma and Louise*'s passionate audience, are no longer silent, passive creatures." The reaction against feminism and against a film like *Thelma and Louise* demonstrates the degree to which women's movements have been successful in challenging traditional assumptions.

Thelma and Louise is a backlash representation but not in the usual sense – not as an instance but as a fantasy enactment of backlash as experienced by women. The film maps women's experience of backlash from the moment in which the two women begin to assert themselves to the moment in which force is used to stop them. In allegorical fashion, the film plays out the process by which women's challenges to authority have resulted in a breakdown of consensus. The film gives symbolic expression to women's worst fears about backlash, before that expression is contained. Like *Basic Instinct* (1992), *Fatal Attraction* (1987) or *The Temp* (1993), *Thelma and Louise* may be reassuring to those who are committed to patriarchal authority and who are, consequently, disturbed by Thelma and Louise's transgression. Like these other films, *Thelma and Louise* may very well be read as an endorsement of backlash, as a warning to women who seek autonomy. Through the two women's deaths, the film does indeed reinforce the status quo. But this kind of conservative reading is rendered problematic because the film draws upon women's experiences as raw material for its fantasy. This is contrary to the backlash films mentioned, which speak solely from, to and about patriarchal anxieties over liberated women. Within this volatile ideological climate, *Thelma and Louise* becomes meaningful for an astonishing array of positions. This paper analyzes the film as a confused and baffled response to its own historical situation.

Along these lines, *Thelma and Louise* displays a consciousness of popularized feminist concerns, and seeks to incorporate such discourses while simultaneously adhering to the contradictory institutional demands of Hollywood filmmaking – that is, the demands for established forms and genres, as well as for novelty and contemporaneity. According to Christine Gledhill, while Hollywood production is indeed formula-bound, the drive to appear contemporary and innovative necessitates that even the most formulaic of plots must address, however obliquely, the topical issues of the day and offer new approaches to old genres.

Besides addressing issues of interest to the women's movement, one of Hollywood's other recent nods to feminism has been to insert women into protagonist roles in traditionally male genres such as the Western (e.g., *Bad Girls* [1994]; *The Quick and the Dead* [1995]) or the detective thriller (e.g., *Black Widow* [1987], *Blue Steel* [1990]; *The Silence of the Lambs* [1991]; *Copy Cat* [1995]). As a road movie, *Thelma and Louise* belongs to this recent trend in Hollywood filmmaking. The road movie thematizes transformation through journey, with the main characters' movement from a familiar context to an unfamiliar space leading to personal discovery. Combining aspects of the buddy film, the outlaw couple film and the Western, the road movie often traces the picaresque adventures of two male friends as they bond across a natural landscape and through their mutual disregard for women and social institutions, in particular the law and community. Whether on the road as in *Easy Rider* (1969) or the wide-open range as in *Butch Cassidy and the Sundance Kid* (1969), these men are romantic outsiders unable to live within society and its rules, rebelliously seeking freedom from social convention. Paradoxically and typically, these characters are conventional themselves. They are hardly transgressive since, ultimately, they help to perpetuate closely held American myths about free will, rugged individualism and self-reliance.

Thelma and Louise draws upon road-movie codes, parachuting women into a traditionally male genre, to mobilize the desires of its contemporary female audience. The intersection of gender and genre inflects this film so that it speaks about ideological struggles in the late '80s/early '90s. The road movie regenerates itself to become a fantasy enactment of recent social conflict over notions of the law, gender and heterosexual relations. *Thelma and Louise* aptly illustrates Gledhill's notion of textual negotiation. As a generic hybrid, this film blends aspects of the road movie and the woman's film, offering gender-bending twists to old Hollywood conventions while also acknowledging popular feminist concerns around male violence against women. Yet genre also socializes us towards specific expectations. What happens when those expectations are not met?

The issue of violence places *Thelma and Louise* and others like it within the context of mainstream battle-of-the-sexes rhetoric. As a hegemonic strategy, "battle of the sexes" works to obscure feminist concerns with structural, gender-based inequalities. Battle of the sexes implies a natural, inevitable conflict abstracted from historical and systemic conditions. Moreover, it suggests a power struggle for the supremacy of one sex over the other, and perpetuates the misogynist stereotype of the feminist as a castrating bitch or – to use a term that had special currency during the release of *Thelma and Louise* – a "feminazi" on and off the screen. This is not the only public discourse in which to situate these films. In recent years, women's movements in Canada and the United States have raised awareness on women's issues. Sexual harassment, date rape and domestic violence have been on the public agenda – they are popular issues that twenty-five years ago had no vocabulary. Women's movements have also brought attention to the ways in which social institutions often fail to protect women against male abuses in the workplace and in the home. Issues once associated with feminism only are now daily concerns in Canada and in the United States, regardless of how women and men situate themselves in relation to feminism. Films like *Thelma and Louise* represent the impact of feminist thought on public discussion.

The film attempts to negotiate the concerns outlined, raising topical questions about male violence against women, women and the law, heterosexual relations, and relationships between women. The film also works within ideological and generic parameters that limit its engagement with these social issues, generating meanings that are, in some cases, contradictory, and in others, clearly hegemonic. The symbolic treatment of gender relations and women's issues is potentially ambiguous – and therefore politically dubious – in that it depends upon an interpretive strategy sensitive to allegory to successfully align viewers' perspectives with the protagonists', creating identification and empathy. Similarly, the interaction of gender and genre confounds expectations and – depending on how wedded one is to convention – produces readings that either decry or celebrate gender/genre transgressions. Given these factors, the diverse and diametrically opposed readings ascribed to *Thelma and Louise*, especially amongst feminists, make it an excellent example for engaging with questions around meaning and polysemy [the ability of a work to have multiple meanings].

The film's reception in particular has been well documented. Here, academic critics as well as film reviewers pay attention to the gendering of readings, showing that interpretations of *Thelma and Louise* have been split along gender lines, with male critics decrying the film as an example of violent, battle-of-the-sexes male-bashing and a threat to American moral standards, and female critics arguing that the film addresses the social experiences of American women, expressing their concerns about sexual harassment and rape, and the law's insensitive treatment of women victimized by such crimes. The latter are issues that, Mia Carter points out, male critics often ignore, focusing instead on the film's representation of men. Indeed, Brenda Cooper's 1999 analysis of student responses to *Thelma and Louise* uncovers the same gender split.

A less-documented aspect of reception has been the split amongst feminists. Some feminist critics such as Alice Cross and Pat Dowell maintain that *Thelma and Louise* is reactionary and even offensive to women (e.g., the film is nothing more than a regressive male-buddy film in female drag; the film acts as a warning to women who challenge the status quo), while others, such as Mia Carter, Patricia Mann, Martha Minow, Susan Morrison, and Elizabeth V. Spelman, assert its progressive qualities, its potential to open readings for female and/or feminist viewers. To make a progressive reading, each of these critics raises important points: Carter suggests that readings must pay attention to what male critics ignore in their interpretations; Morrison argues the film must be read in the context of the woman's film rather than the road movie; Minow and Spelman observe that readings of the film depend on how one situates oneself in relation to the law and authority; and Mann maintains the film must be read allegorically as a parable for our times. She notes that literal readings of the film have resulted in "an anxious and hostile torrent" from "sophisticated reviewers who usually accept the brutality and anarchy of contemporary films as unobjectionable cultural and political tropes [but] found it difficult to respond to the narrative of *Thelma and Louise* metaphorically."

Thelma and Louise engages with each of the ideological agendas various critics impart to it. The result is that *Thelma and Louise* presents us with a layered, polysemic essay on contemporary gender relations. My response to previous writings will be to bear in mind the textual qualities that make both reactionary and progressive claims on the film possible. I want to hold the text accountable, in some measure, for the politically opposed readings it has produced. The focus on reception, specifically on the gender of audience members, overlooks a consideration of the text and the way in which it is itself contradictory and ambiguous – something which individuals involved with the production readily admit.

Production and Publicity

A look at press accounts of the production of *Thelma and Louise* and at promotional publicity surrounding the film and its stars sketches out the apparent conditions under which this film was made. While the circulation of such information would have an impact on readings, I am more concerned with how press accounts may suggest conflicts during the making of *Thelma and Louise* that may have become manifest in the text.

Discussions of the screenplay in mainstream media accounts focus on the feminism of its author, Callie Khouri, and on industry interest in the story. Khouri was a first-time screenwriter when she penned the Oscar-winning screenplay for *Thelma and Louise*. In interviews, Khouri identifies herself as a feminist, but also claims she did not write *Thelma and Louise* with the intention of producing a feminist tract, contrary to what her critics might claim: "I am a feminist, so clearly it is going to have my point of view. But this is a movie about outlaws, and it's not fair to judge it in terms of feminism." Khouri explains that her concern with the lack of respectable film roles for women led her to write the screenplay. In 1989, director Ridley Scott, known for his genre-twisting in films such as *Alien* (1979) and *Blade Runner* (1982), optioned her script with plans to use it as a project for his production company. According to *New York Times* writer Larry Rohter, "[Khouri's script] became the talk of Hollywood – or at least of agents with female clients," and "attracted the attention of the four big studios and big stars like Goldie Hawn, Cher and Michelle Pfeiffer." Scott says he had no plans to direct the film himself, until he shopped the screenplay around to various top directors and found their reactions so positive, he decided he would take it on as director.

Reports in popular magazines and newspapers suggest that the screenplay's circulation within the industry did not generate controversy but genuine interest. Given that *Thelma and Louise* was the first screenplay of a virtual unknown, such interest is remarkable and speaks to industry confidence in the wide appeal the film could garner. From the perspective of female stars, the screenplay no doubt was refreshing in that it featured not one but two female roles in a narrative that put women front and centre. As actor Geena Davis, who plays Thelma, comments, "I had been hearing about this great script with not one but two great parts for women, which is a very unusual event … [I] just loved both the parts. Its not often you see parts for two fully realized women characters and have a movie be about women's adventures and journey." This discourse around the screenplay suggests there were no concerns that the film would alienate audiences. In a 1996 interview, actor Susan Sarandon, who plays Louise, comments that at the time she was making *Thelma and Louise*, she had no idea it would inspire the heated debate that it did, implying that outcry over the film came as a surprise. According to Sarandon, "I don't quite understand what happened, because I thought it was just a cowboy movie with trucks and women instead of guys and horses." Khouri expresses similar dismay, stating, "I couldn't keep up with the number of people who attacked me. I didn't think what I wrote was even mildly offensive, and all these people were calling me a fascist."

Relying on hindsight and media accounts of the film's production is problematic. On the one hand it may be that publicity was controlled so as to contain any mention of conflicts over the script during the filming. On the other hand, it may be that confidence in the script was so high that concerns, if there were any, were minor. In any case, press coverage gives a picture of an ordinary, routine and uneventful production – surprising considering the controversy the film subsequently generated. Rohter even reports that MGM/Pathe, the studio that took on Scott and *Thelma and Louise*, "promised not to force Ms. Khouri and Mr. Scott to tinker with the script or change the dramatic conclusion."

While this is somewhat astonishing, it isn't if one considers just how ambiguous Khouri's screenplay is. As Harvey R. Greenberg puts it, "Khouri's script … enhances the film's ambiguous openness for interpretation by sharply scanting information of the protagonist[s'] prior lives, except for a few bold strokes. What one gets of the women is what one sees." Indeed, interviews with Sarandon suggest the script was so full of holes the actors "had to come up with so much backstory" in order to find motivation for the characters. Discussing the emotional logic behind Louise's shooting of Harlan, Sarandon explains that a backstory had to be constructed: it was decided that Louise was re-living her rape in Texas, after seeing her friend humiliated in a similar way. In the same interview, Sarandon cites other scenes that were either rewritten or supplied as backstory, including Thelma and Louise's different methods of packing, as well as the actual shooting. According to Sarandon, there was discussion as to whether or not the shooting should be interpreted as an assassination, indicating anxiety with the scene, an anxiety that would later be echoed more vociferously in the film's critical reception. "What I didn't want it to be, which was discussed, was an assassination; I didn't feel [Louise] was together enough to do that," explains Sarandon. "When she says, 'Buddy, you keep your mouth shut,' after he's obviously dead, it shows she's gone off a bit." In a later interview, Sarandon states, "In the script, she takes a stance and executes him. I couldn't imagine her taking that stance. I wanted to change it so she just brings the gun up and it goes off – which is what happens sometimes with guns." Sarandon's comments are revealing. While there doesn't appear to have been concern over the screenplay in the sense that it might be offensive or alienating, there was nonetheless a concern with its ambiguity and with how the shooting might be read. Significantly, this concern is framed in terms of character motivation rather than ideology or politics.

Knowing Me Knowing You

Independence and freedom are central to *Thelma and Louise*. The film's opening sequence sets up the primary conflict that motivates the narrative: a woman's desire for freedom from male authority. The sequence cuts between Louise working at the restaurant and Thelma trying to contend with her domineering, loudmouthed husband, Daryl. The mise-en-scène of the opening sequence suggests the entrapment of the two women. Louise winds her way between tables and customers, and Thelma contends with the domestic chaos of her cramped suburban kitchen. Both women move in spaces that are cluttered, and both women are tightly framed by the camera.

On the telephone, Louise tells Thelma she wants to get out of town to punish her boyfriend who is unwilling to make a commitment to her. As Daryl, who cannot find his socks, blusters in the background, Louise cajoles Thelma, calling her a "little housewife," in an effort to persuade her to abandon Daryl for the weekend. Thelma replies that she has not asked his permission yet, prompting Louise to inquire impatiently and accusingly, "Is he your husband or your father?" Louise's question signals the film's first challenge to traditional gender relations. While in another historical context, one might have answered there is no difference, in a '90s context the question brings attention to the ongoing re-definition of heterosexual relations occurring in the wake of second-wave feminism. However, Daryl is characterized as a buffoon rather than a menace, and this sets off several possible meanings.

Mann comments that Daryl's blustering "suggests the empty quality of patriarchal authority" in contemporary America. This characterization of Daryl also lessens the threat the film poses to sexist male audience members, who can breathe a sigh of relief: they are not him since Daryl's sexism is excessive and comical while theirs is reasonable and normal (read: invisible). Cooper sees the film's "mockery" of "macho stereotypes" as constructing a female gaze that challenges patriarchal authority. While I agree that male stereotypes such as Daryl, as well as others (e.g., the working-class rapist, the obnoxious truck driver, the arrogant cop, the seductive cowboy), invite women's recognition, I am not convinced these pose a challenge, but instead, may be recuperative. The stereotypes have the potential to distance the men on the screen from men in real life and from those sitting in the audience, rendering the fantasy safe. The problem becomes some men rather than an entire society founded on patriarchal assumptions, and criticism is rechanneled so that it is directed at male caricatures like Daryl.

Moreover, the conflicts that emerge from Thelma's oppressive domestic situation, however comical, help trigger her search for autonomy, suggesting that a woman's desire for self-determination is in need of exterior justification – In this case, an extreme jerk for a husband. The implication is that if Daryl had been different, Thelma's inclination toward female autonomy might never have existed. As Thelma later says to a police officer who has a wife, "You be sweet to her. My husband wasn't and look how I turned out." However, Daryl's demands on Thelma, even if they appear ideologically contradictory and are stretched to the point of ridiculousness, still speak to frustrations expressed in many other examples of women's popular cultural practices such as the soap opera, the fashion magazine and the woman's film. The familiarity and recognizability of the question Louise asks ("Is he your husband or your father?") is important, then, in that it links up with a host of heterosexual women's frustrations – from unsatisfying relationships with men to an unfair share of the housework to the vague feeling that there could be more to life – and opens space for a negotiation of meanings that may relate allegorically to broader women's experiences.

While Louise starts off as the stronger, more experienced, and independent-minded of the two women, the story belongs to Thelma and her transformation from a meek, obliging housewife who has never been out of town without her husband, to a (quasi-) feminist, gun-wielding, whiskey-drinking outlaw. Still, Louise is set up, initially, as Thelma's older, more knowledgeable role model. At the beginning of the road trip, Thelma, with unlit cigarette, emulates Louise smoking. "Hey, I'm Louise," she says to her friend, signifying her desire to be like Louise, to know what she knows. The naive woman's fascination with the experienced woman links Thelma and Louise to previous examples of the woman's film such as *Rebecca* (1939), *All About Eve* (1950) and *Desperately Seeking Susan* (1985). While the first two films render this fascination problematic, the latter one like *Thelma and Louise* valorizes it and encourages it.

Indeed, after Thelma's admission of wanting to be like Louise, the film works as wish-fulfillment, much like the bump on the head Roberta/Rosanna Arquette receives which makes her believe she is Susan/Madonna. It is not surprising, then, that Daryl refers to Louise as a "bad influence" on Thelma. Moreover, the two women resemble each other from the start (both have red hair, with Geena Davis dying hers for the part of Thelma), and increasingly so as the narrative progresses. At the outset of the trip, Thelma wears big hair and a frilly dress, while Louise sports a tidy hairdo and chic spangled jacket. While on the run, each woman discards the accoutrements of femininity – Thelma, her frilly dress and Louise, her jewelry and lipstick. Through a process of deglamorization, they come to look more and more like each other, in jeans, T-shirts and loose hair.

Journalists writing about Davis and Sarandon at the time of the film's release want to strongly identify the two actors with their respective characters. Writers often construct Sarandon as a rarity in Hollywood: a mature woman who still gets good jobs and is allowed to be sexy and smart; and a positive role model and inspiration for younger women. This latter discourse around Sarandon frames media accounts of the relationship between Davis and Sarandon during the film's making. *People Weekly*'s Jim Jerome reports that the film represented a "chance for Davis to bond with a fellow actress" and claims "Sarandon became a role model for Davis." Both these comments are interesting given that the film is about female bonding and about the naïve Thelma's transformation into her role model, the worldly and wise Louise. Davis is quoted speaking admiringly of her co-star: "She's great and strong and wonderful. I used to tease her and say, 'When can I be like you?' " *Premiere*'s Rachel Abramowitz goes so far as to imply that Davis's feminist consciousness was raised because of her experiences making this film: "Ever since *Thelma and Louise*, Davis has been more politically engaged, speaking mostly on women's rights. When Faludi's *Backlash* appeared [the same year as *Thelma and Louise*], Davis sent out copies to a number of Hollywood colleagues. She's taken more public stands." Parallels between Davis and Thelma seem hard to resist, and Davis is sometimes described in words that could be used to describe Thelma, particularly around her desire to be free and in charge of her life. As Jerome writes, "[F]or Davis – as for Thelma – the name of the game is independence ...."

Key to Thelma's transformation is the acquisition of the knowledge that Louise possesses, while the knowledge that passes from Louise to Thelma is never explicitly spoken in the film. What Louise knows (from an experience in Texas to which she refuses to refer) and what Thelma subsequently learns at the road house, where she narrowly escapes a rape, can be read symbolically as a female initiation into patriarchal relations. Feminist critics such as Rhona Berenstein, Karen Hollinger, Alison Light, Susan Morrison, and Tania Modleski have written about *Rebecca* in this way, suggesting that the girl (we never learn her name) comes into maturity once she learns the terrible truth about the position of women in a patriarchal culture, and subsequently must choose between the worldly and independent Rebecca, the image she wishes to become and who threatens patriarchal authority, and Maxim, who represents that authority and whose approval the girl seeks. In the end, she chooses the latter. While comparing the narrative of a gothic romance to that of a road movie may seem like a stretch, it may be that feminizing a male genre involves the incorporation of narrative codes that are familiar to female audiences, that draw from women's genres, and that speak in some way to shared anxieties arising from similar social experiences.

Thelma learns the terrible truth about patriarchal dominance of which Louise never speaks. With this knowledge, she rejects her husband, her former self as a "little housewife" and chooses Louise over patriarchal authority. More correctly, the women choose each other, an aspect of the film that appealed strongly to female viewers, as Cooper was able to prove in her reception study. Moreover, Thelma and Louise's rejection of patriarchal authority and their refusal to give heterosexual relations primacy over their friendship has led to readings of the film as a lesbian coming-out story, which not only widens the film's address, but further accentuates the threat the women's relationship poses to patriarchal authority, as represented in the narrative by the law.

Rape and Allegory

The road to Thelma's transformation is a treacherous one placing her further and further outside the law. It begins at the road house where the two women have stopped to have a drink on their way to their destination. Here, an increasingly drunk Thelma dances and flirts with the stranger Harlan, much to Louise's annoyance. Later, Harlan beats and tries to rape Thelma in the parking lot, until Louise comes to the rescue with the gun Thelma packed for the trip in case of "psycho killers." Thelma's frightened imagination at the start of the trip illustrates what Carter calls "the truth of women's grim social awareness; too often we are afraid." Indeed, Thelma's fears at the beginning of the trip become manifested in the form of the rapist Harlan. When Harlan shows no remorse for his attack, and instead hurls sexual insults at the women, Louise shoots him dead.

Harlan's murder is one of the more difficult scenes to read in the film and has produced the most controversy, generating conflicting interpretations. The scene produces at least two possible readings, one literal, the other allegorical, each with different political implications. The literal reading interprets the attempted rape and subsequent murder as an advertisement for vigilantism: the scene advocates that individuals take the law into their own hands, acting as judge, jury and executioner. That Louise shoots Harlan in response to verbal rather than physical abuse makes it difficult, according to these accounts, to justify the punishment she metes out. Moreover, the scene draws an equivalence between the violence of language and the violence of rape so that two key feminist concerns – male violence against women and the power of language to perpetuate misogyny – become conflated instead of remaining separate but connected. This conflation gives grounds to criticize feminists as politically correct, humorless feminazis who take everything too seriously (e.g., you can't say anything these days for fear a feminazi might slap you with a harassment suit). In addition, the popular recognition of rape as a feminist issue links the scene to radical feminism's "kill-your-rapist" rhetoric, which has been attacked in the mainstream, interpreted in a battle-of-the-sexes context, and has served to further marginalize feminisms of all kinds.

This literal reading may be further divided into those that are feminist and those that are anti-feminist, with both, ironically enough, rejecting the film as dangerous and reactionary. In a literal feminist reading, the scene is damaging to feminism and to women because it misrepresents feminist concerns with language and violence, and plays into the hands of conservatives who fear that the feminazis are going too far and must be stopped (by film's end, they are). In a literal anti-feminist reading, the scene validates hegemonic anxieties about unruly, hysterical feminists who are getting out of control and must be reined in (by the conclusion, they are). As Dowell remarks, "Thelma and Louise have made their most indelible mark as cautionary figures for men. (Less noted is the fact that they serve as a warning to women.)"

When read allegorically, however, the scene has altogether different ideological implications. Rather than conflating issues of sexist language and male violence against women, an allegorical reading sees these two feminist concerns as metonymic representations in the film. Metonymy works by using a part or element of something to stand in for the whole. Metonyms depend upon our skill at constructing the rest from the part we have been given. In *Thelma and Louise*, the attempted rape and the subsequent verbal attack are parts that make up the whole of women's social experiences in a sexist society. With this in mind, Harlan's death takes on particular connotations and acts as a lightning rod drawing to it social questions that the film wants to explore. As Putnam explains it, the murder is committed

> ... to avenge not only this outrage [the verbal assault after the sexual assault] but all of the little rapes, the everyday usurpations of female autonomy that all women know. Viewed allegorically, the scene portrays the ritual re-enactment of cultural conflicts at the heart of women's everyday lives. The actual social world is magnified, symbolized, throughout this sequence of crime and redress.

Harlan represents every misogynist we have ever encountered. In the role of feminist avenger, Louise shoots Harlan for Thelma, and as we later learn, for herself in reaction to a past trauma of which she will not speak. Harlan is symbolically exorcised, cast out, by Louise's bullet in punishment for all the times a woman's agency has been denied, either through violence or language. The film illustrates in larger-than-life proportions the interconnectedness of sexist language and male violence against women, and the ways in which women are routinely dismissed, silenced, or humiliated. Read allegorically, the scene demonstrates Thelma and Louise's right to say no to all forms of misogyny and to be heard rather than ignored. The actual use of this reading strategy bears up in Cooper's research. She found that female students interpreted the shooting "as the desire to overcome powerlessness" in a system that leaves women with "no voice" and "few choices." Most male students in the study were unable to make the metonymic links necessary for an allegorical reading. To put it another way, the female students, like the actors, supplied the backstory the film needed, while the male students could not.

Along these lines, the waitress at the road house offers the best reading of Harlan's murder. Interpretations of the crime depend upon the degree to which the viewer is willing to metonymically relate the waitress's comments to the experiences of Thelma and Louise and women generally. During the police investigation, the waitress tells the key investigator that she "hope[s] it was his wife who did it" and that "I coulda told you he'd end up buying it." Without saying anything explicit, the waitress knows (and presumably, the women in the audience know) what kind of man Harlan is, and that sooner or later (we hope) he would pay for it. In this reading, the experiences of women are the focus and not the murder itself (which, conversely, tends to be the case in the literal readings). As Minow and Spelman state, "[Louise] shoots in judgment; she has judged that he will not stop this behaviour and that even if Thelma gets away, other women will be victimized."

Elayne Rapping has written that Louise's shooting of Harlan during the verbal attack instead of the sexual assault "muddies the political waters hopelessly." As it is, the shooting opens *Thelma and Louise* to various interpretations, resulting in a relativism that renders feminist, oppositional claims on the film as legitimate as hegemonic ones. Still, to see a man punished by a woman for his sexism rather than a woman for her sexuality gives the film a unique political resonance. While the fate of the femme fatale rarely inspires the righteous indignation of male film reviewers, it is interesting that the death of a misogynist asshole could inspire an outpouring of moral outrage. Comments by Davis and Khouri aptly sum up the situation: defending the film against charges of male-bashing, Davis argued, "If you're feeling threatened, you are identifying with the wrong character," and Khouri, maintaining that the film is not hostile toward men, stated, "I think it is hostile toward idiots."

Women and the Law

Thelma and Louise flee the crime scene because of Louise's conviction that they cannot go to the police. At various points the option of turning to the police for help is presented either by Thelma or by Hal/Harvey Keitel, the sympathetic cop, who wants to help the women at the same time that he is tracking them down, bringing with him the force of the law. *Thelma and Louise* displays a consciousness of contemporary feminist critiques of the law and its insensitive, inadequate treatment of women who have experienced male violence. Moreover, the film suggests that Louise has been mishandled by the law previously in Texas. She knows they will not be believed. They have been drinking and Thelma was seen flirting with Harlan. When Thelma first mentions the idea of going to the police and explaining to them what happened, Louise says the police wouldn't believe her because "a hundred goddamn people saw you dancing cheek to cheek ... We don't live in that kind of world!" *Thelma and Louise* works from our knowledge of recent, publicized rape trials where women have been required to prove they did not provoke or deserve the assault. As Carter points out,

> The sad truths of the real world and the disappointing scenarios of too many recent rape trials have taught women that they will not be believed, however battered and bruised and no matter how well-witnessed the crime .... Many women understand all too well why Thelma and Louise fled.

The question of whether or not Thelma was asking for it echoes public discussions of where the blame lies in rape cases. In this way, the women's personal and private conversation become a social conversation. Their conversations inside the car work in the same way that conversations do in the soap opera, with characters recounting dramatic events through fragments of conversation in an attempt to make sense of them and give them meaning. *Thelma and Louise* attempts to blend (masculine) action with (feminine) conversation which is indicative of the textual negotiations the film enters into as it tries to feminize the road movie through codes more familiar in women's genres such as the soap opera and the woman's film. Minow and Spelman comment that

> Although the law put them beyond its ken and beyond its protection, Thelma and Louise engage in a continual discussion about blame and guilt, and about responsibility and obedience. Placing at the center these outlaws' views of law and morality displaces societal images of the outlaw as amoral. Their own moral judgments afford a critical perspective on law and conventional morality.

Considerable negotiation occurs between differing viewpoints on issues of blame and responsibility. However, both Thelma and Louise eventually reject the notion that a woman's behaviour is in any way culpable in her own assault. Furthermore, despite the best intentions of individuals like Hal, the film is firm in its conviction that institutional law does not work on women's behalf, but instead, turns the victims into criminals, forcing Thelma and Louise to take the law into their own hands.

The law works to define notions of criminality and justice, which are often gendered concepts. To stress the point, the film sets up a contradiction between the way in which the film's police and legal discourses define Thelma and Louise, and the way in which the two women are constructed for the audience. We are given two views of Thelma and Louise, which complicates our relationship to the women and to the law, no matter where we may stand on the issues portrayed. The events leading up to and including Thelma's robbery of the convenience store provide a good example. Here, Thelma and Louise pick up a charming hitchhiker named J.D./Brad Pitt, with whom Thelma has a fling (the film's way of demonstrating what consensual sex between strangers looks like), during which he explains to her the patter he uses when conducting an armed robbery. The morning after, J.D. steals Louise's $6,700 in savings, the money the two women were using to get to Mexico. When the women discover the theft, Louise is devastated, about to give in to the law, until Thelma takes charge, and robs a convenience store. When the hold-up occurs, the audience is positioned outside the store with Louise, who is unaware of Thelma's actions until she comes running out of the store telling Louise to start the car. Thelma's behaviour here is unexpected since, up until this point, she has been passive with Louise making all the plans. Thelma's crime is captured on the store video. The first time the audience actually sees the crime is on this video, which the police investigators and Thelma's husband are watching as evidence of the two women's criminal inclinations. The scene makes us privy to the kinds of interpretations that the spectacle of Thelma – conducting an armed robbery using J.D.'s self-assured patter – can produce. When read through the lens of the law, Thelma, and by extension Louise, are criminals, armed and dangerous. But an alternative reading presents itself, arising from the viewer's role as witness to the social experiences that led to their criminal behaviour (i.e., Harlan's murder, the convenience-store robbery, the destruction of the truck driver's rig, the locking of the officer in the trunk of his cruiser). By positioning the viewer as witness to the crimes, the film presents a reading of Thelma and Louise as women misdefined by the law and wronged by a sexist society. As Minow and Spelman point out,

> The law has its own rules about what are the relevant and irrelevant facts about people's lives. The price of being protected by the law in court is to surrender control over the telling of your story .... Had Thelma and Louise turned themselves over to the law – whether to the sheriff or to an attorney – they would have become subject to constraints much like those from which they found themselves fleeing, constraints which among other things make their versions of themselves and of the world irrelevant.

The law attempts to seize control of Thelma and Louise's story, in order to put in its place a version of the two women that is in keeping with received notions of criminal women. "I almost feel like I know you, Louise," says detective Hal. "I know what happened to you in Texas." Quick to reply, Louise says, "You don't know me," challenging Hal's claim to knowledge of her story. To further accentuate the conflicting versions available of Thelma and Louise, the scene of the police watching the spectacle of the robbery on video is followed by a scene in which Louise admonishes Thelma not to litter. While this is a minor incident, its inclusion serves to illustrate a point: these women are not without morals nor a sense of social responsibility.

Making the audience privy to Thelma and Louise's points of view complicates viewers' attitudes towards the law and other social institutions. Louise is keenly aware of how the law is defining her and positioning her in relation to the rest of society, whereas Thelma has difficulty in apprehending the shift that has taken place in her social position. "We're fugitives now," says Louise to Thelma, "Start behaving like that." But what constitutes fugitive behaviour, and who gets to decide are questions that always hover on the surface and that also illustrate the film's strong links to the outlaw-couple film.

The Female Outlaw Couple

The outlaw-couple film has its origins in the American, Depression-era gangster film, where the gangster is sympathetically portrayed as someone who overcomes class limitations and defies the class hierarchy of capitalist society. These films ask: who is the bigger criminal, the gangster or the capitalist society? And where does responsibility for criminal behaviour lie, in the individual or the society? *Thelma and Louise* works in similar ways but as an indictment against patriarchy (as well as, though to a lesser degree, capitalism). *Thelma and Louise* demonstrates the way in which a Hollywood genre renews itself to become an enactment of contemporary social conflict. According to Glenn Man,

> Analogous to such forbearers as Rico (Edward G. Robinson, *Little Caesar* 1930) and Tony Camonte (Paul Muni, *Scarface* 1932), who dare to disturb the hierarchy of class in society through criminal violence, Thelma and Louise disrupt their gendered placement in society and therefore must be brought to task or eliminated as threats to the status quo, the traditional fate of all movie gangsters … What once passed as social/class oppression in the genre now becomes a social/gender oppression in the 1990s.

In gangster films featuring outlaw couples, the pair is forced to live outside society but not by choice. In films such as *They Live By Night* (1948), *Gun Crazy* (1949), *Bonnie and Clyde* (1967) and *Thieves Like Us* (1974), social forces are portrayed unsympathetically and the outlaw couples are romanticized because they are presented as victims of a corrupt society. As *Ms. Magazine* film reviewer Kathy Maoi states, "Thelma and Louise become outlaws not because they love violence, but because men won't leave them be." As an outlaw couple film, *Thelma and Louise* exposes the inadequacies of patriarchal society. In the end, society wins out and, as is traditional, the outlaw couple is destroyed.

Moreover, as a female same-sex outlaw couple, Thelma and Louise's threat is magnified. While their flouting of the law threatens authority in general terms, the fact of their femaleness increases their threat. Like (Arbuthnot and Seneca's argument about) *Gentlemen Prefer Blondes* (1953), *Thelma and Louise* is unique in that it presents us with a female friendship that is not tainted by jealousy or competition but instead is based on loyalty, caring, and mutual admiration. This is a departure from films that portray women in competition with each other for the attention of men or that render female same-sex identification as narcissistic or even pathological, as in *All About Eve* (1950) or *Single White Female* (1992). By contrast, *Thelma and Louise* emphasizes the women's allegiance to each other in a positive way, and as such, poses the ultimate threat to patriarchy – lesbianism and the elimination of the male, or more symbolically, of a reassuring patriarchal presence. Men may bond with other men (with the unstated rule that they never have sex with each other) in the interests of shoring up misogyny and male dominance, as they do in the male buddy film or the film noir, but women are not to bond with other women, either as friends or especially as lovers, and they are not to put their relationships with women (if they are misguided enough to have any) above those with men. Doing so makes outlaws of women.

Discussing the outlaw in American mythology, Minow and Spelman argue that our ability to accept outlaws as noble depends on how we judge the outlaws' worldview and their actions:

> Viewers of *Thelma and Louise* who are ready to regard the two women as noble outlaws have to be able to think about both the women and those affected by their actions in fairly specific ways. Thelma and Louise have to be seen as acting, preferably self-consciously, in accordance with a just principle or concern. The would-be rapist Harlan and others directly affected by the women's actions have to be seen as in some sense deserving what they got, whether or not the law prohibits their being treated that way.

Minow and Spelman's conclusions aptly account for the competing readings available of *Thelma and Louise*, and bring us back to literal versus allegorical readings: in order to justify Louise's shooting of Harlan, the viewer is required to make metonymic links between other aspects of the film and the social world in which Thelma and Louise, and the female audience members, live. Producing a reading that justifies Harlan's punishment is impossible without a sense of that social world, as Cooper found in her analysis of student responses to the film.

On their road trip, the women encounter a "miscellany of masculinity" from the would-be rapist Harlan, to the obnoxious truck driver, to the paternalistic Hal. As Ann Putnam notes, the two women travel through "a landscape awash in waves of pumping testosterone: spouting steam, spraying planes, spilling hoses, pumping oil riggers, and men pumping iron and pumping gas." Thelma and Louise's personal moral code is not in keeping with that of the male-dominated world in which they live but rather reflects their social experiences as women. Their defiance of conventional expectation is rendered all the more transgressive because they are women who reject traditional femininity. Because Thelma and Louise refuse to passively accept the routine victimization of women, they threaten patriarchal authority – an authority dependent, in part, upon women's quiescence. If a viewer is committed to the gender status quo, then *Thelma and Louise* is bound to be discomfiting, as its critical reception has indicated.

Along these lines, and as Minow and Spelman maintain, who the outlaw is also determines their status as noble or ignoble. In Thelma and Louise's case, we are referring to two, straight, white women from working- to lower-middle-class backgrounds. What is the effect of their gender and social status on possible readings and on viewers' relationships to the two characters? The importation of women into a traditionally male genre requires a degree of genderbending accompanied by a sense of gender transgression. In this case, women, usually defined as having nurturing, non-violent, passive qualities, are committing crimes at gun-point, including acts of violence against domineering men. If one is committed to male dominance, a certain amount of discomfort will be connected to the punishments Thelma and Louise mete out, making the two characters anything but noble in their affront to patriarchal authority. As Maoi comments, "Women can shoot a gun for the government and blow away anyone who threatens their men or their kids, but any 'heroine' who packs a pistol against systematic male violence is going to take some heat." In this reading, even the deaths of Thelma and Louise may not be enough to quell fears of unruly women because the spectre of their example lingers, long after the projector stops. Thelma and Louise's gender transgression exceeds closure, and this is best exemplified by the way in which the film, after the two women have (presumably) plunged to their deaths in the Grand Canyon, reverts to a montage of narrative high points during the end credits, reminding the audience of the women's strength and exuberance.

Even if one is not committed to the status quo, it still may be difficult to produce a progressive reading. Thelma and Louise's gender transgression may work to produce diametrically opposed feminist readings which jeopardizes their status as noble outlaws, and which, broadly speaking, indicates struggles amongst feminists over issues of gender and representation. Are the characters' gender transgressions justified as an allegory for contemporary feminist concerns? Or are they an insult to women because the film masculinizes the female characters so that they resort to stereotypical masculine forms of behaviour – in this case, aggression and gun-related violence – which feminists want to challenge? As an example of the latter concern, Dowell remarks that the film "does little more than fill a male formula with female forms." In light of this comment, it is difficult to regard Thelma and Louise as noble – never mind, feminist – outlaws.

My criticism of concerns such as Dowell's is not meant to invalidate them but to consider their implications. The concern with women behaving like men invites a discussion of notions of femininity and masculinity, as well as popular fantasy. The question is not whether or not Thelma and Louise are indeed behaving like men, but rather, how do definitions of appropriate gender behaviour impact on one's reading of the film as progressive or reactionary? And how might genre socialize us towards particular gender expectations? Comments such as Dowell's suggest there is behaviour acceptable for and essential to women and other behaviour that is not; and that there are genres more preferable for dramatizing women's fantasies than others. Taking the argument that Thelma and Louise are women in male drag suggests there is an essential femininity beneath their genre-induced masculine masquerade. While feminist concerns with violence and aggression are not to be dismissed, comments about Thelma and Louise's masculinization inadvertently perpetuate patriarchal and essentialist-feminist myths about a feminine essence that is non-violent, self-sacrificing, nurturing, passive, non-aggressive. It is easy to see why the film produced unfavorable responses from both feminist/oppositional and conservative/hegemonic perspectives, making temporary and inadvertent allies out of the unlikeliest political groupings.

Certainly, Thelma and Louise's class positions additionally impact on readings with contradictory effects. For instance, Minow and Spelman argue that the women's class backgrounds make the fantasy "more palatable to the middle-class audiences to whom the film is directed than if the heroines were solidly middle- or upper-middle class." The same can be said for the race of the two women, as well as their sexuality. (Imagine critical reception if Thelma and Louise had been black or explicitly identified as lesbians.) However, I am not convinced that the film's address works with respect to class in the way Minow and Spelman suggest. On the contrary, rather than being directed specifically at a middle-class audience, the film seeks to cut across class lines by speaking in classless terms about adult disillusionment – a problem in itself in that it feeds into the American myth of a classless society, and distracts from the economic and societal constraints on youthful hopes for the future.

Resistance and Address

Thelma's fugitive status is directly proportional to her new-found self-determination. Each of Thelma's self-determining actions increases her threat to the social order: she decides to run to Mexico with Louise after she phones Daryl and tells him he is her husband not her father; she chooses to have sex with J.D., after which she "Finally understands what all the fuss is about"; she takes control of her situation by robbing the store to make sure she and Louise have money to complete their escape. She is no longer the woman Louise accused of "flaking out" every time she was in trouble. Having made the full transition to Louise-ness, Thelma wears her friend's jacket when, over the phone, she tells Daryl "to go fuck [him]self."

Thelma's transformation is made all the more transgressive given the class positions of the two heroines. Louise is a lower-income food-service worker while Thelma is a middle-income housewife. Their class status and social environment limited the choices they can make, leading to frustration and boredom. As Cathy Griggers points out,

> They've been around long enough to know they haven't been far enough – not yet. And so they've got cabin fever – the desire to get out and to get away – if only for the weekend … [Moreover, t]hey have cabin fever for different reasons. Thelma is fed up with housework, Louise with the salary-wage exchange. The tips don't make up the difference. There's something missing, something left unmarked in the political economy of both the contemporary working single-woman and the domestic housewife.

Like the gangsters of Depression-era Hollywood, who also come from working- or lower-class backgrounds, Thelma and Louise transgress against the limitations of their class, as well as gender. Their flight from their social and economic positions is a fantasy that opens up the film's textual address for at least two reasons: first, it connects with the lived realities of its intended female audience in ways that acknowledge both the diversity of female social experiences and the commonalities that can bring women like Thelma and Louise together; second, it expands its address to include both women and men by tapping into adult fears that life has not lived up to society's promises. Feminist film critic Carol J. Clover rightly argues that

> To focus, as the debate about *Thelma and Louise* did, on those men who disliked it is to miss what I think is the far more significant fact that large numbers of men both saw and did like it … lots of men were evidently happy to enter into that very American fantasy [the buddy-escape plot] even when it is enacted by women, even when the particulars are female-specific (rape, macho husband, leering co-worker), and even when the inflection is remarkably feminist. And although the film showed signs of defensiveness on this point (the niceness of the Harvey Keitel figure struck me as something of a sop to men in the audience), it was on the whole surefooted in its assumption that its viewers, regardless of sex, would engage with the women's story.

Clover maintains that attention to the gendering of readings has ignored this film's appeal for men. Even screenwriter Khouri points out that "during test screenings prior to the film's release, it scored the highest points amongst 25-year-old males." Indeed, the sheer popularity of the film would indicate not all men found it difficult to relate to the story of Thelma and Louise. The film's confidence that it could appeal to viewers of both sexes is evidenced in the initial interest Hollywood heavyweights paid to the screenplay of Khouri, an unknown entity at the time.

As the narrative moves towards its conclusion, the film increasingly comes to speak about adult disappointment because, contrary to popular belief, we are not masters of our own destiny. There are forces beyond our control that limit our lives and the choices we can make. For instance, in a set of close-ups of the two women, whose faces dramatically fade into each other's, a Marianne Faithful song plays on the sound-track: "At the age of 37, she realized she'd never ride through Paris in a sports car with the warm wind in her hair." This melancholy song comments on the plight of Thelma and Louise, whose choices in life have been radically curtailed. Lost youth becomes a metaphor for the drudgery of taking up our roles in the social world. This metaphor is focused around Louise, the older of the two women who notices the sad, resigned faces of the elderly people she encounters on the road.

Read in general terms that widen narrative address, *Thelma and Louise* becomes an allegory for breaking free. In publicity interviews, comments about the film from direc-tor Ridley Scott and actor Geena Davis speak to the theme of freedom and offer an explanation as to why people who worked on the film believed in its universal appeal. According to Scott, "The film's not about rape. It's about choices and freedom," and according to Davis, "This is a movie about people claiming responsibility for their own lives." My intention here is not to challenge the film's address to women, but to sug-gest there are aspects that speak to an audience of women and men. The film's impres-sive box-office suggests that it appealed to a wide audience, despite the wrath it elicited from some male film reviewers. Its economic success would appear to confirm John Fiske's thesis that the more popular a text is, the more polysemic it will be [that is, the more possible meanings it will have], and therefore, capable of accommodating a range of diverse readings. So the acknowledgment of adult disillusionment that comes to the surface closer to the end of *Thelma and Louise*, coupled with the reckless excitement that it may not be too late to change things, renders it difficult not to go along with the ride, even if one seriously minds women with guns.

The class and gender (as well as generational) implications of Thelma and Louise's escape become increasingly poignant, particularly in the scene in which the women are driving in the desert at night, on the lookout for police. The spaces in which the two women move open up. The framing, and the panning and tracking shots accom-modate the wide-open vistas and big sky of the frontier. Traditionally, the desert has been the landscape of the Hollywood western. The cowboy doesn't just ride into the sunset in the closing credits – he rides into the desert landscape, choosing the com-pany of his horse, maybe a male buddy, over civilization and all the social conventions entailed (marriage in particular). But the desert frontier is no longer the traditional preserve of white masculinity, as the black Rasta cyclist and the two fugitive women prove. "I've always wanted to travel but I never got the opportunity," says Thelma. No longer content to be left behind singing sad ballads at the local saloon, Thelma and Louise have elected to go to the desert, metaphorically speaking, even if it means dying. As Thelma says later, when she is afraid Louise might make a deal with the cops, "Something's crossed over in me. I can't go back. I just couldn't live."

Thelma has been married since she was eighteen, but only now does she feel "wide awake ... everything looks different, like I got something to look forward to." For the heroine of the woman's film, the very presence of a desire for something else is literally better than nothing. To be in possession of desire in spite of the oppressive social circumstances in which the heroine finds herself makes life somewhat livable – there is something to hope for. The narrative of *Thelma and Louise* is as much about awakening desires and hopes in the women on the screen as it is about their adventures on the road. As a woman's film *Thelma and Louise* draws upon several social experiences that women may share in common (e.g., sexual harassment, the threat of male violence, housework, the salary-wage exchange) as raw material, and then articulates the day-to-day desires and frustrations of its intended female audience in fantasy form. Moreover, there is a sense in which the expression of these female frustrations and resentments via masculine road-movie conventions marks the fantasy as especially illicit, and therefore, all the more pleasurable (and dangerous). Like Thelma, I, too, "am glad I came with you, no matter what happens." Maybe not entirely.

Gender, Genre, and Closure

The ending of *Thelma and Louise* has produced almost as much controversy and has generated almost as many conflicting responses as Louise's killing of Harlan. After eluding the police for many days, the two women eventually find themselves cornered, trapped between Hal and his police officers at one end, and the Grand Canyon at the other. The showdown represents the final struggle to contain Thelma and Louise in a definition of femininity and criminality that shores up patriarchal interests. Thelma expresses surprise at the magnitude of force marshaled on their behalf. "All this for us?" she asks. Her incredulity marks her lack of understanding of the threat she and her friend represent. Thelma and Louise like the audience are faced with the consequences of gender transgression.

Hal becomes a personification of the contemporary struggle to re-define gender. He mediates between legal hegemonic discourses around Thelma and Louise and the two women's experiences of the social world. He desperately wants to arrive at a compromise between the two perspectives. Hal is also a familiar figure in popular film these days: the local cop who attempts to understand the situation in all its complexity and ambiguity, unlike the institutionalized authority of the FBI who see the case in simplistic terms. Hal knows about Louise and Texas, and he wants the policemen to refrain from shooting at the two women. Despite his best intentions, Hal doesn't really get it – he is still trying to work within institutions founded on gender-biased assumptions. Moreover, he believes in his ability to act as an individual and to bring about justice within existing institutions. The two women must be apprehended and held accountable because those are the rules under which Hal operates. He does not represent a challenge to the law in the way that Thelma and Louise do, for they are not willing to compromise. Hal, on the other hand, is the symbol of compromise, a kinder, gentler patriarch.

Mann maintains that Hal "shows the future possibility for male desire to alter itself ...." In other words, Hal represents an emergent masculinity which works in at least two contradictory ways. First, Hal offers a way out for those male audience members made uneasy by the questions around gender and power that the film asks. Hal offers a vision of a patriarchy that is tempered by feminine (not feminist) concerns but that is still in the right. To use a relevant cliché, he is a reformist not a revolutionary. Moreover, as the only positive male stereotype in the film, the implication is that what may be needed are more gentlemanly patriarchs like Hal. Men like him know how to be sweet to their wives, so they won't turn out like Thelma. (Father still knows best, even if no one seems to be listening at the moment.) Second, his struggles to negotiate various ideological interests and beliefs signifies a social order in transition where consensus on a definition of femininity that bolsters male dominance has been irretrievably lost. The last resort is force.

Unlike Hal, the cops represent old-style, status-quo masculinity. Their response to Hal's request to not shoot is that the women are armed. Over a speaker a male voice intones, "Failure to obey is an act of aggression against us," which aptly summarizes the film's primary, motivating conflict: the failure of women to obey will be interpreted by men as an act of aggression against them. And to the end, Thelma and Louise refuse to obey. "Let's not get caught. Let's keep going," says Thelma, and Louise agrees, as the two women clasp hands and kiss in a shot-reverse shot, which, says Putnam, "elevates the friendship between women to the status of heterosexual romance, the end toward which everything is always working in a traditional Hollywood film." As they go racing towards the canyon in the blue convertible, Hal runs after them futilely, for the car goes sailing over the cliff. A freeze frame shows the car suspended in mid-air, the shot fades to white, and then, a montage of past scenes showing the women alive and happy rolls during the end credits.

Many critics have argued that one's reading of the ending is genre-dependent. For instance, Man and Morrison maintain that reading *Thelma and Louise* as an example of the woman's film means the ending works as a critique of patriarchy, and as such carries subversive connotations. The woman's film is centered around a female protagonist, who in her search for personal fulfillment finds she must contend with societal constraints on her desires. According to Morrison,

> What the majority of these female protagonists quickly discover ... is that in the patriarchal society of their diegetic world, there is no place for an active, independent woman .... [I]t is, time and again, only through renunciation and sacrifice that they achieve their ultimate goal; indeed, have any hope of achieving it. Those women who refuse to forgo their active desires in effect refuse the possibility of recuperation. Consequently, they almost always are punished by a kind of filmic moral trajectory that brings a double closure, to the woman's life and to the film's narrative. This is not to imply that the cinema is not fascinated with "bad" women; only that it makes sure that they are not rewarded for their "crimes" against society.

Both Man and Morrison argue that Thelma and Louise, in refusing to compromise their personal desires, reject recuperation by patriarchy. Their suicide is their final act of female self-determination, providing transcendence of the social world. While Morrison sees the two women's deaths "as a victory rather than defeat," Man is more cautious, saying that "Thelma and Louise triumph and they do not."

Man's comment encapsulates the contradictory quality of Thelma's and Louise's Pyrrhic victory over patriarchy. To what degree can the ending be read as progressive, as critical of the status quo? While Thelma and Louise's suicides represent their refusal to capitulate with male dominance, simultaneously, patriarchy's worst fears about disobedient women are excised. Moreover, their deaths suggest there are no alternatives to the existing order. The film can only offer a solution that complies with existing definitions of reality, the law, and gender. This is where *Thelma and Louise* most demonstrates that it is a hegemonic female fantasy, for it cannot offer a vision of a social world transformed. This begs the question, to what extent is Thelma and Louise's decision to die actually of their own making or to what extent is it socially predetermined?

In other words, even in suicide, Thelma and Louise might not be masters of their own destiny. Instead, they, like this fantasy, accept the limits placed on women rather than fighting to transform their reality. Yet *Thelma and Louise*'s difference from other backlash representations is its genuine interest in women's social experiences, and its desire to express their fears and frustrations. Even if the film eventually eliminates any alternatives to the status quo, it still envisions a different state. For instance, its critical stance towards the law and its treatment of women victimized by male violence argues that institutional changes are needed. Moreover, *Thelma and Louise* presents, however fleetingly, a utopian vision of a life other than the one Thelma and Louise have left behind, a life where the two women put their friendship, their responsibility to each other in solidarity against a common foe, patriarchal authority. As Manohla Dargis says, "Thelma and Louise create a paradigm of female friendship, produced out of their willful refusal of the male world and its laws. No matter where their trip finally ends, Thelma and Louise have reinvented sisterhood for the American screen." This is the potentially feminist reading *Thelma and Louise* produces despite its closure, and that accounts largely for the moralistic, conservative backlash against the film. The images of Thelma and Louise shown during the end credits resonate more powerfully than the vision of their suicidal leap. As the bumper sticker says, "Thelma and Louise live."

Nonetheless, *Thelma and Louise*'s refusal of the male world and its laws is pessimistic. I am left uncomfortable by the need for two women's deaths in order to make a point about patriarchal injustice. At the same time, seeing *Thelma and Louise* sipping margaritas in Mexico would not be the point either. In the end *Thelma and Louise* presents us with the difficulty of envisioning a feminist future in a time when we in Canada and the United States are desperately fighting to keep the gains women's movements have made in the last twenty years – never mind imagining new possibilities. *Thelma and Louise*'s pessimism speaks to this disillusionment. In a time of backlash, the possibility of social transformation may very well require women to join hands and take a leap of faith. While the film is one of the brighter moments in contemporary Hollywood representations of women, it is a rare example, which perhaps suggests the desperation of those of us who were eager to embrace any Hollywood offering that did not feature the woman as the male psycho-killer's object of desire, or as a male-bashing psycho-killer herself, or as the girlfriend of the male lead (who may/may not be a psycho-killer, depending on the genre). Because it is an exception to the usual Hollywood fare, *Thelma and Louise* may be regarded as an instance of accommodation, a momentary acknowledgment of women's anger and frustration. To put it another way, *Thelma and Louise* aside, what has Hollywood cinema done for women or for feminism lately?

28

Hollywood Remembers World War II
Saving Private Ryan *and Postwar Memory in America*

John Bodnar

Growing up in post-World War II America was never much further away than the movie house down the street. Millions of boys and girls were raised on war movies. The actions of heroes and heroines, the sounds of machine guns, the sight of blood, and the iconic images of flags and burials are part of Americans' shared cultural baggage. Indeed, Ron Kovic, the paralyzed Vietnam War veteran whose memoir Born on the Fourth of July *traces how he was influenced by war movies, recounts how, inspired by John Wayne and* Sands of Iwo Jima, *he charged off to battle and came home a broken, disillusioned man. War, he discovered, was not like the movies. In the following essay, John Bodnar discusses the war movie in American culture and questions the political values such films instill. He also discusses how collective memories are invented and reinvented over time.*

The release in 1998 of *Saving Private Ryan* by Hollywood director Steven Spielberg has revived again the debate over war and remembering. In this case, audiences have flocked to see a story of American troops, led by a dedicated captain, John Miller (Tom Hanks), attempt to rescue a young private from the field of battle just after the Allied invasion of Normandy in 1944. Some reviewers have stressed how Spielberg's film is the first to truly show the horror of battle, especially in its opening scenes, which depict the American landing on Omaha Beach, June 6, 1944. Modern technology has allowed the filmmaker to reproduce the frightening sound of German gunfire and the brutal reality of exploding body parts. American soldiers are shattered and maimed on the beachhead, and some fall apart emotionally from the stress of battle. As many reviewers have suggested, the movie counters images of heroic warriors by disclosing the real terror of combat and is in many ways an antiwar story.

Ironically, while the Spielberg film reveals the brutality of war, it preserves the World War II image of American soldiers as inherently averse to bloodshed and cruelty. The war was savage; the average American GI who fought it was not. American men in this story are destroyed by war, and only a few actually enjoy killing Germans. At its rhetorical core, the story's argument would have seemed very familiar to audiences in the 1940s: the common American soldier was fundamentally a good man who loved his country and his family. He went to war out of a sense of duty to both, and he wanted to get it over with as quickly as possible. Rather than being a natural-born killer, he was a loving family man who abhorred the use of extreme force but could inflict it when necessary. This point is made well in the figure of John Miller. A high school teacher and part-time baseball coach from Pennsylvania, he disdains brutality and says that every time he kills another man he feels "farther from home." Traumatized himself at times by battle, this common man still has heroic potential and is always up to the task of taking on the German war machine. It is a model found in dozens of wartime films that depicted average guys from Brooklyn or Texas who loved their everyday life in America or the girl next door. Miller is ultimately a representation of the brand of common-man heroism that infused the culture of wartime America. Without a doubt, a platoon of men like him could save Private Ryan and win the war. Norman Corwin's famous radio broadcast of May 8, 1945, on the occasion of Germany's surrender, makes the case for the courageous possibilities of the ordinary person. "Take a bow, GI. Take a bow, little guy," Corwin told his listeners. "The superman of tomorrow lies at the feet of you common men this afternoon."

Although anguish and bravery share narrative space in this film, they do not do so on an equal basis. The pain of the American combat soldier is revealed but is ultimately placed within a larger frame of patriotic valor. Some American soldiers in this story question the war effort and their superiors' decisions, but in the end the nation and its warriors are moral and honorable. The fact that combat was so frightening serves mainly to reinforce our admiration for these soldiers and their gallantry. The entire narrative, for that matter, is immensely "reverent" toward the nation and its warriors, attempting to uphold its patriotic architecture with opening and closing scenes at an American military cemetery in Europe. The very design of these sites of remembering was originally driven by the desire to proclaim the unity of the American nation, with their rows upon rows of white crosses, and to serve as "permanent reminders to other nations of the sacrifices made by the United States." If other nations were expected to recall their debt to America, Spielberg's film makes the additional claim that survivors of the war (like Ryan) and subsequent generations of Americans need to recognize their obligations to these brave combatants. Thus, at the film's end, Ryan can only look back over his life and the graves of the heroic dead and express the hope that he lived a life that merited the sacrifice his comrades made for him, one that consisted of devotion to family and country. In this veneration of patriotism and self-denial, the story takes us back to dominant political and moral values of the 1940s, which advocated collective goals over individual ones.

But, as Spielberg remembers, he also forgets. Forties' calls to patriotic sacrifice were contingent on assurances of a more democratic society and world. Government leaders such as Franklin D. Roosevelt took pains to make democratic promises in pronouncements like "The Four Freedoms." And the Office of War Information (OWI) told Hollywood producers to make films that not only helped win the conflict but reminded audiences that it was "a people's war," which would bring about a future with more social justice and individual freedom. The democracy for which "the people" fought, in fact, was a cultural blend of several key ideas: tolerance, individualism, anti-totalitarianism, and economic justice. The representation of open-mindedness was aimed particularly at reducing ethnic tensions at home. American individualism was venerated in the call for personal freedoms and even in the rhetoric of military recruiters. They promised that army life would not destroy a man's self-interests but would preserve the same balance between individualism and teamwork that Americans experienced in their sporting endeavors. Frank Capra's series "Why We Fight" (1942–1945) was a vivid example of the use of anti-totalitarian images to encourage support for the war. And slogans like "Freedom from Want" acknowledged the popular desire for economic security after the 1930s.

Spielberg's turn to the moral individual in heroism and in pain at the expense of the moral or democratic community, however, suggests just how much this film is a product of the late twentieth century and not of the 1940s. The attainment of democracy rested in the 1940s on a sense of reciprocity between individuals and the institutions that governed their lives. In a totalitarian state, government and institutions dominated individuals; in a democracy, a relationship of mutual respect existed between citizens and institutions. People served the nation because they believed the nation would serve their democratic interests in return. Narratives that endorsed this relationship, such as those found in many wartime films, effectively linked the fate of the individual with the fate of the nation. Today, however, narratives and images about the destiny of individuals command more cultural space than those about the fortunes of nations. As a result, both political speech and commemoration have more to say about victims or people who have met tragic fates. Spielberg's memory narrative of moral men represents very much the late twentieth century's concern with the singular person in the past, present, and future. Cohesive narratives that effectively link personal stories to collective desires for progress are harder to find. Those that exist are disrupted by images of victims. Heroism and patriotism remain, but they must fight for cultural space with the claims of those who have sorrowful tales from the past or those who insist on redress rather than self-denial. Many believe that, since Vietnam, it is harder to commemorate gallantry and victory or to suppress individual subjectivities at the expense of collective ones. Thus delineations of victims – from Vietnam, from the AIDS epidemic, from racism, from child abusers, from rapists, from drugs, even from World War II – now command more cultural space. Statements of what was lost now eclipse expressions of what was gained.

This tension between the old patriotic narrative about the fate of the nation and the new expression of individual suffering and loss is expressed clearly on the Washington Mall, a central site of American cultural memory. In recent times, the process of nationalizing the representation of emotional shock and private pain appears arrested. The images of the old public history, dominated by powerful statesmen who were devoted to the nation, have been substantially modified by the appearance of victims. Names (and possessions) of dead soldiers constitute the 1982 Vietnam Veterans Memorial, known simply as "The Wall." Statues of American troops reveal men moving cautiously through a battlefield scene from Korea (1995); they appear fearful that they could be killed or hurt at any moment. Figures standing in Depression-era bread lines or listening for words of hope command attention at the Franklin Delano Roosevelt Memorial (1997), and, nearby, thousands of images pertaining to Holocaust victims have been mounted for exhibit (1993). Explanations for this transformation remain elusive. Some attribute the change to the impact on American culture of the Vietnam War and traumatic events such as the AIDS epidemic. The overall effect of the Holocaust cannot be discounted. Certainly, the nation's ability to manage discourse about the past has withered, as many more voices – including the mass media – have joined in the production of culture.

Contests over public remembering were certainly not pervasive in most nations after World War II. Many countries were able to limit the representation of war trauma and homegrown victimization in their societies for a very long time after the war. In Japan, a long-term effort to conceal that nation's culpability for atrocities in China or for starting the war in the Pacific has fallen apart only in recent years. To some extent, this campaign was sustained by silences in Japanese history books and by memorials to the Japanese dead that tended to remember them as innocent victims, not brutal warriors. In postwar Germany, the Holocaust was substantially denied in public; in many instances, Germans referred to themselves as "victims" of Nazi aggressors, denying the realities of German-sponsored brutality toward others. In France, for some two decades after the war, citizens tended to recall the conflict in terms of a patriotic narrative: brave French Resistance fighters under Charles de Gaulle waged an unrelenting campaign to free their captured nation from the Germans. This version of the war had elements that were true, but it failed to acknowledge completely the role of some French citizens who collaborated with the Nazis in sending French Jews to death camps. In much of the Western world, in fact, the contemporary memory of the Holocaust as an act of unparalleled barbarism did not emerge fully until the 1960s: publicity surrounding Adolf Eichmann's trial and the Arab–Israeli Six-Day War for a time recalled images of the death of Jews.

In this essay, however, I want to argue that the narrative of heroism, patriotism, and democracy that permeated wartime America – the story that *Saving Private Ryan* seeks to restore only partially – began to decompose immediately in the aftermath of World War II. This would not be so apparent if one looked only at official commemorations and public monuments, such as the one dedicated in 1954 to the costly American victory at Iwo Jima. Mass culture, however, was more responsive to the range of personal emotions and recollections that resided in the hearts and minds of the people, and it frequently challenged "reverent" narratives by the late 1940s. Although limitations of space prevent a full discussion of the impact of mass culture on society, the central point must be made that mass cultural forms undermined disciplinary institutions (such as governments or churches) in their goal of managing the public expression of human wants. Films, for instance, thrived because they were able to broadcast the full range of human desires and emotions.

Long before *Saving Private Ryan* or even the Vietnam War, American mass culture was flooded with a torrential debate over the violence unleashed by war and, more importantly, over the turbulent nature of American society itself. Scholars have documented both political opposition to the American atomic build-up in the late 1940s and cultural expressions of anxiety over the possibility of world destruction by atomic weapons throughout the Cold War era. But this line of analysis is grounded too much in Cold War issues and fails to sufficiently appreciate the overall impact of World War II and the memory of violence and trauma that it generated. The war showed Americans that their fellow citizens were as capable of inflicting brutality as citizens of other nations, and it led them to search for the sources of such behavior within the home front itself. Public anxiety over victimization was as likely to be grounded in fears of dangerous impulses in the hearts and souls of fellow citizens as in fears about powerful weapons. The anxiety that linked popular nervousness over brute force in both wartime and peacetime America was articulated especially in the cinema and in literature. There, writers and directors challenged the sentimental views of the nation and the perspectives of the Office of War Information. In this oppositional view, American men and, for that matter, women were not inherently patriotic and loving but were domineering and ruthless. In its recognition of evil in the hearts and souls of "the people," this construction of the nation and its citizens worked against the hope of a more democratic and prosperous future. Once it was demonstrated that violence could be homegrown and did not reside only in the visions of dictators, it followed that America itself could produce victims as well as patriots, treachery as well as loyalty.

From its inception in the eighteenth century, the nation-state has been haunted by visions of degeneration, chaos, and anarchy. Those potentially responsible for such destructiveness have been located both inside and outside national boundaries. Ideally, the nation was imagined as a united community that would protect its members, grant them rights, and foster their material progress. In the consciousness of nations, citizens entrusted powerful men with civic affairs and the defense of boundaries. Serving as statesmen, patriarchs, or dedicated warriors, these men merited the admiration and gratitude of females and others dependent on them. It was understood that leaders and warriors might sometimes need to suppress savages on the frontiers of the nation or even minorities within it. But hints that they themselves were bloodthirsty or cruel could not only weaken their elevated status but threaten the cultural stability of the nation itself. Consequently, war always involves cultural risks even if the nation wins. Omer Bartov has observed that modern warfare and the massive trauma it generated incited feelings of anxiety in all participants and prompted a wide search for enemies and victims. This is what happened in much of the domestic politics of Cold War America and in the aftermath of Vietnam.

Even more central to my argument is the point that, after 1945, recognizing the war's incredible scale of brutality caused ordinary Americans and probably people elsewhere to connect the cruelty of warfare with other forms of malevolence in their lives and society. Once war exposed how savage men could be, it did not take much of a cultural leap to see that everyone was threatened by warlike behavior wherever it was manifested. This process had distinct implications for remembering the war. Dominick LaCapra suggests that extremely traumatic events often force the imagination to employ extravagant metaphors, invoking terms such as in one's "wildest dreams or most hellish nightmares." In a sense, both the mind and the culture must find ways to confront the "unimaginable magnitude" of what took place. Thus the search for extraordinary models of enemies and victims displaced the wartime representations of a democratic nation and common-man heroism, and it undermined future attempts to represent the national society in a positive manner.

This argument moves away from standard paradigms regarding the relationship between trauma and memory. It accepts and notes that trauma can lead to a "lapse or rupture" in the memory of emotional shock but contends that this form of repression is incomplete. The psychoanalytic study of trauma has revealed that the painful event usually returns against the victim's will and only after an initial period of suppression or "absolute numbing"; the victim must first move away from the event before returning to it. This certainly appeared to happen to some extent in the public culture of the warring nations after 1945. But I will also offer evidence that a substantial amount of the trauma and anxiety, at least in the United States, was not restrained as much as it was displaced into the narratives of mass culture. One scholar has written that "the historical power of trauma is not just that the experience is repeated after its forgetting, but that it is only in and through its inherent forgetting that it is first experienced at all." I would amend this position by claiming that, to a considerable extent, both the personal anxieties and the collective concerns over the violence of war never really left American culture at all.

Some observers who have studied the impact of the Holocaust on postwar culture are impressed by the fact that the cultural suppression of trauma involved in "acting-out" the past in a nostalgic sense (something that suppresses the reality of pain) now appears to take place alongside the practice of working-through or confronting emotional disturbances. Nostalgia and mourning coexist. In looking at the films of postwar America and a modern feature like *Saving Private Ryan*, we clearly see what LaCapra calls "interaction, reinforcement, and conflict" between the need to forget and the desire to confront what happened. In its opening scenes, *Saving Private Ryan* confronts the horror; in later scenes, when GIs go off on an adventure to save one individual, it often lapses into play acting and a desire to fight the war over again. The same sort of tension was noticeable in American films about the war in the decade after 1945, although the narrative resolution of contradictions was not always the same. In *Ryan*, patriotic sacrifice as a frame of remembrance stands above both trauma and democracy. But in the immediate postwar era, some films effectively contested patriotic ideals. They often displaced the representation of trauma from the combat zone to American society or to a distant past, but the discourse over the pain of war was real. Thus, between 1946 and 1949, hardly any combat films of the war were made. Many features, however, were issued about the devastating consequences of the war on Americans as well as the potential Americans had to inflict harm on others. Moreover, combat did not disappear completely but was often exiled into the genre of the Western. The most thoughtful of these latter films actually located savagery in the character of the American cavalrymen and not Native Americans.

Wartime films were not without their own set of contradictions, to be sure, although patriotism, unity, and democracy dominated the stories. In tales about the war and gender relations, women were assigned crucial roles of support for the men they loved with devotion. This point was made clear in films such as *Since You Went Away* (1944) and *Pride of the Marines* (1945). Ethnic cooperation was fostered in numerous depictions of American platoons, such as *Bataan* (1943). Hatred for authoritarian regimes was certainly prevalent in movies such as *Sahara* (1943), and patriotic sacrifice was venerated in films such as *Wake Island* (1942), which evoked memories of American heroism at Valley Forge and the Alamo. The grim reality of war, the random and unheroic nature of much death, and the sometimes futile plight of the common soldier broke through in creative stories such as *A Walk in the Sun* (1945), but its cynicism was rare. More common was a film like *Air Force* (1943), which effectively merged personal interests and collective needs. In this film, men love their mothers and wives, naturally want to defend their nation, kill the treacherous Japanese, and fight bravely in the Pacific. A tailgunner who feels that he has not been treated fairly in the past eventually lets go of his anger as he joins the fight. The entire film is framed by a preamble from Abraham Lincoln's Gettysburg Address, suggesting that the military struggle is ultimately about "a new birth of freedom" and the need to preserve "government of the people, by the people, and for the people." *Saving Private Ryan*, by contrast, invokes the memory of Lincoln as an expression of the ideal of patriotic sacrifice, not as a call to work for more democracy.

Postwar films moved away from wartime censorship and immediately into a discourse over how the violence unleashed by the war could wreak havoc with the

American future. The suggestion that dangerous impulses resided in the souls of Americans themselves was at the core of film noir features of the later 1940s. In both mood and story, these films countered sentimental and optimistic assessments not only about the future but about Americans themselves. The 1946 film *The Killers* made evident the "ubiquity" of viciousness and victimization in everyday American life. The central character, played by actor Burt Lancaster, is drawn into a life of crime, betrayed by a woman, and gunned down in the symbolic space of American democracy – the small town. So much for the potential of stable gender relations. Dana Polan has argued that the war was a "disciplinary moment" in which diverse discourses came together to "empower a particular social reality." But it was increasingly clear in the immediate postwar period that critical images of America and Americans could no longer be domesticated and that, as Polan writes, "discourses of commonality" had reached the limits of their persuasiveness.

The productions of film noir did not always connect despair directly to the event of World War II, but the popular classic by William Wyler, *The Best Years of Our Lives* (1946), certainly did. In this story, servicemen return home with deep emotional and physical scars. One is haunted not only by the memory of flying bomber runs over Germany but by the realization that his wife has been unfaithful while he was away. In other words, he was victimized by events both abroad and at home. Another veteran, who drinks excessively upon his return, manages to advance the cause of a just society; through his job at a bank, he makes it easier for ordinary veterans to get loans that will help them rebuild their lives. Trauma is acknowledged; the hope of a democratic future still persists.

The most powerful cultural attack on the sentimentality and heroic quality of wartime culture came in Norman Mailer's 1948 novel *The Naked and the Dead*. Mailer was a veteran himself who had served in the Pacific and had seen firsthand some of the destruction caused by the atomic bomb in Japan. His narrative is one that centers not so much on the war as on the nature of American society and the patterns of male behavior it engendered. Stationed on a fictional island in the Pacific, Mailer's GIs are not particularly capable of patriotism or virtue. Rather, they are consumed by personal quests of power and destructiveness. A minor character on the island expresses the Roosevelt administration's view that the conflict is a "people's war" that will lead to a more democratic world for all mankind, a point that the OWI worked assiduously to inject into wartime films. However, General Edward Cummings, a major character in the story, envisions a postwar world dominated not by democracy but by the "Right" and the "Omnipotent Men" who will lead America. Clearly, Mailer saw an innate drive for power and dominion in American men that Spielberg does not. For Mailer, this drive was realized not only in the massive retaliation against the Japanese but in the lives of domineering men like Cummings, whose father had sent him to military school to make him "think and act like a man."

Cummings's perspective frames the novel's unflattering portrayal of American manhood, and Mailer contends that the male drive for dominance could be found in democracies as well as dictatorships. When someone suggests to Cummings that men would fight out of love for their country, he dismisses the notion as a "liberal historian's attitude." For Cummings, it is not democracy that motivates American men to fight. Instead, they learned to be aggressive from living in a society of unequals in which most men were trying to climb upward from humble origins.

Mailer's story is important not only because it represents a critique of the official views of why America fought and of the romantic images of the American fighting men but because it connects narratives of victimization from the 1930s with those of the 1940s. That is to say, he suggested that both experiences, economic conflict and war, can destroy lives. American culture in the postwar era still reverberated with the after-shocks of the Depression and with notions that revealed the pitfalls of capitalism. In fact, many conservatives had attacked the OWI during the war precisely because of its liberal orientation, which connected the idea of a "people's war" to the need to respect labor as much as business in narrative films. Numerous films continued to reveal the manner in which the nation's fundamental economic system destroyed as many individuals as it rewarded. In *All My Sons* (1948), an industrialist decides to place prof-its before patriotism, resulting in the production of planes with faulty parts. When American airmen lose their lives as the result of his decisions, the man is traumatized enough to take his own life. In *Champion* (1949), a man throws away relationships with people who care about him for a chance to become a boxing king. In this story, the boxing ring becomes a metaphor for the marketplace pursuit of wealth and fame.

Remembering war as the progenitor of victims rather than heroes was central to a number of films in the late 1940s. In *Crossfire* (1947), soldiers bring their brutal ways back home. Some are described as capable of going "crazy" once there is no one around to give them orders. They engage in drunkenness and murder and even acts of anti-Semitism. In general, they do not seem to have the clear sense of purpose that soldiers in *Saving Private Ryan* exhibit regarding the desirability of resuming domestic arrangements or serving their country. Before *Crossfire* ends, one soldier even kills another.

Two years later, *Home of the Brave* (1949) connected the respective trauma-induc-ing abilities of war and society. In this tale, an African-American soldier, James Moss, suffers severe emotional distress due to the brutality of racism in the United States and the effects of combat. Moss undergoes treatment for what a military psychiatrist calls "traumatic shock." (In reality, the discovery of psychiatric stress during the war had a profound influence on the way the military treated this problem. Entering the war, the common assumption was that emotional breakdowns in battle were the result of a weak or less than manly character.) Moss is depicted as deeply disturbed by the insults he received in civilian life and from racist soldiers in the military. When he hears his good friend being tortured by the Japanese on a secret mission and is forced to leave his partner to die on an island in the Pacific, he breaks down and cries. The psy-chiatrist gives him a drug that allows him to relive and, therefore, to come to terms with his combat experience. He realizes that war trauma is shared equally by people of all races. As he goes back home to open a bar with a white friend, we get a hint that the success of a postwar future will depend not only on putting the trauma behind us but on resolving inequality and prejudice as well.

Even more traditional war films of the period were reluctant to temper the anguish of battle with simple images of bravery and valor. In *Battleground* (1949), the point of view of the ordinary fighting man was stressed. War for these "battered bastards" was confusing and painful. Some are looking for a "good clean flesh wound" that will get them out of battle and back to a field hospital and, perhaps, home. As Private Holley, actor Van Johnson claims that the PFC, or private first class, in his military rank stands only for the fact that he is "praying for civilian" status. In this film, there is no cataclysmic battle or talk of democracy or patriotism, only an intent focus on fighting to stay alive or to take a small piece of ground. There is dogged determination on the part of American troops in this film against superior enemy forces and bitterly cold weather, but *Battleground* tries hard to say that the average GI was uninterested in putting any sort of political frame on an experience that he detested.

By 1950, a popular war film such as *The Sands of Iwo Jima* went a bit farther than the cynical commentary articulated in *Battleground* by mounting a direct attack on some of the men who won the war, even as it sustained heroic notions about them. John Wayne starred as a dedicated Marine sergeant capable of training soldiers and leading them into battle. This film was supported extensively by the Marine Corps, which supplied it with an array of military hardware, and it is often seen as a pivotal representation of the heroic American war myth. But there is considerable irony in this narrative. Shots of brave American fighting men attacking the Japanese on Tarawa and Iwo Jima are countered by expressions of regret over the fact that men like Wayne (Sergeant Stryker in the movie) ultimately elect the ideals of military life over those of domestic life. Unlike John Miller in *Saving Private Ryan*, Stryker is a zealous soldier who has little interest in maintaining close ties to his wife and family. War is brutal in this film, and men get killed, although 1950s film technology could not achieve the sense of fear that Spielberg's does. *The Sands of Iwo Jima* also made a much more determined attempt to work through the impact of war on men and to address the concern that military life exacerbated natural impulses toward violence, which would have devastating consequences for American society. Unlike the Spielberg film, *The Sands of Iwo Jima* made a specific plea to American men to put the violence of wartime behind them. Audiences watched as a young Marine tells Stryker that he wants to raise his son to read Shakespeare, not the Marine manual. And they saw Stryker come to regret the way he mistreated his wife and son. Film historians astutely note that when Stryker is killed near the end, the heroic and violent warrior of World War II is symbolically destroyed. Ryan only asks us to honor these men and "earn" the freedom they have left us. Presumably, pacifistic pleas are unnecessary because in Spielberg's world these men are not inherently violent.

By the middle 1950s, it was clear that a far-reaching contest over how to recall and forget the war was under way. At the dedication of the Iwo Jima Memorial, citizens gathered to venerate victory and the men who earned it. This was by no means a suppression of popular sentiment. The memorial represented well the belief that ordinary men fought gallantly, that the war was worth the sacrifice, and that the trauma could be put behind us. The same point is made in the film *To Hell and Back* (1955), which depicts a brave and decorated soldier who is close to his family. But members of the wartime generation continued to represent some veterans as brutes who had no place in peacetime America in films such as *A Streetcar Named Desire* (1951), *Peyton Place* (1957), and *No Down Payment* (1957). During the war, women had already expressed fears that military experiences incited men to misogynistic behavior. In 1954, Harriet Arnow articulated another critique by writing a novel, *The Dollmaker*, of how the war (and capitalism) destroyed the independence of a woman.

For a time in the 1960s and 1970s, Cold War pressures reinvigorated heroic images of American men and quelled some of the cultural divisions that had marked the immediate postwar era. In 1962's *The Longest Day*, the prowess of the American military and men of all ranks was validated. This movie of epic proportions lavished attention on the planning that went into the Allied invasion of Europe in 1944 and the extent to which the "biggest armada the world has ever known" was firmly under American leadership. A small amount of space was turned over to the heroics of the British and the French resistance, but the "star" of the feature was the collective effort of the Americans. The Nazis in this feature were disorganized; the sons of democracy were eager and united in purpose. Heroism crowded out serious discussion here of personal trauma or the emotional and political longings of ordinary soldiers.

In 1970, the release of *Patton* again reaffirmed the brilliance of American military strategy and leadership, although this film also took an extended look at the psychological traits of a heroic leader as well. Neither *Patton* nor *The Longest Day* paid much attention to 1940s concerns about democracy or the potential for brutality of Americans themselves. For General George Patton, war was less an act to save democracy than it was an opportunity to realize his dream of becoming a brave combatant – a certain type of man. "All real Americans love the sting of battle," he reportedly told his men. He was famous for his intolerance of subordinates who were traumatized by battle, who failed to relish killing the enemy as he did, and who lacked the fighting spirit to be a brave warrior. That is why he loved so much leading the triumphal parades of victors into liberated towns in Europe. Cheering crowds reaffirmed his sense of what war and men were all about.

Catch-22 (1970) appeared at the same time *Patton* did, however, and it suggested that the cultural effort to laud the World War II experience of Americans was in deep trouble. Certainly, the impact of Vietnam was crucial here, but it should be recalled that the story was drawn from a novel authored by a World War II veteran (Joseph Heller), as was the film of *The Naked and the Dead* (1958). This cynical view of the American military in World War II Italy completely debunked not only the integrity of military leadership but any effort to look at the war in heroic or sentimental terms. In this story, American soldiers use their spare time looking for cash or sex and actually question orders to drop bombs on innocent civilians. One U.S. serviceman kills and rapes an Italian woman. The central premise of the narrative is an antiwar statement, pure and simple. Captain Yossarian, the central figure, wants doctors to declare that he is insane so he can get out of the war completely. The "catch" is that the wish to escape from war is a perfectly sane idea and, therefore, cannot be a basis for judging someone to be insane.

Today, stories of glorious rises and tragic falls dot the landscape of American cultural memory. The celebration of personal dreams is discussed more widely than collective destinies. Images of a proud nation are contested by those of a society capable of inflicting pain and suffering. In this culture of contradictions and silences, cultural memory is subjected, in the words of Griel Marcus, to "an anarchy of possibilities" and, in the terms of Pierre Nora, to a "series of initiatives with no central organizing principle." But that "anarchy" is fiercely contested in the Spielberg film, not to restore the vision of a democratic nation but to rehabilitate traditions of good fathers, patriotic men, and self-sacrifice. Miller and Ryan do not challenge moral conventions, are not inherently violent, and are willing to relinquish personal dreams. They recognize that the fortunes of the nation take precedence over their own futures. The film *Saving Private Ryan* does not say that personal sacrifice is glorious as does *Patton*, or that wars are free of death and trauma as does the Iwo Jima Memorial. Distinct boundaries between cultural categories, like the tropes of heroic soldiers and personal pain, have generally been difficult to maintain since 1945. But the film chooses to take sides in the modern culture of opposites by protecting a sentimental view of American men that was seriously disrupted by both World War II and Vietnam. In fact, it basically suppresses a critical view of American society as well, preferring to suggest that the American future will best be fashioned by moral individuals rather than by democratic reforms.

Postwar films tended to treat the American warrior and American society in a more evenhanded way. They shared with *Saving Private Ryan* a tendency to remember the turmoil and stress. This is not an invention of the 1990s. Postwar films and culture actually went further, however, in exploring the consequences of the war, which is exactly what Bartov argued when he claimed that the acknowledgment of victims impelled individuals to find reasons for the suffering. Because the Spielberg film attempts to preserve the memory of patriotic sacrifice more than it desires to explore the causes of the trauma and violence, however, it is more about restoring a romantic version of common-man heroism in an age of moral ambivalence than about ending the problem of devastating wars.

The failure of *Saving Private Ryan* to evoke the memory of "a people's war," moreover, reveals the film's conservative politics. Past, present, and future are now contingent on standards of individual behavior rather than on democratic ideals such as the quest for equality, a just capitalism, or citizen participation in political life. Spielberg's film about trauma and patriotism suggests why the contemporary turn to memory, anguish, and the testimony of victims is about more than the demise of the cultural power of the nation. It also has a great deal to do with a sense of disenchantment with democratic politics and with turning political life over to "the people." Visions of a democratic community are feeble in this story, which remembers individuals in a more exemplary way than they were understood by their own generation.

29

East Meets West
The Asian Invasion (of Multiculturalism) in Hollywood

Minh-Ha T. Pham

From the birth of cinema, moviemakers have been interested in the interactions between cultural "insiders" and "outsiders." Perhaps because they flourished in the hands of immigrants in the United States, American films have always been concerned with the clash of peoples and cultures. From The Jazz Singer *to* The Godfather, *from* Birth of a Nation *to* Malcolm X, *filmmakers have explored how American multi-culturalism works. They have traced stereotypes and bigotry, cultural legacy and social change, the persistence of the old and the arrival of the new. During the last several decades, as more immigrants arrived in the United States from Asia, Africa, and the Middle East, a new wave of films has examined the process of cultural exchange. In the following essay, Minh-Ha T. Pham details how the film industry is treating Asians and multicultural values.*

When Ang Lee's *Crouching Tiger, Hidden Dragon*, a subtitled, epic Chinese drama, was released to American movie theaters in December 2000, the film marked the peak of what many American film reviewers and film critics have been calling an "Asian invasion" in Hollywood. The so-called invasion began when John Woo started filming *Broken Arrow* in 1995 and gained momentum in 1998 with *Rush Hour*, a Hollywood-produced film starring Jackie Chan. The invasion continued with *Romeo Must Die* (2000), *Rush Hour 2* (2001), *Kiss of the Dragon* (2001), and Quentin Tarantino's re-release of Tsui Hark's *Iron Monkey* (2001). Although Ang Lee is taking a break from the martial arts genre (at the time of this writing, he had just released *The Hulk*, starring Australian actor Eric Bana and American actors Nick Nolte and Jennifer Connelly), the Asian invasion is not quite over. Recently released were Chow Yunfat's *Bulletproof Monk* (2003) and *Cradle 2 The Grave* (2003) starring Jet Li, Kelly Hu, and rap artist DMX. *Rush Hour 3* is scheduled for release in 2004.

Scholars across a range of disciplines are debating what these films say about Hollywood and its audiences, the processes of globalization in Asia and the United States, and the state of the Hong Kong film industry. Shu-mei Shih, a Chinese studies scholar, argues that Taiwan's history of colonialism and imperialism has "accidentally and ironically become a historical benefit" for cultural producers such as Ang Lee whose knowledge of American culture – an inevitable byproduct of America's cultural hegemony in Taiwan – enables him to translate himself and his work easily to the American mainstream. Steve Fore, a film studies scholar, observes that the marketing and editing strategies employed in all of Jackie Chan's films emphasize action at the expense of the plot to ensure increased traffic at the box office. Whereas Fore argues that "universal marketability is the signature of the international blockbuster," Yingjin Zhang, a scholar of comparative literature, argues that these films are neither universal nor translatable. Instead, Zhang suggests that films such as those mentioned above make it possible for us to "screen China in a more meaningful way; not exclusively in a Western theoretical context, nor merely in one of 'authentic' Chinese culture and history, but ultimately in the context of cross-cultural, multiethnic, and transnational aspects of film making, film viewing, and film criticism in the contemporary world." All of these American-based scholars and many others, including those from Europe and Australia, have made important contributions to what Zhang calls the emergence of "Chinese film studies in the West."

Curiously, Asian American studies scholars have been relatively quiet witnesses to the phenomenon of Chinese transnational films. Whereas fanzines and online chatrooms reveal that amateur Asian American and Asian film critics have a lot to say about Jackie Chan, Chow Yun-fat, and Ang Lee, there has been little Asian American scholarship to date that investigates the Asian invasion or its impact on Asian American representational politics. One reason for this relative silence might be a point Roger Garcia makes in the introduction to *Out of the Shadows: Asians in American Cinema*, a catalog published to accompany a retrospective series by the same name at the Fifty-Fourth International Film Festival at Locarno, Switzerland. Distinguishing Asian American cinematic representation from the Asian presence of Jet Li and Chow Yun-fat in Hollywood films, Garcia writes:

> [Despite] developments in the independent realm, and the greater presence of Asian film-makers in the mainstream industry, the struggle for the representation of the Asian American experience in the media continues. This is different from recognizing an Asian presence on American screens where movies like *Romeo Must Die* or *Crouching Tiger, Hidden Dragon* have brought Chinese heroes and legends to American audiences. Asian America is a distinct and discrete entity – it is not a subset of China, Japan or Vietnam, but a constituency that has lived, breathed and contributed to the nation for over a century. It has its own achievements, artists, stories, and traditions that have grown separate from its various Asian roots.

Garcia's introduction echoes a point Asian American cultural nationalists such as Frank Chin and Jeffery Paul Chan made during the inaugural moment of Asian American studies in the mid-1970s. Both Garcia and the Asian American cultural nationalists of the 1970s speak to the long history of cultural marginalization, legal exclusions, and social rejection that Asian Americans have had to bear as a consequence of the dominant culture's conflation of Asian Americans' lived experiences and Hollywood's exoticized representations of Asians. Such conflation continues today. As Asian American historian Ronald Takaki puts it, "People come up to me and assume I must know karate. Most of us haven't studied the martial arts. It's not something we inherit. *Crouching Tiger* and other Americanized representations of Asia aren't so innocent. They reinforce our identity as outsiders and strangers."

Takaki's statement is an important reminder that the Asian invasion itself is an American construct. Since the mid-1800s, America has imagined Asia to be a homogenous continent of cultural and economic marauders whose presence in America had to be quarantined and regulated by immigration exclusion acts, segregation, internment camps, and auditors. Unlike the other Asian invasions, however, the Asian invasion of Hollywood is framed by an increasingly popular discourse of multiculturalism, a discourse that, in Lisa Lowe's words, "levels the important differences and contradictions within and among racial and ethnic minority groups according to the discourse of pluralism ... while simultaneously masking the existence of exclusions by recuperating dissent, conflict. and otherness through the promise of inclusion." In the Asian invasion, multiculturalism functions to abate the paranoia that has traditionally accompanied the other Asian invasion scares and, at the same time, to re-present and reactivate a particularly American drama of assimilation and socialization at both the national and international levels.

Unlike prior renditions of the Asian invasion, Hollywood is not threatened by the increased presence of Asian and Asian American actors and filmmakers; instead, the so-called Asian invasion enhances Hollywood's image as a racially inclusive, equal opportunity, global industry. Moreover, Asian actors and filmmakers are not invading Hollywood as much as they are finally being admitted into Hollywood under very specific conditions and for very specific roles. Despite the increased presence of Asian actors in Hollywood, the struggle for equitable and fair Asian American representation in Hollywood has not ended. Asian American filmmaker Wayne Wang has noted in several interviews that the mainstream success of *Crouching Tiger, Hidden Dragon* "only helps Kung Fu action films," not Asian American films.

Even so, an Asian American studies analysis of Hollywood's Asian invasion is useful to determine the influence of multicultural discourse on Hollywood's representations of Asians – whether they are transnational subjects becoming American national subjects, such as Jackie Chan's character in *Rush Hour*, or national subjects who are transnationally conceived, such as the characters in *Crouching Tiger*. Transpacific migrations. in the form of cinematic plots, financial investments, and on-screen and off-screen labor, are undeniably Asian American issues because these issues require the field to rethink and reposition many of its political and social commitments from the nation to the diaspora. At the same time, the transpacific migrations within and of Hollywood continue to perpetuate the myth that any marker of Asianness is synonymous with foreignness. Jackie Chan and Chow Yun-fat never play Asian Americans and are never in Asian American films; yet, as Takaki's experience demonstrates, Asian Americans are often confused with the Asian characters they play.

In *Rush Hour* (1999), a conventionally produced Hollywood film set in post-riot Los Angeles, multiculturalism is represented as a discursive and bodily meeting of the East and West. The movie uses Jackie Chan's and Chris Tucker's bodies to externalize the differences between the East and the West as an unavoidable binarism. Where Chan's Inspector Lee is overly modest and unassuming, Tucker's Detective Carter is overly boastful and presumptuous: where Lee is quiet and reserved, Carter is loud and obnoxious; where Lee is asexual, Carter is sexually aggressive; and where Carter's ability to speak the street slang of Los Angeles gives him access into the community, Lee's failed attempts to mimic Carter's slang constantly bar him from Los Angeles and remind us that Lee is a foreigner, Against the backdrop of LA's racial tensions,

Rush Hour offers a reconciliatory multiculturalist utopia that reenvisions the American topography of race relations.

Unlike *Rush Hour*, the nineteenth-century mythicality of *Crouching Tiger, Hidden Dragon* does not offer a national narrative of racial reconciliation but instead offers a transnational model of global feminism. Instead of "the fastest hands in the East meeting the biggest mouth in the West," as articulated in *Rush Hour*'s tagline, ancient Chinese masculinist tradition meets global feminism in *Crouching Tiger, Hidden Dragon*. In both films, Hollywood's multiculturalisms revitalize an old East meets West paradigm, which presupposes that the East and the West are always dialectically opposed in binaries of ancient and modern, exotic and familiar, and feminine and masculine, only to disavow these differences in melting-pot narratives of discursive and bodily assimilation. Using these two articulations of multiculturalism, both films effectively and profitably hook large American audiences by appealing to neo-liberal, cosmopolitan America, a powerful social, if not political, community.

"The Fastest Hands in the East Meet the Biggest Mouth in the West" Meets Multicultural Commodification

The tagline New Line Cinema used to advertise *Rush Hour*, "The Fastest Hands in the East Meet the Biggest Mouth in the West,' establishes, even at the paratextual level, a multicultural logic that operates throughout the film. The East and the West, personified by Inspector Lee and Detective Carter, are dichotomous entities with distinct characters. At one end of this dichotomy is Inspector Lee, a police detective in the Hong Kong Royal Police Department whose position in the Chinese heritage is established at the beginning of the movie when we see – but do not hear – Lee recovering 5,000-year-old Chinese artifacts stolen by the Juntao criminal organization, a British-run operation. Moving stealthily and quietly across the screen, Lee epitomizes the ninja hero whose greatest asset is his silence.

At the other end of the East-West dichotomy is Detective Carter, an African American police officer with the Los Angeles Police Department. Unlike Lee, whom we see before we hear, we hear Carter long before we see him. In our first "meeting" with Carter, he is honking and yelling at other drivers to "get the hell out of the way!" Soon, we learn that Carter is on his way to meet an illegal arms dealer, Clive Cod (Chris Penn), whom Carter is trying to arrest. Unlike Lee's capture of the Juntao criminal organization, Carter's arrest is less than effective. Two white police officers who happen to be walking through the parking lot in which Clive and Carter are meeting do not recognize Carter as a police detective and think they are witnessing a real transaction. Even though Carter attempts to signal to them that he is a police detective, they arrest both Carter and Clive. By the time Carter successfully makes his arrest, one police officer is shot and Clive's car blows up, as does an entire city block. Unlike Lee, who is a credit to his government, Carter is not an esteemed member of the Western heritage or the Los Angeles Police Department. The relationship between the LAPD and the African American community, as American audiences are well aware, has been particularly strained since the videotaped beating of Rodney King and the acquittal of the officers who beat him. Carter's status as an African American man in the LAPD is an uncomfortable one, as he reveals to his partner, Tania Johnston

(Elizabeth Pena), "My own mama's ashamed of me. She tells everybody I'm a drug dealer." The LAPD appears equally ashamed of Carter.

The central plot of *Rush Hour* begins when Chinese Consul Han's young daughter is kidnapped by the Juntao. The FBI's investigation of the kidnapping is stymied when Han requests that the FBI bring one of Hong Kong's finest, Inspector Lee, into their investigation. To keep Lee – "the Chunking cop" – away from its investigation, FBI agents Russ and Whitney devise a "bullshit assignment" designed to both humiliate a member of the LAPD as well as protect their case. Carter is immediately given this "bullshit assignment." Throughout the rest of the movie, Lee's misplacement in the West is matched by Carter's displacement.

Carter's reassignment effectively transforms him from a police officer into a cultural guide (for Lee as well as Hollywood audiences), but Carter's tour does not include Beverly Hills or Santa Monica, locations highlighted in most films set in Los Angeles. Instead, Carter takes Lee to a seedy pool hall, a liquor store, and a jail. Through Carter, Lee meets convicted criminals such as Clive Cod, Carter's shady cousin Luke (Clifton Powell), and an ex-drug dealer (Jason Davis). Carter's itinerary suggests that he is an insider not of the mainstream but of the periphery. The liquor store and the jail, peripheral sites in America, have been particularly condemned by African Americans as sites that cripple African American communities as well as aid in their criminalization. That Carter's tour of Los Angeles focuses on these peripheral sites suggests that, despite his status as an officer, Carter belongs in the liquor store and the jail rather than in the FBI. In addition, Carter's tour introduces Lee to the racial politics of the United States.

There are two "educational" scenes that highlight Lee's foreignness during this introduction. Frustrated because Carter rebuffs all of Lee's attempts to get to Consul Han. Lee turns on Carter's car radio without Carter's permission.

Lee: The Beach Boys!
Carter: Ah, man, hell no! You didn't just touch my goddamn radio!
Lee: The Beach Boys are great American music.
Carter: The Beach Boys are gonna get you a great ass whoopin'. Don't you ever touch a black man's radio, boy! You can do that in China but you can get your ass killed out here, man.

After teaching Lee that "you never touch a black man's radio," Carter quickly displaces Lee's idea of "great American music" by replacing the Beach Boys with Jay-Z, a commercially successful African American hip hop artist. Like the connection between the 5,000-year-old artifacts that Lee recovers and Lee's heritage, Carter's radio, the only "artifact" he guards and protects, signifies a connection to an African American heritage of which the Beach Boys are not a part.

A second educational opportunity arises when Carter takes Lee to Azteca Billiards for a "shakedown." Following Carter's orders that Lee "follow [his] lead and do what [he does]," Lee imitates Carter by greeting the African American bartender with, "What's up, my nigga?" Lee is, of course, completely unaware that the term carries distinctly different connotations depending on who is speaking. When the bartender asks Lee to repeat himself, Lee assumes, in his ignorance, that the bartender just doesn't understand his English. After repeating the greeting again, this time, more slowly, the bartender responds by grabbing Lee by the collar of his jacket and punching him.

A barroom brawl ensues, and Lee is forced to rely on his "fast hands" to compensate for his cultural ignorance. Besides providing Lee with another lesson on racial politics, this scene reiterates the differences between Lee and Carter established paratextually by the tagline. The difference between the East and the West is a difference between the nonspeaking but laboring hands of the East and the expressive and affective culture of the West. Speaking gets Lee into trouble at the pool hall, whereas speaking gets Carter into the pool hall, further establishing the pool hall as a black space. Lee's hands are the only things that save him from his cultural ignorance. After beating up eight or nine men (and apologizing to them profusely), Lee leaves the pool hall with Carter.

Lee's mistakes accentuate his foreignness and reconfirm the distinctions between East and West. At the same time, Lee is able to quickly learn from his mistakes, which minimizes the significance of his foreignness and underscores the myth that Asians learn fast and are assimilable. This is the promise and appeal of multicultural discourse. Racial differences exist but are easily overcome. In this ideal multicultural meeting of East and West, both the East and the West benefit from the meeting. Not only does Lee learn valuable lessons from Carter, Carter learns from Lee as well.

From the first moment that Carter and Lee meet, Carter's bigotry against all things Eastern is obvious. He expresses many of the same kinds of stereotypes that all Asians, whether native born or foreign born, in America are subjected to at one time or another. Carter assumes at their first meeting, for example, that Lee cannot speak English. When he meets Lee at the airport, Carter asks in a condescendingly slow and loud tone, "Please tell me you speak English. I'm Detective Carter. Do you speak any English? Do you understand the words that are coming out of my mouth?!?" When Lee responds only with a smile, Carter says to himself, "I cannot believe this SHIT! First I get a bullshit assignment, now Mr. Ricearoni doesn't even speak American." It is not until a few scenes later when a white cab driver pulls a gun on Carter and Lee that Carter realizes Lee can speak English. Carter's amazement is punctuated by the cliché of a gong that sounds when Carter realizes his mistake.

Carter: All of it sudden you speaking English now, huh!
Lee: A little.
Carter: A little my ass – you lied to me.
Lee: I didn't say I didn't speak English. You assumed I didn't.
Carter: Assume I kick your little Beijing ass right now, man.
Lee: I'm not responsible for your assumption.
Carter: You full of shit, you understand that, you full of shit.
Lee: Not being able to speak is not the same as not speaking. You seem as if you like to talk. I like to let people talk who like to talk. It makes it easier to find out how full of shit they are.
Carter: What the hell did you just say? […] So I'm the one full of shit, right?
Lee: We're both full of shit.

When Lee tells Carter that he is "not responsible for Carter's assumption," Lee is speaking for all Asian Americans. Asian Americans are not responsible for the assumptions African Americans or anyone else has about Asians in America. After explaining that "not being able to speak is not the same as not speaking," Carter is demonstrably shocked at both Lee's ability to speak and his eloquence. Carter's only comeback is to mock Lee's English. The racial tensions might have been elevated by Lee's accusation that Carter is full of shit, but Lee quickly defuses the tensions by sharing the blame for Carter's assumption: "We're both full of shit." After Lee accepts partial responsibility for the racial tensions between them, Lee and Carter are on their way to multicultural harmony. This scene, twenty-seven minutes into the movie, is the first sign that the differences between Lee and Carter – between Asian and African American, between East and West – may not be insurmountable after all. Throughout the last half of the movie, Lee and Carter's differences, always racialized, are resolved through the medium of multicultural exchange.

In a classic situation of multicultural resolution, Lee and Carter's friendship begins when they share a meal. Carter's initial disdain for the Chinese takeout food Lee offers him reflects his bigotry, but once he discovers that he actually likes the food, he and Lee become friends. In other words, Lee is finally accepted by Carter, a representative of one part of the West, via Chinese takeout.

> *Carter*: Damn, Chin, this is some greasy shit. You ain't got no better food, like some chicken wings, some baby back ribs, some fries or something?
> *Chin*: Chinese food, no soul food here!
> *Carter*: I didn't say nothin' 'bout no soul food, I said you got some better food. I don't want that greasy shit. How you gonna sell a big box of grease?
> *Carter*: Man, what you got me eatin'?
> *Lee*: That's eel.
> *Carter*: Is it good?
> *Lee*: Very good.
> *Carter*: What you got?
> *Lee*: Camel's hump.
> *Carter*: Mmm! Kinda good. Need a little hot sauce but it's kinda good though.

Although food is always a cultural and ethnic signifier, the significance of Chinese food is elevated in this movie in which East meets West. Within the East-West paradigm, Chinese food operates as a sign for Chinese culture. It is no wonder that a *Newsweek* article claiming that "Hollywood was destined to discover Hong Kong" is titled "Chinese Takeout." The allusion to manifest destiny ("destined to discover") speaks volumes about the colonial relationship structured into the East-West paradigm. The eel and the camel's hump that Lee "has Carter eating" reify the strangeness of the East. The exotic East is only made acceptable in the West when it is turned into a consumable commodity, as it is when Carter decides eel is "kinda good" even if it does "need a little hot sauce." The conflation of Lee and the Chinese food is what finally makes the West's acceptance of the East (and Lee) possible. The appreciation of Chinese food suggests at least one common denominator that connects this biracial odd couple.

Besides food, however, Lee and Carter, or rather Jackie Chan and Chris Tucker, have one more important thing in common: the ways that the commodification of racial difference influences their representation as Asian and African American men. The economic strands of multiculturalism are nowhere more revealing in *Rush Hour* than in the consistent manner in which both men are described only in terms of their fragmented body parts. "The fast hands of the East" carries with it two well-known stereotypes of Asians as martial artists and laborers. On one level. the "fast hands of the East" refer to Inspector Lee's martial arts skills (or one facet of his skills given that

Lee uses more than just fast hands when he is fighting). Because Lee is representative of the East, we can assume that Lee's martial arts skills are not unique to him but shared by many in the East as well. As noted by Takaki, there is an assumption that most Asians know martial arts.

On another level, the "fast hands of the East" refer to a widely circulating stereotype used to exploit the labors of Asian workers globally. Large multinational corporations as well as global sex service industries (here, I am referring to the fantasies surrounding Oriental massage parlors) have long targeted Asians for their supposed manual dexterity. Although Chan is not a "manual laborer" in either of these senses, the tagline does permit us to redefine the "manual laborer" to include the martial artist. By emphasizing Chan's hands, the East-West binary employed in the tagline and in the movie operates on a long and broad history of Asian stereotypes in America that recognizes the Asian immigrant not as a fully embodied human being but as a set of laboring hands, the part of the Asian body that traditionally produces the most profit and, therefore, the part that is most vulnerable to exploitation. The meeting of East and West, within a multicultural frame, is beneficial not only for cultural appreciation but for the profits that such a meeting produces for the West. Jackie Chan's laboring hands are, after all, one of the main attractions of the movie.

Similarly, Carter's character is reduced to the site of his (big) mouth. It is not just that Carter is loud and obnoxious, however. Carter's mouth defines him and confines him within stereotypically racialized parameters of blackness. His slang situates him not just in the West but in the streets of the West. The streets, often a euphemism for the ghetto, are a liminal national space, which are both geographically inside but culturally outside the nation. Carter's peripheralized position can be described in similar terms. Carter's mouth, the most playful and privileged site on his black body, registers loudly within the global economy of black male bodies. In his book *Yo' Mama's Disfunktional* Robin Kelley has noted that "[i]n a nation with few employment opportunities for African Americans and a white consumer market eager to be entertained by the Other, blacks have historically occupied a central place in the popular culture industry." While Kelley's observation gently references American's long obsession with black bodies that range from Step'n Fetchit to Michael Jordan, it is possible to extend this history to Carter's character as well. Carter's mouth is his most entertaining and most obvious feature. Although Carter's character is not defined by the protruding lips that other black bodies historically have been defined by, Carter's mouth does over-reach and over-step social standards or propriety, and it is this overstepping that makes Carter funny. Without his obnoxious but colorful language, Carter is nothing but an inefficient, bad cop. We like him because he makes us laugh; that is, we like him because he entertains us. Carter's mouth not only produces the most laughter in this film, it also produces the most profits in Hollywood. Just as Inspector Lee's broken English heightens his foreignness, and greatly adds to the comic value of the film, Carter's big mouth also marks him as a racial Other, a mark that is absolutely essential to the multicultural and comic value of the movie. Carter is nothing without his mouth and *Rush Hour* is nothing without Carter. As I have already noted, the importance of this particular body part is underscored when we first meet Carter. Both Carter and Lee represent racialized laboring bodies in Hollywood's global industry; the difference between them is not so much their race but how their race translates as labor in the racially segmented global economy.

Although the racial tensions between Lee and Carter are so central to this film that they often overshadow the plot, these differences are never so important or so substantial that they lead to any real problems, certainly nothing that could compare to the Los Angeles riots in 1992. Although Carter often threatens to "kick Lee's ass," these threats are never realized. Post-riot Los Angeles is rescripted in *Rush Hour* as a multicultural utopia and a capitalist's dream. Thus, the multicultural moral of this biracial odd coupling is that racial differences are never so significant that they cannot be overcome and are never so insignificant that they cannot be turned into a profit .... "The Tucker-Chan pairing" reifies a multicultural fantasy of racial pluralism; at the same time, such a pairing also displaces this fantasy. That Lee enters America via the cultural routes of African Americans (by the end of the movie, Lee has adopted Carter's taste for music, imitates Carter's dance moves, and uses Carter's slang) suggests that Asian (im)migrants have an alternative means or assimilation, a path that is distinctly non-white. Asian (im)migrants can gain access into the nation – at least into the nation's widening periphery – by approximating blackness (or brownness or redness, for that matter) rather than whiteness. Moreover, their coalition offers them both a way to challenge their marginalization in America. After all, despite Carter and Lee's exclusion from the big FBI investigation, they are ultimately responsible for safely rescuing Consul Han's daughter, Soo-Young.

Because Hollywood films are made not only for American audiences, it is important to note that although there are embedded in *Rush Hour* multicultural "handles" for American audiences to grab onto, these handles are not accessible to all audiences in other parts of the world. For audiences outside of America, Lee and Carter probably do not represent the East and West in the same way that I have represented them. In this sense. the "East" and "West" are historically contingent constructs. Nonetheless, because Lee and Carter are the racial underdogs who successfully challenge two white FBI agents, they represent globally sympathetic figures. The appeal of the underdogs is further increased when Carter remains loyal to his partner even when he has the opportunity to join the ranks of those who once marginalized him. Instead of taking the FBI badge Agents Russ and Whitney offer him, Carter tells them, "Why don't y'all take that badge and shove it up your ass? All up in your ass." All audiences can appreciate Carter's loyalty as well as the momentary power reversal that allows the underdog to tell off his bullies. More important for Hollywood and Hollywood's global audiences, Carter's loyalty to Lee means that we can expect *Rush Hour* sequels as well as *Rush Hour* imitations.

Crouching Tiger, Hidden Dragon: Multicultural Breakthrough or Breakdown?

Salman Rushdie, literary author and critic, has argued that the popularity of *Crouching Tiger, Hidden Dragon* signals a major paradigm shift in Hollywood's repertoire as well as in the tastes of American audiences. In an article written for the *New York Times*, Rushdie claims that the staggering number of multicultural moviegoers to *Crouching Tiger*, including Asian Americans, delegitimizes any possible accusations of Orientalism. Instead, he is optimistic that *Crouching Tiger* is evidence of a new and more tolerant American audience. Rushdie calls *Crouching Tiger* a "breakthrough movie that has taught Americans to accept subtitled foreign films" and calls its critics "killjoys." Rushdie goes on to say that "It may just be that the mass audience is ready, at long last, to enjoy rather more diversity in its cultural diet." The success of *Crouching Tiger* – and more broadly, the Asian invasion – demonstrates America's growing multicultural sensibilities. Implicitly, Rushdie's glowing evaluation is also an appraisal of Hollywood, whose multicultural track record has been bleak at best. Thus, *Crouching Tiger* is a breakthrough movie on many levels. Besides teaching Americans to read at the movies, as Rushdie's review suggests, the film is a breakthrough for Asian American actors in Hollywood as well as a breakthrough for multicultural discourse in Hollywood. Although it is important to investigate whether these breakthroughs will result in any longterm and more consistent changes in the film industry, the answers to these kinds of questions have a frustrating way or falling back on either pessimistic or optimistic speculation depending on one's own stakes in representational cultural politics. Instead, a more useful approach may be to focus on the ways that multiculturalism functions in *Crouching Tiger*. What does multiculturalism do for Hollywood films? What does it do to and for Hollywood audiences?

In the previous section, I argued that *Rush Hour* repositions Los Angeles as a site where multicultural fantasies of racial pluralism are still possible against the backdrop of "real" racial tensions between African Americans and Korean Americans as well as Asian Americans in general. *Rush Hour* recuperates Los Angeles' recent dystopic past by offering an alternative narrative or multicultural harmony through an altered process of socialization in which new Asian (im)migrants enter the nation culturally via African American-based cultural routes. That is, contemporary Asian roots are cultivated on the grounds of African American routes. By forcing Jackie Chan's character and Chris Tucker's character together in contemporary Los Angeles, *Rush Hour* offers an alternative relationship between Asian American and African American people in the "post-riot" period.

Crouching Tiger is an entirely different kind of Asian invasion film. *Crouching Tiger* is not a traditional Hollywood film. Unlike other major Hollywood blockbusters, *Crouching Tiger*'s budget was a modest $15 million and it was filmed entirely in China and in Mandarin. The total cost of production was shared by nine American and Chinese companies, including Sony Pictures Entertainment, Edko Film Limited, which is based in Hong Kong, and Ang Lee's own production company, Good Machine. The eleven companies in charge of distribution for *Crouching Tiger* are headquartered in Germany, Argentina, Canada, Slovenia, Hong Kong, the Netherlands, Spain, France, and the United States. Moreover, *Crouching Tiger* is set in mythical nineteenth-century China rather than contemporary America or contemporary China. That *Crouching Tiger* is set in the mythical past means that it has no real-life baggage attached to it. Without the boundaries and burdens of recuperation, *Crouching Tiger* is freer to imagine multicultural harmony not between racialized minorities but between ancient Eastern philosophy and modern Western discourse, *Crouching Tiger*'s success is due in large part to the film's ability to offer its audience the best of both the East and the West.

Unlike *Rush Hour*, Ang Lee's film lacked a catchy tagline. However, the film's brilliant promotion team more than made up for this lack. As Tom Bernard, co-president of Sony Picture Classics, explains, this movie's success depended on its popularity with diverse communities of film audiences. "We targeted five different groups – the art house crowd, the young, females, action lovers, and the popcorn mainstream." This broad-based marketing strategy ensures the film's success in mainstream venues. If men aren't interested in the romantic aspects of the film, they will be interested in the special effects and action. If women aren't interested in the martial arts action, they will enjoy this film as a love story or as a profoundly feminist story. Those who have never taken an interest in the low-budget feel of Kung fu films will embrace *Crouching Tiger* as a film that raises the martial arts genre from low- to highbrow. However, because *Crouching Tiger* is an Asian film with Asian actors, to target American audiences, all of the marketing strategies must ultimately appeal to America's desire for cultural diversity. The film has to appeal, in other words, to American multiculturalism.

The multicultural value of *Crouching Tiger* comes from the carefully controlled way in which racial difference is displayed and contained. Sony Picture Classics successfully promoted the foreignness of *Crouching Tiger* while also familiarizing the foreignness, making it palatable for mainstream America's "cultural diet." Following the logic of this marketing "master plan," both Sony's marketing team and Ang Lee have described this movie in terms of its approximation to well-known Western cultural products. Widely circulating descriptions of the movie include "a mix of Jane Austen lovemaking with Bruce Lee butt-kicking" and "a kung fu Titanic." Ang Lee explains the hybridity of the film in this way, " 'Family dramas and *Sense and Sensibility* are all about conflict, about family obligations versus free will." The martial arts form "externalizes the elements of restraint and exhilaration. In a family drama there is a verbal fight. Here you kick butt." By invoking *Titanic* and *Sense and Sensibility*, Lee neutralizes the foreignness of *Crouching Tiger* by reframing *Crouching Tiger*'s storyline as a derivative of these Western narratives. *Crouching Tiger*, in the logic of Sony's marketing, is part of a Western tradition of film. As one reviewer describes the movie, "While undeniably exotic to Western eyes, Ang Lee's film is not entirely foreign. The landscapes and costumes speak a universal language, the Taoist acrobatics suggest a refinement of *The Matrix*, and the adventure in the desert conjures up any number of classic westerns." Mainstream American audiences. like this film critic, could only link *Crouching Tiger*'s martial arts tradition back to *The Matrix* (1999), a Hollywood-produced, science fiction film starring Keanu Reeves. Although Yuen Wo Ping was involved in both *The Matrix* and *Crouching Tiger*, Lee's decision to use Yuen was based not on his work in *The Matrix* but on his long career directing and choreographing Kung fu films in Hong Kong.

Sony's marketing strategy could not ensure that all American audiences would love the movie, but it did succeed in piquing their interest enough to buy a ticket. Box-office figures for *Crouching Tiger* reached record-breaking numbers, with a large boost after the Academy Awards ceremony where it won [the award] for Best Foreign Picture. As of this writing, *Crouching Tiger* has grossed nearly $150 million in the United States alone, making it the highest grossing foreign language film ever. But why was this "foreign" or Asian film so commercially successful with Hollywood audiences when similar films have enjoyed only art house success? Although Lee claims that he and James Schamus, a writer involved in all of Lee's films, "didn't exactly have [*Crouching Tiger*] in mind for a western audience," Lee does admit that he wanted "to tell a story with a global sense." This "global sense" is accomplished in large part by making a particularly palatable form of ethnic feminism central to the movie, an ethnic feminism that privileges a globally universal rather than locally and temporally specific kinship among women.

Zhang Ziyi's character, Jen, the young and dangerously talented protagonist of the film, struggles with many kinds of "crouching tigers and hidden dragons," but perhaps her biggest personal struggle is her struggle to define herself as her own woman. If we emphasize Jen's struggles and personal growth, we can add one more Western genre to the descriptions of *Crouching Tiger*, the genre of the bildungsroman [the coming of age story]. Like so many narratives of this genre, *Crouching Tiger*'s Tom Jonesian protagonist, after unintentionally disrupting the social order in her understandable if misguided desire to create her own identity, learns difficult life lessons and redeems herself by the narrative's end, thereby restoring and reaffirming the dominant social order. That Jen is a young woman with modern feminist ideas only slightly changes the classically masculinist bildungsroman to a superficially feminist narrative in which even the most legendary swordswomen are powerless to escape the traditional male gaze of Li Mu Bai.

Although Lee's film has been positively received by female audiences because of the large amount of screen time devoted to highlighting the ability of very talented swordswomen, Lee's female heroines are not unique to the martial arts genre. There is, in fact, a long tradition of *nüxia* (female knight-errant) films dating back as early as the 1900s, which have their cultural basis in Chinese legends, such as the story of Fa Mu Lan. Describing the basic formula of the *nüxia* subgenre, Zhang Zhen writes:

> In the *nüxia* subgenre as a whole, the heroine is usually pushed onto [the] "stage" by default, due to either the absence or enfeebled condition of a male heir in the family. Having assumed the role of the avenger for an unjust death in the family and of the guardian of a community under external threat. the heroine takes up the responsibility and renounces or postpones her sexual desire.

In *Crouching Tiger*, the female heroines are not "pushed onto [the] stage" but actively clear a feminist space in the male-dominated Giang Hu world. Even Jade Fox, the most clearly defined female villain, seems to be motivated in part by anti-sexist ideals. As she tells Li Mu Rai before their fight, "Your master underestimated us women. Sure, he'd sleep with me, but he would never teach me."

Jade Fox's admonition speaks to the sexism of the Giang Hu world and, at the same time, emphasizes the exceptional skill of Jade Fox, Shu Lien, and Jen, who have had some impact on Giang Hu, however minimal. Nonetheless. these three very talented swordswomen only matter in the film insofar as they affect Li Mu Bai's life. Jade Fox's sexual oppression may justify her rage against Li Mu Bai's master, but because these women are defined so tightly through Li Mu Bai, audiences have little choice but to hate Jade Fox for hurting the more sympathetic Li Mu Bai. Our disgust for her is further heightened by her unappealing physical characteristics. When not undercover as Jen's governess, Jade Fox is always represented as a bitter old hag. She hunches over when she walks, her hair is always stringy and matted, and she is reviled by women and men of all social classes. We may recognize and even empathize with the misogyny of which Jade Fox accuses Li Mu Bai's master, but we cannot side with her.

On the other end of *Crouching Tiger*'s spectrum of female characters is Shu Lien, an older and more traditional *nüxia*. Shu Lien respects and abides by the social codes that Jade Fox and Jen revile, even when these codes stand in the way of her own self-fulfillment. It is her fidelity not only to her dead fiancé and Li Mu Bai but also to Giang Hu's dominant social order that makes Shu Lien so likable. Although she pines for Li Mu Bai, she does so quietly without imposing her personal desires on Li Mu Bai. Thus, the true hero of the film is free to follow his own life's path, even when Li Mu Bai's attachments to the Giang Hu world, his need to avenge his master's death and his personal desire for an apprentice outweigh his desire for her.

Finally, even Jen, who refused to submit to Li Mu Ba (as an apprentice or sexual partner), ultimately bows down to the world for which he stands when she kneels before Shu Lien in the aftermath of Li Mu Bai's death. This is the moment of feminism's failure. When the most active feminist figure, the young woman who once dreamed of the freedom "to live my own life, to choose whom I love," and the modern woman who embraced her individual rights even at the expense of her communal and family obligations – an archetypically feminist subject – submits to the traditions that Shu Lien lives by, not only has feminism failed, but the social order against which Jen's feminist ideals were in struggle prevails. That Jen kneels for Shu Lien rather than Li Mu Bai or Jade Fox demonstrates the final phase of Jen's development in which she atones for both the death of Li Mu Bai and the sins of her master, Jade Fox. And yet, for many audiences, Jen still represents a modern feminist figure:. There are good reasons for this.

Jen's ability to befriend both Shu Lien and Jade Fox, two women who do not share Jen's aristocratic social class, makes her an appealing global feminist figure. Even Shu Lien, who remains fond of Jen throughout the movie, cannot overlook their social differences, as she tells Li Mu Bai, "She's an aristocrat's daughter. She's not one of us." Jade Fox also warns Jen against befriending Shu Lien because "[Her] mother would not want [Jen] consorting with [Shu Lien's] kind." Despite these warnings, Jen welcomes Shu Lien and begs her. "Don't distance us. From now on, let's be like sisters." Jen is most recognizable as a feminist to Hollywood audiences because of her pluralism. Her willingness to create sisterhood with those unlike her invites female audiences to relate to Jen despite differences in race, culture, nation, and temporality, which is perhaps why Elaine Showalter observes that *Crouching Tiger* "speaks with luminous directness to the aspirations of contemporary women."

In fact, it is the differences (racial, cultural, class, and temporal) between Jen and female audiences that make her an attractive feminist figure. A nineteenth-century Chinese woman, Jen is an authentic racial Other. Her ability to embrace pluralism affirms the value of pluralistic feminism as not exclusively Western and modern but universal and global. Jen's character suggests that class boundaries, such as race, nation, and culture, cannot keep women apart. Jen's sisterhood evokes a brand of contemporary global feminism in which Western middle-class and upper-middle-class women claim a "sisterhood" with women in the Third World. The same erasures of history and culture must be made for this "sisterhood," whose power is unevenly distributed, to function. Jen's appeal for sisterhood is unlikely but nevertheless compatible with Rushdie's assessment of the multiculturality of this film because both multiculturalism and pluralistic feminism offer the possibility of transcending the limitations of one's own social and geographic position to try on or test an Other's position. Herein lies the fantasy of multiculturalism: Differences in race, class, and history are flattened out, making movement across race and class much less problematic. As multiculturalism homogenizes difference by making all differences the same, so too does global feminism, according to Karen Kaplan, "homogenize economic and cultural difference in favor of a universalizable female identity." Jen's "sisterhood" offers another marker of multiculturalism in this movie whose box-office success depends on Hollywood's ability to sell itself and the movie in a global economy in which multicultural products are valuable commodities.

If we are to understand fully these films in their material and historical context, a critical dialogue between Asian American studies scholars and the scholars of "Chinese film studies in the West" is extremely important. Asian Americanists can help articulate the relationships between transnational Chinese cultural producers and Asian American cultural consumers that the scholars of "Chinese film studies in the West" have not been able to do. Although non-Asian Americanist film scholars such as Gina Marchetti have provided important contributions to the study of Chinese films, without a more sustained attention to Asian American identity politics, the effect of these transnational films on Asian American audiences is lost.

30

Immigration at the Movies
The Immigrant in Film:
Evolution of an Illuminating Icon

Carlos E. Cortés

Immigration has long been a popular cinematic theme. The birth of film coincided with an unprecedented wave of global migration, and immigrants formed a large share of film's early audience. Not surprisingly, many early films, including the first "talkie," The Jazz Singer, dramatized and personalized the immigrant experience. The movies explored immigration's human meaning: what it means to be uprooted, voluntarily or involuntarily, from one's homeland; the perils of voyage by sea or land; the disorientations following arrival; and the traumas of resettlement and problems of acculturation. In the movies, we can see how immigration altered generational relationships, since the young often found it easier to learn a new language and pick up new customs than did their parents. We also see whether women or men were more successful in adjusting to a new environment, and the extent to which the new environment posed a threat to the immigrant's morality, faith, or traditions. The movies provide vivid glimpses of immigrant neighborhoods and enclaves, and valuable insights into immigrants' aspirations and how these have changed over time. As Carlos E. Cortés shows, sometimes movies have celebrated assimilation and praised characters who overcome the pressure to maintain ethnic and religious traditions. Sometimes, movies were optimistic about immigrants' ability to achieve material success through a combination of optimism and hard work. Yet at other times, the movies have taken a very different view, emphasizing the problems of poverty, prejudice, and discrimination that immigrants faced as they entered a new society.

In the 1984 motion picture, *Moscow on the Hudson*, Soviet saxophonist Vladimir Ivanoff defects while touring with a Russian circus in New York City. Here he is in the United States of America, yet everywhere he encounters other cultures, other languages, and other immigrants or American-born minorities – his Cuban immigrant lawyer, his Italian immigrant girlfriend, a Korean cab driver, the black family that adopts him. Acculturation, 1980s style, means adjusting to a multi-ethnic, multi-lingual society of immigrants and other ethnics.

Paul Loukides. BEYOND THE STARS 1. © 1990 by the Board of Regents of the Univeristy of Wisconsin System. Reprinted by permission of the University of Wisconsin Press.

In its portrayal of immigration, *Moscow on the Hudson* provided the screen antithesis of Hollywood's oft-expressed melting-pot film vision of the United States. Rather, it posited an America in which cultural differences coexist with societal commonalities, in which pluribus and unum continuously interact. In *Moscow on the Hudson*, Hollywood had once again made convenient use of immigrants to simultaneously entertain, provide alternative perspectives on America, and address changing societal concerns.

American movies have drawn heavily on the theme of immigration, using the immigrant as a stock figure to explore issues and disseminate ideas. With their power to personalize, to dramatize, and to magnify, American films have served as a kind of public textbook on immigrants as individuals and on immigration in general. Native-born Americans, many of whom have had little significant contact with immigrants, have learned about them through their screen experiences. By watching movies, immigrants, too, have gone to school – becoming aware of other immigrant groups, receiving lessons on acculturation to America, internalizing modes of social behavior, and observing both the possibilities of and obstacles to becoming full-scale Americans.

Since the early silent era, American movies have used immigrants as metaphors for aspects of the real and mythical America, both past and present. By massaging immigrants as stock characters and modifying their usage over time, American movies have addressed evolving issues, supported patterns of behavior, and proclaimed continuing American hopes. Based on my analysis, I have concluded that filmmakers have developed five basic types of immigrant stock characters:

1 *The Incomprehensible Alien* – *as* examples of foreignness (strangeness and alienness) in our midst;
2 *The Cultural Bumbler* – *as* targets of humor, usually butts of cultural jokes;
3 *The Dream Seeker* – *as* embodiments of the process of seeking to become American and grasp the American Dream;
4 *The Societal Victim* – *as* pawns, sometimes victims, sometimes combatants, in the struggle to resolve U.S. societal issues, including prejudice, discrimination, and exploitation; and
5 *The Alien Threat* – *as* subverters of American life, often as personifications of incomprehensible and mysterious evil.

Arrival of the Silent Alien

The five basic types of immigrant stock characters emerged quickly. From the beginning, movie immigrants served as Incomprehensible Aliens. With their foreign roots, odd (to native-born Americans) customs and values, unintelligible languages (unheard but imagined in silent movies), and garbled English, these immigrants personified strangeness – sometimes cute and quaint, sometimes mysterious and forbidding.

In addition, these same movie immigrants tended to be Cultural Bumblers. Burdened by alien customs and restricted by language, they made silly mistakes while trying to function in American society. Filmmakers soon found that bumbling immigrants could draw predictable laughs, even from immigrant audiences.

Charlie Chaplin's lauded 1917 film, *The Immigrant,* illustrated these two stock character usages, The Incomprehensible Alien and The Cultural Bumbler. An immigrant

Figure 15 *The Immigrant* (1917). Mutual Film Corporation. Directed by Charles Chaplin. Mutual Film Corporation. Author's screenshot.

of unspecified origin, Chaplin sails to the United States on an ocean-buffeted ship filled with other immigrants of varying backgrounds. Even Chaplin's immigrant finds the others odd. Once in the United States, he bumbles along, slowly learning from error and observation to function as an American.

Although perceived as odd and culturally bumbling, many screen immigrants strove to immerse themselves in the process of Americanization and pursue that most American of quests, the American Dream. Thus emerged the third immigrant stock character, The Dream Seeker, whom Hollywood used to send Americanizing messages to immigrants who flocked into movie houses. Films like the 1915 *Regeneration*, in which education becomes an avenue for Jewish personal and familial advancement, illustrated Hollywood's early use of dream-seeking stock immigrants to preach the messages of opportunity, effort, and Americanization.

Yet the road to The Dream contained obstacles. Poverty, prejudice, and other societal restrictions often thwarted immigrants' efforts. Thus moviemakers created the fourth immigrant stock figure, The Societal Victim, sometimes passive, other times a victim despite heroic efforts.

The powerful 1914 film, *The Italian*, typified the blending of these two stock characters, The Dream Seeker and The Societal Victim. Ambitious Venetian gondolier Beppo Donnetti seeks his fortune in "the golden land" (according to one title card).

Becoming a bootblack on New York City's Lower East Side, Beppo earns extra money by getting his "wop friends" (so termed by the local Irish-American political boss) to vote for the machine's candidates. Beppo's Italian fiancée joins him, but their dream turns into a nightmare when their baby becomes ill and dies, as poverty prevents them from obtaining the needed hygienic food. The young Dream Seekers had become Societal Victims.

Most movie immigrant Dream Seekers and their offspring came from European extraction. Yet while movie European immigrants strode toward Americanization, Asian immigrants retreated into their cultural and linguistic enclaves. While European immigrants rose through hard work, Mexican immigrants remained subservient.

But non-European immigrants did more than seek The Dream. They also preyed on others. Thus emerged the fifth and final major immigrant stock character – The Alien Threat. Although silent movies sometimes presented European immigrants as threats, colored immigrants (as defined by US racial perceptions) and US-born minorities provided the silent screen with its main source of villainy.

The old West furnished the ideal locale for these colored immigrant villains. The westward movement of white (mostly) Americans into a region inhabited by Mexicans (implicitly treated although not always explicitly labeled as immigrants) and Indians established the basis for conflict. Building from decades of western "dime novels," filmmakers quickly adopted the novelistic tradition of using Mexicans and Indians as "convenient villains." Anti-Mexican epithets even climbed onto movie marquees in such films as *The Greaser's Gauntlet* (1908), *The Greaser's Revenge* (1914), and *Guns and Greasers* (1918). Asian immigrants provided a less aggressive threat. Operating in their ethnic enclaves, they plied their evil within limited boundaries (*The Fatal Hour* – 1908).

By the middle of the 1910s, then, American moviemakers had established Hollywood's five basic types of immigrant stock characters. These types have reappeared consistently to the present, but historical forces have both solidified and modified the manner of usage. The types have continued, but the concerns they represented and the messages they embodied have evolved with the changing national and global environment.

The Immigrant as an Americanizing Icon

War has periodically influenced the movie depiction of immigrants. With the onset of World War I, the government clamped down on German-language media and organizations, while states passed laws restricting the use of foreign languages in schools. Hollywood, too, joined in this campaign by making films that encouraged more rapid Americanization. During the 1920s, immigrant stock characters increasingly moved from Cultural Bumblers to Dream Seekers, who role-modeled Americanism and Americanization.

Hollywood movies proclaimed two paths to accelerated immigrant Americanization – intermarriage and effort. Movies propounded intermarriage as a way of eroding ethnic isolation by blending immigrant heritages in such films as *The Cohens and the Kellys* (1926), *His People* (1927), and *Abie's Irish Rose* (1929). Movies also celebrated European immigrants who used industriousness and initiative to advance economically. The 1924 *Manhandled* personified this vision in the character of Jimmy Hogan, an enterprising Irish-American mechanic-cab driver who, in his spare time, develops an invention that improves the operation of automobiles.

Symbolically, the first "official" sound film, the 1927 *The Jazz Singer*, integrated these two themes, focusing on the ethnic maintenance-Americanization crossfires racking Jakie Rabinowitz, a Dream-seeking cantor's son. From one side came pressures for ethnic conformity – to follow his father's vocation, to maintain Jewish tradition, to marry a Jewish girl. From the other side came the pull of the melting-pot dream – through a musical career and intermarriage.

The ethnic dilemmas of *The Jazz Singer* reflected struggles within U.S. filmmaking itself involving Jewish immigrants and their offspring. On one side stood Hollywood's Americanizing Jews – studio heads and producers who dominated Hollywood and had become champions of its public textbook on melting-pot Americanization. Determined to demonstrate their Americanness, they used immigrant stock characters as icons for their message.

In opposition stood the Jewish immigrant-led Yiddish film movement. Using this popular language spoken by many Eastern European immigrant Jews, Yiddish films emphasized the importance for Jewish immigrants to celebrate Jewish culture, resist assimilationist enticements, and strengthen ethnic bonds even in the face of melting-pot societal pressures. However, the Yiddish film movement (like the temporally parallel black film movement) proved to be only transitory due mainly to limited audiences. Inadequately financed and lacking the expensive production values that film audiences (including Jewish moviegoers) had come to expect, these motion pictures also suffered from the declining use of Yiddish among American Jews. Yiddish-language films virtually disappeared by the end of the Great Depression.

Immigrants as Role Models

During the Great Depression, numerous filmmakers used movies to examine the roots and expressions of America's social dilemmas, including the problems faced by immigrants and their offspring. Moreover, in 1934 the movie industry adopted its Motion Picture Production Code (Hays Code), which ruled American filmmaking until the mid-1950s and was not officially buried until 1966. Some of the Code's provisions addressed issues critical to the screen depiction of immigrants, with three provisions of particular importance.

First, the Code cautioned against the use of negative national and ethnic group epithets – "Chink, Dago, Frog, Greaser, Hunkie, Kike, Spig, Wop, Yid" – on the grounds that these words were "obviously offensive to the patrons of motion pictures in the United States and more particularly to the patrons of motion pictures in foreign countries." Second, to warn immigrants (in fact, all Americans) against the pitfalls of choosing inappropriate avenues for upward mobility, the Code mandated that the treatment of "crimes against the law ... shall never be presented in such a way as to throw sympathy with the crime as against law and justice or to inspire others with a desire for imitation." Third, while intermarriage offered an Americanization avenue for white immigrants, the Code ordained that "miscegenation (sex relationship between the white and black races) is forbidden." In practice, "black" was usually interpreted broadly as "colored," encompassing Asian and "dark" Latino immigrants.

Addressing the social contradictions of the Depression and guided by the Hays Code, filmmakers increasingly used movies to distinguish between appropriate and inappropriate avenues to The Dream. As a metaphor for this moral lesson, Hollywood often turned to its convenient icon, the stock character immigrant. While celebrating The Dream Seeker who chose proper avenues, movies sometimes combined The Dream Seeker and The Alien Threat into a negative role model of how not to behave.

The popular urban gangster film became a basic movie textbook. Hollywood often featured immigrants and their descendants as criminals, who inevitably paid the price. In particular, movies targeted three immigrant groups: Italians (as in *Little Caesar* – 1931 and *Scarface* – 1932); Irish *(Public Enemy* – 1931 and *Angels with Dirty Faces* – 1938); and Chinese immigrants (*Chinatown Nights* – 1930 and *The Hatchet Man* – 1932).

Movies continued to recommend intermarriage as an appropriate road to Americanization ... with limitations. The Hays Code had prohibited this avenue for Asian and most Latino immigrants (a few light-skinned, Spanish-type Latin lovers might qualify). Moreover, even some European immigrants tended to remain outsiders when it came to screen intermarriage with mainstream Anglos.

This dilemma formed the core of one of the era's more instructive immigrant films, the 1935 *The Wedding Night*. To recharge his creative batteries, Anglo society novelist Tony Barrett takes refuge in rural Connecticut, near a Polish immigrant farming community. There he meets and falls in love with Mania Novak, a beautiful young Polish woman, who helps with his recharging. However, she has been promised to Frederick Sobieski, an oafishly portrayed Polish farmer. The film celebrates Anglo superiority, contrasting the urbane, sensitive Tony with the crude, cloddish Frederick. When Mania rejects Frederick's drunken advances on their wedding night, he becomes an Alien Threat, seeking revenge on Tony. But even here Frederick bumbles, accidentally killing Mania by knocking her down a flight of stairs as she tries to protect her Anglo beloved.

But while Cultural Bumblers and criminal Alien Threats abounded in movies of the 1930s, Hollywood also used immigrants and immigrant offspring to demonstrate the attainability of The Dream through positive avenues. Such characters ranged from an industrious, loyal Jewish immigrant department store manager in *Sweepings* (1933) to an illiterate but intrepid Polish immigrant miner who successfully challenges an Anglo-controlled mining company in *Black Fury* (1935), from a compassionate Swedish-American lumberman in *Come and Get It* (1936) to a sensitive Portuguese-American fisherman in *Captains Courageous* (1937), from *In Old Chicago's* (1938) flamboyant Irish-American O'Leary clan to a prosperous California Italian immigrant grape grower in *They Knew What They Wanted* (1940). However, the foremost Depression-era ethnic film hero was that master sleuth, the unflappable Charlie Chan, beginning with *The House Without a Key* (1926). (Justifiably criticized by members of the Asian-American community for their caricaturing of Chinese-Americans, these movies became popular in China, as Chan epitomized Chinese intellectual superiority, with Number One Son typifying the negative cultural impact of Americanization.)

While movies used immigrant stock characters to preach the imperative and proper process for becoming good Americans, Hollywood also instructed immigrants that they had to be willing to fight for their adoptive nation. Enlisting in the World War II national effort, Hollywood cranked out movies calling on Americans of all races, religions, and national origins to sacrifice for their country. In wartime-made war movies, Hollywood instituted its first "affirmative action" policy, with nearly every movie military unit becoming an ethnic mosaic. While at times these movies merely suggested foreign heritage through surnames – often with a Kowalski, a Gomez, a Cannelli, a Swenson, a Weinberg, and a Mulcahy fighting side by side – at other times they made that immigrant status explicit.

Of course, one immigrant group – Japanese – did not merit such treatment. Most spent much of the war in internment camps, this treatment justified in the 1942 *Little Tokyo, U.S.A.*, which portrayed Los Angeles as a hotbed of disloyal Japanese Alien Threats. Japanese-Americans ultimately served in the military – in segregated units, of course – but not until 1951, with *Go For Broke!*, did these Japanese-American war heroes receive feature film recognition for their valorous military contributions.

The Rise of Immigrant Victimization

While Hollywood has continuously featured all five movie immigrant types, these stock characters have alternated in screen prominence. Incomprehensible Aliens and Cultural Bumblers served as the principal immigrant stock characters of the 1910s. Dream Seekers dominated the 1920s. Alien Threats, usually urban criminals, took center stage in the 1930s. But the post-war era would bring The Societal Victim to the forefront.

In the euphoria following World War II, Hollywood turned its attention from the evil that the United States had been fighting abroad to the evils that had to be confronted within. Many films focused on problems faced by immigrants and other ethnic Americans. These obstacles included oppressive socio-economic conditions, anti-ethnic prejudice, and, for would-be Americans, the difficulty of gaining legal entry into the United States.

Challenging, often soul-destroying conditions dominated the lives of post-war movie immigrants. *Give Us This Day* (1949) dramatized the plight of poor, industrious Italian immigrants. The film follows the decades-long struggle of Geremio, an industrious bricklayer, and his courageous, determined immigrant wife, Anunciata, to escape the congested tenements of New York City's Little Italy and fulfill their dream of buying a home in Brooklyn. Anunciata valiantly tries to amass the needed purchase price, but the birth of three children slows their quest and the Great Depression erodes their savings. The long-unemployed Geremio finally finds work, but he dies in an on-the-job cave-in. When a government investigation reveals contractor negligence and awards financial compensation to Anunciata, the grief-stricken widow laments, "At last Geremio has bought us a house."

Prejudice provided a special type of victimization. Slavic immigrants find justice difficult to achieve in the American legal system in *Call Northside 777* (1948). Puerto Ricans (who are not immigrants, but who have been treated metaphorically as such in movies) face not only inner-city poverty but the taunts of classmates, who make fun of their use of English in *The Blackboard Jungle* (1955). Japanese immigrants become the victims of war-intensified hatred in *Bad Day at Black Rock* (1954) and *Japanese War Bride* (1952).

Hollywood even set immigrant dilemmas to music with adaptations of Broadway hits. In the 1961 *West Side Story*, Puerto Ricans face the prejudice of New York City whites in a struggle over limited urban turf. Other times the problems arise internally, as in the 1961 *Flower Drum Song*, which highlights the conflicting traditions and intra-ethnic tensions among Chinese-Americans and Chinese immigrants.

Possibly the most pan-ethnic example of the immigrant anti-prejudice film was the brilliant *12 Angry Men* (1957), which deals with a white male jury's deliberations concerning the fate of a young man on trial for the murder of his father. The jurors' discussion makes it explicit that he is one of "them," either an immigrant or the off-spring thereof, although the defendant's ethnicity is never specified – making him the ultimate Incomprehensible Alien. Yet the defendant's acquittal suggests that, in America, even "they" can obtain justice.

Particularly during the 1950s and early 1960s, a new type of Dream Seeker-Societal Victim emerged, as movies examined still another immigrant issue, the problem of gaining entrance to the United States. Undocumented immigrants, particularly undoc-umented Mexican workers, received special attention. In line with that era's critique of social ills, post-war movies addressed the exploitation of Mexican undocumented workers in such films as *Border Incident* (1949) and *The Lawless* (1950). Generally faceless stock pawns, perfect examples of the passive Societal Victim, these immigrants mainly provided a rationale for showdowns between Anglo heroes and villains.

At times movies humanized undocumented immigrants. For example, the 1962 adaptation of Arthur Miller's play, *A View from the Bridge*, addressed this experience in a far more personal fashion than the Mexican worker films, while also examining ethnic intra-group conflicts, in this case between Italian-Americans and Italian undoc-umented immigrants. Even the problem of would-be immigrants received film attention, whether they came from Italy (*The Glass Wall* – 1953), from Japan (*Sayonara* – 1957), or from Greece (*America, America* – 1963).

But yet another war created still further variations for immigrant stock characters. The Cold War brought a surge of super-patriotic (including anti-communist) films. Acting American was not enough; you had to proclaim your Americanism. Immigrants again served as convenient icons, with Dream Seekers also becoming Dream Proclaimers, voicing their passionate Americanism.

The 1950 *Gambling House* provides a striking example. Marcus Furiani, a never-nat-uralized Italian immigrant, is about to be deported as an undesirable alien. Sent to Ellis Island to await deportation action, he observes how deeply immigrants crave to become Americans. At his deportation hearing, instant-patriot Furiani presents his mea culpa:

> I never cared for anybody or anything. I never cared for my country. I never even thought of it. I deserve to be thrown out of this country. What I'm trying to say is it's the words that man said. He said that the idea of this country was to give every man his chance, regardless of his birth. The right to live, and to work, and to be himself. He said that this was the promise of America. And, your honor, I'm sorry that I didn't understand that a long time ago.

Emotionally moved, the judge rejects deportation and permits Furiani to stay in the United States and seek naturalization.

Return of the Alien Threat

The acceleration of the civil rights movement in the 1960s brought ethnicity into increasing vogue as a film subject. Unfortunately, the ethnic screen experience was often couched in criminal terms. Moreover, with the demise of the Hays Code and the institution of a far more permissive rating system (G, PG, R, or X), that criminal search became more violent than ever, while screen criminals frequently went unpunished.

Films on the immigrant experience, from the serious and sensitive to the erotic and exploitive, poured out of Hollywood. As in the 1930s, the Alien Threat returned as the prominent immigrant stock character. Italian-Americans led the parade, becoming nearly synonymous with the immigrant criminal.

Francis Ford Coppola created the archetype for the new Alien Threat with the two installments of his masterful *The Godfather* (1972, 1974). Italian-American protest groups rightfully criticized Hollywood's repeated depiction of Italian-Americans as violent and criminal So when the two *Godfather* films came to television in 1977 in revised, expanded, chronological form as *The Godfather Saga*, the following words, both emblazoned on the screen and intoned by a solemn voice, introduced the movie:

> *The Godfather* is a fictional account of the activities of a small group of ruthless criminals. It would be erroneous and unfair to suggest that they are representative of any ethnic groups.

Of course, following this warning came the violent, multi-generational saga of the Corleone family, with much of the action set against the background of New York City's Italian immigrant community. The gratuitous and ineffective "Godfather disclaimer" soon became the model for filmmakers proclaiming self-absolution in their negative treatment of immigrants. Its clones appeared in other movies that criminalized immigrant groups, like the 1983 *Scarface* (Cubans) and the 1985 *Year of the Dragon* (Chinese).

While Italian-Americans assumed the lead among screen immigrant criminals, other groups took their turns as contemporary Alien Threats. By the 1980s, Latino drug dealers, in particular, had joined Italian-Americans as screen icons for violent criminality in such films as *Scarface, Code of Silence* (1985), *Running Scared* (1986), and *8 Million Ways to Die* (1986). Chinese immigrants made a criminal comeback in a manner reminiscent of the films of the 1930s, whether in serious form (*Year of the Dragon*) or in comic-strip escapism (*Big Trouble in Little China* – 1986). After years of using Arabs as convenient overseas antagonists, Hollywood now adopted Arab immigrants as an internal terroristic enemy in the 1987 *Wanted: Dead or Alive*.

But the renewed Alien Threat went beyond criminality. Movies now also portrayed immigrants as another type of Alien Threat, an economic one. Reflecting growing American unemployment angst, screen immigrants now became competitors for jobs and scarce resources. For example, the *1985 Alamo Bay* examined the economic challenge generated by recent Asian immigration, as embodied in the conflict between industrious Vietnamese immigrant fishermen and equally industrious native Texans on the gulf coast.

Economic competition sometimes erupted between ethnic groups. In a non-musical variation on *West Side Story* (or *Romeo and Juliet*), the 1987 *China Girl* focused on the tragedy-bound love between an Italian-American boy and a Chinese immigrant girl in New York City. Its powerful opening credit sequence deftly reveals the almost-inevitable conflict created by the expansion of the Chinese immigrant community into an old Italian-American neighborhood. This sequence encapsulates the tensions by showing a proud Chinese immigrant family taking down the sign of an old

Italian store and erecting a sign for their new Chinese restaurant, while old Italians watch with nostalgia and young ones glare with hatred.

Movies sometimes blended the new theme of immigrant economic competition with the 1950s theme of undocumented workers. Gregory Nava's engrossing *El Norte* may be the quintessential contemporary immigrant film, bringing together all five of the stock character types and adding a unique linguistic twist. Enrique and Rosa, a young brother and sister, escape from military oppression in their native Guatemala and traverse both a threatening Mexico and the formidable U.S.–Mexican border to reach Los Angeles. Incomprehensible Aliens, they also encounter inevitable moments as Cultural Bumblers – Rosa gets a job as a maid but cannot operate the automatic clothes washer. Both are Dream Seekers, but ultimately suffer defeat as Societal Victims – Rosa dies, Enrique must flee from his restaurant job when a fellow worker sees him as an economic Alien Threat and reports him to U.S. immigration authorities. Moreover, beyond synthesizing all five immigrant character types, Nava audaciously creates a trilingual film – English, Spanish, and a Guatemalan Indian language, with English subtitles. That such a film became a critical and a surprise box-office hit in itself makes *El Norte* a landmark in the screen characterization of immigrants.

El Norte also symbolizes recent efforts to reinvigorate U.S. filmmaking with a significant use of foreign languages to help capture the essence of the immigrant experience. Such films as *Hester Street* (Yiddish – 1975), *El Super* (Spanish – 1979), *The Mission* (Farsi – 1983), *Stranger Than Paradise* (Hungarian – 1984), and *A Great Wall* (Chinese – 1986) suggest the linguistic richness of contemporary American life. They also may portend the elevation of screen immigrants from stock character status.

Yet to this day immigrants remain a target of derision, even in movies having nothing to do with immigration. In the 1987 *Suspect*, Eddie Sanger, a prominent Congressional lobbyist, is called up for jury duty. When another lobbyist learns of Sanger's obligation, he sardonically chides Eddie, "What are you, an immigrant? Nobody has jury duty!"

31

Movies and the Construction of Historical Memory
Movies, History, and the Disneyfication of the Past: The Case of Pocahontas

Steven Mintz

In today's video culture, how do we learn history? From the Alamo to the Titanic, from Gettysburg to the Watergate break-in, most Americans have learned the essentials of important historical events on television or at the movies. Such documentary filmmakers as Ken Burns and such television outlets as the History Channel have provided a classroom where millions of Americans have learned about their history. But perhaps no purveyor of popular culture has played a more important role in shaping impressions of our past than the Walt Disney Corporation. Walt Disney's movies have long been staples of American childhood. From Snow White and the Seven Dwarfs *(1934) and* Fantasia *(1940) to* The Little Mermaid *(1989) and* Beauty and the Beast *(1991), the Disney studio has created many of the best-loved animated films in American history. The studio has also helped to define and shape American history. Disney films and television shows featuring the American Revolution and western expansion have taught a particularly slanted view of American history to millions of viewers. In the following essay, Steven Mintz asks the important questions: Are the products of the Disney studios good history? What is good film history? And does it matter if Hollywood's treatment of history is accurate or not?*

More than any other company, Walt Disney has demonstrated an ongoing interest in American history. From the adventures of Davy Crockett to the animatronic Abraham Lincoln robot at Disneyland and the attempt to build an American history theme park near the Bull Run battlefield, Disney has long looked to American history as a source of entertainment, edification, and profit. Yet despite its fascination in history, Walt Disney has been a corporation historians love to hate.

Why don't historians like Disney? Is it because historians fear competition and are eager to monopolize control over the past? Perhaps. But it is also because Disney epitomizes the way that popular culture sentimentalizes and caricatures American history, stripping it of its complexity, conflict, drama, and meaning.

To understand the ways that a particular Disney film, *Pocahontas*, distorts and sanitizes the past, it is helpful to understand the various forms historical films have taken and the changing way they have been perceived. It is at the movies that many viewers obtain their most vivid images of the past. From the beginnings of motion pictures, moviemakers have turned to history for many of its most compelling stories. And from the beginning moviemakers have misused and abused the past.

Much of the history found in early films was laughable. The 1940 Michael Curtiz film *Santa Fe Trail*, starring Errol Flynn, Olivia de Havilland, and Ronald Reagan, offers a particularly glaring example of how Hollywood played fast and loose with the historical record. Set on the eve of the Civil War, the film looks at the interactions of a group of future Union and Confederate officers, including J.E.B. Stuart, George Armstrong Custer, George Pickett, and Philip Sheridan. It explores their efforts to keep the peace in "Bleeding Kansas" and culminates with the suppression of John Brown's raid on Harpers Ferry Virginia.

Filled with gross historical inaccuracies, the film has nothing to do with the Santa Fe Trail but rather offers a look at the causes of the Civil War. In an effort to offend as few potential moviegoers as possible, the film suggests that the roots of the conflict lay in the provocations of fanatical abolitionists, especially John Brown, who is depicted as a religious zealot and homicidal psychopath rather than as a figure truly committed to the abolition of slavery and a bi-racial society.

In recent years, critics have grown far less tolerant of cinematic inaccuracies. Frequently, critics serve as the accuracy police, taking it upon themselves to identify a film's errors, distortions, and omissions. A 2001 History Channel show, *History vs. Hollywood*, epitomized this approach, judging films' value and significance on the basis of their level of historical accuracy.

Why do present-day critics take historical films so seriously? Partly this is a reaction to technologies which allow filmmakers to achieve an illusion of realism unimaginable in the past. Some critics fear that technological wizardry blinds audiences to manipulations of the historical record. Even more importantly, recent filmmakers have become ever more willing to challenge conventional understandings of the past. No historical film aroused more ire than Oliver Stone's *JFK*, which combined documentary and fictional footage, and suggested that John Kennedy's assassination was the product of a conspiracy hatched by government leaders and members of the military industrial complex, who feared that President Kennedy would end the U.S. presence in Vietnam. Many critics worried that a historically challenged population would readily accept a view that they regard as profoundly misleading.

No one expects a film to be a schoolbook, held to the same standards of accuracy and rigor as a scholarly article. Even the most impressive historical movies, such as *Glory* or *Schindler's List*, engage in dramatic license, inventing dialogue, manipulating or embellishing facts, combining or concocting characters, condensing events, collapsing time, or injecting romance. Nitpicking, however, does little to help us understand why a historical film might resonate with the audience at a particular time. Nor does an obsession with accuracy help us understand how a film might cause us to critically reflect on the past. Despite their factual inaccuracies, we must recognize that there are some things that movies can do better than a historical text. Movies are often better than history books at capturing the atmosphere and look of a particular time. They can help us visualize the past in a way that few scholars can. But great historical movies can do something more: They can illuminate a historical figure's character, clarify moral or political issues, and expose a mass audience to an important but forgotten incident from the past.

Historical films have taken several distinct forms. There are costume dramas, like *Titanic* (1997), which place recognizably modern actors and actresses in an artfully re-created simulation of the past. Apart from the period setting and scenery and carefully crafted costumes, however, the characters themselves feature current values and outlooks.

Closely related to the costume drama is the docudrama, which blends real historical figures and events with fictional characters, dialogues, and incidents. Unlike costume dramas, docudramas claim to be essentially true to the historical record, but seek to fill in gaps in the surviving documentation. One example of a docudrama is the 2006 film *United 1993*, which re-creates the story of the passengers and crew aboard a hijacked United Airlines flight on September 11, 2001, who succeeded in preventing a group of terrorists from crashing the plane into the U.S. Capitol.

Docudramas are not necessarily the innocent creations they seem on the surface. Myths and falsehoods often lurk just beneath such films' surfaces. Perhaps the most influential docudramas in American film history are *Birth of a Nation* and *Gone With the Wind*. Both allowed the former Confederacy to achieve in peacetime what it had failed to do during the Civil War: to win the ideological Civil War. Intended to reunify North and South, these films presented the Civil War as an immense human tragedy even as they obscured the conflict's origins in the debates over slavery. The films romanticize the Old South, present Confederates as heroic figures, and reinforce a mythology that dominated Americans' views of race relations until the 1960s: that slave life was "idyllic" and, unless manipulated by white fanatics, slaves were loyal, docile, ignorant, and childlike. This tendency to minimize the role of slavery in the past reappears in some recent historical films, including Mel Gibson's *The Patriot* and the cinematic adaptation of the novel *Cold Mountain*.

Many earlier historical films were intensely ethnocentric, presenting history from a narrow and unreflective point of view. These include not only films like John Wayne's *The Alamo*, which is oblivious to the Mexican and Tejano (Mexican Texan) perspectives on the Texas Revolution, and the many World War II films that omitted America's allies and treated the war as if it only involved U.S. soldiers. Even *Saving Private Ryan* (1998), one of the most poignant and powerful World War II movies ever made, implicitly seems to suggest that the British and Soviets were only bit players in the defeat of Nazi Germany.

Presentism – a tendency to impose present-day perspectives and preoccupations upon the past – is a characteristic found in many historical films. Since Hollywood rarely believed that audiences were interested in history for its own sake, many historical films often have a present-minded agenda. Thus the 1942 epic *They Died with Their Boots On*, a sympathetic screen biography of George Armstrong Custer, glorified the valor of men fighting in a lost cause at a time of repeated American defeats in the Pacific. A somewhat more recent example, *Bonnie and Clyde*, transformed the story of two Depression-era bank robbers into a present-minded tale of youth revolt and women's liberation.

Recent years have witnessed a new kind of historical film that brings largely ignored historical incidents or topics to the audience's attention. We might call this cinematic social history. Examples include *Reds*, which looked at the Progressive-era American bohemians, socialists, and pioneering feminists; *Matewan*, which explored labor unrest in the West Virginia coal fields during the 1920s; and *Glory*, the story of the

Massachusetts 54th Volunteer Infantry and black participation in combat during the Civil War. The goal of cinematic social history has often been to use past incidents to show that contemporary concerns involving class struggles or the quest for racial justice or the movement for women's equality have deep historical roots.

Not all examples of cinematic social history are successful. From the historian's vantage point, Steven Spielberg's *Amistad* was deeply flawed. In telling the story of a group of African captives who staged a revolt on a Spanish slave ship, the film portrayed the white abolitionists as racially condescending hypocrites and religious fanatics and mistakenly focused on the court case rather than on the captives themselves.

In addition to revisionist historical films, such as Oliver Stone's *JFK*, which attempt to refute dominant interpretations of history, there are a handful of films that genuinely grapple with the meaning of historical change. Early examples include *Return of the Secaucus Seven* and *The Big Chill*, both of which look at the reunion of a group of friends and use this encounter to explore issues of aging and memory and the shift in mood from the activist and idealistic1960s to the more cynical, self-centered 1970s and '80s.

A particularly striking example of a film concerned with the meaning of history is Oprah Winfrey's cinematic version of Toni Morrison's *Beloved*, which examines slavery's psychic legacy. Perhaps the most successful cinematic exploration of the meaning of change was *Forrest Gump*, which uses computer animation to allow its protagonist, a man with an IQ of 75, to meet three presidents and to take part in the court-ordered desegregation of the University of Alabama, the Vietnam War and the antiwar movement, and the apprehension of the Watergate burglars. The film uses Gump as a vehicle for understanding the impact and meaning of such events as the assassination of President Kennedy, the murder of the former Beatle John Lennon, and the violence associated with the Vietnam War.

The 1995 animated musical *Pocahontas* offers Walt Disney's take on the early seventeenth-century encounter between the English and the Powhatan Indians near Jamestown in Virginia. Featuring romance, anthropomorphized animals, and a talking tree, the film contains a handful of problems, some big and some little. We might begin with a minor example. The Disney film shows a youthful, clean-shaven, blond John Smith with the voice of Mel Gibson. The real John Smith was a bearded Renaissance soldier in his forties, who had been a pirate, a beggar in Ireland, and a mercenary for the kingdom of Hungary. Pocahontas herself was just 12 to 14 at the time she first encountered John Smith, not the older teenager depicted in the film.

Then there are major problems. *Pocahontas* illustrates five psychological mechanisms that Americans have used to evade the true meaning of our collective past. One such mechanism is a screen memory. An important concept in Sigmund Freud's system of psychoanalysis, a screen memory is a recollection of early childhood that is falsely recalled or magnified in importance, masking other memories of deeper significance.

Nations, like individuals, can have screen memories. As schoolchildren, we all learned a series of legends that suggest that relations between the English and the indigenous people were more cooperative and less acrimonious than they actually were. Each Thanksgiving, schoolchildren recite the story of Squanto, the Patuxet Indian who taught the Pilgrims how to plant corn. And all schoolchildren are familiar with William Penn, the founder of Pennsylvania, who promised fair dealings with his region's native people. But the most famous legend of all involves Pocahontas' rescue of Captain John Smith.

Figure 16   Portrait of Pocahontas, from a painting by William Sheppard, dated 1616. Courtesy of Prints and Photographs, Library of Congress.

The Pocahontas legend, like the story of Squanto and of William Penn, allows present-day Americans to evade the ugly realities of relations between English colonizers and the indigenous people. The true story of English settlement in Virginia was a revolting story of conflict, failed negotiations, and cultural and racial warfare. Pocahontas' brief life illustrates the stomach-churning collision of cultures that occurred when English colonists arrived in colonial America.

Born about 1595, Pocahontas was a daughter of Powhatan, the leader of a powerful Indian confederacy. Comprised of some 30 tribes totaling about 20,000 people, the confederacy occupied much of what is now known as Virginia. She was about twelve years old when the English established their first permanent America settlement at Jamestown and when she purportedly rescued John Smith.

When she was about 14, she reportedly married a chief in her tribe. Temporarily, she disappears from the colonial records, only to reappear in 1613, when she was lured aboard an English ship and held captive. Her marriage in 1614 to John Rolfe, the Virginia settler who learned how to cure tobacco, helped bring a temporary peace between the English and the Powhatan confederacy. After her marriage, Pocahontas converted to Christianity and adopted an English name, Rebecca.

Her story ended tragically. In 1616 she went with her husband to London to help raise funds for the struggling colonists in Virginia. The English celebrated her as an

Indian "princess," but while she was waiting to return to America, she contracted smallpox and died in 1617 – one of countless Indians to die from European diseases.

According to a story told by Captain John Smith in an account published years after the purported event, he was captured while exploring the Virginia countryside. Powhatan was about to have him executed when Pocahontas intervened. We do not know if the episode took place. If it did, it is unlikely that it occurred as John Smith described it. Its meaning and significance were almost certainly far different than the film portrays. Pocahontas' rescue of John Smith from beheading was most likely a staged event. It was a ritual of adoption – not an actual execution. The Powhatans used mock executions as a symbolic way to incorporate vassals or subordinates into their society. To sentimentalize and romanticize Pocahontas' rescue of John Smith is to misunderstand its true cultural meaning.

A second basic defense mechanism is known as "splitting." It involves dividing a complex reality into dualities or polar opposites. Splitting has played a critical role in European perceptions of Indians. In early accounts, Indians were depicted as either noble children of nature or as bloodthirsty savages. Such stereotypes have been updated, with native peoples depicted as either proto-ecologists or as a primitive people. The realities, of course, were far more complex, and do not conform to such simplistic categories.

A third basic defense mechanism is projection or displacement. This involves attributing one's own feelings, ideas, or attitudes onto some other people or objects. Today, Americans feel very uneasy about race relations, the environment, and the materialism of our society. One way to deal with these anxieties is to displace them into the distant past. The film *Pocahontas* projects present-day concerns about ethnic relations, tolerance, and environmentalism into the distant past, obscuring the difference between the past and the present.

A fourth psychological mechanism involves transference – a process in which certain emotions and desires are inappropriately shifted elsewhere. The story of a European colonizer, depicted as strong, white, and intensely masculine, who is rescued from savages by the love of a dark, sensual, deeply feminine princess, is a repeated theme in the literature of colonization. This is a common fantasy about colonialism – that the people whose land is being colonized eagerly embrace their conquerors.

A final psychological defense that Americans frequently resort to might be termed "depersonalization." It treats events as inevitable, as the product of impersonal forces rather than of human agency. It involves the externalization of blame, guilt, or responsibility. Along with slavery, the nation's treatment of Native Americans stands out as among the most shameful aspects of this country's past. One way that many present-day Americans have dealt with the mistreatment of Native Americans is by depicting Indians as the passive victims of an impersonal and inevitable process of modernization, or what used to be called "the march of civilization." Indeed, this is a way that American society has commonly dealt with its losers, from the Populist farmers who found themselves pushed off the land in the late nineteenth century to the steelworkers and autoworkers who lost their jobs in the last quarter of the twentieth century. These people are treated as the inevitable and tragic victims of an ongoing process of social change, fated for extinction.

This view, I would argue, is a gross distortion of history. Far from being passive victims, Native Americans were active agents who responded to threats to their cultures through negotiation, physical resistance, and cultural adaptation. Pocahontas herself was no mere passive figure. In real life, she played a critical mediating role between two cultures. She was what anthropologists and ethnohistorians call a cultural intermediary and interpreter. In colonial encounters, some women have often played a critical mediary role: to forge alliances, to facilitate communication, and to instruct both sides in diplomacy.

Pocahontas is a wonderfully well intentioned movie. It is a plea for tolerance and ecological awareness in a world torn by ethnic strife and environmental degradation. It transforms the Pocahontas legend into cultural critique – a critique of ethnocentrism, materialism, possessiveness, and greed. Who could possibly be opposed to this?

Yet the film is historically misleading. It omits the larger context of colonial expansion and violent resistance. It does not suggest that Pocahontas' future husband, John Rolfe, was apparently the first Englishman to grow tobacco in Virginia – which stimulated a rush for Indian land. Nor does the film mention that in 1622, Pocahontas' brother led an assault that killed a third of the English settlers, including Pocahontas' English husband. It is inconceivable that Disney could create a heartwarming cartoon musical based on the story of Anne Frank. Yet this is precisely what the studio has done with *Pocahontas.*

Bibliography of Recent Books in American Film History

Reference Works

Bibliographies

Bowles, Stephen E. *The Film Anthologies Index*. Metuchen: Scarecrow, 1994.
Ellis, Jack C. et al. *The Film Book Bibliography, 1940–1975*. Metuchen: Scarecrow, 1979.
Manchel, Frank. *Film Study: An Analytical Bibliography*. Rutherford, NJ: Fairleigh Dickinson University Press, 1990.
Morgan, Jenny. *Film Researcher's Handbook*. London: Routledge, 1996.

Biographical Dictionaries

Andrew, Geoff. *The Director's Vision: A Concise Guide to the Art of 250 Great Filmmakers*. Chicago: A Cappella, 1999.
Liebman, Roy. *From Silents to Sound: A Biographical Encyclopedia of Performers Who Made the Transition to Talking Pictures*. Jefferson, NC: McFarland, 1998.
Thomson, David. *The New Biographical Dictionary of Film*. Revised and expanded edn. New York: Alfred A. Knopf, 2004.

Chronologies

Brown, Gene. *Movie Time: A Chronology of Hollywood and the Movie Industry from its Beginnings to the Present*. New York: Macmillan, 1995.

Dictionaries

Beaver, Frank Eugene. *Dictionary of Film Terms: The Aesthetic Companion to Film Art*. New York: Peter Lang, 2006.
Blandford, Steven, Barry Keith Grant, and Jim Hillier. *The Film Studies Dictionary*. New York: Oxford University Press, 2001.
Bognar, Desi K. *International Dictionary of Broadcasting and Film*. 2nd edn. Boston: Focal, 2000.

Pearson, Roberta E. and Philip Simpson, eds. *Critical Dictionary of Film and Television Theory.*
    New York: Routledge, 2001.
Schatz, Thomas, ed. *Hollywood: Critical Concepts in Media and Cultural Studies.* New York:
    Routledge, 2004.

Document Collections

Brown, Gene. *New York Times Encyclopedia of Film.* New York: New York Times, 1984.
Gardner, Gerald. *Censorship Papers: Movie Censorship Letters from the Hays Office, 1934–1968.*
    New York: Dodd, Mead, 1987.
Mast, Gerald. *The Movies in Our Midst: Documents in the Cultural History of Film in America.*
    Chicago: University of Chicago Press, 1982.

Encyclopedias and Handbooks

Abel, Richard, ed. *Encyclopedia of Early Cinema.* New York: Routledge, 2005.
Cartmell, Deborah and Imelda Whelehan, eds. *The Cambridge Companion to Literature on
    Screen.* Cambridge: Cambridge University Press, 2007.
Grant, Barry Keith, ed. *Schirmer Encyclopedia of Film.* Detroit: Schirmer Reference, 2007.
Hayward, Susan. *Cinema Studies: The Key Concepts.* 3rd edn. New York: Routledge, 2006.
Katz, Ephraim. *The Film Encyclopedia.* Revised by Ronald Dean Nolen. 6th edn. New York:
    Collins, 2008.
Law, Jonathan et al. *Cassell Companion to Cinema.* Revised and updated edn. London: Cassell,
    1997.
Miller, Blair. *American Silent Film Comedies: An Illustrated Encyclopedia of Persons, Studios,
    and Terminology.* Jefferson, NC: McFarland, 1995.
Rollins, Peter C., ed. *The Columbia Companion to American History on Film: How the Movies
    have Portrayed the American Past.* New York: Columbia University Press, 2003.

Film Guides

Curran, Daniel. *Guide to American Cinema, 1965–1995.* Westport, CT: Greenwood Press,
    1998.
Film Index International. Paris: Chadwyck-Healey-France, n.d.
Goble, Alan. *International Film Index on CD-ROM.* West Sussex: Bowker-Saur, 1996.
Halliwell, Leslie. *Halliwell's Filmgoer's Companion.* 12th edn. London: HarperCollins, 1997.
Magill, Frank N. *Magill's Survey of Cinema.* Englewood Cliffs: Salem, 1980, 1981, 1985.
Whissen, Thomas R. *Guide to American Cinema, 1930–1965.* Westport, CT: Greenwood Press,
    1998.

Filmography

Fetrow, Alan G. *Feature Films, 1950–1959: A United States Filmography.* Jefferson, NC:
    McFarland, 1999.
Klotman, Phyllis Rauch and Gloria J. Gibson. *Frame by Frame II: A Filmography of the African
    American Image.* Bloomington: Indiana University Press, 1997.
Martin, Len D. *The Republic Pictures Checklist.* Jefferson, NC: McFarland, 1998.
Ranucci, Karen and Julie Feldman, eds. *A Guide to Latin American, Caribbean, and U.S.
    Latino Made Film and Video.* Lanham, MD: Scarecrow Press, 1998.
Richards, Larry. *African American Films through 1959.* Jefferson, NC: McFarland, 1998.

Journals

American Film
Cineaste
Cinema Journal
Classic Images
Film Comment
Film & History
Film in Review
Film Quarterly
Film Reader
Historical Journal of Film, Radio, and Television
Image
Journal of Popular film and Television
Journal of the University Film and Video Association
Jump Cut
Literature/Film Quarterly
Marquee
Quarterly Review of Film Studies
Screen
Sight and Sound
SMPTE Journal (Society of Motion Picture and Television Engineers)
Variety
Velvet Light Trap
Wide Angle

Quotations

Bloch, Jeff. *Women's Book of Movie Quotes*. Secaucus: Carol, 1995.
Corey, Melinda. *Dictionary of Film Quotations*. New York: Crown, 1995.
Nowlan, Robert A. and Gwendolyn W. Nolan. *Film Quotations*. Jefferson, NC: McFarland, 1994.

Research Guides

Mehr, Linda. *Motion Pictures, Television, and Radio: A Union Catalogue of Manuscript and Special Collections in the Western United States*. Boston: G.K. Hall, 1977.
Rowan, Bonnie G. *Scholars' Guide to Washington D.C. Film and Video Collections*. Washington: Smithsonian Institution Press, 1980.

General Interpretations

Belton, John. *American Cinema, American Culture*. 2nd edn. Boston: McGraw-Hill, 2005.
Bordwell, David and Kristin Thompson. *Film Art: An Introduction*. 8th edn. Boston: McGraw Hill, 2008.
Cook, David A. *A History of Narrative Film*. 4th edn. New York: W.W. Norton, 2004.
Geiger, Jeffrey and R.L. Rutsky. *Film Analysis: A Norton Reader*. New York: W.W. Norton, 2005.

Giannetti, Louis D. *Understanding Movies*. 11th edn. Upper Saddle River, NJ: Pearson Education, 2008.

Hill, John and Pamela Church Gibson, eds. *American Cinema and Hollywood: Critical Approaches*. Oxford: Oxford University Press, 2000.

Hill, John and Pamela Church Gibson, eds. *The Oxford Guide to Film Studies*. New York: Oxford University Press, 1998.

Ross, Steven J., ed. *Movies and American Society*. Malden, MA: Blackwell, 2002.

Sklar, Robert. *A World History of Film*. New York: Harry N. Abrams, 2002.

Thompson, Kristin and David Bordwell. *Film History: An Introduction*. Boston: McGraw-Hill, 2003.

Wexman, Virginia Wright. *A History of Film*. 6th edn. Boston: Pearson, 2006.

Eras

Silent Era to 1920

Abel, Richard. *Americanizing the Movies and "Movie-Mad" Audiences, 1910–1914*. Berkeley: University of California Press, 2006.

Abel, Richard. *The Red Rooster Scare: Making Cinema American, 1900–1910*. Berkeley: University of California Press, 1999.

Bowser, Eileen. *The Transformation of Cinema, 1907–1915*. New York: Scribner, 1990.

Brownlow, Kevin. *Behind the Mask of Innocence*. New York: Knopf, 1990.

Corkin, Stanley. *Realism and the Birth of the Modern United States: Cinema, Literature, and Culture*. Athens: Georgia, 1996.

Elsaesser, Thomas. *Early Cinema: Space, Frame, Narrative*. London: British Film Institute, 1990.

Everson, William K. *American Silent Film*. New York: Da Capo Press, 1998.

Hansen, Miriam. *Babel and Babylon: Spectatorship in American Silent Film*. Cambridge, MA: Harvard University Press, 1991.

Keil, Charlie. *Early American Cinema in Transition: Story, Style, and Filmmaking, 1907–1913*. Madison: University of Wisconsin Press, 2001.

Kobel, Peter. *Silent Movies: The Birth of Film and the Triumph of Film Culture*. New York: Little, Brown & Co., 2007.

Koszarski, Richard. *An Evening's Entertainment: The Age of the Silent Feature Picture, 1915–1928*. New York: Scribner, 1990.

Koszarski, Richard. *The Rivals of D. W. Griffith*. New York: New York Zoetrope, 1980.

Leyda, Jay and Charles Musser. *Before Hollywood*. New York: American Federation of the Arts, 1986.

Maland, Charles J. *Chaplin and American Culture*. Princeton, NJ: Princeton University Press, 1989.

Musser, Charles. *Before the Nickelodeon: Edwin S. Porter and the Edison Manufacturing Company*. Berkeley: University of California Press, 1991.

Musser, Charles. *The Emergence of Cinema: The American Screen to 1907*. New York: Scribner, 1990.

Musser, Charles. *Thomas A. Edison and his Kinetographic Motion Pictures*. New Bruswick: Rutgers University Press, 1995.

Robinson, David. *From Peep Show to Palace: The Birth of American Film*. New York: Columbia University Press, 1996.

Slide, Anthony. *Early American Cinema*. Revised edn. Metuchen: Scarecrow, 1994.

Sloan, Kay. *The Loud Silents: Origins of the Social Problem Film*. Urbana: University of Illinois Press, 1988.

1920s

Jacobs, Lea. *The Decline of Sentiment: American Film in the 1920s.* Berkeley: University of California Press, 2008.

1930s

Bergman, Andrew. *We're in the Money: Depression America and Its Films.* New York: NYU, 1971.

Hanson, Philip. *This Side of Despair: How the Movies and American Life Intersected during the Great Depression.* Madison, NJ: Fairleigh Dickinson University Press, 2008.

Hark, Ina Rae, ed. *American Cinema of the 1930s: Themes and Variations.* New Brunswick, NJ: Rutgers University Press, 2007.

Maland, Charles. *American Visions: The Films of Chaplin, Ford, Capra, and Welles, 1936–1941.* New York: Arno, 1977.

Shindler, Colin. *Hollywood in Crisis: Cinema and American Society, 1929–1939.* London: Routledge, 1996.

1940s

Dixon, Wheeler Winston, ed. *American Cinema of the 1940s: Themes and Variations.* New Brunswick, NJ: Rutgers University Press, 2006.

Friedrich, Ott. *City of Nets: A Portrait of Hollywood in the 1940's.* New York: Harper & Row, 1986.

Schatz, Thomas. *Boom and Bust: The American Cinema in the 1940s.* New York: Charles Scribner's Sons, 1997.

Shindler, Colin. *Hollywood Goes to War: Films and American Society, 1939–1952.* Boston: Routledge & Kegan Paul, 1979.

1950s

Barranger, Milly S. *Unfriendly Witnesses: Gender, Theater, and Film in the McCarthy Era.* Carbondale: Southern Illinois University Press, 2008.

Biskind, Peter. *Seeing Is Believing: How Hollywood Movies Taught Us to Stop Worrying and Love the Fifties.* New York: Pantheon, 1983.

Booker, M. Keith. *The Post-Utopian Imagination: American Culture in the Long 1950s.* Westport, CT: Greenwood Press, 2002.

Casper, Drew. *Postwar Hollywood, 1946–1962.* Malden, MA: Blackwell, 2007.

Chopra-Gant, Mike. *Hollywood Genres and Postwar America: Masculinity, Family and Nation in Popular Movies and Film Noir.* New York: Palgrave Macmillan, 2006.

Dixon, Wheeler W. *Lost in the Fifties: Recovering Phantom Hollywood.* Carbondale: Southern Illinois University Press, 2005.

Lev, Peter. *Transforming the Screen, 1950–1959.* New York: Charles Scribner's Sons, 2003.

Pomerance, Murray, ed. *American Cinema of the 1950s: Themes and Variations.* New Brunswick, NJ: Rutgers University Press, 2005.

Sayre, Nora. *Running Time.* New York: Dial, 1982.

Sikov, Ed. *Laughing Hysterically: American Screen Comedy of the 1950s.* New York: Columbia University Press, 1994.

Smoodin, Eric and Ann Martin, eds. *Hollywood Quarterly: Film Culture in Postwar America, 1945–1957.* Berkeley: University of California Press, 2002.

1960s

Bapis, Elaine M. *Camera and Action: American Film as Agent of Social Change, 1965–1975.* Jefferson, NC: McFarland, 2008.

Biskind, Peter. *Easy Riders, Raging Bulls: How the Sex-Drugs-and-Rock-'n'-Roll Generation Saved Hollywood.* New York: Simon & Schuster, 1998.

Grant, Barry Keith, ed. *American Cinema of the 1960s: Themes and Variations.* New Brunswick, NJ: Rutgers University Press, 2008.

Harris, Mark. *Pictures at a Revolution: Five Movies and the Birth of the New Hollywood.* New York: Penguin Press, 2008.

Hoberman, J. *The Dream Life: Movies, Media, and the Mythology of the Sixties.* New York: New Press, 2003.

James, David E. *Allegories of Cinema: American Film in the Sixties.* Princeton: Princeton University Press, 1989.

Krämer, Peter. *The New Hollywood: From Bonnie and Clyde to Star Wars.* New York: Wallflower, 2005.

Man, Glenn. *Radical Visions: American Film Renaissance, 1967–1976.* Westport, CT: Greenwood, 1994.

Monaco, Paul. *The Sixties, 1960–1969.* New York: Charles Scribner's Sons, 2001.

Mordden, Ethan. *Medium Cool: The Movies of the 1960s.* New York: Knopf, 1990.

1970s

Bernardoni, James. *The New Hollywood: What the Movies Did with the New Freedoms of the Seventies.* Jefferson, NC: McFarland, 1991.

Cagin, Seth and Philip Dray. *Hollywood Films of the Seventies.* New York: Harper & Row, 1984.

Cook, David A. *Lost Illusions: American Cinema in the Shadow of Watergate and Vietnam, 1970–1979.* New York: Charles Scribner's Sons, 2000.

Elsaesser, Thomas, Alexander Horwath, and Noel King, eds. *The Last Great American Picture Show: New Hollywood Cinema in the 1970s.* Amsterdam: Amsterdam University Press, 2004.

Friedman, Lester D., ed. *American Cinema of the 1970s: Themes and Variations.* New Brunswick, NJ: Rutgers University Press, 2007.

Hogan, Ron. *The Stewardess is Flying the Plane! American Films of the 1970s.* New York: Bulfinch Press, 2005.

Lev, Peter. *American Films of the '70s: Conflicting Visions.* Austin: University of Texas Press, 2000.

O'Brien, Tom. *The Screening of America: Movies and Values from Rocky to Rain Man.* New York: Continuum, 1990.

Wood, Robin. *Hollywood from Vietnam to Reagan – and Beyond.* Expanded and revised edn. New York: Columbia University Press, 2003.

1980s

Brode, Douglas. *The Films of the Eighties.* Secaucus: Carol, 1990.

Corrigan, Timothy. *A Cinema without Walls: Movies and Culture after Vietnam.* New Brunswick, NJ: Rutgers University Press, 1991.

Grunzweig, Walter et al. *Constructing the Eighties: Versions of an American Decade.* Tubingen: G. Narr, 1992.

Hanson, Peter. *The Cinema of Generation X: A Critical Study of Films and Directors.* Jefferson, NC: McFarland, 2002.

Miller, Mark Crispin. *Seeing Through Movies.* New York: Panthon, 1990.

Nowlan, Robert A. *The Films of the Eighties: A Complete, Qualitative Filmography*. Jefferson, NC: McFarland, 1991.

Palmer, William J. *Films of the Eighties: A Social History*. Carbondale: Southern Illinois University Press, 1993.

Prince, Stephen, ed. *American Cinema of the 1980s: Themes and Variations*. New Brunswick, NJ: Rutgers University Press, 2007.

Ryan, Michael and Douglas Kellner. *Camera Politica: The Politics and Ideology of Contemporary Hollywood*. Bloomington: Indiana University Press, 1988.

Traube, Elizabeth G. *Dreaming Identities: Class, Gender, and Generation in 1980s Hollywood Movies*. Boulder: Westview, 1992.

Vineberg, Steve. *No Surprises, Please: Movies in the Reagan Decade*. New York: Schirmer Books, 1993.

1990s

Austin, Thomas. *Hollywood, Hype and Audiences: Selling and Watching Popular Film in the 1990s*. New York: Palgrave, 2002.

Lewis, Jon, ed. *The End of Cinema as We Know It: American Film in the Nineties*. New York: New York University Press, 2001.

Wyatt, Justin. *High Concept: Movies and Marketing in Hollywood*. Austin: University of Texas Press, 1994.

Genres

Adventure Films

Tasker, Yvonne. *Spectacular Bodies: Gender, Genre, and the Action Cinema*. London: Routledge, 1993.

Taves, Brian. *The Romance of Adventure: The Genre of Historical Adventure Movies*. Jackson: University Press of Mississippi, 1993.

Animation

Crafton, Donald. *Before Mickey: The Animated Film, 1898–1928*. Chicago: University of Chicago Press, 1993.

Gifford, Denis. *American Animated Films: The Silent Era, 1897–1929*. Jefferson, NC: McFarland, 1990.

Kanfer, Stefan. *Serious Business: The Art and Commerce of Animation in America*. New York: Scribner, 1997.

Lotman, Jeff. *Animation Art: The Early Years, 1911–1953*. Atglen, PA: Schiffer, 1995.

Merritt, Russell. *Walt in Wonderland: The Silent Films of Walt Disney*. Baltimore: Johns Hopkins University Press, 1993.

Sampson, Henry T. *That's Enough, Folks: Black Images in Animated Cartoons, 1900–1960*. Lanham: Scarecrow, 1998.

Smoodin, Eric Loren. *Animating Culture: Hollywood Cartoons from the Sound Era*. New Brunswick, NJ: Rutgers University Press, 1993.

Thomas, Bob. *Disney's Art of Animation*. New York: Hyperion, 1991.

Thomas, Frank and Ollie Johnston. *The Illusion of Life: Disney Animation*. New York: Hyperion, 1995.

Wells, Paul. *Understanding Animation*. London: Routledge, 1998.

Art Cinema

Wasson, Haidee. *Museum Movies: The Museum of Modern Art and the Birth of Art Cinema.* Berkeley: University of California Press, 2005.

Avant-Garde Films

Posner, Bruce. *Unseen Cinema: Early American Avant-Garde Film 1893–1941.* New York: Anthology Film Archives, 2001.

Biblical Films

Babington, Bruce and Peter William Evans. *Biblical Epics: Sacred Narrative in the Hollywood Cinema.* Manchester: Manchester, 1993.
Kreitzer, L. Joseph. *The New Testament in Fiction and Film.* Sheffield: JSOT, 1993.
Kreitzer, L. Joseph. *The Old Testament in Fiction and Film.* Sheffield: JSOT, 1994.
Kreitzer, L. Joseph. *Pauline Images in Fiction and Film.* Sheffield: Sheffield Academic Press, 1999.

Biographical Films

Custen, George Frederick. *Bio/Pics: How Hollywood Constructed Public History.* New Brunswick, NJ: Rutgers University, 1992.

College Life in Film

Hinton, David B. *Celluloid Ivy: Higher Education in the Movies.* Metuchen: Scarecrow, 1994.

Comedies

Babington, Bruce and Peter William Evans. *Affairs to Remember: The Hollywood Comedy of the Sexes.* New York: St. Martin's, 1989.
Byrge, Duane and Robert Milton Miller. *The Screwball Comedy Films: A History and Filmography.* Jefferson, NC: McFarland, 1991.
Cavell, Stanley. *Pursuits of Happiness: The Hollywood Comedy of Remarriage.* Cambridge, MA: Harvard University Press, 1981.
Gehring, Wes D. *American Dark Comedy: Beyond Satire.* Westport, CT: Greenwood, 1996.
Gehring, Wes. D. *Parody as Film Genre: "Never Give a Saga an Even Break."* Westport, CT: Greenwood, 1999.
Gehring, Wes D. *Screwball Comedy.* Westport, CT: Greenwood, 1986.
Harvey, John. *Romantic Comedy in Hollywood from Lubitsch to Sturgis.* New York: Knopf, 1987.
Horton, Andrew. *Comedy/Cinema/Theory.* Berkeley: University of California Press, 1991.
Horton, Andrew. *Laughing Out Loud: Writing the Comedy-Centered Screenplay.* Berkeley: University of California, 2000.
Jenkins, Henry. *What Made Pistachio Nuts? Early Sound Comedy and the Vaudeville Aesthetic.* New York: Columbia, 1992.
Karnick, Kristine Brunovska and Henry Jenkins. *Classical Hollywood Comedy.* New York: Routledge, 1995.
Kendall, Elizabeth. *The Runaway Bride: Hollywood Romantic Comedy of the 1930's.* New York: Knopf, 1990.

Miller, Blair. *American Silent Film Comedies.* Jefferson, NC: McFarland, 1995.

Rubinfeld, Mark D. *Bound to Bond: Gender, Genre, and the Hollywood Romantic Comedy.* Westport, CT: Praeger, 2001.

Sennett, Ted. *Laughing in the Dark: Movie Comedy from Groucho to Woody.* New York: St. Martin's, 1992.

Weales, Gerald. *Canned Goods as Caviar: American Film Comedy of the 1930s.* Chicago: Chicago University Press, 1985.

Winokur, Mark. *American Laughter: Immigrants, Ethnicity and 1930s Hollywood Film Comedy.* Houndmills: Macmillan, 1996.

Documentaries

Ellis, Jack C. and Betsy A. McLane. *A New History of Documentary Film.* New York: Continuum, 2005.

Girgus, Sam B. *America on Film: Modernism, Documentary, and a Changing America.* New York: Cambridge University Press, 2002.

Ethnographic Films

Griffiths, Alison. *Wondrous Difference: Cinema, Anthropology, & Turn-of-the-Century Visual Culture.* New York: Columbia University Press, 2002.

Heider, Karl G. *Seeing Anthropology: Cultural Anthropology Through Film.* 2nd edn. Boston: Allyn & Bacon, 2001.

Loizos, Peter. *Innovation in Ethnographic Film: From Innocence to Self-Consciousness, 1955–85.* Chicago: University of Chicago Press, 1993.

MacDougall, David. *Transcultural Cinema.* Princeton: Princeton University Press, 1998.

Ruby, Jay. *Picturing Culture: Explorations of Film and Anthropology.* Chicago: University of Chicago Press, 2000.

Russell, Catherine. *Experimental Ethnography in the Age of Video.* Durham: Duke University Press, 1999.

Film Noir

Cochran, David. *America Noir: Underground Writers and Filmmakers of the Postwar Era.* Washington, DC: Smithsonian Institution Press, 2000.

Dickos, Andrew. *Street with No Name: A History of the Classic American Film Noir.* Lexington: University Press of Kentucky, 2002.

Gangster Films

Grieveson, Lee, Esther Sonnet, and Peter Stanfield, eds. *Mob Culture: Hidden Histories of the American Gangster Film.* New Brunswick, NJ: Rutgers University Press, 2005.

Horror Films

Freeland, Cynthia A. *The Naked and the Undead: Evil and the Appeal of Horror.* Boulder, CO: Westview Press, 2000.

Heffernan, Kevin. *Ghouls, Gimmicks, and Gold: Horror Films and the American Movie Business, 1953–1968.* Durham: Duke University Press, 2004.

Jones, Darryl. *Horror: A Thematic History in Fiction and Film.* London: Arnold, 2002.

Pomerance, Murray, ed. *Bad: Infamy, Darkness, Evil, and Slime on Screen*. Albany: State University of New York Press, 2004.
Prince, Stephen, ed. *The Horror Film*. New Brunswick, NJ: Rutgers University Press, 2004.

Independent Film

Holmlund, Chris and Justin Wyatt, eds. *Contemporary American Independent Film: From the Margins to the Mainstream*. New York: Routledge, 2005.
King, Geoff. *American Independent Cinema*. New York: Palgrave Macmillan, 2005.
Mann, Denise. *Hollywood Independents: The Postwar Talent Takeover*. Minneapolis: University of Minnesota Press, 2008.
Pribram, E. Deidre. *Cinema & Culture: Independent Film in the United States, 1980–2001*. New York: P. Lang, 2002.

Musicals

Altman, Rick. *The American Film Musical*. Bloomington: Indiana University Press, 1987.
Barrios, Richard. *A Song in the Dark: The Birth of the Musical Film*. New York: Oxford University Press, 1995.
Cohan, Steven. *Hollywood Musicals: The Film Reader*. New York: Routledge, 2002.
Knapp, Raymond. *The American Musical and the Performance of Personal Identity*. Princeton, NJ: Princeton University Press, 2006.
Rubin, Martin. *Showstoppers: Busby Berkeley and the Tradition of Spectacle*. New York: Columbia University Press, 1993.

Political Films

Coyne, Michael. *Hollywood Goes to Washington: American Politics on Screen*. London: Reaktion Books, 2008.
Davies, Philip John and Paul Wells, *American Film and Politics from Reagan to Bush Jr*. New York: Palgrave, 2002.
Feeney, Mark. *Nixon at the Movies*. Chicago: University of Chicago Press, 2004.
Rollins, Peter C. and John E. O'Connor, eds. *Hollywood's White House: The American Presidency in Film and History*. Lexington: University Press of Kentucky, 2003.

Science Fiction

Hendershot, Cynthia. *Paranoia, the Bomb, and 1950s Science Fiction Films*. Bowling Green, OH: Bowling Green State University Popular Press, 1999.
Kuhn, Annette. *Alien Zone: Cultural Theory and Contemporary Science Fiction*. New York: Verso, 1990.
Penley, Constance. *Close Encounters: Film, Feminism, and Science Fiction*. Minneapolis: University of Minnesota Press, 1991.
Schelde, Per. *Androids, Humanoids, and Other Science Fiction Monsters: Science and Soul in Science Fiction Films*. New York: New York University Press, 1993.
Sobchack, Vivian Carol. *Screening Space: The American Science Fiction Film*. 2nd edn. New Brunswick, NJ: Rutgers University Press, 1997.
Telotte, J.P. *Replications: A Robotic History of the Science Fiction Film*. Urbana: University of Illinois Press, 1995.

Social Problem Films

Aitkin, Ian. *Film and Reform: John Grierson and the Documentary Film Movement.* London: Routledge, 1990.

Braendlin, Bonnie and Hans Braendlin. *Authority and Transgression in Literature and Film.* Gainesville: University Press of Florida, 1996.

Roffman, Peter and Jim Purdy. *The Hollywood Social Problem Film.* Bloomington: Indiana University Press, 1981.

Sloan, Kay. *The Loud Silents: Origins of the Social Problem Film.* Urbana: University of Illinois Press, 1988.

War Films

Rollins, Peter C. and John E. O'Connor, eds. *Why We Fought: America's Wars in Film and History.* Lexington: University Press of Kentucky, 2008.

Westerns

Buscombe, Edward, ed. *The BFI Companion to the Western.* London: A. Deutsch, 1988.

Canfield, J. Douglas. *Mavericks on the Border: The Early Southwest in Historical Fiction and Film.* Lexington: University Press of Kentucky, 2001.

Cawelti, John G. *The Six-Gun Mystique.* Bowling Green, OH: Bowling Green State University Popular Press, 1971.

Cawelti, John G. *The Six-Gun Mystique Sequel.* Bowling Green, OH: Bowling Green State University Popular Press, 1999.

Coyne, Michael. *The Crowded Prairie: American National Identity in the Hollywood Western.* New York: St. Martin's Press, 1997.

French, Philip. Westerns: *Aspects of a Movie Genre.* Revised edn. New York: Oxford University Press, 1977.

Lenihan, John H. *Showdown: Confronting Modern America in the Western Film.* Urbana: University of Illinois Press, 1980.

McDonald, Archie P., ed. *Shooting Stars: Heroes and Heroines of Western Film.* Bloomington: Indiana University Press, 1987.

Mitchell, Lee Clark. *Westerns: Making the Man in Fiction and Film.* Chicago: University of Chicago Press, 1996.

Nachbar, John G., comp. *Focus on the Western.* Englewood Cliffs, NJ: Prentice-Hall, 1974.

Nachbar, John G. *Western Films: An Annotated Critical Bibiliography.* New York: Garland, 1975.

Nachbar, John G., Jackie R. Donath, and Chris Foran. *Western Films 2: An Annotated Critical Bibliography from 1974 to 1987.* New York: Garland, 1988.

Pilkington, William T. and Don Graham, ed. *Western Movies.* Albuquerque: University of New Mexico Press, 1979.

Roberts, Randy, and James S. Olson. *John Wayne: American.* New York: The Free Press, 1995.

Rollins, Peter C. and John E. O'Connor, eds. *Hollywood's West: The American Frontier in Film, Television, and History.* Lexington: University Press of Kentucky, 2005.

Sarf, Wayne Michael. *God Bless You, Buffalo Bill: A Layman's Guide to History and the Western Film.* Rutherford, NJ: Fairleigh Dickinson University Press, 1983.

Slotkin, Richard. *Gunfighter Nation: The Myth of the Frontier in Twentieth-Century America.* New York: Atheneum, 1992.

Sullivan, Tom R. *Cowboys and Caudillos: Frontier Ideology of the Americas.* Bowling Green, OH: Bowling Green State University Popular Press, 1990.

Tompkins, Jane P. *West of Everything: The Inner Life of Westerns.* New York: Oxford University Press, 1992.

Walker, Janet, ed. *Westerns: Films through History.* New York: Routledge, 2001.

Walle, Alf H. *The Cowboy Hero and its Audience: Popular Culture as Market Derived Art.* Bowling Green, OH: Bowling Green State University Popular Press, 2000.

Wallmann, Jeffrey M. *The Western: Parables of the American Dream.* Lubbock, TX: Texas Tech University Press, 1999.

Wills, Garry. *John Wayne's America: The Politics of Celebrity.* New York: Simon & Schuster, 1997.

Wright, Will. *Six Guns and Society: A Structural Study of the Western.* Berkeley: University of California Press, 1975.

Age, Class, Ethnicity, Gender, Religion, and Sexuality in Film

General Works

Benshoff, Harry M. and Sean Griffin. *America on Film: Representing Race, Class, Gender, and Sexuality at the Movies.* Malden, MA: Blackwell, 2004.

Davies, Jude and Carol R. Smith. *Gender, Ethnicity and Sexuality in Contemporary American Film.* Chicago: Fitzroy Dearborn, 2000.

African Americans

Bogle, Donald. *Toms, Coons, Mulattoes, Mammies and Bucks: An Interpretive History of Blacks in American Films.* 3rd edn. New York: Continuum, 1994.

Cripps, Thomas R. *Black Film as Genre.* Bloomington: Indiana University Press, 1978.

Cripps, Thomas R. *Making Movies Black: The Hollywood Message Movies from World War II to the Civil Rights Era.* New York: Oxford University Press, 1992.

Cripps, Thomas R. *Slow Fade to Black: The Negro in American Film, 1900–1942.* Oxford: Oxford University Press, 1993.

Gabbard, Krin. *Black Magic: White Hollywood and African American Culture.* New Brunswick, NJ: Rutgers University Press, 2004.

Gaines, Jane M. *Fire & Desire: Mixed-Race Movies in the Silent Era.* Chicago: University of Chicago Press, 2001.

George, Nelson. *Blackface: Reflections on African Americans and the Movies.* New York: HarperCollins, 1994.

Iverem, Esther. *We Gotta Have It: Twenty Years of Seeing Black at the Movies, 1986–2006.* New York: Thunder's Mouth Press, 2007.

Leab, Daniel J. *From Sambo to Superspade: The Black Experience in Motion Pictures.* Boston: Houghton Mifflin, 1975.

Reid, Mark A. *Redefining Black Film.* Berkeley: University of California Press, 1993.

Arabs

Khatib, Lina. *Filming the Modern Middle East: Politics in the Cinemas of Hollywood and the Arab World.* New York: Palgrave Macmillan, 2006.

Semmerling, Tim Jon. *"Evil" Arabs in American Popular Film: Orientalist Fear.* Austin: University of Texas Press, 2006.

Asian Americans and Asians

Hamamoto, Darrell Y., and Sandra Liu, eds. *Countervisions: Asian-American Film Criticism.* Philadelphia: Temple University Press, 2000.

Hsing, Chun. *Asian America through the Lens: History, Representations, Identity.* Walnut Creek: AltaMira, 1998.

Marchetti, Gina. *Romance and the "Yellow Peril": Race, Sex and Discursive Strategies in Hollywood Fiction.* Berkeley: University of California Press, 1993.

Masavisut, Nitaya et al. *Gender and Culture in Literature and Film East and West.* Honolulu: East-West Center, 1994.

Boys

Pomerance, Murray and Frances Gateward, eds. *Where the Boys Are: Cinemas of Masculinity and Youth.* Detroit: Wayne State University Press, 2005.

Children

Ayesworth, Thomas G. *Hollywood Kids: Child Stars of the Silver Screen.* New York: Dutton, 1987.

Bazalgette, Cary and David Buckingham. *In Front of the Children: Screen Entertainment and Young Audiences.* London: British Film Institute, 1995.

Bell, Elizabeth et al. *From Mouse to Mermaid: The Politics of Film, Gender, and Culture.* Bloomington: Indiana University Press, 1995.

Cantor, Joanne. *Mommy, I'm Scared: How TV and Movies Frighten Children and What We Can Do To Protect Them.* New York: Harcourt Brace, 1998.

Flanagan, Victoria. *Into the Closet: Cross-Dressing and the Gendered Body in Children's Literature and Film.* New York: Routledge, 2008.

Jackson, Kathy Merlock. *Images of Children in American Film.* Metuchen: Scarecrow, 1980.

Jowett, Garth et al. *Children and the Movies: Media Influence and the Payne Fund Controversy.* New York: Cambridge University Press, 1996.

Keller, Marjorie. *The Untutored Eye: Childhood int he Films of Cocteau, Cornell, and Brakhage.* Rutherford, NJ: Fairleigh Dickinson, 1986.

Kinder, Marsha. *Playing with Power in Movies, Television, and Video Games.* Berkeley: University of California Press, 1991.

Moss, Joyce and George Wilson. *From Page to Screen: Children's and Young Adult Books on Film and Video.* Detroit: Gale, 1992.

Pecora, Norma Odom. *The Business of Children's Entertainment.* New York: Guilford, 1998.

Schober, Adrian. *Possessed Child Narratives in Literature and Film.* New York: Palgrave Macmillan, 2004.

Sinyard, Neil. *Children in the Movies.* London: Batsford, 1990.

Staples, Terry. *All Pals Together: The Story of Children's Cinema.* Edinburgh: Edinburgh University Press, 1997.

Wojik-Andrews, I. *Children's Films: History, Ideology, Pedagogy, Theory.* New York: Garland: 2000.

Class

Bodnar, John E. *Blue-Collar Hollywood: Liberalism, Democracy, and Working People in American Film.* Baltimore: Johns Hopkins University Press, 2003.

Gandal, Keith. *Class Representation in Modern Literature and Film.* New York: Palgrave Macmillan, 2007.

Ross, Steven J. *Working-Class Hollywood: Silent Film and the Shaping of Class in America.* Princeton: Princeton University Press, 1998.

Ethnicity

Hamilton, Marsha J. and Eleanor S. Block. *Projecting Ethnicity and Race: An Annotated Bibliography of Studies on Imagery in American Film.* Westport, CT: Praeger, 2003.
Summerfield, Ellen and Sandra Lee. *Seeing the Big Picture: Exploring American Cultures on Film.*Yarmouth, ME: Intercultural Press, 2001.

Femininity

Basinger, Jeanine. *A Woman's View: How Hollywood Spoke to Women, 1930–1960.* New York: Knopf, 1993.
Doane, Mary Ann. *The Desire to Desire: The Woman's Film of the 1940s.* Bloomington: Indiana University Press, 1987.
Kaplan, E. Ann, ed. *Feminism and Film.* New York: Oxford University Press, 2000.
Kuhn, Annette. *The Women's Companion to International Film.* Berkeley: University of California Press, 1994.

Gender

Brosh, Liora. *Screening Novel Women: From British Domestic Fiction to Film.* New York: Palgrave Macmillan, 2008.
Grossvogel, David I. *Marianne and the Puritan: Transformations of the Couple in French and American Films.* Lanham, MD: Lexington Books, 2005.
Matthews, Nicole. *Comic Politics: Gender in Hollywood Comedy after the New Right.* Manchester: Manchester University Press, 2000.
Pomerance, Murray, ed. *Ladies and Gentlemen, Boys and Girls: Gender in Film at the End of the Twentieth Century.* Albany: State University of New York Press, 2001.

Girls

Gatewood, Frances and Murray Pomerance, eds. *Sugar, Spice, and Everything Nice: Cinemas of Girlhood.* Detroit: Wayne State University Press, 2002.
Hentges, Sarah. *Pictures of Girlhood: Modern Female Adolescence on Film.* Jefferson, NC: McFarland, 2006.

Irish Americans

Curran, Joseph M. *Hibernian Green on the Silver Screen.* New York: Greenwood, 1989.
Gribben, Arthur. *Images of the Irish & Irish Americans in Commercial & Ethnographic Film.* Boston: Northeastern University Press, 1987.
Lourdeaux, Lee. *Italian and Irish Filmmakers in America.* Philadelphia: Temple University Press, 1990.

Italian Americans

Giordano, Paolo A. and Anthony Julian Tamburri. *Beyond the Margin: Readings in Italian Americana.* Madison: Fairleigh Dickinson University Press, 1998.
Lourdeaux, Lee. *Italian and Irish Filmmakers in America.* Philadelphia: Temple University Press, 1990.

Jews in Film

Cohen, Sarah Blacher. *From Hester Street to Hollywood*. Bloomington: Indiana University Press, 1983.

Desser, David and Lester D. Friedman. *American-Jewish Filmmakers: Traditions and Trends*. Urbana: University of Illinois Press, 1993.

Erens, Patricia. *The Jew in American Cinema*. Bloomington: Indiana University Press, 1984.

Gabler, Neal. *An Empire of Their Own: How the Jews Invented Hollywood*. New York: Crown, 1988.

Goldman, Eric A. *The American Jewish Experience through the Lens of Cinema*. New York: American Jewish Committee, 2008.

Rogin, Michael Paul. *Blackface, White Noise: Jewish Immigrants in the Hollywood Melting Pot*. Berkeley: University of California Press, 1996.

Latinos/Latinas

Berumen, Frank Javier Garcia. *The Chicano/Hispanic Image in American Film*. New York: Vantage Press, 1995.

Fregoso, Rosa Linda. *The Bronze Screen: Chicana and Chicano Film Culture*. Minneapolis: University of Minnesota Press, 1993.

Keller, Gary D. *Chicano Cinema: Research, Reviews, and Resources*. Binghamton: Bilingual Review/Press, 1985.

Keller, Gary D. *Hispanics and United States Film*. Tempe: Bilingual Press, 1994.

List, Christine. *Chicano Images: Refiguring Ethnicity in Mainstream Film*. New York: Garland, 1996.

Noriega, Chon A. *Chicanos and Film*. New York: Garland, 1992.

Noriega, Chon A. *Shot in America: Television, the State, and the Rise of Chicano Cinema*. Minneapolis: University of Minnesota Press, 2000.

Noriega, Chon A. and Ana M. Lopez. *The Ethnic Eye: Latino Media Arts*. Minneapolis: University of Minnesota Press, 1996.

Pettit, Arthur G. *Images of the Mexican American in Fiction and Film*. College Station: Texas A&M University Press, 1980.

Reyes, Luis, and Peter Rubie. *Hispanics in Hollywood: An Encyclopedia of Film and Television*. New York: Garland, 1994.

Richard, Alfred Charles. *Contemporary Hollywood's Negative Hispanic Image*. Westport, CT: Greenwood, 1994.

Richard, Alfred Charles. *The Hispanic Image on the Silver Screen*. New York: Greenwood, 1992.

Masculinity

Bruzzi, Stella. *Bringing Up Daddy: Fatherhood and Masculinity in Post-War Hollywood*. London: British Film Institute, 2005.

Caster, Peter. *Prisons, Race, and Masculinity in Twentieth-Century U.S. Literature and Film*. Columbus: Ohio State University Press, 2008.

LaSalle, Mick. *Dangerous Men: Pre-Code Hollywood and the Birth of the Modern Man*. New York: Thomas Dunne Books/St. Martin's Press, 2002.

Powrie, Phil, Ann Davies and Bruce Babington, eds. *The Trouble with Men: Masculinities in European and Hollywood Cinema*. New York: Wallflower Press, 2004.

Stephen, John, ed. *Ways of Being Male: Representing Masculinities in Children's Literature and Film*. New York: Routledge, 2002.

Trice, Ashton D. and Samuel A. Holland. *Heroes, Antiheroes, and Dolts: Portrayals of Masculinity in American Popular Films, 1921–1999*. Jefferson, NC: McFarland, 2001.

Native Americans

Bataille, Gretchen M. and Charles L.P. Silet. *Images of Amerian Indians on Film: An Annotated Bibliography.* New York: Garland, 1985.

Bataille, Gretchen M., and Charles L.P. Silet, eds. *The Pretend Indians: Images of Native Americans in the Movies.* Ames: Iowa State University Press, 1980.

Churchill, Ward. *Fantasies of the Master Race: Literature, Cinema, and the Colonization of American Indians.* San Francisco: City Lights Books, 1998.

Kilpatrick, Jacquelyn. *Celluloid Indians: Native Americans and Film.* Lincoln: University of Nebraska Press, 1999.

O'Connor, John E. *The Hollywood Indian.* Trenton, NJ: New Jersey State Museum, 1980.

Owens, Louis. *Mixedblood Messages: Literature, Film, Family, Place.* Norman: University of Oklahoma Press, 1998.

Rollins, Peter C. and John E. O'Connor, eds. *Hollywood's Indian: The Portrayal of the Native American in Film.* Expanded edn. Lexington: University Press of Kentucky, 2003.

Religion

Bergesen, Albert, and Andrew M. Greeley. *God in the Movies.* New Brunswick, NJ: Transaction Publishers, 2000.

McDannell, Colleen, ed. *Catholics in the Movies.* New York: Oxford University Press, 2008.

Martin, Joel W. and Conrad E. Ostwalt, Jr. *Screening the Sacred: Religion, Myth, and Ideology in Popular American Film.* Boulder, CO: Westview, 1995.

Miles, Margaret Ruth. *Seeing and Believing: Religion and Values in the Movies.* Boston: Beacon, 1996.

Parish, James Robert. *Ghosts and Angels in Hollywood Films.* Jefferson, NC: McFarland, 1994.

Sexuality

Doherty, Thomas Patrick. *Pre-Code Hollywood: Sex, Immorality, and Insurrection in American Cinema, 1930–1934.* New York: Columbia University Press, 1999.

Pennington, Jody W. *The History of Sex in American Film.* Westport, CT: Praeger, 2007.

Youth

Doherty, Thomas Patrick. *Teenagers and Teenpics: The Juvenilization of American Movies in the 1950s.* Revised and expanded edn. Philadelphia: Temple University Press, 2002.

Kaveney, Roz. *Teen Dreams: Reading Teen Film from Heathers to Veronica Mars.* New York: Palgrave Macmillan, 2006.

Lewis, Jon. *The Road to Romance & Ruin: Teen Films and Youth Culture.* New York: Routledge, 1992.

Shary, Timothy. *Teen Movies: American Youth on Screen.* New York: Wallflower, 2005.

American History in Film

History in Film

Barta, Tony, ed. *Screening the Past: Film and the Representation of History.* Westport, CT: Praeger, 1998.

Burgoyne, Robert. *Film Nation: Hollywood Looks at U.S. History.* Minneapolis: University of Minnesota Press, 1997.

Burgoyne, Robert. *The Hollywood Historical Film.* Malden, MA: Blackwell, 2008.

Cameron, Kenneth M. *America on Film: Hollywood and American History*. New York: Continuum, 1997.

Carnes, Marc C., ed. *Past Imperfect: History According to the Movies*. New York: H. Holt, 1995.

Chopra-Gant, Mike. *Cinema and History*. London: New York: Wallflower, 2008.

Croteau, Melissa, ed. *Reel Histories: Studies in American Film*. Hollywood: Press Americana, 2008.

Crowther, Bruce. *Hollywood Faction: Reality and Myth in the Movies*. London: Columbus Books, 1984.

Custen, George Frederick. *Bio/pics: How Hollywood Constructed Public History*. New Brunswick, NJ: Rutgers University Press, 1992.

Edgerton, Gary R. and Peter C. Rollins, eds. *Television Histories: Shaping Collective Memory in the Media Age*. Lexington: University Press of Kentucky, 2001.

Eldridge, David. *Hollywood's History Films*. New York: I.B. Tauris, 2006.

Francaviglia, Richard and Jerry Rodnitzky, eds. *Lights, Camera, History: Portraying the Past in Film*. College Station: Texas A&M University Press, 2007.

Grindon, Leger. *Shadows on the Past: Studies in the Historical Fiction Film*. Philadelphia: Temple University Press, 1994.

Guynn, William Howard. *Writing History in Film*. New York: Routledge, 2006.

Hughes-Warrington, Marnie. *History Goes to the Movies: Studying History on Film*. New York: Routledge, 2007.

Landy, Marcia. *Cinematic Uses of the Past*. Minneapolis: University of Minnesota Press, 1996.

Landy, Marcia, ed. *The Historical Film: History and Memory in Media*. New Brunswick, NJ: Rutgers University Press, 2001.

Lewis, Jon and Eric Smoodin, eds. *Looking Past the Screen: Case Studies in American Film History and Method*. Durham: Duke University Press, 2007.

Lorence, James J. *Screening America: United States History through Film since 1900*. New York: Pearson Longman, 2006.

McCrisken, Trevor B. and Andrew Pepper. *American History and Contemporary Hollywood Film*. Edinburgh: Edinburgh University Press, 2005.

Marcus, Alan S. *Celluloid Blackboard: Teaching History with Film*. Charlotte, NC: IAP-Information Age, 2007.

Niemi, Robert. *History in the Media: Film and Television*. Santa Barbara: ABC-CLIO, 2006.

Pitts, Michael R. *Hollywood and American History: A Filmography of over 250 Motion Pictures Depicting U.S. History*. Jefferson, NC: McFarland, 1984.

Pucci, Suzanne R. and James Thompson, eds. *Jane Austen and Co.: Remaking the Past in Contemporary Culture*. Albany: State University of New York Press, 2003.

Rebhorn, Marlette. *Screening America: Using Hollywood Films to Teach History*. New York: P. Lang, 1988.

Rollins, Peter C., ed. *Hollywood as Historian: American Film in a Cultural Context*. Lexington: University Press of Kentucky, 1983.

Roquemore, Joseph H. *History Goes to the Movies: A Viewer's Guide to Some of the Best (and Some of the Worst) Historical Films Ever Made*. New York: Main Street Books, 1999.

Rosenstone, Robert A. *History on Film/Film and History*. New York: Longman/Pearson, 2006.

Rosenstone, Robert A. *Visions of the Past: The Challenge of Film to our Idea of History*. Cambridge, MA: Harvard University Press, 1995.

Rosenthal, Alan, ed. *Why Docudrama? Fact-Fiction on Film and TV*. Carbondale: Southern Illinois University Press, 1999.

Russell, James. *The Historical Epic and Contemporary Hollywood: From Dances with Wolves to Gladiator*. New York: Continuum, 2007.

Sanello, Frank. *Reel v. Real: How Hollywood Turns Fact into Fiction*. Lanham, MD: National Book Network, 2003.

Schablitsky, Julie M., ed. *Box Office Archaeology: Refining Hollywood's Portrayals of the Past.* Walnut Creek, CA: Left Coast Press, 2007.

Schultz, Deanne. *Filmography of World History.* Westport, CT: Greenwood Press, 2007.

Slocum, J. David. *Hollywood & War: A Film Reader.* New York: Routledge, 2006.

Smyth, J.E. *Reconstructing American Historical Cinema: From Cimarron to Citizen Kane.* Lexington: University Press of Kentucky, 2006.

Toplin, Robert Brent. *Reel History: In Defense of Hollywood.* Lawrence: University Press of Kansas, 2002.

Tracey, Grant Annis George. *Filmography of American History.* Westport, CT: Greenwood Press, 2002.

Wilson, Wendy S. and Gerald H. Herman. *American History on the Screen: A Teachers' Resource Book on Film and Video.* Portland, ME: Walch Education, 2002.

Colonial Era

Österberg, Bertil O. *Colonial America on Film and Television: A Filmography.* Jefferson, NC: McFarland, 2001.

Civil War

Chadwick, Bruce. *The Reel Civil War: Mythmaking in American Film.* New York: Knopf, 2001.

Gallagher, Gary W. *Causes Won, Lost, and Forgotten: How Hollywood & Popular Art Shape What We Know about the Civil War.* Chapel Hill: University of North Carolina Press, 2008.

Sachsman, David B., S. Kittrell Rushing, and Roy Morris, Jr., eds. *Memory and Myth: The Civil War in Fiction and Film from Uncle Tom's Cabin to Cold Mountain.* West Lafayette, IN: Purdue University Press, 2007.

Slavery

Davis, Natalie Zemon. *Slaves on Screen.* Cambridge, MA: Harvard University Press, 2000.

World War I

Campbell, Craig. *Reel American and World War I.* Jefferson, NC: McFarland, 1985.

DeBauche, Leslie Midkiff. *Reel Patriotism: The Movies and World War I.* Madison: University of Wisconsin Press, 1997.

Dibbets, Karel and Bert Hogenkamp, eds. *Film and the First World War.* Amsterdam: Amsterdam University Press, 1995.

Isenberg, Michael T. *War on Film: The American Cinema and World War I.* Rutherford, NJ: Fairleigh Dickinson University Press, 1981.

Kelly, Andrew. *Cinema and the Great War.* London: Routledge, 1997.

Rollins, Peter C. and John E. O'Connor, eds. *Hollywood's World War I: Motion Picture Images.* Bowling Green, OH: Bowling Green State University Popular Press, 1997.

Ward, Larry Wayne. *The Motion Picture Goes to War: The U.S. Government Film Effort During World War I.* Ann Arbor: UMI, 1985.

World War II

Basinger, Jeanine. *The World War II Combat Film: Anatomy of a Genre.* Middletown, CT: Wesleyan University Press, 2003.

Doherty, Thomas Patrick. *Projections of War: Hollywood, American Culture, and World War II.* New York: Columbia University Press, 1999.

Fyne, Robert. *Long Ago and Far Away: Hollywood and the Second World War*. Lanham, MD: Scarecrow Press, 2008.

Koppes, Clayton R. and Gregory D. Black. *Hollywood Goes to War: How Politics, Profits, and Propaganda Shaped World War II Movies*. New York: Free Press, 1987.

Korean War

Lentz, Robert J. *Korean War Filmography: 91 English Language Features through 2000*. Jefferson, NC: McFarland, 2003.

Vietnam War

Anderegg, Michael. *Inventing Vietnam: The War in Film and Television*. Philadelphia: Temple University Press, 1991.

Auster, Albert and Leonard Quart. *How the War Was Remembered: Hollywood & Vietnam*. New York: Praeger, 1988.

Dittmar, Linda and Gene Michaud. *From Hanoi to Hollywood: The Vietnam War in American Film*. New Brunswick, NJ: Rutgers University Press, 1990.

Gilman, Owen W., Jr. and Lorrie Smith. *America Rediscovered: Critical Essays on Literature and Film of the Vietnam War*. New York: Garland, 1990.

Hellmann, John. *American Myth and the Legacy of Vietnam*. New York: Columbia Univrsity Press, 1986.

Rowe, John Carlos and Rick Berg. *The Vietnam War and American Culture*. New York: Columbia University Press, 1991.

Recent American History

Toplin, Robert Brent, ed. *Michael Moore's Fahrenheit 9/11*. Lawrence: University Press of Kansas, 2006.

Toplin, Robert Brent, ed. *Oliver Stone's USA*. Lawrence: University Press of Kansas, 2000.

Special Topics

Alcoholism and Film

Cook, Jim and Mike Lewington. *Images of Alcoholism*. London: British Film Institute, 1979.

Denzin, Norman K. *Hollywood Shot by Shot*. New York: A. de Gruyter, 1991.

Atomic Bomb

Shapiro, Jerome Franklin. *Atomic Bomb Cinema: The Apocalyptic Imagination on Film*. New York: Routledge, 2002.

Audiences

Barker, Martin. *Knowing Audiences: Judge Dredd, its Friends, Fans and Foes*. Luton: University of Luton, 1998.

Casetti, Francesco. *Inside the Gaze: The Fiction Film and its Spectator*. Bloomington: Indiana University Press, 1998.

Dixon, Wheeler W. *It Looks at You: The Returned Gaze of Cinema*. Albany: State University of New York Press, 1995.

Lesley Stern and George Kouvaros, eds. *Falling for You: Essays on Cinema and Performance*. Sydney: Power, 2000.

Scheiner, Georganne. *Signifying Female Adolescence: Film Representations and Fans, 1920–1950*. Westport, CT: Praeger, 2000.

Sedgwick, John. *Popular Filmgoing in 1930s Britain: A Choice of Pleasures*. Exeter: Exeter University Press, 2000.

Staiger, Janet. *Perverse Spectators: The Practices of Film Reception*. New York: New York University Press, 2000.

Stempel, Tom. *American Audiences on Movies and Moviegoing*. Lexington: University Press of Kentucky, 2001.

Stokes, Melvyn, and Richard Maltby. *Identifying Hollywood's Audiences: Cultural Identity and the Movies*. London: British Film Institute, 1999.

Biographies

Slide, Anthony. *American Racist: The Life and Films of Thomas Dixon*. Lexington: University Press of Kentucky, 2004.

Celebrity

Orgeron, Marsha. *Hollywood Ambitions: Celebrity in the Movie Age*. Middletown, CT: Wesleyan University Press, 2008.

Censorship

Black, Gregory D. *The Catholic Crusade Against the Movies, 1940–1975*. New York: Cambridge University Press, 1998.

Couvares, Francis G., ed. *Movie Censorship and American Culture*. 2nd edn. Amherst: University of Massachusetts Press, 2006.

Doherty, Thomas Patrick. *Hollywood's Censor: Joseph I. Breen & the Production Code Administration*. New York: Columbia University Press, 2007.

Grieveson, Lee. *Policing Cinema: Movies and Censorship in Early-Twentieth-Century America*. Berkeley: University of California Press, 2004.

Leff, Leonard J. and Jerold L. Simmons. *The Dame in the Kimono: Hollywood, Censorship, and the Production Code*. Lexington: University Press of Kentucky, 2001.

Phillips, Kendall R. *Controversial Cinema: The Films that Outraged America*. Westport, CT: Praeger, 2008.

Smith, Sarah. *Children, Cinema and Censorship: From Dracula to the Dead End Kids*. New York: I.B. Tauris, 2005.

Cities and Towns in Film

Clarke, David B. *The Cinematic City*. London: Routledge, 1997.

Levi, Emanuel. *Small-Town America in Film: The Decline and Fall of Community*. New York: Continuum, 1991.

MacKinnon, Kenneth. *Hollywood's Small Towns*. Metuchen: Scarecrow, 1984.

Directors

Birchard, Robert S. *Cecil B. DeMille's Hollywood*. Lexington: University Press of Kentucky, 2004.

Bliss, Michael. *Justified Lives: Morality and Narrative in the Films of Sam Peckinpah*. Carbondale: Southern Illinois University Press, 1993.

Durgnat, Raymond and Scott Simmon. *King Vidor*. Berkeley: University of California Press, 1988.

Freedman, Jonathan and Richard Millington, eds. *Hitchcock's America*. New York: Oxford University Press, 1999.

Gehring, Wes D. *Populism and the Capra Legacy*. Westport, CT: Greenwood, 1995.

Girgus, Sam B. *Hollywood Renaissance: The Cinema of Democracy in the Ear of Ford, Capra, and Kazan*. Cambridge: Cambridge University Press, 1998.

Gunning, Tom. *D.W. Griffith and the Origins of American Narrative Film*. Urbana: University of Illinois Press, 1991.

Jacobs, Diane. *Christmas in July: The Life and Art of Preston Sturges*. Berkeley: University of California Press, 1992.

Kapsis, Robert E. *Hitchcock: The Making of a Reputation*. Chicago: University of Chicago Press, 1992.

Kolker, Robert Phillip. *A Cinema of Loneliness: Penn, Kubrick, Coppola, Scorsese, Altman*. New York: Oxford University Press, 1980.

Koszarski, Richard. *Hollywood Directors, 1914–1940*. New York: Oxford University Press, 1976.

Koszarski, Richard. *Hollywood Directors, 1941–1976*. New York: Oxford University Press, 1977.

Langman, Larry. *Destination Hollywood: The Influence of Europeans on American Filmmaking*. Jefferson, NC: McFarland, 2000.

Lourdeaux, Lee. *Italian and Irish Filmmakers in America: Ford, Captra, Coppola, and Scorsese*. Philadelphia: Temple, 1990.

Mahar, Karen Ward. *Women Filmmakers in Early Hollywood*. Baltimore: Johns Hopkins University Press, 2006.

Morrison, James. *Passport to Hollywood: Hollywood Films, European Directors*. Albany: State University of New York Press, 1998.

Petrie, Graham. *Hollywood Destinies: European Directors in America, 1922–1931*. Revised edn. Detroit: Wayne State University Press, 2002.

Phillips, Gene D. *Major Film Directors of the American and British Cinema*. Bethlehem: Lehigh, 1990.

Quarles, Mike. *Down and Dirty: Hollywood's Exploitation Filmmakers and their Movies*. Jefferson, NC: McFarland, 1993.

Sikov, Ed. *On Sunset Boulevard: The Life and Times of Billy Wilder*. New York: Hyperion, 1998.

Studlar, Gaylyn and David Desser. *Reflections in a Male Eye: John Huston and the American Experience*. Washington: Smithsonian Institution Press, 1993.

Disability and Film

Fleming, Michael and Roger Manvell. *Images of Madness*. Rutherford, NJ: Fairleigh Dickinson University Press, 1985.

Klobas, Lauri E. *Disability Drama in Television and Film*. Jefferson, NC: McFarland, 1988.

Norden, Martin F. *The Cinema of Isolation: A History of Physical Disability in the Movies*. New Brunswick, NJ: Rutgers University Press, 1994.

Schuchman, John S. *Hollywood Speaks: Deafness and the Film Entertainment Industry*. Urbana: University of Illinois Press, 1988.

Economics

Balio, Tino. *Grand Design: Hollywood as a Modern Business Enterprise, 1930–1939.* New York: Scribner, 1993.
Balio, Tino. *United Artists.* Madison: University of Wisconsin Press, 1987.
Sedgwick, John and Michael Pokorny. *An Economic History of Film.* New York: Routledge, 2004.

Family and Film

Harwood, Sarah. *Family Fictions: Representations of the Family in 1980s Hollywood Cinema.* Basingstoke: Macmillan, 1997.
Leibman, Nina C. *Living Room Lectures: The Fifties Family in Film and Television.* Austin: University of Texas Press, 1995.
Rueschmann, Eva. *Sisters on Screen: Siblings in Contemporary Cinema.* Philadelphia: Temple University, 2000.
Williams, Tony. *Hearths of Darkness: The Family in the American Horror Film.* Madison, NJ: Fairleigh Dickinson University Press, 1996.

Film Exhibition

Fuller-Seeley, Kathryn H., ed. *Hollywood in the Neighborhood: Historical Case Studies of Local Moviegoing.* Berkeley: University of California Press, 2008.
Waller, Gregory A., ed. *Moviegoing in America: A Sourcebook in the History of Film Exhibition.* Malden, MA: Blackwell, 2002.

Film Music

Buhler, James, Caryl Flinn, and David Neumeyer, eds. *Music and Cinema.* Hanover, NH: University Press of New England, 2000.
Donnelly, K.J., ed. *Film Music: Critical Approaches.* New York: Continuum, 2001.

Immigrants and Immigration

Cull, Nicholas J. and Davíd Carrasco, eds. *Alambrista and the U.S.–Mexico Border: Film, Music, and Stories of Undocumented Immigrants.* Albuquerque: University of New Mexico Press, 2004.
Naficy, Hamid. *Home, Exile, Homeland: Film, Media and the Politics of Place.* New York: Routledge, 1998.

Journalism and Film

Good, Howard. *Girl Reporter: Gender, Journalism and the Movies.* Metuchen: Scarecrow, 1998.
Langman, Larry. *The Media in the Movies.* Jefferson, NC: McFarland, 1998.
Ness, Richard R. *From Headline Hunter to Superman: A Journalism Filmography.* Lanham: Scarecrow, 1997.

Labor Relations in the Motion Picture Industry

Horne, Gerald. *Class Struggle in Hollywood, 1930–1950.* Austin: University of Texas Press, 2001.

Law and Film

Denvir, John. *Legal Reelism: Movies as Legal Texts.* Urbana: University of Illinois Press, 1996.

Literary Adaptations

Jeffers, Jennifer M. Britain *Colonized: Hollywood's Appropriation of British Literature.* New York: Palgrave Macmillan, 2006.
Willson, Robert Frank, Jr. *Shakespeare in Hollywood, 1929–1956.* Madison, NJ: Fairleigh Dickinson University Press, 2000.

Marketing

Jarvie, I.C. *Hollywood's Overseas Campaign: The North Atlantic Movie Trade, 1920–1950.* New York: Cambridge University Press, 1992.
Segrave, Kerry. *American Films Abroad: Hollywood's Domination of the World's Movie Screens from the 1890s to the Present.* Jefferson, NC: McFarland, 1997.
Trumpbour, John. *Selling Hollywood to the World: U.S. and European Struggles for Mastery of the Global Film Industry, 1920–1950.* New York: Cambridge University Press, 2002.

Motherhood in Film

Fischer, Lucy. *Cinematernity: Film, Motherhood, Genre.* Princeton: Princeton University Press, 1996.

Philosophy and Film

Allen, Richard. *Projecting Illusion: Film Spectatorship and the Impression of Reality.* Cambridge: Cambridge University Press, 1995.
Allen, Richard and Murray Smith. *Film Theory and Philosophy.* Oxford: Clarendon Press, 1997.
Freeland, Cynthia A. and Thomas E. Wartenberg. *Philosophy and Film.* New York: Routledge, 1995.
Sobchack, Vivian Carol. *The Address of the Eye: A Phenomenology of Film Experience.* Princeton: Princeton University Press, 1992.

Scandals in the Motion Picture Industry

McLean, Adrienne L., and David A. Cook, eds. *Headline Hollywood: A Century of Film Scandal.* New Brunswick, NJ: Rutgers University Press, 2001.

Sound

Geduld, Harry M. *The Birth of the Talkies.* Bloomington: Indiana University Press, 1975.
O'Brien, Charles. *Cinema's Conversion to Sound: Technology and Film Style in France and the U.S.* Bloomington: Indiana University Press, 2005.

The South and Film

Campbell, Edward D.C., Jr. *Celluloid South: Hollywood and the Southern Myth.* Knoxville: University of Tennessee Press, 1981.

French, Warren. *South and Film.* Jackson: University Press of Mississippi Press, 1981.

Graham, Don. *Cowboys and Cadillacs: How Hollywood Looks at Texas.* Austin: Texas Monthly, 1983.

Williamson, Jerry Wayne. *Hillbillyland.* Chapel Hill: University of North Carolina Press, 1995.

Williamson, Jerry Wayne. *Southern Mountaineers in Silent Films.* Jefferson, NC: McFarland, 1994.

Sports and Film

Dickerson, Gary E. *The Cinema of Baseball.* Westport, CT: Meckler, 1991.

Tudor, Deborah V. *Hollywood's Vision of Team Sports: Heroes, Race, and Gender.* New York: Garland, 1997.

Stereotypes

Loukides, Paul and Linda K. Fuller. *Beyond the Stars: Stock Characters in American Popular Film.* Bowling Green, OH: Bowling Green State University Popular Press, 1990.

Studio System

Anderson, Christopher. *Hollywood TV: The Studio System in the Fifties.* Austin: University of Texas Press, 1994.

Davis, Ronald L. *The Glamour Factory.* Dallas: SMU, 1993.

Mordden, Ethan. *The Hollywood Studios: House Style in the Golden Age of the Movies.* New York: Knopf, 1987.

Schatz, Thomas. *The Genius of the System: Hollywood Filmmaking in the Studio Era.* New York: Henry Holt, 1996.

Staiger, Janet. *The Studio System.* New Brunswick, NJ: Rutgers University Press, 1995.

Suspense and Film

Howard, Tom. *Suspense in the Cinema.* Wyong, NSW: John Howard Reid, 1995.

Vorderer, Peter et al. *Suspense: Conceptualizations, Theoretical Analyses, and Empirical Explorations.* Mahwah, NJ: Erlbaum, 1996.

Teachers and Film

Joseph, Pamela Bolotin and Gail E. Burnaford. *Images of Schoolteachers in Twentieth-Century America.* New York: St. Martin's, 1994.

Index

Academy Awards, 1
Academy of Motion Picture Arts and
    Sciences, 1
Addams, Jane, 3, 39
African Americans in film, 100–11,
    272–80
All Quiet on the Western Front, 1
Arbuckle, Fatty, 14
Armat, Thomas, 10
Asians and Asian Americans in film, 340–53

Beard, George M., 2
Bergman, Andrew, 93
Birth of a Nation, 29, 43–51, 53, 55, 69–70,
    101, 104, 366
Black, Gregory D., 162
Blackboard Jungle, 23, 275, 360
Blumer, Herbert, 13
Bogart, Humphrey, 133, 134, 136, 137,
    146, 162, 180, 181
Bok, Edward W., 6
Bonnie and Clyde, 25, 241, 255, 258, 366
Born on the Fourth of July, 27, 281, 292–4,
    295, 297, 300, 329
Brando, Marlon, 24, 187
Breen, Joseph I., 78, 116, 140–1
Breen Office, 17, 18
Brownlow, Kevin, 13
Bugs Bunny, 19, 129

Cagney, James, 1, 16, 84, 146, 150
Capra, Frank, 18, 19, 80, 148, 269, 331

Casablanca, 1, 133–43
Chaplin, Charlie, 1, 31, 56, 59, 146,
    355–6
Cicognani, Most Reverend Amleto
    Giovanni, 17
Citizen Kane, 1
Clarke, Mae, 1, 84
Cohn, Harry, 11, 20
Coney Island, 4, 7, 222, 225, 227, 228
Confessions of a Nazi Spy, 18, 184
Cooper, Gary, 16, 146, 147, 149,
    150, 180
Crane, Stephen, 6, 40
Crawford, Joan, 146, 159, 160, 163,
    164–5, 167, 168
Crouching Tiger, Hidden Dragon, 340,
    343, 348–53

Daguerre, Louis, 9
Day, Doris, 24
De Forest, Lee, 16, 112, 113
De Sica, Vittorio, 22
Denby, David, 27
Dickson, William K. L., 9
Dirty Harry, 260, 262–3
Disney, Walt, 21, 80, 180, 225–8, 364
Disneyland, 219, 225–33
Double Indemnity, 175–7, 224
Doubleday, Frank, 5
Dr. Strangelove, 243–54
Dreiser, Theodore, 3, 6
Duck Soup, 17, 78

Easy Rider, 259, 305
Edison, Thomas Alva, 6, 8, 9, 10, 11, 15, 63, 64, 65, 100
El Norte, 363

Fail Safe, 253–4
Fairbanks, Douglas, Sr., 52–62, 84
fallen woman film, 86–90
Faludi, Susan, 309
Fields, W. C., 17
film noir, 22–3, 175–7, 219, 223–5
Fonda, Henry, 19, 147, 150, 151, 253
Footlight Parade, 71–2, 79
Ford, John, 19, 103, 147–8, 150, 151
42nd Street, 71–3, 79
Fox, William, 12
French Connection, 260, 262–3

Gable, Clark, 19, 146, 148, 151
gangster film, 76, 77, 82–6, 88
Garbo, Greta, 13, 15, 88, 146, 159
Garcia, Roger, 341
genteel tradition, 5
Gibson Girl, 4
Gold Diggers of 1933, 71–2, 79, 109
Gold Rush, 1
Goldwyn, Samuel, 12, 20
Gomery, Douglas, 112
Gone with the Wind, 91–3, 95–9, 110–11, 366
Graduate, 255, 257–8
Grapes of Wrath, 81, 91, 93–6, 99
Great Depression, x, 16, 71–3, 75–81, 82–90, 91–9, 108, 202–3
Great Dictator, 19
Great Train Robbery, 6, 209
Green Berets, 26, 281
Griffith, David Wark, 11, 13, 29–30, 41, 43–51, 52, 53, 55, 69–70, 101, 104, 105
Guess Who's Coming to Dinner?, 273, 278–9

Haskell, Molly, 167
Hays, Will, 14, 16, 78, 81, 116
Hearst, William Randolph, 5, 33
Hellman, Lillian, 22
Higham, John, 3
Hill, Anita, 309

Hofstadter, Richard, 24
Hollywood, location of film industry in, 15
Hollywood Ten, 21
Horse Feathers, 17
Howe, Frederic, 35, 36
Huston, John, 19, 148
Huygens, Christiaan, 8

I am a Fugitive from a Chain Gang, 1, 17, 81, 110
I Was a Teenage Werewolf, 24
Immigrant, 355–6
immigrants in film, 354–63
Intolerance, 29–30, 55
Invasion of the Body Snatchers, 198–206
It Happened One Night, 18, 80

Jacobs, Lewis, 12, 84
James, William, 3
Jazz Singer, 16, 358
JFK, 281, 295–7, 299, 365
Jolson, Al, 16

Kazan, Elia, 187, 189–92, 196
Keaton, Buster, 31
Khouri, Callie, 309, 312–13
Klein, Maury, 18
Koppes, Clayton, 162
Kubrick, Stanley, 243, 246–52

Laemmle, Carl, 10, 11, 12, 105
Lamarr, Hedy, 15, 146
Lardner, Jr., Ring, 21
Lawrence, Florence, 11
Lee, Ang, 340
Lindsay, Vachel, 39, 40
Lingerman, Richard R., 19
London, Jack, 5
Lord, Father Daniel, 17
Lowell, James Russell, 5
Lubitsch, Ernst, 15, 92
Lumière, Auguste and Louis, 10

McClure, Samuel Sidney, 6
Magnificent Seven, 207–18
Marconi, Guglielmo, 6
Marey, Etienne Jules, 9, 63, 64
Marx Brothers, 17, 18, 78, 146
May, Lary, 13

Mayer, Louis B., 12, 20, 159
Medved, Michael, 27
Micheaux, Oscar, 106–7
Miller, Arthur, 189, 192, 361
Miller, Mark Crispin, 25
Miracle case, 22, 238–9
Mission to Moscow, 182–3
Mix, Tom, 15, 79
Moore, Colleen, 13
Moscow on the Hudson, 354–5
Moten, Etta, 72
Muni, Paul, 1, 84
Munsterberg, Hugo, 39
Mutual case, 67–8
Muybridge, Eadweard, 9
My Man Godfrey, 18

National Association for the Advancement
    of Colored People (NAACP),
    47–8, 49–51, 69, 100, 101–2
neurasthenia, 2, 3
nickelodeon, 10, 14, 65–7
Niépce, Joseph Nicéphore, 8
Nixon, 298–9

Office of War Information (OWI), 19–20,
    152, 156, 159, 160, 330, 335, 336
Olmsted, Frederick Law, 4
On the Waterfront, 187–97

Palance, Jack, 1
Paramount case, 21, 234, 274
Peiss, Kathy, 7, 13, 227
persistence of vision, 8
Pickford, Mary, 11, 52–62
Platoon, 27, 281, 286, 287, 288, 289,
    290–2, 295
Pocahontas, 364, 367–70
Poitier, Sidney, 272–80
Porter, Edward S., 6, 101, 209
Preminger, Otto, 22
Production Code, 17, 22, 78–9, 116,
    119–28, 140–1, 358
Progressive era, 12, 14, 31, 33, 34
Ptolemy, 8
Pulitzer, Joseph, 5, 6

Ray, Robert, 16
Rebel Without a Cause, 23

Reid, Wallace, 14
Riesman, David, 201, 203
Robert, Etienne Gaspar, 8
Robinson, David, 12
Rocky, 25, 264–71
Rogers, Ginger, 71, 93, 167, 176
Rogers, Will, 80–1
Roosevelt, Franklin, 19, 94, 129, 136, 152,
    179, 330, 331
Roosevelt, Theodore, 3, 54, 57, 101
Ross, Edward A., 41
Rossellini, Roberto, 22
Rush Hour, 340, 342–8, 349

Santayana, George, 5
Saving Private Ryan, 329–39
Sayre, Nora, 24
Schenck, Joseph, 12
Schulberg, Budd, 148, 192–6
science fiction film, 198–206
screwball comedy, 18
Selznick, David O., 12
Sennet, Mack, 13
Shane, 210–11
silent film, 12–14, 31–42
Sinclair, Upton, 38
Sontag, Susan, 200
sound, 15–16, 112–16
Spielberg, Steven, 329, 337, 367
Splendor in the Grass, 23
Stallone, Sylvester, 265, 266, 267
Stanford, Leland, 9
Stanwyck, Barbara, 163, 167, 176
Sternberg, Josef von, 15
Stewart, Jimmy, 19, 146, 148, 151
Stoheim, Erich von, 10
Stone, Oliver, 281–300
Straw Dogs, 260–1, 262
Sunset Boulevard, 1
Supreme Court, 14, 21, 67–8, 230, 234,
    238–9
Swanson, Gloria, 1, 15, 147

Takaki, Ronald, 241–2
Tarbell, Ida, 38
Taylor, Desmond, 14
theaters, 15
Thelma and Louise, 26, 309–28
Treasure of the Sierra Madre, 1

Uchatius, Baron Franz von, 8
Un-American Activities Committee, 21–2,
    179–86, 187, 190–5, 235–8, 274
Unforgiven, 1

Valentino, Rudolph, 13
Victorian culture, x, 3, 4, 5, 6, 7, 12, 28, 52,
    54, 56, 60, 62
Vietnam War, x, 25, 26–7, 256, 281–300,
    331, 332
Virginian, 4

Warner, Harry, 172–3
Warner, Jack, 19, 137
Warshow, Robert, 84
Wayne, John, 144–62, 329

West, Mae, 17, 18, 78, 90
Western, the 1, 25, 207–18
Why?, 34–5, 36
Wilson, Woodrow, 48, 70
Wister, Owen, 3, 4
woman's film, 163–9
Wood, Robin, 90
World War I, 1, 19
World War II, 19–20, 23, 129–62, 170–3,
    329–39
World War II combat film, 129–31
World's Columbian Exposition, 4, 233

Zanuck, Darryl F., 12, 20, 93, 95,
    146, 148
Zukor, Adoph, 11, 12, 78